PLANNED GIVING
ADMINISTRATION

NACUBO

Forrest C. Brostrom, J.D.

Library of Congress Cataloging-in-Publication Data

Brostrom, Forrest C., 1953–
    Planned giving administration : the business officer's guide / Forrest C. Brostrom.
        p. cm.
    Includes bibliographical references and index.
    ISBN 1-56972-029-0
    1. Universities and colleges—United States—Endowments. 2. Education, Higher—United States—Finance. 3. Deferred giving—United States. I. National Association of College and University Business Officers. II. Title.

LB2336.B76 2004
278.1'06—dc22

                                                            2004053895

National Association of College and University Business Officers
Washington, DC
www.nacubo.org

Printed in the United States of America

CONTENTS

APPENDICES

ACKNOWLEDGMENTS

No book is written in a vacuum and there are many people who have had an impact (either knowingly or unknowingly) on this book.

I would like to thank my wife, Josie, for her love and support in this endeavor. I probably would have given up long ago but for her constant encouragement and assurances that someone somewhere would appreciate the effort.

I would like to acknowledge my friends and colleagues at the University of Southern California Office of Planned Giving. They have provided me with wonderful examples of professional development officers and gift administrators who work with their business officers for the betterment of the entire university.

In particular I want to thank my colleague Geoff Gilchrist, who wrote the book on real estate gifts and was kind enough to provide his last copy to me. It was an invaluable resource for those discussions of real estate contained in this book. I am indebted to him.

I would like to thank Dennis Dougherty, senior vice president for administration at the University of Southern California. He asked me to write this book. He also told me that business officers needed a glossary of terms. Hopefully the glossary meets his expectations.

Thanks also to Carol Campbell, vice chancellor for finance and administration at Texas Christian University, for permitting the use of the university's planned giving policy statement as well as for her valuable input on this book in general.

Special thanks to Anna Marie Cirino on NACUBO's staff, who has worked with me over a long period of time without impatience (expressed or implied) and with great understanding. And I would also like to thank Donna Klinger on NACUBO's staff and Karen Colburn and Ellen Hirzy for their editorial assistance and insight.

INTRODUCTION

Your office door bursts open, and an out-of-breath development officer rushes in. "We've got a big one!" he says, gasping for air from the two-story climb up the stairs. "It's all together. Old Fred Johnson has decided to give us a million dollars. It's gonna be real estate, but in a trust with some other things thrown in. We'll name a building for him. It'll be great. Here are the papers you need to sign. Right there and there and there. He's waiting downstairs in his car to take the papers to his lawyer." The development officer stops for a moment to catch his breath. Before you can answer, the development officer pulls out a pen and hands it to you. "He's in kind of a hurry."

What would you do? If you have no prior information about this gift, it seems that you have three options. You could say, "Sure, no problem," and sign. Of course, you don't know what you're signing or the risks you may be assuming for your institution. You could say, "No," and possibly cost your college $1 million. You could say, "Maybe," and slow the process down by asking questions, looking the proverbial gift horse in the mouth, and then making a decision.

While your third choice is the best, what exactly do you need to know to make an informed, well-reasoned decision? What are the issues that you must examine? Where are the hidden pitfalls you must guard against? If you do not know the answers to these questions, then this book is for you.

Many business officers have faced the type of situation described here. For some people, the response is easy. Just say, "No." That's safe (you hope) and is a standard, risk-averse response. But it is also a shortsighted response that will cost you money in the long run. Not all good gifts look good on first impression. Only a business officer who understands the basic administrative issues surrounding planned giving and individual planned gifts can separate Seabiscuit from the old gray mare, to continue our gift horse analogy.

This book will help you analyze individual planned gifts and planned giving programs. It is written with the busy person in mind and can be read from beginning to end, end to beginning, or simply sampled anywhere you like. This book offers practical guidance, covering common issues and the most reliable options for dealing with these issues. While the book is comprehensive, it is not exhaustive. The intent is to provide business officers with the tools they need in establishing and collaborating with development staff in administering a planned giving program.

Part One (Chapters 1 through 10) deals with the establishment of new planned giving programs. What are the issues involved in setting up an entire program or adding a new giving technique, such as gift annuities or pooled income funds? What are the pitfalls? How can you give your program a solid footing from the beginning?

Chapter 9 is for programs that have existed for some time, and perhaps have been dormant. They may simply need an overhaul to become truly comprehensive programs. Older programs have different problems and challenges than start-ups do. You probably did not create the problems. It's more likely that you inherited them from prior administrations. But that doesn't make them go away. You are the one who needs to solve them. Solving these problems and getting your program on the right track are covered here.

Chapter 10 provides some pointers for working with the development staff. If you try to understand what makes development officers tick and how they get their jobs done, your planned giving program and your relationships with donors will run much more smoothly. Remember that both the business office and the development office have the institution's best interests in mind. You may sometimes have different working styles, but you're both in the business of ensuring the financial health of your college or university.

For business officers who are new to the area of planned giving, Chapters 11 through 17 in Part II are for you. They provide a brief explanation of the techniques of planned giving, including trusts, annuities, pooled funds, outright gifts, and gifts through estate plans. They also discuss how planned gifts are marketed, including how an individual planned gift is developed and how a planned giving officer works. Appendix A covers general marketing approaches for planned gifts. Read this section for an overview.

At the request of a good friend and longtime university business officer, an extensive, if opinionated, glossary of terms is also included. The language of planned giving is filled with jargon and abbreviations that are sometimes difficult to translate. The glossary will help you to speak the language, and perhaps communicate better with your planned giving officer.

I have written this book as if I were your planned giving consultant sitting across from you in your office. Your position makes you responsible for some portion of your planned giving program, whether it is all administrative duties or merely investment oversight. I know from experience that a well-informed business officer who is supportive of a planned giving program can give that program wings to reach new heights. I have been blessed to work with several such business officers, and I can tell you that every development officer in the country wants similar working relationships. After reading this book, perhaps you, too, can raise your planned giving program to new heights.

PART ONE

STARTING OR EXPANDING A PLANNED GIVING PROGRAM

Successful planned giving programs require oversight and intelligent management to maximize the potential for large, planned gifts while minimizing the institutional risks inherent in a planned giving program. Business officers can't devote full time to administering these programs, though their importance to an institution's economic livelihood is clear. The following discussion will help business officers make the most of their limited time by reviewing the major administrative issues for each type of planned gift technique and offering suggestions for the most effective way to handle certain common problems faced by all nonprofit institutions. Each chapter concludes with suggested actions for business officers to take to ensure a successful planned giving program.

Donor relations is assumed to be an institutional priority and much of the discussion is written with an eye toward developing the best possible administrative operations that will keep donors happy and contributing. As part of that discussion, the business officer's relationship with the development office is also discussed, since development officers are the first line of contact with donors and can prove to be invaluable.

Another section discusses methods for evaluating individual planned gift proposals. It's important to take responsibility for looking the "gift horse" in the mouth, without becoming the roadblock to legitimate, but difficult gifts. The overall discussion suggests some methods for developing an institutional approach that involves all departments in an effective and successful planned giving program.

Part One is written for those business officers who are already knowledgeable about the techniques of planned giving and how they work. If you do not feel confident in your own knowledge, stop right now and turn to Part Two, which contains a brief discussion of each type of gift, how they work (with examples), and why a donor might want to make a gift by that method.

UNDERSTANDING PLANNED GIVING

Some people associate planned giving with fancy trusts and exotic tax plans. The truth is far simpler and more profound. Most fully developed planned giving programs account for 66 percent or more of their funds through bequests. Gifts through wills, revocable living trusts, beneficiary designations on retirement plans, insurance policies, and even bank accounts usually provide the majority of funds received by a fully developed planned giving program, sometimes as high as 80 to 90 percent. What this means for the institution considering planned giving is that even with modest technical expertise, an effective planned giving program can be developed.

Why Start a Planned Giving Program?

The key reasons to start a planned giving program are fairly straightforward:

- **The timing is right.** Demographers suggest that the largest single wealth transfer in American history will occur in the next 30 to 40 years. This trillion-dollar transfer will be done primarily through estate plans as the parents of the Baby Boom generation pass their accumulated assets on to children and grandchildren. Charities that are actively involved in promoting gifts through estate plans cannot help but benefit.

- **A new source of funding.** For institutions beginning a formal program, planned gifts will provide new money from a source not currently being tapped. Many institutions do receive bequests from their constituency but seldom on an organized or consistent basis. An institution may receive very large gifts in one year, only to have three years of little or no giving before the next big gift. An organized program of planned giving creates a consistent funding source for the institution.

- **More and larger gifts.** Planned giving programs usually produce larger than average gifts. In highly developed programs, planned gifts may register in the high six figures or even seven figures. Planned giving discussions may also result in larger annual gifts because of a careful discussion of the donor's giving options.

- **Low-cost funds.** Planned giving traditionally has been a low-cost area. Unlike the annual fund, which relies on high volume and large budget, planned giving programs are often the smallest portion of a development office budget. The cost per dollar raised can be between 8 and 10 cents for an institution with an established program.

- **Easy to start.** While it is important to have a high level of expertise available to a planned giving program, it is not essential to have that expertise on staff when the program begins. A large percentage of planned gifts will come through bequests, usually in wills, revocable living trusts, and other estate planning vehicles. Any institution with a rudimentary understanding of what a will is and the ability to encourage gifts by will may have a successful planned giving program with little or no expertise required from staff. It is only when programs become wider ranging that more expertise is needed to address the planning needs of people considering life income plans and complex estate planning.

Tax Advantages to the Donor

If you are just beginning to study planned giving and its potential benefits for your institution, a quick review of the tax advantages of a planned gift will be useful. Gifts that are made outright provide maximum tax benefits to a donor. However, they also mean that the donor irrevocably relinquishes all right, title, and interest in the property contributed. Frequently, a planned gift is in the form of a life income plan, an irrevocable gift that has as one of its primary features an income paid back to the donor or to a person the donor designates. There are four principal reasons that donors make planned gifts of this type.

First, a gift to a life income plan creates an income tax charitable deduction. The amount of the charitable deduction is not the full fair market value of the property transferred, but rather an actuarially calculated value based on the amount of income the donor is to receive, the length of time the donor is to receive that income, and the ages of the donor and any other beneficiaries.

The higher the income paid to the donor or beneficiary, the lower the deduction. The longer the term of the life income plan, the lower the deduction. The character of the property transferred to the life income plan can also affect the value of the deduction. Gifts of tangible personal property, for example, do not receive the same treatment for tax purposes as gifts of cash, appreciated stocks, or bonds.

Second, appreciated assets contributed to a life income plan may be sold without realizing any capital gains. In other words, the donor avoids the capital gains tax on the sale of the asset as long as it is inside a life income plan, such as a charitable remainder trust. This provision is a great advantage when a donor contributes highly appreciated low-yield assets such as growth stocks or vacant real estate. Because of this feature, appreciated assets may be sold and then reinvested for higher income with no reduction in value due to the capital gains tax. The result: higher lifetime income for the donor.

Third, assets transferred to a life income plan can often be removed from the donor's estate. This advantage is particularly attractive for high-net-worth individuals who are subject to the gift and estate tax.

Fourth, a life income plan is advantageous in the case of real property. A person may manage real property but no longer enjoy the activity. By contributing assets to a trust that then sells the property, the donor has effectively eliminated the management headaches. The same can be said for an active investor who is aggressively buying and selling stocks and bonds. He or she may eventually tire of this activity and be eager to pass on the duties to someone else. A properly administered charitable remainder trust is the perfect solution.

The most frequent type of planned gift, however, is through a will or living trust. These gifts occur through a person's estate rather than during his or her lifetime. Under current estate tax law, a contribution to charity is 100 percent deductible. Therefore, a donor making a gift through an estate plan effectively eliminates any tax on the value of the gift.

The Gift Cycle

Just as planned giving is part of the overall cycle of giving, the individual planned gift has its own cycle. The cycle usually begins when a representative of a college or university has a discussion with a donor who is interested in planned giving. A long period of gestation—often several years—usually follows. Eventually, the prospective donor has more formal discussions with his or her advisors (an attorney or accountant, for example) or

with a representative of the institution. These technical discussions may take days, weeks, months, or even years before the donor is ready to move forward.

After the donor has reached the decision point, he or she is usually eager to complete his or her planning process and see the gift realized. Many different professionals can be involved—attorneys for legal drafting, accountants for number crunching and tax analysis, and university representatives for developing the gift agreement that designates what programs the gift will support and what, if any, recognition or naming opportunities the institution might grant.

The key to understanding the planned giving cycle is to realize that it is not a quick process. It takes patience, consistency, and willingness on the part of the institution to stay with the donor for many years.

The final phase in the planned giving cycle—the fulfillment phase—actually occurs *after* the gift is made. The donor has been intrigued, enticed, and promised many different benefits from the planned gift, from immortality to complete avoidance of all income taxes, estate taxes, and gift taxes. During the fulfillment phase, the income from a life income plan must be paid to the donor, investments must be made, tax returns must be filed, and filings with state regulatory agencies may be necessary. All of these responsibilities fall upon the business officer. It is not enough to have the gift signed. For the complete satisfaction of everyone involved, a strong fulfillment program must be in place.

What the Donor Expects

As you create a planned giving program, it is important to keep in mind how things look to the donor. If you develop a program that meets most of the donor's needs, you will be successful and run a highly effective program.

Simple and Easy to Understand

Too often in planned giving, we are caught up in professional jargon. We forget that donors do not know the jargon; nor do they care. You will hear a planned giving officer talk about CRUTs, CRATs, NIMCRUTs, FLIP-CRUTs, CGAs, FLPs, LLCs, and so on. Nobody understands this but other planned giving officers and some professional advisors.

Instead of calling it a charitable remainder unitrust with net income and makeup provisions, call it a "life income plan." Keep it easy enough for your grandmother to understand. The explanatory materials that you provide should be equally easy to understand. You don't need a 12-page treatise from a lawyer to convince your grandmother that a life income plan might be useful. Explain that she gets the income for life and that the income may be guaranteed (only for gift annuities; see Chapters 4 and 14), and tell her how much she will receive. The more technical aspects can be addressed during the overall process.

Planned giving programs often lack this kind of simplicity because well-meaning attorneys and CPAs emphasize the complexity of the gift techniques before showing people the benefits of a gift.

Ease of Access

You should also give your donors easy access to your program. All information related to planned giving should be available from one office, preferably from one or more professionals who work full-time in the area of planned giving. Ease of access also means a simplified way for donors to communicate their interest to your institution. Many planned giving programs offer toll-free telephone numbers. They provide response mechanisms such as business reply envelopes or cards in all mailings. Magazines published by the institutions frequently contain information about how to inquire about planned giving, including mail-in envelopes, mailing addresses, phone numbers, and even e-mail and Web site addresses. The more ways you are accessible to someone who is interested, the more planned gifts you will receive.

Prompt Response Time

When someone contacts your institution to express an interest in planned giving, you should respond promptly. "Prompt" is a relative term and need not be rigidly determined. In planned giving, years often elapse between the first conversation and the final gift. Any salesman will tell you, however, that if you can respond quickly to someone who is thinking about making a gift, you may find him or her in the "white heat" of interest and more likely to begin a positive conversation. The norm usually is some form of contact within a 24-hour period, primarily by phone. At a minimum, you should respond no later than a week after the inquiry.

Friendly Even When Saying No

Many gifts offered to institutions are simply not feasible for one reason or another. Often, the donor's intent is so high that the gift is simply not in his or her best interest and must be declined on ethical grounds. Sometimes the assets that are offered carry liability, such as toxic problems with a piece of real property. Whenever anyone from the institution (including and especially the business officer) communicates with a donor, he or she should provide a friendly and reasoned response to the offer. Even when the response is not positive—when the representative tells the donor that a particular piece of property is unsuitable or a certain type of gift structure is not within comfortable parameters for the institution—the message should be delivered with the utmost sensitivity to the donor and with respect for the possibility of a long-term relationship. A donor may propose a gift that is declined politely but then offer a different asset as the gift. Emphasis on donor relations is critical not just for the development officer but also for others involved in the planned gift, including the business officer.

The Business Officer's Role

From the donor's point of view, the business officer has a critical role in the entire relationship. This role will vary slightly from institution to institution. For smaller institutions, the business officer may have direct, ongoing contact with the donor and his or her advisors regarding all facets of the gift, from appraisal through final distribution of assets. For larger, more decentralized management structures, the business officer may be responsible for only one specific area, such as investment management or trust accounting.

The business officer is responsible for living up to any promises or commitments made to the donor in securing the planned gift. A knowledgeable business officer with good people skills can be a tremendous asset to an institution. Often the business officer provides the final element in the completion of a planned gift.

Seeking the Board's Approval

The first step in creating a new planned giving program is to seek the governing board's approval and endorsement. Usually, the development office makes a formal presentation to the board that outlines the benefits of a planned giving program and the likely institutional investment required to be successful. Frequently, business officers are included in the presentation, but the development office usually has primary responsibility. The board presentation should be viewed as an opportunity to educate board members on the benefits of planned giving. You can be persuasive by showing that planned giving offers a low-cost opportunity for increased cash flow, that tangible results will be seen within a short time, and that the next 20 years will be a boom time for planned gifts. Be prepared to answer these frequently asked questions.

How Long Will the Program Take to Pay Off?

Board members worry about the lag time between the establishment of the planned giving program and the eventual payoff. While there is no denying that the first couple of years may show few results, it is clear that most bequest programs, if run at an optimal level, will begin to see payoff in the third or fourth year. This payoff will rise to a steady stream of gifts, usually by the seventh year. Thus, the institution needs to make a commitment to forgo immediate payoff in the first two years with the understanding that some payoffs should be seen by the third and fourth years.

As a sideline benefit, it is very common for planned giving efforts to generate outright gifts. Often a donor will decide he or she really doesn't need the tax benefits and simply wants to make a gift to the institution. This is surprising to people who believe all gifts are tax motivated. However, charitable intent is often a major deciding factor for motivated donors. They will frequently make an outright gift instead of a deferred one simply to help the institution or to see a program or project benefit from their gift while they are alive. They will also make a gift that generates tax deductions they are unable to completely use under current tax law. Giving for the joy of giving does happen!

What Investment Is Required?

Although there are many reasons to be enthusiastic about a planned giving program, an investment by the board is required. First, the board must make an investment of time. They must not only be willing to allow the staff to spend time promoting the program, but they must also be ready to devote their own time to promotion. This investment is often shortchanged in a development office where the staff wears many hats. Just as it takes time to grow a garden, it takes time to develop a healthy program of planned gifts.

Second, planned giving requires an investment of cash. Depending on the financial strength of the institution and how quickly it wishes to develop a comprehensive program, the cash investment may be substantial. If you want to hire a full-time planned giving officer and give him or her the budget to market the program and meet with donors and professional advisors, the commitment will be significant. If you are merely considering adding this duty to the many duties of the development staff, it will still require an investment. Mailings, advertising, newsletters, and seminars all cost money.

What Is Our Potential for Success?

Any program can be successful at virtually any institution, but some institutions simply have more potential for success than others. If your institution has been in existence for longer than 20 years or has a constituency that is older than the average, then you may have the potential for much greater success in planned giving. If you are a young institution with mostly younger volunteers, you may have more trouble. Many institutions have to "grow into" a planned giving program. The maturity of the constituency is important. Institutions like Harvard and the American Cancer Society have such successful planned giving programs in part because their constituencies are the right age.

Be realistic in assessing your potential. How many donors do you currently have? How many of these donors are over the age of 60? What is their demographic profile? Are they high income? low income? renters? homeowners? All of these factors enter into the equation for success.

In addition, you should know about success stories in institutions similar to yours. If there are other area institutions with similar purposes or missions, have they been successful in planned giving? If there are other colleges or universities similar in size, structure, and age, have they been successful in planned giving? As part of your board presentation, you may be able to point to these examples as a signal that your program can be successful in a similar fashion.

What Is Our Potential Liability?

The board must be made aware of the potential liability that an institution undertakes when entering into a planned giving program. While the payoffs can be great, you must also look at the potential downside.

From an institutional standpoint, limiting liability is a fairly straightforward matter. If the institution is the beneficiary of an estate plan or another type of deferred gift, it always has the right to refuse the gift. This option should eliminate most of the major liability issues. Too often, an institution incorrectly assumes it must accept a gift. By disclaiming the right to receive a gift through an estate plan, you will be in a position to defend any liability claims that a third party may attach or attempt to attach to your institution.

It becomes more problematic to avoid liability when the institution has decided to serve as trustee, executor, or conservator for a donor or a gift. In California, for example, a trustee may be held liable for certain problems related to assets that are placed in trusts. While this is a very liberal interpretation of the law, this is the way one California court interpreted it. Other states may have less liberal interpretations, but the potential for a court deciding there is trustee liability is ever present. For this reason, it is important to understand that by serving as trustee or custodian of funds given to the institution by donors, especially where there are life income responsibilities, the institution is undertaking a significant duty and a potential liability.

Remember, however, that the number of institutions that have incurred serious liability on planned gifts is relatively small. In most of these cases, the institution has been careless in its administration of the planned giving program. A carefully managed program will not provide an unduly large liability exposure, and because the payoff is so significant, it can seldom be seen as a net liability.

What about the personal liability of governing board members? The answer to this question is less clear. Most planned giving programs operate on the staff level. The board endorses the program, and the staff manages and administers it. The general liability of individual board members usually is that of any individual serving in a fiduciary capacity. Most institutions of significant size carry some type of liability insurance for board members. Only in dire situations will a board member be held personally liable for the actions of an institution. In the case of planned gifts, however, personal liability is a possibility if the institution has not managed the funds carefully and has breached the fiduciary duty imposed on any trustee or executor.

Board members should be kept informed of the status of a planned giving program. How much information to provide board members is an open question. At a minimum, reports should include the number and market value of all planned gifts held on the institution's books. Changes from year to year or quarter to quarter can certainly be included in such reports. Many institutions like to platform their development operations as well and will show revocable gifts that have been confirmed in wills, revocable trusts, insurance policies, and other gift vehicles, even though they are not reflected on the financial statements. Frequently, large bequests are known many years prior to receipt and can be shown to the trustees as a future source of income or endowment. It is not unusual for older institutions to have far more future value in revocable gifts than in the trusts and annuities they include in financial statements.

Trustees should also be kept informed of any unusual arrangements that the institution enters into at a donor's request. These procedures are not intended to give board members veto power over such actions (although the board would always have such power). Rather, they ensure that board members are kept abreast of the risks and rewards inherent in a planned giving program. Even institutions with large governing boards often have a board committee that receives regular staff reports about all fund-raising activity and reports regularly to the full board on planned giving and other areas. This committee also receives regular accounting reports that show all existing life income plans and all income related to planned giving.

The bottom line on liability is fairly simple: When an institution has been careful, prudent, and attentive to its planned giving program, there has been little or no problem with liability, either at the institutional or the personal level. The courts have only attached liability to a governing board when there has been blatant abuse.

The Scope and Structure of a Planned Giving Program

One of the first decisions to be made in establishing a planned giving program is the overall scope. Do you want a comprehensive program or one that focuses only on bequests from wills and revocable trusts? Many programs thrive by focusing only on wills. Others move into the more sophisticated area of charitable trusts, annuities, pool funds, and lead trusts. The scope of the program will determine the costs and staffing needs.

For a smaller institution, the best approach often is to begin with a wills program that the development office can handle. When there is some success, you can begin to expand into life income plans and annuities. Hiring a part-time or full-time planned giving officer will come next.

There really is no one answer to how to approach the scope of your program. Even a fairly well developed program may not offer certain types of planned giving vehicles, such as a pooled income fund. If you have the staff expertise or can add new staff quickly, a full-service program can be established rapidly. Budget will often dictate the scope.

Oversight Responsibilities

One of the most important issues to discuss is responsibility for oversight of the planned giving program. Since most planned giving outreach programs are initiated from the fund-raising side of an institution, usually the vice president for institutional advancement or director of development has oversight for the overall program. While this structure is necessary from a management standpoint, it is not enough.

Since a planned giving program's first priority is to raise new money for the institution, the program also needs involvement from the financial side—ideally, the department that is most immediately affected by planned giving activities. Additional oversight should come from the business officer or, in larger institutions, the office of the treasurer or controller.

5

PLANNED GIVING PROGRAM LEVELS

LOW-LEVEL PROGRAM:

Staffing	No additional staff	
	Area assigned to nonexpert existing staff	
Budget	Less than $10,000	
Marketing	Will language available	
	Articles in in-house publications	
Gifts Sought	Wills	
	Trusts held by others	

MID-LEVEL PROGRAM:

Staffing	0.5–1.0 FTE staff	
	Frequently FTE an outside consultant	
Budget	Less than $50,000	
Marketing	Will language available	
	Articles in in-house publications	
	Direct mail	
	Seminars	
	Some one-to-one follow-up on direct mail respondents	
Gifts Sought	Wills and other revocable gifts	
	Trusts held by others	
	Gift annuities	

HIGH-LEVEL PROGRAM:

Staffing	1.0–5.0 FTE staff with 5+ years' experience	
	Frequently one or more with law degree or CPA designation	
Budget	More than $50,000 (Good staff members usually make $80K–$100K and often more)	
	Estimate for one experienced staff person, one support staff person, and an office and marketing budget of $150K–$200K	
Marketing	Will language available	
	Articles in in-house publications	
	Direct mail	
	Seminars	
	Organized program of one-to-one solicitation of alumni, donors, and direct mail respondents	
	Outreach to professional advisors	
	Web site	
Gifts Sought	Wills and other revocable gifts	
	Trusts held by others	
	Trusts managed by nonprofit	
	Gift annuities	
	Pooled income funds	
	Complex outright gifts	
	Complex estate gifts	

When the planned giving program is plugged in to both the fund-raising side and the financial side, the staff will be more aware of the issues faced throughout the institution. When a donor agrees to a planned gift, the institution is making a commitment for 20, 30, or 40 years. Everyone needs to be on board before these commitments are made. Do not proceed with developing a program if you have not reached agreement on the appropriate reporting requirements.

Gift Approval Process

Every type of gift should have an approval process. For checks and cash, this process is as easy as a written acknowledgment from the development officer. For more involved gifts, including planned gifts, a more formal approval process is necessary.

Gift Acceptance Committees

Many institutions create a gift acceptance committee to deal with one or two specific functions, such as the acceptance of gifts of real property or limited partnership interests. Acceptance committees can be both useful and incredibly bureaucratic, depending on how they are structured.

A large acceptance committee is like having no committee at all. You will be bogged down in too much consensus building within the group, and it will become an institutional waste of time. A small, select committee of three to four knowledgeable people can be very useful. If you are dealing with a sophisticated area such as real property, committee members—who may be board members or active volunteers—should be in that business. If no qualified members are active in the institution, recruit them. You need the expertise, and you need just a few people to make the committee workable.

Acceptance committees are a great help for business officers and development officers who are confronted with a willing (and possibly influential) donor but an inappropriate gift. The ability to tell the donor, "We really appreciate your offer, but the acceptance committee has refused the gift" can be a positive step toward a continuing relationship with the donor.

Staff Approval

The institution also needs a staff process that preapproves all gifts submitted to the acceptance committee. This process will weed out truly bad gifts that can be refused politely without involving committee members. Many institutions substitute staff approvals for a functioning acceptance committee. This is a viable option but exposes you to criticism from influential prospective donors.

Staff approval should begin with the planned giving officer or development officer. The development office must be clear that its job is more than just signing up donors and handing them to the business office for approval. A professional approach to gifting and a skeptical eye toward deals can go a long way toward eliminating bad gifts before they become a nuisance for other staff members. If the development staff feels the gift is viable and in the institution's best interest, there should be sign-off from a second person or office.

Some types of gifts can be streamlined to avoid wasting time. Outright gifts of publicly traded stock probably do not need the approval of the business office. They simply need to be processed and placed in the correct account. Staff approval becomes more important for assets that carry a potential liability for the institution. For example, a proposed gift of real property can often be a simple matter. However, if the property offered is a commercial structure that was used as a dry cleaning establishment, has a garage in the back where mechanics work on cars, and was once an industrial waste dump, the property needs to be reviewed carefully by experts. Real property gifts usually are approved by the office in charge of all properties, often the office of property management but in smaller institutions sometimes the business office. No gift of real property should be accepted until the development or planned giving office and the office of property management or business office have signed off on it. The property management office should do a site inspection, title checks, and other steps to determine whether the property carries any problems. Only after approval by both offices should any gift of real property—either outright or a life income plan—be submitted to an acceptance committee or accepted directly.

General Policies and Procedures

Many people feel that policies and procedures are vital to a planned giving program. Carefully constructed policies and effective, streamlined procedures can be useful, but a large handbook filled with hundreds of pages of minutiae tends to waste time and slow people down. But policies do have a place in a planned giving program. They should help to clarify how the program will function. Statements should be made about what you accept and what you do not accept. Statements should be made about the types of gift vehicles you will work with and the ones you will not. Statements should be made about what types of assets you are willing to consider taking and the ones you will not. Statements should be made about the types of recognition carried by each type of gift. And finally, policy statements need to be made for the edification of the staff regarding those offices and/or persons who are directly responsible for the intake of gifts that have been closed. These objectives can be met by effective, simple policies. Anything beyond that is simply an invitation to more bureaucracy (see Appendix I for a sample gift policy statement).

Gift Acceptance Criteria

Specific gift acceptance criteria for all types of gifts, including outright gifts of difficult assets, are sometimes useful. These criteria will include all procedural steps. If you have worked through a gift approval process when considering a gift, the acceptance criteria will simply reflect the decision that you have already made. For example, the criteria might state that following the approval of the office of planned giving, no gift of real property shall be accepted until the office of property management (or the treasurer's office, or the business office) has reviewed and approved it.

Asset Class Policies

Sometimes a policy is based on the type of asset that is being proposed as a gift. Many policy manuals specifically state that gifts of cash, securities, real property, insurance, mutual funds, and retirement plans shall be encouraged. Each asset class then has its own formal acceptance procedures and policies, which usually are related to the gift acceptance procedures and the mechanisms for formal transfer of the assets to the institution.

Gift Technique Policies

Policies based on gift technique relate to the mechanism used to make the gift. "Outright gifts shall be encouraged" is a famous policy statement that does not need to be in writing. The techniques that most often require policies are gifts in trust, gift annuity contracts, and pooled income funds. A few institutions have policies related to lead trusts.

Technique-related policies are consistent with legal requirements. For example, a pooled income fund may not invest in a tax-free investment, such as a municipal bond. These stipulations are often expressed as policies as a reminder for staff. If the law changes, the policy must be updated.

Where your institution is planning to serve as trustee or co-trustee most policies for charitable remainder trusts suggest the types of trusts that are acceptable (in most institutions, it is usually all types) and state limitations on the level of income donors will receive. This type of policy may appear to be useful, but it may end up being ignored in the pursuit of a gift and thus reduce

the effectiveness of policies overall. If a donor offers a $100 million gift in a charitable remainder trust with a 10 percent payout, it is doubtful that you would turn it down even if your policy limited payouts to 8 percent.

In using policies based on technique, the most effective approach is to create policies only for items that are part of your institution's overall focus. A policy statement that encourages planned gifts has little impact, but a statement that only certain types of planned gifts will be handled has more validity. If you have a specific focus, such as wills, then your policies should state it clearly (see Appendix I for examples).

Recognition Policies

Recognition policies should be incorporated into the same overall policy statements that are developed for asset classes and planned giving techniques. While the development office will be most responsible for these policies, the policies should be incorporated clearly into any overall planned giving plan.

Recognition policies should include the different types of recognition that are available to donors upon the completion of a gift. Outright gifts often are recognized in a more substantial fashion than gifts by will. The reason is simple: The cash is an immediate benefit to the institution, while the will is deferred and may even be changed by the donor later. Recognition for life income plans is a typical feature of many development programs. During campaigns, when every dollar is being counted, charitable trusts and gift annuity contracts often are counted and recognized at face value, even though the recognition probably should be based on the discounted present value of the gift. This policy seems only fair when compared to the outright gift. If someone gives you $1 million in cash today, and another person puts $1 million into a charitable trust that will not mature for 30 to 40 years, should they really be given the same recognition? These kinds of policy decisions should be worked out with the development office. They make everyone's life a lot easier, because staff members will not need to negotiate the recognition for every gift. They will be able to refer to the policy manual to determine what recognition is available for a gift at a particular level.

More information on recognition policies can be found in the third edition of *Management and Reporting Standards: Standards for Annual Giving and Campaigns in Educational Fund Raising*, published by the Council for Advancement and Support of Education (CASE) in 2004.

Intake Policies

Every gift to your institution eventually will be received through the business office. However, it is wise to develop specific intake policies. While cash and checks are fairly easily disposed of by hand delivery to the appropriate business officer, gifts of securities, real estate, assets such as boats, cars, and coins, and intangible assets require specialized handling and processing. Every type of asset should have a clearly identified point of intake that bears some logical connection to the gift being offered. Development officers will readily accommodate any clear procedure that allows them to deliver a gift as soon as it has been closed. Intake policies should also include checks and balances that will eliminate the unwitting acceptance of problem assets.

As you develop intake points, keep in mind that different assets will require different reviews before official acceptance. At a large institution, the office of property management or a similar office will handle most assets. However, the treasurer's office usually is responsible for transfers of securities. Other types of assets require a decision. For example, the property management office or the treasurer might handle an interest in a real estate limited partnership, so a policy must be developed to eliminate any confusion. If there are questions about responsibility, it is best to work them out at the policy level before an asset sits in a holding account waiting for two departments to work out their territorial issues.

Suggested intake points for different assets are as follows:

- Cash: Cashier's office

- Securities: Treasurer's office

- Real estate: Property management office

- Other tangible assets (such as boats, cars, planes, trains, art, coins, and collectibles): Property management office

- Intangible assets (such as copyrights, licenses, and royalties): Property management office

I cannot emphasize enough the need to make the policies and procedures as simple and streamlined as possible. Too many institutions become bogged down in their policies. They waste time writing the policies and arguing about them rather than going out and getting new gifts.

The following chapters describe the gift types and techniques that can be developed to form a comprehensive planned giving program that suits the needs and interests of a variety of donors.

RECOMMENDED ACTIONS

1. Before seeking board approval, determine what your planned giving program is going to look like: full service, limited offerings, or bequests only.

2. Based on #1, project the timeline before a satisfactory volume of gifts will begin to be booked and actually realized as income.

3. Based on #1, estimate the costs to staff and market the program for the timeline determined in #2 above.

4. Seek board approval after determining #1–3.

5. Develop a flow chart for the solicitation, acceptance, processing, and management of each type of planned gift that you plan to offer, including the steps required to terminate a gift either at the request of the donor or due to the death of the last income beneficiary.

chapter two

OUTRIGHT GIFTS

Outright gifts are the most frequent type of gift that a college or university receives. They are also the most desirable, and the only major policy issue is the speed with which you thank the donor.

From the donor's tax standpoint, however, an outright gift of cash is seldom the best method of giving. A more attractive method is to transfer highly appreciated assets such as stocks, bonds, or other securities. These types of gifts require some analysis and a definite institutional policy concerning their acceptance. Gifts of real estate raise even more complex issues, but they are equally advantageous for the donor from a tax standpoint if they have appreciated in value from the date of purchase or if the owner has taken depreciation deductions against them for tax purposes.

Policies

Policies for outright gifts are probably the most useful types of policies since they generally provide for the acceptance of virtually anything that is given outright. They also delineate the institution's basic requirements concerning acceptable risk, liability analysis, and gift crediting.

A general gift policy usually specifies a basic willingness to accept gifts of any type of asset. This approach is preferable, since any asset that has an ascertainable value and can be resold is potentially a good gift. Policies become more important when dealing with assets other than cash.

An outright gifts policy generally includes acceptance of gifts of negotiable securities. Acceptance of all securities, however, is both unnecessary and unwise. For example, a gift of an interest in a bankrupt company or one that may have toxic waste liabilities would need to be analyzed. While corporations generally create liability protection for shareholders, there is the possibility that shareholders will be held liable for the actions of a corporation where public policy demands such accountability. For this reason, gifts of traded securities are preferable to gifts of securities that are closely held. (Closely held companies have shares outstanding but are

not publicly traded and have not qualified under federal or state securities laws.) A statement explaining which types of securities are completely acceptable and which types will be evaluated for possible acceptance is a useful part of any outright gifts policy.

The single most complex outright gift is a gift of real property. An acceptance policy for real property gifts should carry the caveat that properties will be accepted only after approval by either the director of property management, the business officer, or an acceptance committee of volunteer experts. Real property carries heavy liabilities and risks. Once an institution's name is on the title to a piece of property, all future claims against the property may easily run back to the institution, which is likely to be considered a "deep pocket" by potential litigants.

Policy statements should also be in place to clarify the types of tangible personal property that are and are not acceptable as gifts. For example, the University of Southern California has a general policy against accepting boats as gifts—not because boats have no potential value, but because they require a tremendous investment in ongoing maintenance and upkeep that amounts to more than the average value of the gift. Similar decisions can be made for other types of assets, including cars and airplanes.

Assets that are considered intangible personal property—such as copyrights, licenses, and royalties—may also need to be excluded. For example, mineral rights for oil wells may be a wonderful gift, but they may carry a huge potential liability for cleanup of the drilling operation. Often it is simpler to say no than to accept the gift and then face the potential consequences.

Acceptance

Most acceptance committees consider outright gifts only in unusual situations or when there are very difficult assets that need to be analyzed. Usually, the staff analyzes potential outright gifts and makes informed decisions. The acceptance committee is a useful mechanism, however, for politely turning down gifts that the staff recommends not accepting.

Transfer of Cash

For tax purposes, an outright gift of cash is made when the cash or check is placed *under the control of* the college or university—usually, when a staff member or faculty member takes physical possession of the asset. Completion of a gift for tax purposes occurs on the date the donor mails a check via the U.S. Postal Service. Mailing by private mailing service does not trigger completion of a gift. When a private company is used, the gift is completed only upon receipt of the actual check or cash.

Gifts of cash are recorded on the date actually received, either directly or through an agent of the institution, such as the development officer. The gifts are placed in either the general fund or a restricted fund, as determined by the donor and the institution, and a gift receipt is issued to the donor for the amount of the gift.

The receipt does not determine the date of gift for tax purposes; rather it serves simply as verification that a gift was made. It memorializes the gift, indicating the date the institution actually controlled the assets given. The taxpayer must verify the date that a completed gift was made by another means, such as a postmark, check date, or letter from the institution indicating a date of receipt. As anyone who has worked at year-end in a nonprofit institution will tell you, gifts often flood their offices in late December, but receipts are not issued until January or February. This does not mean the gifts were made in January or February, but that the taxpayer will need other verification.

Transfer of Stock

The delivery rules for gifts of stock are somewhat complex, and they vary depending on how the owner holds his or her shares.

Through a Brokerage Firm

The typical method—and the easiest situation for transferring stock—is to hold the shares in "street name," usually at a brokerage firm. The donor writes a letter instructing the broker to transfer shares from the donor's brokerage account to the college or university. The broker consults a representative of the institution—usually the business officer or treasurer—for transfer instructions and then transfers the shares to the appropriate account. It is not unusual for an institution to maintain accounts at all major brokerage firms to facilitate these transfers. The donor's gift is considered made when the broker, under instructions from the donor, starts acting on behalf of the institution—usually when the broker begins the process of transfer to the institution's account.

By Endorsement or Stock Power

The shares may also be held personally, in the donor's name. This may mean that the donor has physical possession, and very often, the shares will have his or her name on the certificates as well as on the records of the corporation. When the donor's name is imprinted on the certificates, there are two basic methods for making a gift. The most common method is for the donor to endorse the back of each certificate, either naming the institution as the new owner or "in blank"(the donor signs the forms but leaves the new owner designation line blank). The other method is to execute a signed stock power authorizing the institution to exercise control and authority over the certificates that are in the name of the donor. Once the donor has signed the certificates, they become negotiable.

Delivery of the endorsed physical shares into the possession of the institution is enough to be considered a gift. For tax purposes, the transfer date sets the date of the gift. The donor may also mail the certificates via the U.S. Postal Service and consider the gift made on the date of mailing. This method is not the best way to make a gift, since it involves a certain risk of loss. If the certificates are endorsed "in blank," they are fully negotiable if stolen; if they are endorsed to the institution, they still may be converted to the use of other people. The wisest way is to transfer the shares by using a signed stock power. The stock power is a form usually provided by brokerage firms, which allows the donor to authorize the charity to exercise control over the shares. The stock power works independently from the share certificates and allows the donor to gift unendorsed certificates to the charity. When making a gift of stock by mail it is best to mail the share certificates in one envelope and the stock power in another envelope, thereby reducing the risk of loss and providing security for the transfer.

Over the last few years, it has become virtually impossible to have a stock power accepted as valid by a brokerage firm without a "medallion guarantee" by a bank. Banks are reluctant to issue a medallion guarantee to someone who is not a customer, causing problems when a donor uses something other than a bank—for example, a credit union—as his or her primary financial institution. Medallion guarantees are as cumbersome as notary stamps to obtain, and even the wealthiest donors can have difficulties. Be aware of possible delays when a donor attempts to transfer securities using a stock power, especially when trying to time a year-end gift.

Through a Transfer Agent

Another method for gifts of personally held securities is to make a formal transfer of ownership on the books and records of the transfer agent for the corporation, a procedure that requires several weeks. Corporate transfer agents are usually large institutions, primarily located on the East Coast, who serve as the official record keeper for all stock ownership. Each share of stock is recorded with the name of a particular owner on it. When stock is held "in street name" the transfer agent indicates the brokerage firm where the stock is held. When the stock is held personally, the actual owners are listed in the transfer agent's records.

To facilitate a transfer of ownership, the owner of the certificates must make a written request to transfer the shares to the college or university, taking the timing of the gift out of the donor's and the institution's control and placing it in the hands of the transfer agent. It is advisable to urge donors to choose a more expeditious method, but sometimes a donor initiates the transaction before talking with the staff. The donor may contact the transfer agent and cancel the transfer, or the institution can contact the agent to encourage quick processing. However, even rapid transfers by transfer agents still take two to four weeks.

By Electronic Transfer

A donor may also transfer securities directly to the custodian (DTC) for the college or university. DTC transfers—the most widespread method currently employed—are fast and efficient. The instructions are fairly simple, requiring account numbers and the appropriate routing numbers. Most financial institutions can accommodate DTC transfers.

Some people are concerned with the actual date of gift on this type of transfer. This is a false problem, since usually the question is directed at when a gift is made *for tax purposes,* not the actual date of gift shown on the records of the institution. The institution does not determine the date of gift for tax purposes. The institution commonly shows a different date of gift than what the donor claims for tax purposes, and each one can be correct for its own purpose. That being said, the IRS will consider the date when the funds are transferred to the charity as the date of gift for the donor, not the date when the donor instructed the bank to make the transfer.

Transfer of Real Property

Executing a Deed

No transfer of real property is valid unless reduced to writing, usually in the form of a deed. A deed describes the property in legal terms and includes a clear statement transferring the property from the current owner (the donor) to the new owner (the college or university).

Types of deeds include:

- Grant deeds, which transfer the fee simple absolute title. Fee simple absolute is the ultimate clear title in a piece of real property. This is the best and clearest form of ownership under law.

- Quit-claim deeds, which transfer only the donor's interest in the property, whatever that title may be. This type of title can be valid but leaves the possibility of third-party claims to the property since the donor is transferring only the rights to the property that they currently own.

- Warranty deeds, common in some but not all states, which guarantee that the title is free and clear of all liens and encumbrances.

Deeds of transfer often include notations concerning qualifications for tax purposes under state laws (California in particular); easements held by third parties, such as easements for environment or historic purposes as well as physical easements from landowners to permit access to and from roads or rivers; or rights to be retained by the donor, such as a retained life estate and lifetime right to usage. A deed must be signed by all property owners and usually requires notarization. Once a deed has been executed, it is valid between the parties to the transaction. It is a simple document to execute and usually requires no more than one page. A deed is not valid as a gift until the new named owner has signed the deed or other acceptance documents. A person cannot transfer property to a charity without it knowing about it and agreeing to it. Lack of acceptance by the charity defeats the claim of a gift by the donor.

Recording a Deed

Many people do not realize that a deed is valid as an instrument of transfer whether or not it has been recorded. However, formal recording is necessary to protect the interest of the college or university against third-party claims to the property. In theory, once the deed has been executed the donor is no longer in possession of the property, but if the donor sells the property to a third party who then records the deed ahead of the institution, the third party would be deemed to be the owner. Recording establishes the date the ownership changed. Once recorded, the college or university is the official owner. It is good policy to routinely record gifts of real property as soon as possible upon execution of the deed.

Title Searches and Title Insurance

Title insurance becomes an important part of a transaction involving a quit-claim deed, which is executed when a donor may not be certain about his or her general rights to a piece of property. Ideally, the donor should transfer clear title to the college or university. However, since this is a gift, not a sale, many donors do not want to bother with this step. Quit-claim deeds are often used on behalf of estates in which the lawyers and executors wish to discharge their duties without worrying about title. Since most gifts of property are considered immediately for resale, property title searches are necessary and title insurance should be issued. Title insurance can cover all contingencies related to title and often help "clean up" the title for the recipient institution. A preliminary title report is sufficient to identify problems with the title. However, such a report is informational in nature and not the same as title insurance. Each institution must decide how much protection it requires prior to acquiring a property.

Gifts of Personal Property

Possession

The best way to facilitate the transfer of personal property is by taking possession. Once the property is in the physical possession of the institution, the gift has been made. A third party may hold the gift if the third party is clear that they take instructions from the institution, not the donor. For example, items such as paintings may require special storage facilities. Frequently owners do not display their entire collection and use such facilities for long-term holdings. A gift is considered completed when such a facility begins to take direction from and to deal with the institution rather than taking instructions from the donor.

Receipts and Deeds of Gifts

When the development officer or business officer takes possession of a gift of personal property, it is customary to issue a receipt or execute a deed of gift. The receipt indicates that a staff member from the institution has accepted possession of the property. The deed of gift is a more formal mechanism for transferring ownership. A deed of gift functions as a quasi-deed (although not usually recorded) and often includes a description of the purposes for which the gift was given and any eventual uses of the gift.

Proof of Ownership

Proof of ownership of tangible personal property is important. If the donor purchased the asset, a copy of a receipt may be available. If not, sometimes there is other evidence, such as a newspaper article describing the donor's purchase of a painting or other artifact. When

a donor has no proof to indicate actual ownership of the assets, problems can result. For example, an owner of pre-Columbian art may be in violation of several international conventions regarding theft of artwork from its country of origin. The date that such an asset was acquired is essential to determine what laws were in effect at the time of acquisition and what rules or laws may govern its eventual resale. Certain assets acquired after prohibitions were passed may need to be returned to the country of origin (often without reimbursement for acquisition costs).

Gifts of Intangible Personal Property

Intangible personal property gifts are infrequent but do occur. Because of their nature, these assets generally are memorialized in writing. Copyrights and patents, for example, are formally recorded by name, and mineral rights are usually formalized through certain types of deeds. Transfers of intangible personal property are executed by deed or instrument of transfer. These documents need not be complex and can be drafted by most attorneys.

Valuation of Outright Gifts

Valuations for the General Ledger

Determining the valuation of an outright gift for tax purposes is fairly simple. For cash gifts, it is the face value. For gifts of publicly traded securities, the valuation is the median value—the high-low average of the stock price on the date of transfer. The stock is deemed to be transferred on the date the donor no longer exercises control of the stock—usually the date the broker transfers the assets from the donor's account to the institution's account. Accountants sometimes argue that the date the institution sells the assets should be the transfer date, an approach that is not accurate from a tax standpoint but may be valid from an accounting standpoint. An institution might delay the liquidation of stock for several days or even weeks, but a donor deserves to have the median valuation on the date closest to the attempted transfer date.

Valuations of gifts of real property are based on a qualified appraisal or, occasionally, on proceeds from the sale of the property. A nonprofit institution is prohibited from being involved in the valuation process. Since weeks or months may pass from the time of transfer to the final liquidation, booking gifts at the proceeds value is seldom appropriate. A qualified appraisal is required for the donor's tax purposes. An institution usually works with a donor on the appraisal. Although the institution can have no formal control over the appraisal process, it can evaluate whether it is willing to accept the appraisal as the value for booking purposes. Appraisers are relatively restrained in their evaluations of real property, since they do have a liability under the current tax laws. If the institution accepts the appraisal, that value becomes the booking value. If the institution does not find the valuation acceptable, a separate internal appraisal is then acquired. This decision may result in a more accurate valuation, but it can be a disaster for donor relations. If a donor believes a property is worth $1 million but the institution wants to book it at $600,000, you can have a difficult and embarrassing situation.

Valuations of gifts of tangible and intangible personal property also require a qualified appraisal for tax purposes. Appraisers who specialize in these areas do exist, but their services can be quite costly. Most institutions make an internal decision about whether an appraisal is acceptable. If an appraisal appears to be overstated, the institution will attempt to get an internal appraisal.

The problem for the business officer is that once a gift has been booked at a particular value, the subsequent sale of the asset will result in a gain or loss on investments for accounting purposes. Since the outright gift has become an asset of the institution, its subsequent sale at a loss is viewed as a loss on an investment. This is a puzzling result but one that seems to be consistent under FASB Statements of Financial Accounting Standards (see Nos. 116 and 117).

Valuations for Development Campaign Purposes

The Council for Advancement and Support of Education (CASE) Management Reporting Standards mirror the valuation issues for the general ledger. CASE values all outright gifts either at face value or at market value, as determined. The only obvious problem arises when assets are overvalued and booked at ridiculously high valuations. CASE standards are more complex for gifts with retained interests, such as life estates or charitable trusts and annuities.

Liquidation of Outright Gifts

Policies

Why should an institution have a policy of immediate liquidation? Large gifts of difficult assets such as real property and tangible personal property frequently carry with them administrative and management headaches that most institutions prefer to avoid. For example, rental real estate must be managed, rents collected, and delinquent tenants evicted. Vacant land can require constant upkeep, such as "weed abatement," or can be used by unauthorized persons, creating potential liabilities for the owner, such as land used for dirt bike races by local teenagers, etc. Tangible personal property creates many of the same problems, such as storage in special facilities for works of art or security systems for collections of rare coins or stamps. Most institutions prefer to receive cash that can then be reinvested in a formal cash management program.

Institutions can make exceptions for income producing assets that may be more valuable than their cash equivalents, for example real estate that has been placed under a very favorable lease. While the same administrative issues mentioned above still apply, it is more efficient to make exceptions to the immediate liquidation rule for special situations than to make decisions about every gift of real or personal property as they are received. Save your exceptions for the truly exceptional opportunities and liquidate the rest.

A policy statement regarding liquidation is useful for donor relations purposes. Most institutions do not want to hold outright gifts of real property and tangible or intangible personal property, but rather wish to access the value these assets represent. When dealing with donors, however, it is critical to clarify that you have a liquidation policy. It is easier for a donor to know before making the gift that a prized collection of butterflies will be sold at auction. That way, the donor will not learn after the fact that the collection is not displayed proudly in the president's office but was converted to cash to buy light bulbs and paperclips. The standard policy for outright gifts should be one of immediate liquidation of any noncash assets. Holding the assets should be an exception to general policy.

An institution's policy should not indicate any willingness or intention to hold an outright gift of property for any length of time at the request of a donor. IRS rules governing the sale of contributed assets by nonprofit institutions require the nonprofit to report on Form 8282 the sale of any asset that it has received during the prior two-year period. This report is compared to the donor's Form 8283, which claims a charitable deduction for the value of the gift. Obviously, Form 8282 highlights for the IRS any wide discrepancies between valuation and actual sales price. Any strings that are attached to a gift negate the tax deductibility of that gift. The implication that this practice is followed in your institution could jeopardize the charitable deductions of donors who have made good-faith efforts to make outright gifts following the law.

Private Inurement Issues

The term "private inurement" refers to any benefit a private individual may receive from the activities of a nonprofit charitable institution. This usually refers to some type of business transaction, rather than to the salaries or reasonable fees paid to professionals for their services. Any time a private individual "profits" from the activities of a nonprofit institution, it is possible that the issue of private inurement will be present. Private inurement can cause great harm to an institution and jeopardize its tax-exempt status. It is of particular concern when liquidating gifts of property. If your policy is to liquidate properties immediately upon receipt, it is very clear that you must be careful about who purchases the property. You cannot accept a gift from a father and then quietly resell it to his son at a low value.

Where you receive assets with the intent to liquidate, you should liquidate through normal business channels. Real estate should be listed with a real estate agent or a brokerage firm that is actively engaged in that business. Tangible or intangible property should be sold through an auction house or another mechanism that does not benefit one individual or family. The liquidation activity must be scrutinized carefully to ensure that anyone in the public domain can buy the property and that there is no attempt to exclude potential buyers through prior arrangement with the donor. The concept of a "prearranged sale" is common in tax law, and it negates the charitable gift. When party A contributes a property to a nonprofit institution to be resold to party B, the sale is considered prearranged if party A and party B both knew that this was the intent of the gift and the agreement was in writing or the institution either fails to market the property to the general public or takes steps to limit the number of potential buyers in such a way as to ensure that party B is the purchaser. The IRS will rule that the sale constitutes private inurement because the institution sold the property by prearrangement to party B. The donor will not receive a charitable deduction and, if the property has been sold for a profit, will be viewed as receiving ordinary income or capital gains income on the sale. This result is not positive for the donor and certainly will cause harm to the institution's standing with the IRS. (This concern should not stop an institution from working with donors who wish to contribute property that already has an interested buyer. Prearrangements must usually be in writing when dealing with real property. Verbal agreements are not legally binding with respect to real property and seldom cause a problem with private inurement, unless other factors are present, such as "insider status" with the charity or the third party being a family member of the donor, etc.)

Keep in mind that the IRS conducts institutional audits that review a nonprofit's activities from A to Z. By suggesting that the institution is involved in less-than-appropriate activities, you may open the door for the IRS to audit everything in your operations, from executive salaries and benefits to gift acquisition methods. An institutional audit is an onerous and trying experience that can consume huge amounts of time and money.

RECOMMENDED ACTIONS

1. Your general acceptance policies should be broad. Focus specifics on those types of assets you do not want, such as boats, livestock, game mounts, etc. You can always make exceptions when prudent.

2. Keep your acceptance procedures streamlined and respond quickly to donors.

3. Educate development officers on the key acceptance issues for difficult assets such as real estate or closely held corporate stock. They can prescreen gifts.

4. Keep open accounts at most active brokerage firms in your community. Ask for reduced fee arrangements (institutional rates) for the sale of gifts of securities.

chapter three

BEQUESTS

Bequests are usually the single largest source of planned gifts. Most, if not all, institutions are ready to accept gifts by bequest at any time, and a general policy statement to this effect is usually included in overall gift acceptance policies. As with other gifts, however, it is not mandatory to accept a bequest. Therefore, any relevant policy should indicate that while the institution encourages gifts through estate plans, the institution reserves the right to refuse any such gift for any policy reasons. These reasons may include the difficulty of the asset that the donor proposes to give. For example, a herd of livestock, while perhaps valuable, may be too much of a bother for an inner-city institution to deal with. The laws of every state allow charities to "disclaim" a gift attempted to be made through an estate plan. That asset then remains in the estate and is distributed under the estate's provisions. If the charity is the residual beneficiary of the entire estate or a portion of it, the property usually is either passed on to other institutions at the discretion of the executor or escheats to the state.

Speaking with One Voice

When dealing with a gift by bequest, the institution should charge one person with the responsibility for oversight of outside attorneys, executors, and other professionals who are involved in the final distributions from an estate. As a beneficiary, the institution has legal rights to information regarding an estate. As a first step, it should be routine practice for the institution to contact the attorney for the executor and request all the pertinent legal documents related to the estate. As an estate is probated, the executor will be required to file an accounting of all assets and to inform the court on a regular basis of progress toward the completion of the probate. An institution that monitors the progress will be in a position to question excessive fees charged by the attorneys or executor; observe obvious underprice sale of major assets, such as real estate; or identify missing assets that the institution knew were in the donor's possession before death.

The routine can be condensed into several form documents. A standard letter requesting information should be sent immediately upon notification of probate. A system should be established for contacting the executors or attorneys every two to three months. Most probates will take six to eight months to complete; difficult assets can take longer. If it appears that the probate is taking an excessive amount of time and continuing to incur attorneys' and accountants' fees, it is the beneficiary's right to take legal action seeking an explanation for this delay. Often a court appearance is not necessary, because the delays are reasonable and understandable. If the delays are not reasonable, the court has the power to replace the executor or attorney.

Suggested Bequest Language

It is useful to provide suggested bequest language that prospective donors can use to create a bequest by will. Include the legal name of the institution, wording to create a named fund and/or endowment fund for the gift, and wording to authorize handling of the gift in a certain way, such as authorization to commingle funds for investment purposes. You may also include suggested language for creating various types of gifts, such as an endowed scholarship fund, an endowed professorship or chair, and special funds for research and teaching. The planned giving advisory committee, especially the attorney members, can develop this language.

Authority for Legal Documents

One or more staff members must have clear signing authority for gifts from estates. This requirement may appear obvious, but many institutions have not made this assignment. When a development officer or other staff member receives a check along with a receipt to be signed, it is easy to sign the document and return it to the estate, an action that may result in a reduction in the total amount of money the institution receives.

Signing authority should be given to the offices that are directly related to the administration of the bequest program, preferably either the general counsel's office or the business office. In rare instances, it may be appropriate for an experienced development office to have signing authority. It should be clear throughout the institution that only certain offices or individuals may sign for bequests on behalf of the institution.

Rights of Beneficiaries

The beneficiary of an estate has rights to full disclosure and timely accounting for all activities in and during the probate. These rights, as delineated under state law, are protected by the probate court. Beneficiaries usually receive notification of inclusion in a probate estate, all filings made by the executor on behalf of the probate estate with the court, and full disclosure of any issues relating to the probate estate. These general rights are stronger when the beneficiary is receiving a larger portion of the estate. In the case of a small bequest of a specified amount of money, with no assets attached to the gift, your institution's standing in terms of influencing the probate is probably small, although a court will certainly make sure that you are fully informed. If your institution is the residuary beneficiary of the entire estate, with large dollar amounts and significant assets at stake, you will have a lot more influence with the court.

The institution's standing in the probate is the same as that of a family member who is receiving information from the executor. While you do not want to be a nuisance, you do want the institution to receive the assets that the deceased has given it. This is not something to be shy about; simply be sensitive to the people who are involved in the process. The institution has rights, and you should not hesitate to assert them where it appears that these interests are not being considered in the overall administration of the probate estate.

Right to Documents from the Estate

Once an estate has entered probate, the beneficiaries have the right to receive all related documents, including the will or trust that is the primary estate planning vehicle, along with all codicils and amendments to those documents that are on file in the probate court. These documents should be reviewed to determine the type of gift the donor has made to the institution. Estates often provide bequests of specific assets. This stipulation can be important in the overall resolution of an estate and needs to be monitored carefully.

Right to an Accounting

Along with a right to documents, beneficiaries have the right to review all accounting documents filed with the probate court. These documents include the initial asset inventory along with accountings of expenditures and income received by the estate during the probate period. Small estates may have just one or two documents, but larger estates may provide continual accountings over a period of years.

The business office or the general counsel's office should review the accounting reports to determine if they are reasonable and necessary expenses for the estate. Many states allow percentage fees to attorneys and executors. Other states have recognized the abuses inherent in this system and require billing statements from attorneys and other professionals that must be approved by the court. Be aware of which system is in place in your state, along with the allowable percentage rates. Review the bills along with any accountings filed by the attorneys for an estate.

The beneficiary has the right to seek an accounting through the probate court if information is not forthcoming from the executor or attorneys for the executor. Nonprofits rarely exercise this right, but it is important to know that you have this right. Any executor who is not forthcoming with information should be viewed suspiciously and monitored carefully.

Liquidation of Assets

It is not unusual for an executor, especially in a smaller estate, to wish to deed over to an institution real estate that has been left in a probate estate. The executor or the executor's attorney may be unwilling to spend time on an estate that will generate low fees. Your institution needs a policy specifying whether you will accept gifts of real property or prefer to have the executor liquidate such assets before distribution to you.

There are obvious advantages to having the executor liquidate the assets and hand over the proceeds to the institution. You will not have any of the administrative headaches related to the liquidation of property or any of the general issues related to holding costs and the administration and upkeep of properties before their sale. For difficult assets, you will not have responsibilities related to evaluation and valuation, including the handling of appraisals for purposes of booking the gifts as assets and for validation for any future sales of the assets. On the other hand, you will not control the liquidation of the assets and may find the executor's process to be less than optimal.

If you decide that the institution will liquidate the assets, you will accept the headaches. However, if the executor is not a professional executor or an attorney frequently involved in probates, it may be in the institution's best interest to handle the liquidation, especially if the assets require some attention. Maximizing the value of an estate can yield additional benefits in the form of higher prices and better terms if handled by the institution.

The institution may make the final policy decision on an ad hoc basis. If you have a small staff and are not equipped to handle bequests of real property, liquidation of assets by the executor is usually the better choice. But if you have a high volume of bequest income, it may be better to assign a staff member full-time to this activity and develop a systematic way of liquidating assets. The result may be additional revenue for the institution.

RECOMMENDED ACTIONS

1. Have preprinted bequest language and tax ID number available for all who ask.

2. Assign responsibility for monitoring open estates to a specific person.

3. Develop procedures and form letters to initiate contact with, and request pertinent documents (including all accountings) from, executors and attorneys.

4. Make clear to internal constituencies—including development officers, deans, and faculty—who is responsible for signing all legal documents related to any estate gift.

5. Publicize internally your procedures for handling estates, including the person who should receive all notices of probate and other documents that may be sent to someone at your institution.

chapter four

CHARITABLE GIFT ANNUITIES

Charitable gift annuities, which originated in the Middle Ages, are a highly popular type of life income plan because of their relatively high payout rates and the simplicity of the annuity concept. The American Council on Gift Annuities (ACGA) provides suggested payout rates for nonprofits. The ACGA rates use conservative actuarial assumptions and are designed to provide a residual gift to the institution of approximately 50 percent, assuming certain internal rates of return on investments and standard overhead charges against the accounts. The council meets regularly and adjusts the payout rates to reflect the current investment climate of the national and international markets (see Appendix B for contact information).

Policies

Gift annuities require certain policies to ease the administration of the program. First, you must decide whether to use the ACGA's suggested rates. The ACGA has been in existence since the 1920s and has proven to be conservative and fairly accurate as to eventual result. Following these gift annuity rates is not required under state laws or by the IRS but is strongly recommended.

Second, you need a policy related to what types of assets will be accepted. Restricting the gift annuity program to cash and negotiable securities is recommended unless the asset is particularly valuable and worth the risk. Illiquid assets are difficult to handle because the institution is committed to making regular fixed payments to an annuitant with no guarantee that it will be able to liquidate the asset in a timely fashion.

Third, some institutions have policies setting a minimum age for annuitants, but such policies are more appropriate for charitable remainder trusts. The lower the payout, the better the long-term chances for the institution to benefit from the assets placed in the gift annuity program. There is no reason for age minimums, except for the potential problem created by a statutory reserve based on age; ACGA payout rates include children. In California, more than 100 percent of the value of the gift annuity may be required to be placed in a statutory reserve account. This requirement effectively limits the ages of individuals to whom California institutions can offer annuities, unless they are willing to assign non-gift annuity assets to the reserve to cover the shortfall. If a large enough gift annuity is proposed, however, an institution probably would figure out a way to cover the statutory reserve with other assets.

Some institutions create age minimums and maximums to reduce their administrative costs. This approach solves a false problem and also puts your institution at a competitive disadvantage. All ACGA rates assume an administrative cost factor that is determined by the ACGA from surveys of its membership. Every rate it endorses contains this factor. In other words you are already charging the annuitant a small fee to cover administration of the annuity. Secondly, if you limit the maximum ages, it means you will offer lower rates than other institutions following the full ACGA rate system, making you second best in any competitive situation. Your institution could also be accused of gouging your donors to squeeze extra money out of them. Any savings you might realize from these minimums and maximums would be more than offset by the lost gifts and bad will created among donors and advisors.

The final policy decision—and a straightforward one—is whether to offer more than an immediate-pay gift annuity. The deferred gift annuity is a better vehicle because it allows the institution to have the funds available for investment for several years before being obligated to make payments. In states that permit a "total return" approach to the investment of gift annuity reserve assets, the institution has an excellent opportunity to grow the pool beyond the internal investment return assumed by the ACGA gift annuity rates. Deferred annuities are treated as immediate-pay gift annuities for most statutory and reporting requirements. They have some outstanding planning features that can benefit younger donors, which may allow an institution with a younger alumni or donor base to develop an effective planned giving program.

Licensing

Most states have adopted some form of licensing for institutions that offer gift annuities. Frequently the state insurance commissioner is the regulatory agency assigned to oversight of charitable gift annuities. Recently more states are considering legislation related to gift annuities. Some are seeking clear regulation of licensees, and others are exempting licensees from oversight. The National Association of Insurance Commissioners has prepared a model for consideration. Many states—California and New York in particular—heavily regulate gift annuity programs.

In establishing a gift annuity program, the most important first step is to determine your state's statutory requirements. At a minimum, most states require some type of filing by the institution, with an application and a small licensing fee. In heavily regulated states, the application process can be cumbersome. Many states also require annual reporting. College and university colleagues in your state can suggest attorneys or consultants who specialize in helping to establish gift annuity programs. Investing in experienced professional assistance is worthwhile and can save you time and aggravation.

Contracts

A gift annuity is in fact a contract between the donor and the institution. The gift annuity document provides for the donor to transfer assets to the institution and for the institution to provide him or her with income for life in return. These contracts are simple documents of no more than one or two pages. In heavily regulated states, specific formats must be followed. In other states with less regulation, consistency of documents is all that is required.

A standard set of annuity contracts, to be used by all donors, is recommended. These documents will usually be filed with the state regulatory agency. If your institution offers annuities in more than one state, you will need to make sure your documents conform to each state's law. This may result in multiple standard sets for each state in which your institution is active. The key is that any donor from a particular state gets the same contract as anyone else from that state.

The contract, in its essential elements, recites the transfer of assets by the donor to the institution, including the amount and frequency of payments to the donor (at least annually). Usually, the contract states the ages of the donor or donors at the time of the transfer, as well as the dollar value of the assets. In some states, the assets must be listed on the contract, while in other states it is enough to indicate the dollar value and attach a supplemental listing. Your attorney or planned

giving consultant can suggest contract language. Books on planned giving also cover this topic (see Appendix B). At this time several software companies are attempting to provide current contracts for all 50 states, including Crescendo software and PG Calc (see Appendix B).

Accounting

Most states that regulate gift annuities require the institution to hold in a special reserve account—often a trust account—a certain amount of the money given to it through the gift annuity program. Reserve amounts usually are the actuarially determined value of the assets necessary to fulfill the payment commitments made under the gift contracts based on the life expectancies of the annuitants.

In addition to the required statutory reserves, it is general practice to create additional reserves for an annuity program. A simple approach is to place all monies received in a gift annuity program in a statutory reserve account or a supplemental reserve account. Distributions from these accounts occur only upon the death of the annuitant. This method achieves two goals: It simplifies the matter for accounting purposes, and it provides an additional security reserve in case investment performance lags behind the underlying assumptions of the gift annuity contract.

Investing

It is important to evaluate the overall investment approach for your annuity program and determine a simple, straightforward, and conservative investment methodology. If you are following the ACGA rates, there is an internal return assumption used to develop the payout rates for income beneficiaries. Knowing this anticipated rate of return will assist you in developing your overall investment approach. Investment results that exceed these assumptions may create an available pool of assets (in excess of reserve requirements) that the perceptive business officer will be able to make use of for overall cash management purposes.

Statutory Requirements

Heavily regulated states often have statutory limitations on the types of investments that can be made with reserve funds. In California, for example, at one time 90 percent of the total portfolio had to be invested in bonds and cash instruments. (This was deemed to be too difficult a requirement to achieve the overall earnings assumptions underlying the gift annuity payout rates and was recently changed to permit up to 50 percent of the total portfolio to be invested in U.S. equities.) Careful review of your own state's authorizing statutes should reveal any restrictions that will impact your overall investment approach.

One reason that institutions put 100 percent of the funds in reserve is to provide a higher percentage of equity investments in the overall portfolio. When a statutory reserve is 70 to 90 percent of the overall value of the gift, the additional 10 to 30 percent invested in equities is the only way to achieve the overall return assumed by the gift annuity contracts.

Total Return Approach

In a state that is relatively unregulated, the total return investment approach is always a more desirable way to handle annuity funds. Investment advisors use various asset allocation models to achieve a high total return on investments. If the earnings assumptions on gift annuity contracts are relatively low, and you are able to have significant equity exposure in your investments, a sound conservative asset allocation can net a much better return on gift annuity funds over time. The earnings assumptions on gift annuity contracts aim for a residual gift of 50 percent of initial asset value. With a sound investment approach and proper asset allocation, it may be possible for an institution to achieve a return of 100 percent of face value on annuity funds, if not higher.

Prudent Man Rule

Many states have a so-called "prudent man rule" that requires trustees to invest funds as a prudent man would do. Any institution that invests too heavily in a single asset class is technically in violation of the law. Some states have not codified this rule, but if your state is not among them, you should become aware of the requirements. Should your investment program not prove successful, you may have some liability. In several states, statutory requirements for investing annuity funds put an interesting twist on the prudent man rule, because close adherence to the statutory requirements would appear to force the institution to violate the rule by triggering an overweighting of fixed-income investments in the reserve portfolio.

Reporting to State Authorities

Almost every state requires some form of reporting by licensees that offer gift annuities. The type of reporting varies. Heavily regulated states often require not only financial reporting of assets held in gift annuity reserve accounts, but also overall financial reporting that indicates the financial health of the institution. Filing requirements can include the mission statement, a list of governing board members, full financial statements, and detailed reporting of investments and investment results in all annuity reserve accounts. Reporting is a necessary part of the gift annuity process that should be handled by a designated staff member who can become knowledgeable in this area. (See Planned Giving Resources, Appendix B.)

Disclosure Requirements

In the early 1990s, an elderly woman in Texas executed a charitable gift annuity. Later, a distant relative of the woman found out about the gift and, probably because she was a disappointed heir, instituted legal proceedings when the woman was declared incompetent. These proceedings sought rescission of the contract and return of the funds transferred to charity. The relative's attorneys decided that all charities in the country were involved in a "price-fixing" scheme perpetrated by the American Council on Gift Annuities and the suggested rates provided by the council. They filed a class action lawsuit that dragged on for a number of years, with all charities in the United States named as potential defendants.

Nonprofits throughout the country were outraged at this attempt to seek damages for what was inherently a benign effort to allow them to compete on mission rather than on how high a rate they could pay. The direct result of this lawsuit was the enactment by Congress of the Philanthropy Protection Act. This law eliminated the plaintiff's antitrust claims and created full-disclosure requirements. Institutions must now give donors a clear disclosure statement explaining the features of the gift annuity (as well as charitable remainder trusts and pooled income funds) and providing information about the nature of the gift annuity contract. Disclosure statements have reached a relative level of sophistication. Some institutions prefer very short disclosure statements, while others have extensive statements (see Appendix H for a sample document). Disclosure statements are a requirement, not an optional feature of your gift annuity program. They should be developed and approved by legal counsel as meeting the requirements of the Philanthropy Protection Act.

Nonstatutory Reserves

Placing all gift annuity assets into a gift annuity reserve even when only a portion is required by statute has an extra benefit for the business office. Although all statutory reserves must be maintained as per statute, the excess reserves can be tapped from time to time for cash flow purposes. If your annuities are accounted for separately, you may wish to "borrow" money from the excess reserves at interest to keep from being criticized by the eventual beneficiary of the annuity, such as your School of Business or athletics department. But, where this is not an issue, the excess funds can be used when needed. In addition, the excess reserve funds can be invested more freely and will soften the blow of any adverse investment outcomes occurring to the gift annuity statutory reserves. Some institutions choose to immediately spend every dollar that is not required for the statutory reserves, but from a conservative standpoint, it would appear wiser to maintain the reserve until the underlying annuity obligation has terminated.

Reinsurance

A gift annuity is a contract, but it resembles an insurance product typically known as a commercial annuity. Commercial annuities act exactly like gift annuities, but there is no gift involved. Because there is no gift involved, it is possible to purchase a commercial annuity paying the exact amount as the gift annuity contract but for less money. In other words, if you wanted to, you could take the money from the gift annuity that has been given to you, buy a commercial annuity, and net a positive sum as the difference between the cost of the gift annuity and the cost of the commercial annuity.

In most states, reinsurance is authorized for annuity contracts and should be investigated when you do not want to have the financial liability for the gift annuity contract itself. Remember, however, that insurance companies are not in the business of losing money. Every commercial annuity product has a profit margin for the company, and sometimes a very large one. When you fully reserve all funds received under a gift annuity and invest them for growth, theoretically you should be ahead of the reinsurance approach in overall total return. Only your investment experience will be able to verify this for you. The University of Southern California reserves 100 percent of each gift annuity split between the statutory or nonstatutory reserve. A portion of the statutory reserve and all of the nonstatutory reserve is invested for total return. However, it may be easier for an institution that does not have a diversified investment program to reinsure its annuities and allow the insurance companies to worry about the overall investment return on its annuities. The positive side of reinsuring is that the difference between the cost of the commercial annuity and the face amount of the gift received is available for immediate expenditure. Prices for commercial annuities will fluctuate with the prevailing interest rates, so checking on their cost effectiveness is necessary at all times.

Reinsuring can be difficult to administer. Insurance companies will want to issue 1099-R forms and frequently they are inaccurate, in particular where the funding assets were appreciated assets. Some institutions end up having all checks and 1099-R forms issued by the reinsurer sent to them and then resent to donors in order to double-check their accuracy. You must evaluate the administrative strengths of any reinsurer as well as its financial strength before entering into a program of reinsurance.

RECOMMENDED ACTIONS

1. Have your attorney review your license to offer gift annuities in your state. If you are establishing a new program, retain legal counsel who specializes in obtaining appropriate licenses to offer gift annuities in your state. Do not try to do this yourself.

2. Have the attorney review your contracts for compliance with state laws.

3. Have the attorney review your disclosure documents for compliance with federal and state laws.

4. Have the attorney review your system for handling gift annuity funds, including any statutory trusts that may be required by law.

5. Join the American Council on Gift Annuities. Most members follow its suggested payout rates on all gift annuities.

6. If you choose to set your own payout rates, hire an actuary to determine the appropriate payout rates for your program, based on your investment experience.

7. Determine the appropriate investment mix for your gift annuity assets based on state laws and the current investment climate. Some states limit your investment options.

8. Determine what types of assets you will accept for a gift annuity. Illiquid assets are usually not desirable for this type of gift vehicle.

24

chapter five

CHARITABLE REMAINDER TRUSTS

Policies

A policy statement about charitable remainder trusts should encourage this form of planned giving and offer full cooperation with financial and legal professionals in the establishment of charitable remainder trusts that benefit the institution. The policy should also state whether the institution will serve as trustee. If the institution does serve as trustee, it is appropriate to include further statements about limitations that you will place on trusts in these cases. For instance, the institution may require that it serve as trustee when all beneficiaries of the trust are above a certain age, such as 50 or 60. You may also include provisions that limit the types of assets that will be accepted, although there are no limitations under the tax laws for such contributions (see Appendix I for sample policy documents).

The Key Decision: To Trustee or Not to Trustee

The single most important decision that an institution needs to make before offering or encouraging charitable remainder trusts is whether it will serve as trustee of the trust. In most jurisdictions, a nonprofit institution is entitled to serve as trustee. Banking and trust company laws are so complex, however, that it is not necessarily appropriate to charge standard trustees' fees or investment management fees that are paid directly to the institution. It is possible that trustee services could be a cost center of the institution, though not a large one.

Serving as trustee can be advantageous for several reasons. The most important reason is for donor relations, because the institution remains in close contact with the donor from the establishment of the gift until the termination. There are many opportunities to continue the relationship with the donor and to pursue future gifts based on the relationship. In addition, the institution as trustee can keep close tabs on the trust's investments and control the investment mix—an important role when a trust has a high payout that threatens to erode the principal. Serving as trustee also allows the institution access to all information in a timely fashion.

There are a number of reasons why an institution might not wish to serve as trustee, the principal one being the lack of expertise in the planned giving or business office regarding the administration of charitable trusts. The trustee relationship has a built-in conflict of interest that, while relatively mild, requires the institution to be particularly scrupulous about administrative practices, following all of the rules and sometimes even making decisions that go against its own interests but benefit the donors and beneficiaries. For example, it always benefits the institution if the assets in a charitable trust are invested for maximum growth, but in several types of trusts, a total return investment approach is a decided handicap to providing the beneficiaries with adequate income. In many instances, the institution will forego a certain amount of investment growth to generate a higher degree of income for the beneficiaries.

A second reason to consider not serving as trustee is the strain on donor relations that might occur when investments are not successful. If the institution is serving as trustee and the investments prove to be disappointing, the donors may hold the institution responsible. While this is always a risk, it can be overcome to a certain degree by employing an investment advisor—usually a bank or trust company—to make the general decisions on investment approach and day-to-day buying of individual stocks and bonds.

A third reason to hesitate about trusteeship is the potential liability for the handling of assets. Accepting trusteeship gives the institution a fiduciary duty to handle all assets for the benefit of the beneficiaries and the remainderman. Since the institution is the remainderman, there is an assumption that investments will seek to benefit the institution (although some state attorneys general are beginning to ignore this assumption and assert their oversight authority for the benefit of nonprofits, even when the nonprofit is trustee). The liability issues can also run to the assets themselves. In one instance in California, a trustee was held liable for the costs of an environmental cleanup problem on an asset placed in trust. The trustee did not create the trust, nor did the trustee own the assets before putting them into trust, but the court basically attached liability to the trustee anyway. While this situation is an exception, it does suggest that a trustee must be prepared to deal with a certain liability exposure. This risk can be mitigated by a good set of acceptance policies regarding assets placed in trust. It is entirely reasonable for a trustee to refuse to accept assets to trust that carry liabilities for toxic cleanups, for example.

Documents

Form Documents for Attorneys' Review

Some professional advisors, primarily attorneys, seek form documents showing examples of charitable remainder unitrusts and charitable annuity trusts. Several vendors nationwide—attorneys in practice in this area—have prepared sets of documents. Form documents are not the formal practice of law and do not carry with it that type of liability.

There are two reasons to provide form documents. First, this practice allows you to control the content to a point. A good sample document will ensure the inclusion of all necessary and important provisions, including those that are not specified in the Internal Revenue Service Code and regulations. For example, you may want a specific provision that allows you to appoint a co-trustee for investment advisory purposes. If you are seeking to appoint a bank or trust company, you will want to include their language in your documents, which are then translated into the trusts executed by attorneys. By having form documents, you can easily insert the appropriate language.

Secondly, many of the attorneys that you will be dealing with lack experience with charitable remainder trusts, lead trusts, or other sophisticated planned giving arrangements. By providing state of the art documents, you provide them with a template to follow. This makes it easier for them and ensures you a more soundly drafted document that hopefully contains the key terms that you seek, such as an irrevocable designation of the charitable beneficiary.

Document Preparation

Many institutions have attorneys on staff or on retainer who provide documents to donors for execution. This practice should be carefully considered, because it carries with it a number of inherent problems.

The first problem is relatively obvious: An attorney hired by or on the staff of the institution has a conflict of interest in developing documents for a donor. The attorney's client is the person paying the bills—in this case the institution. Some attorneys will argue that full disclosure of their relationship with the institution is enough. Although some practitioners may be able to hold that ethical fine line, it is unlikely that a court would agree that they are completely without bias, especially when a decision appears not to be in the donor's best interests. Moreover, there is a liability risk associated with the preparation of documents. When the institution foots the bill, it may be liable for any mistakes made by the attorney. While most attorneys are required to carry liability insurance, they sometimes leave the profession or are no longer able to pay liability judgments. In those cases, an institution would appear to be a "deep pocket" suitable for suing.

A further problem is the question of full disclosure. If the institution is paying the attorney who has prepared the documents, can one actually be satisfied that full disclosure was given to a donor who subsequently complains or sues claiming lack of knowledge of certain techniques? Every development officer encounters donors who have "selective memory" about the negotiations on a charitable trust. An argument that full disclosure was made would be suspect simply because the institution's attorney was doing the disclosing. Fortunately, the Philanthropy Protection Act's requirements for written disclosure documents have mitigated this problem in recent years (see Appendix H).

Some institutions deal with the problem of document preparation by providing a list of advisors. Many bar associations now have lists of specialists in various areas, including estate planning and trusts. Some donors may appreciate a list based on geography, especially if they are elderly and unable to travel significant distances for their legal work. This approach is certainly appropriate when attempting to provide counsel for a donor and involves limited liability for the institution.

The critical issue, however, is not who recommended a particular attorney but whether that attorney is paid by the donor or the institution. The institution should consider paying attorneys' fees only in special situations when provision of this service is in some way critical to the completion of the gift or is the most effective way to help a donor achieve his or her goals. For example, an institution retained an attorney in the case of an elderly donor who did not know any advisors capable of providing the services to him. The donor was asked to execute a liability waiver agreement (often called a "Hold Harmless" agreement) to protect the institution.

Life Income: Who Decides How Much to Pay?

The payout rate on a charitable remainder trust is negotiable and established at the creation of the trust. The trust terms must require a payout of no less than 5 percent and no more than 50 percent annually. The rate is also limited by the requirement that a charitable remainder trust must have a minimum charitable remainder value at its creation equal to 10 percent of the initial funding assets. An institution can influence the trust payout only by its decision to serve as trustee.

It is prudent to consider refusing to serve as trustee of a charitable remainder trust if the payout is so high that you believe in good faith that it will erode the principal value. It is much better to refuse to serve as trustee on a high payout trust than to serve as trustee, fail to achieve investment results that meet the stated payout rate, and then have the donor complain about your performance.

Just how high should a payout be? If your institution is the trustee and has some influence over the decision, it is recommended that rates be market driven, and, when you have the opportunity, they should lean to the low side. Lower payouts increase the chance for principal growth. In an annuity trust, a low rate can appear to be an effort to featherbed for the institution. But in a charitable remainder unitrust—in which the assets are revalued annually and the payouts are determined based on that valuation—a low payout encourages asset growth, which creates a rising income stream over time for the donor. If the donor has a long life expectancy, this is a prudent and appropriate approach.

Different types of trusts may have different payout rates simply because the trustee and/or donor is attempting to achieve different results. High current income is not the only goal for a trust. Trusts may be established to create large income tax deductions rather than current income. Trusts may be established to fund college education for a beneficiary or to increase retirement income at some date in the future. Net income unitrusts will usually need to consider lower payout percentages because the trust must pay out "income" and cannot invade principal to meet its expected payout requirements. Standard unitrusts can be set for higher payout amounts since the trustee is able to use a total return investment approach.

A curious issue related to charitable remainder trusts is the "competition effect" on rates. Sometimes institutions learn that a crosstown rival is "paying" a higher rate on its charitable trusts. This perception is wrong because a donor can establish a charitable remainder trust at any payout percentage he or she chooses. If an institution chooses to be trustee of a trust, it has the right to choose which trusts it will handle, and the stated payout rate will be a consideration. However, anyone can set up a trust at any payout rate between 5 percent and 50 percent (provided there is a 10 percent remainder value for charity). The only sensible approach is to be open to handling trusts that you feel have reasonable income expectations or trusts where erosion of principal over time still leaves your institution with a worthwhile gift.

Administration of Charitable Trusts

There are two main approaches to the administration of charitable trusts: handling all administration in-house and outsourcing the function to banks, trust companies, and other types of vendors. Depending on the size of your institution and the commitment that it is making to planned giving, either choice can be productive.

Much like choosing whether to serve as trustee of a charitable remainder trust, in-house administration has both positive and negative points. On the positive side, administering a trust brings the institution closer to donors and to any problems they may be experiencing from their charitable trusts. This is a wonderful opportunity to serve donors and keep in close contact with them. However, trust administration requires a high degree of expertise, knowledge that can only be developed by handling a large volume of charitable trust work on a regular basis. If your institution does not have a large number of charitable trusts and a staff member who is at least dedicated to learning the area—whether full-time or not—it may be wiser to use outside administrators.

Custody

No matter what decision you make about administration, charitable remainder trusts hold assets that need a custodian. Banks and trust companies are the most common types of custodians and provide this service for a fee, which is usually expressed as a certain number of basis points of total assets held in trust. Other fee arrangements may also be entered into, but generally, custodial costs are a fairly low-cost service. Many banks have minimum amounts that they will service, and any amount below the minimum is refused or charged higher fees.

If you have decided to outsource the administration of charitable trusts, then the vendor probably will have its own custodial relationship, often at a good rate due to the volume of business the vendor provides. If the institution is aggressively entering the planned giving field, most companies offering custodial services will be eager to have you as a client.

Tax Returns and Accounting

Every charitable remainder trust must file IRS Form 5227, the basic tax return for split-interest trusts. This form is quite complex, but computer software is available to minimize the amount of work required. Every beneficiary receives IRS Form 1065-B (Schedule K-1), a less complex form that reports annual income and the character of that income. The donor must file Form 1041-A, U.S. Income Tax Return for Estates and Trusts. The state of domicile for the trust will usually require reporting as well.

The single most complex part of charitable trust administration is accounting for the transactions of the individual trusts. Charitable trusts are governed by the "four-tiered" system. A trust may distribute up to four different types of income that must be determined and accounted for: ordinary income, capital gains income, tax-free income, and return of principal. Determining which type of income is being distributed to a donor depends on the accuracy of the accounting. For effective accounting, the trustee needs a master list of all transactions; the dates the transactions occurred; whether the transactions occurred within one year of the purchase of the asset; and the cost basis of the stock and other contributed assets. This precise accounting is necessary to determine whether any asset that was sold has generated income and, if so, whether the income is short term or long term. Long-term and short-term losses are computed as well, resulting in the necessity of having the cost basis of all assets, their holding periods, and their net sales gains or losses.

As long as the reporting from the bank or trust company is detailed, it is possible to handle the accounting and tax preparation for charitable trusts in-house without undue hardship. With a simple spreadsheet program and proper reports from banks or other custodians, you can reconcile the transactions to determine the appropriate amount to be paid to a donor and the character of those payments. Based on the accounting, Schedule K-1 shows the donor the types of income received during the prior tax year.

Assigning the accounting and tax preparation to an outside vendor involves a certain amount of risk. Trust accounting for charitable trusts is not something that most institutions typically do, so careful oversight and some type of auditing are necessary. Be sure to inquire about the extent of expertise provided by the vendor in this area. Sometimes larger institutions actually outsource this function to smaller companies that you have never heard of or talked with. Do they know what they are doing? Try to avoid finding out the hard way that they were learning on the job with your trusts.

Investments

The assets of charitable trusts need to be invested or managed. In the case of investments in stocks, bonds, and other securities, it is prudent to retain investment counsel. If you have several charitable trusts and a significant pool of assets, virtually any bank or trust company will be eager to serve as investment advisor. Investment counsel is also available from independent firms. Investments must follow the "prudent man rule," because the trustee has a fiduciary duty to ensure that the investment mix is reasonable and sound. High-risk investing in charitable trusts is a formula for disaster, not only for donors but for the institution that will undoubtedly be sued.

When dealing with a number of trusts and an active planned giving program, it is useful for your investment advisor to help develop several investment scenarios. These approaches should emphasize various types of investments, such as long-term growth, high income, or balanced approaches. Each one will appeal to a different demographic segment. Older donors will seek a higher income, while younger donors will appreciate long-term growth and assets for the future. Those who are within five years of retirement or at retirement age will probably appreciate a more balanced approach that will grow the asset base over time during the retirement years but provide some immediate income. An investment advisor can mold this program into a simple approach that can then be modified for the individual donor.

Investment in large pooled funds is now permitted by law. Before 1986, charitable trust assets could not be commingled, or invested in mutual funds or any type of diversified investment fund internal to a bank or trust company. Consult the actual trust document if you are dealing with a charitable trust established before 1986. Most of these documents contained a provision specifically stating that the assets cannot be commingled. A new planned giving program obviously does not have this problem. Often, it is appropriate to ensure that the assets in trust are in large enough pools of money that they can achieve wide diversification of investments. Some mutual funds are even offering asset allocation mutual funds, which provide total diversification among a number of asset classes, all from the basis of a single mutual fund. Your investment advisors will be able to direct you to the most appropriate funds to achieve the goal of the investment mix.

Frequently, investment advisors forget that many CRTs must be invested in a specific way to achieve donor goals. Pooled funds can cause problems with many of these types of trusts. For example, if a trust donor expects tax-exempt income from a trust, you may disappoint that donor if you invest trust assets in a municipal bond mutual fund rather than individual bonds. An actively traded bond fund will often have realized capital gains from the sale of individual bonds. The trust beneficiary must recognize these distributed gains before receiving tax-exempt income from the trust.

Asset Management and Liquidation

Charitable trusts are often funded with assets such as real estate or other illiquid investments, such as limited partnership interests. Although the trust owns these assets, management is required, especially in the case of real estate that is rented or producing income. "Administration" means property management for real estate and due diligence for limited partnership interests and other illiquid assets. If the institution has a property management program, whether as a part of the business officer's responsibilities or a full-time position, real estate held in trust must be added to the management structure. If there is no ongoing formal program, this function should be assigned in-house or contracted to an outside property management firm.

The liquidation of assets held in trust is handled in a similar fashion to the liquidation of other assets. Real estate usually is listed with a broker and sold in the normal way. Other more difficult assets are handled similarly, although specialization in certain asset classes is often required to analyze their value and market them. These functions are generally outsourced as a matter of policy.

Who Pays for What?

The administrative costs outlined in this chapter can be paid by the institution or paid from the trust assets. Your initial reaction may be to charge the trust for all related expenses, but you should look beyond the obvious immediate impact to other issues.

For one thing, banks often charge significant fees, so the institution serving as trustee that charges charitable trusts for costs can appear to be acting much like a bank. From a marketing standpoint, it is advantageous to advertise a low-cost or no-cost administrative program as part of the inducement to create a charitable trust. If you were going to charge fees like banks and trust companies, why wouldn't a donor simply go there to set up a trust, removing the institution from the equation completely? In many jurisdictions, nonprofit institutions serving as trustees are not permitted to charge trustee fees for their services. This means that you are already lowering the donor's cost of creating the gift.

Keep in mind that there is an impact on the donor when fees are charged to the trust. Most costs of trust administration are usually charged against trust assets and taken out of income first. Therefore, if a trust is to pay out 7 percent and it is earning 7 percent, any charges against that 7 percent will reduce the income stream below the expectations of the donor, resulting in problems from a donor relations standpoint. These problems are increased if the donor's perception is that the institution is gouging the income stream from the trust to the donor's detriment simply to pay costs that he or she feels are really costs of doing business for your institution. Some institutions find it more satisfactory to maintain an account that keeps track of the costs incurred in the administration of a charitable trust and to reimburse themselves from trust proceeds at the termination of the trust.

Changes in Beneficiaries

From time to time, the beneficiaries on charitable trusts may change, especially when donors name themselves or their spouses as primary beneficiary and someone else as successor beneficiary, either for life or for a term of years. When the primary beneficiaries either no longer wish to receive the income or have died, it is necessary to change to the new beneficiaries for purposes of payment. Usually a death certificate or a written waiver of right to income is required before changing beneficiaries. Sometimes this process becomes a problem if the institution is not notified immediately of the death of an income beneficiary. This situation emphasizes the need for regular communication with all beneficiaries, if for no other reason than to determine which ones are no longer alive or receiving mail at their old addresses. Checks can be sent with address correction requested and often come back with notations from friends and neighbors that a person has died. Encouraging the development office to stay in touch with beneficiaries is also another good way to ensure timely notification of changes.

Reformation of Faulty Trusts

Reformation of a charitable remainder trust requires legal counsel. If a trust has been set up incorrectly, there are two mechanisms for correcting the faults. If language in the trust document allows for changes to conform to Title 26, section 664 of the Internal Revenue Code, which deals with charitable remainder trusts, reformation of faulty trusts is fairly easy. Your counsel can execute a simple document that is signed by the trustee, stating that certain errors were determined that are being corrected under the provisions of the trust document allowing for reformation to conform to the code.

The second reformation method is a court proceeding that follows the IRS rules and regulations relating to trust reformation. Some states allow for trust reformation independent of the Internal Revenue Code. However, the fact that a charitable trust is reformed under state law does not necessarily mean that it is a qualified trust under federal tax law. If a trust has been set up incorrectly from the beginning, a state reformation of the document is probably not enough to salvage its tax-exempt status. There are extensive rules related to trust reformation that are beyond the scope of this book. However, no institution should attempt a reformation without legal counsel.

Termination Procedures

Upon the death of the last living income beneficiary, a charitable trust terminates and the assets are distributed to the institution for the purposes agreed to by the donor and the institution. Termination procedures should be in place to handle this distribution.

These procedures can be fairly simple. A certified copy of the death certificate of the last living beneficiary (and all other beneficiaries acquired before the death of the last beneficiary) should be on file. Once proof of death has occurred, the terms of the trust direct that within a reasonable number of days, the trust be terminated and all assets distributed to the charitable remainderman. A clear paper trail should be maintained showing a request for distribution to the custodian, followed by a transfer to the appropriate account at your institution.

You may be asked for information by the estate of the income beneficiary. This information usually is requested to comply with the requirements for asset valuation of the trust on the date of the beneficiary's death. As you handle the termination procedures, it is wise to make sure that you get this valuation from the custodian so that you can have it available when it is requested.

The termination procedures should also include a notification that is sent to the development office encouraging it to contact the family of the donor to express thanks for the gift in question. By notifying the development office of the termination of the trust, you may update it on the current situation with a particular donor, prospect, or family member. This will allow the institution to be sensitive to the family's situation and to stay in touch with the donors and/or family in an appropriate way.

RECOMMENDED ACTIONS

1. Determine if your institution is going to serve as trustee of CRTs where it is named as beneficiary or as one of several beneficiaries.

2. If you choose to serve as trustee, then you must decide whether to administer the trusts or have them administered by an outside provider, such as a bank or trust company.

3. Assign management responsibility to one person whether you plan to administer the trusts in-house or outsource the work. Monitoring the administration of the trusts is critical, no matter who is trustee.

4. Develop suggested form documents that can be shared with donor's counsel. Whether you are trustee or not, include in the forms all items that you want included in the trust, including the provision making the gift irrevocable for your institution.

5. Determine the payout rates you are comfortable with as trustee and let your development staff know what they are. These rates should reflect current interest rates and the best advice from your investment advisors. Make special exceptions when the situation warrants.

6. Have legal counsel review all disclosure documents for each type of CRT that you are offering. If you are not serving as trustee, you may want to provide disclosure documents to donors anyway.

7. Trusts must be invested individually because each trust is trying to achieve different goals. Investments must be customized for each trust and your investment advisor must be aware of this requirement to avoid future problems.

chapter six

POOLED INCOME FUNDS

In the 1980s, pooled income funds were marketed to nonprofit institutions by many banks, trust companies, and other financial institutions. They were promoted as "the poor man's unitrust" and a more democratic way to offer the benefits of life income plans to larger groups of small donors. Many institutions entered into pooled income fund arrangements, but very few were successful.

The basic problem with pooled income funds is that they are variable income options being marketed to older donors as income options for retirement. The fund is therefore in direct competition with the fixed-income option known as a charitable gift annuity. Elderly people place a premium on income security. Unlike charitable gift annuities, pooled income funds were not guaranteed by institutions. In addition, charitable gift annuities routinely paid significantly higher rates to donors than the average pooled income fund was earning.

As interest rates dropped during the late 1980s and early 1990s, pooled income funds were in a double bind. They were not necessarily attractive to older donors due to their variable income nature and nonguaranteed arrangement and, because they are limited to generating income from interest and dividends, the drop in interest rates created a decline in overall earnings.

When considering a pooled income fund, it is important to realize that the average fund has not been successful. To warrant the effort required to establish a pooled income fund, along with the associated costs, you must understand where your market is for this type of fund and whether it is a large enough market to make the fund viable overall.

Evaluating the Market

It is pointless to establish a pooled income fund simply to have it available to a group of people who don't plan to make gifts. You need to know the market and how it will react. Before you begin, do a thorough analysis of the donor base, and consider your options carefully. Otherwise, you will be saddled with a gift vehicle that will not accumulate a large pool of assets for your institution. It will become a management headache that you will wish you had never created.

The characteristics of your target group will affect the investment strategy of the pooled income fund and the likely success of any marketing effort. The one thing to keep in mind is that it is not necessary to offer every type of planned giving vehicle to have a "comprehensive" planned giving program. If you can't sell it, it is not worth the effort or time to establish it, manage it, report on it, and perform all related duties concerning donor relations. Don't be afraid to say no.

The good news about pooled income funds is that there is no limitation on investment approach. There are only limitations on the types of investments. For example, a pooled income fund cannot invest in tax-exempt bonds. It probably should not handle investments in any type of property that would be considered depreciable, such as real estate. (Real estate depreciation can be passed through to income beneficiaries along with income earned by the fund. However, if the fund takes depreciation, it must offset the depreciation in calculating the distributable income. In other words, it must maintain a sinking fund that must be funded dollar for dollar against any depreciation. This has the negative result of reducing income to the beneficiaries and has discouraged the use of pooled income funds for investing in real property.) However, the fund can invest for specific beneficiary needs, either high income, income and growth, or just growth using either a balanced or a growth approach to a diversified investment portfolio mix.

Creative investment ideas appear to be the future of pooled income funds. Different approaches are appropriate for different age groups, enabling you to tailor a pooled income fund to a particular category of donor. A high-income fund will be attractive to older people who are not particularly interested in growth of principal. Younger donors will be interested in a balanced portfolio or a growth portfolio that will increase their assets over time and provide a higher degree of income in the future.

The current regulations governing pooled income funds do not prohibit investment approaches that vary over time. Experts in the field believe that a pooled income fund can be tailored to provide a retirement savings program for younger donors. A fund that invests for growth for the first 20 years can switch over gradually to a high-income fund. Donors in their 40s and 50s would see this as a good way to supplement their retirement with a charitable gift. For the institution, this type of pooled income fund may open doors to gifts from an age group that traditionally is not involved in planned giving.

Choosing a Custodian

A pooled income fund is established with the creation of a pooled income fund trust. A trust must have a trustee, which usually is the charitable institution. The trustee routinely arranges with a bank or other fiduciary entity to handle all custodial duties related to investments, contributions, and reporting. Banks across the country offer turnkey pooled income fund programs.

If the institution prefers not to serve as trustee, it must still exercise control over the trust, which usually means it retains the right to replace the trustee at any time the pooled income fund is in existence. Only one charity may be the remainder beneficiary of a particular pooled income fund.

When establishing a pooled income fund, consider having a reputable institution handle the administrative duties. Pooled income funds require extensive disclosure documents under the current securities law, and handling this work on your own will result in high legal fees. Banks usually have standardized disclosure statements, transmittal statements, and prospectuses for the fund that they can offer to you at no additional cost. They are also equipped to handle unitized accounting, which is not a simple record-keeping method, and they will be able to issue timely standardized reports. Fiduciary institutions will also be able to assist in the preparation of the pooled income fund tax return that is required annually by the Internal Revenue Service.

Documents and Disclosure Requirements

An outside custodian will provide all the documents required of a pooled income fund. If you are administering the program in-house, you will need to have a number of documents prepared.

The *pooled income fund trust document* creates the fund and agrees that its monies will be held in trust for the benefit of your institution. This document is usually complex, although the IRS has issued "safe harbor" documents (see Appendix J). *Documents of transmittal* typically take the form of an application that the donor completes, along with asset transmittal documentation

for stocks and bonds or a check or cash. These documents usually are simple to prepare and cover the information needed to calculate the income tax deduction of the donor and to determine where a check should be sent and where the eventual gift may be directed.

The most important document for a pooled income fund is probably the *prospectus*, which is required under securities laws. This document is similar to the prospectus issued by mutual funds or companies marketing their stock to the public. A bank or other fiduciary institution will have a prepared prospectus. If you are creating your own, the prospectus should disclose fully all the features of the pooled income fund, the method by which income and charitable deductions are calculated, the inherent risk, the fact that the funds are not guaranteed by the institution, and various other information. Prospectuses prepared for other pooled income funds can serve as models.

What to Do with Preexisting Pooled Funds

Many institutions have pooled income funds that are sitting dormant and unfunded or contain a small asset base with only a handful of donors receiving income. Most such funds were set up in the 1980s when pooled income funds were new. If you have not been growing this fund, what should you do?

Some institutions are letting their funds die a slow death, waiting for the last few income beneficiaries to die so that they can close the fund out. Other institutions have taken the more proactive approach of converting the pooled fund donors into gift annuity recipients and then closing down the fund. A very few are looking at reviving the funds and developing new marketing approaches for their constituencies.

Many institutions are simply not putting new donors into pooled income funds, opting to promote gift annuities exclusively to small donors.

Recently, many charities have aggressively attempted to shut down their pooled income funds. Usually, the development staff approaches donors and asks them to consider gifting their income interest outright to the institution. If this is not successful, then the institution offers to convert the income interest into a gift annuity, providing fixed income to the donor for life, just like the pooled fund, but not limited to the actual earnings from the fund but rather the generous payout rates provided for gift annuities under the ACGA guidelines. Valuation of the interest being given for the gift annuity can be tricky, but the net result is the pooled income fund donors are converted to gift annuity donors (hopefully at higher income rates than before) and the institution is freed from the administrative costs associated with managing a pooled income fund.

A very few institutions are reviving existing pooled income funds and adjusting them for their particular markets, as discussed above. While developing new marketing approaches for existing pooled income funds is exciting, the business officer needs to keep in mind the existing donors (if any) already in the fund. How was the pooled income fund presented to them when they first signed up? What promises and assurances were they given by the development staff? Will the new and improved pooled income fund meet these expectations? If not, how are you going to try and meet the preexisting expectations?

RECOMMENDED ACTIONS

1. Have your legal counsel review any existing pooled income fund for compliance with existing federal and state law. Be sure to retain someone who works with pooled funds and is knowledgeable in this area.

2. If you are considering a pooled fund or have an existing one with few donors and/or assets, work with your development office to determine the potential market for the fund. Try to determine the minimum acceptable level of funding for such a program. If there is little chance for the fund to reach an acceptable level of funding based on the market, consider not offering it at all or closing off the fund to new donors.

3. If an existing fund has been dormant for longer than three years and has few donors, consider closing the fund.

chapter seven

RETAINED LIFE ESTATES

The concept of the retained life estate is simple and easily explained to potential donors. The donor gifts the property in question to the institution while keeping the legal right to live in the property or use the land for his or her lifetime or, in some cases, for a term of years. Although the institution is deeded the property at the beginning of the life estate, the fee interest in the property is held subject to the donor's retained interest until the conclusion of the life estate. The life estate concludes either at the end of the term of years specified or at the death of the life estate holder. Life estate holders may also give their interest to the charity during their lifetime and receive an additional tax deduction for the current value of their interest.

Most institutions have a policy of accepting life estate gifts, although very few of these gifts occur. On the transfer of the gift, the institution's name goes on the title, creating potential liability should there be problems with the property that are not covered adequately by insurance. For example, a farm might have storage tanks that have been buried in the ground for many years, and the toxic cleanup may be beyond the financial ability of the life estate holder. Because your institution is on the title, it will be the logical deep pocket.

A retained life estate can be established for a personal residence, second home, vacation home, farm, or ranch. However, most life estate agreements are written on single-family residences and condominiums, usually negating big-ticket liability issues. With adequate homeowner's insurance and/or general liability insurance, your institution will be protected. Your policy statement should include a general assertion about the institution's willingness to accept retained life estates and more specific information about what types of properties are appropriate (see Appendix I).

The Life Estate Agreement

Life estate agreements come in all shapes and sizes. Some are merely written letters of one or two pages, and others are extensive legal documents. A standard agreement contains a clear statement that the donor intends to make a gift of the residence while retaining the right to live in it for his or her lifetime. It outlines the donor's responsibilities for maintenance, insurance, and property taxes. It also specifies that the donor may not enter into high-risk activity on the property and must notify the institution of any change in circumstances, including the vacating of the property. The agreement usually provides for a termination mechanism at a time earlier than the death of the life estate holder.

The document is signed by the donor and countersigned by an authorized representative of the institution. A notarized deed is attached, and the deed is recorded (usually by the institution) to complete the gift.

Acceptance Policy

It is not necessary to accept all forms of life estate. The most reasonable approach is to encourage such gifts but to have some clear parameters in mind when dealing with donors.

Condition of the Property

The acceptance of a gift of property with a retained life estate should be contingent on a thorough evaluation of its current condition, just as you would require if you were buying a property. A site inspection should be conducted by a professional who is knowledgeable about structural issues and can spot potential hidden problems. The condition of a residence's foundation and roof, for example, can indicate possible trouble. Phase I or Phase II environmental studies usually are not necessary unless problems are visible or suggested by the history of the property. But most life estate agreements are more modest—such as a single-family residence or vacant farmland—so it is unlikely that you will be dealing with issues related to previous industrial use. If the value of the gift is small in relation to its potential problems, it is best to say no. A $15 million property would warrant significant effort even if there were environmental or structural problems. Most environmental problems are quantifiable and, where the property is of significant value, due diligence in evaluating the costs of these problems may yield some outstanding gifts for your institution.

Potential Marketability

Another issue to consider carefully is the potential for resale upon the termination of the life estate. If the property is three states away and requires a lot of attention, it may be difficult to market. Too often, one hears of colleges and universities that hold properties in the desert, in swamplands, or on flood plains. Sometimes it is easy to determine that a property will sell easily, but often this is not the case. It is fine to receive a gift of property, but if you can't dispose of it at the end of the life estate, the institution may carry the cost for years.

The potential marketability of both structures and land should be analyzed. The property may have an inferior structure but a superior location that argues for good future land value. The property may also be acquired for the long-term growth of the institution's fiscal plant, another version of marketability.

Maintenance

The policy of the institution toward the maintenance and upkeep of a property is critical to the success of this type of gift. Most agreements assign all responsibility for maintenance to the life estate holder. Problems can arise when the life estate holder does not keep the property up to the expected standards. Before entering into a life estate agreement, you should have a clear idea of the level of maintenance normally required to keep the property in reasonably good condition. It is not unusual for an institution to step in and perform maintenance duties on a property subject to a life estate if the life estate holder is unwilling to or incapable of seeing to this activity.

As with structural or environmental problems, it is acceptable to set minimum dollar values for certain types of properties to minimize the administrative problems for the institution. You may not be used to dealing with farms or ranches, but if the ranch is worth $5 million, you'll learn how to handle it because of the benefit. But if the property is a 10-acre farm with marginal value located in a remote area far from your institution, you may want to decline the donor's offer.

Rental of the Property

The life estate holder has certain rights, often including the right to use the property as a rental property. This right can be eliminated from the life estate agreement, and it is wise to do so. It is one thing to deal with the donor, but it is another thing to deal with a third-party tenant who may have entered into a restricted agreement with the life estate holder. When the life estate terminates, it may be unclear who has the right to occupy the property. While legally you will be on sound ground, it

is advisable to eliminate this potential problem at the inception of the gift.

Purchase of a Life Estate

After a life estate has been held for a number of years, the holder may become unable to live in the residence and may want to sell the property to support the expenses of long-term care. The holder may approach you suggesting that the institution purchase the life estate. From an evaluation standpoint, the development office should be able to determine the value of the remaining life estate for the donor. This relatively simple tax calculation can be done using planned giving software. You could also do your own discounted present value calculation using your own discount rates. However, this can cause problems with donors if they get a different number from their accountant or the development office when they do their tax returns, especially if you discounted the value more than the IRS tables do.

Purchasing a life estate is no different from purchasing real property. You will pay the life estate holder, and he or she will execute documents deeding the life estate to the institution. This transaction completes your fee simple title and allows you to liquidate the property in a normal fashion. The purchase of a life estate is usually an acceptable and often a desirable step. You turn an illiquid asset into a liquid asset and can immediately begin to market a previously unmarketable property.

Gift of a Life Estate

When a life estate holder is considering giving up his or her retained life estate, you should consider what a gift of the life estate would do for the donor. Giving the life estate outright to your institution results in another gift for tax purposes and creates another income tax charitable deduction for the present value of the life estate interest.

To determine how much of a deduction would be created, you will need to do another life estate gift calculation using current ages on the life estate holder(s) and a fair market value of the property. Most calculation software will show you the charitable deduction for the *remainder* interest. What you are looking for is the reciprocal value, i.e., the life estate value. Simply subtract the remainder interest as calculated from the fair market value of the property. The resulting sum is the value of the retained life estate as of the date of your new calculations. Frequently donors will choose to make an outright gift of their life estate once they see the tax benefits.

Potential Problems with Retained Life Estates

Life estates in general cause very few problems after they have been established. The problems tend to occur either toward the end of the life estate or after it has terminated. You should anticipate two major types of problems and develop appropriate strategies to deal with them.

In the first scenario, the life tenants do not want to leave the property even though they have become physically or mentally incapacitated. A person who is not in good health will not be up to the task of maintaining the property, and its condition will deteriorate. It would appear better for the institution to offer to take over these responsibilities, and it seems appropriate to expect the life estate holder to pay for a reasonable amount of maintenance and care. However, the institution cannot expect the homeowner to pay for everything that it deems necessary for property maintenance. An overzealous property manager can end up looking like Simon Legree while trying to do the life estate holder a favor. While you should not provide this service from the beginning of the life estate, regular property inspections and stewardship visits to the life estate holders (as donors) should keep you in touch with the overall condition of the property and give you advance warning of a need to step in with some type of assistance.

The second problem—and the most frequent one in my experience—occurs after the death of the life estate holder. The scenario usually develops like this: A life estate holder becomes physically and/or mentally incapacitated. To help the person remain in his or her home, a paid caregiver or a volunteer moves in to assist with day-to-day living. When the life estate holder dies, the resident caregiver either asserts a promise by the donor that he or she can live permanently on the property or refuses to vacate when the institution gives appropriate notice. It is an unfortunate situation, since the recent death of the life estate holder tends to make the issues emotional. We have on occasion sent the county sheriff to evict caregivers who refuse to vacate properties based on vague promises or their claims to some property right. This situation can be confused further when the institution is the sole beneficiary of the life estate holder's estate. An adversarial relationship can result, with an individual claiming that the deceased promised them money, possessions, or the right to live on the property.

There is no perfect solution to this problem, but there seems to be a better chance of an amicable resolution when the institution has maintained a strong relationship with the donor, including making regularly scheduled visits to his or her home. While you have the right to inspect the property at any time, a carefully orchestrated development effort with the donor to continue the stewardship of the gift usually will keep you fully apprised of the donor's physical condition as well as whether any caregivers or outside parties are exercising influence over the donor.

Rental of Property

The life estate holder owns the right to use the property during his or her lifetime. This means that a life estate holder has the right to rent the property to third parties unless that right has been specifically reserved to the remainderman (i.e., the charity). If a donor has a financial need—long-term care or medical expenses, for example—the idea of renting the property is a viable economic alternative. However, the institution will end up dealing with a renter the life estate holder has chosen, and it could be subject to agreements between the life estate holder and the renter that may not be in the best interests of the institution.

One alternative is to stipulate in the life estate agreement that any attempt to rent the property would be subject to consultation and perhaps approval by the institution. Another option is to suggest that the life estate holder specifically waive this right in favor of the institution's purchase of the life estate. With this type of restriction, you should eliminate potential problems. If a particularly important donor requests the ability to rent the property, the institution can grant this request on an informal basis.

RECOMMENDED ACTIONS

1. Develop procedures to review and inspect all life estate properties on a regular basis (at least yearly).

2. Develop a life estate agreement form that covers all issues that are of concern to the institution. Make sure the document spells out rights and duties of all parties.

3. Develop procedures for property inspection, review, and acceptance.

4. Develop clear policies concerning the type and condition of properties that are appropriate for life estate agreements as well as any limitations on the number and ages of life estate holders.

chapter eight

EVALUATING THE PLANNED GIFT

At some point in the acceptance process, you will be faced with the potentially difficult task of evaluating the planned gift arrangement. On the one hand, you want to encourage the completion of as many planned gifts as possible to benefit your institution. On the other hand, you do not want to approve a gift arrangement that may prove to be a problem. A planned gift can go either way, so evaluation is critical.

Keep in mind that the failure to make a correct evaluation of a planned gift is the biggest criticism that development officers level toward business officers. Repeatedly, development officers complain about business officers' lack of flexibility and understanding when dealing with planned giving arrangements. Your goal should be to bring to the table a business eye toward the gift arrangement and a development officer's enthusiasm for the completion of as many gifts as possible. By acquiring a certain level of expertise in the evaluation of planned gifts, your relationship with the development office should improve and, over time, that office will begin to include you at an earlier stage in gift negotiations.

Several points will aid in the analysis of a planned giving arrangement. Keep each point in mind as you consider the terms and conditions that the donor wishes to impose on a gift.

The Time Value of Money

Any investor will tell you that a critical piece in the analysis of an investment is the time value of money. This point is equally true for most deferred gift arrangements. A dollar that you receive a year from now is not worth a dollar; it is worth some smaller sum because of your lack of ability to use the dollar during the year.

As you consider a planned gift, keep in mind the discounted present value of the proposed gift. A large gift may be wonderful for the institution, but if the donor is 35, then you will need to consider what long-term benefit there is for the institution. Is the gift worth enough—from a financial standpoint or a public relations standpoint—to warrant incurring the accompanying costs, risk, and liability? What is the gift worth in today's dollars (its discounted present value)?

Determining the "present value" of a deferred gift requires a discounting process. Discounting to present value is a standard mathematical analysis that depends largely on the "discount rate." The federal government sets discount rates for planned gifts based on the applicable federal rate, which for trusts is 120 percent of the federal midterm rate for funds. These discount rates, used in calculating charitable deductions, also are frequently used in evaluating charitable gifts from a business standpoint. These midterm rates are published frequently in the *Wall Street Journal*. They can be accessed on the Internet at the Planned Giving Design Center (www.pgdc.com/usa/rates).

Institutional Liability

Another key aspect of the analysis is an evaluation of the potential institutional liabilities. Keep a simple mental checklist of questions about liability issues. If you have concerns analyze them closely to determine whether they are serious. Every planned gift has a certain element of risk, but usually it is very small in relation to the benefit to the institution.

For example, the trustee has potential liability for failure to act or follow the rules that govern the actions of a fiduciary. Liability may also be created by assets such as contaminated real estate, which may have toxic waste or Superfund costs that may be imposed on a trustee where there is no other party capable of handling cleanup.

The Philanthropy Protection Act contains disclosure requirements for nonprofit institutions, with potential liability for failure to do proper disclosures. Most planned giving disclosures are standard and easily done. However, when a planned giving arrangement becomes complex, a disclosure either may not be completed or may be difficult to adapt from standard documents.

Institutional liability can also come in the form of a private inurement problem, which may put the tax-exempt status of the institution at risk. Consider whether the proposed arrangement appears to send benefits back to the donor that exceed those contemplated in a standard life income arrangement. For example, does the donor expect to sell the contributed asset and receive a commission for the sale even though he or she is not in the real estate business?

Institutional Financial Risk

Planned gifts seldom bring a financial risk to the institution because most are outright gifts, which carry little risk; bequest gifts, which come with few strings attached; and charitable trusts, which are limited in scope to the assets held in the trust. Pooled income funds are similar to charitable trusts from an institutional risk perspective and must satisfy the donors' expectations strictly from funds held in trust.

The largest area of financial risk is the charitable gift annuity program. A gift annuity is a contract with the institution rather than a trust. The institution guarantees that payments will be made whether or not there are sufficient funds in any statutory reserve account, creating a larger degree of long-term liability. Under FASB rules, gift annuities are shown as an asset with a corresponding liability (adjusted annually) on the institution's books and financial statements.

In analyzing the financial risk of planned gifts, the key question is, "What is our downside?" In most cases, the usual answer is "very little." However, donors and their advisors often propose unusual gift arrangements that create a more significant level of risk. In these cases, you must look closely for possible costs and evaluate the likelihood that they may occur. Being risk-averse is an understandable thing for most institutions, but being totally risk-averse is simply not rational in a business environment.

Institutional Administrative Obligations

Another key question to ask is what administrative duties a gift may require of your institution and whether you are willing to commit to them. For example, a donor asked an institution to handle the accounting for a charitable trust that she was establishing. This trust was worth several hundred thousand dollars, but she wished to serve as trustee and manage the investments. The institution decided that the request was reasonable under the circumstances and agreed to do the accounting. Unfortunately, the institution failed to ask exactly what type of investor the donor was. Only months later, it became clear that she was a day trader who by the end of the first year had made more than 1,800 trades. Each one required separate accounting, cost basis information, and determination of the type of gain or loss incurred (short term or long term), adding up to days of full-time work for a staff member in the accounting office. The gift has proven to be a time-consuming task on an annual basis.

As you analyze a planned gift, you should remind yourself of the administrative tasks required and decide whether it can be accommodated within the systematic handling of all planned gifts or whether it will require special handling. Special handling is not necessarily a bad thing, but it can be a far bigger task than you anticipate.

Institutional Benefits

Although there may be definite negatives to a particular planned giving arrangement, you also need to be clearly focused on the benefit to the institution. The development officer, whose job is to encourage gifts, is likely to be totally focused on this issue. The business officer should not stand in the way of a wonderful benefit simply by focusing on negatives.

The analysis of tangible benefits is straightforward. What type of benefit will your institution receive, and how long will you have to wait to receive it? Even with the costs attached to a planned gift, there may be tremendous advantages to accepting it. Business officers are roundly criticized for throwing the baby out with the bath water. You should balance a skeptical attitude with the willingness to consider gifts that may be difficult but have significant tangible benefits.

Keep in mind that some planned gifts may have few if any tangible benefits but important intangible benefits. For example, one university was just beginning to establish a planned giving program. The institution was relatively new, so it had a young alumni base and very few alumni of planned giving age. A wealthy young alumnus set up a charitable remainder trust and funded it with $1 million. The net present value of the trust was minimal, but the donor was the first alumnus to make a charitable remainder trust gift to the institution and also its first seven-figure donor. With the donor's permission, the institution promoted the gift to the alumni base as a worthy example. This marketing effort identified numerous potential planned giving donors, many of whom were not even alumni.

Be conscious of the possibility that there can be many intangible reasons for accepting a gift. It is likely that the development staff will be aware of these benefits, and they will be happy to answer any questions about the precedent-setting nature of a gift that may open new doors for the institution in the future.

A War Story

To put this section in perspective, consider a situation that two institutions found themselves in. An individual approached them who had no affiliation with either institution. He was a donor to virtually no charities. He had a 15-acre parcel of land located in a very desirable area. The land was covered with post-World War II Quonset hut buildings that were leased to artists and small manufacturing firms. The individual was single and wanted income for life and also wished to reside in the properties for the remainder of his life (he was in his 80s). Analysis of the properties found that 50 percent were vacant and that there appeared to be a toxic waste problem. However, the property's estimated market value was $15 million if cleaned up and rented. The individual wanted a high payout rate for his lifetime. At this point, one institution decided that it was too difficult a gift to consider and dropped out of the competition.

The other institution decided to analyze the gift more thoroughly. They brought in an environmental hazards expert, who did Phase I and Phase II studies for toxic problems and provided an estimated cost for the cleanup, which he was confident would eliminate any toxic problems on the property. The institution also contracted with an expert on commercial leasing, who did a market analysis and found that the properties were highly desirable. He recommended adopting a strategy that would increase the number of tenants occupying the buildings.

Based on these experts' analyses, the institution went to the donor and outlined a plan that provided him everything that he wanted. He agreed to make the gift and transferred the $15 million property into a charitable arrangement that included charitable trusts and other more complex entities that the institution's lawyers developed. The toxic cleanup was completed within six months, and the buildings were 100 percent leased within nine months. The net result was a cost to the institution of approximately $200,000 and a gift that, at a discounted present value, was still valued at more than $7 million. A clearheaded analysis of the risks resulted in a gift larger than anything this institution had ever seen. The other institution, being totally risk-averse, walked away from the gift before truly analyzing the risks and rewards. The business officer's job is to make sure that the institution walks away from deals that are clearly losers and accepts gifts that are potential winners, even if they carry some type of risk.

Evaluating Charitable Remainder Trusts

The charitable remainder trust is the most flexible instrument in planned giving. In particular, the unitrust provides more options for donors and advisors than any single vehicle available to them. As a result, you are likely to find that the most complex questions about university policies and acceptance of gifts will involve charitable remainder trusts.

It is possible for a charitable remainder trust to be used not only as a simple life income plan, but also as a supplemental retirement plan for younger donors. Several generations may be involved in a unitrust, which can run for up to 100 years, according to some planners. Income from charitable trusts, which theoretically should be paid on an annual basis, can be manipulated to turn on and off like a "spigot," providing income almost on demand. Investment vehicles within charitable trusts can vary widely as well. Many individuals place assets in trust only to reinvest them in some type of insurance product, usually a variable annuity. These diverse approaches to charitable remainder trusts will cause the business officer to be faced with various analytical chores related to these gifts.

While you must protect the institution's financial well-being, you must also keep a flexible attitude. If you do not, you will cost your institution large amounts of money. Because a trust can be written in a variety of ways, you must be able to analyze the benefits and look beyond any unusual drafting. The key will be to ask the right questions.

Who Is the Trustee?

The critical issue is exactly who serves as trustee of the charitable remainder trust (see Chapter 4). If your institution is not the trustee, you need not be too concerned about the structure of a gift except when it is clearly illegal or so poorly drafted as to create a gift that is unusable. Frequently you will find documents that are improperly drafted and do not achieve the goals that the donor has expressed. Attorneys often draft faulty documents because they do not know the area but are loathe to give up the client to another attorney.

If your institution is being asked to serve as trustee of the charitable trust, you are in a position to impose stringent requirements on the documents presented to you. You should be cautious, however, about limiting the donor's options under any proposed plan. Although as trustee you must be able to function under the terms of the trust, and the trust needs to be a qualified charitable remainder trust, you must keep an open mind. Donors are giving you their assets; it is their money. If they want a high payout, that is their prerogative. It is your prerogative to refuse to serve as trustee should you feel that the terms of the trust are reducing the value to the institution so severely that it no longer warrants your time and energy.

41

When asked to serve as trustee, it seems prudent to require that the trust be a qualified charitable remainder trust and that the payout rate be within a reasonable range. When my university serves as trustee, we often seek a low payout, not only to benefit our institution, but also because we feel that our investment program may not be able to meet the donor's income expectations. Should the donor want a very high payout rate, we often simply suggest that he or she seek another trustee. We do this in part because we do not charge for our services as trustee, and therefore it is an expense for us. That being said, it is also true that we have accepted high-payout trusts, which clearly will erode assets over time, when the donor was adamant about the payout rate and it was unlikely that we would see any gift if we refused to serve as trustee. The incentive became a simple remainder value calculation to determine what the net present value of the benefit to our institution was. When satisfied that there is enough value to warrant our activity on the trust, we agree to serve as trustee.

You may also wish to consider unusual trusts where you can shift the costs of administration from your institution to the trust itself. Instead of refusing to serve on a 15 percent payout trust, perhaps you should suggest that you are willing to serve at no cost, provided that all costs of administration are covered by the trust, such as investment costs and tax return preparation. Then you have some staff time invested, but no out-of-pocket costs and you have closed another trust for your institution.

Who Is the Beneficiary?

While your institution need not care about who is to receive the income from a charitable remainder trust, it is important to know the ages of the beneficiaries. Many institutions have an age minimum on income beneficiaries. They do not want to serve as trustee for a trust that has a three-year-old grandson as a life-income beneficiary. On the surface, this policy seems reasonable, but it can be faulty in the case of larger gifts. If someone offered you a gift of $50 million with an 18-year-old grandson on the trust, but the trust was a 5 percent payout net income unitrust, would you take the gift? A simple remainder value calculation would indicate a sizable remainder to your institution, notwithstanding the fact that $50 million started in the trust. With the new trust rules requiring a minimum 10 percent charitable remainder value, this particular trust probably does not qualify as a CRT. But a good business officer identifying this as a problem with this trust would not simply say no, but would suggest other options. For example, a deferred gift annuity may be a good alternative for someone that young. A deferred annuity would allow

the donors (who are probably parents or grandparents) to postpone the grandson's income until he is older and, hopefully, wiser about money. This might appeal to the donors. A deferred annuity would also allow the institution to invest the funds and build up the account prior to beginning payments to the grandson. And, if your investments perform better than the underlying earnings assumptions reflected in the gift annuity payout rate, you will be creating an even bigger gift for the institution than originally planned. If the trust is being set up for multiple individuals who require income, either drop the 18-year-old from the trust or split it into two different gifts. One gift could be a deferred annuity, and the other could be a charitable remainder trust based on the lives of the parents or grandparents.

The emphasis again is on insight and flexibility. Don't just say no; analyze the situation and suggest to your development officer methods that you would be willing to use with this type of gift. If the money is substantial, you must make it work if possible.

Who Is the Remainderman?

As you analyze a charitable remainder trust, one of the most important considerations is to name your institution as the charitable remainderman. Identify two issues from the start: You may not be the only remainderman, and you may not be named irrevocably as remainderman.

The most important issue from the institution's standpoint is whether you are named irrevocably as remainderman. Donors need not name a charity when establishing charitable remainder trusts. Most donors name at least one charitable beneficiary, but they can reserve the right to name the charity in their will or even assign the trustee of the trust the power to name a qualified 501(c)(3) organization upon their death. In the naming of the charity, attorneys commonly recommend that donors leave the designation revocable, giving them the power to change the charity with the stroke of a pen. From your standpoint, this is not a satisfactory result. The naming of your institution irrevocably is the only way to be certain you will eventually receive the gift. Unless you are doing a large volume of charitable remainder trusts, this is the single most important thing to check on any charitable remainder trust that you are presented, especially where you are being asked to serve as trustee.

If a donor has left the designation of the charity revocable, I would hesitate to agree to serve as trustee. The time and expense involved in serving as trustee warrant some type of permanent gift to your institution. We have found that simply pointing out to the donor that he or she has not made an irrevocable gift to the institution is sufficient to justify either refusing to serve as trustee or encouraging the donor to make it irrevocable so that you will serve as trustee. Most donors find this an entirely reasonable request where they are asking you to perform services on their behalf.

The issue of split remaindermen is one that is growing in frequency. Many donors are seeking to make one gift that satisfies many of their philanthropic goals. It is not unusual for two, three, or more charities to be named as remaindermen. When you are not asked to serve as trustee, this is simply a piece of information that you can file away. When you are asked to serve as trustee, you need to make some decisions about how you will handle multiple remaindermen. It is recommended that you willingly accept multiple remaindermen and agree to serve as trustee in those cases where you are the single largest beneficiary of the charitable remainder trust and when your institution's gift, whatever the percentage of the entire gift it may be, is adequate to meet your minimum standards for charitable trusts. If someone asks you to serve as trustee of a trust that is going to 10 different institutions, but your share of the trust is worth $2 to $3 million, it is advisable to do everything you can to facilitate this gift for the donors. If one institution is receiving $20 million of the trust assets, however, I would suggest that they be the ones who serve as trustee of the trust, if they are capable of doing it well. Usually, donors who make large gifts through charitable remainder trusts have much larger asset bases that are not being placed into trust. By performing a service for a donor in this manner, you cement the relationship and often put yourself in a position to receive a much larger gift later—outright, in trust, or through the estate.

What Assets Are Being Placed in Trust?

If the assets being placed in trust are cash, negotiable securities, or easily marketable real estate, we can classify them as easy assets. Your existing policies will allow you to handle them in an expeditious fashion, assuming you are serving as trustee. You may want to know precisely what assets are being transferred simply to be aware of any needs that the assets may have for maintenance, marketing, or underlying financial risks, such as high-flying growth stocks that probably need to be liquidated immediately versus blue-chip long-term hold stocks that may even be left as part of the underlying trust investment mix.

Difficult assets come in many different categories, but I would generally put them in the categories of difficult to manage, difficult to value, difficult to market or sell, and difficult to define.

Assets that are difficult to manage will need analysis before you agree to serve as trustee of a charitable remainder trust. This area can be the single biggest time drain for a business officer. If you are accepting an apartment building, for example, you may want to be sure that it is not 500 efficiency studio units. The sheer volume of management activity on such a property may force you to hire a staff person to handle it. If the assets appear to be tremendously difficult, you may need to negotiate with the donor as to how management will be handled. If the apartment building is large enough, you may be able to hire a property management firm to take care of day-to-day decisions. However, most real estate investors seem uncomfortable with the hiring of property management firms, feeling that they take too much money for the services rendered. This issue can easily turn into a donor relations problem should you wish to farm out management completely. The best solution is to determine the management needs of the asset and then sit down with the donor before the gift to outline how you intend to handle it. If the donor has any trouble with your proposed plan, he or she will speak up, letting you know about potential donor relations issues. If the donor agrees to your proposal, you stand a much better chance of giving him or her satisfactory service, since the donor's expectations will be clearly in line with your intent.

Assets that are difficult to value become a bit of a headache in terms of knowing whether your institution should even be agreeing to serve as trustee of the trust. The values may be so low that spending time and money on the management of the trust is not warranted. By carefully structuring your overall handling of planned gifts, you should have established a committee of experts who are available to provide advice, expertise, and assistance on difficult or politically sensitive decisions. One of these experts should be someone who knows how to value difficult assets, or at least knows people who can do so. You can assign difficult evaluation issues to experts, who will then give you the information you need to make a decision. Just because an asset is difficult to value doesn't mean that you should not take the gift, however. Too often business officers appear willing to choose the easy option, turning up their noses at gifts that have tremendous potential but are difficult to value. This is a shortsighted approach that will simply cost your institution money in the end.

Assets that are difficult to sell or market are a completely different matter. If you cannot determine that there is an active market for the assets being considered for gifting to trust, you may want to alert the donors up front. You definitely should ensure that the trust is structured so that you are not obligated to make payments on an asset that is not generating income before the liquidation of the asset. You don't want to take in raw land in a charitable remainder annuity trust or gift annuity contract, for example, unless you know you have a buyer or can easily sell the property. In this critical area, you can be relatively straightforward with donors. You can tell them that you estimate it may take two years or more to sell the property. You should structure the agreements to reflect the difficulty of marketing and to avoid disappointing donors by not liquidating the asset in a timely fashion and creating an income stream for them. By discussing the difficulties with donors from the start, you will diffuse most problems that would arise from disappointed expectations.

The final type of difficult asset is one that is difficult to define. For example, rights in real property other than fee simple rights can be quite confusing and difficult to define as well as to value. Another example is intangible property rights, which may be less than 100 percent of the rights to a property, such as a copyright that has already had certain serialization rights sold to magazines, first American rights sold on publication as a book, and some but not all theatrical rights sold. In these cases, you should spend some time determining what specifically is being given to the trust so that you can try to place a value on it and determine whether it is of enough value to warrant the time and trouble that it may cause.

Who Will Manage the Assets?

If the institution serves as trustee, you will be charged with managing the assets. If cash or negotiable securities are involved, your preestablished standard investment program will suffice. You will hire either a custodian or an investment manager to handle the assets, and it should be an efficient system with little extra trouble for you.

What will be your policy concerning assets that require more active management? If you are given a piece of real estate inside a charitable trust and you intend to liquidate it, you still may have management and administration needs for six months to a year or longer. Will you handle this management, or will someone else?

What about other more difficult assets? If you are receiving oil and gas leaseholds, who will do the due diligence on these leaseholds and then continue to monitor them after they are in the name of the trust? These assets are being given with the expectation that they be sold, invested, or held for the generation of income. Who will ensure that they are in fact generating income?

In most cases, your institution will manage the assets. First, you must ensure that there is a clear understanding of how the management of the assets will be handled. If third parties are involved, for example, everyone should be aware of that so there is no surprise on the part of the donors or staff. Keep in mind that you will be dealing with your donors for 20 or 30 years on all of these decisions, so they must be fully informed.

What Terms Are Different than Usual?

One thing you will find in dealing with charitable remainder trusts is their incredible flexibility. They can serve many purposes for the donor. While it is most common to have charitable trusts set up for simple purposes of life income and avoidance of capital gains taxes, you should be aware of a number of techniques that have been employed over the last few years. These techniques are not "tax dodges," nor will they reduce the value of a trust to your institution. In fact, many of the techniques will enhance the long-term value without undue administrative hardship.

"Spigot" Trusts

One feature of a charitable remainder trust is a payout to a donor no less than annually. Some trusts are set up for net income and will pay income earned up to the stated percentage limitation. Many planners have sought ways around this rather restrictive mechanism to fit more closely with their clients' varying needs regarding regular income.

The "spigot" trust allows the trustee to provide income to a donor as the trustee may choose. Obviously, the trustee is given total discretion or there would be no trust in the first place. The donor cannot legally demand that the trustee invest in a certain way (other than following the prudent man rule), but the reality is that most institutions will attempt to accommodate a donor if the request for income is a reasonable one. It is to the institution's advantage to agree to any withholding of income that the donor may request.

Spigot trusts have usually worked hand in hand with investments in variable annuity products. Variable annuity products have recently been recognized in an IRS letter ruling as acceptable assets for investment in charitable remainder trusts. A variable annuity product under trust tax law is considered the source of the income that is generated by the trust and then passed on to the donor. Inside the variable annuity product, however, there are frequently multiple investment options, including stock mutual funds that can invest for high growth and other diversified investment vehicles. In a variable annuity, there is no income to distribute to beneficiaries unless the owner (the trustee) requests it. This means that since there is no income in certain years, there is no distributable income to the donor. A trustee with knowledge of the beneficiaries' income needs can control the amount of income distributed each year. This might appear to be a terrible power to have if you are a remainderman, but in fact it's just the opposite. The beneficiaries will sometimes tell you that they wish to defer income for a period of four or five years, perhaps until they retire. This means that the assets accumulate tax free in the variable annuity within the trust and continue to build up the residual value to your institution.

Some negative outcomes with this technique must be considered as well. First, income that is received from the variable annuity is considered ordinary income even though it may be generated by capital gains realized within the annuity contract itself. This means that income to the beneficiaries will be ordinary income and taxed at higher rates than normal capital gain income under the four-tier system. Second, the insurance company issuing the variable annuity contract may restrict the types of investments permitted, which the more sophisticated donor may find unattractive.

By approving the investment vehicle of the variable annuity inside the trust, the IRS has basically acquiesced to this type of technique, provided that no written guarantees are made to donors as to what you as the trustee will do regarding the investment mix or the income stream to them. This can be an excellent way to grow the asset base held inside the trust.

Retirement Trusts

A kindred type of trust to the spigot is a "supplemental retirement plan" trust. This type of trust is intended to allow an individual to accumulate assets over time that pay little or no income until retirement age, at which point the trust switches to an investment mix high in income-producing assets and increased income stream. Charitable remainder unitrusts are particularly well suited for this type of technique, since they allow for contributions on any schedule you care to follow and the trust enjoys a buildup of principal value. The trust provides a mechanism to revalue the assets annually and increase the potential payout to a donor over time.

A retirement trust works very much like a spigot trust, but it is usually invested in high-growth, low-yield assets. Consider, for example, a 60-year-old donor who wants to retire at age 65. She is maxing out her retirement funding under federal law through either a 401(k), Keogh, or 403(b) plan. She wants to increase her retirement savings and is looking for something that would provide at least partial deductibility for the savings. Enter the charitable remainder trust or supplemental retirement plan trust.

The donor begins contributing to a unitrust that is invested entirely for growth, providing virtually no dividend income. The trust, being a net income trust (perhaps with a makeup provision), does not pay out any more than it actually earns in dividends during the five-year period before retirement. On the date that she wishes to retire, the beneficiary notifies the trustee that, if possible, she would like to receive more income than she has been receiving from the trust. The trustee considers this request and, assuming it is acceptable, restructures the investment portfolio to include high-income assets such as bonds and cash instruments. The donor has had five years of tax-free accumulation of assets from which to draw the income. The institution has been allowed to grow the assets, which it will eventually receive, for over five years without having to deplete them at all by any type of income payment. The switch is allowable if there is no legal obligation on the part of the trustee to invest in any particular way or by any method that the donor has demanded.

The numbers, when calculated on a retirement trust, can prove to be very good when compared with taxable alternatives. This technique, however, never can be as good as a 100 percent–deductible retirement plan such as the 401(k) or 403(b).

Tuition Assistance Trusts

This type of trust, unique to education, develops income for a specified period of years for students attempting to complete their education. A tuition assistance trust is usually a charitable remainder unitrust set up for a term of years. It is also a net income unitrust with a makeup provision, which is critical to the overall success of the plan.

In a tuition assistance trust, the initial investments are handled exactly as you would in a retirement trust or a spigot trust. The assets are invested for growth and not income. The donors are usually parents or grandparents, but the beneficiaries are usually children or grandchildren. During a specified period (usually coinciding with the number of years before a child or grandchild enters college or turns 18) the investment strategy is strictly for growth, attempting to build a large asset base and also to accumulate a large "deficiency" of unpaid income for beneficiaries that can be "made up" at a later date.

When the income beneficiary reaches a certain age, usually 18, the trust assets are repositioned to produce income. Ideally, the assets have grown in value and have capital gains within them. When the switch occurs, any gains or large ordinary income recognition that may occur is distributed under the terms of the makeup provision. This results in a large distribution far greater than the original payout rate for a period of time. How long these large payments go on can be predetermined in the investment mix using timed-payout investments. The best technique seems to be zero coupon bonds, which have total predictability of income and result in a large recognition of ordinary income when they mature.

While this can be an attractive plan, in the last few years this plan has had reduced interest due to the rising use of charitable deferred annuities in place of the charitable remainder trust. A deferred annuity can be structured exactly as the tuition assistance trust can be structured, is simpler, and provides for total predictability of income, since the annuity is a contract that can specify exactly how much will be distributed at what time during the course of the annuity. There are some problems with annuities in this strategy, since they do require the acquiescence of the beneficiary to function as a tuition assistance plan. Only a small number of people do these annuities, however, and the problems with annuitants are extremely few. Most young people going to school want the money and are happy to agree to any terms related to the annuity.

Term of Years and/or Life Trusts

As this chapter has explained, a charitable remainder trust can be set up with a term measured by the lives of one or more people, or for a specified term of years not to exceed 20. What about the donor who wants it both ways? It is possible and legal to establish a charitable remainder trust for a term of years or the measuring lives of one or more donors. Usually, this term comes with the added statement "whichever is greater in length," since the intent is to create a trust that pays out a minimum number of years, no matter whether the life income beneficiaries survive. Frequently, the successor beneficiaries on such a trust will be children whose parents feel that they should receive at least a minimum benefit from the assets transferred.

It is possible to set up a trust for the term of years or the life of an income beneficiary, whichever is less. The only purpose for this arrangement appears to be that the donor may have been planning to do a straight term-of-years trust and then decided that if he or she died and did not receive income for 10 years, there was no one else who needed to get the income, and the donor was happy to terminate the trust in favor of the nonprofit institution.

The key here is that the deductions for a term-of-years or life trust are calculated based on the longer life expectancy. If a donor has a 12-year life expectancy and is setting up a 15-year trust, the calculation for deductibility will be based on the 15-year trust, not on the life of the donor.

Sprinkling Trusts

Although charitable remainder trusts are seldom set up this way, a sprinkling trust can be written to give a trustee the power to "sprinkle" income between several income beneficiaries. Donors may not serve as trustee of a sprinkling trust, whether or not they are income beneficiaries of the trust. Only an independent trustee as defined by Reg. 1.664-1 is permitted. This is a problem because often the donors are concerned that some beneficiaries may need a larger proportional share of total trust income due to health or mental disabilities or because they are spendthrifts. The donors may wish to exercise some control over this allocation process, which is not permitted under the regulations. Sprinkling trusts are a dicey thing for a nonprofit institution to become involved in from a trustee's standpoint, although they would certainly not be any different than other types of trusts if your institution were merely the remainderman.

An institution should study carefully sprinkling trusts before agreeing to serve as trustee. Potential donor relations problems can be created if you, as trustee, are placed in the position of having to decide who gets income and who does not.

Who Is Profiting from the Deal?

As you analyze a potential charitable remainder trust gift, often you will become involved with charitable advisors, such as attorneys, CPAs, life insurance agents, brokers, and financial planners. Each one of these professionals is being paid by the donor directly or through commissions on the transactions within the trust. While it is not advisable to treat all advisors as potential "pirates" and "profiteers," it is important to analyze how advisors are being paid and whether that compensation is reasonable. In one case, a simple charitable remainder trust was executed for a donor who was charged $25,000 for the services. Most charitable remainder trusts do not cost 20 percent of that amount.

For brokers, obviously the sale of stock or underlying assets is expected to generate commissions. Insurance agents are looking to sell an insurance policy that would generate commissions. Financial planners tend to handle commission-based sales of a range of financial products and may be paid in a number of ways. Attorneys usually are paid by the hour but are often in a referral network that may include other advisors, such as brokers, insurance agents, and financial planners. It is important to ensure that their compensation is fair but not excessive.

While concern over compensation may lead one to suspect an advisor's motivations, in many instances advisors can be supportive professionals. With the compensation clearly stated and understood by all parties to a transaction, everyone can reach agreement as to what is fair and equitable. Many advisors play a crucial role in the successful completion of a charitable gift, and you want to encourage them to continue writing trusts for your institution's benefit. Keep an open mind, look for good people in the advising world, and develop relationships with them for the future.

Conversely, if you encounter an advisor who is simply out to make a buck at the expense of the client, you should expose that person, point out the problem to the donor, and make sure that the advisor does not do business with you again. You will be tarred with the same brush should you become involved in a problem gift or an unethical situation, even if you did not cause the problem or act in an unethical manner.

Beware the "Free" Gift

One of the most difficult gifts to say no to—but one that causes consistent problems—is the "free" gift. These deals tend to have been prepackaged by outside parties and brought to the institution for its involvement. Sometimes it is assumed that you will pay for services rendered by other advisors and professionals.

Buying gifts is a very unwise thing for an institution to do. It looks easy on the surface, since the deal is prepackaged, you already have your donor, you already know the amount of the gift, and it looks like a good deal. However, often the fees requested by the gift "brokers" are excessively high when you consider the true discounted present value of the gift. Keep in mind that the cost of raising funds for a nonprofit, especially in the planned giving field, run 8 to 10 cents on the dollar, much less than the fees requested by brokers.

In addition, you do not know what promises have been made to the donor. You end up with a potential liability situation when you agree to "purchase" the gift and along with it all of the representations made by people you don't know to donors you don't know. This double combination is a lawsuit waiting to happen, especially when a donor has expectations of a trust that are not met—and perhaps could never have been met from the inception of the trust.

The National Committee on Planned Giving has determined that paying any type of finder's fee for a charitable gift is unethical. Because of the potential risks involved, you should say no to most of these propositions. However, not every person who packages planned gifts is unethical and irresponsible. If it is a gift of significant value with a reasonable fee, you should perform due diligence research, meet with the donors, and do full disclosures to everyone concerned. If all the

parties are still willing to go forward with the gift, do the deal. No matter how the gift came to you, you are an advocate who is looking out for your institution's best interest. You can't have a strict policy in this area without bypassing useful gifts to your institution.

Many institutions feel that the downside risks are simply too large to ignore, and most such gifts that have been offered are not large enough to cause a change in existing policies. However, if someone walked in the door and said they had a donor interested in giving $50 million in a CRT that they had already packaged, you should take a look at it anyway.

Pooled Income Funds

In analyzing a pooled income fund gift, it is difficult to provide too much generic advice. Most pooled income funds only accept gifts of cash and negotiable securities. They do not accept real estate, closely held stock, or thinly traded stock. These restrictions make it easier to manage a pooled income fund. The few problems seem related to investments and to the expectations of the donors regarding income.

The key issue in establishing a pooled income fund is what type of investment program you will pursue. You can pursue a program for high income, growth, or a balanced portfolio approach. Any competent investment manager can develop this type of investment program. Your problems will probably arise in the donor relations area, where donors expect one type of program and you develop another.

Historically, the older PIF programs were sold to donors as a poor man's unitrust, emphasizing high income levels. This approach has proven problematic for most institutions. If you have established a program recently or can move a program either to a growth mode or a balanced mode, you may find that marketing is improved and problems are reduced. As long as the donor's expectations are for a modest degree of income, you are likely to have few difficulties, assuming you have a reasonable investment approach. Needless to say, if your fund starts losing money due to bad investments, you will have donor problems, but this would be true for any type of investment program.

Retained Life Estates

A gift of real estate with retained life estate can be made with a primary residence or a second home. Special issues related to farms and ranches are discussed later in this section. When a life estate gift is offered to your institution, it must be analyzed on several levels. First, look at the real estate itself as if it were an outright gift, and determine whether you want to have your institution on the title (see Appendix F for a suggested checklist). Assuming that the property is acceptable, decide whether you are comfortable assigning the life estate holder (the donor) responsibility for property maintenance, insurance, and property taxes (see Chapter 7). Most life estate holders are committed to this responsibility, but as they age, it becomes a burden. With a follow-up plan in place, the development office in conjunction with the business office should be able to identify problems and allow for friendly resolution of any issues. Also determine whether caregivers are currently living in the residence. If so, talk with them about what the retained life estate agreement will mean. Sometimes serious problems arise when a caregiver refuses to vacate a residence after the life holder's death (see Chapter 7).

The final aspect of your analysis should concern the property's marketability. It is entirely legitimate to refuse a life estate gift of a property that you are concerned may be unmarketable or that you may not be able to liquidate easily. If holding costs appear to be a major issue, you should not enter into the agreement unless you are comfortable the overall benefit to the institution (perhaps from other gifts made simultaneously by the donor) outweighs the hard costs and nuisance factors that would be associated with a long holding period.

Special Issues Related to Farms and Ranches

Far less frequently, you may be offered a farm or ranch subject to a retained life estate. Since these properties are not only residences but also operating businesses, the issues related to them are somewhat different. Obviously, the first level of analysis is the physical condition of the property and buildings, which should be held to the same standards as a personal residence. Farms and ranches require additional analysis to identify environmental problems. It is very common for farms and ranches to have underground storage tanks for gasoline and oil. They may also have had heavy industrial usage that has contaminated the ground. A careful analysis is critical to avoid possible future cleanup liability, especially when water contamination is involved.

Farms and ranches are also operating businesses that may be involved in programs that could convey with the land. For example, the owner may have participated in programs that pay farmers for planting—or refraining from planting—certain crops. Are these agreements binding on all owners of the land, or are they merely binding on the original owners? You will want to investigate this matter if you are considering a gift of a farm or ranch. What obligations will you assume based on commitments made by the current owners?

Easements on farms and ranches are a more critical element than on residential properties. Large acreages may run in many different directions, or portions may be separated. It is important to make sure that the easements on the properties will not limit marketability. A title search is essential to determine what, if any, easements are on file and whether the deed reflects these easements when the gift is made. Easements are not necessarily a bad thing, but they may affect the value of the property by limiting its use for certain purposes, such as roads.

Cost-Benefit Analysis

After determining that the property is acceptable and carries no unreasonable risk or liability, a cost-benefit analysis based on the ages of the life estate holders will contribute to your decision about whether to accept the gift. Donors will propose life estates at various times in their lives and, while the deductions can be quite small, you should determine whether you wish to be involved with the donors for an extended period of time. Many institutions do not accept life estate agreements with donors who are under 60, because they are reluctant to enter into an extended relationship with people who may live another 30, 40, or 50 years.

Donors commonly propose that the institution pay them an income as well as allow them to live on the property for their lifetimes. This arrangement can result in a decent gift to the institution even with the financial commitment, but it requires careful analysis.

Institutions can determine the viability of a retained life estate with lifetime income by calculating the remainder value of the life estate gift. To create an income stream, this remainder value is then treated as if it were a gift to the institution in exchange for a charitable gift annuity. The remainder value of the gift annuity calculation, not the life estate calculation, is the income tax charitable deduction a donor is entitled to for creating the life estate with lifetime income. The income stream created by the annuity is based on the smaller remainder value of the life estate, not the property's fair market value. Many donors are not satisfied with this amount, since they have based their income expectations on a percentage of the fair market value, not the discounted present value. I recommend against this practice except in the case of very elderly donors in their 80s or 90s because it is usually far too high a cost for the institution. Most donors who are eager to have a high income from a life estate would be better served by looking at other options, such as reverse mortgages. You may want to reconsider entering into an agreement with anyone who is so in need of income that he or she is seeking help from home equity. Retained life estate gifts are best suited for financially secure donors who will never need to depend on the income from the life estate to maintain a comfortable lifestyle.

RECOMMENDED ACTIONS

1. Do look a "gift horse" in the mouth.

2. Always keep in mind the "time value" of money. A dollar in 40 years isn't worth a dollar today.

3. Consider the potential institutional liability. How much risk are you undertaking in the deal?

4. Consider the institution's financial risk. Are you putting money in to the deal? Why?

5. Consider the long-term administrative obligations to which you are committing the institution. Are they manageable? Are they worth the eventual gift?

6. Is the gift to your institution irrevocable? Beneficiary designation on many gifts can be changed if the documents provide for it or are silent on the subject. Are you sure that you will get the gift in the end? But don't say no too quickly. Remember you want to facilitate a gift if possible.

7. Beware of the "free gift." Complex charitable gifts that have been prepared without your involvement carry big risks for the institution. Frequently institutions are asked to pay for the costs in return for being named as a beneficiary of the gift arrangement. Ask yourself who is getting paid in this type of deal. Are the costs consistent with charitable gifts developed by your staff (or those of other institutions, if you are just starting a program)? Are the payouts reasonable? What are the ages of the beneficiaries? Who will be asked to take on long-term administrative duties? What fees will be assessed? Just say no if you have any concerns or unanswered questions.

chapter nine

REVIEWING OR EXPANDING A PLANNED GIVING PROGRAM

Your institution may have been involved in planned giving for many years. For most colleges and universities, planned gifts in the forms of bequests have probably been coming to the institution almost from its inception. How do you know whether you have a comprehensive planned giving program working at an optimal level? Periodic review of any program is advisable—particularly a planned giving program, which must stay on the cutting edge of law and finance issues to remain a viable and competitive operation. You can analyze your program from a number of different perspectives, each of which will offer a partial picture of the overall program and help you decide how much time you need to spend improving or overhauling it.

Program Comparisons

The obvious first question is how active your program is in comparison with those of other institutions of similar size and character. By looking at some institutions that you view as your peers, you should gain some perspective on how you measure up.

Three organizations provide resources to help you. The Council for Aid to Education (CFAE or CAE) produces comprehensive annual reports on fund raising by institutions of all sizes, from large research universities to small colleges. These reports include data on life income plans, bequests, and general fund-raising success. Keep in mind when evaluating the CFAE reports that the planned giving office has more control over life income plans than bequests. The gestation period for bequests makes it difficult to know whether a current program has yielded the high number of bequests or whether someone was particularly active 20 years ago in seeking bequests. Life income plans, on the other hand, tend to be in the control of the development office, so these data are a better measure of program productivity.

The National Committee on Planned Giving (NCPG) is a professional association that has chapters in almost every metropolitan area in the United States, representing all of the major planned giving operations. NCPG has embarked on a series of research projects related to planned giving and its function. In particular, it has been seeking information related to the staffing; salaries; gift frequency, type, and technique; and dollar value. With the data, you will be able to compare, for instance, the average size of a gift annuity to your institution with the average size nationwide and by type of institution. You can easily become a member of NCPG or access its research directly (see Appendix B).

NACUBO also prepares annual lists of endowments and life income plans currently held by institutions of all sizes. These lists may suggest where your program should or could be in comparison with institutions of comparable size and maturity (see next page).

Recent Gift Activity

As you analyze your program, it is important to look at actual experience. You should compile information on planned giving activity for at least the last five years. How many planned gifts were executed during that time period? What types of planned gifts were executed? What was the average size by type? How many bequests were received?

You should begin to see a picture of what program areas are most popular with your donor base and what current techniques do not seem to hold much interest for potential donors. In addition, you may find that the apparent success of a program has been predicated upon a heavy dose of bequest income that might or might not be the result of recent work. It is important to know where the money is coming from and what techniques are most successful.

Program Staffing

It is critical to determine the number of staff members (on an FTE basis) who work on planned giving to get a feel for the resources being allocated to this function. Some institutions have no planned giving staff whatsoever. Others have four, five, or more people actively

Average Endowment and Life Income Funds

Endowment Assets	Endowment ($000)	Life Income ($000)
Greater Than $1.0 Billion	3,459,437	97,540
> $500 Million to ≤ $1.0 Billion	727,829	27,404
> $100 Million to ≤ $500 Million	231,716	14,820
> $50 Million to ≤ $100 Million	70,083	6,510
> $25 Million to ≤ $50 Million	36,905	3,120
Less Than or Equal to $25 Million	13,443	2,024
Public	331,413	15,587
Independent	373,563	16,185
Full Sample Average	360,651	16,017

Based on 741 institutions providing endowment data and 594 institutions providing life income data. Table data are dollar-weighted.

Average Values of Life Income Fund Components

Endowment Assets		Charitable Remainder Trusts ($000)	Charitable Gift Annuities ($000)	Pooled Income Funds ($000)	Other ($000)
Greater Than $1.0 Billion	$	44,703	8,381	19,576	18,614
	%	44.1	18.1	19.3	18.4
> $500 Million to ≤ $1.0 Billion	$	17,341	9,296	1,900	1,900
	%	57.0	30.5	6.2	6.2
> $100 Million to ≤ $500 Million	$	8,424	3,620	1,257	1,524
	%	56.8	24.4	8.5	10.3
> $50 Million to ≤ $100 Million	$	3,532	1,482	937	493
	%	54.8	23.0	14.5	7.7
> $25 Million to ≤ $50 Million	$	1,830	947	74	268
	%	58.7	30.4	2.4	8.6
Less Than or Equal to $25 Million	$	748	1,134	147	7
	%	36.7	55.7	7.2	0.4
Public	$	9,927	3,206	294	1,863
	%	64.9	21.0	1.9	12.2
Independent	$	7,368	3,923	2,666	2,010
	%	46.1	24.6	16.7	12.6
Full Sample Average	$	8,095	3,720	1,993	1,968
	%	51.3	23.6	12.6	12.5

592 institutions provided data on asset values of life income fund components. Table data are dollar-weighted.

SOURCE: 2004 NACUBO Endowment Study, copyright 2005

engaged in soliciting planned gifts. Where are you in the spectrum? You should know not only how many different people are involved, but also how the staffing compares to that in peer institutions. This information is not readily available, so you may need to do your own informal survey.

Obviously, you should know who your director of planned giving is, but there may be other people working on the program that you are not aware of. A person in the business office or support staff may spend time on planned giving responsibilities. A development officer other than the planned giving director may work in this field even though his or her title may not indicate an involvement. If you have no one currently working full-time in planned giving, then who is handling the planned gifts that are being completed? How much of his or her time is involved?

Successful planned giving programs have a minimum of one full-time person. Programs with large dollar volume tend to have more than one person, often two or three, actively involved in planned giving on a full-time basis. Staffing often is not a function of the size of the donor base, budget, or endowment. The greater the financial and time commitment, the more effort and time that can be spent on the function and the more successful you will be.

Program Goals

As you review your current program, you should consider what the goals for the program have been in the past. If the goals have been modest, they may have been fully achieved, but there may be institutional dissatisfaction in the low goals that were set. If you are in the process of setting new goals, you will need to factor in the increased funding and staffing that would be required to achieve them. If the old goals were unmet due to staffing problems, then this issue obviously needs to be addressed. If the problem was ridiculously high expectations without a corresponding commitment by the institution, then this situation should be evaluated and addressed.

In establishing your planned giving goals, your review of the CFAE (CAE) reports and your recent activity should give you a good feel for what to expect. Perhaps your program has been viewed as successful but, compared to your peer institutions, it is clearly lagging. Perhaps the reason is inadequate staffing or the wrong staff placed in positions within the program.

Goals are somewhat difficult to establish in planned giving. To set a dollar goal does not seem terribly useful. Planned gifts happen by accident as well as by activity. Many donors begin to discuss a gift only after setting a clear goal or having a particular asset in mind. If some-

one walks in the door in January and drops a large gift on an unsuspecting planned giving officer, have they really achieved their goals for the year? The goals for a planned giving program, while including a nominal dollar target, should focus more on controllable activities. You cannot control the size of the gifts that come into planned giving. But you can control the number of face-to-face calls on donor prospects. You can control the number of proposals you submit to qualified prospects. You can control the number of pieces of mail you send to prospective donors. You can control marketing activities, from mailings to seminars. The dollars will follow if these goals are being met at a satisfactory level.

What is a satisfactory level? The answer to this question has eluded planned giving professionals for a long time. Efforts to analyze what a productive planned giving officer does have focused on statistical elements such as number of calls, proposals, and mailings. Unfortunately, no two institutions are exactly alike, and the goals of one institution may be inappropriate for another. For example, some institutions set high goals for face-to-face contact with new donors. This approach gets staff out of the office to meet alumni and friends of the institution, but it tends to be unfocused and untargeted, especially for institutions with a limited number of prospects. If you have a large alumni or donor base, this method may serve your purposes. However, for institutions with high dollar expectations, it is not important to see a lot of people; it is important to see the *right* people.

Anecdotal information suggests that the average planned giving officer meets with donors once or twice a week, for about 100 face-to-face meetings in a typical year. At the University of Southern California, where the dollar expectations are very high, staff focus on fewer visits with high-end potential donors. The average planned giving officer would meet with 75 to 100 different donors during the year. However, the resulting solicitations were expected to be in the mid to high six figures as often as possible, and preferably in the seven figures. Smaller institutions or institutions with less affluent donor bases will have to determine their own optimal levels, but it remains true that dollar goals are useless in terms of evaluating or motivating planned giving officers. Allow them to control their destiny by setting goals for face-to-face meetings and proposals, and, if they are doing the right things, the money will follow.

Compiling Data

One of the best ways to evaluate your planned giving program is to look at current statistics. Some development officers report regularly on their various activities during a given period, usually monthly or quarterly. This activity report typically will indicate the number of visits made to donor prospects, gifts that may have resulted, and the type and value of the gifts. If your development officer does not do quarterly or monthly reports, you would want to ask for the following information:

- Number of gifts closed during the last year (preferably two to three years for a better perspective)

- Type of gift by technique (such as trusts, gift annuities, wills, or life insurance policies)

- Estimated dollar value of gifts closed (both fair market value and, when appropriate, discounted present value)

- Number of gifts that your institution manages versus number of gifts managed by others (if applicable)

- Payout rates for life income plans by type of gift (for example, 7 percent trusts, 8 percent trusts, and 10 percent trusts)

- Funding assets by type (such as cash, securities, and real estate)

- Number of donor contacts made by staff (annually, quarterly, and/or monthly)

- Number of formal proposals and/or solicitations to donor prospects

- Number of gifts directly attributable to staff proposals versus gifts initiated by donors or advisors

- Number and frequency of direct mail marketing pieces, size of official planned giving mailing list, and any demographic information used to select the group

- Other types of marketing methods employed (for example, articles and/or ads in institutional publications, ads in newspapers and other commercial publications, and seminars)

Historical data are also useful in this analysis. You may want to ask for some of the following:

- Total number of trusts and/or annuities currently in place to support the institution, by type of gift and dollar value

- Length of time the institution has offered each type of technique (You may have a successful program that appears small merely because it started recently.)

These key data provide three different methods of analysis: statistical data concerning the dollars and cents of the current program; personnel data related to the number of people and the type of activity they are en-

gaged in; and marketing data concerning the actual marketing activity of the planned giving program. All three methods will be useful in evaluating the program.

Evaluating Data

Segmenting the data gives you a better feel for the overall program. If you have already done the peer institution review, you have a ballpark idea what institutions of your size and character are doing in terms of total dollar production. Now you can evaluate this information and compare your institution with others.

Keep in mind that planned giving is a "feast or famine" activity. There are boom years and there are bust years, and only over several years can you accurately evaluate the effectiveness of your program. A larger estate can come in one year and make you look wonderful on paper, but the reality may be that your program is nonfunctional. Conversely, you may have a highly functional program that simply has not managed to hit a big-dollar gift for several years. As you analyze the gifts, it is important to segment those that have come from wills, revocable living trusts, life insurance policies, and other types that are often beyond the control of the development staff. That way you can ascertain which gifts were expected and which were surprises.

Your information will also allow you to evaluate the number of irrevocable instruments that have been executed, including charitable remainder trusts, charitable gift annuities, pooled income fund gifts, retained life estates, and charitable lead trusts. The activity reports from your development staff can be useful here in evaluating the overall success of the program. If the number of irrevocable instruments matches the number of solicitations made for these instruments, it appears that you have an effective program. If solicitations do not seem to be resulting in any of the gifts that you are closing (that is, the gifts are being generated by advisors or donors) then you may have a fine reputation in the community that causes people and professional advisors to seek you out, but your planned giving program may be less than optimal.

By looking at the total number of solicitations and the number of solicitations that are converted to gifts, you can determine the "closing ratio" as a percentage of the total solicitations made. A ratio of 33 percent proposals to closed gifts is solid; 50 percent is exceptional. If the program receives more then 30 percent of its irrevocable instruments from professional advisors, your staff may not be meeting and talking with enough of the right people. This does not mean they have to be the sole initiator of any kind of gift, but they must be involved at an early stage in discussions to ensure that gifts come to your institution in the manner you desire and are directed to areas where you are seeking gift support.

Correcting Structural Problems

A program may be very well run from the development side and still have major problems. These problems tend to be of a structural nature. It is essential for the business officer to analyze and eliminate any possible structural problems to optimize the planned giving program.

Legal Issues

Licensing

Charitable remainder trusts do not require licensing at any level. They are creatures of statute (Internal Revenue Code, section 664) and are governed by the regulations therein. Charitable gift annuities are a different story. They usually fall under the regulatory arm of the state in which the annuities are issued, often the state insurance commission. Gift annuities resemble commercial annuities offered by insurance companies and have been lumped into that same regulatory pattern in most states. Each state has different licensing and reporting requirements that must be met in order to offer gift annuities legally and to continue managing them after they have been acquired. Failure to license can result in severe legal penalties as well as a public relations disaster should the state make the issue public. In addition, failure to report adequately to the state in the required manner can result in revocation of an existing license or penalties as well as public relations problems.

The business officer must be completely knowledgeable about licensing requirements for a charitable gift annuity program in your state. It is recommended that you acquire a copy of the state law authorizing gift annuities and any relevant regulations, as well as any information and all reporting forms from the appropriate regulatory department, probably the state insurance commissioner.

Under the Philanthropy Protection Act, the federal Securities and Exchange Commission (SEC) regulates gift annuities. This means licensing becomes a major issue. In addition to licensing, you should be completely comfortable with your knowledge of all requirements relating to your institution's disclosure documents, which are necessary to offer gift annuities under SEC regulations. (See Appendix H for a sample of a disclosure document.) The various disclosure documents provided by a nonprofit are usually similar in nature. Gift annuity contracts require more disclosure because they are contracts with the in-

stitution. When an institution is serving as trustee of a remainder trust, the same information provided for the gift annuity is usually included in the disclosure materials to increase the confidence and understanding of the donors not only in the gift, but the institution.

Tax-Exempt Status

The nonprofit status of your institution is, of course, the most important legal status you need to maintain as the business officer. This status can be jeopardized if your planned giving program is not conducted correctly. The issue is usually raised when private inurement is suspected. Private inurement occurs when a nonprofit—through the conduct of its business and other activities—generates a benefit (usually financial in nature) enjoyed by a private individual. (Paying an individual a salary or fair compensation for work rendered is not included.) In a planned giving context, donors may not benefit financially from their charitable giving activities except as prescribed by law. Thus, a donor to a life income trust enjoys a tax deduction for the gift and the avoidance of capital gains tax. But he or she may not continue to operate the property that is contributed to the trust; charge fees or receive commissions on the sale of the property; or sell the property to a third party and receive a finder's fee. These are all examples of private inurement. Charitable trusts probably pose less of a risk to the institution than gift annuities, which are a direct obligation of the institution.

While these problems sound terribly onerous (and they can be), they are easily managed with careful policies and procedures. It is not difficult to eliminate most, if not all, private inurement issues up front with any donor, and then they become a nonissue during the gifting process. If a donor insists on certain extra financial benefits, the wisest policy is to simply say no, cite risk to your tax-exempt status, and, if necessary, close the door on the gift.

The most recent example of the risk of private inurement was the life insurance technique known as "charitable split-dollar insurance," which allowed a donor to convert after-tax payments on life insurance premiums into tax-deductible charitable gifts while keeping personal life insurance in effect. The IRS has ruled this technique illegal, and it is clearly an issue of private inurement.

A donor either makes a gift or not. A gift that will in fact benefit the donor simply is not a gift unless structured according to generally accepted rules governing charitable remainder trusts, charitable gift annuities, and pooled income funds. No matter how good the financial picture on a charitable trust or life income plan, there is always an element of gift in the structure. Without this gift element, it is merely a financial transaction, and that is not what your institution is all about.

Unlicensed Practice of Law

From time to time, this issue pops up when institutions aggressively seek planned gifts and in the process the planned giving office advises donors on the tax benefits of their gifts. Few, if any, major lawsuits have resulted from such situations, but the risk always exists. Most state bar associations prohibit the practice of law by anyone who is not licensed. If an attorney is on the planned giving office staff, you are probably safe, but this is rarely the case.

It is inevitable that a planned giving officer will attempt to explain to prospective donors how planned giving techniques will affect them from financial and estate planning standpoints. This is not the unauthorized practice of law in anything but the most technical of interpretations. You begin to cross the line when you insist on preparing final documents for a donor without insisting that the donor's legal counsel review them. This practice is common when sample documents are converted into finished documents ready to be signed.

The solution is to avoid going too far as you try to provide legal advice to donors. Insist that no life income plan of any sort be executed by a donor without adequate legal counsel. This approach will reduce the risk of unauthorized practice of law since you are admitting up front that you are not able to provide adequate legal counsel and that you wish the donor to have counsel.

Prudent Man Rule of Investing

The prudent man rule of investing, which has been made statutory in many states, relates primarily to the handling of a charitable remainder trust by a trustee or the custodian for a trustee (see Chapter 5). If your institution is not acting as trustee, you probably need not worry about this rule. If you serve as trustee, however, then it applies to you. Failure to handle your investments in a prudent fashion or consistent with the common thinking of the investment community may put you in violation of the rule. The most frequent violation occurs when the trustee places too much of the total portfolio in one asset class or one individual stock holding.

Avoiding this problem is a fairly simply structural issue. Institutional policies regarding investment of trust assets must state specifically that you will attempt to follow the prudent man rule, which in general means a diversified investment portfolio. Through the years this concept will change as the investment climate changes,

but if you approach your investments conservatively you are not likely to have a problem as long as you pay careful attention.

Practical Issues

Insufficient Oversight of Acceptance of Gifts

A critical structural problem can result when there is insufficient oversight of the acceptance process for gifts. Development officers by their nature are eager to complete a gift. This is their job, and this is what they receive recognition for doing. Someone else usually has to "look a gift horse in the mouth." The institution needs a clearly defined acceptance procedure that calls for evaluating the gift for business purposes and liability exposure.

Institutions often have acceptance committees of volunteers who are available to evaluate any proposed gift. In a large institution, it may be easier to create acceptance procedures that require the approval of two or more departments. Keep in mind that you do not want to bog down your program in bureaucracy. Do not require six or eight different people to sign off on a gift. If the development office recommends the gift, having approval from one or two other offices on the business side would seem appropriate, prudent, and efficient.

Often gifts must first be approved by the Office of Planned Giving and then, depending on the asset class, by either the Office of Property Management or the Treasurer's Office. This procedure allows staff to apply their expertise on every gift that appears to be unusual, while at the same time not slowing down the gift when a donor wishes to move rapidly. It has proven an effective and efficient system.

Insufficient Oversight of Investments

If your institution does not serve as trustee of any charitable trusts, you still may be concerned with oversight of investments for your gift annuity program. For institutions acting as trustee, it is vital that oversight be maintained on all life income plans. One or more people must be specifically assigned the responsibility for regular review of all investments in all life income plans offered by the institution. The obvious reason for this practice is the high expectations that donors carry concerning their income streams, as well as the high expectations of your institution for future benefit from the assets held in these plans.

It is helpful *but not safe* to rely on the money management people for oversight of these investments. They are usually more concerned with looking good than with a specific analysis of what is going on with different life income plans. In addition, they frequently lack the expertise to understand the effects their decisions may have on the plans. For example, one institution established several charitable remainder trusts, with the donors requesting that the assets be invested in tax-free municipal bonds. Under the prudent man rule of investing, the institution refused to invest 100 percent in municipal bonds but kept the bond exposure in the trusts in the 80 to 90 percent range to satisfy the donors. Over the first few years of this arrangement things were fine, but during a market growth period the 10 percent equity position in the trusts ballooned in value. The investment managers were then faced with a situation in which it was necessary to liquidate assets to make income payments on the newly raised value of the trusts. However, the sale of highly appreciated assets inside the trusts created taxable capital gains income for the donors, which is exactly what they did not want to receive. Then the managers moved the funds into municipal bond funds within the custodial bank. This decision also proved ineffective, since bond funds trade bonds actively and regularly trigger capital gains. Once again, the investments resulted in taxable income for the donors. Although the problem was fixed eventually, if the investments within the trusts had been monitored more closely from the beginning, perhaps the money managers would have been prevented from moving the funds into inappropriate investment vehicles like municipal bond funds.

The staff member who is assigned this task should be required to issue a regular internal report on all life income plans for distribution to the investment and business officers and the development staff. The development staff usually is far more tuned in to the donor's expectations, and they can be helpful in adjusting the investment mix based on their knowledge of the donors.

Insufficient Oversight of Tax Filing and Reports

Every type of life income plan requires some reporting and often tax filings. Tax reporting to donors is also part of this responsibility, especially when the institution serves as trustee. The best practice is to assign a staff member in the business office the responsibility for all filings and reports required by licensing agencies and the IRS. As an alternative, these duties can be outsourced to a firm in the business of handling regular reporting, such as a reputable CPA firm or trust administration company.

Failure to make timely filings of the tax returns or reports to state regulatory agencies can easily result in fines and interest penalties. The staff member responsible for oversight should develop a filing calendar that is distributed to relevant personnel in the business office and the development office. This calendar should include filing deadlines for all types of reports that the institution is responsible for, along with tax deadlines that may be important to donors.

This staff member must also be charged with keeping the development staff informed. Donors frequently request information on these issues, especially when an institution serves as trustee and is responsible for federal K-1 and W-4 forms. By keeping development staff up to date, you will allow them to work with donors more effectively and keep the number of inquiries to the business office to a minimum.

Correcting Procedural Problems

Many problems related to planned giving programs can be the result of simple procedural problems rather than structural problems. It is important to review all procedures related to planned giving for elimination of possible problem points.

Acceptance Procedures

Gift acceptance can be a sticking point if you do not have clear procedures for acceptance of all gifts. Whether you use an acceptance committee or a sign-off system within departments, some type of system needs to be in place. Even when there is a system, problems can develop.

Procedures for handling the intake of gifts must be clearly stated and clearly understood by all parties—both the business side and the development side. Gifts that are generated by development officers should have an effective, efficient way of being evaluated and either approved or rejected. To this end, your acceptance system should contain a checklist of steps that must be followed with any accepted gift. The steps can be as simple as having sign-off from one department in addition to the office of planned giving, or as involved as a sign-off by a committee after a committee vote.

Acceptance procedures need to be streamlined so they do not waste the time of the parties involved. You should set parameters and agree that if a proposed gift falls inside them, staff can dispense with steps in the acceptance process beyond the development office. For example, if a donor proposes a cash gift to fund a charitable remainder trust on an 80-year-old with a 5 percent payout rate, and you have set a minimum age of 60 and a maximum payout rate of 8 percent, then the development office should accept this gift without further sign-off. On the other hand, if the trust involved a 42-year-old, it would be outside the standard parameters and require the evaluation of at least one other office and possibly a meeting of the acceptance committee. If the 42-year-old is planning a $100 million gift, you will probably accept the gift unless it is terribly onerous to do so. If, on the other hand, the 42-year-old is offering merely a $10,000 gift, your overall management costs over his life expectancy will far outstrip any potential benefit that your institution might derive.

Liquidation Procedures

A policy should be in place concerning liquidation of assets transferred to your institution, either outright or in trust. Most policies probably specify immediate liquidation of contributed assets, and the development staff must communicate this policy to donors. Some donors give assets to charities with the admonition that the assets be held for a specific period because they will grow in value significantly. Often this assumption is not true, but when it is true you must be able to tell a donor up-front that if the gift is made, you are likely to liquidate the assets immediately. If the donor has a problem with this policy, then you may be able to reach an accommodation and waive the policy in a particular instance. For example, if a trustee is the potential donor and suggests that you hold the assets for future growth, you would be well advised to consider this request seriously.

You should have a standard liquidation procedure that may be as simple as notifying the custodian or brokerage firm to liquidate the stock upon receipt or as involved as receiving RFPs from brokerage firms to market a gift of real property. Each type of activity can have a simple checklist of procedures. In the case of unusual or difficult to value property, due diligence may require that you investigate the property before liquidation to determine its accurate market value. You would not want to liquidate an obscure painting that turns out to be a Van Gogh or a Rembrandt.

Investment Procedures

Investment procedures, like other planned giving procedures, need not be involved, but they do need to be very specific. Donor relations issues enter into any investments that you make on behalf of life income beneficiaries.

Intake Policies

Simple intake policies are necessary for the physical or electronic transfer of assets. When transferring stock, the person who serves as custodian for your institution should have clear directions for handling the gift. In the case of real estate, the office of property management or the property manager should have procedures in place for the timely deeding of the property to the institution or to the institution as trustee of a life income plan. These procedures, while not necessarily onerous, should be

spelled out to avoid mistakes in the transfer of assets. In the case of year-end giving, the transfer date is critical. Appropriate intake policies can expedite the matter by explaining the approximate time it will take to process the gift. They will also allow development officers to warn donors in advance that they need to consider making their gifts earlier rather than later.

Investment Policies

Investment policies are perhaps the most involved area of procedural problems that need to be addressed. These policies and procedures must indicate several points for the benefit of both staff and donors. For example, the types of acceptable investments can be specified. Certain types of assets are inappropriate under current requirements for fiduciaries. Banks spend a great deal of their time analyzing whether a particular bond is "investment grade." Your stated investment policies can direct your investment advisor as to what is appropriate and what is not. For instance, a trust investment in triple-C bonds is simply inappropriate, no matter how high the payout rate. You would do well simply to eliminate this issue by saying that you will only invest in triple-A and double-A bonds.

In addition, your investment policies must reflect the prudent man rule, described earlier in this chapter. This rule applies to individual stock issues as well as general-sector investments. No matter how attractive Internet stocks were at one time, it would not have been wise to invest all the funds in a life income trust for a 90-year-old in high-flying technology stocks.

Asset allocation is a critical element to an investment program and requires clearly stated policies. Especially from a marketing standpoint, such policies can have attractive results for fund raising. For example, if you have two or three different asset allocation models designed for donors interested in high income, growth, or a balanced portfolio, the development staff can explain to donors and prospects how you approach the investment of assets in a charitable life income plan.

Procedures for Changes in Investments

Investment mixes change, as does the financial climate, necessitating a change in investment policies from time to time in response to market conditions. Any change in an investment mix will have a direct bearing on the results, and thus on the donors and beneficiaries of life income plans and annuities. Before you make any changes in your investment program, it is imperative that you take care of several issues.

First, you need to know how trusts and annuities work in order to understand how a change in investment approach will affect donors. Recall the example, given earlier in this chapter, of donors who expected a tax-free income only to find that because of the large growth in the equity side of the portfolio, they had taxable income. This change had tremendous impact on the donors. Luckily, it was not a positive action on the trustee's part that created the problem, but a huge run-up in the stock market. It would have been just as easy to trigger this same problem by a bad choice of investment vehicles, such as switching from individual bonds to a municipal bond fund.

Before making a procedural change that may be prudent in the current investment climate, you need to determine what the donor's expectations are. The first step may be simply talking with the development officer most closely associated with the donor. You may need to send a letter to the donor about the possible change and the likely impact that it will have on him or her. It is a useful donor relations tool for the business officer or investment advisor to sit down with the development officer and the donor to outline the situation, explain why the contemplated move is deemed important and prudent, and describe how it will affect him or her. This meeting can be beneficial because the donor feels taken care of and positive toward the institution. At the very least, you are taking the time and personal effort to explain why a change is appropriate, even though the donor may be adversely affected.

If an institution works closely with outside advisors, it is not unusual to involve them in meetings with donors, especially if the advisors are capable of effectively presenting options to donors. Donors are often highly complimentary of an institution's willingness to introduce them to the people who handle the transactions for their trust portfolios.

Tax Returns and Reporting

Tax returns and reporting are a critical part of any planned giving program, particularly when the institution serves as trustee. While the forms themselves can be a challenge, procedural problems arise in this area as well. The single biggest flaw is the failure to assign this responsibility to one person. It is too easy to try to separate parts of the reporting requirements and assign them to different offices or people, with no one taking full responsibility for the completion of the task.

When you have assigned responsibility, it is important to provide the appropriate training on how to complete the task. IRS instructions are often inadequate or confusing, as anyone who has filled out an income tax return can confirm. If necessary, hire a CPA or management firm that has some expertise in this area to provide critical support to the staff member. In addition to training, the staff member should have the resources to do the work—from enough desk space to the most sophisticated software available to complete the task. One university that handles several hundred charitable life income plans invested heavily in tax return software that enables the director of trust management to complete all the tax returns for all the charitable trusts for which the university serves as trustee. Your staff member should receive the same type of resource support, whether you are a small or a large office.

In addition, it is critical that your procedures include a calendar of deadlines for tax returns and state reports. It would be wise to prepare a quarterly task list related to all of the deadlines. A big part of filing these returns is the time-consuming task of accumulating data for the reports. If you know that you have to file certain returns in a certain quarter, you can make it a priority of the previous quarter to assemble as much data as possible or to prime the data deliverers that you need the information in a timely fashion. Distribute this quarterly task list to the appropriate people in the business office and the development office so that everyone knows what is going on and what the timeline is.

In addition, a system should be in place to check and update all licenses and reports with the appropriate regulatory agencies. License information is likely to be the most common type of information you will need to update on a regular basis. Licenses can lapse if there is a failure to do something as simple as pay an annual fee or make a filing. For example, in California a small fee is submitted with the filing of reports for the charitable gift annuity licensees. The failure to send this check can result in the license lapsing. The license itself is very difficult to get, and having to reapply could cost you dearly in cash and lost gift opportunities. Again, if a staff member is in charge of licenses and reports and is educated on the tasks, this should not be a major problem. Procedurally, you should have a simple tickler system to ensure the timely filing of all reports, returns, and license fees.

RECOMMENDED ACTIONS

1. Conduct an audit of your planned giving program to determine both weaknesses and strengths.

2. Review current statistical data on gifts in existence from inception as well as current gifts received. Review statistical data on activity of staff and/or volunteers currently responsible for the program. Is staff activity related in some way to a portion of the gifts received? How big a correlation is there?

3. Review program staffing. Who is working in the area now? Who are they? Do volunteers play a role? Are outside vendors, such as attorneys, accountants, and bank trust officers involved in developing new business? Servicing old business?

4. What are the goals for the program? Are you stressing endowment gifts, capital project gifts, or current operations? What would you like the program to achieve in the future?

5. Review your program for structural problems. Are licenses up to date? Are policies appropriate? Is there adequate oversight and management?

6. Review your program for procedural problems. Are gift inquiries responded to quickly? Are gift assets reviewed in a timely manner? Are asset liquidation policies clearly communicated to donors prior to acceptance?

Author's note: These activities can be viewed as the job of your development staff. Who performs these recommended actions is not as important as the fact that they are done and you are given the results to review and consider. Planned giving can be a profit center for the institution with the right support from the business side, but you should know your program's current level, how it compares to others, and its growth potential.

chapter ten

WORKING WITH DEVELOPMENT STAFF

A critical relationship for any business officer is with those who represent the institution out in the real world. The development staff, especially planned giving officers, meet every day with donors and other members of the public. It is important to the success of the business office that they be out there saying the things that you wish to be said and presenting the concepts in a way that you will be able to live with should the gifts come in. The business officer's relationship with development officers will be most effective if you understand how they think, what motivates them, and what you can bring to the relationship. If you can reach a meeting of the minds on major issues, you will find your life is a lot easier. You will seldom be confronted with deals that you must turn down.

Emotion Is the Basis for Action

If you take the time to analyze the type of people who are most successful in development, you will find that they have a strong bias toward emotion rather than analysis. There are plenty of technicians in the planned giving field, but most truly successful development officers have a wonderful sense of enthusiasm and emotional connection not only with the mission of the institution they serve, but also with the donors. This motivation may be somewhat alien to the business officer, who tends to be more bottom-line oriented. But it is important to acknowledge and to couch your discussions with development officers in terms that are more emotional than analytical.

For example, you may be confronted with a marginal gift that you would just as soon not take. If you say you can't make any money on the deal, you may be technically correct. But the development officer's more emotional relationship with the donor and the institution may not allow him or her to accept this as a reasonable response. He or she may react in a negative way, since it seems you are merely a business "hack" worrying about two cents on a balance sheet. If you couch the rejection in terms of the gift failing to achieve the goals that the donor has set or the institutional goals and mission, you are likely to get a more understanding response. The development officer may even be willing to go back to the donor to explain that the gift doesn't quite get the job done and perhaps needs to be enhanced, for example by reducing a payout rate or increasing the total dollar value of the gift itself.

While it is not advisable to attempt to manipulate development officers by couching everything in emotional terms, you do need to understand their motivations. They have a high-stress, active job that requires a lot of commitment to be effective. They will warm up very quickly to someone who speaks their language and seems as excited about the institution's purpose and mission as they are. If you remember that they are passionately supportive of the institution, you will be able to work with them more effectively.

Salesmanship Comes First

Fund raisers tend to be high-energy people as they aggressively seek out individuals who will give to your institution. They approach every deal as something that should be done and can be done if they simply structure it correctly and are enthusiastic enough about it with the donors. They are looking to make the sale, so you must view every gift they bring to you with a certain degree of skepticism, since they are clearly seeing the "rosy scenario" for every gift. They want the deal to happen because that's their job. Your job is to look at the deal as a businessperson and come back to them with a good response.

Development officers are often quite competitive with each other. They want to make every sale, and they want to convert every prospect into a donor. For the business officer, this means that every time you reject one of their deals, they may simply begin to find ways to work around you if you do not couch the rejection in terms that they can understand and react to. You should get them thinking with you about ways you can work together to benefit the institution.

Technical Expertise Varies Widely

Development officers come in all shapes and sizes, with different degrees of expertise in the field of planned giving. Colleges and universities require varying levels of expertise to perform the planned giving function. One institution, for example, requires its planned giving officers to pitch the concepts to donors and encourage them to make gifts. As soon as the donor is ready to make a gift, the development officer turns the individual over to a lawyer or CPA and hopes that the gift is concluded in a satisfactory manner. Other offices, however, follow the gift from the initial donor contact all the way through closing and administration. They are heavily involved in working with outside counsel to draft documents, and they advise CPAs and financial planners of the impact of the gift on the donor's financial situation. Some serve as trustee and also administer the life income plans that they close and may, therefore, be knowledgeable about every aspect of planned giving.

You need to ascertain exactly what level of expertise is available on your planned giving and development staff. You will not find many people who are so technically proficient that they can assert with conviction what the appropriate documents should look like in a given case or what the overall impact of a gift on a total estate plan might be. Some do have that expertise and are virtually attorneys, whether or not they have the formal training. (Several come to mind who are able to correct attorneys on the interpretation of tax law.) When you know your planned giving officers' strengths, you'll have a higher degree of confidence and also a clearer idea about how much analysis you will need to provide on a proposed gift. If someone is not an attorney and is not an expert in the more technical areas, you will need to rely more on an advisory committee and outside resources.

How can you determine the level of expertise? A good step is to simply talk with a development officer about his or her relative level of confidence in different areas. You may also want to arrange a lunch between the development officer and a technical expert, such as an attorney or CPA, who can assess the development officer's strengths. You could develop some kind of test, but you would need a high degree of expertise yourself before attempting to do so. Most planned giving officers will be comfortable talking about most basic concepts, and by inquiring as to whether they have worked in drafting of documents or final negotiations with attorneys and CPAs, you should learn more about their true level of expertise.

What the Development Officer Wants from the Business Officer

The Good Ones

The good planned giving officers know what they want from the business officer: a positive professional who is supportive of their endeavors and understands what they are trying to do. A good business officer:

- Brings a solid sense of business to the table, along with a commitment to make things work, if he or she is convinced that the institutional goals are being met by the proposed gift.

- Brings expertise and money to the table when a deal warrants it.

- Provides a sounding board for the development officer when he or she is considering how a deal might be structured.

- Wants the deal to happen, but only if it's a win for the institution. This is what the planned giving officer wants as well.

- Inspires trust. When the fund raiser believes that you are on his or her side, he or she will be as protective as you are of the institution and will work with you collaboratively.

The Clueless Ones

The clueless fund raisers are unclear about the concepts but eager to get a gift. They are wary of the business officer because they are afraid you may kill their deals and fear that you might find out they don't know what they are doing. When you are insecure in your knowledge, it is only human nature to want to hide your shortcomings. The trouble is that this type of person may get you into a deal that will come back to bite the institution five or 10 years later. Sometimes the bite amounts to hundreds of thousands of dollars.

Your own evaluation of such a person will help you to know how much oversight and control you will need to exercise. Keep in mind that trying to exert total control will eventually drive away talented people, so simply following this policy all the time is counterproductive for the institution. You should push for more intensified training for the planned giving officer. Urge that he or she take training sessions or work with a qualified planned giving consultant.

The clueless planned giving officer, when left to his or her own devices, will potentially run amok, putting bad gifts together in order to look productive. If you treat this person as incompetent, you force him or her to work around you. If you try to function as a colleague, however, the planned giving officer will welcome your input and be willing to accept your suggestions. Your people skills will be critical here.

The Dangerous Ones

The dangerous planned giving officers are a problem. They are distinguished from the clueless ones, who are a problem because of their lack of knowledge. If they knew the field better, they would not create problem gifts. They want what is best for the institution; they just don't quite know how to achieve it. The dangerous ones are a different breed. They may have a well-developed sense of expertise, but they are convinced that their job is to put together deals—any deals—and that it is up to the business officer to tell them no. They feel that if you are willing to accept it, then it's a good deal.

People with this attitude are the exception, not the rule, when it comes to planned giving officers. However, they do pose a different problem for the business officer. They tend to be more oriented to the short term and want to look good in the moment, no matter what the long-term benefits to the institution. They want to talk about how much money they have raised, even though the future benefit may be zero or, worse, a negative number for the institution. They seem to change jobs fairly frequently, even though they lay claim to major fund-raising successes. They are adept at working around the business officer, seeking support for their deals from their bosses and even donors or trustees. They are more willing to put you in the position of saying no to the "great gift" that they have put together.

Learning who you are dealing with is especially important in these cases. Having an expert test the person's expertise wouldn't hurt either. You might also want to do a little digging and find out how the business officers perceived the person at his or her former places of employment.

If you think you may have a dangerous planned giving officer on your hands, it is obvious that you will have to scrutinize the gifts brought to you very carefully. You may be forced to learn even more about planned giving in order to handle the gifts effectively and protect the institution from risk and long-term problems.

Controlling the Operation without Destroying the Program

The key concept for the business officer is always control. Just as you have controls on spending and purchasing decisions, you always want control of the planned giving program. But the more you try to exercise control, the more difficult it will become, since the fund-raising programs are usually not in your area of responsibility and the pressure to get new gifts will continue in the years to come. How should you proceed?

Communication Is Key

The first thing to do is get to know the key players as individuals. It is my impression that the average busi-

ness officer does not think much about developing good relationships with development staff. After all, what does that have to do with you? The answer is, a lot, as this book has explained. The better you get to know them, the easier it will be to work with them and to make sure that they implement your controls.

Make sure that the development officers involved know and understand your needs and concerns. Review with them the overall institutional budget and how they fit into your world. As you discuss specific gifts that they may be developing, let them know what you are looking for in the terms of the gift, the type of assets, and other key items that you have identified. Let them react and respond to your concerns. Invite them to discuss how your issues affect their ability to close gifts. You may find that what you want is not feasible in the current economic climate or in the competitive climate of tax-advantaged gifts. You may want to limit the payout rate on trusts to 5 percent, but if a charitable institution down the street is willing to handle higher payouts, you have a competitive disadvantage that your development staff will likely be aware of and want to talk about.

Be assured that most of the business officer's concerns are also the concerns of the development staff. A good development officer wants to put together good gifts, not bad ones. Let them know your needs and preferences, and they will work with you as a team because they will know in advance how you will respond.

Establish Simple Oversight and Approval

You should establish approval controls for all planned gifts, but this does not mean that you have to approve every gift as it comes in. Create working parameters for all forms of planned gifts and communicate them to all development officers likely to be working with complex gifts. These parameters should include acceptable gift types, assets, and payout rates. Discount rates should be clearly stated, even if you follow IRS rates. The clearer you are about these basics, the less you will have to worry about the types of gifts coming in. You should also identify the key areas in which you want "green light" approval—usually complex asset gifts such as real estate (especially commercial properties or those most likely to have environmental issues) and gifts that are structured in unusual ways or that may require cash outlays by the institution.

It is recommended that you be at least one of the signatures required on all gift instruments, whether they are trusts, gift annuities, or life estate agreements. Usually a simple transmittal form filled out by the development office can show you the basics of the agreement and, assuming it fits within the parameters you have set earlier, is merely a quick signature on your part.

Although you are working to protect the institution and have no direct interaction with the donor, your control system must be donor centered. Donors have been asked to consider a complex gift. They may be giving away assets that they have owned for 20, 30, or even 50 years. The transaction is very significant to them. Responsiveness and personal sensitivity are key elements for any program. Whether you say yes or no to a gift, how you say it is as important as what you say. Keep the donors in your thoughts. How would you want to be responded to if you were the donor?

Quick Response to All Gift Proposals

If there is one recurring problem between the business office and the development office, this is it. Repeatedly development officers complain that they cannot get a quick response to gift proposals from the business office. There probably are several reasons for this delay.

First, everyone is in a hurry. Many times the business officer is confronted by an out-of-breath development officer eager to get immediate approval on a complex gift and worried that if they delay even a day, the donor may change his or her mind. On the other hand, you are busy and don't necessarily have the time to drop everything to handle the proposed gift analysis and due diligence required of you. The donor usually is also eager to complete the gift, putting added pressure on the development officer and the business officer. And, if the donor is a high-profile donor, such as a trustee, you will also be getting calls from the president and trustees wanting to know when the gift will be completed and how you are responding to the donor.

Responsiveness is critical here, and your busy schedule seldom will be a good reason for delaying the analysis of a gift. Your systems will aid you in handling this task, and your relationship with the development office will also help. Being cautious is a good thing, as long as you are cautious in a timely way.

Lost in the internal systems for planned gift analysis is the consideration of donor gift timing, which only adds to the pressure. Obviously, a donor will be concerned about gift timing regarding taxes and the tax year. All individual donors are on the calendar year for tax purposes, so year-end gifts will require acceptance and transfer by December 31. If a gift is being made through a corporation, the tax year may be a fiscal one—for example, July 1–June 30. You should ask about the tax year when being asked to consider a gift. Pressure may come at you unexpectedly due to a different tax year than you expected.

Other gift timing issues may cause you to expedite gift acceptance. A donor may be receiving a gift through a bequest from a family member and need to expedite his or her own gift to allow for the closing of the estate. The donor may wish to make the gift in order to increase income—for example, a piece of undeveloped real estate with high value. Donors may simply be in a hurry because they are leaving on an extended vacation. You need to ask about the donor's timeline to make sure you are not viewed as the bottleneck on a large gift simply because you were unaware of the timeline.

Another reason for quick response to gift acceptances is the competition for charitable gifts. Every institution faces some type of competition, whether it is Harvard or the small private day school around the corner. This competition is usually felt in the area of payout rates on life income gifts and the liberality of acceptance policies sometimes forced on institutions.

Because you do not live in a vacuum with donors who give exclusively to your institution, your responsiveness can play a role in the completion of a gift. There are numerous instances of donors approaching an institution with a gift proposal and, due to the slow response time, the donors going to their second-choice institution with the same proposal.

You must keep timeliness of your response in mind as you perform your due diligence work on a gift proposal. It is easy to make it a medium or low priority, but you will be doing the institution (and yourself) a disservice if you do not make every effort to ensure a quick analysis and reasoned response to all gift proposals of any merit.

RECOMMENDED ACTIONS

1. Take the time to try and understand the type of people who work in development.

2. Meet with the development staff formally or informally on a regular basis to discuss the program.

3. Explain to the development staff how the business office evaluates proposed gifts, in particular gifts of difficult assets such as real estate, limited partnership interests, and tangible personal property. If possible, develop a list of assets that you do not want to deal with unless the value is very large.

4. Work with the development staff to develop standard procedures for the evaluation and acceptance of a gift. If possible, determine the types of gifts that can be accepted without consultation, such as cash gifts or trust gifts within specific payout and age ranges.

5. Emphasize to the development staff that you do not want to say no to creative arrangements, so long as they benefit the institution. Encourage them to seek your advice while the gift is being negotiated, not after.

6. Try to be timely in responding to gift proposals. And, when you must decline the proposal, suggest alternative terms or assets that would be acceptable.

PART TWO

A FINANCIAL OFFICER'S GUIDE TO PLANNED GIVING VEHICLES

The average business officer is too busy to become a walking, talking expert on all phases of planned giving. In these chapters, you'll find a concise overview of planned giving techniques that gives you the basic information you need to understand and evaluate your institution's current planned giving programs.

In a nutshell, there are four types of planned gifts: outright gifts, gifts of income but not the assets, gifts of the assets but not the income, and finally, deferred gifts. Most people understand outright gifts, whether in the form of cash, checks, or outright gifts of assets such as stocks, bonds, and real estate. Deferred gifts, such as gifts through wills, revocable trusts, and life insurance death benefits are also fairly clear. Most of the complexity in planned giving centers on "split-interest" gifts of assets in which either the income or the asset is retained or controlled by the donor during a specified period of time. Gifts of income without assets are usually completed through charitable lead trusts. Gifts of assets without income are the largest area of activity for the average program and include charitable remainder trusts, charitable gift annuities, and pooled income fund gifts.

chapter eleven

TAX ADVANTAGES OF PLANNED GIVING

Planned gifts offer donors three basic income tax advantages. First, donors giving appreciated assets avoid capital gains tax on the transfer to charity. This is frequently a major factor in deciding to create a planned gift. Second, they are allowed an income tax charitable deduction for a portion of the value of their gift depending on whether the gift is outright or deferred. Outright gifts of appreciated assets are deductible at the full fair market value of the gift, subject to the 50 percent/30 percent limitation. Life income plans are allowed a deduction but it is discounted to net present value. Any gift to charity is deductible under the federal alternative minimum tax as well; state laws may vary. Third, a gift to charity removes the contributed assets from the donor's estate thereby reducing the donor's overall estate tax liability.

Capital Gains Tax

The average taxpayer is subject to tax on any gain from the sale of any asset. Profit from assets held for less than one year is considered short-term capital gain. Profit from assets held for longer than one year (a year and a day) results in long-term capital gain. The tax is levied on the gain, that is, the difference between the basis of the asset (usually the purchase price) and its selling price. Short-term capital gains are taxed at ordinary income rates, which are the highest tax rates. Long-term capital gains are taxed at capital gains rates, which usually are much lower than ordinary income rates. Assets sold at a loss are not subject to the tax.

An appreciated asset that would be subject to capital gains tax if sold may be given to charity with no tax liability. This feature, while true for outright gifts to charity, has heightened value for a donor who wishes to establish a life income plan. The donor would not only avoid the capital gains tax, but also receive an income based on the fair market value of the asset, undiminished by tax (see the discussion of charitable remainder trusts in Chapter 12).

An Example of a Gift of Appreciated Assets

Giving appreciated assets is one of the best ways to get the maximum tax advantage from a charitable gift.

When donors give assets like stocks, bonds, and real estate, they not only create an income tax charitable deduction—they also avoid capital gains tax on the appreciated asset itself.

Over the past several years, the tax rate on capital gains has dropped from 28 percent (higher in states with state income taxes in effect) to as low as 15 percent. When the tax rate was 28 percent or higher, the numbers looked far more persuasive than in this example. The following example illustrates the difference in tax outcomes between outright gifts of appreciated assets and selling the assets and giving the proceeds. It also shows what would happen if a person sells the assets with no intention of making a gift.

A potential donor, Charlie Potts, is considering how to handle a block of Microsoft stock that he purchased when the company first went public. He bought 1,000 shares at $2.00 each. His current holdings, including stock splits, have a fair market value of $1.26 million. He has a $1.258 million capital gain, which will be subject to tax if he tries to sell the stock (fair market value of $1.26 million less cost basis of $2,000 = capital gain of $1.258 million).

Should he sell the stock, pay the tax, and keep the proceeds? Should he sell the stock and give the proceeds to charity? Or should he give the stock outright to charity prior to sale? Here are how the numbers look under current tax rates:

	Sell/Keep Proceeds	Sell/Give Proceeds	Give Stock
Fair market value	$1,260,000	$1,260,000	$1,260,000
Cost basis in stock	2,000	2,000	2,000
Capital gains tax @ 15 percent	188,700	188,700	-0-
Income tax deduction	-0-	1,071,300	1,260,000
Tax savings (28 percent tax bracket)	-0-	299,964	352,800
Net cash in hand for donor	1,071,300	299,964	352,800
Net gift to charity	-0-	1,071,300	1,260,000

The answers to our questions are clear from this chart. If the person has no charitable intent, he probably will sell the stock, pay the tax of $188,700 and end up with $1,071,300 in the bank. If, however, our donor has charitable intent and wants to make a gift, the clear advantage is with giving the appreciated assets directly to the charity, rather than selling them first and contributing the proceeds. Our donor will end up with $52,836 more in hand by giving directly before sale of the stock. Not only that, but his net gift to charity is increased by $188,700.

The net cost for our donor to contribute the stock is $907,200 ($1,260,000 fair market value less $352,800 of tax savings). This is a cost of 72 cents on the dollar to make the gift.

Compare our cost of giving with what the nondonor did. He realized $1,071,300 of net cash on hand, but made no gift. Our donor realized $352,800 of net cash on hand. Thus, we can say that it cost our donor $718,500 out of pocket to make a gift of $1,260,000 to charity. This is a cost of 57 cents on the dollar to make the gift compared to not making the gift at all.

When the capital gains tax rates are higher, the net position of the donor after the gift is often very close to the net position of the person without charitable intent who merely sells the stock and keeps the proceeds.

Income Tax Charitable Deduction

The donor receives an income tax charitable deduction for the full fair market value of an outright gift by claiming this amount as an itemized deduction on his or her income tax return. The deduction is limited to a percentage of the donor's income, depending on the type of asset given.

If a donor contributes cash or short-term gain property, the total charitable deduction is limited to 50 percent of the adjusted gross income of the donor. For example, if the donor's income is $80,000, the deduction allowed for total charitable gifts of cash and/or short-term gain property is $40,000 (50 percent of $80,000). In the case of long-term capital gain property, the charitable contribution deduction is limited to 30 percent of the donor's adjusted gross income. For example, if the same donor earning $80,000 per year gave only long-term capital gain property, the deduction in the year of the gift would be limited to $24,000 (30 percent of $80,000).

When a donor is unable to use the total deduction in the year of the gift due to these limitations, he or she may carry the unused portion of the deduction forward to the next year. The "carry-forward" is allowed for up to five years after the year of the actual gift. For example, if

our donor makes cash gifts totaling $50,000, the deduction for the year of the gift is $40,000. The remaining $10,000 of unused deduction is available the next year. If the donor makes a cash gift of $240,000, it is fully deductible over the carry-forward period, assuming no other gifts are made ($40,000 in the year of the gift and $40,000 per year in each of the five carry-forward years). Changes in adjusted gross income from year to year could increase or decrease the total deduction amount available to the donor.

Gift and Estate Tax Advantages

Tax Rates

The gift and estate tax systems have been the subject of much argument over the past several years. The estate tax is on schedule to be reduced and finally repealed in 2010. However, in 2011 it is scheduled to return in its pre-2001 form. It is a relatively safe bet that some form of estate and gift taxation will remain in effect for the near future, and, if repealed, it is very likely to be reinstituted.

Both the estate and gift taxes are graduated (i.e., rates rise with the size of the gift or estate, and are levied against all gifts made during lifetime or through the estate of the donor—with the possible exception of 2010 under the estate tax repeal). Rates begin at 18 percent and rise to a current maximum rate of 47 percent (or less, depending on the year up to 2010, when the estate tax expires). Taxpayers currently enjoy a credit against the gift tax that exempts up to $1 million in lifetime noncharitable gifts and a credit against the estate tax that exempts up to $1.5 million in testamentary noncharitable gifts. While the estate tax exemption amount will rise to $3.5 million by 2009, the gift tax exemption is frozen at $1 million. Prior to 2001, these credits were aggregated in a "unified credit" that applied to all noncharitable gifts made during lifetime and at death. Effective planning now allows couples to shelter as much as $3 million in testamentary noncharitable gifts and $2 million in noncharitable gifts during their lifetimes. The estate tax side will gradually increase to $7 million in testamentary transfers by 2009 and becomes unlimited for 2010.

For the purposes of calculating the gift and estate tax (not the income tax), charitable gifts—whether made during a lifetime or through an estate—are 100 percent deductible. This means that an unlimited dollar amount may be given to qualified charities through a person's estate or during his or her lifetime, and the donor is not subject to either the gift or estate tax.

Gifts between spouses are also fully deductible against the gift and estate tax. Taking into account both the charitable deduction and the unlimited marital deduction, it is possible to give everything to a spouse and then to charity with zero tax liability. This 100 percent can be applied successfully to life income gifts as well. The potential for taxation only arises when a donor creates a life income gift in which the income runs to a nonspouse. Drafting appropriate language and using either the gift or estate tax credit can effectively cover this situation.

Transfer Tax Exemptions (Credits)

Prior to 2001 a unified gift and estate tax credit against all noncharitable gifts made by a taxpayer existed. In 2001 the estate tax and gift tax were decoupled and different credit amounts were established for the gift tax and the estate tax. These credits are often referred to as exemptions, but the exemption actually refers to the total dollar amount that the credit effectively shelters from transfer taxes. These credits are available to each taxpayer individually, which allows couples to shelter a significant amount.

Below are the scheduled exemption amounts for gifts made under the gift tax and under the estate tax. In 2010, the estate tax will be repealed. However, it returns in full force at its 2001 rates in 2011.

Year	Gift Tax Exemption	Estate Tax Exemption	Maximum Estate & Gift Tax Rate
2003	$1 million	$1 million	49% over $2 million
2004	$1 million	$1.5 million	48% over $2 million
2005	$1 million	$1.5 million	47% over $2 million
2006	$1 million	$2 million	46% over $2 million
2007	$1 million	$2 million	45% over $1.5 million
2008	$1 million	$2 million	45% over $1.5 million
2009	$1 million	$3.5 million	45% over $1.5 million
2010	$1 million	Repealed	35% gifts over $500K
2011	$1 million	$1 million	55% over $3 million

The Generation-Skipping Tax

The generation-skipping tax (GST) is perhaps the most complex tax, since its application is incredibly obtuse in many instances. The tax is levied on gifts made either during a person's lifetime or at death that attempt to transfer assets from one generation (think grandparents) to another generation (think grandchildren) while skipping a middle generation (think the grandchildren's parents).

This type of transfer usually happens if the middle generation is financially successful and does not want or need more assets, or if they are spendthrifts. A gift by grandparents to grandchildren makes more sense because it arguably skips a round of gift or estate taxation by avoiding the parents and their estates before going to the grandchildren.

For most people, this doesn't seem like such a bad thing. But if a Bill Gates were to do this, the government would lose a substantial amount of tax money if it didn't somehow make this situation a taxable event. Enter the generation-skipping tax. Without going into too much detail, the GST treats the transfer to a "skip" generation (grandchildren) as if it were first transferred to their parents (even though it wasn't) and then from the parents to the children (the grandchildren of the donor). This legal fiction makes the skipped "transfer" a taxable event, and the assets are taxed accordingly. Tax rates on the GST are equal to the maximum estate tax rate (currently 47 percent). It is a flat rate, not a graduated rate like the gift and estate tax.

The good news is that the GST has a credit or exemption amount just like the gift and estate taxes do. Originally, the credit sheltered up to $1 million in gifts to a skip person within a skip generation. For transfers made in 2003 and after, the exemption amounts have been increased and are shown below:

	GST Exemption	Maximum GST Rate
2003	$1.12 million	49% over $2 million
2004	$1.5 million	48% over $2 million
2005	$1.5 million	47% over $2 million
2006	$2 million	46% over $2 million
2007	$2 million	45% over $1.5 million
2008	$2 million	45% over $1.5 million
2009	$3.5 million	45% over $1.5 million
2010	Repealed	Repealed
2011	$1 million	55% over $3 million

Each gift to a skip person is subject to the GST. The GST exemption amount is applicable to each transfer made. Gifts can be made to multiple skip persons and aggregated separately to apply the exemption. In other words, in 2005 gifts totaling $1.5 million could be made to each of several skip persons and all would be completely sheltered from the GST. However, if one person received $2 million, then the $500K over the exemption amount would be subject to the GST.

Alternative Minimum Tax

All taxpayers are subject to the alternative minimum tax (AMT), although most people do not realize it. The tax is an alternative method of calculating income tax that is intended to increase the taxes paid by high-income taxpayers. Under the AMT, certain deductions available under the regular method of calculation are no longer available, including most of the deductions that are available to people who invest in tax shelters. While the AMT is complex and beyond the scope of this book, most high-income taxpayers are forced to deal with it.

The good news from a charitable standpoint is that all gifts to charity are deductible under the AMT, including gifts of appreciated property. Some donors may be under the impression that gifts of appreciated assets such as stocks and real estate are not fully deductible under the AMT. This was true for a few years, but the laws were changed in the early 1990s. Under current law, appreciated assets are deductible at full fair market value with no reductions. State laws generally conform to federal laws, but California law did not change for several years after the federal law was changed. You should check state tax law to make sure your state conforms to the federal AMT rules, especially concerning gifts to charitable organizations.

chapter twelve

CHARITABLE REMAINDER TRUSTS

The charitable remainder trust (CRT) was created by federal statute in 1969 (Internal Revenue Code, sec. 664). Until that time, trusts were drafted to conform to tax law, but it was clear that the field was in confusion concerning the best method to create tax-advantaged trusts. The statute attempted to codify the best practices in the field while at the same time shutting down the abuses.

The CRT comes in two basic types: the charitable remainder annuity trust and the charitable remainder unitrust. Each trust provides an income to one or more income beneficiaries for a period of time known as the term of the trust. Most remainder trust terms are for the lifetimes of the income beneficiaries, but you can also set up a trust to run for a period of up to 20 years. Clever drafting can combine these two terms to ensure that a trust pays out for a minimum term defined in years or the lifetime of a beneficiary, whichever lasts longer.

When the term of the trust expires, either by the death of all income beneficiaries or the conclusion of the term of years, all trust assets must be paid to a qualified charity. The charity is known as the *remainderman* of the trust. A CRT may name one or more remaindermen. It may also remain silent as to the remainderman, provided that it defines a mechanism for naming one at the termination of the trust. Frequently a trust provision gives the donor the power to name a remainderman by will and, if the donor fails to do so, gives the trustee the power to name a remainderman.

When a charity is named the remainderman on a trust, this designation is revocable, absent specific language in the document making it irrevocable. Charities prefer otherwise, but attorneys frequently counsel their clients to leave it revocable in case donors change their minds. Revocable designations make the gift the equivalent of a will and should not be booked as a gift or an asset of the charity. In accordance with FASB, revocable trusts are conditional transfers and should be reflected both as an asset and a refundable advance. There is no effect on net assets. There is no basis in GASB literature that would allow an entity to record and report these assets. Thus, public institutions that follow GASB do not record revocable trust arrangements. However, public institu-

tions with affiliated organizations [whereby the affiliated organizations are usually 501(C)(3) entities that follow FASB] may have a reporting event if the affiliated organization is a significant component unit and "blended" into the financial statements of the public institution in accordance with GASB Statement 39, which addresses affiliated organizations.

All trusts must have a trustee, either the remainderman or someone else. The trustee can be a person or an institution, such as a bank or trust company or a nonprofit institution. The trustee has fiduciary obligations and requirements that may vary from state to state. The trustee is, for example, responsible for all investment decisions made for assets held in trust. Usually the trustee is responsible for the sale of the funding assets and the reinvestment of the cash to generate income for the income beneficiaries. Donors can name themselves as trustee, but it should only be done under special circumstances. It is difficult to serve as a trustee if you have never done so before, and the risk of self-dealing increases when a donor acts as trustee. Nonprofit institutions seldom act as trustee on trusts unless they are named irrevocably as charitable remainderman of the trust. In many states, nonprofit institutions may be prohibited from receiving compensation as trustee for services rendered and must look to the remainder for remuneration.

A CRT is created when a donor irrevocably transfers assets to a trust that complies with Internal Revenue Code section 664. Under the terms of the trust, the donor must be paid an income for a term, either life or years. The stated income percentage amount must be at least 5 percent but no more than 50 percent of the value of the trust. At the end of the trust term, the assets are given to the charity that is designated remainderman of the trust. To qualify as a CRT under section 664, the remainder value of the trust must be at least 10 percent of the total value of the trust assets at the time the trust is established. This rule was put in place due to taxpayer abuse of the old rules, which were silent as to the minimum value of the charitable remainder.

By transferring assets irrevocably to a qualified charitable remainder trust, the donor is allowed to take an income tax charitable deduction. The deduction amount is *not* the full fair market value of the assets. It is the full fair market value of the assets *discounted to present value*. This means the deductions, which are calculated according to IRS tables, are based on the payout rate of the trust and the life expectancies of the income beneficiaries. In other words, how much you pay the beneficiaries and how long you expect to pay them is taken into account when determining the charitable deduction amount that the donor is allowed to use. The calculations are complex, and most charities and accounting firms have computer software that makes them easier to determine.

The assets held in charitable remainder trusts may be invested in pooled investment funds, including mutual funds and investment trusts. However, the trustee must be sure that any pooled investment avoids generating any unrelated business income (UBI) as defined by trust tax law. This risk is usually caused by debt financing of investments within the pooled investment fund. Prospectuses should be reviewed to determine if the fund is allowed to leverage investments with borrowing. This practice will cause significant problems for any charitable remainder trust.

Charitable Remainder Annuity Trusts

The charitable remainder annuity trust (CRAT) is a fixed-income trust. The amount to be paid to the income beneficiaries is determined when the trust is first established, by stating a specific dollar amount or by stating a percentage amount that is then applied to the value of the funding assets to determine a specific payout amount. Whether stated as a dollar amount or a percentage, the payout must be at least 5 percent and no more than 50 percent of the fair market value of the trust's funding assets. This payout amount remains fixed for the term of the trust or until all assets in the trust are exhausted. (Compare this feature with the variable nature of unitrust payments in the next section.)

This fixed payment choice can be a two-edged sword for the charity and the donor. If you have good fortune in your investments, the principal can grow. Since the payout remains fixed, the donor notices no change, and the principal growth can accrue to the benefit of the charity. I have witnessed at least three trusts that accumulated millions of dollars in excess principal due to a low payout on an annuity trust and very successful investment results.

However, if you do not have good investment results (especially in the early years of the trust term), your principal base is eroded and you begin a slow downward spiral toward zero. The payments are fixed, so each year a larger percentage of the asset base is required to meet

the obligation to the beneficiaries. This in turn means that an even higher investment return is required each year to stay even or bring the trust back to its original funding amount.

To qualify for tax purposes as a charitable remainder annuity trust, the trust is subjected to the 5 percent probability test. This test, governed by IRS rules and tables (see IRC sec. 664 and reg. 1.664(a)(1)), is an attempt to determine if there is more than a 5 percent chance of the trust assets being depleted during the term of the trust. Since most trusts are based on one or more lifetimes, the ages of donors are factored into the calculation along with the payout rate being paid. A high payout rate to younger donors is more likely to fail the 5 percent probability test than, say, two 80-year-olds with a 5 percent payout. This test also is affected by the discount rate applicable in the month of the gift. (See Glossary—midterm rate.)

The income tax deduction for an annuity trust historically has been larger than for a unitrust. However, in low interest rate environments where earnings assumptions drop below 5 percent, the reverse is true. The annuity trust will have a smaller income tax charitable deduction than the unitrust in a low interest rate environment because all trusts must pay at least 5 percent. In a fixed-income instrument, this means built-in erosion of principal for purposes of the tax calculations since the minimum payout (5 percent) is higher than the assumed earnings of trust assets.

Advantages to the Donor

There are several reasons for a donor to establish a charitable remainder annuity trust.

- **Security.** The fixed-income feature of the trust provides a steady income stream that can only diminish if the trust assets are depleted. Donors can achieve certainty with their income, which in retirement becomes important to most people.

- **Tax benefits.** The donor receives an income tax charitable deduction for an amount less than the fair market value of the trust assets. The deduction is calculated using IRS tables that discount the deduction to present value. The donor also avoids capital gains tax on any appreciation in the contributed asset. Because the capital gains tax is avoided, the donors receive income based on the pretax value of the appreciated assets. The contributed assets are also removed from his or her estate for estate tax purposes.

- **Planning benefits.** The donor may use an annuity trust to assist in overall estate planning. Assuming the estate tax remains in effect, a common planning technique is to use the income derived from the trust to make payments on a life insurance policy, which is held in an irrevocable life insurance trust and names the donor's children as beneficiaries. The children receive the insurance money tax free on the donor's death. This provision allows donors to liquidate low-yield assets, reinvest during their lifetime for higher income, and still be able to pass some or all of the value of the assets to their children.

Annuity trusts have fallen out of favor over the past 10 years, primarily due to the huge stock market gains that most investors experienced in the 1990s. Since annuity trusts cannot benefit from such growth, their results look less attractive than the unitrust.

An Example of a Charitable Remainder Annuity Trust

Betty and John Trembly, both 70 years of age, would like to increase their retirement income. Their investments through the years have been quite successful, but they are reluctant to sell their stocks to reinvest because of the large capital gains tax liability. An advisor suggests that they consider creating a charitable remainder annuity trust in order to unlock their capital gains for more income and to receive a predictable income base from this fixed-income vehicle. It will also allow them to make a gift to the college where they met, something they have wanted to do for a long time.

The Tremblys create a two-life 6 percent CRAT funded with $500,000 in publicly traded stock that they have owned for 10 years. They originally paid $50,000 for the stock, which they bought in a single block. The stock has never paid a dividend. The Tremblys will receive annual income of $30,000, prorated from the date of funding of the trust ($500,000 at a 5.8 percent payout rate). This payout will not vary for the term of the trust or until all assets in the trust are exhausted. So, if the Tremblys are looking for an inflation hedge over time, this is not a good choice for them.

When the trustee sells the stock, the Tremblys will avoid all capital gains tax on their $450,000 capital gain in the stock ($500,000 full market value less their cost basis of $50,000). They will be taxed on the income they receive from the trust, either at ordinary income tax rates (the highest) or at capital gains tax rates, until all $450,000 of the capital gain from the funding assets has been recognized. (Basically you avoid gain on sale of the assets, but the IRS does not let you turn around and invest the proceeds in tax-exempt municipal bonds to avoid all income taxes. First, you must treat exempt income payments as if they were capital gain until all gain within the trust has been recognized. The IRS still wants something out of the deal!)

The Tremblys will also be entitled to take an income tax charitable deduction for the discounted present value of their gift to charity. Based on IRS formulas and using current mortality tables, the present value of the gift to charity at the estimated end of the trust term is considered the Tremblys' charitable contribution for which they are allowed a deduction (in this case, $140,183). This deduction will be subject to the 30 percent of AGI limitation discussed earlier because the stock has been held for longer than one year and one day, making it long-term capital gain property. The Tremblys could get 50 percent treatment for their contribution by using the special election (see Glossary), but then they would only be able to deduct the discounted present value of $50,000 (their basis in the stock). They would be entitled to a deduction of only $14,018, which is so low that it would not be attractive.

Here are the numbers and how they look in comparison to simply selling the stock and reinvesting for income:

	Sale/No CRAT	CRAT
Fair market value of stock	$500,000	$500,000
Cost basis of stock	50,000	50,000
Capital gain	450,000	450,000
Capital gains tax (15 percent)	67,500	-0-
Money available for reinvestment (fair market value minus tax)	432,500	500,000
Income (5.8 percent)	25,085	29,000
Charitable deduction	-0-	140,183
Tax savings from deduction (28 percent bracket)	-0-	39,251
Net gift to charity	-0-	500,000

By using the charitable remainder annuity trust, the Tremblys will receive 15.6 percent more income for retirement than they would have realized by selling the stock and reinvesting the proceeds. They have avoided $67,500 in capital gains tax, received an additional $39,251 in tax savings from the charitable deduction ($140,183 x 28 percent), and have made a wonderful gift to charity. The fixed-income feature of the trust also solves their financial planning need for a dependable, predictable income stream to offset the volatility of their other investments. Keep in mind that the tax savings realized from this technique would look even more favorable in states that have an income tax.

The chart above, while accurate, is used to explain the benefits of a CRAT. Keep in mind that the row labeled money available for reinvestment does not distinguish between the money held by the seller in his bank account and the money of the donor that is now tied up in an irrevocable charitable trust benefiting your institution. Yes, the donor will receive income, but he will not be able to access the funds like the seller would.

The charitable gift annuity, although not under discussion here, is another choice that the Tremblys might make. See the discussion of charitable gift annuities starting on pages 21 and 83.

Charitable Remainder Unitrusts

Standard Unitrusts

The standard unitrust (STANCRUT) is a variable-payment charitable remainder trust. The income is variable because, unlike the annuity trust, the unitrust revalues all assets annually and recalculates the amount to be paid to the donor the following year. The revaluation of assets usually occurs on the first day of the new calendar year; some trusts provide for revaluation on the last day of the prior year. The governing documents determine the date. All CRT's must be on a calendar tax year for reporting purposes.

Unitrust payouts must be expressed in percentages, with the usual payout range between 5 and 50 percent. This percentage is applied to the assets held in the trust to determine the new payout amount for the coming year. Once the trustee determines this amount, the trust will pay it to the income beneficiary no matter what the investment experience of the trust is. In other words, the trust will distribute principal, if necessary, to satisfy the annual payment amount. Only at the end of the year or the beginning of the next year will the payout amount be readjusted to reflect the actual investment experience of the trust. For this reason, trust income may go up or down depending on the market environment. Unlike the charitable remainder annuity trust, the unitrust is not subject to the 5 percent probability test. Why would a donor choose a standard unitrust?

- Immediate income tax charitable deduction
- Avoidance of capital gains tax on sale of appreciated assets
- Removal of asset from estate for tax purposes
- Increased income from reinvestment of assets
- Elimination of management responsibilities for assets (in particular real estate, such as apartment buildings)
- Chance to have increasing income over time due to appreciation of trust assets and corresponding increase in trust payout

- Potential inflation hedge
- Certainty of income

Net Income Unitrusts

The net income unitrust (NICRUT) is a charitable remainder trust that provides a variable income stream but is better suited to handling non-income-producing assets or difficult-to-market assets producing low income. As the name implies, the net income unitrust pays the donor a stated percentage amount (5 to 50 percent) of trust assets annually but will only pay actual net income earned by the trust in years when the income earned is less than the stated payout amount.

For example, if a 5 percent, $100,000 trust earns only $4,000 for the year, a net income trust pays out $4,000. At no time will a net income unitrust invade principal to make payments. Theoretically, it is almost impossible to deplete a net income unitrust of all its assets absent a catastrophic decline in asset value over a very short period. If a net income unitrust pays out actual earnings rather than a larger stated amount, the unpaid amount does not carry over to future years. The unpaid amount is never paid to the donor.

Why would a donor choose a net income unitrust?

- Immediate income tax charitable deduction
- Avoidance of capital gains tax on sale of appreciated assets
- Removal of asset from estate for tax purposes
- Increased income from reinvestment of assets
- Elimination of management responsibilities for assets (in particular real estate, such as apartment buildings)
- Chance to have increasing income over time due to appreciation of trust assets and corresponding increase in trust payout
- Potential inflation hedge
- Allows non-income-producing assets to be placed in trust and liquidated without timing considerations

Why have a net income provision? Consider this. If a non-income-producing asset is placed in a standard unitrust or an annuity trust the trust still has an obligation to make payments to the income beneficiaries. If the contributed asset cannot be sold quickly, then the trustee is faced with the problem of making a payment without cash. The trustee is prohibited from borrowing money from a third party or directly loaning the trust cash until the asset is sold (this is considered debt financing and revokes the trust's tax exemption for the year of the sale or longer). Thus, the only option for the trustee in this situation would be to invade principal to make the payments. Since the trust is funded with a non-income-producing asset and, perhaps, one that must be sold in total rather than piecemeal, such as undeveloped real property, the only option left to the trustee would be to make payments of undivided interests in the assets. In the case of real estate this would be deeding a percentage interest in the property back to the donors as an income payment. This is the reason the net income unitrust was created—to solve the problem of difficult assets and their timely liquidation.

Net Income with Makeup Unitrusts

The net income with makeup unitrust (NIMCRUT) is a refinement of the net income unitrust. It operates exactly as the net income unitrust, with the exception that it carries forward any unpaid income to future years. This carry-forward allows the trustee to pay out more than the stated payout amount for a particular year if earnings from assets exceed that amount. The trustee may distribute excess earnings to the extent of any existing deficiencies from all prior years. Thus, if a 5 percent, $100,000 trust has earned less than 5 percent for several years and has unpaid deficiencies of $6,000, then in a year when the trust earns 10 percent, it will be allowed to pay out $5,000 and an additional $5,000 to satisfy part of the deficiency amount, for a total of $10,000. Because it was $6,000 in arrears and paid out only $5,000, it will still have a $1,000 deficiency to carry forward to the following year. If earnings results are better than 5 percent the next year, the rest of the deficiency will be paid out.

NIMCRUTs can be attractive to donors but are seldom as attractive to charities receiving remainder gifts. The net income unitrust (NICRUT) tends to have a greater chance of principal growth over time than the NIMCRUT because it is not burdened by deficiencies that must be made up from prior years. However, donors may find the makeup provisions of the NIMCRUT useful in planning since often income can be timed to occur in a certain year and paid out immediately to satisfy prior year deficiencies.

Why would a donor choose a net income with make-up unitrust?

- Immediate income tax charitable deduction.

- Avoidance of capital gains tax on sale of appreciated assets.

- Removal of asset from estate for tax purposes.

- Increased income from reinvestment of assets.

- Elimination of management responsibilities for assets (in particular real estate, such as apartment buildings).

- Chance to have increasing income over time due to appreciation of trust assets and corresponding increase in trust payout. This income may be more limited than the net income trust, however, due to income distributions under the makeup provision.

- Allows non-income-producing assets to be placed in trust and liquidated without timing considerations.

Why have a net income provision? Consider this. If a non-income-producing asset is placed in a standard unitrust or an annuity trust, the trust still has an obligation to make payments to the income beneficiaries. If the contributed asset cannot be sold quickly, then the trustee is faced with the problem of making a payment without cash. The trustee is prohibited from borrowing money from a third party or directly loaning the trust cash until the asset is sold (this is considered debt financing and revokes the trust's tax exemption for the year of the sale or longer). Thus, the only option for the trustee in this situation would be to invade principal to make the payments. Since the trust is funded with non-income-producing assets and, perhaps, assets that must be sold in total rather than piecemeal, such as undeveloped real property, the only option left to the trustee would be to make payments of undivided interests in the assets. In the case of real estate, this would be deeding a percentage interest in the property back to the donors as an income payment. This is the reason the net income unitrust was created, to solve the problem of difficult assets and their timely liquidation.

The makeup feature provides for eventual payment of all expected income from the trust over time. The difference between actual payments and stated payment amounts create deficiencies in years when actual earnings do not meet the stated payout amount. When earnings are higher than expected, the trust is obligated to pay earnings in excess of the annual payout amount to income beneficiaries until all prior-year deficiencies have been satisfied. This feature increases the chance that the donor's income expectations for the trust will eventually be met.

Flip Trusts

The flip trust (FLIPCRUT) is a hybrid of the net income unitrust and the standard unitrust. It is designed to assist in the contribution and subsequent liquidation of difficult assets while giving the trustee the opportunity to pursue a diversified investment approach. It was created in the 1990s to allow a donor to contribute property that the trustee and/or donors anticipated might be difficult to sell in a timely manner without setting long-term limits on the trustee's ability to invest assets for growth.

At the outset, the flip trust works like a net income unitrust. The assets are contributed to the trust just like any other remainder trust, and while the original funding assets are held in trust, the trust pays out only net income up to the stated percentage payout amount. However, when all or a portion of the assets are sold (or on a specified date set at the establishment of the trust) the net income trust "flips" over to function like a standard unitrust. (But this does not occur immediately. The trust continues to act like a net income trust until the beginning of the next calendar year.) The "flip" event may be a specific date, which makes this type of trust useful in planning. For example, if the assets are non-income-producing assets, but they are appreciating from year to year, a donor may decide to postpone the switch to diversified investing for a period of time either to enjoy the growth being experienced by the contributed assets or to defer the income beneficiaries' enjoyment of the trust income until they are older and perhaps more able to handle the money wisely. This situation may occur when the donors are parents or grandparents and the beneficiaries are children or grandchildren of a young age (either chronologically or emotionally).

The flip trust allows for several things to happen. First, a donor can contribute valuable but difficult-to-market assets, such as vacant land or closely held securities. Second, a donor will have more certainty about the amount of money he or she will receive on an annual basis, since a standard trust will make fixed payments within a particular year, even though it will revalue assets annually. Third, from the charity's perspective, a flip trust allows a total return investment approach, rather than one limited to dividends and interest, as many net income trusts are forced to do. This approach will give the charity a better chance of seeing long-term asset growth in the trust, due to the better long-term performance of diversified investment portfolios.

A FLIPCRUT may be written to act as a net income unitrust with makeup provision. Before the flip date or event, the trust will work exactly like a NIMCRUT and, if needed, record income deficiencies to be paid to beneficiaries in future years. However, when the trust flips to become a standard unitrust, any unpaid deficiency amount is lost to the income beneficiary.

The flip trust is likely to become the predominant type of trust used in charitable giving, since it protects the trust and the trustee by paying only net income as long as the funding assets are held in the trust. Once liquidated, the trust assets may be invested for total return, which benefits the charity as much as it benefits the donors.

An Example of a Charitable Remainder Unitrust

Sally and Fred Bloom, ages 66 and 72, respectively, would like to make a gift to their alma mater, but they are concerned about having enough income to support themselves through retirement. Their investments are primarily their house and a large parcel of undeveloped land located in the growth path of the Portland, Oregon, metroplex. They have received calls for years from developers eager to buy the land, but they are reluctant to sell their property to reinvest because of the large capital gains tax liability. An advisor suggests that they consider creating a charitable remainder unitrust to avoid the tax liability and to provide an income stream that may grow through the years. While there are no guarantees, the unitrust has the chance to offset inflation and the erosion of their buying power during retirement.

The Blooms create a two-life, 5 percent charitable remainder unitrust funded with their undeveloped land, which is appraised at $1 million. Sally Bloom inherited the land from her grandmother in the 1970s when it was valued at $250,000. Assuming the land is sold immediately, and the proceeds renvested in the first year the Blooms will receive income prorated from the date of their gift based on an annual income of $50,000 ($1 million fair market value of the property x 5 percent payout rate = $50,000 annual income). This payout will last until the end of the tax year in which the trust is created. At the beginning of the next year, the assets held in trust will be revalued, and a new payout amount will be determined by applying the 5 percent payout rate to the new trust principal balance.

This procedure creates an income stream that will go up or down from year to year. The annual change will allow income to grow as principal in the trust grows. However, it will also cause the income stream to decline if investments are not successful. If the Blooms are looking for certainty of income, this is not a good technique for them. But, since they are relatively young, with a combined life expectancy of more than 20 years, they are likely to need a rising income stream over time. By setting the trust payout at the lowest legal limit, they have given the trustee the best chance of making this happen.

When the trustee sells the land, the Blooms will avoid all capital gains tax on their $750,000 gain. Instead, the income they receive from the trust will be taxed at either ordinary income tax rates (the highest) or at capital gains tax rates until all $750,000 of the capital gain from the funding assets has been recognized. (Basically you avoid gain on sale of the assets, but the IRS does not let you turn around and invest the proceeds in tax-exempt municipal bonds to avoid all income taxes. First, you must treat exempt income payments as if they were capital gain until all gain within the trust has been recognized.)

The Blooms will also be entitled to take an income tax charitable deduction for the discounted present value of their gift to charity. Based on IRS formulas, and using current mortality tables, the present value of the gift to charity at the estimated end of the trust term is considered the Blooms' charitable contribution for which they are allowed a deduction. In this case, the allowable deduction is $401,870, which is subject to the 30 percent of AGI limitation related to long-term capital gain property. The Blooms could get 50 percent treatment for their contribution, by using the special election, but they would only be able to deduct the discounted present value of $250,000 (their basis in the property). This would give them a deduction of only $100,467. In this case, if the Blooms cannot use up their larger deduction over the year of the gift and the five-year carry-forward period, the election may be a good choice for them. However, if they are able to use up the full 30 percent deduction over six years, they will enjoy much larger tax savings in the long term by not using the election.

Here are the numbers and how they look in comparison to simply selling the land and reinvesting for income:

	Sale/No CRUT	CRUT
Fair market value of real property	$1,000,000	$1,000,000
Cost basis of real property	250,000	250,000
Capital gain	750,000	750,000
Capital gains tax (15 percent)	112,500	-0-
Money available for reinvestment (fair market value minus tax)	887,500	1,000,000
Income (5 percent)	44,375	50,000
Charitable deduction	-0-	401,870
Tax savings from deduction (28 percent bracket)	-0-	112,523
Net gift to charity	-0-	1,000,000

By using the charitable remainder unitrust, the Blooms have realized 12.67 percent more income for retirement than they would if they had sold the land and reinvested the proceeds. They have avoided $112,500 in capital gains tax, received an additional $112,523 in tax savings from the charitable deduction, and made a meaningful gift to their alma mater. The variable income feature of the trust also solves their financial planning need for a rising income stream to offset loss of buying power due to inflation. Also keep in mind that the tax savings realized from this technique would look even more favorable in states that have a state income tax in effect.

chapter thirteen

CHARITABLE LEAD TRUSTS

The charitable lead trust is best described as the mirror image of the charitable remainder trust. With a charitable lead trust, the assets placed in trust generate income that is paid to the charity. At the end of the trust term, the assets are transferred either back to the trustor or, more commonly, to a third party, usually children or grandchildren.

During the term of the trust, an income is paid to a qualified charity or charities. The amount is established in the trust document as either a stated percentage amount or a dollar amount. Charitable lead trusts come in two varieties: the charitable lead unitrust and the charitable lead annuity trust. These trusts function similarly to the remainder unitrust and annuity trust in that the lead unitrust is a stated percentage amount that varies from year to year, while the lead annuity trust provides for fixed payments to the charity during the term of the trust. The trust term may run for 21 years or longer depending on individual state law governing perpetuities.

Upon the termination of the lead trust, assets may be distributed in one of three ways:

- **To the donor (also called the grantor).** This method is often the case when a high-income donor does not need the income from the assets but does not wish to give up permanent possession of the assets. This designation makes the trust a grantor charitable lead trust (see "Tax Benefits" section of this chapter).

- **To a third party.** This designation is the most common for a lead trust. The assets from the trust are transferred upon trust termination to a third party, usually a family member, making the trust a nongrantor charitable lead trust (see "Tax Benefits").

- **To a charity.** This method is highly unusual and seldom used since a donor could do it without using a charitable lead trust. Should the donor be uncertain that a living beneficiary will outlive the term of the trust, a charity should be a successor beneficiary in this case. Such a trust would also be considered a nongrantor charitable lead trust, although both the income interest and the remainder interest would both be deductible as charitable gifts, assuming the designations to charity are both irrevocable.

Tax Benefits of Charitable Lead Trusts

Charitable lead trusts are not tax exempt. They must pay income tax like any other taxable trust. The trust cannot sell appreciated assets without incurring capital gains on the sale, in stark contrast to the tax-exempt charitable remainder trust, which has as a key feature the avoidance of capital gains tax on the sale of the assets. Lead trusts are allowed to deduct against capital gain income any distributions the trust makes to the income beneficiaries (the charities).

And yet, even though the lead trust lacks the income tax benefits of a charitable remainder trust, people enter into a lead trust, in addition to their philanthropic motives, for the tax benefits derived from such a trust. Because a lead trust defers the enjoyment of the assets by the third-party remainderman (or trustor) until the end of the trust term, the trustor receives certain attractive tax benefits that they may find appealing. In the case of a grantor lead trust, the tax laws allow an immediate income tax deduction in the year of the gift for the present value of the income that is estimated to be paid to the charity during the term of the trust. For example, if a trust is set to last 20 years, the grantor may deduct the discounted present value of all 20 years of payments in the first year—potentially a very large deduction.

However, the benefits are not as good as they appear. Each year the trust receives income and then pays it out to the charity. Because the grantor receives an income tax deduction only in the first year, he or she is then taxed on the income received by the trust in all subsequent years. In other words, each year the grantor must report on his or her income tax return the value of the total income received by the trust, but since the grantor has already enjoyed the immediate income tax deduction in the first year, there is no additional deduction created when the trust pays this income to the charity.

The most common form of lead trust is the nongrantor lead trust, in which the assets are transferred to a third party at the end of the trust term. Under these circumstances, the tax benefits are different from those received when the grantor gets the asset back (as in a grantor charitable leader trust). In this situation, the grantor has irrevocably transferred the assets to the trust and has no expectation of getting them back. There is no income tax deduction given for this type of lead trust. But neither is the income earned from the trust taxable to the grantor, as it is in the grantor lead trust. The real benefit lies in the gift and estate tax savings, which can be created with proper use of this type of trust.

Because the trust is eventually transferring assets to a third party, a gift tax or estate tax liability is incurred depending on whether the lead trust was established during the grantor's lifetime or through the estate plan at death. But because a lead trust defers the third party's enjoyment of the asset during the period the charity receives income (the term of the trust), the IRS permits the grantor to discount the taxable gift to the third party to reflect the postponement of enjoyment. In other words, if the trust term is long enough and the payout to charity high enough, it is possible to discount by 50 percent, 75 percent, or even 100 percent the taxable value transferred to the third party. For this reason, people with high net worth like this technique. It allows them to transfer their wealth to the next generation of their family (or other "objects of their bounty," as the common law has described them) with significantly reduced estate or gift tax liability.

How big a discount the grantor can take is up to them and their accountant. As with remainder trusts, the IRS provides a formula to calculate the deductions, but accountants are not bound to use these deduction amounts. However, an auditor would rely on it in examining your tax return, so using other discounting methods is not recommended.

Two Examples of a Charitable Lead Trust

Harry "The Horse" Wiggins has been in the real estate business for five decades. His company has thrived and expanded to the point where it now holds several hundred urban acres of property throughout the country. Harry personally owns many of the properties, which his company manages and leases for him. Harry's brother Walt asked him to become a major donor to his alma mater and help it complete a new building for its business school. Harry grudgingly agreed to meet with a planned giving officer at the college. After a few icy minutes, the meeting warmed up as the planned giving officer began to ask Harry questions about his business and how he got his start. Harry didn't think much of MBAs, but the planned giving officer told him about the new "entrepreneurs program" at the business school. This intrigued Harry, because he didn't think that stuff could be taught. Harry visited the campus, talked with the faculty, and met several successful retired business

executives who were now teaching in the new program. Harry even agreed to be a guest lecturer when he had the time.

Once Harry was enthused about the program, it wasn't too difficult to get him excited about making a gift. The planned giving officer suggested that he create a charitable lead trust, which would last for seven years and then any assets would be returned to Harry. To Harry, this seemed like a simple "loan" of assets, with the trust making payments to the college to support the entrepreneurs program. He decided to place a large downtown parcel he owns in Baltimore in the trust. The property has a market value of $15 million and yields about $750,000 in rental income annually. The trust is set up to pay out 5 percent to the college, for a total gift of $5.25 million over seven years.

Since the trust is irrevocable, the day Harry creates the trust and transfers the property to it he is deemed to have made a gift to the college. Because Harry will get the property back at the end of the trust term, there is no gift to a third party and therefore no gift tax liability. Harry does receive an income tax deduction of $4,538,132 for the discounted present value of all seven years of gift payments. Harry may use that amount to offset any income he may receive in the year of the gift—a tax savings of up to $1,797,100 for Harry from his gift. The deduction will be subject to the 30 percent limitation rule since the property transferred was long-term capital gain property. If Harry is unable to use the entire deduction in the year of the gift, he will be allowed to use the five-year carryforward period to maximize his deduction.

The downside for Harry is that he must report all income earned by the trust during the seven years the trust is in existence, and there are no corresponding deductions to offset this "phantom income" during those years. In essence, what Harry has been allowed to do is accelerate the deductions for all seven years of gifts to the college from the trust and use them in the year of the gift. But the IRS is now making him show as income the money the trust earns in later years. However, the time value of money works to his advantage since he will enjoy the benefits of all his deductions years before the gifts have actually been made. In addition, he has created an unusually large income tax deduction that can be used to offset other realized income earned in the gift year. It also means that Harry can receive increased income in the early years of the trust (and therefore a move up to a higher income tax bracket) without having to pay higher income taxes, due to the charitable deduction. Dollars in to dollars out, Harry could be much better off using the lead trust for these reasons.

Consider another example, this time of a nongrantor lead trust. Joe Bauble's highly successful business, Baubles, Bangles and Beads, has expanded from one store to 300 over the past 30 years. Joe's estate is estimated to be worth $100 million, most of it in company stock. Joe also owns several apartment buildings that he bought to diversify his investment portfolio. The apartments are valued at $10 million and generate annual income of $700,000. Joe has two children—Gina, 20, and Bert, 18. Both are in college, have no significant assets, and tend to spend money as fast as their father gives it to them. Joe would like to begin passing assets on to his kids, but knows they are not ready for the responsibility. Joe also plans to make a contribution to his university's capital campaign. He would like to have a building on campus named after him and his late wife.

Joe's advisors suggest that he create a charitable lead trust that would last for 15 years. During that time, the trust would make payments to the university to support the capital campaign and to put the Bauble name on a new building. At the end of the term, the trust would terminate, and Gina and Bert will receive the remaining assets. By that time they will be in their mid-30s and, Joe hopes, more responsible with money.

Joe decides to place the apartment buildings into the lead trust. The trust is set up to pay out 7 percent annually to the university for a total gift of $10.5 million—enough to allow Joe to place the Bauble name on the new building. Since the trust is irrevocable, the day Joe creates the trust and transfers the property to it is the day he has made a gift to his children. However, because the children must wait 15 years to enjoy the gift, the IRS allows Joe to discount the gift to present value. The calculations determine that the value of the gift to the children is $2,205,118 in today's dollars. This amount is reduced by the onetime $1.0 million exclusion amount to which Joe is entitled under the gift tax system. This means that Joe pays gift tax on $1,205,118 to transfer $10 million worth of real property to the children. The tax on this gift amount is $429,898 based on a 47 percent maximum gift tax rate.

Because this is a nongrantor lead trust, Joe does not receive an income tax charitable deduction for the value of the gift to charity. However, neither does Joe have to pay income tax on the annual income earned by the apartment buildings while they are in the trust. From a tax standpoint, Joe gets a wash on the income tax side of the deal. However, Joe has avoided up to $4,775,800 in gift and/or estate tax on the transfer to Gina and Bert. Compare the tax of $4,775,800 if Joe gave the assets directly to the kids immediately with the $429,898 tax when using the lead trust. This amounts to a savings of $4,345,902. His out-of-pocket cost to transfer this amount to the children is $429,898.

Joe has also made a very large gift to the university and placed his and his late wife's names on a beautiful new building that will last for many years.

chapter fourteen

CHARITABLE GIFT ANNUITIES

Charitable gift annuities are the oldest known life income plans. They are also the least complex type of giving arrangement from a legal standpoint, but not from a tax standpoint. The gift annuity is a simple contract (not a trust) between the donor and the charity. Under the terms of the contract, the donor transfers assets directly to the charity. In return, the charity agrees to pay a specified amount to one or two income beneficiaries for their lifetimes. The contract is a general obligation of the charity and can be satisfied by any and all assets of the institution. (Compare this to a charitable trust, where the donor must look only to the trust assets for income payments. The charity and/or the trustee are not obligated to make trust payments from other assets of the institution.) For this reason, marketing materials refer to gift annuity payments as being "guaranteed" by the issuing institution, which literally backs the annuity with all of its assets.

Charitable gift annuity payment rates are structured to ensure at least a 50 percent residual gift to the charity at the end of the life income term, provided that earnings from the funds contributed are equal to the earnings assumptions used in the calculations. The payout rates are based on the ages of the income beneficiaries, and deductions are determined by the current interest rate assumptions used by the IRS. The American Council on Gift Annuities provides suggested payout rates for charitable gift annuities based on the latest actuarial assumptions. These rates change as interest rates change, although adjustments tend to be made every one to two years. While most mainstream charities follow the suggested rates, some prefer to use their own assumptions to calculate the payout rates.

Gift annuity payments are unique. Each payment potentially has three types of tax treatment: ordinary income, capital gain income, and tax-exempt income. How a payment is treated for tax purposes depends on the type of asset originally contributed for the gift annuity and the age of the income beneficiary at the time he or she receives a payment.

When a donor contributes cash or short-term capital gain property, the income payments will generally be ordinary income or tax-exempt income. When a donor contributes appreciated assets that have been held long term (one year and one day), the income will usually consist of part ordinary income, part capital gain income, and part tax-exempt income. When the asset has been depreciated down to zero basis, the payments frequently will be all ordinary income or capital gain income.

The important thing to remember is that ordinary income rates are usually higher than capital gain rates. Therefore, any giving vehicle that offers capital gain treatment or tax-exempt treatment for income is good for the donor. From a more technical perspective, the after-tax benefit of a charitable gift annuity payment may be much greater than the actual payment percentage used to determine the dollar payout. For example, assume that you have a 6 percent payout that is treated as 75 percent ordinary income and 25 percent tax-exempt income. What would someone need to earn from a taxable investment to equal the after-tax benefit from a 6 percent annuity payment, assuming he or she is in a 28 percent tax bracket? The answer is 6.58 percent. From a marketing perspective, this can be a very powerful incentive to create a charitable gift annuity.

Deferred Annuity Payments

Most gift annuities begin making payments within a few weeks of their creation. These are called immediate-pay gift annuities. A donor may also defer the beginning of payments to a date in the future. These are called deferred payment gift annuities. A deferred annuity has several features that can be attractive to donors. First, they offer higher payments than immediate-pay annuities, due to the deferral period. The longer the deferral of income, the higher the payments become. The deferred annuity also carries a higher income tax charitable deduction than an immediate-pay gift annuity, again as a result of the deferral period. Finally, the ability to plan when income will be received in the future is valuable for retirement planning, college tuition financing, and various other needs of the typical donor.

Advantages to the Donor

A donor might want to establish a charitable gift annuity for these reasons:

- **Security.** The annuity provides a fixed income backed by the assets of the institution. Many states also require a segregated account or trust fund to hold enough assets to equal the estimated liabilities for all annuities issued by the charity.

- **Tax benefits.** The donor receives an income tax charitable deduction for an amount less than the full market value of the contributed assets, calculated using IRS tables that discount the deduction to present value. Capital gains are prorated over several years and are distributed with each income payment, resulting in a lower tax liability due to the favorable treatment of capital gain income when compared with ordinary income. Each payment is part ordinary income, part capital gain income and, for some donors, part tax-exempt income. This increases the after-tax income of the donor. In addition, the asset is effectively removed from the estate for tax purposes. (Technically, it is included in the estate at the time of death, but there is a corresponding charitable deduction for the remainder value, thus negating any estate tax liability.)

- **Planning benefits.** A gift annuity may assist a donor in estate planning. Assuming the estate tax remains in effect, the donor may use the income derived from the annuity to make payments on a life insurance policy, which is held in an irrevocable life insurance trust with the donor's children as beneficiaries. On the donor's death, the children receive the insurance money tax free. Donors are able to liquidate low-yield assets, receive higher income, and still be able to pass some or all of the value to their children at their death.

An Example of a Charitable Gift Annuity

Bertha Parks is an 88-year-old widow living in a retirement community in Fresno, California. She and her husband, Fred, ran a small hardware store for 50 years. Fred died in 1985, leaving Bertha with her house and some life insurance. Bertha took the insurance death benefit and invested it on her own in a small company called Microsoft Corporation, which had gone public shortly before she bought stock. Her $10,000 investment has become a $900,000 nest egg, which has provided Bertha with a sense of security but absolutely no income. She is concerned about the volatility in the stock market in recent years, but she does not want to pay capital gains tax on the sale of the stock. She also is seeking security for her income.

Because of her age, a planned giving officer suggests a charitable gift annuity. Not only will it provide above-average income for her (due to her age), but it carries income payments backed by the full faith and credit of the local university that the planned giving officer represents. The one-life gift annuity rate suggested by the American Council on Gift Annuities is 10.6 percent. If Bertha exchanged $400,000 of her $900,000 nest egg for a charitable gift annuity, she would receive $42,400 annually. This payment could be monthly, quarterly, or annual and would not vary. It would last for the rest of her lifetime.

Bertha will not have to pay capital gains tax at the time when the stock is transferred to the university in exchange for the gift annuity (it will be recognized pro-rata over her life expectancy). In addition, because Bertha is making an irrevocable gift to charity, she receives an income tax deduction for the present value of her eventual gift. In this case, her deduction is calculated to be $215,055. This deduction will be available for Bertha to use, up to 30 percent of her adjusted gross income, in the year of the gift. Any unused portion may be carried forward for up to five more years (a total of six years to use up the deduction). In the 28 percent tax bracket, Bertha would enjoy savings of up to $60,215, assuming she could use up the entire deduction amount. Each payment that Bertha receives will also receive favored tax treatment. In her case, since she has contributed highly appreciated property, her annual income of $42,400 will be treated as $9,370.40 of ordinary income, $32,658.90 of capital gain income, and $370.70 of tax-exempt income. Since capital gains are currently taxed at a lower rate than ordinary income rates and exempt income is not taxed at all, Bertha will enjoy increased after-tax income due to this treatment.

The taxable equivalent yield is often a helpful comparison for donors to make. In this case, we can assume a flat 28 percent income tax bracket for the donor and a 15 percent capital gains tax rate. Based on the above numbers, Bertha's after-tax income would be $34,877.45 [$6,746.69 ($9,370.40–28%) + $27,760.06 ($32,658.90–15%)+$370.70($370.70–0%)= $34,877.45]. To achieve this level of after-tax income on $400,000 Bertha would need to achieve a return of 12.11 percent before tax or $48,440.90. Bertha's income is guaranteed by the issuing institution.

Since a gift annuity is a contract rather than a trust, the money given to the charity can be used immediately, if the charity wishes. Most charities tend to place the donated assets into some form of reserve fund to make sure there is enough money available to make income payments. Money is only made available for use after the death of all the income beneficiaries. In Bertha's case, she has designated that the funds be used to support scholarships at the university named for herself and her late husband.

chapter fifteen

POOLED INCOME FUNDS

The pooled income fund, known as the "poor man's unitrust," allows donors to pool their various gifts for investment purposes. The pooled income fund holds all assets together and invests them without regard to individual donor preferences. Most pooled income funds invest exclusively in marketable securities and cash instruments. Pooled income funds are not permitted to invest in tax-exempt instruments. They are permitted to invest in real estate, but few do.

A pooled income fund pays out all earnings from the fund each year on a prorated basis. Income is paid to income beneficiaries based on the value of the gifts they contributed to the fund. Earnings are defined as interest and dividends. Capital gains on the sale of assets within the pooled fund are generally added to principal. At no time is principal invaded to make income payments.

Unlike the assets of a unitrust, pooled income fund assets are not revalued annually, nor is there a stated percentage amount that must be paid. Effectively, however, every time a new donor contributes to the fund, the fund is revalued to determine the new gift's interest in the pooled fund. Most pooled funds do not accept gifts of real or personal property due to valuation and marketability problems.

Deductions to pooled funds are calculated using IRS formulas that factor in standard mortality tables. The payout rate for these calculations is the highest income the pooled fund has earned in the prior three years. New funds or those in existence for less than three years use an assumed rate of earnings set by the IRS. Currently, the assumed rate is equal to the highest annual average federal midterm rate from the previous three years, less 1 percent.

Pooled funds are considered securities under federal securities laws and must strictly comply with disclosure laws. They must file tax returns and are often required to make state as well as federal filings. The complexity involved in administering pooled funds, including unitized accounting requirements, usually causes charities to outsource the administration. Banks and trust companies frequently offer "turnkey" pooled funds programs.

Pooled funds have never achieved the popularity that banks and trust companies originally hoped they would. The problem is that they are generally marketed to older people who often want certainty of income, which the pooled income fund does not provide. More sophisticated donors may see the value of the pooled fund, but often charities have chosen to invest the funds strictly for income, which freezes their long-term value, eliminates their value as an inflation hedge, and causes the fund to become a risky version of a charitable gift annuity. Donors have not found this attractive.

Many charities, as a result, have not started pooled income funds or have elected to shut them down. Closing a pooled income fund is a complex legal issue but can be accomplished.

Advantages to Donors

A donor may want to give to a pooled income fund for these reasons:

- Immediate income tax deduction
- Avoidance of capital gains tax on the sale of appreciated assets
- Increased income from the reinvestment of low-yield or non-income-producing assets
- Removal of assets from the taxable estate, resulting in estate tax savings
- Variable income that has the potential to grow over time and serve as an inflation hedge

An Example of a Pooled Income Fund

Jim Poole, a graduate of the East State University, wants to make a gift to support the football scholarship program. (Jim played defensive tackle on the team for three years.) He has a good job but is not in a position to make a large gift. Jim is single and 48 years old. He works as an engineer, but his firm does not provide a very good retirement plan, which concerns him.

The planned giving director at ESU approaches Jim about making a gift for the football program. After discussing Jim's situation, the director suggests that he consider making a gift to their pooled income fund 2020. This fund is designed to minimize income and invest for growth until the year 2020, at which time the fund managers will shift investments to emphasize income for the duration of the fund. Jim is intrigued by this fund, since it allows him to make a gift to ESU while helping to increase his income during retirement.

Jim decides to place $10,000 cash into the pooled income fund. The fund has been earning less than 3 percent annually due to its investment approach, which increases Jim's charitable deduction. He will receive a deduction of $4,297 for his gift, which in Jim's 28 percent tax bracket amounts to $1,203 saved. He will receive his share of the actual earnings for the pooled income fund each year. The earnings will vary from year to year. In the prior full year, he would have received $300 (3 percent of $10,000) of income. He will receive income from the fund for his lifetime and fully expects that the fund will grow in value through the years and his income will grow with it. Note that growth is hoped for, not guaranteed; the income could also decrease. When the investment switch occurs in 2020, Jim expects to be retired, and the increase in income will be very welcome.

Jim could also have given appreciated securities to the pooled income fund. He would have received the same benefits, but he would also have avoided the capital gains tax on the appreciation in the securities—a good reason to give appreciated assets instead of cash, if possible, when making a charitable gift.

Jim will also be able to add to his pooled income fund account at any time in the future. As his career and income progress, he will be able to increase his contributions, build his supplemental retirement fund, and expand his gift to ESU. Perhaps someday he will have enough in the fund to create a named endowed scholarship fund.

Jim was lucky. He found a pooled income fund that met his need for some growth in income to help with retirement. Most pooled income funds invest exclusively for income, resulting in greater current income but far less opportunity for principal growth. Taking this approach will reduce the buying power of the income stream over time (assuming a degree of inflation). The lack of principal growth also means that Jim would have no incentive to participate in the fund since he would be better off paying tax on the money and then investing it in growth assets to save for retirement. As a further disincentive, the higher income reduces the donor's income tax charitable deduction.

chapter sixteen

GIFT OF PERSONAL RESIDENCE OR FARM WITH RETAINED LIFE ESTATE

The gift of a residence or farm with retained life estate is one of the more underutilized planned giving techniques but one that can be of great value to an institution's long-term success. When a donor contributes a residence or farm to charity with retained life estate, the donor contributes the fee simple interest in the property but retains in the deed the right to occupy the residence for the remainder of his or her life. This right to occupy includes the right to rent the property should the donor no longer wish (or be able) to live there.

Before acceptance, the charity usually requires the donor to sign an additional agreement stating that the holder of the retained life estate is responsible for the care and upkeep of the property and for keeping homeowner's insurance in force at all times. The agreements may also give the charity the right of property inspection at any time. Further terms vary from institution to institution. When a donor creates a retained life estate gift, he or she is entitled to an immediate income tax deduction for the discounted present value of the gift to charity at the end of all intervening interests.

As an inducement, some charities agree to pay the donor an income based on the value of the life estate created, usually by adding a charitable gift annuity to the gift. The annuity is valued based on the discounted value of the original remainder interest to charity. In other words, you calculate the remainder value for the life estate and then treat it as if the donor had contributed this amount in return for a charitable gift annuity. (Note that this technique will reduce the value of the donor's deduction to the value of the gift annuity remainder value.) This technique can be effective, but it must be made available only to very elderly donors. Anyone younger than 80 years of age is potentially a risk with this technique, since younger life estate holders have too long a life expectancy to make the cash investment worthwhile for the charity. Keep in mind the time value of money when looking at this type of arrangement.

Advantages to the Donor

A donor might give a residence or farm with retained life estate for the following reasons:

- Immediate income tax charitable deduction for the discounted present value of the gift to charity

- Removal of the residence or farm from the taxable estate

- A gift to a charity with no change in the donor's living arrangements or lifestyle

- With the addition of a gift annuity, an opportunity to unlock capital appreciation in a home or farm to increase income without leaving or selling it

An Example of a Gift of Residence or Farm with Retained Life Estate

Joe and Helen Hernandez are farmers, as were their parents and grandparents. They have owned their farm for more than 60 years. Joe is 82 and Helen is 78. They have no living children. Joe is planning to sell part of the farm to a larger farming operation but wants to continue living on a portion of the farm and keep his hand in with a small crop of wheat and a truck garden. Joe is concerned that they will have to pay capital gains tax on the sale of the land but is unsure what to do about it.

Joe and Helen are very active in the church they have attended for 60 years. They would like to make a gift to the church but are uncomfortable giving something outright since they might need the money for their old age. The minister suggests that they talk to someone from the national church foundation for their denomination.

After talking with the Hernandezes, the planned giving officer suggests they make a gift of their reduced-size farm to the church but retain the right to live on the property for both their lifetimes. The planned giving officer explains that a gift of their farm with retained life estate makes a wonderful gift without touching their liquid assets. The gift is made with a simple document and a deed. There would be no change in their lifestyle or living arrangements.

He also tells them that because such a gift is irrevocable, they will be allowed to take a charitable deduction for the present value of the eventual gift to the church. An appraisal of the reduced-size farm indicates that it is worth $450,000. Based on their ages, the planned giving officer determines that they would be entitled to an income tax charitable deduction of $275,686.

The deduction would be available up to 30 percent of their adjusted gross income to offset income received from the sale of their other parcel of land. Assuming they could use up the entire deduction amount, they would save $77,192 in taxes in the 28 percent tax bracket ($275,686 deduction x 28 percent tax bracket = $77,192).

The Hernandezes are told that they would still be responsible for the upkeep and maintenance of the property as long as they lived there. They could also rent the property to someone else should the time come when they no longer want to or are able to live on the property.

The gift of residence or farm with retained life estate is a good way for donors to make a gift to charity without affecting their lifestyle, but it does carry with it some possible problems. For instance, what if the Hernandezes run out of money, perhaps due to unexpected medical bills? They have given away the farm and cannot borrow against it or sell it to raise needed cash. Some charities will offer to buy out the remaining life estate on the property, which can provide the needed cash. However, then where do the Hernandezes go to live?

From the charity standpoint, there are also possible problems. For example, what if the Hernandezes fail to keep the property up or maintain insurance? While most life estate agreements give the charity the right to take care of these things and look to the Hernandezes for payment, it can be a sticky situation when the donors lack the resources to pay. Another problem is the possibility of "squatter" caregivers who refuse to leave the property after the donors have died. Eviction actions may be necessary in certain situations.

These problems must be anticipated and may guide the charity in deciding whether to accept this type of gift. But do not think that it is too filled with problems to pursue. Most life estate gifts work smoothly. Donors usually take care of their end of things, and charities only infrequently have to deal with problems after the gift is made.

chapter seventeen

OUTRIGHT GIFTS

Any asset, whether tangible—such as real estate or coins—or intangible—such as copyrights, leases, or mineral rights—can be given outright to a charity. Even unusual assets—a pet zebra, for example—will qualify, although there is an old rule in fund raising never to take a gift that has to eat!

Irrevocable Gifts

When a donor makes an irrevocable gift of an asset, there are tax benefits. The most prominent is an immediate income tax charitable deduction for the fair market value of the gift. To take this deduction, the donor must have proof of the gift. This is usually in the form of a receipt from the charity. Every institution has its own policy concerning receipting and acknowledgment of gifts. Gifts of tangible personal property, for example, are usually acknowledged by the institution as having been received, but are not valued by the charity in the acknowledgment. Gifts of cash, on the other hand, will be receipted for the exact amount.

Real estate is documented through a deed, usually recorded shortly after it has been signed. Most stock transfers are handled primarily through brokerage accounts, and, as a result, the brokerage firm gives the donor the records to document the transfers. The donor may also gift the stock certificates directly to charity. In either case, the charity gives the donor a receipt acknowledging acceptance of the stock but placing no monetary value on it. Copyrights and interests in oil and gas have written documentation as well. These interests plus a deed of gift are enough to prove the contribution and receipt of the gift.

Bargain Sales

A donor can sell an asset to a charitable organization. If the sale price is less than the appraised value of the property, the transaction is called a *bargain sale,* and the donor is allowed to deduct as a gift the difference between the sale price and the market value of the asset. A bargain sale results in an outright gift to the charity (unless it is in the form of a charitable gift annuity; see below).

Consider this hypothetical example of a bargain sale. Bill and Tess Robinson wish to make a $150,000 gift to their favorite charity. In reviewing their assets, they identify a vacant piece of land that they originally intended to use for a second home. They had planned to sell the property, but their advisors suggest that a bargain sale would accomplish several of their goals, including a gift to the charity.

The vacant land was purchased 20 years ago for $50,000. It is now worth $250,000 on the open market. They propose to sell the property to the charity for $100,000 in the form of cash, a note, or a combination of both.

The numbers look like this:

Original purchase price (cost basis)	$ 50,000
Sale price to charity	100,000
Fair market value (FMV) of property	250,000
Bargain portion (FMV–sale price)	150,000

Keep in mind that a bargain sale is actually two pieces: a sale to the charity and a gift to the charity. The difficulty comes in figuring out how capital gains are determined for each part of the transaction. In the Robinsons' case, they will realize a capital gain only on the "sale" portion of the gift. Their original cost basis in the property was $50,000, but they are required by law to prorate this basis between the sale portion and the gift portion before determining the taxable capital gain. The fair market value of the property was $250,000, and the sale price was $100,000. The difference between the sale price and the fair market value is considered the gift portion, or $150,000.

To prorate the basis of $50,000 between the sale portion and the gift portion, we determine the fractional split between each portion. In this case, the sale fraction is 10/25, since the sale price was $100,000 and the market value was $250,000. The gift fraction is 15/25 because the gift was $150,000. This results in a basis proration of $20,000 to the sale (10/25th or 40 percent of the $50,000 cost basis) and $30,000 to the gift (15/25th or 60 percent of the cost basis). The cost basis allocated to the gift portion ($30,000) is *not* available to the donors to help offset their capital gain on the sale portion and is effectively lost to them.

The prorated cost basis on the sale portion of the gift reduces the Robinsons' capital gain to $80,000 (sale price of $100,000 minus prorated cost basis of $20,000). Compare this to the full $200,000 of capital gain they would have realized if they had sold the property at full fair market value ($250,000 minus the cost basis of $50,000).

In addition, the Robinsons have made a $150,000 gift to charity that results in a $150,000 income tax charitable deduction. Since the property was held long term, they will be able to deduct up to 30 percent of their adjusted gross income in the year of the gift. If they are unable to use the entire deduction in the year of the gift, they will be able to carry the unused deduction forward for the next five years (they have a total of six years to use the entire deduction amount). If the Robinsons' adjusted gross income were $266,667 or more, they would be able to deduct $80,000 in the first year ($266,667 x 30 percent = $80,000), offsetting the capital gain realized on the sale portion of the gift and resulting in no tax liability. The unused $20,000 of deduction would be available the next year to offset other income.

The Robinsons have achieved several goals with their gift. First, they have made a $150,000 gift to their favorite charity. From a tax standpoint, they have eliminated a $250,000 asset from their estate, and depending on the size of their estate, they could save up to $117,500 in estate taxes. They have avoided the capital gains tax on 60 percent of the value of the gift, or $120,000. (The bargain portion of the gift, or $150,000, minus the prorated basis of $30,000 equals the gain portion of gift, or $120,000.) They have even more tax savings from the carry-forward deduction amount of $20,000 in future years. The Robinsons also enjoy having $100,000 to use as they please—ideally, to give to another charitable organization.

Revocable Gifts

Wills

The gift by will accounts for the majority of planned gifts, not only in number but also in value. An institution with a fully developed planned giving program rarely has less than 55 percent of its planned gifts in a given year come from wills.

A charitable gift by will is 100 percent deductible under the estate tax. There are no income limitations as there are with outright gifts. A gift by will can be made in several ways:

- **Specific bequest**. Language in a will gives the charity a specific piece of real and/or personal property, a block of stock, or a clearly identified property that

can be distinguished from other similar property: "I leave the house located at 135 Sycamore Lane, Austin, Texas, to ABC University."

- **General bequest**. A bequest of a dollar amount that does not name a particular asset to be given: "I give to ABC University the sum of $10,000."

- **Residuary bequest**. A bequest that usually comes after all specific bequests have been satisfied from the estate and is stated only as a percentage of the entire estate: "I give 30 percent of the residue of my estate to ABC University," or "All the rest and residue of my estate I give to ABC University."

- **Contingent bequest**. A form of bequest activated upon the occurrence of some specific event. The language provides only the possibility of a gift for charity. For example: "If my son shall predecease me, I give my estate to ABC University." If the son does not predecease the testator, the charity receives nothing.

Revocable Living Trusts

Revocable living trusts are a popular form of trust being used in estate planning today. A donor transfers most or all of his or her assets, including house, car, securities, and personal property, to the trust. The trust becomes the titleholder of all the property transferred to it. The trust then is administered for the benefit of the donor (the trustor) or for persons the donor may designate. (Anyone who receives income or principal, including the donor, would be considered a beneficiary of the trust.) A revocable trust usually is set up for a couple, although their children (especially children with special needs) and sometimes even grandchildren commonly are included. It is more unusual to see nonfamily members included in a revocable living trust, but it does happen from time to time.

Most often, a trustor will also serve as the trustee of the trust. Frequently, couples name each other jointly, with the survivor and then either another family member or an institution as successor trustee. The trustee administers the trust for the benefit of the named beneficiaries, which usually includes the trustor(s) themselves, children, and other family or friends. The trustee always has the right, with rare exceptions, to invade principal and even exhaust all trust assets, if necessary, in providing support to the beneficiaries. In most cases, there is no change in lifestyle or control during the lives of the trustor(s).

Control is a key issue with a revocable living trust. That is why the trustor retains the right to revoke all or a portion of the revocable living trust during his or her lifetime. Sometimes a trust will become partially or totally irrevocable upon the death of a spouse, especially when it is a second marriage and there are multiple sets of potential beneficiaries. Once the trust has become irrevocable, the trustee may have only limited powers to invade principal for the benefit of surviving beneficiaries.

Revocable living trusts are *not* tax-advantaged trusts. They are not charitable remainder trusts and carry no income tax deductions or avoidance of capital gains tax on the sale of appreciated assets. They do not remove assets from the taxable estate. If properly drafted, however, they do have the ability to avoid probate and the costs associated with that process.

Gifts to charities can be made through a revocable living trust. The gifts usually are written into the trust document and take a form similar to those of wills. The language used in a revocable living trust is identical to the bequest language used in a gift by will. Any gift to charity made through a revocable living trust is deductible under the estate tax for 100 percent of its fair market value, assuming that the revocable living trust does not make a gift using a charitable remainder trust, pooled income fund gift, or charitable gift annuity. In these cases, the charitable deduction would be for the net present value of the gift based on the ages of the income beneficiaries at the time of the gift. There would also be potential tax liability for any income interests created.

Life Insurance and Annuities

Charities will promote life insurance gifts as long as there are life insurance agents available to push them. Gifts of life insurance are seldom attractive to a charity unless the donor is someone who would not make a gift any other way. However, they are relatively easy to accept from the charity's standpoint.

A donor may name the charity as a beneficiary under the terms of most life insurance policies. This designation of the beneficiary is made much like a will, with the donor placing the name of the charity in the beneficiary designation section of the life insurance policy application. If the policy is already in effect, then the donor could make the designation by filling out the appropriate insurance company form naming the charity as beneficiary. This type of gift does not create a charitable deduction for the donor. For the charity, it is similar to a will, since the donor has the power to change the beneficiary designation at any time.

Often you will hear about an irrevocable designation of beneficiary being made in favor of a charity. This designation may be binding for the donor. However, if the policy still requires premiums to be paid, it is subject to

effective revocation if the donor simply stops paying the premiums. It also may be revoked if the donor switches from one insurance company to another, creating a new policy in the process.

A donor may receive some tax benefits from a gift of life insurance. If the policy is already paid up and no further premiums are required, the donor can make the charity the owner of the policy, and by retaining no incidences of ownership, the donor will be permitted a charitable deduction for the value of what is called the *interpolated terminal reserve* (ITR). This number is very difficult to ascertain, and even insurance companies have trouble providing it. Most people simply deduct the cash value of the policy, since it is usually a little bit less than the ITR value.

If the policy is new or still requires premiums to be paid, a donor can receive a tax deduction by making the charity the owner of the policy and then continuing to pay the premiums. Premiums are usually paid to the charity, which then makes the payments to the insurance company. IRS letter rulings also suggest that if the donor pays the premium directly to the insurance company, the premiums will also be fully deductible. Transferring ownership of the policy is a simple matter of completing and signing the insurance company's form making the charity the new policy owner. The charity is usually required to sign off on the form as well.

Charities seldom seek gifts of insurance unless an insurance agent close to the organization has sold the board on insurance as a giving program. Insurance programs seldom benefit the charity in the long run although the insurance agent often benefits from the beginning. To be certain that the charity will eventually benefit to some degree, it is necessary that several hundred people be enrolled in such a program. Few, if any, charities have been able to put a hundred people in such a program, and most report little or no benefit from insurance gifts. Some report that the same premiums paid directly into their endowments would have resulted in far larger gifts to the organization over time.

Donors frequently propose gifts of commercial annuities, which carry a tax deferral feature allowing for cash buildup within the annuity without the owner having to pay income tax during the buildup phase. However, when a donor attempts to gift a commercial annuity to charity, the tax-deferred buildup becomes a problem. When an annuity is given to charity (or any third party), the owner must recognize as income in the year of transfer all of the appreciation within the annuity. If the annuity has been held long term, the owner may have a large and unanticipated tax bill. As a result, few annuities are given directly to charity. The key is to look at the amount of appreciation within the account, not the actual cash value. The difference between value and cost basis in the policy will probably determine whether the gift is a good tax move for the donor.

IRA Assets

The individual retirement arrangement (IRA) is a popular method of making a revocable gift to charity. The form that establishes an IRA account provides for the designation of a beneficiary, in case the owner of the IRA dies before all the assets have been taken out of the account. By naming a charity as the beneficiary, the donor makes a potential gift that is fully deductible under the estate tax, including the avoidance of income tax on any income earned after the death of the donor but before distribution to the charity. The latter is called income in respect of a decedent or IRD (see Glossary).

Gifts of IRA assets are revocable, and they are also very uncertain. Even if the donor does not change his or her mind, you will not be able to tell how much you will receive until the gift arrives, since the donor will be forced to deplete the account starting no later than 70½ years of age but starting as early as 59½. It is possible for the gift to disappear completely, but depending on the investment results it is also possible that the assets will not be depleted during his or her lifetime. If the funds grow at a rate equal to or greater than the rate of depletion, the fund may stay stable. This means that while IRA gifts may be good to receive, they are not appropriate vehicles to use when naming opportunities are at stake, such as a name on a building or endowed chair.

Donors frequently ask if it is possible to roll over their IRA assets into a gift annuity or a charitable remainder trust. The short answer is yes, but *it will not be a tax-free rollover.* The gift to charity would provide only a partial offset against the income tax, and the donor would receive no net tax benefit (except for the removal of the assets from the taxable estate).

Bank Accounts

A traditional method of transferring assets to family as well as charity—naming a person or charitable institution as a beneficiary on a bank account—has fallen out of favor over the past 25 years. Sometimes this method is used when the institution is receiving all or a majority of the assets from an estate. In those cases, the donor simply wanted to be sure that the charity got all of the assets.

Retirement Funds

Gifts from 401(k), Keogh, and 403(b) retirement funds will be a growing area for charities over the next 25 years. Currently, a tax-free rollover of retirement fund assets to a charitable life income plan is not allowed. Distributions from these sources are taxed as income to the owner, and any subsequent contribution to charity merely provides an offset to the donor. It is possible to designate a beneficiary for these funds should the owner not live to deplete all of the assets and has not chosen to annuitize the assets. These gifts have problems similar to those of the IRA, since it is almost impossible to determine what you will receive until you finally have the gift. However, the designation allows the owner to make a gift to charity that will enjoy full deductibility from the income tax (under IRD rules) and the estate tax.

MARKETING PLANNED GIFTS

This overview will provide some background to help business officers understand how a planned giving program markets gifts and how planned giving officers develop individual gifts. It illustrates some of the art and science of planned giving so you can examine your own program for areas of strength and areas that could use some improvement.

What Is Your Market?

The most important information you will need to run an effective planned giving program is exactly who you are targeting for planned gifts. Large institutions with a long history will usually focus on their alumni. Younger institutions or those with small student bodies or constituencies will need to expand their focus in order to reach enough people to make their efforts worthwhile. Market the right techniques to the appropriate groups couched in terms that address their concerns and your efforts will yield good results for your planned giving program.

Segmenting the Market by Age

When most people think of planned giving, they think of old people—wills, estate planning, and death. But in the modern world of planned giving, that is not always the case. It is important that you determine the profile of your core supporters and develop age-appropriate marketing approaches. For example, a support base made up primarily of people over 65 is going to respond better to appeals for wills and gift annuities because they are planning their estates and seeking safe, predictable income for their retirement. Knowing the age group you are appealing to will change the emphasis of your message and may force you to focus your appeal far differently than the average nonprofit.

In contrast, an institution with a support base made up of people no older than 50—the case in many younger institutions—will focus on gifts that appeal to a group still in the "acquisition phase" of their lives. These people worry about having enough money to retire and put their children through college. They may also worry about taking care of their aging parents. This group will respond, but only to appeals that consider their concerns. For example, marketing annuities will not appeal to them, but marketing *deferred* annuities that allow them to make a gift while building retirement income might be of interest. This group might also respond more to tax savings benefits than to income security.

Segmenting the Market for Affluence

You should market your program to those people who can afford to make a gift to your institution. But within the upper levels of affluence are segments that need to be approached in different ways with different techniques. Dividing your potential market by levels of affluence will allow you to tailor your message to each subgroup to take into account their concerns and major issues. Since you could create literally hundreds of groups, it is best to limit your market segmentation to three or four, unless you have the luxury of a very large support base that lends itself to further segmentation.

Segmenting your market based on their affluence will save you time and effort.

In approaching the lowest one-third of the market (assuming this is already a subgroup of those who can afford to make a gift), most experts would suggest that revocable gifts, especially wills, should be the main focus of the planned giving appeal. Gifts made through wills and revocable instruments are not realized until the donor's death, but they allow someone of modest means to participate in a planned giving program. Often, these types of gifts can help build the permanent endowment since they cannot be anticipated from year to year.

The middle one-third is probably the group that is most interested in life income plans. Usually this group consists of people of above-average income but not necessarily above-average assets. They have some investments—perhaps a second home or rental unit and some stocks or bonds—but they do not have the asset base to enjoy retirement without careful planning and maximization of all available tax benefits. The unitrust and annuity trust, along with annuities, can be very appealing to this group. Charitable trusts have a special appeal as people seek to unlock the capital gains in their long-term investments. For example, a person with a rental property held for 20 years probably has depreciated the property down to a low basis or even a zero basis. Sale at this point would trigger the capital gains tax that they wish to avoid. Using a charitable trust to liquidate the asset, increase their retirement income, and at the same time support a charity that they already believe in is a win-win situation.

The top one-third of the market holds the greatest interest. But this group will generally be asset wealthy and frequently not proportionately income wealthy. After a certain point, taxable income is to be avoided; untaxed appreciation is preferred. People in this group frequently seek methods to avoid the estate and gift tax, not the income tax. They are attempting to pass assets on to their children or grandchildren in cost-effective ways.

To this group, life income plans are less interesting because they already are trying to minimize their income for tax purposes. If you're sitting on $10 million, you aren't that interested in increasing your income, but you are interested in maximizing your tax benefits to avoid the estate tax or the gift tax. For this group, charitable lead trusts—which allow assets to be transferred from one generation to the next with a reduced estate-tax bite—are far more appealing. Since lead trusts create an immediate income stream for the charity, they are far more interesting from your viewpoint as well.

Segmenting the Market for Affiliation with the Institution

Determining a person's degree of affiliation with your institution and its mission can ensure that your planned giving program is focusing on those who are most likely to support your efforts. Segmenting the market in this way is also helpful if your planned giving constituent base is not immediately identifiable.

Donors are the most logical group. They have already indicated a willingness to support you with their money. This says a lot about their feelings of affiliation. Within this general group, you can segment by size of gift to come up with a prospect list. (Whether it is a good one depends on how successful your fund-raising programs have been in the past. If your largest donor only gave you $50, your prospect list may not be very valuable to you.)

Frequency is a measure of donor affiliation that has major implications for planned giving. A frequent donor, even of very modest amounts, is demonstrating support for you in a very significant way. Long-term support is a strong indicator of planned giving potential. Gifts by will are the single most popular method of planned giving. People with even modest means can turn into major donors through their wills. Robert F. Sharpe Jr. has noted

in his research that frequent modest donors may drop off your giving rolls after they retire, especially if they are of modest means. Someone who has given faithfully for years who suddenly drops down to a lower level of giving or to no gift at all may still be a solid planned giving prospect through a will or revocable living trust. The key is to remain faithful to them: Send them your newsletter, even if they have lapsed after many years of faithful giving. It will pay off in the long run.

Affinity group marketing helps institutions that need to go beyond their existing support base to seek planned gifts, due either to their mission or to their relative youth as an organization. Affinity group marketing has worked for credit card companies, who appeal to your positive attachment to a school, club, or local charity. A similar approach can expand your potential planned giving market by helping you find the people who support all or a portion of your mission. What about research at your university that might affect a large group? What about ways you are helping children or at-risk youth, or doing community outreach to the homeless or helpless? Hospitals are known for using support groups and guilds with members who may have had no direct affiliation with the hospital but simply wanted to be a part of a group that was supporting the hospital. Look for your own "support" groups, and if necessary create them. Build them around a part of your core mission or a major new initiative. Network into the community, and you will be able to identify planned giving prospects no matter how new your organization may be.

Subgroups within the institution are another way to segment prospects. One program or department may have stronger loyalty among constituents, or a particular faculty member may have the drive and ability to develop a strong following in one area of interest. Appealing to the limited interest of a subgroup is an effective way of building a planned giving program. This approach does take more time and money, but it is more effective than a general appeal to these same groups. Do not be afraid to appeal to their passion for a particular part of what your organization does. Passion is a key to most people's giving patterns and one that you should cultivate.

One-on-One Marketing: Still the Best Approach

Most people think of a marketing program as direct mailings, seminars, and big production ideas like videos or awards luncheons. While these approaches are useful in developing a planned giving program, the most important aspect of any marketing effort is the one-on-one contact between planned giving prospects and representatives of your organization. People give to other people, not to letters, brochures, or gimmicks. In the planned giving arena, you are asking people to give you assets they have accumulated over a lifetime. This process requires a lot of thought and information, and the key ingredient is not the best brochure, but the best person—a person who can explain what you are appealing for, answer questions about planned giving techniques, and keep the donor focused on the importance of their gift to your organization.

One-on-one marketing has the added benefit of being the least expensive method of planned giving promotion available. Simply telling donors to include your institution in their wills is one method of planned giving marketing that could be done by virtually anyone who can talk effectively with people. Don't discount the value of this type of one-on-one work, even if your institution cannot afford a full-time planned giving officer.

One-on-one marketing is based on what is commonly called *relationship selling,* in which the salesperson develops a relationship of trust with the prospect. On a more sophisticated level, a development officer seeks to become a trusted advisor, someone the donor respects for his or her opinions about not just planned giving, but other matters as well. Development officers usually consult on organizational matters, but they frequently advise donors on other unrelated issues, such as family relationships, overall estate planning, and even business questions. The donor trusts the development officer's opinion and seeks it out.

The average planned gift follows a cycle of cultivation, education, and the eventual solicitation of the prospect. The cultivation and solicitation portions of the cycle can be repeated through the years, provided the donor maintains an interest in the organization (and, ideally, the development officer stays on the job throughout the time period).

The gift cycle begins with the identification of the prospect and the determination that this person has the capacity to make a significant gift to your organization—in other words, the financial resources necessary to make a significant gift to the organization if properly motivated. Note that *capacity* is not the same as *likelihood.* It will be up to the planned giving officer to generate the interest and motivation to give. The second step is to evaluate the person's interest in your institution or its area of activity, or some type of personal connection through friends or family and whether or not they have the financial capacity to make a significant gift if properly motivated. The development officer makes a decision at this point whether to view the person as a prospective planned giving donor. If the answer is no, this does not

mean that the person is dropped from your mailing list and exiled. He or she should be kept in mind for possible future evaluation. If you can afford it—and the person appears to at least have potential—then add him or her to your informational mailing list. You can reevaluate the person in the future, perhaps after he or she has shown some interest in your program.

Donor Cultivation and Education

If the person is deemed to be suitable, the officer moves forward by developing a cultivation plan for the prospect. The plan can be informal or formal, depending on how your organization works. Usually written plans are more helpful to less experienced development officers who need to clarify their own thinking. Experienced development officers may jot down a few notes, but they won't need to have a written, step-by-step plan. The term *moves management* is a complex term in fashion at the moment for the rather simple process of working a donor through steps to a point where solicitation is viable. The experienced development officer knows the timing of the solicitation is as much a feeling as it is some arbitrary schedule. Moves management helps development officers who are afraid to make the ask by arbitrarily specifying that after three, four, or five different contacts with a prospect, it is time to ask for a gift. This is helpful for less experienced and more reticent people, but a system that forces the solicitation may backfire if the system forces an ill-timed request. The art of planned giving conflicts with the science of management at this point.

Cultivation of a donor has a clear purpose—and it's not what you think. Merely asking people for money is easy. The goal of a proper cultivation plan is the education and involvement of the donor in the life of your organization. Before a donor is willing to write you a big check, he or she will want to believe in your organization's goals and mission and to understand how it works. A key issue is developing the donor's confidence in institutional leadership, from trustees and president to middle management. Most large gifts are given to organizations that have gained the donor's confidence that the money will be used wisely and stewarded well.

The development officer—whether a planned giving officer or general fund raiser—will be working to bring about this education and involvement, trying everything in the book to do so. These activities are what people most closely associate with development work. Social functions, sporting events, lectures, and other intellectual gatherings all may prove useful as the development officer tries to bring the prospective donor closer to the organization. This process may take weeks, months, or years depending on the hoped-for level of giving and the degree of preexisting knowledge and interest the prospect may have. For example, Harvard doesn't need to educate many people as to what the university does or how well it does it. But a brand-new organization with little or no track record or donor base will have a larger challenge. Good development work can still bring gifts to your organization, but it may take a little longer to build up the knowledge and confidence in the organization. After all, Harvard has been doing it for five centuries.

At some point in the cultivation process, the development officer will decide that the donor is ready for a solicitation. A solicitation is usually made face to face in a meeting between the donor (and ideally the donor's spouse) and a representative of the institution. The most straightforward solicitation technique is for the development officer, CEO, or a trustee (or some combination of them) to join in asking the donor to make a gift. Exactly who makes "the ask" is often determined by the size of the request, with larger gifts commanding the attention of the CEO. Usually the gift appeal is for a specific amount. For larger gifts, the appeal will be made verbally, but the prospect will also receive a written proposal that reiterates the amount and explains why the institution needs this gift. There may also be a discussion or a written suggestion concerning the naming opportunities available to the donor.

Some view the solicitation as the most difficult part of the process, but I have found it to be one of the easier parts. Unless you are dealing with an unsophisticated person—and most wealthy people are not unsophisticated—the person being cultivated knows that the time will come when you will ask him or her for a gift. The wealthier they are, the more in tune they are with the process, and the less time is necessary between the initial cultivation activity and the solicitation. The key issue for the institution is how well you do the "dance" of cultivation.

The key to successful solicitation lies in being donor-focused during the cultivation process. Too often, the institution falls into the trap of thinking that what is important to it is just as important to other people, especially people who have supported it in the past. The truth is that most people are aware that you need money, but they don't really care, since it is a constant problem for almost every institution. Otherwise, you wouldn't be fund raising. You need to learn through your contacts with prospects what *they* feel is important. Why do they like your institution or find your work interesting? What personal motivations are you dealing with? If you are a large university, you do many different things and pro-

vide knowledge in many areas. Chances are the donor is not interested in all of them. So the key question is, what are they attracted to? If it is research, what area? If it is teaching, what excites them about teaching? Maybe it's your football team, or your theater department or music department. You need to have this information and make it part of your solicitation. Too many gifts have been lost when an institution fails to identify the donor's motivations and asks for gifts based on what the institution thinks it needs at the time. You may need new concrete for parking structures, but most donors don't care. You must present them with the opportunity to support their own area of interest. If you do that, you will have success with large gifts.

Many planned giving officers use a more subtle approach in their efforts to close big gifts. Because of the more technical nature of planned giving, often prospects begin to consider a planned gift based on mailings they have received from your institution or other nonprofits. When they contact you, it is frequently to get more information and to learn how some form of planned gift (usually a life income plan) might help their specific situation. The planned giving officer usually talks with them on the phone and arranges either to meet them (a suggestion that is often met with reluctance on the part of the prospects) or send them more information. At this point a good planned giving officer can actually make a subtle appeal, couched in the guise of sending more information. The planned giving officer gets key information on assets, income, and current financial goals (for instance, do they need more income or are they worried about getting money to their children with little or no estate tax?). Based on the answers to these questions, the planned giving officer will send the prospect a detailed letter that outlines the options they believe fit the prospect's situation and gives them estimated results from income and tax-savings points of view. This communication usually sets the framework for a follow-up visit. But, if this appointment is made, the ask has already been made as well. During the appointment, the discussion will center on how to make the gift and any key questions the donor has about the techniques involved or the likely financial or tax results. In sales, they refer to an *assumed close*, which moves past the question "Would you consider a gift?" all the way to "How can we make this gift work?" A good planned giving officer will further cement the deal by discussing where the donor would like to designate the gift within the institution and what types of naming opportunities are available. This type of solicitation is nonthreatening and has a high success rate.

After the solicitation, the development officer must handle any follow-up and determine the next step to take. Frequently, donors do not make a decision when the solicitation is made, especially when the gift is for an amount over $10,000 (for under $10,000, the response seems to be an easy yes or no for almost all qualified prospects). The hesitation may occur because the development officer failed to get the spouse in the room (a vital step, especially for large gift appeals and for prospects living in community property states), or because they are cautious about major commitments of money. No one gives away assets accumulated over a lifetime without some thought. And if you have asked for an amount that is a major gift by your standards and you do get an immediate yes, seasoned fund raisers will tell you that you probably didn't ask for enough.

The larger the gift, the longer you may be kept waiting for an answer. Institutions will have to decide for themselves how long to wait before contacting the prospect again. Some donors will attempt to say no by not telling you anything at all. To wait in this situation will simply slow you down. Others will want to think about it for a few days or even weeks just to make sure they are making a well-reasoned, thoughtful decision. My experience has been that most people who eventually say yes do so within six months, even for the largest gifts. Sometimes large gifts are resolved more quickly because people who are excited about a project or program usually want to see their money at work as soon as possible.

Staffing the Planned Giving Program

For one-on-one donor contact and solicitation, most organizations rely on a paid full-time professional development officer. A growing number of professionals in the field provide part-time planned giving services. The answer to the question of whether to use a full-time or a part-time person is "It depends." It depends on the size of your organization, the budget, and the size of your prospect list. A large organization that has a complex mission or structure needs a person who can explain to the layperson what you do and how you do it. It is difficult for even the best part-time staff member to develop enough knowledge about a large institution to be effective talking with prospective donors. It is not impossible, especially if the person is a quick study and doesn't represent many other clients, but it will be more difficult and will require support from other staff to sell the organization. A full-time person, on the other hand, will become knowledgeable about every aspect of the organization, the things that you do, and the manner in which you do them. He or she will be able to present you in the best possible light to your prospective donors because you are his or her only "client" and he or she has the time and inclination to study you more thoroughly.

But a full-time person costs more, and a planned giving officer is one of the more expensive people to add to your development staff. The budget that you can dedicate to planned giving is obviously the key factor. If you're worried about meeting your existing payroll this month, you cannot afford a new planned giving officer. On the other hand, if you don't make an investment in planned giving and give someone the time to develop the program you will never have the long-term benefits that a good program can provide.

The part-time option has grown more popular over the last decade. Most major metropolitan areas have planned giving professionals—usually former planned giving officers for local institutions—who work part-time for several institutions. The financial attractiveness of this arrangement must be weighed against the limitations. First, the person will never know your organization as a full-time staff member would. Second, he or she will charge a high hourly rate so that your costs, while less than full-time staff, may not actually save you that much money. Third, part-time professionals vary dramatically in expertise. A well-qualified person can turn a small, but effective program that can grow over time into a full-time position for your organization. But you can also get someone who only knows the basics of planned giving and may not be that much help with anything other than sending out mailings and calling up people to make appointments.

It is critical to get a clear idea of the prospective part-timer's technical and professional qualifications. Talk to references, especially the last few employers who hired the prospective part-timer full-time. Other clients will be helpful to a point, but it will be the full-time employers who can speak to their expertise and effectiveness. People who provide part-time planned giving services measure their work with clients in months, not years, but a planned giving program takes three to seven years to get off the ground.

Other consultants work in the planned giving field on a regional or national basis. They have classic consulting practices in which they educate and advise institutions on how to develop, promote, and conduct a full planned giving program. In certain instances, they will even call on key high-end prospects with someone from your institution. However, they do not run the programs, nor do they follow up on your inquiries or handle your mailings; that is what the local planned giving consultants offer to do for you. National consultants can bring a broad

97

perspective to your program. They can run program audits and provide you with best practices information. In some instances, they can help you hire full-time staff to run your program. This type of planned giving consultant can move your program forward quickly and save you administrative headaches, but their services are expensive.

Whether you have a full-time or part-time planned giving officer, support staff are required; they are critical if you decide to hire a part-time person. The support staff will often be the first telephone contact that potential donors have with your office in response to marketing efforts. They must have a friendly and helpful manner and be well versed in the basics of planned giving. Their role is to request information from the caller, emphasize that your institution is eager to talk with them, and explain that someone will be calling to discuss their situation as quickly as possible. The last thing you want is for someone to call in, excited about the possibility of making a gift, only to be told that the planned giving officer won't be in for a couple of days and can they take a message. A short list of questions to ask is a good first step in this process. Training in planned giving for the support staff person is helpful to provide an overview of issues that will be critical to the prospective donor. This is not to say that support staff should be placed in the position of answering technical questions. But uninformed or unhelpful support staff will kill more potential deals than you can imagine, and you may never know that they have done so.

A support position is a good point of entry for people who are interested in moving up in an organization. Planned giving is the most sophisticated form of fund raising, and it has great appeal for those who are considering careers in the field. It is often possible to interest a motivated person in taking on a very substantial role in the office with the hope that he or she will eventually work his or her way into a role in development, possibly even in the planned giving field.

Getting the Appointment

Although readers of this book work on the business side of the operation, knowing some of the logistics of one-on-one fund raising helps with an understanding of planned giving operations. Getting an appointment with a prospective donor is as simple as calling someone and inviting them to lunch or asking to meet with them at their home. However, the "cold call" has a low probability of success. Usually there have been other contacts of a less intimidating nature with the prospects over a few months or even years—at sporting events, cultural

events, educational events, or in written communications that suggest a possible giving method of interest to the prospect. Ideally, the prospect has responded to your marketing either by phone or mail, and you are responding to their contact. It is more difficult to say no when you are the one who started the conversation in the first place.

No matter how you slice it, however, eventually the development officer must call the prospect and suggest an appointment. Often the prospect asks for a reason, and this question can leave the development officer short. You really want to talk to them about giving money to your institution, but by baldly stating this fact it is difficult to get an appointment. A blunt answer can result in a negative response, and the atmosphere can get quite cold.

When people talk about call reluctance, this is usually where it occurs. No one likes to be told no. It is a difficult word for most people to hear, and many development officers run from the situation. Only the true professional has the willingness to continue the conversation, seeking out the reasons and hoping to identify an issue that he or she can address and possibly overcome. This is not to say that manipulation or outright lying is the way to overcome the problem. It does mean that a professional development officer will either get the appointment or attempt to determine if the prospect's reluctance is connected directly to supporting the institution or whether it is a result of other things, such as illness, travel plans, a pending divorce, business problems, or problems with children or grandchildren. If it is the former, the professional will move on to another prospect. If it is the latter, the professional will regroup and develop a longer-range plan that takes into account the problems that the donor may be facing.

Each development officer perfects his or her own techniques through years of experimentation. One of the best planned giving officers I have worked with suggests that the good development officer will play—as he calls it—"drop the hanky," to develop intriguing hooks to drop in casual conversation, usually about how certain planned giving techniques can be used to solve financial or estate planning problems. He will study how a simple technique can be turned into a problem-solving tool—for example, showing people how to structure a charitable remainder trust to make a gift to the institution while at the same time providing income for a grandchild during his or her college years. The application to funding college tuition is a creative technique that intrigues prospective donors enough that they want to learn more. The appointment to discuss it is made, and the process begins. He tells me that if he does things correctly during the process, there is no time at which he actually asks the donor for the gift. The assumed close brings the gift to conclusion as the prospect adopts the giving technique to solve a financial or estate planning problem.

Another colleague has perfected his own personalized technique that has proven wonderfully successful over a 20-year period. This development officer seeks to interview alumni from his college for purposes of a history project. (He is a historian by training and frequently writes articles on the history of the college for the alumni magazine.) He calls both people he knows and people he has never met and asks them to meet with him to answer his questionnaire. No discussion of giving or planned giving techniques occurs during these survey meetings. Once he has completed his conversation, which he prefers to conduct in their own homes, he walks away with a clear idea of their personal history, their connection to his college, and the level of their wealth. From this information, he develops his own strategy for further cultivation of those he believes have giving capacity and an interest in the college. His future calls are usually well received, not only because he is a truly charming person, but also because they now have at least one person at the college whom they know and, if he has done his part, an interest in the institution.

Cold calling is seldom employed in planned giving, but it does have a place. Recently, telemarketing firms have been offering to make cold calls on alumni or donor base prospects. The costs per call are high, but these firms argue that the payoff is so high on a single planned gift that if they uncover any gifts at all, it will more than pay for the up-front costs of their programs. Cold calls to get appointments have merit, if you can get someone else besides the planned giving officer to do them. An experienced planned giving officer is too valuable a person to spend time on such low-yield activities. They would be better off hanging out at the local golf or country club talking with the older club members. However, a system of taking prescreened leads from a cold-calling operation may have great potential. Unfortunately, most nonprofits have neither the money nor the staff time to devote to such a program. For them, cold calling, if done at all is done by the planned giving officer and is therefore not an optimum use of staff.

The Planned Giving Call

The rubber meets the road when the planned giving officer meets with the donor prospect. This is known as a *call* or a *donor call*, not to be confused with calling someone on the telephone for an appointment. The call *is* the appointment. If the planned giving officer has done her homework, she is meeting with a person or a couple who has the capacity to make a gift, an interest in the organization's mission, and an openness to hearing what the planned giving officer has to say. Preparation is invaluable; development officers are known for keeping records of their contacts with donors through the years. Having one key piece of information on hand may make the difference between a successful outcome and a terminated discussion. (For example, is the woman in your meeting the first wife or the second wife? Is their giving history specific to one area of your university?)

Many practitioners feel that this meeting must achieve certain goals, and they even have a checklist of items that they must go through with the prospect. Depending on whether the meeting is a first meeting or a solicitation meeting, they have a plan. This approach is laudable in the sense of wanting to make the meeting a productive one. Unfortunately, they don't seem to ask the question "Productive for whom?" Too often, a mechanistic approach to development work is less productive than it could be because it is institution centered, not donor centered, and this becomes quite clear to the donor.

For an experienced planned giving officer, the face-to-face meeting is a time to get to know the prospect better and to find out exactly what they are thinking of doing—or, in the case of an initial meeting, whether they have an interest in the institution and its mission. During the meeting, the planned giving officer will wait for opportunities or cues to speak about the institution and its successes (either recent or historic) or about a particular planned giving technique that might be used to solve a problem that the prospect has alluded to—for example, needing to rebalance investments for retirement income.

Often, though, the "feel" of the meeting is wrong for a strong attempt to close on a gift. Knowing when this is the case requires instinct and sensitivity. The great fund raisers go into these meetings with all their "antennae" out and ready to read the prospect's body language, tone of voice, what they say, and the way they look at you and, in the case of couples, each other, to determine what the next step is and when it should be introduced into the discussion. A checklist approach would simply force an arbitrary template onto what is inherently a fluid situation. Remember that the donor is in a stressful situation, too. Giving away hard-earned money is an unsettling idea. A development officer who pushes for a decision may easily push into a quick no, since the prospect may be able to rationalize a refusal based upon the crass approach to the discussion. Large gifts take time and patience. Staying donor focused allows regular contact with donors without seeming pushy. Providing further information, answering technical questions, and referring the prospect to a good attorney or CPA are attentive, not pushy, ways of moving the gift along.

The Proposal

When a planned giving officer is in discussions with a prospect, the most common method of showing how a planned gift would affect the donor's financial situation is the letter proposal. This document is in letter form, but it contains the information that would be placed in a formal proposal for an outright major gift.

The letter proposal usually is submitted to the prospect following either a phone conversation or a meeting. It usually restates all pertinent data provided by the donor that have been used as the basis of tax calculations. It states the donor's goals and reviews the appropriate and relevant planned giving techniques, including a clear description of how the technique works, its estimated tax results for the donor, and the steps necessary to complete the technique. Charts, graphs, and other documentation are often included to fully educate the prospect. In addition, the letter proposal frequently contains a discussion of how the gift will be used, any unusual requests from the donor concerning the gift, and a mention of recognition that the donor would receive on completion of the gift—for example, becoming a member of a legacy society or planned giving recognition group.

A letter proposal should also state clearly the downside of the proposed gift. This is not just a sales document; you are trying to help the prospect make an important financial decision. An honest discussion of all the pros and cons is the best way to build the prospective donor's confidence and trust. It will also protect you from disgruntled heirs, because you will have written proof that you did disclose everything and that the donors went forward anyway.

Some institutions give prospects a more elaborate, customized proposal that looks and sounds more like a grant proposal than the personal, conversational type of communication the letter proposal provides. The letter proposal makes the donor feel less a target and more a friend of the institution, one whom you are trying to educate and help to make a wonderful gift to your institution.

The ultimate key to an effective planned giving proposal is to keep it centered on the donors' needs. If you help them solve their problems and achieve their goals, you will be in a good position to receive a gift. The more successfully you help the donors, the more connected you become to them, and the easier it will be to

influence how the gift is designated to your institution. Your willingness to see things their way will be reciprocated by the donors, and you will have much better luck ensuring that the gift comes to you in a way best suited to its use, whether as an endowment gift or a gift to current operations.

Broader Marketing Approaches

Direct Mail

Direct mail is the single largest planned giving marketing activity, employed by virtually all types of institutions attempting to develop planned gifts. Many vendors sell planned giving direct mail pieces, either individually or in an organized series, to nonprofit institutions. Depending on the size of the mailing list used, nonprofits devote a large percentage of their marketing budgets to direct mail. Why direct mail? The key reason is the difficulty and complexity of the subject matter. Planned giving is not something that can be completely explained over the phone to a prospect. The amount of information needed to make an intelligent, informed decision, coupled with this complexity, lends itself well to direct mail marketing.

With direct mail marketing, you are attempting over time to raise the knowledge level of a large group of people. This is complex stuff, and it takes people a long time to absorb the information. Frequently we have found people who take years or even decades to make a planned gift. This long lead time is part of the reason it takes so long to establish a successful program.

How effective is direct mail? Response rates for planned giving vary from institution to institution and from list to list. Generally speaking, if your planned giving mailings are generating 0.5 percent return, you are in the average response range. It is common for newer programs to pull a higher return initially from their lists, so 1 percent is common in the early years. Well-developed programs that have been marketing for years will have more modest rates of return unless they are adding significant numbers of new names to their mailing lists regularly.

Direct mail techniques include:

- Newsletters that develop awareness and provide a consistent reminder to prospects about planned giving

- Single-piece mailings that focus on one planned giving technique

- "Statement stuffers," or planned giving reminders that accompany all of your mailed communication pieces

In-House Publications

The least expensive and most effective way to reach your natural constituency is through articles and advertising in your publications—a newsletter, alumni magazine, or, in larger institutions, publications aimed at alumni of particular departments and schools. Some are low-key messages that remind people about your mission and how they can help you achieve it. Others are more informational, discussing planned giving techniques and their tax impact on a donor's financial situation, or possibly gifts of certain assets, such as real estate.

It is critical to the success of a planned giving program that each issue of an institution's publication contains a planned giving message. This marketing method adds minimal cost and reaches those most likely to support you through a planned gift. Failure to communicate to this group is a wasted opportunity.

Planned Giving Seminars

Educational seminars are a common method for institutions to reach out to prospective donors. However, the success rates vary dramatically. Some institutions report great success with their seminars and many gifts received as a result. Others report that prospects "stay away in droves" when invited to a planned giving seminar.

Running a few planned giving seminars on a trial basis is a good idea. If you have a good turnout, you will be able to meet and talk with people who have indicated by their attendance that they are considering some type of financial decision, whether it is a gift to your organization, an investment decision, or an estate planning problem. Planned giving seminars are usually not promoted as such. Most organizations like to talk about a "Financial Planning Seminar" or an "Estate Planning Seminar." One organization runs a "Wills Clinic," which obviously is focusing on people creating or updating their wills and estate plans.

A college or university would not be alone in running this type of seminar. Stockbrokers and insurance agents have made extensive use of seminars on financial planning and estate planning topics. Their dogged use of seminars in their marketing implies that the seminars are working for them in generating new business.

Advertising in General Publications

The decision to advertise in general publications, such as local newspapers and magazines, is usually a budgetary decision. The problem with general interest publication advertising is that it tends to be unfocused. The people most likely to support you may read the publication, but so will lots of people who have no interest in you. So this approach should be taken only *after* you have communicated with your core constituency through every means possible.

Most institutions that advertise in general publications emphasize the tax and financial benefits of a planned gift. Charitable intent is downplayed in the overall discussion, although we should probably assume they are glad their money will eventually do some good after they are gone. The emphasis on tax and financial benefits means that the decision is more of a buying decision and less of an emotional, gift-giving decision for the prospective donor.

What if you were told that you could launch a planned giving program, but you could not solicit or mail to the board of trustees, volunteers, or alumni? Although this is hard to believe now, back in the 1950s Pomona College development officers were given this "go-ahead" to their proposal to start a program to encourage gifts in trust and through annuities. Faced with this rather unenthusiastic "approval," the development people at Pomona decided to market their planned giving program to the only group left to them: strangers. They began to purchase display ads in the *Wall Street Journal* and other publications, advertising what they called the "Pomona Plan." The ads promoted life income, tax savings, and reduced estate taxes as some of the benefits from participation. They developed marketing materials, booklets, and brochures that explained the plan to prospective donors who responded to the ads—and the response was amazing. Little Pomona College created the first comprehensive planned giving program in the country (and probably the world). Their success through the years has grown to legendary proportions, and their endowment has grown to $1 billion. Many other institutions through the years have imitated their approach.

Television and Radio Advertising

As with print advertising, radio and television advertising tend to reach a large but unfocused group. Public radio and television stations, as you might imagine, have been doing this type of advertising for some time. They claim to have had good results from their promotional messages, but other organizations have tried this method without much success.

Colleges and universities, like other nonprofit institutions, have a complex message that is difficult to communicate in the limited time that an average radio or television advertisement lasts (usually no more than one minute). Longer ads are costly and may not even be available on certain stations. The television medium is very powerful, however, and radio can be as well. The right ad with a simple response mechanism might prove useful to a planned giving marketing effort, but other than public television and radio, no one has reported results that justify the large expense. A few other institutions are experimenting with this approach, and it may begin to show better results over the next few years.

Marketing on the Web

The Internet provides a cost-effective way to communicate with donors and advisors and, if properly developed, will be a growing source of referrals and gifts for the visionary college or university. The fastest growing Internet user segment is the over-65 age group, which shows a healthy annual percentage growth, so the future of this type of marketing looks bright.

There is some value to these tools right now for your organization, but you should think of them primarily as long-term marketing tools with small immediate payoffs but potentially huge payoffs in the future. If you have an effective Web site in place and a reliable mechanism for responding to e-mail messages, you have the basic framework. A popular add-on to Web sites is the ability to receive gifts by credit card. Institutions that have this feature report good results, especially when collecting annual fund pledges and support group memberships. It does not mean much for planned giving now, since most planned gifts are too large to put on a credit card and frequently are made with noncash assets.

Web sites, however, are passive vehicles that may not be proactive enough for fund raising. There are effective ways to use e-mail to reach prospective donors. An electronic version of your newsletter sent to subscribers can be a positive Web-based marketing vehicle. Another technique that is gaining ground is a specialized e-mail—either regular, like a newsletter, or episodic, when you have important news to share—that keeps donors and prospective donors informed on the latest financial or estate planning news. The text can be written in-house or outsourced. As you develop an electronic mailing list, you will be able to reach out to many of your constituents in an intimate way.

This approach also works for professional advisors. Vendors can provide up-to-date information on tax law changes or planned giving techniques that you can send to attorneys, accountants, and financial advisors in a contemporary version of the advisors' outreach programs that organizations once used.

These types of e-mails should make it clear how to contact your organization directly. Since confidentiality is crucial, a private, secured link to the planned giving officer or development director is the best approach.

Telemarketing

Telemarketing of planned gifts is a recent phenomenon in the field. Most telemarketing programs attempt to interest people enough to be willing to meet with a planned giving officer, not to explain planned giving techniques or answer questions about taxes. The companies who market this service to charities rely heavily on mailings before and after the telephone contact to ensure that prospects are not annoyed or made to feel like mere chips in a very large numbers game. The standard program relies on a preliminary "opt-out" letter that explains the purpose of the call and gives the prospect the opportunity to say that he or she would prefer not to be called. This letter is intended to reduce the annoyance factor among otherwise loyal supporters and friends and to eliminate the false leads that are not going to turn into a gift anyway.

Telemarketing of planned gifts holds intriguing possibilities for larger institutions, especially those with huge donor bases. Those that have a wide geographic reach with donors in many different areas may also find that telemarketing is perfect for them as they organize "road trips" to see prospects in different regions.

Telemarketing is also expensive, so the question of cost-effectiveness becomes crucial. You must examine how much money you spend on your other marketing efforts and what type of return you are getting. Very often, for example, you will realize that for the cost of a telemarketing program you can double or even triple your mailing budget, which you already know has a certain return rate. But what about trying to reach the groups that have not been receiving your mailings? Telemarketing might be an efficient way to touch all of these people and determine whether they have the potential to turn into planned giving donors.

Another problem with telemarketing is that it is telemarketing. Is your institution ready to risk annoying your donor base by allowing strangers to call them? Never forget that the callers, whomever they are, are representing your organization to your supporters. A bad telemarketing program risks this relationship.

The recent law passed by Congress to limit telemarketers and provide opportunities for individuals to limit or eliminate phone solicitations has been enthusiastically embraced by the public and indicates the risk inherent in this type of operation. Even if these laws are eventually deemed unconstitutional, they are a good gage of public sentiment at the moment.

PLANNED GIVING RESOURCES

Administrative Guides

Jordan, Ronald R., and Katelyn L. Quynn, with legal advice from Carolyn M. Osteen. *Planned Giving: Management, Marketing, and Law.* 3rd ed. New York: John Wiley & Sons, 2003. Annual supplements; includes CD.

This book is one of the best in the field on planned giving. Its impressive scope, plus the 300 forms, make it a must. It contains sample gift acceptance policies and many other worthwhile forms. Its limitation is that it speaks mostly to development officers. There is limited coverage of administrative issues, and these discussions are often buried in the different sections. Luckily, the index is a strong point.

Teitell, Conrad. *Planned Giving: Starting, Marketing, Administering.* Old Greenwich, CT: Philanthropy Tax Institute, 2004. Annual supplements.

Very few volumes touch on administration of charitable trusts, annuities, and other planned giving vehicles. This is the best one available. Conrad Teitell is a legend in the planned giving field, and this book is very useful, especially for new programs. Much of the book deals with start-up and marketing issues, but the administrative section is very strong. If there is a weakness, it is the lack of an adequate index, which makes things difficult to find at times. The table of contents can be used as an index to a certain extent.

Tax Law

Charitable Giving and Solicitation. New York: Research Institute of America, 2004. Monthly updates.

This is the best one-volume tax service available in the charitable giving field, covering all phases of tax law and estate planning law related to charitable giving. A monthly update includes news from the planned giving field, content updates, and articles by professionals in the field on topics ranging from estate planning to the best way to run charity events and direct mail appeals. If your space is limited, this book will give you all the tax information you will need. Some forms and worksheets are included. The index is comprehensive.

Charitable Giving Tax Service. Willow Springs, IL: R & R Newkirk, Inc., 2004. 4 vols., monthly updates.

This service provides a comprehensive review of the law related to charitable giving, including exhaustive discussions of all types of planned gifts, outright gifts, and estate planning law. All types of taxes that may be involved in a charitable gift are discussed. The monthly service includes a newsletter with reports from the planned giving field as well as updates to reflect the current law. It is easy to read (although the subject matter is complex), and the index is a great help.

Tax Economics of Charitable Giving. 2003–2004 edition. RIA (Thomson-RIA), New York, 2004.

This new edition takes the place of the title by the same name published through 13 editions by Arthur Anderson and Company. Each chapter is well researched and provides a concise review of the tax impact of each type of charitable gift with footnotes and case citations. This book is a must-have for anyone dealing with planned gifts.

Teitell, Conrad. *Deferred Giving: Explanation, Specimen Agreements, Forms.* Old Greenwich, CT: Philanthropy Tax Institute, 2004. 2 vols., annual updates.

This is the first treatise in the planned giving field and probably the most widely sold. It is a thorough discussion of the techniques of deferred giving. There is limited discussion of outright methods of giving (covered in Teitell's *Outright Charitable Gifts)*. The book covers the basic law related to each technique along with extensive discussions of recent IRS letter rulings and opinions. It is clearly written when discussing the techniques, but many people find the extensive discussions of letter rulings useless in their day-to-day activities. The volumes are severely limited by poor indexing. The table of contents can be used to locate topics.

Teitell, Conrad. *Lead Trusts: Explanation, Specimen Agreements, Forms.* Old Greenwich, CT: Philanthropy Tax Institute, 2004. Annual updates.

This is the best treatise on the lead trust available. Teitell handles this volume much like his two-volume *Deferred Giving*, with a solid discussion of the basics of the technique along with a thorough review of the tax issues. He includes many IRS letter rulings and opinions, which are summarized separately from the text. The indexing is weak, but the table of contents usually helps locate topics. Because of its uniqueness, this book is viewed as a must for most major planned giving programs.

Teitell, Conrad. *Outright Charitable Gifts: Explanation, Substantiating, Forms.* Old Greenwich, CT: Philanthropy Tax Institute, 2004. Annual updates.

This volume focuses exclusively on outright gifts and the tax law related to them. The discussion of substantiation rules for charitable gifts is extremely thorough. This volume follows the format of Teitell's other books. It is strong on content, although it gets bogged down in letter rulings and opinions. The index is weak, but the table of contents can be used as an index.

General Books on Planned Giving

Fink, Norman S., and Howard C. Metzler. *The Costs and Benefits of Deferred Giving.* New York: Columbia University Press, 1982.

This book is the only formal study of the actual costs and benefits of having a planned giving program. Obviously, the conclusions are very supportive of planned giving, or it would not still be in print. The study looked at the first truly comprehensive planned giving program in higher education (at Pomona College in Claremont, California) and attempted to do a formal cost-benefit analysis with all appropriate research formalities. It is useful to read this book and get a feel for how long it takes to see a return on investment. The book also gives you an idea of what your actual fund-raising costs might be once the program is fully developed. A somewhat historic document in the field, it is well worth reading.

Leimberg, Stephan R., et al. *The Tools and Techniques of Charitable Planning.* Erlanger, KY: National Underwriter Co., 2001.

This is a relative newcomer to the planned giving literature, but it is clearly one of the best overviews available. Written for the professional planner, it reviews the tech-

niques and the situations where they are best applied. The appendices are very good, as is the index. The tax information in the book is also solid. A strong thumbs-up on this book.

Moerschbaecher, Lynda S. *Start at Square One: Starting and Managing the Planned Gift Program.* Chicago: Precept Press, 1998.

A good basic how-to book for institutions establishing planned giving programs for the first time. In particular, the section on presenting the program to the board of trustees is very useful. Getting the leadership of the organization behind the initial efforts is critical to long-term success.

Sharpe, Robert F., Sr. *Planned Giving Simplified: The Gift, the Giver, and the Gift Planner.* New York: John Wiley & Sons, 1999.

Robert F. Sharpe Sr. was one of the founders of the field of planned giving. He worked in the field for 40 years. Intended for people just getting into planned giving, this book discusses the basic techniques and their tax impact, the way planned gifts are developed and solicited, and the role of the development officer or "gift planner" in the process. It also touches on the philosophy behind philanthropy. It is a good starting point.

Spitz, William T. *Selecting and Evaluating an Investment Manager.* Washington, DC: NACUBO, 1992.

This book provides an overview of the selection process for investment managers. It is written with an eye toward endowment managers, but the same principles apply for selection of a trust investment manager.

Periodicals

***Charitable Gift Planning News.* Little, Brown & Co., monthly.**

This very effective newsletter attempts to cover tax law and IRS rulings. It provides thorough information about actual planning problems and the application of charitable giving techniques to real cases. The section called "Planner's Forum" is especially good at examining real-life situations. Linda Moerschbaecher and Terry Simmons, both well-known national experts, are involved with this publication as writers and editors.

Planned Giving Today. G. Roger Schoenhals, monthly, www.pgtoday.com.

Planned Giving Today is the most popular newsletter in the country for planned giving officers and those who actively market gifts. It features planned giving marketing ideas and general information, with less focus on tax law (although from time to time there are good discussions of new techniques). If you are seeking the latest in marketing how-to or want to learn more about the cutting-edge issues in the field, this publication is a must. Many of the articles and informational pieces are available on CD through the publisher.

Taxwise Giving. **Philanthropy Tax Institute, monthly. Taxwisegiving.com.**

Conrad Teitell's monthly newsletter on planned giving is the oldest planned giving periodical, and it is always entertaining and informative. The content focuses on tax law, letter rulings, and new IRS opinions affecting the field. It has also been a leading voice on issues before the Congress related to charitable giving and charities in general.

Online Resources

There are many Web sites in the planned giving field, but separating the knowledgeable from the rest is a bit of a trick. You can trust the following sites to provide quality information from expert sources.

Death and Taxes, www.deathandtaxes.com

This site is sponsored by J. J. McNabb, a consultant to the insurance industry and to charities working with insurance products. It has become a national resource center for planned giving. The links are outstanding, as is the content. It is worth bookmarking to keep abreast of new developments. It is also helpful when dealing with insurance gifts or proposed programs.

Planned Giving Design Center, www.pgdc.com

This site is a national proprietary site created by the same company that produced PhilanthroCalc planned giving software. It is the best Web source currently available, with updated information on all types of planned gifts, including tax law citations and links to other useful sites. The site can be used by donors, administrators, attorneys, accountants, and trust officers. The center is licensed to different charities around the country that pay to have "exclusive rights" to a geographic area. Log in to the national site, and you will be referred automatically to the local sponsor site. The content at all PGDC sites is the same. Best of all, the sites are free, although users are asked to register.

Planned Giving Resources, www.pgresources.com

Planned giving consultant James B. Potter's Web site covers all areas of planned giving but emphasizes charitable gift annuities and the state regulations related to their issuance and management. It follows the latest law changes on gift annuities, both federal and state.

Tax Calculation and Administration Software

Every planned giving office has some type of computer software that allows it to provide tax information to donors regarding proposed gifts. There are many vendors, but those listed below are currently the major players.

Crescendo Interactive
110 Camino Ruiz
Camarillo, CA 93012
800-858-9154
805-388-2483 (fax)
www.crescendointeractive.com

A popular provider of tax calculation software that is very well thought of in the industry. Their software provides numbers for all types of planned gifts. Crescendo also has developed Web-based products that are available to clients.

5227 Tax System, Inc.
Temo A. Arjani & Co.
301 East Colorado Blvd., Suite 426
Pasadena, CA 91101
626-578-1978
800-592-5227
626-578-1639 (fax)
info@5227taxsystem.com
www.5227taxsystem.com

The 5227 tax system is recognized as one of the best, if not the best, computer accounting systems for charitable remainder trusts. This easy-to-use software handles all calculations required for IRS Form 5227 as well as Form 1041 and other forms required for CRTs. Annual update seminars are conducted for anyone responsible for trust administration.

PG Calc, Inc.
129 Mount Auburn St.
Cambridge, MA 02138
888-497-4970
617-497-4970 (in Massachusetts)
info@pgcalc.com
www.pgcalc.com

PG Calc is one of the largest vendors of tax calculation software in the planned giving field. The software provides calculations for all types of planned giving vehicles. It is recommended by Blackbaud, a major provider of gift accounting software to the nonprofit industry.

Philanthrotec, Inc.
10800-D Independence Pointe Pkwy.
Mathews, NC 28105
800-332-7832
704-845-5528 (fax)
info@ptec.com
www.ptec.com

Sophisticated software for use in all planned giving calculations. This company's products can be accessed online or downloaded for use on your own computer. The company also runs the Planned Giving Design Center.

Money Management and Trust Administration

Every financial institution with a trust department claims to be able to provide support and service for the management of charitable remainder trusts, gift annuities, and pooled income funds. Only a few work on a large regional or national scale and have the experience necessary to handle these complex giving vehicles as a group. Program management is different from individual trust management, which is what so many institutions want to base their claims of expertise on. The following have provided program support to many nonprofit institutions.

Clifford Associates
200 South Los Robles, Suite 320
Pasadena, CA 91101
626-792-2228
626-792-2670 (fax)
info@clifford1915.com
www.clifford1915.com

Clifford Associates has worked successfully with smaller programs in Southern California and elsewhere. They offer money management services and backroom support

for trust administration. While they do handle large accounts, they have shown good sensitivity to the smaller shop that hopes to grow.

Kaspick & Company
Redwood Shores
203 Redwood Shores Parkway, Suite 300
Redwood Shores, CA 94065-1175
650-585-4100
650-595-1400 (fax)
Contact: C. Alan Korthals
akorthals@kaspick.com
www.kaspick.com

Kaspick and Company has grown into a major trust management player over the past 20 years. They have proven to be a solid performer for many clients around the country. They offer money management services as well as full trust administration services.

Northern Trust
50 South LaSalle Street
Chicago, IL, 60675
312-444-4732
beth.douglass@northerntrust.com
www.northerntrust.com

Northern Trust understands the complexities of planned giving administration and provide organizations with the service they need to achieve their goals. Northern Trust provides a comprehensive range of donor, legal, tax and gift administration solutions that sophisticated planned giving programs require.

Renaissance, Inc.
6100 West 96th Street, Suite 100
Indianapolis, IN 46278
800-843-0050
317-843-5417 (fax)
info@reninc.com
www.reninc.com

Renaissance is a leader in charitable trust administration. They offer full-service "backroom" support for trusts. They do not offer money management services, but work with most major money management firms. They now service an enormous number of trusts. They are plugged into Web-based management systems and continue to be innovators in this area.

State Street Global Advisors
One Lincoln Street, 24th Floor
Boston, MA 02111
Contact: Caitlyn O'Keefe
617-664-2069
617-664-4672 (fax)
caitlyn_o'keefe@ssga.com
www.ssga.com

State Street Bank is another of the major players in trust administration for charitable giving vehicles. Their size and scope has made them the choice of a large number of major charities. They tend to have an East Coast concentration of clients but are seeking to reach further west. They have experience in all phases of money management and trust administration.

Wells Fargo Bank
Charitable Management Group
333 S. Grand Ave., Suite 1110
Los Angeles, CA 90071
Contact: Janice Burrill
213-253-3162
213-689-4109 (fax)
janiceb@wellsfargo.com

Wells Fargo has expanded its charitable management group into virtually every state where it does banking business. They offer full-service administrative support and are a major player in the field.

Vendors

An entire service industry provides support to nonprofit organizations that sponsor planned giving programs. The following vendors are the major ones, although many reputable local and regional firms also provide good products.

Bipster, LLC
P.O. Box 3022
Salem, MA 01970
888-588-BIPS (2477)
978-744-3180 (fax)
info@bipster.com
www.bipster.com

Bipster's freestanding software program tracks bequests from expectancy to completed probate. For larger development offices, keeping track of gifts placed in wills is challenging, especially when many do not become actual gifts for 20, 30, or 40 years or more. This system allows you to organize and track all known gifts in wills and other revocable instruments, providing a method to keep on top of and in touch with bequest donors.

Pentera, Inc.
8650 Commerce Park Place, Suite G
Indianapolis, IN 46268
317-875-0910
317-875-0912 (fax)
info@pentera.com
www.pentera.com

Pentera offers full-service marketing materials for planned giving, including brochures, newsletters, and response pieces. Consulting services and training for development officers are also available.

Planned Giving Today
P.O. Box 1598
Edmonds, WA 98020
800-525-5748
425-744-3837
425-744-3838 (fax)
www.pgtoday.com

The publisher of *Planned Giving Today* newsletter also issues other planned giving marketing publications.

R & R Newkirk
8695 S. Archer, #10
Willow Springs, IL 60480
800-342-2375
708-839-9207 (fax)
inquiries@rrnewkirk.com
www.rrnewkirk.com

Newkirk offers full-service marketing materials for planned giving, including brochures, newsletters, and response pieces. They also offer consulting services and training for development officers and publish the *Charitable Giving Tax Service*.

RIA (Thompson)
395 Hudson St.
New York, NY 10014
212-367-6300
800-950-1216
212-367-6305 (fax)
www.riahome.com

RIA is the publisher of *Charitable Giving and Solicitation* as well as a large number of tax publications.

Robert F. Sharpe & Company, Inc.
(The Sharpe Group)
6410 Poplar Ave., Suite 700
Memphis, TN 38119
800-238-3253
901-680-5300
901-761-4268 (fax)
www.sharpenet.com

One of the oldest planned giving vendors, Sharpe offers full-service marketing materials for planned giving, including brochures, newsletters, and response pieces. They also offer consulting services and training for development officers. Customers receive *Give and Take*, the in-house newsletter, which often contains articles on demographic research conducted by the firm as well as testimonials on the efficacy of Sharpe products.

The Stelter Company
10435 New York Ave.
Des Moines, IA 50322
800-331-6881
515-278-5253
515-278-5851 (fax)
www.stelter.com

Stelter broke into the planned giving field more than 20 years ago with stunning full-color marketing pieces employing reproductions of Old Master paintings. Since then, they have expanded into a full-service vendor of planned giving marketing materials. They have shown great innovation in Web-based marketing and offer Web products on planned giving designed for donors.

Taxwise Giving/Philanthropy Tax Institute
13 Arcadia Rd.
Old Greenwich, CT 06870
203-637-4553
203-637-4572 (fax)
info@taxwisegiving.com
www.taxwisegiving.com

Owned by Conrad Teitell and featuring materials that he either writes or edits, TWG/PTI offers a full range of brochures, newsletters, and informational booklets. It is also the source of an extensive array of papers and publications. Many of the offerings involve Teitell as a speaker and trainer for prospective donors, donors' advisors, and development officers.

National Associations

American Council on Gift Annuities
233 McCrea St., Suite 400
Indianapolis, IN 46255
317-269-6271
acga@acga-web.org
www.acga-web.org

Before there was NCPG, there was the American Council on Gift Annuities. The primary activity of ACGA is to provide recommended, actuarially sound gift annuity rates for member charities. Since most charities subscribe to the recommended rates, ACGA has a great deal of influence. ACGA also offers an excellent training meeting. It is involved with monitoring state regulation of gift annuities and has been influential in regulatory legislation around the country.

National Committee on Planned Giving
233 McCrea St., Suite 400
Indianapolis, IN 46255
317-269-6274
ncpg@iupui.edu
www.ncpg.org

The national trade association for the planned giving world, NCPG is the hub of all activities in the field, including legislation and lobbying, research, national training programs, certification, and even job hunting assistance for members. NCPG sponsors GIFT-PL, the national members-only online discussion group. NCPG is an excellent information clearinghouse and referral center. Someone at every nonprofit institution should be a member to keep up with changes in the field.

GLOSSARY

$11,000 annual exclusion. See annual exclusion amount.

10 percent rule. The rule that no charitable remainder trust will be qualified for tax purposes unless the remainder value to charity is 10 percent or more of the total value of the funding assets of the trust.

1031 exchange. A technique used by real estate investors to transfer the equity they have in one property into another similar property, deferring all capital gains taxes until the actual sale of the property by the owners. This type of 1031 exchange usually involves two or three property owners who are looking to change their position in the real estate they own. The parties frequently select a target property to purchase as part of the exchange since one party may not own a property that another party to the transaction wishes to acquire. Charities can be involved in these transactions when a gift of real property to the charity matches a need that the 1031 exchange participants have. This technique may block a charitable gift when a prospect with low charitable intent finds out he or she can simply defer the gain on the sale of his or her property rather than giving it to a charitable remainder trust. See IRC 1031.

1099 form. See Form 1099.

30 percent charity. A private charity or foundation. The term refers to the limitation on the deductibility of cash gifts to private charities and private foundations of up to 30 percent of the donor's adjusted gross income.

30 percent/20 percent limitation. Refers to limitations on the ability to deduct contributions to private foundations. Gifts of cash or short-term capital gain property are deductible up to 30 percent of the donor's adjusted gross income. Gifts of long-term capital gain property are deductible up to 20 percent of adjusted gross income. No special election is allowed for gifts to private foundations.

306 stock. Stock issued to stockholders in lieu of a taxable dividend. When the stock is sold, the income is taxed as ordinary income to the stockholder, even if the stockholder has held the stock for more than one year and would normally treat the sale proceeds as long-term capital gain income.

401(k) plan. A tax-deferred retirement savings plan available to employees of for-profit corporations. A 401(k) plan is funded by employee contributions and sometimes matching contributions from the employer. Earnings on assets in the 401(k) plan are not taxed until they are withdrawn from the plan. Plan assets may be given to charity through an estate plan, but planning for the gift can be complex and tax benefits often minimal.

403(b) plan. A tax-deferred retirement savings plan similar to a 401(k) plan but available to employees of nonprofit organizations. Earnings on assets in the 403(b) plan are not taxed until they are withdrawn from the plan. Plan assets may be given to charity through an estate plan, but planning for the gift can be complex and tax benefits often minimal.

50 percent charity. A public charity. The term refers to the limitation on the deductibility of cash gifts to public charities of up to 50 percent of the donor's adjusted gross income.

50 percent/30 percent limitation. Refers to limitations on the ability to deduct contributions to public charities. Gifts of cash or short-term capital gain assets are deductible up to 50 percent of the donor's adjusted gross income. Gifts of long-term capital gain property are deductible up to 30 percent of adjusted gross income. A special election allows a taxpayer to treat gifts of 30 percent property under the 50 percent rules, but the taxpayer is limited to deducting the basis rather than the fair market value of the asset. This is a useful election when a taxpayer wants a larger deduction in a particular year and the assets that they contributed had only a small amount of appreciation. See also special election.

501(c)(3) organization. As stipulated in section 501(c)(3) of the Internal Revenue Code, a nonprofit, tax-exempt public benefit charity that may receive tax-deductible gifts.

509(a) organization. See supporting organization.

5227 form. A form that must be filed annually for all qualified split-interest trusts. Every charitable remainder trust must file this form.

5 percent–50 percent rule. The requirement that a qualified charitable remainder trust must have a stated payout of no less than 5 percent and no more than 50 percent. This requirement is independent of the rule that the charitable remainder be 10 percent or more.

5 percent probability test. Using IRS tables, this calculation attempts to determine if there is more than a 5 percent probability that the assets of a charitable remainder annuity trust will be exhausted before the death of the final income beneficiary. If a trust fails to show that there is less than a 5 percent chance of exhausting the trust assets, the trust fails as a remainder annuity trust and no tax benefits are allowed to the donors.

8282 form. See Form 8282.

8283 form. See Form 8283.

Accelerated charitable remainder trust. A type of trust used in the 1990s that attempted to take advantage of accounting rules allowing income payments from a charitable remainder trust to be paid in different tax years. The IRS challenged this technique by issuing new rules creating the 10 percent minimum gift to charity rule and the 50 percent maximum payout rule for CRTs. See also 10 percent rule; 5 percent–50 percent rule.

Acquisition indebtedness. Any debt that is incurred by a nonprofit organization in order to purchase or acquire an asset. Income generated as a result of this indebtedness is taxable unrelated business income. This rule attempts to limit unfair competition by tax-exempt nonprofits with for-profit businesses. Any use of debt by a remainder trust will destroy the tax-exempt status of the trust.

Adjusted gross income (AGI). A taxpayer's total annual income, after certain adjustments but before deductions are subtracted. AGI is used in planned giving marketing to provide a basis from which to estimate the tax benefits to be received from a planned gift technique.

Administrator. The person responsible for the administration of an intestate estate.

Alienation. A legal term to describe the transfer, usually by sale, of real property. Gifts are a form of alienation.

American Council on Gift Annuities (ACGA). Provides technical support and training concerning gift annuities and sets suggested payout rates for one- and two-life gift annuities based on actuarial projections and interest rate assumptions. Rates are set at least every three years, although throughout the 1990s and beyond the rates were reset more often. See also uniform gift annuity rates.

Annual exclusion. Provision allowing a taxpayer to make gifts of up to $11,000 per person per year with no gift tax liability. For example, a couple may give up to $22,000 annually to each of their children, grandchildren, or even unrelated persons. Estate planners use the exclusion to move estate assets from one generation to the next.

Annuity. A contract between two parties in which one party, usually in exchange for a lump-sum payment or transfer of assets, promises to pay the other party (the annuitant) an income for his or her lifetime and often the lifetime of his or her spouse. Two individuals may also create such a contract privately (this practice is very common in Europe). The commercial form of this contract is sold widely by insurance companies in the United States and elsewhere and is highly regulated. See also annuity trust; charitable gift annuity.

Annuity trust. A charitable remainder trust created under section 664 of the Internal Revenue Code that provides for a fixed-income payment to donors for the term of the trust. See also unitrust; term.

Appraisal. A professional opinion of the market value of an asset. An appraisal is necessary when trying to prove the value of a charitable contribution. To qualify for tax purposes, a qualified appraiser must perform the appraisal. The donor does not need the appraisal before contributing the property, although many charities prefer to have an appraisal before acceptance. There are specific criteria that must be met before someone is considered a qualified appraisor.

Appraisal summary. The summary form attached to Form 8283 substantiating the deduction claimed on the taxpayer's income tax return. The summary form includes key information about the donor and nature of the gift. See IRC reg. 1.170A-12, ff.

Appreciated property. Property worth more than its cost basis. See also cost basis.

Arm's-length transaction. The legal concept that two parties to a contract or sale must agree to all terms without undue influence or coercion. This concept is most often discussed with regard to the receipt and resale of an asset used to fund a charitable remainder trust. All asset sales must be arm's-length transactions and cannot be prearranged by the donor.

Assignment form. A form used to transfer ownership of a security. See also stock power.

Assignment of income rule. In tax law, the stipulation that a person who has the right to receive income cannot avoid tax on the income by assigning it to a third party. In charitable giving, the most common situation arises when an individual attempts to have income from personal services sent directly to a charity as a gift, a practice the IRS does not allow.

Audit. In planned giving, an audit usually refers to a complete review by an outside third party of the entire planned giving program, from marketing practices to policies governing administration of life income plans. An audit can help pinpoint areas of needed improvement and possible new investments to grow the program.

Bank account, gift of. See also Totten trust.

Bargain sale. A tax term referring to a gift that is part gift and part sale of the contributed asset. There are two common bargain sales: the sale of an asset to a charity at less than fair market value (the difference between the sale price and the fair market value is considered a gift for tax purposes) and a charitable gift annuity, with the estimated residual gift to charity deemed to be deductible.

Bearer. One who holds possession, usually of a bond or stock certificate.

Bearer instrument. A legal document showing ownership, usually of stock shares or bonds, which does not indicate an owner. If a stock certificate does not specify the name of the owner, then the bearer of the instrument is considered the owner. A bearer instrument is convenient for brokerage firms, but risky if it should fall into the wrong hands.

Beneficiary. The person or persons who receive the benefits from the assets of a trust (usually income or use of assets) for the term of the trust, or the person or institution (also called the remainderman) that will receive the residual amount in the trust at the end of the trust term (the remainder interest).

Bequest. The disposition of assets by will, originally describing only personal property but now broadened to include real property.

Blown trust. A charitable remainder trust that has lost its tax-exempt status through self-dealing, debt financing, acquisition indebtedness, or other illegal acts by the trustee, donors, or income beneficiaries.

Bond. A form of security that is considered a debt of the issuing corporation or public entity. A bond usually pays a stated rate of interest and is usually issued in a $1,000 denomination that is called the "face amount." A bond is a secured creditor to the issuing corporation or public entity, and in the event of liquidation, would be paid before any stockholders. Bonds are traded publicly. Valuations of bonds, since they are fixed-income instruments, are affected by the fluctuation in interest rates on general investments.

C Corp. A corporation that is subject to corporate tax rules and rates. See also ordinary corporation and subchapter S corporation.

Call. Refers to either a meeting or a phone contact with donors or prospective donors. You "call on" a donor, which implies a face-to-face meeting, or you "call" a donor, which implies merely a verbal contact via phone or e-mail. A "cold call" is usually a phone call (although it could be face to face) to someone who has little or no connection with your institution, but someone whom your development officer feels could have the capacity to make a gift if properly motivated. See Appendix A for information on call techniques.

Capacity. The financial ability of a prospective donor to make a large gift either outright, in a life income plan, or through an estate plan. Development officers evaluate all prospects for this ability and make key management decisions based on their evaluation. Frequently, development research efforts are focused on determining the capacity of major donor prospects for possible solicitation.

Capital campaign. A fund-raising campaign that has as one, if not its only goal, the raising of funds for capital projects, including the building or renovation of structures owned or used by the nonprofit organization. In higher education, the term capital campaign now describes almost any large (for the institution) fund-raising effort, whether the primary goal is endowment, current operations, or capital needs.

Capital gain. The difference between the cost basis of an asset and its fair market value. When an asset is sold, the gain from the sale is subject to tax. Gains and losses are characterized as either short term (one year or less holding period) or long term (one year and one day or longer).

Capital gains tax. The tax on gain that results from the sale of a capital asset. If the asset was owned for one year or less, the capital gain is considered short term and is taxed at ordinary income tax rates. If the asset was held for at least one year and one day, the capital gain is considered long term and is taxed under the capital gains tax rates. This tax usually has a lower rate than the ordinary income tax rate; therefore, it is more desirable income to recognize.

Capital loss. The loss realized on the sale of a capital asset for less than the cost basis of the asset, which is deductible against income. For example, the resale of securities on which the price has dropped results in a capital loss. When contributing unappreciated assets, it is better to sell the assets first and contribute the proceeds. The loss amount creates a deduction, and the cash contributed creates a charitable deduction. This means the donor receives full deduction value from the stock purchase, even though it was a loser. Capital losses can be either short term or long term, depending on whether the asset was held for one year or less or one year and a day.

Carry-forward. In tax law, the use of an unused tax deduction in succeeding years, even though the deduction was created in only one tax year. The carry-forward rules for a charitable gift allow a charitable deduction to be used in the year of the gift (up to 50 percent/30 percent limitations for public charities and 30 percent/20 percent for private foundations), and any unused portion may be carried forward for up to five years.

Carry-over. The rules governing the basis in contributed assets, especially contributed assets to a charitable remainder trust. The carry-over basis is the basis in the asset that the donor held before the contribution to the

trust. The trust must use this basis in determining the character of the income paid to the income beneficiaries.

Case statement. A written document that gives all the reasons for philanthropic support from donors, friends, the community, and all interested persons and constituencies. It is intended to be a persuasive sales document. Case statements are a chance for the institution to share its vision with its core constituents.

Cash surrender value. The value of an insurance policy, usually a life insurance policy, if the policy is given back to the insurance company before the death of the insured and all money not used to provide actual insurance is returned to the policy owner. Any cash value buildup inside an insurance policy is not taxed until actually received by the owner. This amount is not the interpolated terminal reserve amount. See also interpolated terminal reserve.

Certified financial planner (CFP). An individual who has successfully completed the certification requirements of the Certified Financial Planner Board of Standards, Inc. Qualifications for receiving the certificate include successful completion of an examination, experience, ethics, and continuing education.

Certified public accountant (CPA). An accountant certified by a state examining board as having fulfilled the requirements of state law to be a public accountant.

Charitable family limited partnership (CHAR-FLP). A family limited partnership (FLP) that includes a charitable organization as one of its partners. This type of FLP (CHAR-FLP) attempts to create increased tax advantages to the other family members by using the charitable organization's tax-exempt status. It is not illegal, but it causes concern. The gift to charity is seldom large enough to matter, but the charity's potential exposure in the event of challenge from the IRS or business reversals of the partnership seems significant. Only if there is a significant gift should a charity become involved in this type of arrangement. If involved, the charity is wise to retain legal counsel to ensure minimum exposure to the institution. See family limited partnership.

Charitable gift annuity. A contract between the donor (purchaser) and the charity (seller) that guarantees payments for the lifetime of one or two people in exchange for a gift of cash or other assets. State laws authorize and regulate gift annuities, but federal law provides for specific disclosure requirements of all charitable gifts where beneficiaries receive income. Payment rates vary, although most mainstream charities subscribe to the American Council on Gift Annuities' suggested rate schedule. Payment rates are based on the ages of the donors and attempt to provide for an approximate 50 percent residual gift to charity at the end of the life income payments. See also uniform gift annuity rates; American Council on Gift Annuities.

Charitable lead trust. Provides for income to be paid to a charity for a period not to exceed 20 years. At the end of the trust term, the assets are either returned to the grantor (a grantor lead trust) or passed on to a third party or to another charity (a nongrantor lead trust). Most lead trusts are nongrantor lead trusts since the estate and gift tax advantages can be substantial.

Charitable remainder trust (CRT). A split-interest trust in which the income beneficiaries enjoy income from the trust for a term not to exceed 20 years or for a term measured by one or more lives at the time the trust was created. The remainder beneficiary (remainderman) of the trust must be a charitable organization organized and qualified under sections 501–509 of the Internal Revenue Code. See also annuity trust (CRAT); unitrust (CRUT).

Charitable remainderman. The nonprofit charitable organization that is the remainder beneficiary of a trust, usually a charitable remainder trust. A person cannot be a charitable remainderman, especially in the context of a charitable remainder trust. Contrast remainderman.

Charitable reverse split-dollar life insurance. A form of reverse split-dollar life insurance in which a charity is made the owner of a portion of the death benefit on the policy. The idea is that a portion of the premium payments on the policy becomes tax deductible. This technique has been repudiated by the IRS and is not considered legal. Before entering into any such arrangement, you should seek your legal counsel's opinion. Do not rely on the legal counsel of the insurance company or agent. Frequently, insurance companies write "opinion letters" to camouflage major problems with the technique. Be sure to understand exactly what benefits your organization would derive from the "gift." Often they are so small as to make the risk unacceptable. See also reverse split-dollar life insurance.

Charitable set-aside rule. A little-discussed rule that allows pooled income funds to set aside any capital gains to principal rather than treating gains as income and requiring that they be paid out to income beneficiaries. In other words, the gains are set aside for the eventual benefit of the charity. Under pre-1969 law, this rule had more impact, since it applied to all irrevocable trusts. See also pooled income fund.

Charitable split-dollar life insurance. A form of split-dollar life insurance in which a charity is made the owner of a portion of the death benefit on the policy. A portion of the premium payments on the policy becomes tax deductible. This technique has been repudiated by the IRS and is not considered legal at this point. See also split-dollar life insurance.

Chartered life underwriter (CLU). A professional designation granted by the American College (formerly the American College of Life Underwriters). Those seeking the designation must successfully complete 10 college-level courses and examinations in insurance, investments, taxation, employee benefits, estate planning, accounting, management, and economics.

Clifford trust. A short-term trust that used to provide tax advantages to the trustor. Pre-1986, if a trustor funded a short-term trust (10 years or less) that paid income to a third party and the asset returned to the trustor at the end of the trust term, trust income was taxed to the trust beneficiary. The trustor could effectively shift income tax liability from himself or herself to another person with this technique. This technique permitted shifting income within families, including shifting income to spouses and children, which effectively reduced the income tax liability of the trustor. The 1986 Tax Act shut this technique down by making the income taxable to the trustor if the reversionary interest is worth 5 percent or more of the value of the assets used to fund the trust.

Closed-end investment fund. A form of commingled investment fund that invests in a specified manner and accepts only a limited number of investors. The fund is then closed to new investors, but the shares in the fund are traded on major exchanges, thus creating liquidity for the purchaser. Once the fund has been closed, it will issue no new shares. Share values will be based on the market and the success of the underlying investments in the fund. See also pooled investment fund; open-end investment fund.

Closely held stock. Corporate stock in a privately owned business. Closely held stock has no market except for other shareholders (if any) in the corporation itself or individuals who may be interested in buying into the company. There is no exchange on which the stock is traded. A charity that has accepted closely held stock as a gift may find it difficult to market.

Codicil. A traditional amendment to a written will that changes the terms of the will in some way. Some states recognize a handwritten codicil as legal even if it does not observe the other formalities of a will. Other states only recognize codicils that observe all of the formalities of a will, as required in that state. Codicils are a low-cost way to adjust and update a will, usually due to changed circumstances, such as the death of a beneficiary under the will or a change in the assets held in the estate. Charitable gifts can easily be added to any will using a codicil. See also will.

Cohan rule. Refers to a court decision, which stated that a court could take evidence other than receipts and cancelled checks into consideration when seeking substantiation for a charitable deduction claimed by the taxpayer.

Commingling. To put together in one group or mass. Commingling is of particular concern for charitable remainder trust (CRT) investments. Commingling of trust assets, permitted since 1986, is the most common method for charities to handle their CRTs with the exception of those over $1 million, which are still frequently invested on a noncommingled basis. Commingling allows total diversification of assets in even the smallest CRT. Some older trusts may still have the noncommingling language and should be followed or amended by court order to protect the nonprofit trustee from liability should investments not meet donor expectations.

Community foundation. A charitable organization formed expressly to raise money to benefit other nonprofit organizations. The community foundation has grown in popularity over the past 30 years to a point where almost every midsized or larger community in the United States has at least one. They operate like other charities, but serve as a pass-through for donations to other organizations. They offer all of the same planned giving vehicles that other charities offer to their donors, and they have popularized the donor-advised fund. See also donor-advised fund.

Community property. A form of property ownership in which the husband and wife share all assets equally during the marriage. Assets owned before marriage and assets received as bequests are usually excluded. However, the appreciation on assets held before marriage can be considered community property unless there is a prenuptial agreement to the contrary. Because this concept is very complex in its application, gifts made by one

spouse to a charity usually should have the written approval of the other spouse. Only legally married couples are allowed to own community property.

Conservatorship. A court-approved legal arrangement in which a person unable to handle his or her own affairs (the conservatee) has a court-appointed representative (the conservator) act on all legal and domestic matters.

Contribution base. In income tax law, the income base from which the 50 percent/30 percent (or 30 percent/20 percent) limitation amounts are calculated. For most (but not all) people in most years, the contribution base is equal to the adjusted gross income.

Corporation. An incorporated business; company. A corporation must have at least one shareholder, unless it is a public benefit nonprofit corporation. All shareholders have limited liability for the actions of the corporation, protecting shareholders from risking their personal assets. Shares may be given to another individual or corporation or sold. See also subchapter S corporation.

Corpus. The principal sum or capital, as distinguished from interest or income. In trust law, the corpus of the trust is the amount used to fund the trust (along with any later additions). If a trust is funded with $400,000, then $400,000 is considered the trust corpus.

Cost basis. The amount originally payed for a particular asset adjusted for certain tax benefits received by the owner. Usually cost basis will reflect the actual cost of the asset less any deductions taken by the owner for depreciaton (very common in real estate investing and limited partnerships). Increases in cost basis are caused by the owners raising the value of the asset through improvement, for example, a home owner adding on a new bedroom to the house.

Credit. Any amount that can be subtracted directly from the tax amount due from the taxpayer. The credit is a dollar for dollar reduction in the tax liability. See also deduction.

Credit shelter trust. A trust that is set up to accept an amount of assets equal to the value of the unified estate/gift tax exemption amount available to the trustor. This type of trust is usually set up through an estate plan. The trustor funds the trust with an amount equal to his or her exemption amount. The trust pays income to the spouse of the trustor. At the death of the surviving spouse, the assets then go automatically to a third person named in the trust. This transfer then avoids any gift/estate tax, since it will be covered by the unified exemption amount (or the unlimited marital deduction for the income interest).

Crummey trust. A trust that allows the grantor to make gifts to family members in a way that permits them to take advantage of the annual gift tax exclusion while not making gifts directly to the recipients. The recipients have a limited right to withdraw trust amounts, about which they must be notified.

Cultivation. The variety of methods employed by organizations to educate a potential donor about the institution and bring him or her closer to the institution. Cultivation includes, but is not limited to: mailings, invitations to events, personal contacts by staff or volunteers, sending information to prospects on giving techniques and the organization, asking prospects to serve as advisors to the institution, asking them to serve as liaisons to other organizations or constituencies, sending them gifts, and sending them cards on special occasions such as birthdays or anniversaries.

***Cy pres* doctrine**. A rule derived from English common law that is used as a method for interpreting documents (usually of deceased persons) to carry out as closely as possible the intent of the donor when it would be impossible or illegal to carry out the person's wishes as actually stated. Thus, if a devise by will created a perpetuity (an interest that violates the legal rule against perpetuities in real property), then the court will attempt as fairness allows to complete the devise, adjusting it so as not to violate this rule. In practical terms, the *cy pres* doctrine affects charities when a donor's gift goes to something that is no longer legal, practical, or possible. For example, a gift is designated for scholarships limited to premed students who are only from one elementary school. If that school has closed, the court would probably open the scholarships to students from the same geographic area. Sometimes charities attempt to use this doctrine to change the purposes of a gift that they simply do not like or want to move to a more general purpose. Courts are reluctant to do this without a compelling reason to second-guess the testator.

***De minimis* rule**. If a charity receiving gifts of tangible personal property for a related use sells a small part of the overall amount of personal property donated (for example, a few pieces from a large coin collection), then the deduction is still considered for a related use and is deductible at fair market value. The sale is considered *de minimis* in relation to the overall size of the collection. A caution: it is possible for the charity's actions in liquidating the tangible personal property to cause the donor's contribution to be considered for an unrelated use. If so, applying the *de minimis* rule will reduce the deduction to basis or fair market value, whichever is lower. The best practice for the charity is to hold the collection for a period of time (preferably two years) before liquidating or, if liquidation is necessary, then to make sure that only a small portion of the collection is liquidated. A mass liquidation by the charity may cause problems for donors.

Death taxes. An outdated term for the tax levied on all testamentary transfers between individuals. Frequently, it is used to distinguish state estate taxes from the federal estate tax.

Debt financing. Any trust investment that uses some form of borrowing in the production of income. Debt financing is death to the tax-exempt status of a charitable remainder trust due to the private foundation rules that prohibit this type of investment. The most common situation for debt financing is when a trust takes in a gift of real property subject to a mortgage. If this debt is recourse debt, it will result in disqualification of the trust. Nonrecourse debt does not have the same result. See also recourse debt; nonrecourse debt.

Debt relief. When a person owing money to a lender has that obligation removed. Usually debt relief occurs in the context of giving away an encumbered property to charity. To the extent that the donor is relieved of the obligation to repay the loan, he or she has been given debt relief. This may be a taxable event for the donor. See also phantom income.

Deduction. An amount that can be subtracted from the adjusted gross income (or gross estate) to reach the amount known as the taxable income (or taxable estate). A deduction is not subtracted directly from the tax due amount. It reduces the amount that the tax is calculated against. Compare credit.

Deferred giving. See also planned giving.

Deferred payment charitable gift annuity. A gift annuity that begins payments at least one year after its creation. This future date frequently coincides with a crucial date in the life of the donor or income beneficiary, such as retirement or the beginning of college. The charitable deductions created by a deferred gift annuity are larger than an immediate-pay gift annuity, since the income beneficiary must wait to begin receiving payments. This larger deduction can also make the deferred annuity more attractive to donors. See also charitable gift annuity; immediate-pay charitable gift annuity.

Deficiency. In a net income with makeup unitrust, the difference between the stated payout amounts for all years and the actual payout amounts for all years. A deficiency, once created, will be carried on the books from year to year, and, when investment performance exceeds the stated payout amount for a given year, additional payments may be made up to the full amount of any unpaid deficiencies for all prior years.

Deficiency balance. The total of all unpaid carry-forward amounts from a net income with makeup unitrust.

Depreciation recapture. There are several methods of taking depreciation deductions for a capital asset. The most common one is called the straight-line method. Accelerated methods tend to make the early-year deductions much larger than the later-year deductions. If the taxpayer wants to sell or give the asset away and has been using an accelerated depreciation method, to the extent that depreciation deductions exceeded the amount that would have been deducted using the straight-line method, this excess amount must be "recaptured" and recognized as income in the year that the asset is sold or given away. In the case of a gift to charity, this recapture will be recorded as income to the donor, and any income tax deduction will be used to offset the recapture income, thereby reducing the value of the deduction to the donor. It is not always possible to avoid recognizing recapture income due to the 50 percent/30 percent deduction limitations imposed upon taxpayers.

Development research. An organized effort to determine the capacity and interests of potential donors. Large institutions maintain departments devoted to gathering information on alumni, donors, and donor prospects in the hope that this information will aid their development officers and senior staff in successfully identifying major donor prospects and getting the right proposal in front of them. Confidentiality is critical to a development research program and may be required by privacy laws. Clear confidentiality policies should be maintained and published to all staff that may have access to the information or use the information in their own jobs.

Devise. A disposition of real property assets by will or other estate planning instrument.

Devisee. The person to whom lands or other real property are given by will.

Devisor. The person who gives land or other real property through their will or estate plan.

Direct mail. In planned giving, mailings to alumni or constituents to promote the idea of making a planned gift to the institution. The standard mailing package contains a letter explaining what you want, a brochure explaining one or more gift techniques, and a response mechanism. Many vendors offer mailing programs to charities, providing them with brochures, reply pieces, and even copy for letters and the brochures.

Director of development. The staff member who raises philanthropic gifts. Frequently, a director of development may be assigned the development of planned gifts along with other duties, including annual fund, major gifts, and alumni programs. See also planned giving officer.

Disclosure. The attempt to reveal to a potential donor, especially a donor considering a life income plan, all the key information that a reasonable person would need to make an informed decision. The Philanthropy Protection Act requires charities to provide disclosure statements to all donors choosing gift annuities or remainder trusts. (Pooled income funds are regulated under securities laws and have required disclosure documents for a long time.) The content of disclosure documents is still an open question. Charities doing a high volume of planned gifts have of necessity sought legal counsel. Smaller institutions may not have been able to afford this expense and have attempted to draft their own, using other institutions' documents as examples. To date, the IRS has issued no "safe harbor" disclosure documents. The best practice, assuming an inability to get legal counsel, is to provide enough information on both the good and bad points of each technique so that a reasonable person would know what he or she is getting into, without making the document so complex that no one would read it. Most institutions require that the disclosure document be signed by the donor and made a part of the permanent file for the gift. (See Appendix H.)

Discount rate. See also midterm rate.

Disqualified person. Under private foundation rules (IRC sec. 4946), certain people may not be involved in the creation, funding, or management of a private foundation. They also may not do business with the foundation or receive compensation from the foundation. Typically disqualified persons include the donor(s), people related to the founding donors, and/or employees of the founding donors. The rules attempt to limit the abilities of the founders to pass income or other assets on to family members and employees free from transfer taxes. To the extent that a charitable remainder trust is subject to the private foundation rules, the trust must also avoid dealing with disqualified persons. Most problems arise when donors try to handle trust assets like they had not given them to trust, including setting up management deals for their family and friends.

Diversification. Investments within trusts must follow the prudent man rule. This rule suggests that the trustee must follow a prudent investment approach. Modern portfolio theory suggests that a widely diversified investment mix will result in above average performance over time with a reduced risk of volatility. Currently this is considered the most "prudent" method of investing. Diversification in this context means spreading investments over several asset classes to reduce the risk for the overall portfolio. A standard portfolio will be diversified not only between assets such as stocks, bonds, cash, and real estate, but also within asset classes themselves. For example, stock investments will be spread between domestic equities and foreign equities, and within these classes they will be subdivided by industries to take advantage of cyclical and noncyclical stocks and industries.

Diversified investment fund (DIF). Similar to a pooled investment fund but usually held by banks and large trust companies exclusively for their clients. These funds are not marketed directly to the public, but are used to handle investments for bank customers requiring wide diversification of their investments. They usually require the bank to be a trustee of the assets invested in the fund, or at least a co-trustee for investment purposes. They are acceptable investments for charitable remainder trusts.

Dividend. A proportional share of the profits of a corporation, which the corporation periodically distributes to shareholders. Dividends from stocks are the most common form and can be paid in cash (most common) or in additional shares of stock in the corporation. Dividends are taxed at ordinary income rates.

Donor-advised fund. A fund held by a nonprofit, frequently a community foundation, that offers a donor a chance to voice his or her preferences with regard to where the money is distributed and how it will be used. Most donor-advised funds permit distributions to other charities. Donor-advised funds provide the ability to separate the tax motivations for giving from the charitable and mission-driven reasons for giving. The donor can give to the fund at any time, usually for tax reasons, without being forced to pick a charitable beneficiary at that time. The donor will receive an income tax charitable deduction for a gift to the advised fund, since the institution holding the money (usually a community foundation) is a qualified charity. He or she can then request that money from the advised fund be given to specific charities at any time. However, the donor gives up all legal rights to the fund, including the right to force the fund to distribute the money at all, let alone to a specific charity. However, a donor-advised fund administrator very rarely refuses to pass money on as the donor advises. Any qualified charity can operate donor-advised funds; community foundations are the pioneers in the field. However, in the past decade large for-profit financial institutions have created nonprofit corporations that offer donor-advised funds to investment clients. The nonprofit community views this negatively since it places a third party between the donor and the charity. See also community foundation.

Earmarked gift. A charitable gift stipulating that the money is used for the benefit of an individual being provided services by the charity. Usually this type of gift occurs when a donor wants to pay the tuition of a particular student by setting up a scholarship for that purpose. An earmarked gift needs to be distinguished from a donor designation, which may restrict the use of the money to a particular program at the institution or a particular group of constituents. Earmarked gifts attempt to single out one or two people for benefits. Designated gifts attempt to help a particular class of people that is large enough to result in public benefit (for example, scholarships to graduates from a particular city or high school). But you cannot designate it exclusively for people from a particular high school with the surname of Brostrom.

Easement. A property right usually involving real property. An easement typically means that a third party, not the owner of the property, has the right to use the property, either generally, or more commonly for a specific purpose. An example of an easement is where one property owner has the right to use a portion of another owner's property to gain access to his or her own property. Landlocked parcels of land frequently have easement rights in another person's property so the landlocked owners can get to and from their own property. Easements can be affirmative or negative in nature. A negative easement is one that prohibits another property owner from using their property in a particular way. A common negative easement is the right to a view, which prohibits another property owner from building a fence or structure that might impede the view from the owner's property. The right to cross another's property to get to your own would be an example of an affirmative easement.

Employee stock ownership plan (ESOP). A plan that permits employees to acquire stock in a corporation, commonly used by corporate founders who hold all or a majority of the stock and wish to partially divest themselves without losing control. ESOPs can be used to facilitate charitable gifts of closely held or thinly traded corporate stock. The transactions are complex, but the result is often a good way for a founder to make a gift to charity of his company stock without losing control of his company. At the same time, the donor can reduce his or her holdings for estate planning purposes or succession planning within the company. When the charity sells the stock to the ESOP, the charity receives the cash and the donor maintains control of the company.

Endowed chair. A position of recognition and esteem bestowed upon a worthy faculty member that has the support of a specific, restricted endowment fund to help pay for the expenses associated with the chair holder such as salary, benefits, secretarial, research assistants, lab space, etc. Frequently the donor(s) who established the endowed chair is honored by having the chair named after him or her.

Endowment. A gift to a charity that has as a condition of its acceptance that the charity keep the money permanently. Only earnings from an endowment are usable by the institution, absent a specific written provision by the donor permitting the invasion of the endowment principal. Institutions frequently charge management fees and costs against endowment earnings, but are not allowed to use principal to satisfy these expenses. Endowment gifts are frequently designated by donors to support specific activities of the charity and exclude support for general expenses of the organization. Gifts of this nature are called restricted endowments. A permanent endowment that does not limit the uses of the income from the fund is considered an unrestricted endowment. See also quasi-endowment.

Endowment investment policy. The goals and strategies, usually in writing, that a nonprofit institution has for its endowment pool investments. A policy typically includes a list of acceptable investments and a discus-

sion of the risk tolerance level for the fund overall and sometimes by asset classes. See also endowment pool; spending rule.

Endowment policy. A life insurance policy that pays a death benefit for a period of years, during which time the policy owner makes premium payments. If the insured is still living at the end of the premium payment term, he or she is paid the face amount of the policy.

Endowment pool. A group or pool of assets that are combined for investment purposes to improve overall investment performance and diversification. Most endowment pools use a unitized accounting method in which each share has equal ownership of all assets in the pool. The value of holdings in the pool is usually given in market value per share. Gains and losses are shared equally by all shares. Endowment pools give even small endowments wide diversification across many different asset categories. Since earnings are pooled, all gains, losses, and types of income are included in each shareholder's account. This can cause major problems for charitable remainder trusts, which cannot have debt-financed income from assets without losing their tax-exempt status. For this reason, charitable remainder trusts are seldom put in general endowment pools. Either they are managed individually or they are placed in a special investment pool that protects them from this danger. See also spending rule.

Entire interest. All rights, titles, and interests in a particular asset that are held by an individual. When making a gift, a person must give his or her entire interest in the property, except for certain specific exceptions, such as a split-interest gift. This does not mean that the interest is the complete interest in a property. If you own a leasehold interest and give it away, then even though the leasehold interest is only a partial interest in the underlying real property, for the donor it is his or her entire interest. A gift of the donor's entire interest qualifies the donation for income tax deductibility as well as estate/gift tax deductibility. See also split interest.

Estate. The real and personal property owned by an individual. Anyone living or dead has an estate. Sometimes corporations and trusts are considered as having estates, but this use is not widespread and is somewhat misleading. See also estate tax.

Estate tax. A tax levied on all testamentary transfers between individuals. The estate tax is aimed at high-net-worth individuals and is part of a unified gift/estate tax that attempts to tax all transfers between individuals.

Excess business holdings. Prohibited investments for private foundations under IRC 4943. This is usually not a factor for charitable remainder trusts unless the trust life is extended beyond the life income beneficiary interests, in which case it becomes a simple charitable trust and is subject to these prohibitions. Excess business holdings are defined as holdings in excess of 20 percent of the outstanding voting stock in a corporation (including the shares held by disqualified persons). These rules are complex and are aimed at stopping a person from giving away stock to a private foundation while still keeping control of the corporation. Holdings of 2 percent or less are considered *de minimus* holdings and create a "safe harbor" for the trustee or foundation. See also safe harbor.

Exclusion ratio. The ratio applied to payments from charitable gift annuities to determine the amount that is deemed return of principal and, therefore, tax free to the income beneficiary. The exclusion ratio is applied only for the life expectancy of the income beneficiary. If an income beneficiary lives longer than projected, the income payments cease to be subject to the exclusion ratio and become taxable. If an income beneficiary dies before his or her projected life expectancy term, the deceased is entitled to a deduction for the portion of exempt income that they would have received (if they had lived the full term) on their final estate tax return.

Executor. The person or institution charged with the responsibility of ensuring that the wishes of the deceased, as expressed in a will and/or trust, are carried out. A female executor usually is called an executrix. An executor is not a trustee, but is held to the same fiduciary duty to follow the wishes of the deceased faithfully. An executor is usually named in the will and/or trust and is approved by the probate court, which gives him or her the legal standing to handle all issues related to the estate as if he or she were the testator. The court usually issues letters testamentary that officially acknowledge the legal standing of the executor. Executors are allowed to charge fees for their services.

Exempt. In planned giving, can refer to either an organization exempt from income tax or to the character of actual income received by an income beneficiary of a charitable gift annuity or charitable remainder trust. Organizations are referred to as exempt organizations when they have been officially recognized by the IRS as public benefit organizations. See IRC section 501(c)(3) for common types of exempt organizations.

Fair market value. The value that a willing buyer would pay a willing seller in an arm's-length transaction; the standard term used to describe the value of assets given to charity (for example, real estate). This term does not describe postsale value of an asset, since most gifts to charity involve first the transfer to charity by the donor and second the sale of the asset by the charity. The term applies primarily to pregift valuation of assets and is not net of selling costs and administrative fees.

Family limited partnership (FLP). A popular form of estate planning and a method of exploiting tax rules governing partnerships to reduce or eliminate the transfer taxes usually incurred upon the transfer of beneficial ownership. Older family members frequently create FLPs that make younger family members partners. The older members contribute assets to the FLP that then are used to facilitate the transfer of beneficial ownership to the younger partners. Frequently, the FLP keeps or increases the income already being earned by the older family members, while at the same time moving the equitable ownership of the income-producing assets to the younger partners. With careful planning and drafting, an FLP allows families to keep their assets, such as business and real estate holdings, in the family while reducing or avoiding the transfer taxes normally associated with gifts to family members. See also charitable family limited partnership.

Farm, gift of. A farm may be deeded to charity with a retained life estate and qualify for an immediate income tax charitable deduction for the discounted present value of the fee interest given to charity. See also personal residence; retained life estate.

Feasibility study. A formal process to determine whether or not a particular fund-raising goal or project, typically a capital campaign, has a high probability of success. A feasibility study usually takes the form of an extensive series of interviews between a consultant hired to run the study and trustees and other high-profile supporters of the institution. These interviews center on the case for such a campaign and the willingness (or lack thereof) of the interviewee to participate financially in the campaign. A good feasibility study not only "presells" key donors on the main purposes and needs for the campaign, but also helps identify areas of weakness for the institution, which may need to be fixed prior to embarking on an extensive capital campaign.

119

Fee simple absolute. A legal term used to describe complete and undisputed ownership of a piece of property, usually real property.

Fiduciary. A person having duty, created by his undertaking, to act on behalf of and in the best interests of another. The term implies scrupulous good faith and candor. A fiduciary is a person holding the character of a trustee. Trustees and nonprofit board members act in a fiduciary capacity. Attorneys, physicians, and other professionals often act in this capacity as well. See also trustee.

Finder's fee. A fee paid to someone who has facilitated the acquisition of an asset, agreement, or gift by a third party. In planned giving, a finder's fee is sometimes requested by a person who has control over the designation of a gift to charity. Finder's fees are considered unethical by the planned giving community but are sometimes paid and viewed as the cost of doing business. See also gift broker.

Fixed payment. A payment to an income beneficiary where the amount does not vary from payment to payment or year to year. Charitable remainder annuity trusts and charitable gift annuities make such fixed payments. A standard unitrust (Type 1) makes fixed payments in a given year, but will not make fixed payments from year to year. Net income unitrusts pay variable income even within the specific year.

Flip trust (FLIPCRUT). A charitable remainder unitrust that starts out as a net income or net income with makeup unitrust, but on the sale of a majority of the funding assets or upon a certain fixed date, flips to become a standard unitrust.

For the use of. Legal term describing gifts that benefit charities, even though the donors generally have controlled the mechanism for distribution and to some extent the purposes for which the gift will be used. Gifts "for the use of" charities will be deductible for tax purposes. Earmarked gifts, which are too restrictive as to the charities' use of the money, are not deductible. See also earmarked gift.

Forced heir. A person or persons whom the testator or donor cannot deprive of a portion of the estate by law. This usually applies only to spousal shares of estates. Most state laws create a presumption that, absent a prenuptial agreement, the spouse is entitled to a share of the deceased spouse's estate. This share is often one-third of the total estate, but percentages vary by state.

Form 1040. The income tax return completed by individuals. This is the form used for taking income tax charitable deductions.

Form 1099. A tax form issued by a nonprofit institution to all charitable gift annuity income beneficiaries. This form details the amount of income received for the tax year and the character of that income (i.e., ordinary, capital gain, or exempt).

Form 706. The federal estate tax return, typically handled by tax professionals.

Form 8282. This IRS form is required to be filed by the donee-charity for any gift of noncash assets (except for publicly traded stock) sold within two years of receipt. This reporting requirement attempts to limit the overstatement of asset value on appraisals by creating a mechanism to check on the actual value of the assets contributed. This is also why institutions are frequently asked by donors to hold an asset for two years before liquidating it.

Form 8283. IRS tax form that a donor must file when taking a tax deduction for a gift of a noncash asset to a charity. The form must be filed when aggregate gifts to a particular charity for the year exceed $500. Gifts of noncash assets (except for publicly traded securities) exceeding $5,000 must include a qualified appraisal. An exception exists for gifts of nonpublicly traded stock and certain publicly traded stock valued between $5,000 and $10,000, but this exception still requires a partially completed appraisal summary form under IRC reg. 1.170A-13.

Four-tier system. Used to determine the character of income received by income beneficiaries from charitable remainder trusts The four-tier system prioritizes income as (1) ordinary income, (2) capital gain income, (3) exempt income, and (4) return of principal. Before income can be characterized as a lower tier of income, all upper-tier income must be recognized for tax purposes. For example, assume that a 10 percent $100,000 trust was funded with property worth $100,000 with a $90,000 basis (i.e., a $10,000 capital gain was avoided). Then assume that the trust earned $6,000 in dividends and interest and $4,000 in tax-exempt income during the year. The income beneficiary receives $10,000, but the character of the income on the Form K-1 would be $6,000 of ordinary income and $4,000 of capital gain income. Why? Because the 2nd-tier income must be recognized before you can move to a lower level. Since there is $10,000 of unrecognized gain inside the trust it must be recognized before there can be tax-exempt income because capital gain is a higher tier than exempt income. See IRC sec. 664(b) for definition and IRC reg. sec. 1.664-1(d)(1)(i) for application.

Fractional interest. A complete interest in property (usually real estate) that does not represent the entire property itself. For example, if five people each own one-fifth of an apartment building, they are each considered to have a fractional interest in the apartment building. A fractional interest is a complete fee interest, but only for a portion of the property itself. See also undivided interest; fee simple absolute; tenancy in common.

Frequency. Refers to the regularity with which a particular donor makes gifts to an organization. Annual gifts over a period of time may indicate a strong interest in an organization, even if the gifts have been relatively modest ones. Multiple gifts each year for several years mark a person as a likely prospect for a larger planned gift.

Future interest. An interest in property that a person will receive in the future, not an immediate right to possess the property now. See also present interest.

Generation-skipping tax. A tax levied on transfers from one generation of a family to another generation that skips one or more intervening generations. For example, if grandparents transfer assets to their grandchildren directly without first giving the assets to their children, the transfer is subject to the tax. Currently there is a credit against this tax that shelters up to $1.5 million (2005) in value transferred. (This credit will gradually increase to $3.5 million by 2009.) This credit is available for each transfer to a different person. Thus, only transfers in excess of $1.5 million to a skip generation member are subject to tax. Transferors can transfer as much as they want without tax liability provided they give no single person more than $1.5 million. Gifts to nonfamily members are not subject to this tax.

Gift acceptance committee. A formal committee that approves all gifts to an institution. As a practical matter, this group primarily focuses on gifts that are difficult to evaluate or value and gifts that may carry some potential liability for the institution.

Gift broker. A for-profit planned giving person who solicits clients and has them place their assets in remainder trusts. The broker then asks charities to pay a fee for the right to be named irrevocably as a remainder ben-

eficiary of the trust. This type of transaction is viewed as unethical by the planned giving community. See also finder's fee.

Gift planner. A generic title for planned giving officer and deferred giving officer.

Gift tax. A tax on lifetime gifts. The gift tax is intended to tax transfers made by wealthy individuals during their lifetime. Gifts made by will or other testamentary transfers are taxed under the estate tax. The lifetime exclusion amount under the gift tax is $1 million. This means that a donor may make tax-free gifts of up to $1 million total during his or her lifetime. When total gifts exceed this amount, they are taxed under gift tax rates. Gifts made to charity are considered taxable gifts, but are 100 percent deductible under the gift tax and do not require the donor to use up a portion of his or her lifetime exclusion amount. See Estate tax; Generation skipping tax.

Governing instrument. The underlying written agreement governing a planned gift. Tax law is very clear that it will look to local law and the governing instrument to interpret the tax rules in areas where the code and regulations are silent.

Grantor. The person who creates and funds a trust. See also charitable lead trust; grantor retained income trust.

Grantor retained income trust (GRIT). A noncharitable trust that is used to reduce or eliminate estate and/or gift taxes; a version of a noncharitable remainder trust. The grantor sets up a trust that pays the grantor income for a period of years. At the end of this term, the assets are transferred to a third party or parties, usually family member(s). The grantor is allowed to discount the gift to the third party since there is deferred enjoyment of the assets during the period of time the grantor receives income. The hook in this technique is that the grantor must live to the end of the trust term. If he or she dies during the trust term, the assets are included in the estate for estate tax purposes.

Holding period. For tax purposes, the length of time that a taxpayer was the owner of a particular asset. See capital gain.

Holographic will. A will that has been written entirely in the hand of the testator and shows no changes or interference on the part of third parties. Many states require formalities to be observed when creating a will and do not recognize any document that fails to follow these formalities, including a holographic will. Other states treat holographic wills with greater flexibility. See also will; codicil.

Honorary gift. A gift made in honor of a living person. Larger nonprofits tend to discourage this type of giving since it requires additional handling and the size of the gifts is usually small.

Identification. The process of finding prospective donors. In planned giving, the term includes identifying those most likely to make a larger gift, whether deferred or outright.

Immediate-pay charitable gift annuity. A gift annuity that begins making payments to the income beneficiaries within one year from the creation of the annuity. See also charitable gift annuity; deferred payment charitable gift annuity.

In-kind. A gift other than gifts of cash. Usually, fund raisers refer to this type of gift when they receive a gift of a tangible asset that is like the kind of asset they were trying to raise money to purchase. For example, if the organization is trying to raise money to refurbish a student lounge and someone donates the carpet and furniture, this would be viewed as an in-kind gift.

Incident of ownership. Any right or interest in a life insurance policy, such as the right to change beneficiaries or borrow from the cash value of the policy. If a person dies with any incident of ownership in an insurance policy, then the value of the entire policy is includible in the estate for tax purposes. If a person contributes a life insurance policy to charity and retains even one incident of ownership, then he or she cannot deduct the gift for tax purposes. Because of this rule, donors will set up an irrevocable life insurance trust as part of a charitable remainder trust gift. See also irrevocable life insurance trust.

Income beneficiary. Recipients of the payments made by a charitable remainder trust; can also refer to the recipients of payments from charitable gift annuities and pooled income funds.

Income characterization. Under IRS rules, all income is either ordinary income, capital gain income, tax-exempt income, or return of principal. Declaring income to be of one type or another is to characterize the income for tax purposes.

Income in respect of a decedent (IRD). Income received by a deceased person during the course of his or her estate administration (i.e., before their assets and interests can be distributed under their will or trust). An example is the final distribution from a standard IRA. IRD is subject to the personal income tax and must be included on the decedent's final income tax return.

Incomplete gift. An attempted gift that has not been completed. In tax law, this usually means that the donor has not complied with one of the requirements for making a gift. Either the donor has not completed the documentation necessary to show clear intent (for example, has failed to sign a check when sending in an annual fund donation or failed to give up possession of the property). An incomplete gift does not create any tax benefits for the donor. A different form of incomplete gift occurs when the donor makes the gift revocable either completely or as to the naming of a beneficiary. In this case, the gift is completed only when the gift becomes irrevocable. Some people consider failing to name a beneficiary on a trust as an incomplete gift, but this assumption is incorrect from a tax standpoint, since the donor has irrevocably transferred the asset to the trust and gets full tax benefits.

Individual retirement account (IRA). A tax-deferred savings account that allows donors to make fully deductible contributions until they reach the age of 70½, at which time they must begin to take distributions from the account. The contributions are subject to tax when they are withdrawn. (Cf. Roth IRA.) Assets held in an IRA may be given to charity, but it is preferable that they be given through the estate rather than during a lifetime because only a gift of IRA assets to charity receives total deductibility under the income tax (IRD is taxed at the taxpayer's income tax rate) and the estate tax. Amounts given during lifetime would be taxable to the donor upon withdrawal. Although the corresponding charitable contribution provides an offsetting deduction for the charitable contribution, the donor is left with no net tax benefit from the gift. See also estate tax.

Installment note. The written document that describes the terms and conditions upon which an installment obligation will operate. Usually contains payment amounts, interest charges, penalties for default, methods to cure defaults, the rights of the parties in the case of default, provisions for recovering of attorney fees, and other matters pertinent to the agreement.

Installment obligation. An obligation to pay money on a prorated basis over an agreed-upon time period. (In tax law the term must extend at least until the next tax year of the taxpayer.) Car loans, house loans, and purchase contracts are all forms of installment obligations. Any gain on the sale of the asset through an installment sale is recognized pro-rata as the payments are received. This is generally considered favorable tax treatment because the seller does not have to recognize all of the gain in one year while waiting years for the actual payments to arrive. However, if the owner of the obligation sells or gives the note away, either to charity or to a noncharitable third party, he or she must "accelerate" the gain and recognize all of it in the year of the transfer.

Insurable interest. In general, the interest or benefit that one person derives from the continued life of another person, usually a family interest or a business interest. If this interest in the life of another exists, then it follows that the loss of this life is worthy of some form of compensation, such as the death benefit on a life insurance policy. When a charity is made the owner and beneficiary of a life insurance policy, most states recognize that a charity has an insurable interest in a policy that is set up by the insured.

Inter vivos. Distinguishes something given or taken during lifetime versus through succession or death. An inter vivos trust, for example, is a trust that is created by the trustor during the trustor's lifetime.

Interest. 1. A general term to describe a right to have the advantage accruing from anything; any right in the nature of property, but less than title; a partial or undivided right; a title to a share. For example, a person is said to have an interest in real estate when he or she is a partner in a real estate holding such as an apartment building. 2. Compensation allowed by law or fixed between parties for the use or forbearance or detention of money. For example, a bond pays out at a rate that is set prior to the owner's purchase of it. Interest is usually taxed at ordinary income rates, although municipal bonds frequently pay out tax-free interest.

Internal Revenue Code (IRC). The federal laws governing the tax system. The code is the "black letter law" concerning all forms of taxes. Extensive regulations have also been issued that explain the black letter law and offer examples for taxpayers to follow. Regulations have the full force and effect of law and can be relied upon by the taxpayer.

Internal Revenue Service (IRS). A division of the Treasury Department responsible for the collection of all taxes in the United States.

Interpolated terminal reserve (ITR). The amount allowed to be deducted as a charitable gift when an insurance policy is contributed to a qualified charity. This amount is calculated and used by insurance companies and is not readily available. Frequently, the insurance company staff themselves have not heard of the term and are unable to provide the accurate information. Donors usually deduct the cash value of a policy rather than trying to find the actual ITR, since the cash value is usually slightly less than the ITR and is easier to determine.

Intestate. To die without a will or other document to direct the distribution of all assets owned at death. Most states have statutes that determine "intestate succession" when a testator leaves no will. These statutes provide a prioritized list of persons who can benefit from the estate. If no beneficiaries can be found, most intestate statutes provide for the state to be the final beneficiary of an intestate estate.

Inventory. Any property held for sale in a trade or business. Inventory when given to a charity is deductible only to the extent of the basis in the asset, not its fair market value. Thus, a dealer in computers could only deduct his actual investment in the machines, rather than the market value, if he donated them to charity.

Irrevocable. A misleading term in planned giving, because state laws sometimes allow for changes to irrevocable instruments, even when the instruments themselves declare them to be irrevocable. For example, in California, an irrevocable trust can in fact be amended if all parties to the trust agree to the changes.

Irrevocable life insurance trust. A trust set up specifically to hold a life insurance policy, usually by a donor who wants to transfer assets to family members. A third party, usually the beneficiaries, pays premiums on the policy. (Frequently the trustor will make outright gifts to the third party, which are then used to pay the premiums.) Upon the death of the insured, the trust terminates and the life insurance proceeds are transferred to the beneficiaries free from all estate taxes. This type of trust is often used in conjunction with a charitable remainder trust.

IRS revenue procedure ruling. A formal ruling by the IRS on a point of procedure. These rulings are used to clarify any confusion on particular issues and to state the IRS's position regarding procedural matters. Revenue procedure rulings are binding on the IRS until rescinded or amended.

Jeopardy investments. An investment that jeopardizes the tax-exempt status of a nonprofit organization. Under private foundation rules, these types of investments are prohibited. Charitable remainder trusts, charitable lead trusts, and pooled income funds are also prohibited from holding these types of investments.

Joint tenancy. A form of ownership of real property where all parties are deemed to own the entire property. Each joint tenant has a right of survivorship in the property, which means that upon the death of one tenant, the other tenants automatically become the owner of the property. This is a popular form of ownership for real property, particularly among families, since it negates the need for probate of the interest.

K-1 form. A form required to be sent to all income beneficiaries of split-interest trusts that tells them how much income they received during the prior tax year and what character that income had (i.e., ordinary income, capital gain income, or exempt income).

KEOGH plan. A tax-deferred savings plan for self-employed people and employees of smaller companies. Contributions to a KEOGH plan are tax deductible up to a maximum amount set by statute. Earnings on assets in a KEOGH plan are not taxed until they are withdrawn from the plan. Withdrawals are taxed as ordinary income. Plan assets may be given to charity through an estate plan with positive tax results, but planning for the gift can be complex.

Leasehold interest. A temporary interest in real or personal property that usually gives the leaseholder the right to exclusive use and possession of the property subject to the lease. Examples include leases in buildings, individual units within buildings, equipment, and software. The lease must be in writing.

Legatee. The person to whom a legacy is given.

Legator. One who makes a will or leaves a legacy to someone.

Letters testamentary. Formal court document acknowledging that a person or persons have been given the powers of the deceased in order to handle the distribution of an estate according to the wishes of the deceased as expressed in a will or trust. See also executor.

Life estate. See also retained life estate.

Life expectancy. The period estimated by mathematical models that a person has left to live, based on the current age of the person. In planned giving, life expectancy is used to determine the value of the charitable deduction for all forms of deferred gifts.

Limitation on deductibility. Gifts of cash or short-term capital gain property to private foundations are deductible up to 30 percent of the donor's adjusted gross income; gifts of long-term capital gain property are deductible up to 20 percent (the 30 percent/20 percent limitation). Unlike the rules for contributions to a public charity, there is no special election allowed for gifts to private foundations. Gifts to a public charity are deductible up to 50 percent of the donor's adjusted gross income for gifts of cash or short-term capital gain property or up to 30 percent of adjusted gross income for gifts of long-term capital gain property (the 50 percent/30 percent limitation). A special election allows a taxpayer to treat gifts of 30 percent property under the 50 percent rules, but the taxpayer is limited to deducting the basis of the asset, not its fair market value. A special election is useful when a taxpayer wants a larger deduction in a particular year and the contributed assets had only a small amount of appreciation. See also special election.

Limited liability corporation (LLC). A hybrid form of corporation that combines the limited liability that a normal corporation provides shareholders with the tax benefits and flexibility that a partnership provides. LLCs were popularized by real estate practitioners who utilized the form to provide better tax results and more flexibility for real estate investors. LLCs provide the same benefits as standard limited partnerships, but add the limited liability that a formal corporate structure normally offers. Shares in LLCs can be given to charities and frequently are used by donors to solve estate and tax planning problems. It is possible to have only one shareholder in a LLC.

Limited partnership. In a limited partnership, one or more partners are made "general partners" of the partnership. The general partner(s) accept the liability risk for the activities of the partnership and frequently take on all management responsibilities for the partnership. Other partners are deemed "limited partners," who generally are not responsible for, nor liable for, the management of the partnership's activities and any error or omissions that might occur. Usually the limited partners contribute cash or other assets to the partnership in exchange for the rights to a share of the profits, if any, that the partnership may make during its existence. They also will frequently have the rights to tax benefits earned by the corporation, such as a share in any depreciation deductions that the partnership may have available. The general partners usually receive some payment from the partnership for their management activities and a share in any profits that the partnership may enjoy. Shares in a limited partnership can be given to charity. They are, however, potentially risky assets to own, since they may have deferred tax liabilities and/or other types of liabilities that the charity may become responsible for when the gift is accepted. Due diligence in investigating limited partnership interests is critical for the nonprofit institution.

Long-term capital gain. See also capital gain.

Long-term capital loss. See also capital loss.

Major gift. In development, a gift that is larger than an average-size gift to the institution. Within the profession, the term major gift has come to indicate a large outright gift rather than one that is deferred through a trust or will. Since many planned gifts are outright in nature, it is difficult to distinguish a major gift from a planned gift in many instances. A major gift officer is usually a person who is focused on outright gifts, but often lacks the sophistication with tax-advantaged techniques that a planned giving officer possesses.

Makeup provision. In a net income with makeup unitrust, the provision stipulating that in years when earnings are not sufficient to meet the stated annual payout amount, the unpaid amount is deemed a deficiency and must be made up from future earnings in any year in which the earnings are in excess of that year's stated payout amount. Any deficiency amounts are accumulated and carried forward from year to year for up to the entire term of the trust.

Mandatory minimum distributions. Distribution rules that require private foundations to divest a portion of their assets annually to qualified nonprofits or risk losing their tax-exempt status. These rules can apply in limited circumstances to charitable remainder trusts, especially when the life income beneficiaries' interests have terminated and the trust plans to continue on as a charitable trust, rather than terminating and distributing all assets to charity.

Marital deduction trust. A trust that tries to take advantage of the marital deduction to maximize overall estate/gift tax benefits. This type of trust is not as important as it once was, because the creation of the unlimited marital deduction made all gifts between spouses completely free from estate and gift taxes.

Memorial gift. A gift made to a charity in memory of a deceased person.

Midterm rate. The discount rate applied by the IRS to all split-interest gifts to determine the deduction amount. It is 120 percent of the federal midterm rate on government bonds. The rate is also used in calculating the 5 percent probability test for charitable remainder annuity trusts. This rate, plus life expectancy and payout rates, are combined in an IRS formula to determine the eventual gift to charity in present dollars.

Mortgaged property. Any property that secures a debt of the owner. Almost all mortgaged property discussed in the planned giving field is real property. Gifts of mortgaged property, whether in trust or outright, carry with them tax issues for the donor and potential problems for a trustee or charity. Any gift of mortgaged property creates "phantom income" that is taxable to the donor in the year of transfer. This phantom income is equal to the mortgage debt. This has the effect of minimizing or even eliminating the tax deduction from their gift. If the property is transferred to a charitable trust, it may cause that trust to become taxable due to the rules governing debt-financed income and unrelated business income (UBI). Recourse debt causes a CRT to become taxable; nonrecourse debt does not. See also recourse debt; nonrecourse debt; phantom income.

Mortmain statutes. Laws that limit the ability of a testator to make a gift to charity within a certain period before death. These types of statutes were intended to reduce the influence exerted upon the dying, especially by the church, when deciding their charitable giving plans. Some states still have these types of statutes on the books.

Moves management. A systematic method of bringing donors to a point where solicitation for a gift is viable. This system attempts to quantify the development activities regarding a particular donor. Activity is broken down into steps or moves that the development officer makes to bring the prospect closer to the organization in the hopes that he or she will eventually be ready to make a gift. This system is somewhat controversial, since it takes the instinctive part of development out of the equation in favor of a more mechanistic approach.

125

Municipal bond. A debt security issued by a government entity, usually a state, county, or city, although water districts, school districts, and many other government entities can issue bonds that are treated in the same manner. A municipal bond is usually exempt from state taxation, and is frequently exempt from federal taxation. Municipal bonds may be contributed outright or in trust to charities. They are also acceptable investments in charitable remainder trusts (but not in pooled income funds). However, when contributed to trust, the income may not be characterized as tax exempt to the income beneficiaries, depending on the four-tier system and its application to the income payments. See also four-tier system.

Mutual fund. A form of investment where a person purchases shares in the mutual fund, which in turn invests the money in an agreed-upon manner. Mutual funds allow small investors to achieve wide diversification of investments to reduce risk and enhance performance. The Securities and Exchange Commission regulates mutual funds. See also pooled investment fund.

Net income unitrust (NICRUT). A charitable remainder unitrust that provides that payments shall be the stated payout amount for the year or the net income earned by the trust for the year, whichever is less. This trust is used commonly when the funding assets are producing no income and their sale will require an unknown amount of time, as in the case of undeveloped land. Also known as a NICRUT or a Type 2 unitrust. See also net income with makeup unitrust.

Net income with makeup unitrust (NIMCRUT). A charitable remainder unitrust that, in addition to providing a payout based on a stated percentage payout amount or net income, whichever is less, also provides a mechanism for beneficiaries to receive unpaid amounts from prior years when investment results exceed the stated payout amount for a given year. Used frequently when the funding assets are non-income-producing assets, such as undeveloped land. Also known as a NIMCRUT or a Type 3 unitrust. See also net income unitrust.

Net operating loss. A loss incurred in the operation of a business. This is deductible and can be used to offset income taxes in other tax years. Net operating losses may be carried forward to a future tax year. If they are, then the contribution base of the taxpayer is reduced by the amount of the carry-forward. They may also be "carried back" to offset taxes already paid in a prior tax year. If they are, the contribution base of the taxpayer is not changed.

Nonrecourse debt. A debt that has as one of its terms the limitation that the lender must look to satisfaction of the debt only from the secured assets. If these assets are not enough to satisfy the debt, the lender cannot seek repayment from other assets of the debtor. For example, in California a mortgage on a personal residence is by law a nonrecourse debt. The lender must look only to the residence itself to satisfy the loan amount. If the property sells for less than the loan amount, the lender has no recourse against the borrower. See also recourse debt; debt financing.

Open-end investment fund. A form of commingled investment fund that continues to accept new investors during its operation. See also pooled investment fund; closed-end investment fund.

Option. In planned giving, the legal right to buy or sell an asset, usually securities or real estate. Options were once popular as a way to deal with potential problems with a gift of encumbered property to a charitable remainder trust. They continue to be promoted as a method to gift stock, since many executives receive stock options as part of their compensation packages. The problem with compensation-related stock options is that most of them are nonqualified options, or options that the executive has not paid income tax on yet. When transferred to a charity, a nonqualified stock option immediately is deemed exercised, and the gain in the option is taxed at ordinary income rates to the executive. A qualified option, on the other hand, is one that the executive has paid tax on when issued. It is a true capital gain asset and can be given to charity without triggering any capital gains tax.

Ordinary corporation (C Corp.). A corporation incorporated under state statutes that complies in all ways with corporate structure and rules. In tax parlance, an ordinary corporation is one subject to corporate income tax and all the tax rules pertaining to it. Also referred to as a C Corp. See also subchapter S corporation.

Ordinary income. Income received from wages, tips, interest, and dividends. Ordinary income is taxed at the highest rates under the tax code and is, therefore, less desirable than other types of income such as capital gain income or tax-exempt income. Profits from the sale of assets held for less than one year are called short-term capital gains, but are taxed at ordinary income rates.

Ordinary life. See also whole life.

Partial interest. An interest in property that is not the full fee interest. A partial interest can be any type of interest in property, whether real or personal. For example, if a father retains the income interest in a property but gives the remainder interest to his son, he has retained a partial interest in the property. It is a legal interest, but does not permit the owner of it to pass on complete ownership of the property to another person. A gift of a partial interest is not deductible, at least until all intervening interests are eliminated. In our example, if the son gave his interest in the property to charity, he would not receive a deduction until his father's interest in the property had terminated.

Partnership. A legal entity that is made up of two or more partners. The partnership is a common form for small business to take. The partnership is transparent for tax purposes. All partners are treated as having the earnings and expenses of the partnership and pay tax as individuals on the profits of the partnership. There is no requirement that all partners be treated in the same way on all things. This creates opportunities for financial and estate planning. See also limited partnership; family limited partnership.

Payout rate. The amount, stated as either a percentage or a dollar amount, that is to be paid out by a charitable remainder trust, pooled income fund, or charitable gift annuity. This amount may or may not actually be paid out, depending on the type of life income plan.

Perpetuity. Any condition or limitation that may suspend or take away an owner's power of alienation over property for a period beyond life or lives in being plus 21 years plus gestation period (9 months). See also rule against perpetuities.

Personal property. Any type of property that is not in some way part of real property. Personal property usually refers to those items that have physical presence that a person can carry away or remove from any location; it also refers to representations (usually in writing) symbolic of a legal possession or right. There are two types of personal property: tangible and intangible. Gifts of tangible personal property are subject to different rules than gifts of intangible personal property, in particular when they are used to fund a life income plan.

Personal residence. An individual's primary or secondary residence, generally means a place that the individual occupies for at least six months per year and lists as his or her residence on income tax returns. A personal residence may be deeded to charity with a retained life estate and qualify for an immediate income tax charitable deduction for the discounted present value of the fee interest given to charity. For tax purposes, a second home may be considered a personal residence and can be given to charity with the same tax benefits as the primary personal residence. See also farm; retained life estate.

Phantom income. Income that a donor must recognize and pay tax on even though the donor has not actually received the income in that tax year. For example, when a donor gives away real property subject to a loan and the recipient assumes the loan as an obligation, the donor has received debt relief. The dollar value of the debt relief—that is, the outstanding loan balance—is treated as income to the donor and he or she must report this as income in the year of the gift. Thus, he or she is treated as having received income that he or she has not actually received in the year of the gift. This is called phantom income. See also debt relief.

Phase I report. A type of environmental report that evaluates the possible environmental problems a particular piece of real property may have. The report is based upon a sight inspection of the property and a review of ownership records. Phase I reports are not necessary for all properties, but some institutions make it a policy to perform Phase I inspections for all gifts of real estate.

Phase II report. A type of environmental report that goes beyond the Phase I level. This inspection includes taking samples of soil or water to determine contamination levels and possible cleanup issues that may be associated with the property. Phase II reports are usually done only after a property has had a Phase I inspection that has revealed possible problems. They are more costly than a Phase I report and are usually reserved for problem properties of great value.

Philanthropy Protection Act of 1995. Created the requirement that nonprofits provide disclosure to potential donors regarding charitable remainder trusts and gift annuities. Pooled income funds were already providing disclosure documents before this act. See also disclosure.

Planned giving. Tax-advantaged charitable giving techniques, including annuities, trusts, retained life estates, pooled income funds, and wills and complex forms of outright giving, usually involving difficult assets, such as real property, securities, and personal property.

Planned giving officer. Title of the professional who works with donors and potential donors considering a planned gift on behalf of one or more charitable organizations. This person is usually on the payroll of the nonprofit institution, although some organizations retain planned giving officers on contract. A planned giving officer's job is to identify, cultivate, solicit, and close planned gifts for the institution, conducting himself or herself at all times in an ethical manner. These officers are expected to take into account the needs of the donors as well as the institutions they represent. The National Committee on Planned Giving is the major professional association for planned giving officers. Other titles might include director of planned giving, director of deferred giving, or director of estates and trusts.

Pledge. A promise by a person to contribute cash or other assets to a charity. Pledges are frequently used to secure donor commitments for amounts that are larger than they are prepared to pay in a lump sum. For accounting purposes, a pledge must be for a period not to exceed five years and must be for a specific amount before it should be shown as a pledge on the institution's financial statement. A pledge to make a charitable gift is almost never legally binding upon the donor. If it were, the IRS would consider it a contract, and the charitable deduction for the gift might be disallowed. Only if a charity has relied on the donor's pledge to the financial detriment of the institution will a pledge be considered legally binding. For example, if you receive a pledge for $10 million to construct a building and build it with the expectation that the gift will pay for the expense, then you have relied on the pledge to your financial detriment and a court will enforce the pledge against the donor if he or she attempts to back out. What constitutes detrimental reliance is an open question. Costs incurred are clearly detrimental reliance. One court felt that the fact that an institution used the pledge from a well-known executive to solicit gifts from other donors in the business community was enough to make the pledge enforceable.

Pooled income fund. A split-interest trust that allows for multiple donors and income beneficiaries; created under IRC sec. 662(c)(5). All gifts are pooled and invested for a return that is distributed proportionately to all income beneficiaries based on the gifts that they have made or benefit from. Payouts must equal the actual earnings of the pooled fund and are not subject to minimum payout standards required of remainder trusts. Capital gains from the sale of assets are not considered income for the purposes of determining the annual payout. Pooled income funds are not allowed to invest in assets that produce state or federal tax-free income. Most institutions do not allow gifts of real property or personal property to their pooled funds due to difficulty of administration. The IRS has issued sample pooled income fund safe harbor documents, similar to those issued for charitable remainder trusts.

Pooled investment fund. Funds that pool assets from multiple investors and seek to use economies of scale to benefit all parties. Pooled investment funds are sold to the public under various names, including mutual funds, closed-end investment funds, and open-end investment funds. They are acceptable investments for charitable remainder trusts but must be examined carefully to avoid funds that use borrowing to leverage investments. Such borrowing is considered debt-financed income, which is not allowed in a CRT.

Prearranged sale. A sale that was agreed to before the gift of property to charity. See also step transaction.

Precatory wishes. Legally nonbinding wishes expressed by a person, usually a decedent.

Present interest. An interest in property that is owned by a person and where their possession of the property is immediate. An outright gift of a home from parents to daughter is a gift of a present interest in the home. If the parents gave the daughter the home subject to a life estate for themselves, then the gift is no longer a gift of a present interest since she cannot take possession of the property immediately. See also future interest.

Present value. The value today of a right to receive income or an asset at some point in the future. All income tax charitable deductions for life income plans are based on the present value of the remainder interest to charity created by the split-interest gift. Using actuarial tables and earnings assumptions, the IRS has created a mathematical formula to determine present value, which is the official deduction amount. The concept of present value is simple although its calculation is not. The IRS tables give the taxpayer a safe-harbor deduction amount, not the only deduction amount that may be claimed in a particular circumstance. Using different earnings assumptions and different life expectancy tables, a taxpayer can come up with a different deduction amount. However, most taxpayers choose to use the IRS tables.

Private charity. Refers to charities and foundations that are controlled by specific individuals and groups. Private charities can receive deductible contributions from donors, but the deductions are limited to 30 percent of AGI for cash and short-term gain property and 20 percent of AGI for long-term gain property. See 30 percent charity; private foundation.

Private foundation. An organization that functions as a nonprofit organization, but is controlled by one or more persons and does not meet the requirements for a public charity. Private foundations are set up by people who wish to exercise more control over their gifts than a public charity will allow. Private foundations commonly "pass through" gifts from a wealthy founder or family to public charities that they want to benefit. In the 1990s private foundations became popular "vanity" items for the wealthy. Private foundations are closely regulated and are governed by separate rules not applicable to public charities. (See IRC sec. 4941–4948 and regs. for detailed rules.) Deductions for gifts to private foundations are limited. See also 30 percent/20 percent limitation.

Private inurement. Benefits received from a public charity by an individual who has not performed services that are usually compensated. This term is distinguished from benefits received for services rendered, such as those of an employee or vendor. The rule against private inurement is intended to avoid unscrupulous people taking control of a public charity and then looting it for their own personal gain. Private inurement can cause a public charity to lose its nonprofit, tax-exempt status. To protect against it, you must look at any benefits that a private person derives from the assets of the institution. If these benefits are not compensation for services rendered or products sold to the institution, you may have a private inurement issue. This situation is usually not associated with high compensation levels for top nonprofit executives, but at some point could be alleged in that situation as well.

Private letter ruling. Rulings issued by the IRS at the request of taxpayers. These letter rulings bind the IRS to honor any actions taken by the taxpayer based upon the ruling. Letter rulings are not binding on the IRS for anyone other than the taxpayer who sought the ruling. However, practitioners in the field use them to gage the way the IRS feels at the moment on specific issues. The IRS in turn uses letter rulings, also referred to as no action letters, to unofficially announce new positions, clarify existing ones, and address new issues that have not been dealt with in the code and regulations. Letter rulings are published on a regular basis.

Probate. The legal process for the transfer of title in assets owned by a deceased person to heirs or beneficiaries. Probate is required for the transfer of title in real property that was held by the deceased at death, except where the title was held by the entirety or in joint tenancy. Executors must file reports and accountings with the court and are subject to severe penalties if they fail to perform their fiduciary duties on behalf of all beneficiaries of the probate estate. Legal fees are also approved by the court, which limits the excessive charges that lawyers sometimes attempt to get from probate estates. Once an asset has been through the probate process, the new owner has clear title to the asset, provided the deceased had clear title to the property on his or her death.

Proof of use. See related use; unrelated use.

Proposal. The verbal or written request for a gift that is presented to the donor by a volunteer or representative of the institution. In planned giving, the proposal is almost always in writing and contains information on the financial and tax impact a charitable gift will have for the donor. The proposal usually attempts to explain the particular techniques suggested along with how this will affect the financial situation for the prospective donor. Proposals can be important in providing a written record of the representations made to a donor during the cultivation and solicitation process and are potentially valuable protection for the charity from third parties or donors who are disappointed with the results of the gift.

Prudent man rule. The court-approved standard to which a trustee is held when investing the assets of a trust. Under this standard, the trustee must use the intelligence and diligence that a prudent person would use in investing his or her own assets. Banks and trust companies have developed complex policies to adopt this rule into their own approach to investing trust assets. Charities that actively manage trusts for individuals are held to the same standard. It is often helpful to have investment policies that emphasize the prudent man rule formalized in writing to share with potential donors.

Public charity. A charitable organization that is organized and operated for the benefit of the public. The public charity is usually controlled by a board of directors or trustees where only a minority of the members are disqualified persons. Disqualified persons include the founder, his or her family, the founder's employees,

129

and others who would be viewed as controlled by the founder. Contributions to a public charity are deductible at the maximum rates (i.e., 50 percent of AGI for cash and short-term gain property, 30 percent of AGI for long-term gain property). See 50 percent charity; compare private charity, private foundation.

Qualified conservation contribution. A gift that certain types of qualified charities may receive of a qualified interest in real property given exclusively for conservation purposes. It is also called a qualified conservation easement. Conservation purposes generally include preserving land areas for outdoor recreation; natural habitat for wildlife or vegetation; historic areas or structures; and open space and scenic areas.

Qualified domestic trust. A trust similar to the QTIP trust. The assets are taxed on the death of the surviving spouse. See also qualified terminable interest property trust.

Qualified terminable interest property trust (QTIP trust). A trust set up for the benefit of a surviving spouse funded with qualified terminable interest property, generally most assets owned by the testator, including most real estate, securities, and personal property. The QTIP trust provides for the care and support of the surviving spouse and then goes on to heirs as designated in the trust. This technique is frequently used when the marriage is a second marriage and one spouse wants to make sure that his or her assets go on to children from a previous marriage or family members rather than the spouse or the spouse's children or family. Charities can also be named as the remainder beneficiary of a QTIP trust. If a charity is named, then all the assets in the trust will avoid estate tax, since there is an unlimited marital deduction and an unlimited charitable deduction available. The problem from a charity's viewpoint is that a QTIP trust is generally one that gives some discretionary power in the trustee to invade principal for the benefit of the surviving spouse. This makes the eventual gift to charity difficult to determine before actual receipt.

Quasi-endowment. A mechanism for setting aside excess capital for long-term needs. It functions like a permanent endowment and is invested like permanently endowed funds. Quasi-endowment may be created by action of the governing board and may be completely exhausted at its discretion. A less well known rule created by the Uniform Management of Institutional Funds Act or UMIFA (adopted in most states) requires that only the original gift amount of permanent endowment

funds is considered truly permanent (absent donor permission to invade principal). This means that any capital appreciation in a permanent endowment fund is not, in fact, permanent endowment. The appreciation is generally considered quasi-endowment and is available to an institution, if needed. For institutions with very old endowments that have grown over the years, a large percentage of the endowment funds may actually be quasi-endowment funds. Quasi-endowment may also be referred to as funds functioning as endowment.

Quid pro quo gift. A gift to charity in which the donor receives something of value in return. Quid pro quo gifts cannot be deducted at full fair market value. The deduction must be reduced by the value of what the donor has received in return. The only situation in which this does not apply is when the value of what the donor receives back is *de minimis*. An IRS ruling suggests that if the benefits are worth 2 percent or less and at no time worth more than $50, then they would probably be *de minimis* benefits. See also *de minimis* rule.

Real property. Interests in land and improvements attached to the land. Real property includes fee simple interests in land and all permutations of ownership in land. It also may include certain types of improvements attached to land, such as buildings, and some unexpected types of property, such as windmills and moorage rights in bays and lakes.

Realize. In tax law, ordinary income or capital gains income that has been converted to the use of the taxpayer. Unrealized capital appreciation is not subject to capital gains tax, but realized capital gains are. For example, a rental house bought for $100,000 two years ago has a fair market value of $150,000. The capital gain is $50,000, but it is unrealized. The taxpayer pays no tax on the appreciation in the property. However, if the owner had sold the property for $150,000, then he would have realized a $50,000 capital gain and would be subject to capital gains tax on $50,000 of capital gain income. See also recognize.

Recognize. In tax law, income that is now subject to tax, whether or not it has been realized in the past. To recognize income is to be responsible for reporting the income on the taxpayer's income tax return and paying the appropriate amount of tax. A key question for tax planners is whether a particular item of income must be recognized for tax purposes. Usually this happens when a gain is realized. Some types of income that are realized by the taxpayer are not recognizable by the taxpayer. For example, income generated from tax-exempt municipal bonds is realized when received. However, due to their tax-advantaged status, the taxpayer does not recognize the income. A portion of each income payment from a charitable gift annuity is usually not recognizable either, being return of principal, which is not subject to tax. See also realize.

Recourse debt. A debt, usually on real property, in which the lender has the right to seek satisfaction of the debt from the secured asset and any other assets of the debtor. See also nonrecourse debt; debt financing.

Reformation. Changes made to a charitable remainder trust in which the governing document either violates current law or public policy or the IRS has allowed changes to be made. Reformation of CRTs is not done regularly and is usually reserved for instances when a trust was incorrectly drafted or the laws have changed and caused the CRT to become a nonconforming CRT. In the late 1990s, the IRS permitted the reformation of charitable trusts to change net income trusts to standard unitrusts. At the time, the stock market was growing rapidly while interest rates were plunging, causing many income beneficiaries to become unhappy with their declining incomes in the midst of economic growth. Wholesale reformations were performed on net income trusts throughout the country. This reformation period was eventually closed and is not currently available to net income trusts absent some other form of drafting error or reformation need.

Related use. A gift made to a charity that directly furthers the charity's charitable purpose. The term is especially relevant for noncash gifts of tangible personal property. For example, a gift of a painting by a famous artist to an art museum is considered a gift for a related use. It becomes difficult at times to determine if a gift is for a related use. For example, is a gift of artwork to a hospital for a related use? (The answer happens to be yes.) The determination is critical in that a donation for a related use is deductible at fair market value. If it is considered an unrelated use then it is only deductible for basis. See also unrelated use.

Remainder. The assets left in a trust after the end of the trust term. Also known as a residual or residuary.

Remainderman. The person or institution that will receive the trust remainder at the end of the trust term. In noncharitable trusts, this may be one of the trust beneficiaries or a third party or institution. For charitable trusts, the remainderman must be a qualified charitable organization.

Remoteness test. See also 5 percent probability test.

Reserve. In planned giving, a sum of money that, with estimated accrued interest and dividends, is deemed to be enough to satisfy the potential demands made on the institution by annuitants or policyholders. It is common for states to require that a nonprofit institution issuing charitable gift annuities maintain a reserve fund from which it will be able to make the actuarially determined payments over the life expectancies of all annuitants. Reserve funds in states like New York and California are heavily regulated and are limited in the types of investments that the reserve fund is permitted to hold. This term also refers to the same type of reserve funds that insurance companies are required to keep for the payment of death benefits or other payments under the various insurance contracts that they have issued.

Residual. The assets left in a trust after the end of the trust term. It can also be used to describe the bequest language in a will that leaves what has not been already disposed of to one or more people or institutions. See also remainder.

Residue. That which remains. This is a common term in will drafting. It refers to the assets remaining in the estate after all debts and specific gifts have been made.

Retained life estate. A gift of a donor's personal residence, a secondary residence, or a farm while retaining the right to occupy the property for his or her lifetime. The property is deeded to the charity, and the donor retains the right written into the deed to occupy the property for life or a period of time. The donor is entitled to an immediate income tax charitable deduction for the discounted present value of the eventual gift to charity. See also farm; personal residence.

Return of principal. The payment to the income beneficiary of a portion of the original asset value given to fund the trust or annuity. In planned giving, it is possible for all or a portion of an income payment from a trust or annuity to be characterized as return of principal for tax purposes. Return of principal is not taxable as income to the recipient of the income payment. However, return of principal in the context of a charitable trust means that the principal balance is being reduced by the amount of the payment attributed to return of principal. This may indicate an eroding principal balance, which will be a problem in the long term if it is not corrected. Charitable gift annuities will usually have a portion of each payment considered return of principal, but since the payments are guaranteed by the charity, there is not the same concern for erosion of principal as there would be with a charitable remainder trust. Return of principal may not occur at all with a particular remainder trust if investments are successful or it is a net income trust. Return of principal may also not occur with a gift annuity, but only if the asset contributed has a large amount of unrecognized capital gain. In this case, the capital gain income must be recognized first, and only after all the gain has been recognized will payments contain return of principal. In addition, with gift annuities the return of principal is limited to the life expectancy of the income beneficiaries. Should the prorated recognition of capital gains last for longer than the life expectancy of the beneficiaries, then there may be no return of principal at any time during the annuity term.

Revenue procedure ruling. An official statement by the IRS related to the procedures and rules applicable to a certain part of the Internal Revenue Code. Procedure rulings are intended to help taxpayers correctly interpret the code and the regulations regarding the correct procedures and methods for computing their taxes and/or filing their tax returns. Revenue procedure rulings are given great weight by practitioners in the field as well as the courts. Taxpayers may rely on revenue procedure rulings.

Reverse split-dollar life insurance. See split-dollar life insurance; charitable reverse split-dollar life insurance.

Revocable gift. A gift that at the donor's discretion can be taken back or revoked. The most well known revocable gifts are those placed in wills. Wills can be changed with a stroke of a pen and provide only the expectancy of a gift, not the certainty of a gift. Trust gifts can have revocable features—for example the revocable living trust, which is completely revocable by the trustors, or a charitable remainder trust where the trustor has retained the right to change the charitable remainderman during his or her lifetime or at death through a will. Revocable gifts are not as attractive to a charity as outright and/ or irrevocable gifts, but frequently the largest gifts an institution receives are from revocable gifts. Revocable gifts are not shown on the institution's financial statements except as a possible footnote and are usually not shown when reporting the amount of money raised by the development office during a particular year.

Right of survivorship. The right vested in an owner of real property in joint tenancy to own the property after the death of another joint tenant. This right runs with the owner until death or divestment of interest in the property or death of all other joint tenants. See also joint tenancy.

Roth IRA. An after-tax savings mechanism in which the owner of the account puts in after-tax dollars that accumulate tax free. Distributions from the account, including any gains from investments, are not subject to income tax.

Rule against perpetuities. In common law, the rule that no interest in real property is good unless it vests title within the lives in being plus 21 years plus gestation period (9 months) from the date of the creation of the interest. This rule is aimed at stopping perpetual ownership of land by a family and also the "dead hand" of the deceased controlling the property after death. Most states have adopted this rule in one form or another. See also perpetuity.

Safe harbor. In tax law, a place from which the IRS cannot challenge the taxpayer's actions if certain steps are followed or actions taken. IRS written guidelines, such as revenue procedure rulings, also create safe harbors in some instances. In the world of charitable trusts, the IRS has published sample charitable remainder trust documents for taxpayer use. They are called safe harbor documents because the IRS will not challenge any taxpayer who follows them as to the legal viability of the trust itself. They do not protect against inappropriate administration of the trusts, however. There are also safe harbor pooled income fund documents. A safe harbor requires a private letter ruling, revenue procedure ruling, or other formal ruling. (See Appendix J.)

Section 170. Refers to the Internal Revenue Code section that states that a gift to a qualified charity is deductible from personal income for tax purposes. (See also 501(c)(3).)

Self-dealing. When a disqualified person uses a charitable vehicle, such as a private foundation or charitable trust, to derive a personal benefit. Self-dealing by a trustor or donor can place the tax-exempt status of the foundation or charitable trust in jeopardy. Self-dealing can range from making a personal loan of trust assets to doing business with a private foundation and receiving compensation. An income beneficiary of a charitable trust can receive the income without it being considered self-dealing. However, if the same person was paid to manage the assets held in the trust, then that may be considered self-dealing since it is a financial benefit, which was not necessarily expected from the vehicle itself. The best rule of thumb is to keep all trustors and beneficiaries at arm's length unless they have such unique skills and abilities that no other person could perform these duties.

Settlement costs. The costs incurred in settling an estate. These costs can include attorney fees, accounting fees, trustee fees, and any selling costs or cleanup costs incurred.

Shares. Usually refers to an undivided partial ownership interest in a business. Shareholders are part owners of the business and hope to receive income and capital appreciation from the business as it profits and grows in value. See also stock.

Short-term capital gain. See capital gain.

Short-term capital loss. See capital loss.

Simplified employee pension plan (SEP). A retirement plan similar to a regular individual retirement account with larger deductible contribution limitations than a normal IRA. This plan is aimed at self-employed people who do not receive pension benefits.

Sole proprietorship. Many businesses are held in the form of a sole proprietorship. The sole proprietorship has no legal or tax benefits. It does not provide limited liability to the owner. It does not provide any special tax benefits. Assets used in the sole proprietorship are the property of the owner of the business, just as they own their house or car. All income and expenses are treated under the income tax sections of the Internal Revenue Code. A gift to charity of a sole proprietorship is possible, but it is essentially the gift of the assets of the company, including "blue sky" assets such as name, reputation, and customer lists. Valuation of sole proprietorships is key to the acceptance of this type of gift, as is standard due diligence to make sure that the assumption of the business by the nonprofit institution does not bring with it unforeseen liability, such as the responsibility for toxic cleanups.

Solicitation. The actual asking for the gift, usually made by the development officer or senior staff or trustees on behalf of the institution. Solicitations can be done by mail or phone, but the most successful method by far for planned giving is face to face.

Special election. Choosing to treat contributed long-term capital gain property as if it were a gift of cash and therefore eligible for 50 percent treatment. To get this treatment, the taxpayer is limited to deducting the basis in the contributed property, not the fair market value of the property. See also limitation on deductibility.

Specialized small business investment company (SSBIC). If an investor realizes a profit on a sale of stock, he or she usually must recognize the profit in the year of sale. But if the investor takes the proceeds from this sale and then reinvests in the stock of a specialized small business investment company, he or she can defer the entire gain. The new shares in the SSBIC are treated as having the basis of the previously sold shares. The shares in the SSBIC may be given to charity just like any other appreciated stock with full deductibility (assuming satisfaction of the holding period requirements for SSBIC stock). When a donor has sold stock before considering a charitable gift, and the tax advantages inherent in such a gift, he or she can recover the tax advantages by reinvesting in an SSBIC and then contributing those shares to the charity. The reinvestment must occur within 60 days from the date of the sale of the stock.

Spending rule. A rule set by the governing board that determines the amount of earnings to be distributed by an endowment pool. This rule is a mathematical formula that should incorporate a growth element in the overall fund to protect against the erosion of buying power due to inflation. It also helps to create predictability of income for all income recipients, since most institutions will set their spending rule and keep it for several years. See also endowment pool.

Spendthrift trust. A trust established to protect a beneficiary who has proven unable or unwilling to manage his or her financial affairs prudently. The trust specifically states that the beneficiary cannot sell or borrow against the trust assets. Sometimes charitable remainder trusts are used for this purpose, although they were not intended as such.

Split-dollar life insurance. A life insurance policy usually taken out by a corporation on behalf of one of its employees. The corporation retains the right to a portion of the death benefit equal to the premium payments made into the policy. The employee or his or her family receives the rest of the death benefit. This benefit is taxable to the employee. See also charitable split-dollar life insurance.

Split interest. An interest in property that is not the complete interest. For example, if a person donates an office building but retains the right to use an office for two days each month, this is a split-interest gift. Such a gift usually is not deductible, unless it meets the Internal Revenue Code requirements. For example, charitable remainder trusts are split-interest gifts that qualify for deductibility. See also split-interest trust.

133

Split-interest trust. A trust with two interests that must be considered by the trustee: the life income interest and the remainder interest. All charitable remainder trusts are considered split-interest trusts. A pooled income fund is actually a split-interest trust.

Spousal remainder trust. See also Clifford trust.

Sprinkling trust. A trust that authorizes the trustee to distribute income, and even principal if the trust document permits it, to one or more income beneficiaries, at the discretion of the trustee. The idea is that by sprinkling the income the most needy members of the class of beneficiaries will receive the benefits they need while those who do not need income can be passed over without losing their rights to income in the future should their circumstances change. The authority to sprinkle puts a certain amount of pressure on the trustee. It can become a problem for a charity acting as trustee on a trust if the charity is hoping to continue in a good relationship with the income beneficiaries as well as the donors.

134

Standard unitrust (STANCRUT). Provides for income to be paid to the donor that is fixed for the year, but is revalued and adjusted at the beginning of each new year. The payments, once determined, must be paid in that year. This means that invasion of principal is possible in a given year in order to make the payments to the beneficiary. Also known as a STANCRUT or a Type 1 unitrust. See also net income unitrust; compare annuity trust.

Step transaction. When a taxpayer attempts to reduce or avoid income tax on the sale of an asset by first assigning the asset to a third party. Charities are frequently at risk for this problem when they accept a property as a gift. If the charity does not negotiate an arm's-length transaction with the third party, the IRS can say that the use of the charity was merely a step in the sale of the property to the third party by the donor and then seek to tax the donor on the capital gain received from the sale of the asset. This problem also occurs with some frequency with charitable remainder trusts.

Stepped-up basis. Under current estate tax law, when a person dies and his or her property is transferred to beneficiaries, the beneficiaries receive a step up in basis. Instead of inheriting the basis of the deceased, they are allowed to claim the fair market value of the property at the date of death of the testator as their basis in the property and are free to liquidate the property received without concerns about the capital gains tax on the sale. As of this writing, stepped-up basis has been made a

victim of recent tax law changes and will disappear when the estate tax law returns in full force in 2011.

Stewardship. Actions taken by the development officer and the institution after the gift has been made to keep the donor connected to the organization. It often involves reporting to the donor on actions taken by the institution because of a gift; handling questions or complaints the donor may have; and trying to keep the donor satisfied with the institution. When dealing with persons who still have the capacity to make further gifts to the organization, it becomes more difficult to determine when you are in a stewardship mode and when you have started the next cycle of cultivation for a new gift.

Stock. The assets of a merchant. More generally, all of the assets of a company. A stock company is a company that gathers investors and in return for their investment of cash or other assets, issues them shares in the company, from which the investors hope to receive income in the form of dividends and capital appreciation as the company profits and grows in value. Stock is what the shares in a company are commonly called, although legally they are considered shares. Stock shares can be privately held (closely held) or they can be publicly traded on an exchange.

Stock certificate. A formal document that shows the name of an owner of corporate stock and the number of shares that the document represents. Stock certificates can be issued for any number of shares. Some certificates do not show a named owner. They are said to be "in blank" and become bearer instruments. The back of most stock certificates contains a form that allows the listed owner of the certificate to assign the shares to a third party. Frequently when donors make gifts of stock, they will fill out the back of the stock certificate and sign it. Some brokerages will not accept this alone, and request a written stock power as well.

Stock power. A form that gives the assigned person the right to sell the stock listed or described on the form. A signed stock power plus the actual stock certificates are usually all that is needed for a donor to make a gift of stock.

Subchapter S corporation. A corporation that has elected to be treated as a partnership for tax purposes under IRC subchapter S. Subchapter S corporations must have only a limited number of shareholders and their shares cannot be traded on public exchanges. Small and midsize businesses often use this structure in order to take advantage of the tax breaks given to partnerships and individuals. Partnerships pay no corporate level of tax. Subchapter S corporate stock can be given to a nonprofit charity, but only outright gifts of stock can be made. The charity also takes over the donor's basis in the stock (which is often $0) and is subject to capital gains tax on the resale of the stock. This reduces the value of a gift of subchapter S stock significantly. This stock cannot be used to fund charitable remainder trusts, and, due to a lack of marketability, is not a good candidate for gift annuities. See also corporation.

Substantiation. Proof or evidence to support a claim or assertion. In planned giving, substantiation usually involves proof of valuation of gifts made to charity. Outright gifts can be substantiated with a simple receipt, cancelled check, or a complete formal appraisal of real estate with all accompanying forms. Taxpayers must be able to prove that they made the gift to charity and that the value claimed for the gift was in fact the actual value of the property transferred.

Successor beneficiary. The person or organization that receives the benefits of a bequest or trust originally intended for the named beneficiary, often a surviving spouse or surviving children. A successor beneficiary steps into the shoes of the beneficiary and has all of the rights and responsibilities attached to the beneficiary. Successor beneficiaries are usually named in the governing documents.

Successor donee. A person who was not the first recipient of the gift property, but due to changes in the circumstances of the original recipient, now steps into the recipient's shoes. Usually a successor donee takes the property in the same manner with the same legal rights as the original donee. This term will often arise when one charity named in a gift is no longer in existence and another charity is given the gift.

Successor trustee. A person who becomes trustee when the original trustee ceases to serve, either by resignation or by removal. Successor trustees are either named in trust documents or designated by the court. Successor trustees assume all of the powers, rights, and responsibilities of the original trustee and are held to the same fiduciary duty.

Supporting organization. An organization authorized under IRC sec. 509(a) that functions like a public charity for tax purposes but offers donors a chance to have more influence over the end use of their gifts. There are three types of supporting organizations, and the rules governing their creation and operation are very complex. They are often used in place of the more cumbersome private foundation for wealthy donors.

Tainted land. Real property that has some form of environmental problem, usually related to toxic waste. Tainted land can still be accepted as a charitable gift, but extreme care must be taken to determine the potential cleanup liabilities that may come with the tainted property. These liabilities can even attach to the trustee of a charitable trust even though the trustee never actually held title to the property. Most cleanup problems can be quantified and costs accurately estimated.

Tattletale report. Refers to IRS Form 8282, which requires a charity to report when it has sold a contributed asset if the asset was received within the past two years. This report is compared with the donor's deduction claimed on Form 8283. If there is a large discrepancy, then the return is flagged for closer inspection. If there is no reasonable explanation for the difference, then it will lead to an audit.

Tax shelter. An investment that enables the taxpayer to enjoy some type of tax benefit. Usually tax shelters are investments that have been designed specifically to take advantage of existing tax laws to maximize the tax savings of the investors. Tax shelters tend to accelerate tax benefits in the early years of the investment, which allows the investors to recoup their initial investment quickly. Because of this acceleration, older tax shelters often have used up their tax benefits and begin to generate taxable income. It is common for charities to be offered these "burned out" tax shelters as gifts. Beware of this type of gift, since it can often carry tax liabilities that the charity may not be able to avoid. Since tax-sheltered investments are often in the form of limited partnerships, there is also the issue of liability for the actual business activities of the partnership itself, which will need to be examined before accepting the gift.

Tax-sheltered annuity. A form of commercial annuity that allows employees of nonprofit institutions to supplement their retirement savings through the purchase of an annuity contract. Earnings are sheltered from tax until taken as payments by the annuitant.

Tenancy by the entirety. A type of joint ownership of real property. Only husbands and wives may hold property through tenancy by the entirety. Tenants by the entirety are deemed to be owners of the entire property

135

and have all rights to alienate the property. Tenants by the entirety have the right of survivorship. When one owner dies, the other owner(s) automatically receives the fee title to the property.

Tenancy in common. A type of joint ownership of real property. Tenants in common own the property together, but they have severable rights in the property, which can be alienated at will. There is no right of survivorship for the other owners, should one owner die. The interest held by the deceased owner is passed on to his or her heirs or other beneficiaries as directed in the will or estate plan.

Term. The length of time that income beneficiaries will receive payments from a charitable remainder trust. The most common term is the lifetime of one or more beneficiaries. Usually, the beneficiaries are a husband and wife, but they can be a single person, two people not married, or a group of people. It is also common to have a term last a period not to exceed 20 years.

Term endowment. An endowment fund that is set up for a specified period of time based on a request in writing from the donor. At the end of the time period the entire balance of the endowment fund becomes available for spending or placement in quasi-endowment.

Term life. A form of life insurance in which there is no buildup of cash value, unlike a whole life or universal life policy. Only a death benefit is paid to the beneficiaries.

Term of years. The number of years that a charitable remainder trust will last before termination. Trusts may have a term of years of between one and 20 years.

Testamentary. Created by will. A testamentary transfer is intended to take effect upon the death of the testator. Frequently charitable trusts are created through the estate plan of a donor. In this case the trust would be considered a testamentary trust.

Testate. One who dies leaving a will. When a person dies leaving a will or other documents that dispose of his or her estate, he or she is considered to have died "testate." The person is referred to as the testator or testatrix.

Tithe. The practice of giving a portion of one's earnings to charity each year (usually the church). Contemporary thinking is that tithing represents a gift of 10 percent of a person's income, but this percentage can vary.

Totten trust. A bank account usually set up by one person, naming another person as either a co-owner or a survivor beneficiary. The person opening the account has complete control during his or her lifetime and may completely deplete the account if he or she chooses. However, upon death of that person, the surviving beneficiary or joint owner owns the assets.

Treasury tables. Actuarial life expectancy tables and other tables that are used in the calculation of tax deductions for gifts made through trusts and other life income plans, as well as gifts of personal residences and farms with retained life estates.

Trust. A common-law concept in which a person (the trustor) gives authority over assets to another person (the trustee) for the benefit of one or more people (the beneficiary[ies]). The concept of trust has been extended to nonliving beneficiaries and is now allowed to run indefinitely in some instances. It is common for trustors to act as trustees and/or beneficiaries of trusts. The most common example in modern times is the revocable living trust, in which couples (the trustors) place assets in trust and then serve as the trustees handling assets for the benefit of beneficiaries (often themselves).

Trustee. The person or institution charged with the fiduciary duty to handle the assets placed in trust for the benefit of the beneficiaries of the trust. This fiduciary duty is often difficult to achieve, since the interests of some beneficiaries may take precedence over others at certain times and some decisions may adversely affect one beneficiary and favor another. The clearest example of this is a charitable remainder trust. Investment decisions that increase income will likely reduce overall growth of trust principal. This benefits the life income beneficiary(ies) at the expense of the charity. See also fiduciary.

Trustor. The creator and funder of a trust.

Undivided interest. Usually refers to an interest in real property, although it could be held in any property. An undivided interest gives to the holder a right in all of the subject property without division. The owner holds title to the entire property, but legally shares this entire ownership with the other owners. The most common form that this takes is when a person owns a property in joint tenancy, which gives each owner a right to the use and enjoyment of the entire property although all rights are shared by the joint tenant in the property. See also joint tenancy; tenancy in common.

Unified transfer tax credit. Historically, a credit allowed to each taxpayer against the unified estate/gift tax. The estate tax and the gift tax were decoupled in 2003 and are no longer 'unified'. There is no unified credit, but rather separate credits against the gift tax and the estate tax. The gift tax credit effectively shelters $1 million in assets gifted during a lifetime. The estate tax credit for 2005 effectively shelters $1.5 million in testamentary gifts and will rise to $3.5 million by 2009.

Uniform gift annuity rates. The rates established by the American Council on Gift Annuities to provide a 50 percent residuum to charity provided the income beneficiaries live their full life expectancy. Income payouts on annuities are set based upon the latest actuarial tables, an assumed small administrative cost per year, and the goal of the 50 percent gift to charity. Rates are uniformly less than those offered by commercial insurance carriers, which do not seek a 50 percent gift from each annuity. Rates are changed periodically to reflect changes in the overall investment climate and the prevailing interest rates, since earnings assumptions are based on the rate of return on interest-bearing instruments, not the stock market. See also American Council on Gift Annuities.

Unitrust. A charitable remainder trust that provides for a variable income to be paid to donors. Payout rates may be between 5 and 50 percent but must also have at least a 10 percent remainder value for charity. See also net income unitrust. Compare annuity trust.

Universal life. A form of life insurance that brokers claimed would require premium payments for three to seven years, after which the policy would be paid up. These policies, like whole life policies, were sold using earnings projections that proved false when interest rates dropped in the mid-1990s. Some charities had gotten into insurance programs that featured this type of policy, and they were faced with going back to donors to ask them to resume making premium payments on the policies.

Unmarketable. An asset that no one is interested in acquiring at any reasonable price. The acceptance of a gift of unmarketable assets can have a detrimental effect on the charity and its financial situation. For example, if an organization accepts a gift of undeveloped land that is unmarketable, it may still have to pay state and local property taxes each year on the property for as long as it holds the property.

Unrelated business income. For tax purposes, any income earned by a charity through activities that are unrelated to its charitable purpose. Such income is taxed as it would be for any for-profit business. If unrelated business income occurs within a charitable remainder trust, the trust will lose its tax exemption; all assets within a trust suddenly become subject to tax, including capital gains tax on the sale of appreciated assets; and the charitable deduction may be lost to the donor.

Unrelated use. A gift to charity, usually of tangible personal property, that does not directly further the charitable purposes for which the organization was founded. This determination does not deal with value of the asset given, but whether the asset in some way furthers the stated purposes of the organization. For example, a gift of a painting by a famous artist to an art museum would clearly be for a related use. But the same gift of a painting to a wildlife conservation organization would be for an unrelated use. A gift to charity for an unrelated use is deductible at basis or fair market value, whichever is lower. See also related use.

Valuation. To place a value on an asset, usually expressed in terms of money. In planned giving, valuation is a general term that describes the attempt to place a value on noncash assets that are being given (or contemplated being given) to charity. The valuation of publicly traded securities and cash is simple—just check the *Wall St. Journal* for prices as of the day of the gift. Valuation of real property and tangible personal property can be very difficult. See also appraisal.

Variable annuity. A commercial annuity that provides for various investment options within the annuity. This means that earnings results will vary from annuity to annuity and from year to year, depending on the investment mix chosen by the purchaser. All cash value buildup is tax-deferred until received by the annuitant. The owner is usually allowed to borrow against the cash value buildup without having to recognize income on the loan.

Variable life. Insurance that features a death benefit and the option of investing the cash buildup in several types of investment vehicles, usually some form of mutual funds. Variable-life products are complex and come in a variety of configurations. The key features are the standard life insurance benefit and the flexible investment feature for the cash value. Any cash buildup in the policy is not taxed until received by the owner.

137

However, the owner has the power to borrow against this cash buildup without having to recognize any of the loan as income. This is the biggest selling point for these types of policies.

Variable payment. The type of payment method used by charitable remainder unitrusts. Due to the annual re-valuation of assets required for unitrusts, their payments to beneficiaries will be adjusted annually. Payments may go up or down depending on investment results, but at no time is the stated payout percentage rate changed on a unitrust (or an annuity trust). The same percentage is applied to the fluctuating trust principal balance.

Wealth replacement trust. An irrevocable life insurance trust, which frequently is used when a donor wishes to give to charity while at the same time passing assets on to heirs. The donor usually sets up a charitable remainder trust and a wealth replacement trust. The CRT converts a highly appreciated low-yield asset into a higher-income investment, and the increased income is in turn used to purchase life insurance held in the wealth replacement trust and payable to heirs as beneficiaries of the policy. See also irrevocable life insurance trust.

Whole life. A form of life insurance that provides, in addition to the death benefit paid to the beneficiaries, a tax-deferred cash buildup inside the policy, based upon company earnings. Premiums usually remain level for the life of the policy. Projections for cash value buildup are based on an assumed rate of earnings. The policy will actually have a minimum guaranteed interest rate, but it is usually significantly below the projected earnings rates used in examples. Also called ordinary life.

Will. A written document expressing the wishes of a deceased person with regard to the disposition of his or her estate. Many states require formalities to be observed when creating a will and do not recognize any document that fails to follow these formalities.

Zero-coupon bonds. A form of corporate and government bond that pays no interest during the term of the bond. Earnings accrue to the owner but are not paid until the end of the bond term; although not received, the earnings are taxed as income. However, if the bonds are held in a charitable trust, IRA, or other retirement plan, the earnings will accrue with no current income tax liability to the owner. They have been used with success to fund charitable trusts that have children or grandchildren as beneficiaries and have usually been timed to pay the income when the children or grandchildren are approximately college age.

AUDIT OF OVERALL CHARITABLE REMAINDER TRUST ADMINISTRATION AND PROCEDURES

A successful administrative program must have clear procedures for handling the intake, administration, and termination of all charitable remainder trusts. This checklist provides a basic review method.

Processing Contributions

1. Review/create initial intake procedures. Who initiates the process? Where is the intake point? Will the intake point be asset-specific (i.e., will only one person handle real property gifts while another person handles all gifts of stock)?

2. Review current procedures for intake of trust instrument—review, acceptance, and signing. Procedures should vary depending upon who serves as trustee.

3. Review current procedures for handling the transfer of assets. When the charity serves as trustee, procedures should include indicating who will sign IRS Form 8283 (as trustee, not as the charity).

4. Review procedures for the physical handling of assets. Who will pick them up? Who will secure them? Will assets be insured? Will different people be responsible for handling different types of assets, or will one person or office have responsibility for all contributed assets (e.g., paintings will need to be stored, insured, and cared for prior to resale)?

5. Review procedures regarding the electronic transfer and handling of assets. Critical to any electronic transfers is careful monitoring. Who will be responsible for monitoring the electronic transfers?

6. Review procedures for the sale of assets by the trustee, including the designation of institutional authority to sell on behalf of the trustee.

7. Verify procedures for correct booking of trust value and basis for book accounting and for the four-tier system. Note: Book accounting and the four-tier system track value and basis in different ways. Make sure you keep track of both methods.

8. Review procedures for proper allocation of sales expense to the trust account.

9. Review your policy regarding whether contribution amount and remainder factors are calculated and sent to donor and, if so, whether calculations are verified.

10. Review the disclaimers by the preparer of any calculations. The disclaimers should also recommend that the donor seek his or her own tax advisor. This disclaimer should appear on all documents given to the donor before or after the trust is established, especially tax calculations and financial models.

11. Review the file for beneficiary information and social security number for distributions and any related matters, such as backup withholding, where applicable.

12. Verify the trust identification number obtained. Have you applied for each trust? Have you received a response from the IRS for each application?

Ongoing Trust Operations

1. What is the procedure for investing cash balances from initial sale of assets? Assignment of responsibility is critical to avoid having money sitting in a non-interest-bearing account.

2. Review the procedure for receiving information from your money manager. Assign monitoring responsibility.

3. What is the procedure for deciding investment changes and communication of these changes to the investment manager? Many institutions delegate day-to-day decision making to investment managers. This procedure does not relieve the trustee from the duty to oversee and review all investment decisions.

4. Evaluate the types of reports received from the investment manager/custodian and the adequacy of reports for accounting controls. For a large group

of trusts, it is useful if the charity and the money manager have compatible software. Hard copies of reports can be lengthy, especially for year-end reporting purposes. Computerized transfers of large amounts of account data are more efficient for everyone.

5. Review procedures for cash sweeps into bank accounts, including monitoring to ensure proper allocation to individual accounts, distribution from individual accounts, reinvestment of excess income, and proper accounting of shortfalls, if any. (Shortfalls may also require a separate procedure for funding the payment of any shortfall when dealing with a standard unitrust.)

6. Review bank statements and reconciliation reports. Implement the necessary policies.

7. Review handling of errors and corrections to bank statements and reconciliation reports, including valuation errors, calculation errors, and improper allocation of income, capital gain, and principal or charges to principal.

8. Review procedures for compliance with IRS Chapter 42 excise tax rules, including monitoring of exposure to rules, correction procedures, payment of taxes (if required), and allocation of tax payment under the four-tier system.

9. Review the preparation policy for IRS Forms 5227 and 1041A (and 1041, if applicable).

10. Review preparation polices for IRS Form K-1.

11. Review preparation policies for IRS Form 8282, including review for compliance with filing requirements and procedures to ensure a timely filing of the form. Sometimes a reminder system is useful with this task.

Trust Termination

1. Review the windup procedures of the trustee. Who is responsible? What tasks are required by governing documents (if any), state law, federal law, or internal institutional policy? Is there a procedure to ensure that the development office is also made aware of a termination?

2. Review the filing of final IRS Forms 5227, 1041A, K-1, and 56.

3. Review the procedure for the distribution of trust assets.

4. Check for any restricted use provisions contained in the governing document. Have these terms been complied with? If not, why not? Review with counsel to determine if it is necessary to seek court approval before changing the restricted use.

5. Verify the handling of endowment funds created through the trust for compliance with gift restrictions, if any, as specified in the governing documents. Only the governing documents matter when making this determination. Outside sources, such as letters or conversations with the donor, are not binding on the institution, absent proof of detrimental reliance on the part of the donor.

Duties of the Trustee

1. Prepare a checklist of fiduciary duties. Fiduciary duties vary from state to state. In general, your checklist will contain standard due diligence duties, emphasis on fulfilling donor wishes and expectations, and following a "prudent man" course regarding all phases of trust administration and termination.

2. Prepare a checklist on investment duties and the standard of care applicable to trustees. Review these items with the nonprofit board, if the nonprofit serves as trustee. Note the significant difference in the standard of care required of a board member and a trustee of a charitable remainder trust.

Prepare a checklist of state and federal reports required for compliance. Who is responsible to make sure these forms are properly handled and filed with the appropriate agencies?

KEY DOCUMENTS NEEDED FOR PROPERTY ANALYSIS

The following documents should be provided by the property owner/donor:

Deed

How is the title vested? Usually the deed can be used to prepare the gift deed to charity.

Appraisal

Preexisting appraisals can be useful in determining fair market value provided they are recent enough in time to the gift date. The appraisal may or may not be a qualified appraisal for tax purposes. Only a qualified appraisal is used when taking tax deductions for gifts of real property.

Property Tax Bill

The tax bill will provide the assessed value of the land and any improvements. It will also verify the actual tax on the property and assessments (if any). Examine and compare with the appraisal you have. Look for costs that will become yours should you accept the property.

Current Mortgage Statement

Debt-encumbered property is difficult to deal with when received as a gift. The statement will assist in determining exactly what you are getting from the donor. It will also show you who the lender is, should you need to work out something to complete the gift.

Notes and Trust Deeds or Mortgages

Can the mortgage be assumed? What will happen if the property is transferred to a third-party charity? Sometimes the only way to determine this information is to review the actual lending documents.

Association Agreement

Many residential properties, especially condominiums and PUDs, are governed by some type of owners' association. The ownership responsibilities and rights are usually expressed in association agreements that bind all owners of the property. Review these documents to determine what rights and responsibilities the charity will assume if you accept the property. Look for any fees or assessments noted. In addition, review a statement as to how large a reserve fund the association maintains for deferred maintenance obligations.

Conditions, Convenants, and Restrictions (CCRs)

Many, if not most, subdivisions require written documentation of all such items. Obtain a copy of the CCRs to determine how the property can be used and the restrictions that may apply.

Lease or Rental Agreements

Review all terms and conditions, including the expiration dates, to better determine marketability of the property. Note any prepaid deposits, as well as obligations for repairs and maintenance for which the owner may be responsible.

Insurance Policy

What type of insurance is maintained on the property? What are the term limits? Are they adequate? Note the cost of the existing insurance and check against market rates. Will your costs go up or down when a transfer of ownership occurs? Can you assume the existing insurance?

Environmental Analyses (If Available)

Environmental analyses are usually not available for proposed property gifts. However, you should ask to see any environmental studies or reports that may have been done on the property or for the area in which the property is located. Some properties have already had problems and others are in areas where known problems exist.

History of Ownership (If Known)

A true history of ownership can be generated during a title search. However, it will help speed up your evaluation if the property owner can provide this information to you. Unfortunately, few property owners can tell you the complete history of a particular property they own.

REAL ESTATE GIFT ANALYSIS CHECKLIST

Getting a clear idea of the value and condition of the gift property is critical to proper analysis. Donors frequently think with their hearts, not their heads, about their properties. You must look a gift horse in the mouth if you are to protect your institution.

Inspect the property.

The charity needs to inspect the property personally. Do not accept a "drive-by" assessment of condition. Walk the property looking for potential problems, such as toxic contamination or likely problems for resale. Consider these areas:

_____   Paint

_____   Plumbing

_____   Roof

_____   Structural cracks

_____   Landscaping

_____   Carpets

_____   Appliances

_____   Water stains

_____   Access, e.g., permanent road access (primarily for rural property)

_____   Utilities installed, e.g., sewer, septic, etc. (rural property/vacant land)

_____   Neighboring properties' use and condition (e.g., is the next-door neighbor running a car repair shop out of his garage?)

_____   Alley access (if any)

_____   Signs of toxic contamination (e.g., pipes indicating underground tanks, darkened patches of ground that look or smell unusual, stains or seepage from foundation walls or basement floors)

Assess the property in relationship to its surrounding neighborhood.

_____   Property overbuilt or underbuilt for surrounding area

_____   Potential liabilities running with the property (e.g., ungated swimming pool or uncapped water well)

_____   Close proximity to desirable locations, such as churches, stores, parks, and schools

_____   Close proximity to undesirable locations, such as taverns, rundown buildings, vacant lots, and noisy or busy streets

Experts in this field suggest that you note any real estate agents or brokers selling property in the area. They may be good sources of information on the area and may also help assess the market value and marketability of the property.

When the property is not close to you, you may wish to consider contacting a nonprofit institution in the area or a local broker to have them do the physical inspection and report back to you. Most nonprofits with qualified real estate people will usually assist fellow nonprofits.

Verify the fair market value.

After reviewing the physical property (and ideally not finding a new Love Canal), you will need to determine the market value of the property.

_____ Review any preexisting appraisals. Be sure to check the actual date of the appraisal. Sometimes appraisals are done later but are for an earlier date in time.

_____ Check appraised value (if any) against comparables currently for sale and also sold in the last three months. Do they seem consistent with the preexisting appraisal?

_____ Determine if there is a need for another, more current (or less biased) appraisal. Who will pay for the appraisal? (Note: If the donor does not already possess a qualified appraisal, then he or she *must* pay for the new, qualified appraisal if planning to use it for tax purposes.)

_____ Review new appraisal (if necessary). Has the new appraisal used relevant, similar comparable sales to determine market value? In fast-moving markets, comps that are six months old may be very far off current market values. Appraisers frequently try to use properties that are too far away geographically for valid comparison or clearly outside of prestigious neighborhoods, especially when there are very few properties being sold within a normal radius of the gift property.

Determine the marketability.

_____ Check with real estate brokers to determine the marketability of the property. Can it be sold in a reasonable time? Is it in the path of urban growth with high long-term potential? Are there future plans that may affect the property value, such as a freeway extension planned to run through the front yard in two years?

Review acquisition and holding costs.

_____ What costs will be incurred by the institution in acquiring the property?

_____ Will cash be required to pay off lenders or to complete a bargain sale? If so, how much?

_____ What is the estimated length of the holding period for the charity?

_____ What is the annual cost of property taxes?

_____ What is the cost of insurance during the holding period?

_____ What is the cost of utilities during the holding period?

_____ What is the cost of maintenance during the holding period?

_____ What is the cost of security during the holding period?

Review outstanding mortgages.

_____ Review all outstanding mortgages and notes. Can they be assumed, or is refinancing required?

_____ What costs will be incurred in refinancing the property?

_____ Who will be responsible for making payments on any assumed mortgages or refinancing?

_____ Which department or division of the institution will provide the payments out of its budget?

Review rental agreements.

_____ Review all existing rental agreements.

_____ Will transfer of the property to a third party affect any existing rental agreement? If so, in what way? Is this a problem?

_____ Is the property subject to rent controls?

_____ Under the rental agreements, are third parties bound by the terms of the agreements?

Transfer marketable title.

_____ Request a binder or preliminary title report from a title company in the area. (Old pros recommend developing a good relationship with at least one title company representative.)

_____ Determine whether marketable title can be transferred to the charity when the gift is made.

_____ If not, review the difficulty of reselling property without marketable title.

Transfer title.

_____ Review the exact names of the owners listed on the current deed to the property.

_____ Insert *exact* language used to describe the owners in the gift deed. This is a critical step. If owners hold property "jointly, as husband and wife," then the deed of gift should read exactly the same. There is no room for inexactitude at this point.

_____ Seek the appropriate deed form from the title company. Different states demand different types of deeds for real property gifts. Some require only quit claim deeds. Others want grant deeds or warranty deeds.

_____ Have the donors execute the title transfer by executing gift deeds with all signing formalities. (The title company can advise here.)

_____ Assign someone to record the gift deed with the county recorder or to oversee the title company's recording of the deed, if it takes on that task.

TRUST REVIEW CHECKLIST

The following checklist is for use when reviewing existing charitable remainder trusts. This checklist is written for the administrator of the trust, but it is a good tool to use when reviewing trusts administered by vendors.

Keep in mind that if your institution is named as trustee or co-trustee of the trusts, you have a fiduciary duty to make sure that the trusts comply with all federal and state laws and that they are handled in all ways as required by law.

If your organization does not serve as a named trustee of the trusts, you still have a vested interest in the proper administration of these gift trusts, since your organization will eventually benefit from the assets held in them. As remainderman, you have the legal right to ask questions concerning the handling of your trust(s).

Trust Review Checklist

Trust Qualification: Is the Trust a Charitable Remainder Trust?

1. Check the trust document for compliance with federal tax law to ensure that it qualifies as a charitable remainder trust.

2. Review any disqualifying or suspect provisions with counsel.

3. Determine appropriate actions to bring the trust into compliance.

Trust Assets: What Is in the Trust and When Did It Get There?

1. List all assets of the trust.

2. Determine or verify the initial value of each asset. It will also be useful to have the donor's original basis in the asset, if this information is available.

3. Determine the value for each year as of the valuation date.

4. Determine the current value of each asset.

5. Review the valuation date and valuation technique, including additional contributions and short-year valuations. Was it done correctly and according to the governing document terms?

6. Review the trust investment objectives based on donor needs, form of trust, and payout requirement, and compare these objectives to the actual results of the investment mix. Are donor needs being met? Have certain asset classes outperformed others inside the trust, requiring rebalancing of the asset mix?

7. Does asset mix meet the prudent man rule for diversification of investments?

8. Compare trust investments with legal and tax requirements for the type of trust. Review investments against any state income and principal laws (many states use the uniform act). Also compare to the actual governing instrument for investment limitations, if any.

9. Review the asset statements produced by the investment manager for accuracy and to determine what fees, if any, are being charged to the trust. Are these fees expected? Reasonable?

Trust Income

1. Determine investment return for each trust by asset category. Is it in line with market performance?

2. Determine investment return for each trust by overall return. Is it in line with market performance?

3. Determine investment return for each trust by comparing capital gain with ordinary income. Types of income affect the donor. Capital gain is treated more favorably than ordinary income under income tax law. Are you doing your best to generate capital gain income for the donor?

4. Review the following trust income payment provisions: the payout amount required by law and/or the governing trust document and whether the trust historically has paid the beneficiaries correctly under the terms of the trust or by law.

5. Check for unusual or different payout terms created by the trust. These types of arrangements may show up when trusts are for multiple lives.

Have these special terms been followed correctly since the inception of the trust?

6. Have investments provided sufficient income to satisfy the donor's expectations? Have the investments allowed for some growth of principal to benefit the remainderman over the long term?

7. Are transaction reports and investment statements adequate to determine the type of income earned? Can they be used easily to provide information required for tax returns and reports?

8. Verify that the income generated by trust assets was in fact received and correctly posted on the books.

9. Verify that the income received was distributed properly to beneficiaries in accordance with trust documents, state law, and federal tax law.

10. Check your master bank account statements or each individual trust bank account statement (if reported separately) to determine if all earned income and realized gains have been deposited to the correct account. Note: It is often considered helpful to cross-check the above records with the financial reports generated for each trust and with the trust's IRS Form 5227.

11. Following your income review, has the asset mix of the trust provided adequate income, or should the mix be revised? What, if any, recommendations does your investment manager suggest?

12. Identify any situations that require corrections for overvaluation or undervaluation. Make the corrections, and note them for future follow-up and review.

13. (Unitrust only)—Review the stated unitrust amount and compare to the trust accounting income (after assets have been determined and income calculated).

14. (Unitrust only)—Check the aggregate stated unitrust amounts against aggregate amounts paid to trust recipients according to the books. Do they match? Have there been underpayments? Overpayments?

15. (Unitrust only)—Check same against reported payments shown on IRS Form 5227.

16. (Unitrust only)—Review four-tier accounting from the inception of the trust. Note income items, classes, and categories as required by federal tax law. Has the four-tier system been followed?

17. Trace expense allocations per item, class, or category, or, if applicable, under the "any tier" allocation or under the corpus allocation as required by federal tax law for specific expenses (losses).

18. Cross-check the interrelationship between the Uniform Principal and Income Act (trust accounting) and four-tier accounting, especially in those areas in which they may be in contradiction.

19. Cross-check four-tier accounting with at least the last three IRS Form 5227s filed for each trust.

20. Recommend necessary changes in trust accounting to comply with IRC sec. 664.

Net Income Unitrusts

Many institutions no longer have net income trusts. If you do have one, it is very likely that it is an older trust that may require close scrutiny.

1. Review records to determine if four-tier accounting has been applied or should have been applied to each net income unitrust.

2. Trace from inception all net income unitrusts with deficiency makeup provisions for compliance with IRC sec. 664(d)(3). Have deficiencies been carried forward each year? Have excess payments been deducted from the deficiency balance, and when have they been paid?

3. Analyze whether the manner of determining distributable amount per payment frequency (month, quarter, semiannual, or annual) is correctly accomplished. If not, what new procedures are necessary, including a procedure for estimating periodic payments?

4. Determine if any fifth adjusting payments were necessary and, if so, whether they were paid. Are monies still owed to beneficiaries? Review each year for possible underpayments, and decide what corrective actions, if any, need to be taken.

SAMPLE CHARITABLE REMAINDER ANNUITY TRUST DISCLOSURE

Author's Note: The disclosure form presented is intended to give you an idea of what a good disclosure form looks like. An arcane example was chosen because disclosure forms should not be copied and used without consultation with your legal counsel. The need for legal counsel is also the reason why this appendix presents only one disclosure form rather than a full set of examples.

Features of Your Charitable Remainder Annuity Trust

Your gift is irrevocable. You cannot change the terms and conditions of your gift after it has been established.

The established payment amount will not change from year to year as long as there are any assets left in the trust. There will be no increase in income even if investment results cause the principal of the trust to grow.

Upon termination of the trust, all assets remaining in the trust will be distributed to the University of XYZ to be used in the manner you have directed.

The university does not guarantee the investments held in the trust. However, professional investment advisors are involved with every investment decision to ensure that the funds are managed in a prudent manner.

You are not permitted to make additional contributions to a charitable remainder annuity trust. If you wish to make an additional gift, a second trust would need to be established.

Tax Considerations

A charitable remainder annuity trust is a tax-exempt trust. Assets that are transferred to the trust and then sold usually will not be subject to the capital gains tax.

A charitable remainder annuity trust provides an income tax charitable deduction to the donor when the trust is funded. The deduction will vary depending upon the amount transferred to the trust, the ages of the income beneficiaries, the term of the trust, the IRS discount rate in effect at the time of your gift, and the stated percentage payout. The university provides estimated deduction calculations for donors and their advisors free of charge.

If you use cash to fund your charitable remainder annuity trust, you can use your deduction to offset up to 50 percent of your adjusted gross income. Any unused portion may be carried forward for up to five years.

If you use appreciated assets (held by you for more than one year) to fund your charitable remainder annuity trust, the value of your gift and income tax deduction is based on the full fair market value of the assets on the date of gift. Your current-year deduction for all gifts of appreciated assets may not exceed 30 percent of your adjusted gross income, with a five-year carryover for any excess. If you are subject to the alternative minimum tax in [your state], your deduction may be reduced.

The tax treatment of distributions made to you and/or your designated beneficiary(ies) will depend on the type of asset used to fund the trust and the income earned by the trust. The trust is required to maintain a historic ledger of income earned and gains realized from year to year. Distributions are treated as consisting first of ordinary income earned by the trust (dividends and interest), then short-term capital gains, then long-term capital gains, then tax-exempt interest, and finally principal.

If your spouse is the only individual beneficiary (other than you), his or her interest will qualify automatically for the gift and estate tax marital deduction. If you name individuals other than yourself and your spouse as beneficiary(ies), you may wish to reserve the right to revoke their interest. Otherwise, the value of that interest will be treated as a taxable gift immediately upon funding the trust.

If you have any questions concerning your trust, its investments, or its administration, you should call our director of trust management, Bob Worthy, at (713) 555-1212.

TRUSTEE
University of XYZ
Office of Planned Giving
Los Robles, CA 94089-0015
Bob Worthy
Director of Trust Management
(713) 555-1212
(713) 555-0000 (fax)

TRUSTEE DESIGNATED CO-TRUSTEE
Reliable National Bank
Charitable Management Section
333 West Is Grand Ave.
Mt. Angeles, CA 94072
Annie Accurate, Trust Administrator
(713) 121-0000
(713) 121-9999

How Trust Assets Are Invested by the University of XYZ

Trust assets may be commingled with the university's endowment and/or invested in diversified investment funds or mutual funds maintained by Reliable National Bank or in such other funds or individual stocks as the university, in its capacity as trustee, chooses at its sole discretion.

The university, as trustee, does not guarantee the payments from a charitable remainder annuity trust. Trust donors and beneficiaries may look solely to the assets held in the trust for all payments required during the term of the trust.

The university has determined that the Reliable National Bank diversified investment funds and mutual funds are appropriate investment vehicles for its charitable remainder trusts. Trust assets may be invested in one or more of these funds, at the sole discretion of the trustee, and may be changed without notice. (A complete list of these funds is available upon request by calling the director of trust management at XYZ; see above.)

Each diversified investment fund or mutual fund has a specific investment objective that is defined in the prospectus for that fund (available on request from the director of trust management). In general, the university, as trustee, invests trust assets to provide wide diversification and growth while attempting to meet the income objectives of donors and beneficiaries. This does not mean that the trustee guarantees a specific rate of return or income level for specific trusts. It does mean that the trustee strives to provide a prudent investment program.

A charitable remainder trust may from time to time be invested in any or all of the following asset classes:

- Domestic equity securities
- International equity securities*
- Domestic debt instruments (including bonds, notes, and debentures)
- International debt instruments (including bonds, notes, and debentures)*
- Government bonds, notes, treasury bills, and similar instruments
- Real estate, real estate investment trusts (REITs), mortgages, notes, etc.
- Cash and cash equivalents

The university Treasurer's Office exercises oversight over all professional investment managers or investment advisors employed by the university directly and in its capacity as trustee of its charitable remainder trusts.

Historic return data from the various diversified funds and mutual funds used by the university are available on request. However, past returns are no guarantee of future results.

Investment in securities and other assets necessarily involves risk, which can be substantial, and it is expected that the value of an annuity trust's investments will fluctuate over time. There can be no guarantee that the net asset value of your charitable remainder annuity trust will not decline significantly, or that the trust will earn any particular level of return. In the case of a charitable remainder annuity trust, as noted above, the amount of distributions to you or your designated beneficiary(ies) will depend directly on the net asset value of your trust at the time it is funded. Distributions from annuity trusts depend on the trust having sufficient assets to make such distributions at the time designated in the trust instrument. In the event of an inability of the trust to make the distributions contemplated by the terms of the trust or expected to be received by the beneficiary(ies), the university would have no obligation to make, nor would it be permitted to make, any distributions or other payments from the university's own assets.

Reports, Tax Returns, Expenses, and Miscellaneous Information

Reports concerning your trust will be sent to you annually by the director of trust management. In addition, you may request updates during the calendar year of the current asset investment strategy for your trust. The director of trust management will also, from time to time, provide additional information concerning your trust, including tax information on a Schedule K-1 detailing the amount and character (ordinary income or capital gain) of the payments you received during the year.

The university, as trustee, is responsible for all tax reporting required for the trust. This does not include the personal income tax returns of beneficiaries or donors.

The consequences of a charitable gift are dependent in significant part on the individual donor's particular circumstances. The general discussion of charitable remainder annuity trusts set forth above does not address every issue, nor does it take into consideration the type of assets you are contributing to your charitable remainder annuity trust, the particular terms of your trust, your individual tax situation, or your estate and gift tax planning objectives. Other factors, such as state and local taxes, may also be relevant to your gift. With respect to these considerations, as well as for a description of other ways to structure charitable gifts, you should consult with your tax and estate planning advisors.

*While investments will be made and managed consistent with sound fiduciary practices, investments made on foreign markets may be somewhat more volatile than domestic investments and are subject to additional risk factors such as fluctuations in exchange rates, global market performance, and investment, credit, political, and market risks associated with particular foreign jurisdictions.

You will receive a separate acknowledgment from the university setting forth the value of the income interest and the remainder interest in your annuity trust in compliance with the charitable deduction substantiation rules.

The University of XYZ serves as trustee at no cost to the trust. Generally, all assets held in diversified investment funds have no management fees assessed to them. Usually, the sale of individual stocks is done at the lowest institutional commission rate available. Fees and expenses related to the maintenance of assets in the trust (for example, costs related to real estate management and upkeep) will be charged to trusts individually. However, only trusts with real estate or other nonliquid assets usually incur substantial maintenance costs.

Pursuant to the terms of the Philanthropy Protection Act of 1995, any commingling of your trust with other such trusts or with the university's endowment is exempt from registration under federal securities laws. Your trust may be commingled as described above, but the university will maintain adequate records to determine the value of the assets of your trust and the income, gain, and loss they produce.

Additional Disclosures (Optional)

None.

I, _____, a representative of the University of XYZ, hereby attest to the fact that I have met with and explained all pertinent features of this charitable remainder annuity trust as contained in this disclosure statement.

Name _____

Title _____

I do hereby agree and attest to the fact that _____ has reviewed this disclosure statement with me and has explained to my satisfaction the pertinent features of my XYZ charitable remainder annuity trust.

Donor _____

Date _____

GIFT ACCEPTANCE POLICIES
OF TEXAS CHRISTIAN UNIVERSITY

Revised September 2001

Introduction

To promote and protect the interests of Texas Christian University (TCU) as well as the persons and other entities who support its programs, these policies are designed to assure that all gifts to or for the use of TCU provide maximum benefits to both parties.

Our goal is to encourage funding of TCU without encumbering the organization with gifts that may generate more costs than benefits, or which are restricted in a manner that is not in keeping with the mission of TCU.

Texas Christian University is qualified to receive tax-deductible contributions under the current IRS code [section 170(b)(1)(A)].

To optimize funding from individuals and other entities, TCU must respond quickly, and in the affirmative where possible, to gifts offered by prospective donors. Except where stated otherwise, these policies are intended as guidelines. Flexibility will be maintained since some gift situations will be complex and decisions can be made only after careful consideration of all related factors.

These policies will therefore sometimes require that the merits of a particular gift be considered by the Gift Acceptance Committee of the University, consisting of the chancellor and vice chancellors of University Advancement and Finance and Business. The Executive Committee of the Board of Trustees will confirm acceptance of gifts of $100,000 or more.

Outright Restricted Gifts

A. Cash

1. Gifts in the form of cash and checks shall be accepted regardless of amount unless, as in the case of all gifts, there is a question as to whether the donor has sufficient title to the assets or is mentally competent to legally transfer the funds as a gift to TCU.

2. All checks must be made payable to "Texas Christian University" and shall never be made payable to an employee, agent, or volunteer for the credit of TCU.

B. Publicly Traded Securities

1. Securities that are traded on the New York, NASDAQ, or American stock exchanges, or other readily marketable securities, shall be accepted by TCU. Donors should expect such securities to be sold immediately by TCU. No employee or volunteer working on behalf of the University shall commit to a donor that a particular security will be held unless approved to do so by an authorized officer of TCU.

2. Securities will be valued at the average of the high and low trading price on the day the gift is legally transferred to TCU.

NOTE: If the securities are subject to restrictions that affect their value to the donor or prevent the securities from being freely traded (e.g., SEC restrictions under rule 145), IRS regulations specify the donor must obtain a qualified appraisal to establish deductibility for federal income tax purposes. When a qualified appraisal exists, TCU gift credit will be limited to the amount of this appraisal. In cases when the donor has not received a qualified appraisal, the amount of gift credit may be approved by the Gift Acceptance Committee of the University.

These restricted securities may be accepted after approval of the chief fiscal officer or the Gift Acceptance Committee of the University.

Exceptions to this policy may only be approved by the chief fiscal officer or the Gift Acceptance Committee of the University.

C. Closely Held Securities

1. Non-publicly traded securities may be accepted only after approval of the chief fiscal officer or the Gift Acceptance Committee of the University.

2. Such securities may be subsequently sold only with the approval of the chief fiscal officer or the Gift Acceptance Committee of the University.

3. Prior to completion of a gift, no commitments by TCU shall be made regarding repurchase of such securities.

D. Real Property

1. No gift of real estate shall be accepted without prior approval by the Gift Acceptance Committee of the University.

2. No gift of real estate shall be accepted without a current appraisal by a qualified appraiser as required by the Internal Revenue Service. In addition, environmental reports appropriate for the type of property to be transferred will be completed before real estate will be accepted by TCU. Transaction screening of residential property shall be made at the expense of TCU.

3. In general, residential real estate located within Tarrant County, with a value estimated by the donor or others to be $50,000 or greater may be accepted, unless the property is not suitable for acceptance as a gift.

4. In general, residential real estate located more than 50 miles from the TCU campus will not be accepted as a gift unless its value appears to be in excess of $50,000 and there is reason to believe it is marketable. The Gift Acceptance Committee will make final decisions to accept or reject such gifts or to make exceptions to this policy.

5. Donors will be asked to make gifts of cash to cover taxes and insurance on gifts of real estate until such property can be sold.

6. No commercial real estate shall be accepted on behalf of TCU without approval of the Gift Acceptance Committee.

7. Real estate acceptability for funding a charitable gift annuity is subject to approval by the Gift Acceptance Committee.

8. Special attention shall be given to the receipt of real estate encumbered by a mortgage, as the ownership of such property may generate unrelated business income and disqualification of certain split-interest gifts unless handled in a proper manner.

E. Tangible Personal Property

1. Jewelry, artwork, certain collectibles, and other personal property are acceptable gifts. However, before the University accepts such gifts, donors will be informed of IRS regulations on such gifts as well as TCU's policy of expeditiously selling property not used by the University at the best available price. Please refer to the policy on Gifts In-Kind for further information.

Artwork shall be accepted by the University following review and recommendation by the Art Acquisition Committee. The Committee shall consist of the following:

- Chair of the Art Department.
- Two other representatives to be appointed by the provost and the chief fiscal officer.

2. Personal property valued at $500 or more shall be accepted by TCU if the property can be used by the University. No personal property shall be accepted requiring ownership in perpetuity without express approval of the Gift Acceptance Committee. No perishable property or property that will require special facilities or security will be accepted without prior approval of the Gift Acceptance Committee.

F. Other Property

1. Other property, including mortgages, notes, copyrights, royalties, and easements, whether real or personal, may be accepted only upon approval by the Gift Acceptance Committee.

Deferred Gifts

A. Bequests

1. Gifts (bequests) through wills shall be encouraged.

2. In the event of inquiry by a prospective legator, future acceptability of property proposed to be left to TCU in a will or through any other deferred gift arrangement shall only be made in accordance with the terms and provisions of paragraphs A through F of this document.

3. Unacceptable gifts of property from the estates of deceased donors shall be disclaimed only by agreement of the appropriate officers of the University. The legal counsel of TCU shall expeditiously communicate the decision of the University to the legal representatives of the estate.

4. Whenever possible, attempts shall be made to discover bequest plans in order to determine whether inappropriate property has inadvertently been left to TCU. For example, intended bequests

of property other than cash or marketable securities should be brought to the attention of the appropriate University officers so the donor can conform his or her plans to TCU policy.

B. Charitable Remainder Trusts

1. In general, TCU will not serve as sole trustee of a charitable remainder trust that benefits the institution.

2. The University will identify a limited number of corporate fiduciaries that hold such trusts. Only when specifically asked may any corporate fiduciary be recommended to a donor. Donors will be encouraged to interview potential trust officers and make their own informed choices.

3. The fees for management of a charitable remainder trust will be paid by the trust and not by TCU.

4. TCU's chief fiscal officer and other employees and volunteers acting on behalf of TCU should be familiar with the types of property generally accepted by corporate fiduciaries as suitable contributions to charitable remainder trusts. Employees or others acting on behalf of TCU shall encourage donors to make gifts of any property to charitable remainder trusts that are in keeping with such guidelines and IRS regulations.

5. No representations shall be made by any employee or other persons acting on behalf of TCU as to the manner in which charitable remainder trust assets will be managed or invested by a corporate fiduciary.

6. Charitable remainder trusts and other life-income gifts shall be encouraged as a method of making gifts to TCU. Such trusts shall not be marketed as tax avoidance devices or as investment vehicles, since such activity may violate federal and/or state securities regulations.

7. Charitable remainder trusts shall be encouraged that name as income beneficiaries individuals older than 60 years and that name one or two income beneficiaries. Exceptions to this guideline may be made by the Gift Acceptance Committee.

The minimum amount required to establish a charitable remainder trust is generally $100,000, although it may vary according to the practice of the trustees selected.

C. Pooled Income Funds

1. TCU will maintain one or more pooled income funds, a gift device established by Congress under the terms of section 642 of the Internal Revenue Code.

2. A corporate fiduciary will be selected to manage the investments of the pooled income fund(s).

3. TCU will pay the administrative fees for managing newly created pooled funds until appropriate officers of the University shall determine otherwise.

4. No income beneficiary in the fund may be younger than 60 years of age without prior approval of the Gift Acceptance Committee.

5. There shall be no more than two income beneficiaries for each contribution to the fund.

6. The minimum initial contribution to the fund shall be $5,000.

7. The minimum additional contribution by a participant in the fund shall be $2,500.

8. The corporate fiduciary shall furnish guidelines governing the acceptance of property other than cash as contributions to TCU's pooled income funds. Such guidelines shall be approved by appropriate University officers.

9. No representation of the fund shall be made that could be construed as marketing the fund as an investment or security of any type. All disclosures required by state and federal regulatory agencies shall be made in a thorough and timely manner. Development officers should be thoroughly familiar with the prospectus of any pooled fund under consideration by a donor.

D. Charitable Gift Annuities

1. No gift annuity shall be accepted that names an income beneficiary under 60 years of age without prior approval of the Gift Acceptance Committee.

2. Deferred gift annuities shall be accepted from younger donors when the income stream begins at age 60 or after.

3. There shall not be more than two income beneficiaries for a gift annuity.

4. The minimum initial contribution for a gift annuity shall be $10,000.

5. The minimum contribution for an additional gift annuity by an individual who has previously entered into a gift annuity agreement shall be $2,500.

6. Gift annuity rates to be offered are those set by the American Council on Gift Annuities.

155

E. Life Estate Gifts

1. The Gift Acceptance Committee may approve gifts in which the donor retains a life interest in real property in situations where the asset involved appears to be a minor portion of the donor's estate, and the Committee is satisfied there has been full disclosure to the donor of the possible future ramifications of the transaction.

F. Gifts of Life Insurance

1. TCU encourages donors to name the University to receive all or a portion of the benefits of life insurance policies that they have purchased.

2. TCU encourages donors to participate in the TCU Life Insurance Program to Endow Athletics ("Frog Life") when such gifts are not replacements for current giving.

3. TCU will not accept gifts from donors for the purpose of purchasing life insurance on the donor's life other than through an approved University program. Exceptions to this policy may be made only after researching relevant state laws to ensure the University has an insurable interest under applicable state law.

4. No insurance products may be endorsed for use in funding gifts to the University without appropriate approval by the Gift Acceptance Committee.

5. Lists of TCU donors will not be furnished to anyone for the purpose of marketing life insurance benefiting donors and/or the University, as this practice constitutes a potential conflict of interest and may be construed as involvement in the marketing of life insurance.

Payment of Fees Related to Gifts to Texas Christian University

A. Finder's Fees or Commissions

1. In general, TCU will pay no fee to any person in consideration of directing a gift to the University. Such fees may or may not be legal and, in the case of irrevocable deferred gifts that involve management of assets, the payment of such fees may subject TCU and its management and Board of Trustees to federal and state security regulation.

2. No commission or finder's fee of any type will be paid to any party in connection with the completion of a gift to TCU.

B. Professional Fees

1. TCU will pay reasonable fees for professional services rendered in connection with the completion of a gift to the University. Such fees will be paid only with prior approval of the chief fiscal officer or the Gift Acceptance Committee.

2. Such fees will be paid only following discussion with and approval by the donor.

3. Fees shall be reasonable and directly related to the completion of a gift. They shall be limited to:

   - appraisal fees by persons who are competent and qualified to appraise the property proposed and who have no conflict of interest,

   - legal fees for the preparation of documents,

   - fees related to providing preliminary opinions related to environmental issues,

   - and accounting fees incident to a transaction.

4. In the case of legal, accounting, and other professional fees, an attempt shall be made to ascertain the reasonableness of fees prior to payment. An hourly breakdown of time should be requested.

5. In cases where TCU is asked to pay fees to persons initially employed by the donor, the donor shall be notified that the payment of such fees may result in taxable income to the donor in the amount of the fees paid.

Restrictions

A. Restrictions on Use and Investment of Gifts

1. Gifts restricted for use by a specific unit of the University or at the discretion of a particular member of the staff may take the same form as those in paragraphs A through F. However, such restricted gifts are acceptable only if they are to be applied to existing programs and uses (e.g., scholarships) and with advance approval by the appropriate officer of the University.

2. Restrictions by the donor on gift use or investment by TCU outside the mission or current programs of the University will not be honored without prior approval by the appropriate officers of the University.

3. Minimum gift levels, as established in the TCU Gift Opportunities Statement, are required unless specific exception is granted by the Gift Acceptance Committee.

B. Gift Credit

1. TCU's policy for crediting donors for gifts is consistent with the guidelines set forth in "Management Reporting Standards for Educational Institutions: Fund Raising and Related Activities" (CASE/NACUBO).

Procedure for Gifts of Securities to TCU/BRITE

A. Hand Delivery

1. Sign "Irrevocable Stock or Bond Power" form without signing the certificate(s) itself. The signature must read exactly as that on the stock certificate.

2. The form requires your signature be guaranteed. A bank officer who knows you may guarantee the signature.

3. DO NOT fill in TCU as the recipient on the stock power form. This requires two transactions before a sale can be made because the stock must first be put in TCU's name and then transferred to the next buyer.

4. Recipient (representative of TCU/Brite) will list the securities on a receipt, including the name of the security, the certificate number, the number of shares, and the purpose of the gift.

5. The recipient signs the receipt and gives it to you.

6. If you have already signed (endorsed) the back of the certificate(s), the transfer forms are not needed. Signed certificates are negotiable as cash and should be handled accordingly. We prefer that you not name TCU as the new owner on the certificate because we will most likely sell the security and this just adds to the paperwork.

7. The effective gift date is the day the physical transfer of paper is made.

A. Mail Delivery

1. Mail unsigned certificates by certified mail (return receipt requested) to TCU, TCU Box 297044, Fort Worth, TX 76129. You should enclose a cover letter stating your name and address and the designation of the gift.

2. In a separate envelope, mail a signed stock transfer form ("Irrevocable Stock or Bond Power") with a copy of the cover letter to the same address.

3. If an endorsed certificate naming TCU as the transferee is mailed (which is risky), the packet should be insured for the fair market value of the stock and a return receipt should be requested. This is the most expensive way to transfer stock.

4. The effective gift date is the date of the postmark on the envelope containing the certificate.

B. Electronic Funds Transfer (account to account)

1. Notify your broker in writing to transfer a specific number of shares (generally those with the lowest cost basis) to TCU's account. Our most active account is with Merrill Lynch. DTC (Depository Trust Company) to Merrill Lynch, DTC #5198, for further credit to Texas Christian University account #552 04092. Deliver to TCU contact Charles Webster at 817-877-9627, fax 817-877-9693, or:

   Merrill Lynch
   201 Main St., #850
   Fort Worth, TX 76102

2. TCU has accounts with other brokers. If you have a particularly close relationship with a broker, you may wish to make the transfer within that company. Please contact TCU (817-257-7524) for further information about TCU's additional brokerage accounts.

   *Please note: Only TCU can issue a sell order for stock transferred to us.

3. A new account in TCU's name can be established easily when necessary, but is not preferred. Please contact Dick Hoban or Mike Mattson to establish a new account. The University's tax ID number will be required.

4. You should notify TCU of an impending or completed transfer. Brokerage firms often do not notify the transferee until the next monthly statement date, which may cause the University to lose money on a timely sale of the securities.

5. The effective gift date is the date on which the transfer is actually made by the broker. If you want the transfer made to take advantage of market prices, you should clearly specify this to your broker.

Information for DTC Stock Transfer to Texas Christian University:

TCU Broker:	Merrill Lynch
	Attn. Charles Webster
Account Number:	552 04092
DTC #:	5198
TCU Tax ID:	75-0827465
Broker's Address:	201 Main Street
	Suite 850
	Fort Worth, TX 76102
Broker's Phone:	(800) 542-7514
	(817) 877-9627
Broker's Fax:	(817) 877-9693
TCU Contact:	Mike Mattson
Address:	TCU Box 297044
	Fort Worth, TX 76129
Phone:	(817) 257-7524
Fax:	(817) 257-7708
E-mail:	m.mattson@tcu.edu

Mutual Fund Transfer Instructions

The transfer of mutual fund shares is a time-consuming process and may take two to six weeks to complete. There are several key points to observe when considering a charitable gift using mutual funds.

- **Transfer in Kind.** Do not sell or redeem. It is important that the mutual fund gift be transferred into the charity's name. If it is sold from the donor's account, then the gift becomes a gift of cash rather than a gift of securities, and the donor will be responsible for the capital gains tax.

- **Timing.** As with other securities, the mutual fund is not considered a gift (for tax purposes) until it has been transferred out of the donor's name and into the charity's name. There is significant variability from fund to fund with regard to how long a transfer will take. Generally, the transfer is dependent upon several variables: how the fund is held, how responsive the mutual fund is to transfer requests, and how complete the transfer request is.

- **Where and How a Mutual Fund Is Held.** Mutual funds can be held in three forms: certificate form (physical), with a broker, or with a fund. When compiling the paperwork needed to accomplish the transfer, it will be important to identify where and how the mutual fund is held.

- **Required Transfer Paperwork.** Most funds will require several documents from the donor and the charity to effect the transfer. The process varies with each fund so it is important to call the fund first in order to determine the appropriate paperwork needed. Individual mutual fund companies may require some or all of the following:

  A. Letter of Instruction from the Shareholder. This should state what he or she is giving, when it should happen, to whom it is being given, the account number from which the mutual fund is coming, and to whom the transfer agent should speak if there are questions. The letter must be signed by the account owner(s) and should be signature-guaranteed.

  B. Letter of Instruction from the Charity. This should confirm the source of the expected gift, convey a new account application and corporate resolution, and provide the name of the contact person at the charity.

  C. New Account Application from the Charity. Most mutual funds will require that the charity complete its own account application. A charity may already have an account with the mutual fund; however, if a gift is to be used to establish a charitable remainder trust, then the account must be in the name of the trust, with the charity as trustee, in order to execute a completed gift for tax purposes.

  D. Corporate Resolution from the Charity. This generally can be obtained from the charity's corporate secretary or gift processing center. It contains the names of the individuals who are authorized to accept gifts on behalf of the charity and is stamped with the charity's corporate seal.

  E. Form W-9 from the Charity. Not all funds will require this, but it contains the charity's taxpayer identification number issued by the Internal Revenue Service.

158

Sample Letter of Instruction: Donor to Mutual Fund

Date

XXXX
XXXX
XXXX

Dear Sir/Madam:

I would like to make a charitable gift to [name of organization] of my shares/units in the [name of fund]. Please transfer (NOT EXCHANGE OR REDEEM) _____number of shares in the fund from my account number (number of account) to a new account in the fund in the name of [name of organization], tax identification number _____. Enclosed is a recent statement of my account with your firm.

Should new account forms need to be completed by [name of organization], you may forward the application to the gift planning office at the address mentioned below. Also, please provide the name and telephone number of the staff person who will be processing the application.

Please send confirmation of this transfer to me and to [name of organization, attention staff person, and address of same]. Thank you.

Sincerely,

Donor's Signature

Signature Guarantee

Date

appendix J

GOVERNMENT "SAFE HARBOR" DOCUMENTS

The following section contains sample "safe harbor" documents issued by the Internal Revenue Service in Revenue Procedure Rulings 90–30, 90–31, 90–32, and 88–53. The rulings contain actual annuity trust, unitrust, and pooled income fund documents that have been preapproved by the IRS. Any taxpayer using these documents *exactly* as written can be certain their trusts will qualify for tax purposes as charitable remainder trusts or pooled income fund gifts.

These documents *are not considered adequate* by practitioners in the area, since they are silent on many provisions that are considered important to include in a remainder trust or pooled income fund document. The IRS recently admitted the problems with these documents and has issued a new series of Revenue Procedure Rulings, 2003–53 through 2003–60. These rulings supercede the examples given in Revenue Procedure ruling 90–32 on annuity trusts. The old ruling is included here to provide a comparison. New rulings are also expected for unitrusts in the near future, but at the present time rulings 90–30 and 90–31 are still in effect.

These rulings are included here to as examples of trust documents or pooled income fund documents. They form a basis for comparison with documents drafted by practitioners, since any document submitted to you for review should, *at a minimum*, contain the provisions included in these samples. Do not be surprised if the documents you see being used are far more lengthy and detailed than these samples.

MODEL DOCUMENTS FOR
CHARITABLE REMAINDER UNITRUSTS

Revenue Procedures
Rev. Proc. 90–30
1990–1 C.B. 534
Reference:

Section 664—Charitable Remainder Trusts
Effect on Other Documents:
Amends Rev. Proc. 89–20.

SECTION 1. PURPOSE

This revenue procedure makes available five sample forms of trust that meet the requirements for a charitable remainder unitrust as described in section 664(d)(2) of the Internal Revenue Code.

SEC. 2. BACKGROUND

The Internal Revenue Service receives and responds to requests for rulings dealing with the qualification of trusts as charitable remainder trusts and the availability of deductions for contributions made to such trusts. In many of these requests, the trust instruments and charitable objectives are very similar. Consequently, in order to provide a service to taxpayers and to save the time and expense involved in requesting and processing a ruling on a proposed charitable remainder unitrust, this revenue procedure allows taxpayers who make transfers to a trust that substantially follows one of the sample forms of trust contained herein to be assured that the Service will recognize the trust as meeting all of the requirements of a charitable remainder unitrust, provided that the trust operates in a manner consistent with the terms of the instrument creating the trust and provided it is a valid trust under applicable local law.

SEC. 3. SCOPE AND OBJECTIVE

Section 4 of Rev. Proc. 89–20, 1989–1 C.B. 841, provides a sample form of trust for an inter vivos charitable remainder unitrust providing for unitrust payments during one life that meets all of the applicable requirements of section 664(d)(2) of the Code. This revenue procedure amplifies Rev. Proc. 89–20 by providing the following additional sample forms of trust.

SEC. 4—Sample Inter Vivos Charitable Remainder Unitrust: Two lives, Consecutive Interests;

SEC. 5— Sample Inter Vivos Charitable Remainder Unitrust: Two Lives, Concurrent and Consecutive Interests;

SEC. 6—Sample Testamentary Charitable Remainder Unitrust: One Life;

SEC. 7—Sample Testamentary Charitable Remainder Unitrust: Two Lives, Consecutive Interests; and

SEC. 8—Sample Testamentary Charitable Remainder Unitrust: Two Lives, Concurrent and Consecutive Interests.

In all cases, the termination of the life interests must be followed by distribution of the trust assets to the charitable remainder beneficiary, and the trust must be a valid trust under applicable local law. If the trust provisions are substantially similar to those in one of the samples provided in sections 4 through 8 of this revenue procedure or in section 4 of Rev. Proc. 89–20, the Service will recognize the trust as satisfying all of the applicable requirements of section 664(d)(2) of the Code and the corresponding regulations. A document will be considered to be substantially similar to one of the samples even though, for example, the wording is varied to comport with local law and practice as necessary to create trusts, define legal relationships, pass property by bequest, provide for the appointment of alternative and successor trustees, or designate alternative charitable remaindermen. Moreover, for transfers to a qualifying charitable remainder unitrust, the remainder interest will be deductible under sections 170(f)(2)(A), 2055(e)(2)(A), and 2522(c)(2)(A) for income, estate, and gift tax purposes, respectively, if the charitable remainder beneficiary otherwise meets all of the requirements of those provisions. Therefore, it will not be necessary for a taxpayer to request a ruling on the qualification of a substantially similar trust. A trust that contains substantive provisions in addition to those provided by sections 4 through 8 of this revenue procedure or by section 4 of Rev. Proc. 89–20 (other than provisions necessary to establish a valid trust under applicable local law) or that omits any of these provisions will not necessarily be disqualified but neither will it be assured of qualification under the provisions of this revenue procedure.

SEC. 4. SAMPLE INTER VIVOS CHARITABLE REMAINDER UNITRUST: TWO LIVES, CONSECUTIVE INTERESTS

On this _____ day of _____ , 19 ___ , I, _____ (hereinafter referred to as "the Donor"), desiring to establish a charitable remainder unitrust, within the meaning of section 4 of Rev. Proc. 90–30 and section 664(d)(2) of the Internal Revenue Code (hereinafter referred to as "the Code") hereby create the _____ Charitable Remainder Unitrust and designate _____ as the initial Trustee. [ALTERNATE OR SUCCESSOR TRUSTEES MAY ALSO BE DESIGNATED IF DESIRED.]

1. FUNDING OF TRUST. The Donor transfers to the Trustee the property described in Schedule A, and the Trustee accepts such property and agrees to hold, manage, and distribute such property of the Trust under the terms set forth in this Trust instrument.

2. PAYMENT OF UNITRUST AMOUNT. In each taxable year of the Trust, the Trustee shall pay to [A LIVING INDIVIDUAL] during his or her lifetime, and after his or her death to [A LIVING INDIVIDUAL] (hereinafter referred to as "the Recipients"), for such time as he or she survives, a unitrust amount equal to [AT LEAST 5] percent of the net fair market value of the assets of the Trust valued as of the first day of each taxable year of the Trust (the "valuation date"). The unitrust amount shall be paid in equal quarterly amounts from income and, to the extent that income is not sufficient, from principal. Any income of the Trust for a taxable year in excess of the unitrust amount shall be added to principal. If for any year the net fair market value of the Trust assets is incorrectly determined, then within a reasonable period after the value is finally determined for federal tax purposes, the Trustee shall pay to the Recipients (in the case of an undervaluation) or receive from the Recipients (in the case of an overvaluation) an amount equal to the difference between the unitrust amount properly payable and the unitrust amount actually paid.

3. PAYMENT OF FEDERAL ESTATE TAXES AND STATE DEATH TAXES. The lifetime unitrust interest of the second Recipient will take effect upon the death of the first Recipient only if the second Recipient furnishes the funds for payment of any federal estate taxes or state death taxes for which the Trustee may be liable upon the death of the first Recipient. [THIS PROVISION IS MANDATORY ONLY IF ALL OR A PORTION OF THE TRUST MAY BE SUBJECT TO SUCH TAXES ON THE DEATH OF THE FIRST RECIPIENT.]

4. PRORATION OF THE UNITRUST AMOUNT. In determining the unitrust amount, the Trustee shall prorate the same on a daily basis for a short taxable year and for the taxable year ending with the survivor Recipient's death.

5. DISTRIBUTION TO CHARITY. Upon the death of the survivor Recipient, the Trustee shall distribute all of the then principal and income of the Trust (other than any amount due either of the Recipients or their estates under the provisions above) to _____ (hereinafter referred to as "the Charitable Organization"). If the Charitable Organization is not an organization described in sections 170(c), 2055(a), and 2522(a) of the Code at the time when any principal or income of the Trust is to be distributed to it, then the Trustee shall distribute such principal or income to such one or more organizations described in sections 170(c), 2055(a), and 2522(a) as the Trustee shall select in its sole discretion.

163

6. ADDITIONAL CONTRIBUTIONS. If any additional contributions are made to the Trust after the initial contribution, the unitrust amount for the year in which the additional contribution is made shall be [THE SAME PERCENTAGE AS IN PARAGRAPH 2] percent of the sum of (a) the net fair market value of the Trust assets as of the valuation date (excluding the assets so added and any income from, or appreciation on, such assets) and (b) that proportion of the fair market value of the assets so added that was excluded under (a) that the number of days in the period that begins with the date of contribution and ends with the earlier of the last day of the taxable year or the date of death of the survivor Recipient bears to the number of days in the period that begins on the first day of such taxable year and ends with the earlier of the last day in such taxable year or the date of death of the survivor Recipient. In the case where there is no valuation date after the time of contribution, the assets so added shall be valued as of the time of contribution.

7. PROHIBITED TRANSACTIONS. The Trustee shall make distributions at such time and in such manner as not to subject the Trust to tax under section 4942 of the Code. Except for the payment of the unitrust amount to the Recipients, the Trustee shall not engage in any act of self-dealing, as defined in section 4941(d), and shall not make any taxable expenditures, as defined in section 4945(d). The Trustee shall not make any investments that jeopardize the charitable purpose of the Trust, within the meaning of section 4944 and the regulations thereunder, or retain any excess business holdings, within the meaning of section 4943(c).

8. TAXABLE YEAR. The taxable year of the Trust shall be the calendar year.

9. GOVERNING LAW. The operation of the Trust shall be governed by the laws of the State of _____ . The Trustee, however, is prohibited from exercising any power or discretion granted under said laws that would be inconsistent with the qualification of the Trust under section 664(d)(2) of the Code and the corresponding regulations.

10. LIMITED POWER OF AMENDMENT. The Trust is irrevocable. The Trustee, however, shall have the power, acting alone, to amend the Trust in any manner required for the sole purpose of ensuring that the Trust qualifies and continues to qualify as a charitable remainder unitrust within the meaning of section 664(d)(2) of the Code.

11. INVESTMENT OF TRUST ASSETS. Nothing in this Trust instrument shall be construed to restrict the Trustee from investing the Trust assets in a manner that could result in the annual realization of a reasonable amount of income or gain from the sale or disposition of Trust assets.

SEC. 5. SAMPLE INTER VIVOS CHARITABLE REMAINDER UNITRUST: TWO LIVES CONCURRENT AND CONSECUTIVE INTEREST

On this _____ day of _____ , 19 ___ , I, _____ (hereinafter referred to as "the Donor"), desiring to establish a charitable remainder unitrust, within the meaning of section 5 of Rev. Proc. 90-30 and section 664(d)(2) of the Internal Revenue Code (hereinafter referred to as "the Code") hereby create the _____ Charitable Remainder Unitrust and designate _____ as the initial Trustee. [ALTERNATE OR SUCCESSOR TRUSTEES MAY ALSO BE DESIGNATED IF DESIRED.]

1. FUNDING OF TRUST. The Donor transfers to the Trustee the property described in Schedule A, and the Trustee accepts such property and agrees to hold, manage, and distribute such property of the Trust under the terms set forth in this Trust instrument.

2. PAYMENT OF UNITRUST AMOUNT. In each taxable year of the Trust, the trustee shall pay to [A LIVING INDIVIDUAL and [A LIVING INDIVIDUAL] (hereinafter referred to as "the Recipients"), in equal shares during their lifetimes, a unitrust amount equal to [AT LEAST 5] percent of the net fair market value of the assets of the Trust valued as of the first day of each taxable year of the Trust (the "valuation date"). Upon the death of the first of the Recipients to die, the survivor Recipient shall be entitled to receive the entire unitrust amount. The unitrust amount shall be paid in equal quarterly amounts from income and, to the extent that income is not sufficient, from principal. Any income of the Trust for a taxable year in excess of the unitrust amount shall be added to principal. If for any year the net fair market value of the Trust assets is incorrectly

determined, then within a reasonable period after the value is finally determined for federal tax purposes, the Trustee shall pay to the Recipients (in the case of an undervaluation) or receive from the Recipients (in the case of an overvaluation) an amount equal to the difference between the unitrust amount properly payable and the unitrust amount actually paid.

3. PAYMENT OF FEDERAL ESTATE TAXES AND STATE DEATH TAXES. The lifetime unitrust interest of the survivor Recipient will continue in effect upon the death of the first Recipient to die only if the survivor Recipient furnishes the funds for payment of any federal estate taxes or state death taxes for which the Trustee may be liable upon the death of the first Recipient to die. [THIS PROVISION IS MANDATORY ONLY IF ALL OR A PORTION OF THE TRUST MAY BE SUBJECT TO SUCH TAXES ON THE DEATH OF THE FIRST RECIPIENT TO DIE.]

4. PRORATION OF THE UNITRUST AMOUNT. In determining the unitrust amount, the Trustee shall prorate the same on a daily basis for a short taxable year and for the taxable year ending with the survivor Recipient's death.

5. DISTRIBUTION TO CHARITY. Upon the death of the survivor Recipient, the Trustee shall distribute all of the then principal and income of the Trust (other than any amount due either of the Recipients or their estates under the provisions above) to _____ (hereinafter referred to as "the Charitable Organization"). If the Charitable Organization is not an organization described in sections 170(c), 2055(a), and 2522(a) of the Code at the time when any principal or income of the Trust is to be distributed to it, then the Trustee shall distribute such principal or income to such one or more organizations described in sections 170(c), 2055(a), and 2522(a) as the Trustee shall select in its sole discretion.

6. ADDITIONAL CONTRIBUTIONS. If any additional contributions are made to the Trust after the initial contribution, the unitrust amount for the year in which the additional contribution is made shall be [THE SAME PERCENTAGE AS IN PARAGRAPH 2] percent of the sum of (a) the net fair market value of the Trust assets as of the valuation date (excluding the assets so added and any income from, or appreciation on, such assets) and (b) that proportion of the fair market value of the assets so added that was excluded under (a) that the number of days in the period that begins with the date of contribution and ends with the earlier of the last day of the taxable year or the date of death of the survivor Recipient bears to the number of days in the period that begins on the first day of such taxable year and end with the earlier of the last day in such taxable year on the date of death of the survivor Recipient. In the case where there is no valuation date after the time of contribution, the assets so added shall be valued as of the time of contribution.

7. ROHIBITED TRANSACTIONS. The Trustee shall make distributions at such time and in such manner as not to subject the Trust to tax under section 4942 of the Code. Except for the payment of the unitrust amount to the Recipients, the Trustee shall not engage in any act of self-dealing, as defined in section 4941(d), and shall not make any taxable expenditures, as defined in section 4945(d). The Trustee shall not make any investments that jeopardize the charitable purpose of the Trust, within the meaning of section 4944 and the regulations thereunder, or retain any excess business holdings, within the meaning of section 4943(c).

8. TAXABLE YEAR. The taxable year of the Trust shall be the calendar year.

9. GOVERNING LAW. The operation of the Trust shall be governed by the laws of the State of _____ . The Trustee, however, is prohibited from exercising any power or discretion granted under said laws that would be inconsistent with the qualification of the Trust under section 664(d)(2) of the Code and the corresponding regulations.

10. LIMITED POWER OF AMENDMENT. The Trust is irrevocable. The Trustee, however, shall have the power, acting alone, amend the Trust in any manner required for the sole purpose of ensuring that the Trust qualifies and continues to qualify as a charitable remainder unitrust within the meaning of section 664(d)(2) of the Code.

11. INVESTMENT OF TRUST ASSETS. Nothing in this Trust instrument shall be construed to restrict the Trustee from investing the Trust assets in a manner that could result in the annual realization of a reasonable amount of income or gain from the sale or disposition of Trust assets.

SEC. 6. SAMPLE TESTAMENTARY CHARITABLE REMAINDER UNITRUST: ONE LIFE

All the rest, residue, and remainder of my property and estate, real and personal, of whatever nature and wherever situated, [ALTERNATIVELY, IF NOT A RESIDUARY BEQUEST, DESCRIBE OR IDENTIFY THE BEQUEST] I give, devise, and bequeath to my Trustee in trust. It being my intention to establish a charitable remainder unitrust within the meaning of section 6 of Rev. Proc. 90-30 and section 664(d)(2) of the Internal Revenue Code (hereinafter referred to as "the Code"), such Trust shall be known as the _____ Charitable Remainder Unitrust and I hereby designate _____ as the initial Trustee. [ALTERNATE OR SUCCESSOR TRUSTEES MAY ALSO BE DESIGNATED IF DESIRES.]

1. PAYMENT OF UNITRUST AMOUNT. In each taxable year of the Trust, the Trustee shall pay to [a living individual] (hereinafter referred to as "the Recipient") during the Recipient's life a unitrust amount equal to [AT LEAST 5] percent of the net fair market value of the assets of the Trust valued as of the first day of each taxable year of the Trust (the "valuation date"). The unitrust amount shall be paid in equal quarterly amounts from income and, to the extent that income is not sufficient, from principal. Any income of the Trust for a taxable year in excess of the unitrust amount shall be added to principal. If for any year the net fair market value of the Trust assets is incorrectly determined, then within a reasonable period after the value is finally determined for federal tax purposes, the Trustee shall pay to the Recipient (in the case of an undervaluation) or receive from the Recipient (in the case of an overvaluation) an amount equal to the difference between the unitrust amount properly payable and the unitrust amount actually paid.

2. DEFERRAL PROVISION. The obligation to pay the unitrust amount shall commence with the date of my death, but payment of the unitrust amount may be deferred from such date until the end of the taxable year of the Trust in which occurs the complete funding of the Trust. Within a reasonable time after the end of the taxable year in which the complete funding of the Trust occurs, the Trustee must pay to the Recipient (in the case of an underpayment) or receive from the Recipient (in the case of an overpayment) the difference between: (1) any unitrust amounts actually paid, plus interest, compounded annually, computed for any period at the rate of interest that the federal income tax regulations under section 664 of the Code prescribe for the Trust for such computation for such period; and (2) the unitrust amounts payable, plus interest, compounded annually, computed for any period at the rate of interest that the federal income tax regulations under section 664 prescribe for the Trust for such computation for such period.

3. PRORATION OF THE UNITRUST AMOUNT. In determining the unitrust amount, the Trustee shall prorate the same on a daily basis for a short taxable year and for the taxable year ending with the Recipient's death.

4. DISTRIBUTION TO CHARITY. Upon the death of the Recipient, the Trustee shall distribute all of the then principal and income the the Trust (other than any amount due the Recipient or the Recipient's estate under the provisions above) to _____ (hereinafter referred to as "the Charitable Organization"). If the Charitable Organization is not an organization described in sections 170(c) and 2055(a) of the Code at the time when any principal or income of the Trust is to be distributed to it, then the Trustee shall distribute such principal or income to such one or more organizations described in sections 170(c) and 2055(a) as the Trustee shall select in its sole discretion.

5. ADDITIONAL CONTRIBUTIONS. No additional contributions shall be made to the Trust after the initial contribution. The initial contribution, however, shall consist of all property passing to the Trust by reason of my death.

6. PROHIBITED TRANSACTIONS. The Trustee shall make distributions at such time and in such manner as not to subject the Trust to tax under section 4942 of the Code. Except for the payment of the unitrust amount to the Recipient, the Trustee shall not engage in any act of self-dealing, as defined in section 4941(d) and shall not make any taxable expenditures, as defined in section 4945(d). The Trustee shall not make any investments that jeopardize the charitable purpose of the Trust, within the meaning of section 4944 and the regulations thereunder, or retain any excess business holdings, within the meaning of section 4943(c).

7. TAXABLE YEAR. The taxable year of the Trust shall be the calendar year.

8. GOVERNING LAW. The operation of the Trust shall be governed by the laws of the State of _____. The Trustee, however, is prohibited from exercising any power or discretion granted under said laws that would be inconsistent with the qualification of the Trust under section 664(d)(2) of the Code and the corresponding regulations.

9. LIMITED POWER OF AMENDMENT. The Trustee shall have the power, acting alone, to amend the Trust in any manner required for the sole purpose of ensuring that the Trust qualifies and continues to qualify as a charitable remainder unitrust within the meaning of section 664(d)(2) of the Code.

10. INVESTMENT OF TRUST ASSETS. Nothing herein shall be construed to restrict the Trustee from ivnesting the Trust assets in a manner that could result in the annual realization of a reasonable amount of income or gain from the sale or disposition of Trust assets.

SEC. 7. SAMPLE TESTAMENTARY CHARITABLE REMAINDER UNITRUST: TWO LIVES, CONSECUTIVE INTERESTS

All the rest, residue, and remainder of my property and estate, real and personal, of whatever nature and wherever situated, [ALTERNATIVELY, IF NOT A RESIDUARY BEQUEST, DESCRIBE OR IDENTIFY THE BEQUEST] I give, devise, and bequeath to my Trustee in trust. It being my intention to establish a charitable remainder unitrust within the meaning of section 7 of Rev. Proc. 90-30 and section 664(d)(2) of the Internal Revenue Code (hereinafter referred to as "the Code"), such Trust shall be known as the _____ Charitable Remainder Unitrust and I hereby designate _____ as the initial Trustee. [ALTERNATE OR SUCCESSOR TRUSTEE MAY ALSO BE DESIGNATED IF DESIRED.]

1. PAYMENT OF UNITRUST AMOUNT. In each taxable year of the Trust, the Trustee shall pay to [a living individual] during his or her lifetime, and after his or her death to [a living individual] (hereinafter referred to as "the Recipients"), for such time as he or she survives, a unitrust amount equal to [AT LEAST 5] percent of the net fair market value of the assets of the Trust valued as of the first day of each taxable year of the Trust ("the valuation date"). The unitrust amount shall be paid in equal quarterly amounts from income and, to the extent that income is not sufficient, from principal. Any income of the Trust for a taxable year in excess of the unitrust amount shall be added to principal. If for any year the net fair market value of the Trust assets is incorrectly determined, then within a reasonable period after the value is finally determined for federal tax purposes, the Trustee shall pay to the Recipients (in the case of an undervaluation) or receive from the Recipients (in the case of an overvaluation) an amount equal to the difference between the unitrust amount properly payable and the unitrust amount actually paid.

2. DEFERRAL PROVISION. The obligation to pay the unitrust amount shall commence with the date of my death, but payment of the unitrust amount may be deferred from such date until the end of the taxable year of the Trust in which occurs the complete funding of the Trust. Within a reasonable time after the end of the taxable year in which the complete funding of the Trust occurs, the Trustee must pay to the Recipients (in the case of an underpayment) or receive from the Recipients (in the case of an overpayment) the difference between: (1) any unitrust amounts actually paid, plus interest, compounded annually, computed for any period at the rate of interest that the federal income tax regulations under section 664 of the Code prescribe for the Trust for such computation for such period, and (2) the unitrust amounts payable, plus interest, compounded annually, computed for any period at the rate of interest that the federal income tax regulations under section 664 prescribe for the Trust for such computation for such period.

3. PRORATION OF THE UNITRUST AMOUNT. In determining the unitrust amount, the Trustee shall prorate the same on a daily basis for a short taxable year and for the taxable year ending with the survivor Recipient's death.

4. DISTRIBUTION TO CHARITY. Upon the death of the survivor Recipient, the Trustee shall distribute all of the then principal and income of the Trust (other than any amount due either of the Recipients of their estates under the provisions above) to _____ (hereinafter referred to as "the Charitable Organization"). If the Charitable Organization is not an organization described in sections 170(c) and 2055(a) of the Code at the time when any principal or income of the Trust is to be distributed to it, then the Trustee shall distribute such principal or income to such one or more organizations described in sections 170(c) and 2055(a) as the Trustee shall select in its sole discretion.

5.   ADDITIONAL CONTRIBUTIONS. No additional contributions shall be made to the Trust after the initial contribution. The initial contribution, however, shall consist of all property passing to the Trust be reason of my death.

6.   PROHIBITED TRANSACTIONS. The Trustee shall make distributions at such time and in such manner as not to subject the Trust to tax under section 4942 of the Code. Except for the payment of the unitrust amount to the Recipient, the Trustee shall not engage in any act of self-dealing, as defined in section 4941(d), and shall not make any taxable expenditures, as defined in section 4945(d). The Trustee shall not make any investments that jeopardize the charitable purpose of the Trust, within the meaning of section 4944 and the regulations thereunder, or retain any excess business holdings, within the meaning of section 4943(c).

7.   TAXABLE YEAR. The taxable year of the Trust shall be the calendar year.

8.   GOVERNING LAW. The operation of the Trust shall be governed by the laws of the State of _____. The Trustee, however, is prohibited from exercising any power or discretion granted under said laws that would be inconsistent with the qualification of the Trust under section 664(d)(2) of the Code and the corresponding regulations.

9.   LIMITED POWER OF AMENDMENT. The Trustee shall have the power, acting alone, to amend the Trust in any manner required for the sole purpose of ensuring that the Trust qualifies and continues to qualify as a charitable remainder unitrust within the meaning of section 664(d)(2) of the Code.

10.   INVESTMENT OF TRUST ASSETS. Nothing herein shall be construed to restrict the Trustee from ivnesting the Trust assets in a manner that could result in the annual realization of a reasonable amount of income or gain from the sale or disposition of Trust assets.

SEC. 8. SAMPLE TESTAMENTARY CHARITABLE REMAINDER UNITRUST: TWO LIVES, CONCURRENT AND CONSECUTIVE INTERESTS

All the rest, residue, and remainder of my property and estate, real or personal, of whatever nature and wherever situated, [ALTERNATIVELY, IF NOT A RESIDUARY BEQUEST, DESCRIBE OR IDENTIFY THE BEQUEST] I give, devise, and bequeath to my Trustee in trust. It being my intention to establish a charitable remainder unitrust within the meaning of section 8 of Rev. Proc. 90-30 and section 664(d)(2) of the Internal Revenue Code (hereinafter referred to as "the Code"), such Trust shall be known as the _____ Charitable Remainder Unitrust and I hereby designate _____ as the initial Trustee. [ALTERNATE OR SUCCESSOR TRUSTEES MAY ALSO BE DESIGNATED IF DESIRED.]

1. PAYMENT OF UNITRUST AMOUNT. In each taxable year of the Trust, the Trustee shall pay to [a living individual] and [a living individual] (hereinafter referred to as "the Recipients"), in equal shares during their lifetimes, a unitrust amount equal to [AT LEAST 5] percent of the net fair market value of the assets of the Trust valued as of the first day of each taxable year of the Trust (the "valuation date"). Upon the death of the first of the Recipients to die, the survivor Recipient shall be entitled to receive the entire unitrust amount. The unitrust amount shall be paid in equal quarterly amounts from income and, to the extent that income is not sufficient, from principal. Any income of the Trust for a taxable year in excess of the unitrust amount shall be added to principal. If for any year the net fair market value of the Trust assets is incorrectly determined, then within a reasonable period after the value is finally determined for federal tax purposes, the Trustee shall pay to the Recipients (in the case of an undervaluation) or receive from the Recipients (in the case of an overvaluation) an amount equal to the difference between the unitrust amount properly payable and the unitrust amount actually paid.

2.   DEFERRAL PROVISION. The obligation to pay the unitrust amount shall commence with the date of my death, but payment of the unitrust amount may be deferred from such date until the end of the taxable year of the Trust in which occurs the complete funding of the Trust. Within a reasonable time after the end of the taxable year in which the complete funding of the Trust occurs, the Trustee must pay to the Recipients (in the case of an underpayment) or receive from the Recipients (in the case of an overpayment) the difference between: (1) any unitrust amounts actually paid, plus interest, compounded annually, computed for any period

at the rate of interest that the federal income tax regulations under section 664 of the Code prescribe for the Trust for such computation for such period; and (2) the unitrust amounts payable, plus interest, compounded annually, computed for any period at the rate of interest that the federal income tax regulations under section 664 prescribe for the Trust for such computation for such period.

3. PRORATION OF THE UNITRUST AMOUNT. In determining the unitrust amount, the Trustee shall prorate the same on a daily basis for a short taxable year and for the taxable year ending with the survivor Recipient's death.

4. DISTRIBUTION TO CHARITY. Upon the death of the survivor Recipient, the Trustee shall distribute all of the then principal and income of the Trust (other than any amount due either of the Recipients of their estates under the provisions above) to _____ (hereinafter referred to as "the Charitable Organization"). If the Charitable Organization is not an organization described in sections 170(c) and 2055(a) of the Code at the time when any principal or income of the Trust is to be distributed to it, then the Trustee shall distribute such principal or income to such one or more organizations described in sections 170(c) and 2055(a) as the Trustee shall select in its sole discretion.

5. ADDITIONAL CONTRIBUTIONS. No additional contributions shall be made to the Trust after the initial contribution. The initial contribution, however, shall consist of all property passing to the Trust be reason of my death.

6. PROHIBITED TRANSACTIONS. The Trustee shall make distributions at such time and in such manner as not to subject the Trust to tax under section 4942 of the Code. Except for the payment of the unitrust amount to the Recipient, the Trustee shall not engage in any act of self-dealing, as defined in section 4941(d), and shall not make any taxable expenditures, as defined in section 4945(d). The Trustee shall not make any investments that jeopardize the charitable purpose of the Trust, within the meaning of section 4944 and the regulations thereunder, or retain any excess business holdings, within the meaning of section 4943(c).

7. TAXABLE YEAR. The taxable year of the Trust shall be the calendar year.

8. GOVERNING LAW. The operation of the Trust shall be governed by the laws of the State of _____. The Trustee, however, is prohibited from exercising any power or discretion granted under said laws that would be inconsistent with the qualification of the Trust under section 664(d)(2) of the Code and the corresponding regulations.

9. LIMITED POWER OF AMENDMENT. The Trustee shall have the power, acting alone, to amend the Trust in any manner required for the sole purpose of ensuring that the Trust qualifies and continues to qualify as a charitable remainder unitrust within the meaning of section 664(d)(2) of the Code.

10. INVESTMENT OF TRUST ASSETS. Nothing herein shall be construed to restrict the Trustee from ivnesting the Trust assets in a manner that could result in the annual realization of a reasonable amount of income or gain from the sale of disposition of Trust assets.

SEC. 9. EFFECT ON OTHER REVENUE PROCEDURES

Rev. Proc. 89-20 is amplified.

SEC. 10. EFFECTIVE DATE

This revenue procedure is effective on and after June 18, 1990, the date of publication of this revenue procedure in the Internal Revenue Bulletin.

DRAFTING INFORMATION

The principal author of this revenue procedure is John McQuillan of the Office of Assistant Chief Counsel (Passthroughs and Special Industries). For further information regarding this revenue procedure, contact John McQuillan on (202) 377-6356 (not a toll-free call).

MODEL DOCUMENTS FOR
CHARITABLE REMAINDER UNITRUSTS

Revenue Procedures
Rev. Proc. 90-31
1990-1 C.B. 539

Reference:
Section 664—Charitable Remainder Trusts

SECTION 1. PURPOSE

This revenue procedure makes available six sample forms of trust that meet the requirements for a charitable remainder unitrust as described in section 664(d)(2) and (3) of the Internal Revenue Code.

SEC. 2. BACKGROUND

The Internal Revenue Service receives and responds to requests for rulings dealing with the qualification of trusts as charitable remainder trusts and the availability of deductions for contributions made to such trusts. In many of these requests, the trust instruments and charitable objectives are very similar. Consequently, in order to provide a service to taxpayers and to save the time and expense involved in requesting and processing a ruling on a proposed charitable remainder unitrust, this revenue procedure allows taxpayers who make transfers to a trust that substantially follows one of the sample forms of trust contained herein to be assured that the Service will recognize the trust as meeting all of the requirements of a charitable remainder unitrust, provided that the trust operates in a manner consistent with the terms of the instrument creating the trust and provided it is a valid trust under applicable local law.

SEC. 3. SCOPE AND OBJECTIVE

The sample forms of trust meet all of the applicable requirements of sections 664(d)(2) and (3) of the Code and include:

SEC. 4—Sample Inter Vivos Charitable Remainder Unitrust: One Life;

SEC. 5—Sample Inter Vivos Charitable Remainder Unitrust: Two Lives, Consecutive Interests;

SEC. 6—Sample Inter Vivos Charitable Remainder Unitrust: Two Lives, Concurrent and Consecutive Interests;

SEC. 7—Sample Testamentary Charitable Remainder Unitrust: One Life;

SEC. 8—Sample Testamentary Charitable Remainder Unitrust: Two Lives, Consecutive Interests; and

SEC. 9—Sample Testamentary Charitable Remainder Unitrust: Two Lives, Concurrent and Consecutive Interests.

In all cases, the termination of the life interests must be followed by a distribution of the trust assets to the charitable remainder beneficiary, and the trust must be a valid trust under applicable local law.

If the trust provisions are substantially similar to those in one of the samples provided in sections 4 through 9, the Service will recognize the trust as satisfying all of the applicable requirements of section 664(d)(2) and (3) of the Code and the corresponding regulations. A document will be considered to be substantially similar to one of the samples even though, for example, the wording is varied to comport with local law and practice as necessary to create trusts, define legal relationships, pass property by bequest, provide for the appointment of alternative and successor trustees, or designate alternative charitable remaindermen. Moreover, for transfers to a qualifying charitable remainder unitrust, the remainder interest will be deductible under sections 170(f)(2)(A), 2055(e)(2)(A), and 2522(c)(2)(A) for income, estate, and gift tax purposes, respectively, if the charitable remainder beneficiary otherwise meets all of the requirements of those provisions. Therefore, it will not be necessary for a taxpayer to request a ruling on the qualification of a substantially similar trust. A trust that contains substantive provisions in addition to those provided by sections 4 through 9 (other than provisions necessary to establish a valid trust under applicable local law) or that omits any of these provisions will not necessarily be disqualified, but it will not be assured of qualification under the provisions of this revenue procedure.

SEC. 4. SAMPLE INTER VIVOS CHARITABLE REMAINDER UNITRUST: ONE LIFE

On this __ day of_____ 19__ , I, _____ (hereinafter referred to as "the Donor"), desiring to establish a charitable remainder unitrust within the meaning of section 4 of Rev. Proc. 90- 31 and section 664(d)(2) and (3) of the Internal Revenue Code (hereinafter referred to as "the Code") hereby create the_____ Charitable Remainder Unitrust and designate _____ as the initial Trustee. [ALTERNATE OR SUCCESSOR TRUSTEES MAY ALSO BE DESIGNATED IF DESIRED.]

1. FUNDING OF TRUST. The Donor transfers to the Trustee the property described in Schedule A, and the Trustee accepts such property and agrees to hold, manage, and distribute such property of the Trust under the terms set forth in this Trust instrument.

2. PAYMENT OF UNITRUST AMOUNT. In each taxable year of the Trust, the Trustee shall pay to [A LIVING INDIVIDUAL] (hereinafter referred to as "the Recipient") during the Recipient's life a unitrust amount equal to the lesser of: (a) the Trust income for the taxable year, as defined in section 643(b) of the Code and the regulations thereunder, and (b) [AT LEAST 5] percent of the net fair market value of the assets of the Trust valued as of the first day of each taxable year of the Trust (the "valuation date"). The unitrust amount for any year shall also include any amount of Trust income for such year that is in excess of the amount required to be distributed under (b) (above) to the extent that the aggregate of the amounts paid in prior years was less than the aggregate of the amounts computed as [SAME PERCENTAGE AS IN (b) ABOVE] percent of the net fair market value of the Trust assets on the valuation dates.

   The unitrust amount shall be paid in quarterly installments. Any income of the Trust for a taxable year in excess of the unitrust amount shall be added to principal. If for any year the net fair market value of the Trust assets is incorrectly determined, then within a reasonable period after the value is finally determined for federal tax purposes, the Trustee shall pay to the Recipient (in the case of an undervaluation) or receive from the Recipient (in the case of an overvaluation) an amount equal to the difference between the unitrust amount properly payable and the unitrust amount actually paid.

3. PRORATION OF THE UNITRUST AMOUNT. In determining the unitrust amount, the Trustee shall prorate the same on a daily basis for a short taxable year and for the taxable year ending with the Recipient's death.

4. DISTRIBUTION TO CHARITY. Upon the death of the Recipient, the Trustee shall distribute all of the then principal and income of the Trust (other than any amount due the Recipient or the Recipient's estate under the provisions above) to _____ (hereinafter referred to as "the Charitable Organization"). If the Charitable Organization is not an organization described in sections 170(c), 2055(a), and 2522(a) of the Code at the time when any principal or income of the Trust is to be distributed to it, then the Trustee shall distribute such principal or income to such one or more organizations described in sections 170(c), 2055(a), and 2522(a) as the Trustee shall select in its sole discretion.

5. ADDITIONAL CONTRIBUTIONS. If any additional contributions are made to the Trust after the initial contribution, the unitrust amount for the year in which the additional contribution is made shall be equal to the lesser of (a) the Trust income for the taxable year, as defined in section 643(b) of the Code and the regulations thereunder, and (b) [THE SAME PERCENTAGE AS IN PARAGRAPH 2] percent of the sum of (1) the net fair market value of the Trust assets as of the valuation date (excluding the assets so added and any income from, or appreciation on, such assets) and (2) that proportion of the fair market value of the assets so added that was excluded under (1) that the number of days in the period that begins with the date of contribution and ends with the earlier of the last day of the taxable year or the day of the Recipient's death bears to the number of days in the period that begins on the first day of such taxable year and ends with the earlier of the last day in such taxable year or the day of the Recipient's death. In the case where there is no valuation date after the

time of contribution, the assets so added shall be valued as of the time of contribution. The unitrust amount for any such year shall also include any amount of Trust income for such year that is in excess of the amount required to be distributed under (b) above to the extent that the aggregate of the amounts paid in prior years was less than the aggregate of the amounts computed as [SAME PERCENTAGE AS IN (b) ABOVE] percent of the net fair market value of the Trust assets on the valuation dates.

6. PROHIBITED TRANSACTIONS. The Trustee shall make distributions at such time and in such manner as not to subject the Trust to tax under section 4942 of the Code. Except for the payment of the unitrust amount to the Recipient, the Trustee shall not engage in any act of self-dealing, as defined in section 4941(d), and shall not make any taxable expenditures, as defined in section 4945(d). The Trustee shall not make any investments that jeopardize the charitable purpose of the Trust, within the meaning of section 4944 and the regulations thereunder, or retain any excess business, holdings, within the meaning of section 4943(c).

7. TAXABLE YEAR. The taxable year of the Trust shall be the calendar year.

8. GOVERNING LAW. The operation of the Trust shall be governed by the laws of the State of _____. The Trustee, however, is prohibited from exercising any power or discretion granted under said laws that would be inconsistent with the qualification of the Trust under section 664(d)(2) and (3) of the Code and the corresponding regulations.

9. LIMITED POWER OF AMENDMENT. The Trust is irrevocable. The Trustee, however, shall have the power, acting alone, to amend the Trust in any manner required for the sole purpose of ensuring that the Trust qualifies and continues to qualify as a charitable remainder unitrust within the meaning of section 664(d)(2) and (3) of the Code.

10. INVESTMENT OF TRUST ASSETS. Nothing in this Trust instrument shall be construed to restrict the Trustee from investing the Trust assets in a manner that could result in the annual realization of a reasonable amount of income or gain from the sale or disposition of Trust assets.

SEC. 5. SAMPLE INTER VIVOS CHARITABLE REMAINDER UNITRUST: TWO LIVES, CONSECUTIVE INTEREST.

On this __ day of _____ 19__, I, _____ (hereinafter referred to as "the Donor"), desiring to establish a charitable remainder unitrust within the meaning of section 5 of Rev. Proc, 90- 31 and section 664(d)(2) and (3) of the Internal Revenue Code (hereinafter referred to as "the Code" hereby create the _____ Charitable Remainder Unitrust and designate _____ as the initial Trustee. [ALTERNATE OR SUCCESSOR TRUSTEES MAY ALSO BE DESIGNATED IF, DESIRED.]

1. FUNDING OF TRUST. The Donor transfers to the Trustee the property described in Schedule A, and the Trustee accepts such property and agrees to hold, manage, and distribute such property of the Trust under the terms set forth in this Trust instrument.

2. PAYMENT OF UNITRUST AMOUNT. In each taxable year of the Trust, the Trustee shall pay to [A LIVING INDIVIDUAL] during his or her lifetime, and after his or her death, to [A LIVING INDIVIDUAL] (hereinafter referred to as "the Recipients"), for such time as he or she survives, a unitrust amount equal to the lesser of: (a) the Trust income for the taxable year, as defined in section 643(b) of the Code and the regulations thereunder, and (b) [AT LEAST 5] percent of the net fair market value of the assets of the Trust valued as of the first day of each taxable year of the Trust (the "valuation date"). The unitrust amount for any year shall also include any amount of Trust income for such year that is in excess of the amount required to be distributed under (b) (above) to the extent that the aggregate of the amounts paid in prior years was less than the aggregate of the amounts computed as [SAME PERCENTAGE AS IN (b) ABOVE] percent of the net fair market value of the Trust assets on the valuation dates.

    The unitrust amount shall be paid in quarterly installments. Any income of the Trust for a taxable year in excess of the unitrust amount shall be added to principal. If for any year the net fair market value of the Trust assets is incorrectly determined, then within a reasonable period after the value is finally determined for federal tax purposes, the Trustee shall pay to the Recipients (in the case of an undervaluation) or receive from the Recipients (in the case of an overvaluation) an amount equal to the difference between the unitrust amount properly payable and the unitrust amount actually paid.

3. PAYMENT OF FEDERAL ESTATE TAXES AND STATE DEATH TAXES. The lifetime unitrust interest of the second Recipient will take effect upon the death of the first Recipient only if the second Recipient furnishes the funds for payment of any federal estate taxes or state death taxes for which the Trustee may be liable upon the death of the first Recipient. [THIS PROVISION IS MANDATORY ONLY II ALL OR A PORTION OF THE TRUST MAY BE SUBJECT TO SUCH TAXES ON THE DEATH OF THE FIRST RECIPIENT.]

4. PRORATION OF THE UNITRUST AMOUNT. In determining the unitrust amount, the Trustee shall prorate the same on a daily basis for a short taxable year and for the taxable year ending with the survivor Recipient's death.

5. DISTRIBUTION TO CHARITY. Upon the death of the survivor Recipient, the Trustee shall distribute all of the then principal and income of the Trust (other than any amount due either of the Recipients or their estates under the provisions above) to _____ (hereinafter referred to as "the Charitable Organization"). If the Charitable Organization is not an organization described in sections 170(c), 2055(a), and 2522(a) of the Code at the time when any principal or income of the Trust is to be distributed to it, then the Trustee shall distribute such principal or income to such one or more organizations described in sections 170(c), 2055(a), and 2522(a) as the Trustee shall select in its sole discretion.

6. ADDITIONAL CONTRIBUTIONS. If any additional contributions are made to the Trust after the initial contribution, the unitrust amount for the year in which the additional contribution is made shall be equal to the lesser of (a) the Trust income for the taxable year, as defined in section 643(b) of the Code and the regulations thereunder, and (b) [THE SAME PERCENTAGE AS IN PARAGRAPH 2] percent of the sum of (1) the net fair market value of the Trust assets as of the valuation date (excluding the assets so added and any income from, or appreciation on, such assets) and (2) that proportion of the fair market value of the assets so added that was excluded under (1) that the number of days in the period that begins with the date of contribution and ends with the earlier of the last day of the taxable year or the date of death of the survivor Recipient bears to the number of days in the period that begins on the first day of such taxable year and ends with the earlier of the last day in such taxable year or the date of death of the survivor Recipient. In the case where there is no valuation date after the time of contribution, the assets so added shall be valued as of the time of contribution. The unitrust amount for any such year shall also include any amount of Trust income for such year that is in excess of the amount required to be distributed under (b) above to the extent that the aggregate of the amounts paid in prior years was less than the aggregate of the amounts computed as [SAME PERCENTAGE AS IN (b) ABOVE] percent of the net fair market value of the Trust assets on the valuation dates.

7. PROHIBITED TRANSACTIONS. The Trustee shall make distributions at such time and in such manner as not to subject the Trust to tax under section 4942 of the Code. Except for the payment of the unitrust amount to the Recipients, the Trustee shall not engage in any act of self-dealing, as defined in section 4941(d), and shall not make any taxable expenditures, as defined in section 4945(d). The Trustee shall not make any investments that jeopardize the charitable purpose of the Trust, within the meaning of section 4944 and the regulations thereunder, or retain any excess business holdings, within the meaning of section 4943(c).

8. TAXABLE YEAR. The taxable year of the Trust shall be the calendar year.

9. GOVERNING LAW. The operation of the Trust shall be governed by the laws of the State of _____. The Trustee, however, is prohibited from exercising any power or discretion granted under said laws that would be inconsistent with the qualification of the Trust under section 664(d)(2) and (3) of the Code and the corresponding regulations.

10. LIMITED POWER OF AMENDMENT. The Trust is irrevocable. The Trustee, however, shall have the power, acting alone, to amend the Trust in any manner required for the sole purpose of ensuring that the Trust qualifies and continues to qualify is a charitable remainder unitrust within the meaning of section 664(d)(2) and (3) of the Code.

11. INVESTMENT OF TRUST ASSETS. Nothing in this Trust instrument shall be construed to restrict the Trustee from investing the Trust assets in a manner that could result in the annual realization of a reasonable amount of income or gain from the sale or disposition of Trust assets.

SEC. 6. SAMPLE INTER VIVOS CHARITABLE REMAINDER UNITRUST: TWO LIVES, CONCURRENT AND CONSECUTIVE INTERESTS

On this __ day of _____, 19__, I, _____ (hereinafter referred to as "the Donor"), desiring to establish a charitable remainder unitrust, within the meaning of section 6 of Rev. Proc. 90- 31 and section 664(d)(2) and (3) of the Internal Revenue Code (hereinafter referred to as "the Code") hereby create the _____ Charitable Remainder Unitrust and designate _____ as the initial Trustee. [Alternate or successor trustees may also be designated if desired.]

1. FUNDING OF TRUST. The Donor transfers to the Trustee the property described in Schedule A, and the Trustee accepts such property and agrees to hold, manage, and distribute such property of the Trust under the terms set forth in this Trust instrument.

2. PAYMENT OF UNITRUST AMOUNT. In each taxable year of the Trust, the Trustee shall pay to [A LIVING INDIVIDUAL] and [A LIVING INDIVIDUAL] (hereinafter referred to as "the Recipients") in equal shares during their lifetimes, a unitrust amount equal to the lesser of: (a) the Trust income for the taxable year, as defined in section 643(b) of the Code and the regulations thereunder, and (b) [at least 5] percent of the net fair market value of the assets of the Trust valued as of the first day of each taxable year of the Trust (the "valuation date"). The unitrust amount for any year shall also include any amount of Trust income for such year that is in excess of the amount required to be distributed under (b) (above) to the extent that the aggregate of the amounts paid in prior years was less than the aggregate of the amounts computed as [SAME PERCENTAGE AS IN (b) ABOVE] percent of the net fair market value of the Trust assets on the valuation dates.

Upon the death of the first of the Recipients to die, the survivor Recipient shall be entitled to receive the entire unitrust amount. The unitrust amount shall be paid in quarterly installments. Any income of the Trust for a taxable year in excess of the unitrust amount shall be added to principal. If for any year the net fair market value of the Trust assets is incorrectly determined, then within a reasonable period after the value is finally determined for federal tax purposes, the Trustee shall pay to the Recipients (in the case of an undervaluation) or receive from the Recipients (in the case of an overvaluation) an amount equal to the difference between the unitrust amount properly payable and the unitrust amount actually paid.

3. PAYMENT OF FEDERAL ESTATE TAXES AND STATE DEATH TAXES. The lifetime unitrust interest of the survivor Recipient will continue in effect upon the death of the first Recipient to die only if the survivor Recipient furnishes the funds for payment of any federal estate taxes or state death taxes for which the Trustee may be liable upon the death of the first Recipient to die. [THIS PROVISION IS MANDATORY ONLY IF ALL OR A PORTION OF THE TRUST MAY BE SUBJECT TO SUCH TAXES ON THE DEATH OF THE FIRST RECIPIENT TO DIE.]

4. PRORATION OF THE UNITRUST AMOUNT. In determining the unitrust amount, the Trustee shall prorate the same on a daily basis for a short taxable year and for the taxable year ending with the survivor's death.

5. DISTRIBUTION TO CHARITY. Upon the death of the survivor Recipient, the Trustee shall distribute all of the then principal and income of the Trust (other than any amount due either of the Recipients or their estates under the provisions above) to _____ (hereinafter referred to as "the Charitable Organization"). If the Charitable Organization is not an organization described in sections 170(c), 2055(a), and 2522(a) of the Code at the time when any principal or income of the Trust is to be distributed to it, then the Trustee shall distribute such principal or income to such one or more organizations described in sections 170(c), 2055(a), and 2522(a) as the Trustee shall select in its sole discretion.

6. ADDITIONAL CONTRIBUTIONS. If any additional contributions are made to the Trust after the initial contribution, the unitrust amount for the year in which the additional contribution is made shall be equal to the lesser of (a) the Trust income for the taxable year, as defined in section 643(b) of the Code and the regulations thereunder, and (b) [THE SAME PERCENTAGE AS IN PARAGRAPH 2] percent of the sum of (1) the net fair market value of the Trust assets as of the valuation date (excluding the assets so added and any income from, or appreciation on, such assets) and (2) that proportion of the fair market value of the assets so added that was excluded under (1) that the number of days in the period that begins with the date of contribution and ends with the earlier of the last day of the taxable year or the date of death of the survivor Recipient

bears to the number of days in the period that begins on the first day of such taxable year and ends with the earlier of the last day in such taxable year or the date of death of the survivor Recipient. In the case where there is no valuation date after the time of contribution, the assets so added shall be valued as of the time of contribution. The unitrust amount for any such year shall also include any amount of Trust income for such year that is in excess of the amount required to be distributed under (b) above to the extent that the aggregate of the amounts paid in prior years was less than the aggregate of the amounts computed as [SAME PERCENTAGE AS IN (b) ABOVE] percent of the net fair market value of the Trust assets on the valuation dates.

7. PROHIBITED TRANSACTIONS. The Trustee shall make distributions at such time and in such manner as not to subject the Trust to tax under section 4942 of the Code. Except for the payment of the unitrust amount to the Recipients, the Trustee shall by designate not engage in any act of self-dealing, as defined in section 4941(d), and shall not make any taxable expenditures, as defined in section 4945(d). The Trustee shall not make any investments that jeopardize the charitable purpose of the Trust, within the meaning of section 4944 and the regulations thereunder, or retain any excess business holdings, within the meaning of section 4943(c).

8. TAXABLE YEAR. The taxable year of the Trust shall be the calendar year.

9. GOVERNING LAW. The operation of the Trust shall be governed by the laws of the State of _____. The Trustee, however, is prohibited from exercising any power or discretion granted under said laws that would be inconsistent with the qualification of the Trust under section 664(d)(2) and (3) of the Code and the corresponding regulations.

10. LIMITED POWER OF AMENDMENT. The Trust is irrevocable. The Trustee, however, shall have the power, acting alone, to amend the Trust in any manner required for the sole purpose of ensuring that the Trust qualifies and continues to qualify as a charitable remainder unitrust within the meaning of section 664(d)(2) and (3) of the Code.

11. INVESTMENT OF TRUST ASSETS. Nothing in this Trust instrument shall be construed to restrict the Trustee from investing the Trust assets in a manner that could result in the annual realization of a reasonable amount of income or gain from the sale or disposition of Trust assets.

SEC. 7. SAMPLE TESTAMENTARY CHARITABLE REMAINDER UNITRUST: ONE LIFE

All the rest, residue, and remainder of my property and estate, real and personal, of whatever nature and wherever situated, [ALTERNATIVELY, IF NOT A RESIDUARY BEQUEST, DESCRIBE OR IDENTIFY THE BEQUEST.] I give, devise, and bequeath to my Trustee in trust. It being my intention to establish a charitable remainder unitrust within the meaning of section 7 of Rev. Proc. 90-31 and section 664(d)(2) and (3) of the Internal Revenue Code (hereinafter referred to as "the Code"), such Trust shall be known as the _____ Charitable Remainder Unitrust and I hereby designate _____ as the initial Trustee. [ALTERNATE OR SUCCESSOR TRUSTEES MAY ALSO BE DESIGNATED IF DESIRED.]

1. PAYMENT OF UNITRUST AMOUNT. In each taxable year of the Trust, the Trustee shall pay to [A LIVING INDIVIDUAL] (hereinafter referred to as "the Recipient") during the Recipient's life a unitrust amount equal to the lesser of: (a) the Trust income for the taxable year, as defined in section 643(b) of the Code and the regulations thereunder, and (b) [AT LEAST 5] percent of the net fair market value of the assets of the Trust valued as of the first day of each taxable year of the Trust (the "valuation date"). The unitrust amount for any year shall also include any amount of Trust income for such year that is in excess of the amount required to be distributed under (b) (above) to the extent that the aggregate of the amounts paid in prior years was less than the aggregate of the amounts computed as [SAME PERCENTAGE AS IN (b) ABOVE] percent of the net fair market value of the Trust assets on the valuation dates.

The unitrust amount shall be paid in quarterly installments. Any income of the Trust for a taxable year in excess of the unitrust amount shall be added to principal. If for any year the net fair market value of the Trust assets is incorrectly determined, then within a reasonable period after the value is finally determined for federal tax purposes, the Trustee shall pay to the Recipient (in the case of an undervaluation) or receive from the Recipient (in the case of an overvaluation) an amount equal to the difference between the unitrust amount properly payable and the unitrust amount actually paid.

2. DEFERRAL PROVISION. The obligation to pay the unitrust amount shall commence with the date of my death, but payment of the unitrust amount may be deferred from such date until the end of the taxable year of the Trust in which occurs the complete funding of the Trust. Within a reasonable time after the end of the taxable year in which the complete funding of the Trust occurs, the Trustee must pay to the Recipient (in the case of an underpayment) or receive from the Recipient (in the case of an overpayment) the difference between: (1) any unitrust amounts actually paid, plus interest compounded annually, computed for any period at the rate of interest that the federal income tax regulations under section 664 of the Code prescribe for the Trust for such computation for such period: and (2) the unitrust amounts payable, plus interest compounded annually, computed for any period at the rate of interest that the federal income tax regulations under section 664 prescribe for the Trust for such computation for such period.

3. PRORATION OF THE UNITRUST AMOUNT. In determining the unitrust amount, the Trustee shall prorate the same on a daily basis for a short taxable year and for the taxable year ending with the Recipient's death.

4. DISTRIBUTION TO CHARITY. Upon the death of the Recipient, the Trustee shall distribute all of the then principal and income of the Trust (other than any amount due the Recipient or the Recipient's estate under the provisions above) to _____ (hereinafter referred to as "the Charitable Organization"). If the Charitable Organization is not an organization described in sections 170(c) and 2055(a) of the Code at the time when any principal or income of the Trust is to be distributed to it, then the Trustee shall distribute such principal or income to such one or more organizations described in sections 170(c) and 2055(a) as the Trustee shall select in its sole discretion.

5. ADDITIONAL CONTRIBUTIONS. No additional contributions shall be made to the Trust after the initial contribution. The initial contribution, however, shall be deemed to consist of all property passing to the Trust by reason of my death.

6. PROHIBITED TRANSACTIONS. The Trustee shall make distributions at such time and in such manner as not to subject the Trust to tax under section 4942 of the Code. Except for the payment of the unitrust amount to the Recipient, the Trustee shall not engage in any act of self-dealing, as defined in section 4941(d), and shall not make any taxable expenditures, as defined in section 4945(d). The Trustee shall not make any investments that jeopardize the charitable purpose of the Trust, within the meaning of section 4944 and the regulations thereunder, or retain any excess business holdings, within the meaning of section 4943(c).

7. TAXABLE YEAR. The taxable year of the Trust shall be the calendar year.

8. GOVERNING LAW. The operation of the Trust shall be governed by the laws of the State of _____. The Trustee, however, is prohibited from exercising any power or discretion granted under said laws that would be inconsistent with the qualification of the Trust under section 664(d)(2) and (3) of the Code and the corresponding regulations.

9. LIMITED POWER OF AMENDMENT. The Trustee shall have the power, acting alone, to amend the Trust in any manner required for the sole purpose of ensuring that the Trust qualifies and continues to qualify as a charitable remainder unitrust within the meaning of section 664(d)(2) and (3) of the Code.

10. INVESTMENT OF TRUST ASSETS. Nothing herein shall be construed to restrict the Trustee from investing the Trust assets in a manner that could result in the annual realization of a reasonable amount of income or gain from the sale or disposition of Trust assets.

SEC. 8. SAMPLE TESTAMENTARY CHARITABLE REMAINDER UNITRUST: TWO LIVES, CONSECUTIVE INTERESTS

All the rest, residue, and remainder of my property and estate, real and personal, of whatever nature and wherever situated, [ALTERNATIVELY, IF NOT A RESIDUARY BEQUEST, DESCRIBE OR IDENTIFY THE BEQUEST.] I give, devise, and bequeath to my Trustee in trust. It being my intention to establish a charitable remainder unitrust within the meaning of section 8 of Rev. Proc. 90-31 and section 664(d)(2) and (3) of the Internal Revenue Code (hereinafter referred to as "the Code"), such Trust shall be known as the _____ Charitable Remainder Unitrust and I hereby designate _____ as the initial Trustee. [Alternate or successor trustees may also be designated if desired.]

176

1. PAYMENT OF UNITRUST AMOUNT. In each taxable year of the Trust, the Trustee shall pay to [A LIVING INDIVIDUAL] during his or her lifetime, and after his or her death, to [A LIVING INDIVIDUAL] (hereinafter referred to as "the Recipients"), for such time as he or she survives, a unitrust amount equal to the lesser of: (a) the Trust income for the taxable year, as defined in section 643(b) of the Code and the regulations thereunder, and (b) [AT LEAST 5] percent of the net fair market value of the assets of the Trust valued as of the first day of each taxable year of the Trust (the "valuation date"). The unitrust amount for any year shall also include any amount of Trust income for such year that is in excess of the amount required to be distributed under (b) (above) to the extent that the aggregate of the amounts paid in prior years was less than the aggregate of the amounts computed as [SAME PERCENTAGE AS IN (b) ABOVE] percent of the net fair market value of the Trust assets on the valuation dates.

   The unitrust amount shall be paid in quarterly installments. Any income of the Trust for a taxable year in excess of the unitrust amount shall be added to principal. If for any year the net fair market value of the Trust assets is incorrectly determined, then within a reasonable period after the value is finally determined for federal tax purposes, the Trustee shall pay to the Recipients (in the case of an undervaluation) or receive from the Recipients (in the case of an overvaluation) an amount equal to the difference between the unitrust amount properly payable and the unitrust amount actually paid.

2. DEFERRAL PROVISION. The obligation to pay the unitrust amount shall commence with the date of my death, but payment of the unitrust amount may be deferred from such date until the end of the taxable year of the Trust in which occurs the complete funding of the Trust. Within a reasonable time after the end of the taxable year in which the complete funding of the Trust occurs, the Trustee must pay to the Recipients (in the case of an underpayment) or receive from the Recipients (in the case of an overpayment) the difference between: (1) any unitrust amounts actually paid, plus interest compounded annually, computed for any period at the rate of interest that the federal income tax regulations under section 664 of Code prescribe for the trust for such computation for such period; and (2) the unitrust amounts payable, plus interest compounded annually, computed for any period at the rate of interest that the federal income tax regulations under section 664 of Code prescribe for the Trust for such computation for such period.

3. PRORATION OF THE UNITRUST AMOUNT. In determining the unitrust amount, the Trustee shall prorate the same on a daily basis for a short taxable year and for the taxable year ending with the survivor Recipient's death.

4. Distribution to Charity. Upon the death of the survivor Recipient, the Trustee shall distribute all of the then principal and income of the Trust (other than any amount due either of the Recipients or their estates under the provisions above) to _____ (hereinafter referred to as "the Charitable Organization"). If the Charitable Organization is not an organization described in sections 170(c) and 2055(a) of the Code at the time when any principal or income of the Trust is to be distributed to it, then the Trustee shall distribute such principal or income to such one or more organizations described in sections 170(c) and 2055(a) as the Trustee shall select in its sole discretion.

5. ADDITIONAL CONTRIBUTIONS. No additional contributions shall be made to the Trust after the initial contribution. The initial contribution, however, shall be deemed to consist of all property passing to the Trust by reason of my death.

6. PROHIBITED TRANSACTIONS. The Trustee shall make distributions at such time and in such manner as not to subject the Trust to tax under section 4942 of the Code. Except for the payment of the unitrust amount to the Recipients, the Trustee shall not engage in any act of self-dealing, as defined in section 4941(d), and shall not make any taxable expenditures, as defined in section 4945(d). The Trustee shall not make any investments that jeopardize the charitable purpose of the Trust, within the meaning of section 4944 and the regulations thereunder, or retain any excess business holdings, within the meaning of section 4943(c).

7. TAXABLE YEAR. The taxable year of the Trust shall be the calendar year.

8. GOVERNING LAW. The operation of the Trust shall be governed by the laws of the State of _____. The Trustee, however, is prohibited from exercising any power or discretion granted under said laws that would be inconsistent with the qualification of the Trust under section 664(d)(2) and (3) of the Code and the corresponding regulations.

9. LIMITED POWER OF AMENDMENT. The Trustee shall have the power, acting alone, to amend the Trust in any manner required for the sole purpose of ensuring that the Trust qualifies and continues to qualify as a charitable remainder unitrust within the meaning of section 664(d)(2) and (3) of the Code.

10. INVESTMENT OF TRUST ASSETS. Nothing herein shall be construed to restrict the Trustee from investing the Trust assets in a manner that could result in the annual realization of a reasonable amount of income or gain from the sale or disposition of Trust assets.

SEC. 9. SAMPLE TESTAMENTARY CHARITABLE REMAINDER UNITRUST: TWO LIVES, CONCURRENT AND CONSECUTIVE INTERESTS

All the rest, residue, and remainder of my property and estate, real and personal, of whatever nature and wherever situated, [ALTERNATIVELY, IF NOT A RESIDUARY BEQUEST, DESCRIBE OR IDENTIFY THE BEQUEST.] I give, devise, and bequeath to my Trustee in trust. It being my intention to establish a charitable remainder unitrust within the meaning of section 9 of Rev. Proc. 90-31 and section 664(d)(2) and (3) of the Internal Revenue Code (hereinafter referred to as "the Code"), such Trust shall be known as the _____ Charitable Remainder Unitrust and I hereby designate _____ as the initial Trustee. [ALTERNATE OR SUCCESSOR TRUSTEE MAY ALSO BE DESIGNATED IF DESIRED.]

1. PAYMENT OF UNITRUST AMOUNT. In each taxable year of the Trust, the Trustee shall pay to [A LIVING INDIVIDUAL] AND [A LIVING INDIVIDUAL] (hereinafter referred to as "the Recipients"), in equal shares during their lifetimes, a unitrust amount equal to the lesser of: (a) the Trust income for the taxable year, as defined in section 643(b) of the Code and the regulations thereunder, and (b) [AT LEAST 5] percent of the net fair market value of the assets of the Trust valued as of the first day of each taxable year of the Trust ("the valuation date"). The unitrust amount for any year shall also include any amount of Trust income for such year that is in excess of the amount required to be distributed under (b) (above) to the extent that the aggregate of the amounts paid in prior years was less than the aggregate of the amounts computed as [SAME PERCENTAGE AS IN (B) ABOVE] percent of the net fair market value of the trust assets on the valuation dates.

Upon the death of the first of the Recipients to die, the survivor Recipient shall be entitled to receive the entire unitrust amount. The unitrust amount shall be paid in quarterly installments. Any income of the Trust for a taxable year in excess of the unitrust amount and which is not paid pursuant to the second preceding sentence shall be added to principal. If for any year the net fair market value of the Trust assets is incorrectly determined, then within a reasonable period after the value is finally determined for federal tax purposes, the Trustee shall pay to the Recipients (in the case of an undervaluation) or receive from the Recipients (in the case of an overvaluation) an amount equal to the difference between the unitrust amount properly payable and the unitrust amount actually paid.

2. DEFERRAL PROVISION. The obligation to pay the unitrust amount shall commence with the date of my death, but payment of the unitrust amount may be deferred from such date until the end of the taxable year of the Trust in which occurs the complete funding of the Trust. Within a reasonable time after the end of the taxable year in which the complete funding of the Trust occurs, the Trustee must pay to the Recipients (in the case of an underpayment) or receive from the Recipient (in the case of an overpayment) the difference between: (1) any unitrust amounts actually paid, plus interest compounded annually, computed for any period at the rate of interest that the federal income tax regulations under section 664 of the Code prescribe for the Trust for such computation for such period: and (2) the unitrust amounts payable, plus interest compounded annually, computed for any period at the rate of interest that the federal income tax regulations under section 664 of the Code prescribe for the Trust for such computation for such period.

3. PRORATION OF THE UNITRUST AMOUNT. In determining the unitrust amount, the Trustee shall prorate the same on a daily basis for a short taxable year and for the taxable year ending with the survivor Recipient's death.

4. DISTRIBUTION TO CHARITY. Upon the death of the survivor Recipient, the Trustee shall distribute all of the then principal and income of the Trust (other than any amount due either of the Recipients of their

estates under the provisions above) to _____ (hereinafter referred to as "the Charitable Organization"). If the Charitable Organization is not an organization described in sections 170(c) and 2055(a) of the Code at the time when any principal or income of the Trust is to be distributed to it, then the Trustee shall distribute such principal or income to such one or more organizations described in sections 170(c) and 2055(a) as the Trustee shall select in its sole discretion.

5.   ADDITIONAL CONTRIBUTIONS. No additional contributions shall be made to the Trust after the initial contribution. The initial contribution, however, shall be deemed to consist of all property passing to the Trust by reason of my death.

6.   PROHIBITED TRANSACTIONS. The Trustee shall make distributions at such time and in such manner as not to subject the Trust to tax under section 4942 of the Code. Except for the payment of the unitrust amount to the Recipients, the Trustee shall not engage in any act of self-dealing, as defined in section 4941(d), and shall not make any taxable expenditures, as defined in section 4945(d). The Trustee shall not make any investments that jeopardize the charitable purpose of the Trust, within the meaning of section 4944 and the regulations thereunder, or retain any excess business holdings, within the meaning of section 4943(c).

7.   TAXABLE YEAR. The taxable year of the Trust shall be the calendar year.

8.   GOVERNING LAW. The operation of the Trust shall be governed by the laws of the State of _____. The Trustee, however, is prohibited from exercising any power or discretion granted under said laws that would be inconsistent with the qualification of the Trust under section 664(d)(2) of the Code and the corresponding regulations.

9.   LIMITED POWER OF AMENDMENT. The Trustee shall have the power, acting alone, to amend the Trust in any manner required for the sole purpose of ensuring that the Trust qualifies and continues to qualify as a charitable remainder unitrust within the meaning of section 664(d)(2) and (3) of the Code.

10. INVESTMENT OF TRUST ASSETS. Nothing herein shall be construed to restrict the Trustee from investing the Trust assets in a manner that could result in the annual realization of a reasonable amount of income or gain from the sale of disposition of Trust assets.

SEC. 10. EFFECTIVE DATE

This revenue procedure is effective on and after June 18, 1990, the date of publication of this revenue procedure in the Internal Revenue Bulletin.

DRAFTING INFORMATION

The principal author of this revenue procedure is John McQuillan of the Office of Assistant Chief Council (Passthroughs and Special Industries). For further information regarding this revenue procedure, contact John McQuillan on (202) 377-6356 (not a toll-free call).

MODEL DOCUMENTS FOR
CHARITABLE REMAINDER ANNUITY TRUSTS

Revenue Procedures
Rev. Proc. 90–32
1990–1 C.B. 546

Reference:
Section 664—Charitable Remainder Trusts

Effect on Other Documents:
Superseded by Rev. Proc. 2003-56, 3003-31 IRB 242; Rev. Proc. 2003-57, 2003-31 IRB 257; Rev. Proc. 2003-59, 2003-31 IRB 268; and Rev. Proc. 2003-60, 2003-31 IRB 274.
Amplifies Rev. Proc. 89–21

SECTION 1. PURPOSE

This revenue procedure makes available five sample forms of trust that meet the requirements for a charitable remainder annuity trust as described in section 664(d)(1) of the Internal Revenue Code.

SEC. 2. BACKGROUND

The Internal Revenue Service receives and responds to requests for rulings dealing with the qualification of trusts as charitable remainder trusts and the availability of deductions for contributions made to such trusts. In many of these requests, the trust instruments and charitable objectives are very similar. Consequently, in order to provide a service to taxpayers and to save the time and expense involved in requesting and processing a ruling on a proposed charitable remainder annuity trust, this revenue procedure allows taxpayers who make transfers to a trust that substantially follows one of the sample forms of trust contained herein to be assured that the Service will recognize the trust as meeting all of the requirements of a charitable remainder annuity trust, provided that the trust operates in a manner consistent with the terms of the instrument creating the trust and provided it is a valid trust under applicable local law.

SEC. 3. SCOPE AND OBJECTIVE

Section 4 of Rev. Proc. 89-21, 1989-1 C.B. 842, provides a sample form of trust for an inter vivos charitable remainder annuity trust providing for annuity payments during one life that meets all of the applicable requirements of section 664(d)(1) of the Code. This revenue procedure amplifies Rev. proc. 89-21 by providing the following additional sample forms of trust.

SEC. 4—Sample Inter Vivos Charitable Remainder Annuity Trust: Two Lives, Consecutive Interests;

SEC. 5—Sample Inter Vivos Charitable Remainder Annuity Trust: Two Lives, Concurrent and Consecutive interests;

SEC. 6—Sample Testamentary Charitable Remainder Annuity Trust: One Life;

SEC. 7—Sample Testamentary Charitable Remainder Annuity Trust: Two Lives, Consecutive Interests; and

SEC. 8—Sample Testamentary Charitable Remainder Annuity Trust: Two Lives, Concurrent and Consecutive Interests.

In all cases, the termination of the life interests must be followed by a distribution of the trust assets to the charitable remainder beneficiary, and the trust must be a valid trust under applicable local law.

If the trust provisions are substantially similar to those in one of the samples provided in sections 4 through 8 of this revenue procedure or in section 4 of Rev. Proc. 89–21, the Service will recognize the trust as satisfying all of the applicable requirements of section 664(d)(1) of the Code and the corresponding regulations. A document will be considered to be substantially similar to one of the samples even though, for example, the wording is varied to comport with local law and practice as necessary to create trusts, define legal relationships, pass property by bequest, provide for the appointment of alternative and successor trustees, or designate alternative charitable remaindermen. Moreover, for transfers to a qualifying charitable remainder annuity trust, the remainder interest will be deductible under sections 170(f)(2)(A), 2055(e)(2)(A), and 2522(c)(2)(A) for income, estate, and gift tax purposes, respectively, if the charitable remainder beneficiary otherwise meets all of the requirements of those provisions. Therefore, it will not be necessary for a taxpayer to request a ruling on the qualification of a substantially similar trust. A trust that contains substantive provisions in addition to those provided by sections 4 through 8 of this revenue procedure or by section 4 of Rev. Proc. 89–21 (other than provisions necessary to establish a valid trust under applicable local law) or that omits any of these provisions will not necessarily be disqualified, but it will not be assured of qualification under the provisions of this revenue procedure.

SEC. 4. SAMPLE INTER VIVOS CHARITABLE REMAINDER ANNUITY TRUST: TWO LIVES, CONSECUTIVE INTERESTS

On _____ day of _____ , 19 __ , I, _____ (hereinafter referred to as "the Donor"), desiring to establish a charitable remainder annuity trust, within the meaning of section 4 of Rev. Proc. 90–32 and section 664(d)(1) of the Internal Revenue Code (hereinafter referred to as "the Code") hereby create the _____ Charitable Remainder Annuity Trust and designate _____ as the initial Trustee. [ALTERNATE OR SUCCESSOR TRUSTEES MAY ALSO BE DESIGNATED IF DESIRED.]

1. FUNDING OF TRUST. The Donor transfers to the Trustee the property described in Schedule A, and the Trustee accepts such property and agrees to hold, manage, and distribute such property of the Trust under the terms set forth in this Trust instrument.

2. PAYMENT OF ANNUITY AMOUNT. In each taxable year of the Trust, the Trustee shall pay to [a living individual] during his or her lifetime and, after his or her death, to [a living individual] (hereinafter referred to as "the Recipients"), for such time as he or she survives, an annuity amount equal to [AT LEAST 5] percent of the net fair market value of the assets of the Trust as of the date of this Trust. The annuity amount shall be paid in equal quarterly amounts from income and, to the extent that income is not sufficient, from principal. Any income of the Trust for a taxable year in excess of the annuity amount shall be added to principal. If the net fair market value of the Trust assets is incorrectly determined, then within a reasonable period after the value is finally determined for federal tax purposes, the Trustee shall pay to the Recipients (in the case of an undervaluation) or receive from the Recipients (in the case of an overvaluation) an amount equal to the difference between the annuity amount(s) properly payable and the annuity amount(s) actually paid.

3. PAYMENT OF FEDERAL ESTATE TAXES AND STATE DEATH TAXES. The lifetime annuity interest of the second Recipient will take effect upon the death of the first REcipient only if the second Recipient furnishes the funds for payment of any federal estate taxes or state death taxes for which the Trustee may be liable upon the death of the first Recipient. [THIS PROVISION IS MANDATORY ONLY IF ALL OR A PORTION OF THE TRUST MAY BE SUBJECT TO SUCH TAXES ON THE DEATH OF THE FIRST RECIPIENT.]

4. PRORATION OF THE ANNUITY AMOUNT. In determining the annuity amount, the Trustee shall prorate the same on a daily basis for a short taxable year and for the taxable year ending with the survivor Recipient's death.

5. DISTRIBUTION TO CHARITY. Upon the death of the survivor Recipient, the Trustee shall distribute all of the then principal and income of the Trust (other than any amount due either of the Recipients or their

estates under the provisions above), to _____ (hereinafter referred to as "the Charitable organization"). If the Charitable Organization is not an organization described in sections 170(c), 2055(a), and 2522(a) of the Code at the time when any principal or income of the Trust is to be distributed to it, then the Trustee shall distribute such principal or income to such one or more organizations described in sections 170(c), 2055(a), and 2522(a) as the Trustee shall select in its sole discretion.

6. ADDITIONAL CONTRIBUTIONS. No additional contributions shall be made to the Trust after the initial contribution.

7. PROHIBITED TRANSACTIONS. The Trustee shall make distributions at such time and in such manner as not to subject the Trust to tax under section 4942 of the Code. Except for the payment of the annuity amount to the Recipients, the Trustee shall not engage in any act of self-dealing, as defined in section 4941(d), and shall not make any taxable expenditures, as defined in section 4945(d). The Trustee shall not make any investments that jeopardize the charitable purpose of the Trust, within the meaning of section 4944 and the regulations thereunder, or retain any excess business holdings, within the meaning of section 4943(c).

8. TAXABLE YEAR. The taxable year of the Trust shall be the calendar year.

9. GOVERNING LAW. The operation of the Trust shall be governed by the laws of the State of _____ . The Trustee, however, is prohibited from exercising any power or discretion granted under said laws that would be inconsistent with the qualification of the Trust under section 664(d)(1) of the Code and the corresponding regulations.

10. LIMITED POWER OF AMENDMENT. The Trust is irrevocable. The Trustee, however, shall have the power, acting alone, to amend the Trust in any manner required for the sole purpose of ensuring that the Trust qualifies and continues to qualify as a charitable remainder annuity trust within the meaning of section 664(d)(1) of the Code.

11. INVESTMENT OF TRUST ASSETS. Nothing in this Trust instrument shall be construed to restrict the Trustee from investing the Trust assets in a manner that could result in the annual realization of a reasonable amount of income or gain from the sale of disposition of Trust assets.

SEC. 5. SAMPLE INTER VIVOS CHARITABLE REMAINDER ANNUITY TRUST: TWO LIVES, CONCURRENT AND CONSECUTIVE INTERESTS

On this _____ day of _____ , 19 __ , I, _____ (hereinafter referred to as "the Donor"), desiring to establish a charitable remainder annuity trust, within the meaning of section 5 of Rev. Proc. 90-32 and section 664(d)(1) of the Internal Revenue Code (hereinafter referred to as "the Code") hereby create the _____ Charitable Remainder Annuity Trust and designate _____ as the initial Trustee. [ALTERNATE OR SUCCESSOR TRUSTEES MAY ALSO BE DESIGNATED IF DESIRED.]

1. FUNDING OF TRUST. The Donor transfers to the Trustee the property described in Schedule A, and the Trustee accepts such property and agrees to hold, manage, and distribute such property of the Trust under the terms set forth in this Trust instrument.

2. PAYMENT OF ANNUITY AMOUNT. In each taxable year of the Trust, the Trustee shall pay to [a living individual] and [a living individual] (hereinafter referred to as "the Recipients"), in equal shares during their lifetimes, an annuity amount equal to [AT LEAST 5] percent of the net fair market value of the assets of the Trust as of the date of this Trust. Upon the death of the first of the Recipients to die, the survivor Recipient shall be entitled to receive the entire annuity amount. The annuity amount shall be paid in equal quarterly amounts from income and, to the extent that income is not sufficient, from principal. Any income of the Trust for a taxable year in excess of the annuity amount shall be added to principal. If the net fair market value of the Trust assets is incorrectly determined, then within a reasonable period after the value is finally determined for federal tax purposes, the Trustee shall pay to the Recipients (in the case of an undervaluation) or receive from the Recipients (in the case of an overvaluation) an amount equal to the difference between the annuity amount(s) properly payable and the annuity amount(s) actually paid.

3. PAYMENT OF FEDERAL ESTATE TAXES AND STATE DEATH TAXES. The lifetime annuity interest of the survivor Recipient will continue in effect upon the death of the first Recipient to die only if the survivor Recipient furnishes the funds for payment of any federal estate taxes or state death taxes for which the Trustee may be liable upon the death of the first Recipient to die. [THIS PROVISION IS MANDATORY ONLY IF ALL OR A PORTION OF THE TRUST MAY BE SUBJECT TO SUCH TAXES ON THE DEATH OF THE FIRST RECIPIENT TO DIE.]

4. PRORATION OF THE ANNUITY AMOUNT. In determining the annuity amount, the Trustee shall prorate the same on a daily basis for a short taxable year and for the taxable year ending with the survivor Recipient's death.

5. DISTRIBUTION TO CHARITY. Upon the death of the survivor Recipient, the Trustee shall distribute all of the then principal and income of the Trust (other than any amount due either of the Recipients or their estates under the provisions above) to _____ (hereinafter referred to as "the Charitable Organization"). If the Charitable Organization is not an organization described in sections 170(c), 2055(a), and 2522(a) of the Code at the time when any principal or income of the Trust is to be distributed to it, then the Trustee shall distribute such principal or income to such one or more organizations described in sections 170(c), 2055(a), and 2522(a) as the Trustee shall select in its sole discretion.

6. ADDITIONAL CONTRIBUTIONS. No additional contributions shall be made to the Trust after the initial contribution.

7. PROHIBITED TRANSACTIONS. The Trustee shall make distributions at such time and in such manner as not to subject the Trust to tax under section 4942 of the Code. Except for the payment of the annuity amount to the Recipients, the Trustee shall not engage in any act of self-dealing, as defined in section 4941(d), and shall not make any taxable expenditures, as defined in section 4945(d). The Trustee shall not make any investments that jeopardize the charitable purpose of the Trust, within the meaning of section 4944 and the regulations thereunder, or retain any excess business holdings, within the meaning of section 4943(c).

8. TAXABLE YEAR. The taxable year of the Trust shall be the calendar year.

9. GOVERNING LAW. The operation of the Trust shall be governed by the laws of the State of _____ . The Trustee, however, is prohibited from exercising any power or discretion granted under said laws that would be inconsistent with the qualification of the Trust under section 664(d)(1) of the Code and the corresponding regulations.

10. LIMITED POWER OF AMENDMENT. The Trust is irrevocable. The Trustee, however, shall have the power, acting alone, to amend the Trust in any manner required for the sole purpose of ensuring that the Trust qualifies and continues to qualify as a charitable remainder annuity trust within the meaning of section 664(d)(1) of the Code.

11. INVESTMENT OF TRUST ASSETS. Nothing in this Trust instrument shall be construed to restrict the Trustee from investing the Trust assets in a manner that could result in the annual realization of a reasonable amount of income or gain from the sale or disposition of Trust assets.

SEC. 6. SAMPLE TESTAMENTARY CHARITABLE REMAINDER ANNUITY TRUST: ONE LIFE

All the rest, residue and remainder of my property and estate, real and personal, of whatever nature and wherever situated, [ALTERNATIVELY, IF NOT A RESIDUARY BEQUEST, DESCRIBE OR IDENTIFY THE BEQUEST.] I give, devise and bequeath to my Trustee in trust. It being my intention to establish a charitable remainder annuity trust within the meaning of section 6 of Rev. proc. 90–32 and section 664(d)(1) of the Internal Revenue Code (hereinafter referred to as "the Code"), such Trust shall be known as the _____ Charitable Remainder Annuity Trust and I hereby designate _____ as the initial Trustee. [ALTERNATE OR SUCCESSOR TRUSTEES MAY ALSO BE DESIGNATED IF DESIRED.]

1. PAYMENT OF ANNUITY AMOUNT. In each taxable year of the Trust, the Trustee shall pay to [A LIVING INDIVIDUAL] (hereinafter referred to as "the Recipient") during the Recipient's life an annuity amount equal to [AT LEAST 5] percent of the initial net fair market value of the assets passing in trust as finally determined

for federal tax purposes, provided, however, that the payout percentage (as adjusted to reflect the timing and frequency of the annuity payments) shall not exceed the percentage that would result in a 5 percent probability that the Trust corpus will be exhausted before the death of the Recipient determined as of the date of my death (or the alternate valuation date, if applicable). [Note: THE PRECEDING SENTENCE IS ONE MEANS OF AVOIDING DISALLOWANCE OF THE CHARITABLE DEDUCTION WITH RESPECT TO A CHARITABLE REMAINDER ANNUITY TRUST FOR WHICH THERE IS A GREATER THAN 5 PERCENT PROBABILITY THAT THE TRUST CORPUS WILL BE EXHAUSTED BEFORE THE DEATH OF THE ANNUITANT. SEE REV. RUL. 77–374, 1977–2 C.B. 329.] The annuity amount shall be paid in equal quarterly amounts from income and, to the extent that income is not sufficient, from principal. Any income of the Trust for a taxable year in excess of the annuity amount shall be added to principal. If the net fair market value of the Trust assets is incorrectly determined, then within a reasonable period after the value is finally determined for federal tax purposes, the Trustee shall pay to the Recipient (in the case of an undervaluation) or receive from the Recipient (in the case of an overvaluation) an amount equal to the difference between the annuity amount(s) properly payable and the annuity amount(s) actually paid.

2. DEFERRAL PROVISION. The obligation to pay the annuity amount shall commence with the date of my death, but payment of the annuity amount may be deferred from such date until the end of the taxable year of the Trust in which occurs the complete funding of the Trust. Within a reasonable time after the end of the taxable year in which the complete funding of the Trust occurs, the Trustee must pay to the Recipient (in the case of an underpayment) or receive from the Recipient (in the case of an overpayment) the difference between: (1) any annuity amounts actually paid, plus interest, compounded annually, computed for any period at the rate of interest that the federal income tax regulations under section 664 of the Code prescribe for the Trust for such computation for such period; and (2) the annuity amounts payable, plus interest, compounded annually, computed for any period at the rate of interest that the federal income tax regulations under section 664 prescribe for the Trust for such computation for such period.

3. PRORATION OF THE ANNUITY AMOUNT. In determining the annuity amount, the Trustee shall prorate the same on a daily basis for a short taxable year and for the taxable year ending with the Recipient's death.

4. DISTRIBUTION TO CHARITY. Upon the death of the Recipient, the Trustee shall distribute all of the then principal and income of the Trust (other than any amount due the Recipient or the Recipient's estate under the provisions above) to _____ (hereinafter referred to as "the Charitable Organization"). If the Charitable Organization is not an organization described in sections 170(c) and 2055(a) of the Code at the time when any principal or income of the Trust is to be distributed to it, then the Trustee shall distribute such principal or income to such one or more organizations described in sections 170(c) and 2055(a) as the Trustee shall select in its sole discretion.

5. ADDITIONAL CONTRIBUTIONS. No additional contributions shall be made to the Trust after the initial contribution. The initial contribution, however, shall be deemed to consist of all property passing to the Trust by reason of my death.

6. PROHIBITED TRANSACTIONS. The Trustee shall make distributions at such time and in such manner as not to subject the Trust to tax under section 4942 of the Code. Except for the payment of the annuity amount to the Recipient, the Trustee shall not engage in any act of self-dealing, as defined in section 4941(d), and shall not make any taxable expenditures, as defined in section 4945(d). The Trustee shall not make any investments that jeopardize the charitable purpose of the Trust, within the meaning of section 4944 and the regulations thereunder, or retain any excess business holdings, within the meaning of section 4943(c).

7. TAXABLE YEAR. The taxable year of the Trust shall be the calendar year.

8. GOVERNING LAW. The operation of the Trust shall be governed by the laws of the State of _____. The Trustee, however, is prohibited from exercising any power or discretion granted under said laws that would be inconsistent with the qualification of the Trust under section 664(d)(1) of the Code and the corresponding regulations.

9. LIMITED POWER OF AMENDMENT. The Trustee shall have the power, acting alone, to amend the Trust in any manner required for the sole purpose of ensuring that the Trust qualifies and continues to qualify as a charitable remainder annuity trust within the meaning of section 664(d)(1) of the Code.

10. INVESTMENT OF TRUST ASSETS. Nothing herein shall be construed to restrict the Trustee from investing the Trust assets in a manner that could result in the annual realization of a reasonable amount of income or gain from the sale or disposition of Trust assets.

SEC. 7. SAMPLE TESTAMENTARY CHARITABLE REMAINDER ANNUITY TRUST: TWO LIVES, CONSECUTIVE INTERESTS

All the rest, residue and remainder of my property and estate, real and personal, of whatever nature and wherever situated, [ALTERNATIVELY, IF NOT A RESIDUARY BEQUEST, DESCRIBE OR IDENTIFY THE BEQUEST.] I give, devise and bequeath to my Trustee in trust. It being my intention to establish a charitable remainder annuity trust within the meaning of section 7 of Rev. Proc. 90–32 and section 664(d)(1) of the Internal Revenue Code (hereinafter referred to as "the Code"), such Trust shall be known as the _____ Charitable Remainder Annuity Trust and I hereby designate _____ as the initial Trustee. [ALTERNATE OR SUCCESSOR TRUSTEES MAY ALSO BE DESIGNATED IF DESIRED.]

1. PAYMENT OF ANNUITY AMOUNT. In each taxable year of the Trust, the Trustee shall pay to [a living individual] _____ during his or her lifetime, and after his or her death, to [a living individual] _____ (hereinafter referred to as "the Recipients"), for such time as he or she survives, an annuity amount equal [AT LEAST 5] percent of the initial net fair market value of the assets passing in trust as finally determined for federal tax purposes, provided, however, that the payout percentage (as adjusted to reflect the timing and frequency of the annuity payments) shall not exceed the percentage that would result in a 5 percent probability that the Trust corpus will be exhausted before the death of the survivor Recipient determined as of the date of my death (or the alternate valuation date, if applicable). [NOTE: The preceding sentence is one means of avoiding disallowance of the charitable deduction with respect to a charitable remainder annuity trust for which there is a greater than 5 percent probability that the trust corpus will be exhausted before the death of the annuitant. See Rev. Rul. 77–374, 1977–2 C.B. 329.] The annuity amount shall be paid in equal quarterly amounts from income and, to the extent that income is not sufficient, from principal. Any income of the Trust for a taxable year in excess of the annuity amount shall be added to principal. If the net fair market value of the Trust assets is incorrectly determined, then within a reasonable period after the value is finally determined for federal tax purposes, the Trustee shall pay to the Recipients (in the case of an undervaluation) or receive from the Recipients (in the case of an overvaluation) an amount equal to the difference between the annuity amount(s) properly payable and the annuity amount(s) actually paid.

2. DEFERRAL PROVISION. The obligation to pay the annuity amount shall commence with the date my death, but payment of the annuity amount may be deferred from such date until the end of the taxable year of the Trust in which occurs the complete funding of the Trust. Within a reasonable time after the end of the taxable year in which the complete funding of the Trust occurs, the Trustee must pay to the Recipients (in the case of an underpayment) or receive from the Recipients (in the case of an overpayment) the difference between: (1) any annuity amounts actually paid, plus interest, compounded annually, computed for any period at the rate of interest that the federal income tax regulations under section 664 of the Code prescribe for the Trust for such computation for such period; and (2) the annuity amounts payable, plus interest, compounded annually, computed for any period at the rate of interest that the federal income tax regulations under section 664 prescribe for the Trust for such computation for such period.

3. PRORATION OF THE ANNUITY AMOUNT. In determining the annuity amount, the Trustee shall prorate the same on a daily basis for a short taxable year and for the taxable year ending with the survivor Recipient's death.

4. DISTRIBUTION TO CHARITY. Upon the death of the survivor Recipient, the Trustee shall distribute all of the then principal and income of the Trust (other than any amount due either of the Recipients or their estates, under the provisions above) to _____ (hereinafter referred to as "the Charitable Organization"). If the Charitable Organization is not an organization described in sections 170(c) and 2055(a) of the Code at the time when any principal or income of the Trust is to be distributed to it, then the Trustee shall distribute such principal or income to such one or more organizations described in sections 170(c) and 2055(a) as the Trustee shall select in its sole discretion.

5.   ADDITIONAL CONTRIBUTIONS. No additional contributions shall be made to the Trust after the initial contribution. The initial contribution, however, shall be deemed to consist of all property passing to the Trust by reason of my death.

6.   PROHIBITED TRANSACTIONS. The Trustee shall make distributions at such time and in such manner as not to subject the Trust to tax under section 4942 of the Code. Except for the payment of the annuity amount to the Recipients, the Trustee shall not engage in any act of self-dealing, as defined in section 4941(d), and shall not make any taxable expenditures, as defined in section 4945(d). The Trustee shall not make any investment that jeopardize the charitable purpose of the Trust, within the meaning of section 4944 and the regulations thereunder, or retain any excess business holdings, within the meaning of section 4943(c).

7.   TAXABLE YEAR. The taxable year of the Trust shall be the calendar year.

8.   GOVERNING LAW. The operation of the Trust shall be governed by the laws of the State of _____. The Trustee, however, is prohibited from exercising any power or discretion granted under said laws that would be inconsistent with the qualification of the Trust under section 664(d)(1) of the Code and the corresponding regulations.

9.   LIMITED POWER OF AMENDMENT. The Trustee shall have the power, acting alone, to amend the Trust in any manner required for the sole purpose of ensuring that the Trust qualifies and continues to qualify as charitable remainder annuity trust within the meaning of section 664(d)(1) of the Code.

10. INVESTMENT OF TRUST ASSETS. Nothing herein shall be construed to restrict the Trustee from investing the Trust assets in a manner that could result in the annual realization of a reasonable amount of income or gain from the sale or disposition of Trust assets.

SEC. 8. SAMPLE TESTAMENTARY CHARITABLE REMAINDER ANNUITY TRUST: TWO LIVES, CONCURRENT AND CONSECUTIVE INTERESTS

All the rest, residue and remainder of my property and estate, real and personal, of whatever nature and wherever situated, [ALTERNATIVELY, IF NOT A RESIDUARY BEQUEST, DESCRIBE OR IDENTIFY THE BEQUEST.] I give, devise and bequeath to my Trustee in trust. It being my intention to establish a charitable remainder annuity trust within the meaning of section 8 of Rev. Proc. 90-32 and section 664(d)(1) of the Internal Revenue Code (hereinafter referred to as "the Code"), such Trust shall be known as the _____ Charitable Remainder Annuity Trust and I hereby designate _____ as the initial Trustee. [ALTERNATE OR SUCCESSOR TRUSTEES MAY ALSO BE DESIGNATED IF DESIRED.]

1.   PAYMENT OF ANNUITY AMOUNT. In each taxable year of the Trust, the Trustee shall pay to [a living individual] _____ and _____ [a living individual] (hereinafter referred to as "the Recipients"), in equal shares during their lifetimes, an annuity amount equal to [at least 5] percent of the initial net fair market value of the assets passing in trust as finally determined for federal tax purposes, provided, however, that the payout percentage (as adjusted to reflect the timing and frequency of the annuity payments) shall not exceed the percentage that would result in a 5 percent probability that the Trust corpus will be exhausted before the death of the survivor Recipient determined as of the date of my death (or the alternate valuation date, if applicable). [NOTE: The preceding sentence is one means of avoiding disallowance of the charitable deduction with respect to a charitable remainder annuity trust for which there is a greater than 5 percent probability that the trust corpus will be exhausted before the death of the annuitant. See Rev. Rul. 77-374, 1977-2 C.B. 329.] Upon the death of the first of the Recipients to die, the survivor Recipient shall be entitled to receive the entire annuity amount. The annuity amount shall be paid in equal quarterly amounts from income and, to the extent that income is not sufficient, from principal. Any income of the Trust for a taxable year in excess of the annuity amount shall be added to principal. If the net fair market value of the Trust assets is incorrectly determined, then within a reasonable period after the value is finally determined for federal tax purposes, the Trustee shall pay to the Recipients (in the case of an undervaluation) or receive from the Recipients (in the case of an overvaluation) an amount equal to the difference between the annuity amount(s) properly payable and the annuity amount(s) actually paid.

2. DEFERRAL PROVISION. The obligation to pay the annuity amount shall commence with the date of my death, but payment of the annuity amount may be deferred from such date until the end of the taxable year of the Trust in which occurs the complete funding of the Trust. Within a reasonable time after the end of the taxable year in which the complete funding of the Trust occurs, the Trustee must pay to the Recipients (in the case of an underpayment) or receive from the Recipients (in the case of an overpayment) the difference between: (1) any annuity amounts actually paid, plus interest, compounded annually, computed for any period at the rate of interest that the federal income tax regulations under section 664 of the Code prescribe for the Trust for such computation for such period; and (2) the annuity amounts payable, plus interest, compounded annually, computed for any period at the rate of interest that the federal income tax regulations under section 664 prescribe for the Trust for such computation for such period.

3. PRORATION OF THE ANNUITY AMOUNT. In determining the annuity amount, the Trustee shall prorate the same on a daily basis for a short taxable year and for the taxable year ending with the survivor Recipient's death.

4. DISTRIBUTION TO CHARITY. Upon the death of the survivor Recipient, the Trustee shall distribute all of the then principal and income of the Trust (other than any amount due either of the Recipients or their estates under the provisions above) to _____ (hereinafter referred to as "the Charitable Organization"). If the Charitable Organization is not an organization described in sections 170(c) and 2055(a) of the Code at the time when any principal or income of the Trust is to be distributed to it, then the Trustee shall distribute such principal or income to such one or more organizations described in sections 170(c) and 2055(a) as the Trustee shall select in its sole discretion.

5. ADDITIONAL CONTRIBUTIONS. No additional contributions shall be made to the Trust after the initial contribution. The initial contribution, however, shall be deemed to consist of all property passing as the Trust by reason of my death.

6. PROHIBITED TRANSACTIONS. The Trustee shall make distributions at such time and in such manner as not to subject the Trust to tax under section 4942 of the Code. Except for the payment of the annuity amount to the Recipients, the Trustee shall not engage in any act of self-dealing, as defined in section 4941(d), and shall not make any taxable expenditures, as defined in section 4945(d). The Trustee shall not make any investments that jeopardize the charitable purpose of the Trust, within the meaning of section 4944 and the regulations thereunder, or retain any excess business holdings, within the meaning of section 4943(c).

7. TAXABLE YEAR. The taxable year of the Trust shall be the calendar year.

8. GOVERNING LAW. The operation of the Trust shall be governed by the law of the State of _____. The Trustee, however, is prohibited from exercising any power or discretion granted under said laws that would be inconsistent with the qualification of the Trust under section 664(d)(1) of the Code and the corresponding regulations.

9. LIMITED POWER OF AMENDMENT. The Trustee shall have the power, acting alone, to amend the Trust in any manner required for the sole purpose of ensuring that the Trust qualifies and continues to qualify as a charitable remainder annuity trust within the meaning of section 664(d)(1) of the Code.

10. INVESTMENT OF TRUST ASSETS. Nothing herein shall be construed to restrict the Trustee from investing the Trust assets in a manner that could result in the annual realization of a reasonable amount of income or gain from the sale or disposition of Trust assets.

SEC. 9. EFFECT ON OTHER REVENUE PROCEDURES

Rev. Proc. 89–21 is amplified.

SEC. 10. EFFECTIVE DATE

This revenue procedure is effective on and after June 18, 1990, the date of publication of this revenue procedure in the Internal Revenue Bulletin.

DRAFTING INFORMATION

The principal author of this revenue procedure is John McQuillan of the Office of Assistant Chief Counsel (Passthroughs and Special Industries). For further information regarding this revenue procedure, contact John McQuillan on (202) 377-6356 (not a toll-free call).

MODEL DOCUMENTS FOR POOLED INCOME FUNDS

26 CFR 601.201: Rulings and determinations letters.
(Also Part I, Sections 170, 642, 2055, 2522; 1.170A-6, 1.642(c)–5,

REV. PROC. 88–53

SECTION 1. PURPOSE.

This revenue procedure makes available a sample form of declaration of trust and instruments of transfer that meet the requirements for a pooled income fund as described in section 642(c)(5) of the Internal Revenue Code.

SEC. 2. BACKGROUND

The Internal Revenue Service receives and responds to many requests for rulings dealing with the qualification of trusts as pooled income funds and the availability of deductions for contributions made to such trusts. In many of these requests, the trust instruments and charitable objectives are very similar. Consequently, in order to provide a service to taxpayers and to save the time and expense involved in requesting and processing a ruling on a proposed pooled income fund, taxpayers who make transfers to a trust that substantially follows the model trust instrument contained herein can be assured that the Service will recognize the trust as rooting all of the requirements of a qualifies pooled income fund, provided the trust operates in a manner consistent with the terms of the trust instrument and provided it is a valid trust under applicable local law.

SEC. 3. SCOPE AND OBJECTIVE

The sample declaration of trust and instruments of transfer made available by this revenue procedure meet all of the applicable requirements for a pooled income fund under section 642(c)(5) of the Code, if the trust document also creates a valid trust under local law. If the public charity responsible for the creation and maintenance of a pooled income fund makes reference in the trust instrument of the fund to this revenue procedure, and adopts substantially similar documents, the Service will recognize the trust documents as satisfying all of the applicable requirements of section 642(c)(5) of the Code and the corresponding regulations. Moreover, for transfers to a qualifying pooled income fund, the remainder interest will be deductible under sections 170(f)(2)(A), 2055(e)(2)(A), and 2522(c)(2)(A) of the Code for income, estate, and gift tax purposes, respectively. Therefore, it will not be necessary for a taxpayer to request a ruling as to the qualification of a substantially similar trust, and the Service generally will not issue such a ruling. See Rev. Proc. 88–54, page 16, this Bulletin.

SEC. 4. SAMPLE DECLARATION OF TRUST

On this ____day of ____, 19___, the Board of Trustees of the _____ Public Charity (hereinafter referred to as a "Public Charity") desiring to establish a pooled income fund within the meaning of Rev. Proc. 88–53 and section 642(c)(5) of the Internal Revenue Code (hereinafter referred to as "the Code"), hereby creates the ___ Public Charity Pooled Income Fund (hereinafter referred to as "the Fund") and designates ___ as the initial trustee to hold, manage, and distribute such property hereinafter transferred to and accepted by it as part of the Fund under the following terms and conditions.

1. Gift of Remainder Interest. Each donor transferring property to the Fund shall contribute an irrevocable remainder interest in such property to Public Charity.

2. Retention of Life Income Interest. Each donor transferring property to the Fund shall retain for himself or herself an income interest in the property transferred, or create an income interest in such property for the life of one or more named beneficiaries, provided that each income beneficiary must be a living person at the time of the transfer of property to the Fund by the donor. If more than one beneficiary of the income interest is named, such beneficiaries may enjoy their shares concurrently and/or consecutively. Public Charity may also be designated as one of the beneficiaries of the income interest. The donor need not retain or create a life interest in all of the income from the property transferred to the Fund and any income not payable to an income beneficiary shall be contributed to, and within the taxable year of the Fund in which it is received paid to Public Charity.

3. Commingling of Property. The property transferred to the Fund by each donor shall be commingled with, and invested or reinvested with, other property transferred to the Fund by other donors satisfying the requirements of this instrument and of section 542(c)(5) of the Code or corresponding provision of any subsequent federal tax law. The Fund shall not include property transferred under arrangements other than those specified in this instrument and satisfying the said provisions of the Code.

All or any portion of the assets of the Fund may, however, be invested or reinvested jointly with other properties not a part of the Fund that are held by, or for the use of, Public Charity. When joint investment or reinvestment occurs, detailed accounting records shall be maintained by the Trustee specifically identifying the portion of the jointly invested property owned by the Fund and the income earned by, and attributable to such portion.

4. Prohibition Against Exempt Securities. The property transferred to the Fund by any donor shall not include any securities whose income is exempt from taxation under subtitle A of the Code or the corresponding provisions of any subsequent federal tax law. The Trustee of the Fund shall not accept or invest in such securities as part of the assets of the Fund.

5. Maintenance of Public Charity. Public Charity shall always maintain the Fund or exercise control, directly or indirectly, over the Fund. Public Charity shall always have the power to remove any Trustee or Trustees and to designate a new Trustee or Trustees.

6. Prohibition Against Donor or Beneficiary Serving as Trustee. The Fund shall not have as a Trustee a donor to the Fund or a beneficiary (other than Public Charity) of an income interest in any property transferred to the Fund. No donor or beneficiary (other than Public Charity) shall have, directly or indirectly, general responsibilities with respect to the Fund that are ordinarily exercised by a Trustee.

7. Income of Beneficiary to be Based on Rate of Return of Fund. The taxable year of the fund shall be the calendar year. The Trustee shall pay income to each beneficiary entitled thereto in any taxable year of the Fund in the amount determined by the rate of return earned by the Fund for the year with respect to the beneficiary's income interest. Payments must be made at least once in the year in which the income is earned. Until the Trustee determines that payments shall be made more or less frequently or at other times, the Trustee shall make income payments to the beneficiary or beneficiaries entitled to them in four quarterly payments on or about March 31, June 30, September 30, and December 31 of each year. An adjusting payment, if necessary, will be made during the taxable year or within the first 65 days following its close to bring the total payment of the actual income to which the beneficiary or beneficiaries were entitled for that year.

On each transfer of property by a donor to the Fund, there shall be assigned to the beneficiary or beneficiaries of the income interest retained or created in the property the number of units of participatior equal to the number obtained by dividing the fair market value of the property transferred by the fair market value of a unit in the Fund immediately before the transfer. The fair market value of a unit in the Fund immediately before the transfer shall be determined by dividing the fair market value of all property in the Fund at that time by the number of units then in the Fund. The initial fair market value of a unit in the Fund shall be the fair market value of the property transferred to the Fund divided by the number of units assigned to the beneficiaries of the income interest in the property. All units in the Fund shall always have equal value.

If a transfer of property to the Fund by a donor occurs on other than a determination date, the number of units of participation assigned to the beneficiary or beneficiaries of the income interest in the property shall be determined by using the average fair market value of the property in the Fund immediately before the transfer, which shall be deemed to be the average of the fair market value of the property in the Fund on the determination dates immediately preceding and succeeding the date of transfer. For the purpose of determining the average fair market value, the property transferred by the donor and any other property transferred to the Fund between the preceding and succeeding dates, or on such succeeding date, shall be excluded. The fair market value of a unit in the Fund immediately before the transfer shall be determined by dividing the number of units then in the Fund. Units of participation assigned with respect to property transferred on other than a [determination] date shall be deemed to be assigned as of the date of the transfer.

A determination date means each day within a taxable year of the Fund on which a valuation is made of the property in the Fund. The property of the Fund shall be valued on January 1, April 1, July 1, and October 1 of each year; provided, however, that where such date falls on a Saturday, Sunday or legal holiday (as defined in section 7503 of the Code and the regulations thereunder), the valuation shall be made on the next succeeding day which is not a Saturday, Sunday or legal holiday.

The amount of income allocated to each unit of participation in the Fund shall be determined by dividing the income of the Fund for the taxable year by the outstanding number of units in the Fund at the end of the year, except that income shall be allocated to units outstanding during only part of the year by taking into consideration the period of time the units are outstanding during the year.

For purposes of this instrument, the term "income" has the same meaning as it does under section 643(b) of the Code or corresponding provision of any subsequent federal tax law and the regulations thereunder.

The income interest of any beneficiary of the Fund shall terminate with the last regular payment of income that was made before the death of the beneficiary. The Trustee of the Fund shall not be required to prorate any income payment to the date of the beneficiary's death.

8. Termination of Life Income Interest. Upon the termination of the income interest of the designated beneficiary (or, in the case of successive income interests, the survivor of the designated beneficiaries) entitled to receive income pursuant to the terms of a transfer to the Fund, the Trustee shall sever from the Fund an amount equal to the value of the remainder interest in the property upon which the income interest is based. The value of the remainder interest for severance purposes shall be its value as of the date on which the last regular payment was made before the death of the beneficiary. The amount so severed from the Fund shall be paid to Public Charity. If at the time of severance of the remainder interest Public Charity has ceased to exist or is not a public charity (an organization described in clauses (i) through (vi) of section 170(b)(1)(A) of the Code), the amount severed shall be paid to an organization selected by the Trustee that is a public charity.

9. Prohibited Activities. The income of the Fund for each taxable year shall be distributed at such time and in such manner as not to subject the Fund to tax under section 4942 of the Code. Except for making the required payments to the life income beneficiaries, the Trustee shall not engage in any act of self-dealing as defined in section 4941(d) and shall not make any taxable expenditures as defined in section 4945(d). The Trustee shall not make investments that jeopardize the charitable purpose of the Fund within the meaning of section 4944 or retain any excess business holdings within the meaning of section 4943.

10. Depreciable or Depletable Assets. The Trustee shall not accept or invest in any depreciable or depletable assets.

11. Incorporation by Reference. The provisions of this document may be, and are intended to be, incorporated by reference in any will, trust, or other instrument by means of which property is transferred to the Fund. Any property transferred to the Fund whereby an income interest is retained or created for the life of one or more named beneficiaries, where this document is not incorporated by reference, shall become a part of the document, unless the instrument of transfer is inconsistent with such terms and conditions, in which case the Trustee shall not accept the property.

12. Governing Law. The operation of the Fund shall be governed by the laws of the State of ___. However, the Trustee is prohibited from exercising any power or discretion granted under said laws that would be inconsistent with the qualification of the Fund under section 642(c)(5) of the Code and the corresponding regulations.

13. Power of Amendment. The Fund is irrevocable. However, Public Charity shall have the power, acting alone, to amend this document and the associated instruments of transfer in any manner required for the sole purpose of ensuring that the Fund qualifies and continues to qualify as a pooled income fund within the meaning of section 642(c)(5).

IN WITNESS WHEREOF ____ [PUBLIC CHARITY] and _____ [TRUSTEE] by their duly authorized officers have signed this agreement the day and year first above written.

[PUBLIC CHARITY]
By _____

[TRUSTEE]
By _____

(Acknowledgements, Witnesses, etc.)

SEC 5. SAMPLE INSTRUMENT OF TRANSFER: ONE LIFE.

On this ____ day of ____, 19___, I hereby transfer to the ___ Public Charity Pooled Income Fund, under the terms and conditions set forth in its Declaration of Trust, the following property: _____.

The income interest attributable to the property transferred shall be paid as follows:

____A. To me during my lifetime.

____B. To _____ during his or her life. However, I reserve the right to revoke, solely by Will, this income interest.

Upon the termination of the income interest, the Trustee of the Fund will sever from the Fund an amount equal to the value of the remainder interest in the transferred property and transfer it to Public Charity:

____A. For its general uses and purposes.

____B. For the following charitable purpose(s): _____

However, if it is not possible for Public Charity in its sole discretion to use the severed amount for the specified purpose(s), then it may be used for the general purposes of Public Charity.

This instrument and the transfer of property made pursuant thereto shall be effective after acceptance by both the Donor and the Trustee.

IN WITNESS WHEREOF ___and ____, [TRUSTEE] by its duly authorized officer have signed this agreement the day and year first above written.

_____

[DONOR]

_____

[TRUSTEE]

By ___

(Acknowledgements, Witnesses, etc.)

SEC. 6. SAMPLE INSTRUMENT OF TRANSFER: TWO LIVES, CONSECUTIVE INTERESTS.

On this ___ day of ___, 19 ____, I hereby transfer to the ___ Public Charity Pooled Income Fund, under the terms and conditions set forth in its Declaration of Trust, the following property:

The income interest attributable to the property transferred shall be paid as follows:

___A. To me during my lifetime, and after my death to ___ during his or her lifetime. However, I reserve the right to revoke, solely by will, his or her income interest.

___B. To ___ during his or her lifetime, and after his or her death to ___ during his or her lifetime. However, I reserve the right to revoke, solely by will, the income interest of either or both beneficiaries.

Upon the termination of the income interest, the Trustee of the Fund will sever from the Fund an amount equal to the value of the remainder interest in the transferred property and transfer it to Public Charity:

___A. For its general uses and purposes.

___B. For the following charitable purpose(s): ___

However, if it is not possible for Public Charity in its sole discretion to use the severed amount for the specified purpose(s), then it may be used for the general purposes of the Public Charity.

This instrument and the transfer of property made pursuant thereto shall be effective after acceptance by both the Donor and the Trustee.

IN WITNESS WHEREOF ___ and ___[TRUSTEE] by its duly authorized officer have signed this agreement the day and year first above written.

_____
[DONOR]

_____
[TRUSTEE]
By ___

(Acknowledgements, Witnesses, etc.)

SEC. 7. SAMPLE INSTRUMENT OF TRANSFER: TWO LIVES, CONCURRENT AND CONSECUTIVE INTERESTS.

On this ___day of ___, 19___, I hereby transfer to the ___ Public Charity Pooled Income Fund, under the terms and conditions set forth in its Declaration of Trust, the following property:

The income interest attributable to the property transferred shall be paid as follows:

___A. ___% to me during my lifetime, and ___% to ___ during his or her lifetime. After the death of the first income beneficiary to die, the right to revoke, solely by will, ____'s income interest.

___B. ___% to ___ during his or her lifetime and ___% to ___ during his or her lifetime. Upon the death of the first income beneficiary to die, the survivor shall be entitled to receive the entire income.

However, I reserve the right to revoke, solely by will, the income interest of either or both beneficiaries. Upon the termination of the income interest, the Trustee of the Fund will sever from the Fund an amount equal to the value of the remainder interest in the transferred property and transfer it to Public Charity:

___A. For its general uses and purposes.
___B. For the following charitable purpose(s): ____.

However, if it is not possible for Public Charity in its sole discretion to use the severed amount for the specified purpose(s), then it may be used for the general purposes of Public Charity.

This instrument and the transfer of property made pursuant thereto shall be effective after acceptance by both the Donor and the Trustee.

IN WITNESS WHEREOF ___ and ___, [TRUSTEE] by its duly authorized officer have signed this agreement the day and year first above written.

_____
[DONOR]

_____
[TRUSTEE]
By ___

(Acknowledgements, Witnesses, etc.)

SEC. 8. APPLICATION.

The Service will recognize a trust as meeting all of the requirements of a qualified pooled income fund under section 642(c)(5) of the Code if the public charity responsible for the creation and maintenance of the trust makes reference in the trust instrument of the fund to this revenue procedure and adopts substantially similar documents, provided the trust operates in a manner consistent with the terms of the trust instrument, and provided it is a valid trust under applicable local law. A trust that contains substantive provisions in addition to those provided by this revenue procedure (other than provisions necessary to establish a valid trust under applicable local law) or that omits any of those provisions will not necessarily be disqualified, but neither will it qualify under the provisions of this revenue procedure.

SEC. 9. EFFECTIVE DATE

This revenue procedure is effective for ruling requests received in the National Office after November 28, 1988, the date of publication of this revenue procedure in the Internal Revenue Bulletin.

IRS SPECIMEN INTER VIVOS CRAT: PAYMENTS FOR ONE MEASURING LIFE

Annotations and Alternative Provisions
Rev. Proc. 2003–53

SECTION 1. PURPOSE

This revenue procedure contains an annotated sample declaration of trust and alternate provisions that meet the requirements of section 664(d)(1) of the Internal Revenue Code for an inter vivos charitable remainder annuity trust (CRAT) providing for annuity payments for one measuring life followed by the distribution of trust assets to a charitable remainderman.

SECTION 2. BACKGROUND

Previously, the Internal Revenue Service issued sample trust instruments for certain types of CRATs. The Service is updating the previously issued samples and issuing new samples for additional types of CRATs; annotations and alternate sample provisions are included as further guidance. In addition to the sample trust instrument included in this revenue procedure for an inter vivos CRAT providing for annuity payments for one measuring life, samples are provided in separate revenue procedures for:

(a) an inter vivos CRAT providing for annuity payments for a term of years (see Rev. Proc. 2003–54);

(b) an inter vivos CRAT providing for annuity payments payable consecutively for two measuring lives (see Rev. Proc. 2003–55, superceding section 4 of Rev. Proc. 90–32, 1990–1 C.B. 546);

(c) an inter vivos CRAT providing for annuity payments payable concurrently and consecutively for two measuring lives (see Rev. Proc. 2003–56, superceding section 5 of Rev. Proc. 90–32);

(d) a testamentary CRAT providing for annuity payments for one measuring life (see Rev. Proc. 2003-57, superceding section 6 of Rev. Proc. 90–32);

(e) a testamentary CRAT providing for annuity payments for a term of years (see Rev. Proc. 2003-58);

(f) a testamentary CRAT providing for annuity payments payable consecutively for two measuring lives (see Rev. Proc. 2003–59, superceding section 7 of Rev. Proc. 90–32); and

(g) a testamentary CRAT providing for annuity payments payable concurrently and consecutively for two measuring lives (see Rev. Proc. 2003–60, superceding section 8 of Rev. Proc. 90–32).

SECTION 3. SCOPE AND OBJECTIVE

Section 4 of this revenue procedure provides a sample declaration of trust for an inter vivos CRAT with one measuring life that is created by an individual who is a citizen or resident of the United States. Section 5 of this revenue procedure provides annotations to the provisions of the sample trust. Section 6 of this revenue procedure provides samples of alternate provisions concerning: (.01) the statement of the annuity amount as a specific dollar amount; (.02) the payment of part of the annuity to an organization described in section 170(c); (.03) a qualified contingency; (.04) the last annuity payment to the recipient; (.05) the restriction of the charitable remainderman to a public charity; (.06) a retained right to substitute the charitable remainderman; and (.07) a power of appointment to designate the charitable remainderman.

For transfers to a qualifying CRAT, as defined in section 664(d)(1), the remainder interest will be deductible by a citizen or resident of the United States under sections 170(f)(2)(A), 2055(e)(2)(A), and 2522(c)(2)(A) for income, estate, and gift tax purposes, respectively, if the other requirements of sections 170(f)(2)(A), 2055(e)(2)(A), and 2522(c)(2)(A) (that is, the requirements not relating to the provisions of the governing instrument) are also met. The Service will recognize a trust as a qualified CRAT meeting all of the requirements of section 664(d)(1) if the trust operates in a manner consistent with the terms of the trust instrument, if the trust is a valid trust under applicable local law, and if the trust instrument: (i) is substantially similar to the sample in section 4 of this revenue procedure; or (ii) properly integrates one or more alternate provisions from section 6 of this revenue procedure into a document substantially similar to the sample in section 4 of this revenue procedure. A trust instrument that contains substantive provisions in addition to those provided in section 4 of this revenue procedure (other than properly integrated alternate provisions from section 6 of this revenue procedure, or provisions necessary to establish a valid trust under applicable local law that are not inconsistent with the applicable federal tax requirements), or that omits any of the provisions of section 4 of this revenue procedure (unless an alternate provision from section 6 of this revenue procedure is properly integrated), will not necessarily be disqualified, but neither will that trust be assured of qualification under the provisions of this revenue procedure. The Service generally will not issue a letter ruling on whether an inter vivos trust created by an individual and with one measuring life qualifies as a CRAT. The Service, however, generally will issue letter rulings on the effect of substantive trust provisions, other than those contained in sections 4 and 6 of this revenue procedure, on the qualification of a trust as a CRAT.

SECTION 4. SAMPLE INTER VIVOS CHARITABLE REMAINDER ANNUITY TRUST -- ONE LIFE

On this ___ day of ___, 20___, I, ___ (hereinafter "the Donor"), desiring to establish a charitable remainder annuity trust, within the meaning of Rev. Proc. 2003–53 and section 664(d)(1) of the Internal Revenue Code (hereinafter "the Code"), hereby enter into this trust agreement with ___ as the initial trustee (hereinafter "the Trustee"). This trust shall be known as the ___ Charitable Remainder Annuity Trust.

1. Funding of Trust. The Donor hereby transfers and irrevocably assigns, on the above date, to the Trustee the property described in Schedule A, and the Trustee accepts the property and agrees to hold, manage, and distribute the property under the terms set forth in this trust instrument.

2. Payment of Annuity Amount. In each taxable year of the trust during the annuity period, the Trustee shall pay to [permissible recipient] (hereinafter "the Recipient") an annuity amount equal to [a number no less than 5 and no more than 50] percent of the initial net fair market value of all property transferred to the trust, valued as of the above date (that is, the date of the transfer). The first day of the annuity period shall be the date the property is transferred to the trust and the last day of the annuity period shall be the date of the Recipient's death. The annuity amount shall be paid in equal quarterly installments at the end of each calendar quarter from income, and to the extent income is not sufficient, from principal. Any income of the trust for a taxable year in excess of the annuity amount shall be added to principal. If the initial net fair market value of the trust assets is incorrectly determined, then within a reasonable period after the value is finally determined for federal tax purposes, the Trustee shall pay to the Recipient (in the case of an undervaluation) or receive from the Recipient (in the case of an overvaluation) an amount equal to the difference between the annuity amount(s) properly payable and the annuity amount(s) actually paid.

3. Proration of Annuity Amount. The Trustee shall prorate the annuity amount on a daily basis for any short taxable year. In the taxable year of the trust during which the annuity period ends, the Trustee shall prorate the annuity amount on a daily basis for the number of days of the annuity period in that taxable year.

4. Distribution to Charity. At the termination of the annuity period, the Trustee shall distribute all of the then principal and income of the trust (other than any amount due the Recipient or the Recipient's estate under the provisions above) to [designated remainderman] (hereinafter "the Charitable Organization"). If the Charitable Organization is not an organization described in sections 170(c), 2055(a), and 2522(a) of the Code at the time when any principal or income of the trust is to be distributed to it, then the Trustee shall distribute the then principal and income to one or more organizations described in sections 170(c), 2055(a), and 2522(a) of the Code as the Trustee shall select, and in the proportions as the Trustee shall decide, in the Trustee's sole discretion.

5. Additional Contributions. No additional contributions shall be made to the trust after the initial contribution.

6. Prohibited Transactions. The Trustee shall not engage in any act of self-dealing within the meaning of section 4941(d) of the Code, as modified by section 4947(a)(2)(A) of the Code, and shall not make any taxable expenditures within the meaning of section 4945(d) of the Code, as modified by section 4947(a)(2)(A) of the Code.

195

7.   Taxable Year. The taxable year of the trust shall be the calendar year.

8.   Governing Law. The operation of the trust shall be governed by the laws of the State of ___. However, the Trustee is prohibited from exercising any power or discretion granted under said laws that would be inconsistent with the qualification of the trust as a charitable remainder annuity trust under section 664(d)(l) of the Code and the corresponding regulations.

9.   Limited Power of Amendment. This trust is irrevocable. However, the Trustee shall have the power, acting alone, to amend the trust from time to time in any manner required for the sole purpose of ensuring that the trust qualifies and continues to qualify as a charitable remainder annuity trust within the meaning of section 664(d)(1) of the Code.

10. Investment of Trust Assets. Nothing in this trust instrument shall be construed to restrict the Trustee from investing the trust assets in a manner that could result in the annual realization of a reasonable amount of income or gain from the sale or disposition of trust assets.

SECTION 5. ANNOTATIONS REGARDING SAMPLE INTER VIVOS CHARITABLE REMAINDER ANNUITY TRUST -- ONE LIFE

.01 Annotations for Introductory Paragraph and Paragraph 1, Funding of Trust, of the Sample Trust.

(1) Factors concerning qualification of trust. A deduction must be allowable under section 170, section 2055, or section 2522 for property contributed to the trust. Section 1.664-1(a)(1)(iii)(a) of the Income Tax Regulations. The trust must meet the definition of and function exclusively as a charitable remainder trust from the creation of the trust. Section 1.664-1(a)(4). Solely for purposes of section 664, a trust is deemed created at the earliest time that neither the grantor nor any other person is treated as the owner of the entire trust under subpart E, part 1, subchapter J, chapter 1, subtitle A of the Code (subpart E), but in no event prior to the time property is first transferred to the trust. Neither the donor nor the donor's spouse shall be treated as the owner of the trust under subpart E merely because he or she is named as a recipient of the annuity amount. Section 1.664-1(a)(4). In addition, funding the trust with certain types of assets may disqualify it as a charitable remainder trust. See section 1.664–1(a)(7) and Rev. Rul. 73–610, 1973–2 C.B. 213.

(2) Valuation of unmarketable assets. If the trust is funded with unmarketable assets, the initial net fair market value of the assets must be determined exclusively by an independent trustee, as defined in section 1.664–1(a)(7)(iii), or must be determined by a current "qualified appraisal" from a "qualified appraiser," as defined in section 1.170A-13(c)(3) and (c)(5), respectively. Section 1.664-1(a)(7).

(3) Income tax deductibility limitations. The amount of the charitable deduction for income tax purposes is affected by a number of factors, including the type of property contributed to the trust, the type of charity receiving the property, whether the remainder interest is paid outright to charity or held in further trust, and the donor's adjusted gross income (with certain adjustments). See section 170(b) and (e); section 1.170A-8; Rev. Rul. 80–38, 1980–1 C.B. 56; and Rev. Rul. 79–368, 1979–2 C.B. 109. See section 6.05 of this revenue procedure for an alternate provision that restricts the charitable remainderman to a public charity (as defined therein).

(4) Trustee provisions. Alternate or successor trustees may be designated in the trust instrument. In addition, the trust instrument may contain other administrative provisions relating to the trustee's duties and powers, as long as the provisions do not conflict with the rules governing charitable remainder trusts under section 664 and the regulations thereunder.

(5) Identity of donor. For purposes of qualification under this revenue procedure, the donor may be an individual or a husband and wife. Appropriate adjustments should be made to the introductory paragraph if a husband and wife are the donors. Terms such as "grantor" or "settlor" may be substituted for "donor."

02 Annotations for Paragraph 2, Payment of Annuity Amount, of the Sample Trust.

(1) Permissible recipients. For a CRAT with an annuity period based on the life of one individual, the annuity amount must generally be paid to that individual and the individual must be living at the time of the creation

of the trust. See Rev. Rul. 2002–20, 2002–1 C.B. 794, for situations in which the annuity amount may be paid to a trust for the benefit of an individual who is financially disabled. An organization described in section 170(c) may receive part, but not all, of the annuity amount. Section 664(d)(1)(A) and section 1.664–2(a)(3)(i). See section 6.02 of this revenue procedure for an alternate provision that provides for payment of part of the annuity to an organization described in section 170(c).

(2) Percentage requirements. The sum certain annuity amount must be at least 5 percent and not more than 50 percent of the initial net fair market value of the assets placed in trust. Section 664(d)(1)(A). Even if the sum certain annuity amount is at least 5 percent and not more than 50 percent of the initial net fair market value of the assets placed in trust, no deduction will be allowable under section 2055 or section 2522 if the probability that the trust corpus will be exhausted before the death of the recipient exceeds 5 percent. Rev. Rul. 77–374, 1977–2 C.B. 329 and Rev. Rul. 70–452, 1970–2 C.B. 199. See sections 1.7520–3(b) and 25.7520–3(b) for special rules that may be applicable in valuing interests transferred to CRATs. In addition, the value (determined under section 7520) of the charitable remainder interest must be at least 10 percent of the initial net fair market value of all property placed in the trust. Section 664(d)(1)(D).

(3) Payment of annuity amount in installments. Paragraph 2, Payment of Annuity Amount, of the sample trust specifies that the annuity amount is to be paid in equal quarterly installments at the end of each quarter. However, the trust instrument may specify that the annuity amount is to be paid to the recipient annually or in equal or unequal installments throughout the year. See section 1.664–2(a)(1)(i). The amount of the charitable deduction will be affected by the frequency of payment, by whether the installments are equal or unequal, and by whether each installment is payable at the beginning or end of the period. See section 1.664–2(c) and section 20.2031–7(d)(2)(iv).

(4) Payment of annuity amount by close of taxable year. Generally the annuity amount for any taxable year must be paid before the close of the taxable year for which it is due. For circumstances under which the annuity amount may be paid within a reasonable time after the close of the taxable year, see section 1.664–2(a)(1)(i)(a).

(5) Early distributions to charity. The trust instrument may provide that an amount other than the annuity shall be paid (or may be paid in the discretion of the trustee) to an organization described in section 170(c). If such a distribution is made in kind, the adjusted basis of the property distributed must be fairly representative of the adjusted basis of the property available for distribution on the date of distribution. Section 1.664–2(a)(4).

.03 Annotations for Paragraph 3, Proration of Annuity Amount, of the Sample Trust.

(1) Prorating annuity amount. To compute the annuity amount in a short taxable year and in the taxable year in which the annuity period terminates, see section 1.664–2(a)(1)(iv)(a) and (b), respectively.

(2) Determining annuity amount payable in year of recipient's death. Paragraph 3, Proration of Annuity Amount, of the sample trust specifies that the annuity amount shall be prorated on a daily basis. See section 6.04 of this revenue procedure for an alternate provision that provides for the termination of the annuity amount with the last regular payment preceding the recipient's death.

.04 Annotations for Paragraph 4, Distribution to Charity, of the Sample Trust.

(1) Minimum value of remainder. As noted in section 5.02(2) of this revenue procedure, the value (determined under section 7520) of the charitable remainder interest is required to be at least 10 percent of the initial net fair market value of all property placed in the trust. Section 664(d)(1)(D).

(2) Designated remainderman. Any named charitable remainderman must be an organization described in section 170(c) at the time of the transfer to the charitable remainder annuity trust. See section 664(d)(1)(C). Any named charitable remainderman also must be an organization described in section 2522(a) to qualify for the gift tax charitable deduction and an organization described in section 2055(a) to qualify for the estate tax charitable deduction. See Rev. Rul. 77–385, 1977–2 C.B. 331. If it is determined a deduction under section 2055(a) will not be necessary in any event, all references to section 2055(a) in the trust instrument may be deleted. The trust instrument may restrict the charitable remainderman to an organization described in sections 170(c), 2055(a), and 2522(a), but grant to a trustee or other person the power to designate the actual

197

charitable remainderman. The gift of the remainder interest will be incomplete for gift tax purposes if, for example: (i) the donor retains the power to substitute the charitable remainderman; or (ii) the trust instrument provides the trustee with the power to designate the charitable remainderman and the donor is not prohibited from serving as trustee. See section 25.2511–2(c). Note, however, that an income tax charitable deduction is available even if the donor has the authority to substitute the charitable remainderman or the trustee has the authority to designate the charitable remainderman. Rev. Rul. 68–417, 1968–2 C.B. 103; Rev. Rul. 79–368, 1979–2 C.B. 109. See section 6.06 of this revenue procedure for an alternate provision in which the donor retains the right to substitute the charitable remainderman. See section 6.07 of this revenue procedure for an alternate provision in which the recipient is granted a power of appointment to designate the charitable remainderman.

(3)   Multiple remaindermen. The remainder interest may pass to more than one charitable organization as long as each organization is described in sections 170(c), 2522(a), and, if needed, section 2055(a). Section 1.664–2(a)(6)(i).

(4)   Alternative remaindermen. The trust instrument of a CRAT must provide a means for selecting alternative charitable remaindermen in the event the designated organization is not qualified at the time any payments are to be made to it from the trust. Section 1.664–2(a)(6)(iv).

.05 Annotations for Paragraph 6, Prohibited Transactions, of the Sample Trust.

(1)   Payment of the annuity amount. Payment of the annuity amount to the recipient is not considered an act of self-dealing within the meaning of section 4941(d), as modified by section 4947(a)(2)(A), or a taxable expenditure within the meaning of section 4945(d), as modified by section 4947(a)(2)(A). Section 53.4947–1(c)(2) of the Foundation and Similar Excise Taxes Regulations.

(2)   Prohibitions against certain investments and excess business holdings. Prohibitions against investments that jeopardize the exempt purpose of the trust for purposes of section 4944, as modified by section 4947(a)(2)(A), and against retaining any excess business holdings for purposes of section 4943, as modified by section 4947(a)(2)(A), are required if the trust provides for payment of part of an annuity amount to an organization described in section 170(c) and gift and estate tax charitable deductions are sought for this interest. See section 4947(b)(3). See section 6.02 of this revenue procedure for an alternate provision that provides for payment of part of the annuity to an organization described in section 170(c).

(3)   Trust to continue in existence for benefit of charity. The governing instrument requirements of section 508(e) must be included in the trust instrument if, after the termination of the annuity period: (i) the trust instrument provides that the trust shall continue in existence for the benefit of the charitable remainderman and, as a result, the trust will become subject to the provisions of section 4947(a)(1); and (ii) the trust will be treated as a private foundation within the meaning of section 509(a), as modified by section 4947(a)(1). Except as provided in paragraph 6 of the sample trust, the trust instrument may limit the application of the provisions of section 508(e) to the period after the termination of the annuity period when the trust continues in existence for the benefit of the charitable remainderman. Note that when the trust provides for the trust corpus to be retained, in whole or in part, in trust for the charitable remainderman, the higher deductibility limitations in section 170(b)(1)(A) for the income tax charitable deduction will not be available (even if the charitable remainderman is restricted to a public charity) because the contribution of the trust corpus is made "for the use of" rather than "to" the charitable remainderman. See section 1.170A–8(b).

SECTION 6. ALTERNATE PROVISIONS FOR SAMPLE INTER VIVOS CHARITABLE REMAINDER ANNUITY TRUST— ONE LIFE

.01 Annuity Amount Stated as a Specific Dollar Amount.

(1)   Explanation. As an alternative to stating the annuity amount as a fraction or percentage of the initial net fair market value of the assets transferred to the trust, the annuity amount may be stated as a specific dollar amount. Section 1.664–2(a)(1)(ii) and (iii). In either case, the annuity amount must be not less than 5 percent nor more than 50 percent of the initial net fair market value of all property placed in trust. Section 664(d)(l)(A).

(2)   Instructions for use.

(a) Replace the first sentence of paragraph 2, Payment of Annuity Amount, of the sample trust with the following sentence:

In each taxable year of the trust during the annuity period, the Trustee shall pay to [permissible recipient] (hereinafter "the Recipient") an annuity amount equal to [the stated dollar amount.]

(b) Delete the last sentence of paragraph 2, Payment of Annuity Amount, of the sample trust concerning the incorrect valuation of trust assets.

.02 Payment of Part of the Annuity to an Organization Described in section 170(c).

(1)   Explanation. An organization described in section 170(c) may receive part, but not all, of any annuity amount. Section 664(d)(1)(A). If a gift tax charitable deduction and, if needed, an estate tax charitable deduction are sought for the present value of the annuity interest passing to a charitable organization, the trust instrument must contain additional provisions. First, the trust instrument must specify the portion of each annuity payment that is payable to the noncharitable recipient and to the charitable organization described in sections 170(c), 2522(a), and, if needed, section 2055(a). Second, the trust instrument must contain a means for selecting an alternative qualified charitable organization if the designated organization is not a qualified organization at the time when any annuity amount is to be paid to it. Third, the trust instrument must contain prohibitions against investments that jeopardize the exempt purpose of the trust for purposes of section 4944, as modified by section 4947(a)(2)(A), and against retaining any excess business holdings for purposes of section 4943, as modified by section 4947(a)(2)(A).

(2)   Instructions for use.

(a) Replace paragraph 2, Payment of Annuity Amount, of the sample trust with the following paragraph:

Payment of Annuity Amount. The annuity amount is equal to [a number no less than 5 and no more than 50] percent of the initial net fair market value of all property transferred to the trust, valued as of the above date (that is, the date of the transfer). In each taxable year of the trust during the annuity period, the Trustee shall pay [the percentage of the annuity amount payable to the noncharitable recipient] percent of the annuity amount to [permissible recipient] (hereinafter "the Recipient") and [the percentage of the annuity amount payable to the charitable recipient] percent of the annuity amount to [an organization described in sections 170(c), 2055(a), and 2522(a) of the Code] (hereinafter "the Charitable Recipient"). The first day of the annuity period shall be the date the property is transferred to the trust and the last day of the annuity period shall be the date of the Recipient's death. If the Charitable Recipient is not an organization described in sections 170(c), 2055(a), and 2522(a) of the Code at the time when any annuity payment is to be distributed to it, then the Trustee shall distribute that annuity payment to one or more organizations described in sections 170(c), 2055(a), and 2522(a) of the Code as the Trustee shall select, and in the proportions as the Trustee shall decide, in the Trustee's sole discretion. The annuity amount shall be paid in equal quarterly installments at the end of each calendar quarter from income, and to the extent income is not sufficient, from principal. Any income of the trust for a taxable year in excess of the annuity amount shall be added to principal. If the initial net fair market value of the trust assets is incorrectly determined, then within a reasonable period after the value is finally determined for federal tax purposes, the Trustee shall pay to the Recipient and the Charitable Recipient (in the case of an undervaluation) or receive from the Recipient and the Charitable Recipient (in the case of an overvaluation) an amount equal to the difference between the annuity amount(s) properly payable and the annuity amount(s) actually paid.

(b) Replace the first parenthetical in paragraph 4, Distribution to Charity, of the sample trust with the following parenthetical:

(other than any amount due the Recipient or the Recipient's estate and the Charitable Recipient under the provisions above).

(c) Add the following sentence after the first and only sentence in paragraph 6, Prohibited Transactions, of the sample trust:

The Trustee shall not make any investments that jeopardize the exempt purpose of the trust for purposes of section 4944 of the Code, as modified by section 4947(a)(2)(A) of the Code, or retain any excess business holdings for purposes of section 4943 of the Code, as modified by section 4947(a)(2)(A) of the Code.

.03 Qualified Contingency.

(1)   Explanation. Under section 664(f), payment of the annuity amount may terminate upon the earlier of the occurrence of a qualified contingency (as defined in section 664(f)(3)) or the death of the recipient. The amount of the charitable deduction, however, will be determined without regard to a qualified contingency. See section 664(f)(2).

(2)   Instruction for use. Replace the second sentence of paragraph 2, Payment of Annuity Amount, of the sample trust with the following sentence:

The first day of the annuity period shall be the date the property is transferred to the trust and the last day of the annuity period shall be the date of the Recipient's death or, if earlier, the date on which occurs the [qualified contingency.]

.04 Last Annuity Payment to the Recipient.

(1)   Explanation. As an alternative to prorating the annuity amount in the taxable year of the recipient's death, payment of the annuity amount may terminate with the last regular payment preceding the recipient's death. However, the fact that the recipient may not receive the last payment shall not be taken into account for purposes of determining the present value of the remainder interest. Section 1.664-2(a)(5)(i).

(2)   Instruction for use. Replace the second sentence of paragraph 3, Proration of Annuity Amount, of the sample trust with the following sentence:

In the taxable year of the trust during which the annuity period ends, the obligation of the Trustee to pay the annuity amount shall terminate with the regular quarterly installment next preceding the death of the Recipient.

.05 Restricting the Charitable Remainderman to a Public Charity.

(1)   Explanation. The amount of the donor's income tax charitable deduction is more limited for gifts to certain private foundations than for other charitable organizations. Specifically, charitable organizations described in section 170(c) include private foundations that are not described in section 170(b)(1)(E). See section 170(b) and Rev. Rul. 79-368, 1979-2 C.B. 109. To avoid these more restrictive limitations, a donor of an inter vivos CRAT may wish to restrict the charitable remainderman to an organization that is described in section 170(b)(1)(A) as well as sections 170(c), 2055(a), and 2522(a) (referred to herein as a "public charity").

(2)   Instruction for use. To restrict the charitable remainderman to a public charity, each and every time the phrase "an organization described in sections 170(c), 2055(a), and 2522(a) of the Code" appears in the sample trust, replace it with the phrase "an organization described in sections 170(b)(1)(A), 170(c), 2055(a), and 2522(a) of the Code."

.06 Retaining the Right to Substitute the Charitable Remainderman.

(1)   Explanation. The donor may retain the right to substitute another charitable remainderman for the charitable remainderman named in the trust instrument. See Rev. Rul. 76–8, 1976–1 C.B. 179. Note, however, that the retention of this right will cause the gift of the remainder interest to be incomplete for gift tax purposes. See section 25.2511–2(c) and Rev. Rul. 77–275, 1977–2 C.B. 346.

(2)   Instruction for use. Insert the following sentence between the first and last sentences of paragraph 4, Distribution to Charity, of the sample trust:

The Donor reserves the right to designate, at any time and from time to time, in lieu of the Charitable Organization identified above, one or more organizations described in sections 170(c), 2055(a), and 2522(a) of the Code as the charitable remainderman and shall make any such designation by giving written notice to the Trustee.

.07 Power of Appointment to Designate the Charitable Remainderman.

(1)   Explanation. The trust instrument may grant the recipient a power of appointment to designate the charitable remainderman. See Rev. Rul. 76–7, 1976–1 C.B. 179.

(2)   Instruction for use. Replace paragraph 4, Distribution to Charity, of the sample trust with the following paragraph:

Distribution to Charity. At the termination of the annuity period, the Trustee shall distribute all of the then principal and income of the trust (other than any amount due the Recipient or the Recipient's estate under the provisions above) to one or more charitable organizations described in sections 170(c), 2055(a), and 2522(a) of the Code as the Recipient shall appoint and direct by specific reference to this power of appointment by inter vivos or testamentary instrument. To the extent the Recipient fails to effectively exercise the power of appointment, the principal and income not effectively appointed shall be distributed to one or more organizations described in sections 170(c), 2055(a), and 2522(a) of the Code as the Trustee shall select, and in the proportions as the Trustee shall decide, in the Trustee's sole discretion. If an organization fails to qualify as an organization described in sections 170(c), 2055(a), and 2522(a) of the Code at the time when any principal or income of the trust is to be distributed to it, then the Trustee shall distribute the then principal and income to one or more organizations described in sections 170(c), 2055(a), and 2522(a) of the Code as the Trustee shall select, and in the proportions as the Trustee shall decide, in the Trustee's sole discretion.

SECTION 7. EFFECT ON OTHER REVENUE PROCEDURES

Rev. Proc. 89–21, 1989–1 C.B. 842, is superseded.

DRAFTING INFORMATION

The principal authors of this revenue procedure are Karlene M. Lesho and Stephanie N. Bland of the Office of Associate Chief Counsel (Passthroughs and Special Industries). For further information regarding this revenue procedure, contact Karlene M. Lesho or Stephanie N. Bland at (202) 622-7830 (not a toll-free call).

IRS SPECIMEN INTER VIVOS CRAT: PAYMENTS FOR A TERM OF YEARS

Annotations and Alternative Provisions
Rev. Proc. 2003–54

SECTION 1. PURPOSE

This revenue procedure contains an annotated sample declaration of trust and alternate provisions that meet the requirements of section 664(d)(1) of the Internal Revenue Code for an inter vivos charitable remainder annuity trust (CRAT) providing for annuity payments for a term of years followed by the distribution of trust assets to a charitable remainderman.

SECTION 2. BACKGROUND

Previously, the Internal Revenue Service issued sample trust instruments for certain types of CRATs. The Service is updating the previously issued samples and issuing new samples for additional types of CRATs; annotations and alternate sample provisions are included as further guidance. In addition to the sample trust instrument included in this revenue procedure for an inter vivos CRAT providing for annuity payments for a term of years, samples are provided in separate revenue procedures for:

(a) an inter vivos CRAT providing for annuity payments for one measuring life (see Rev. Proc. 2003–53, superceding Rev. Proc. 89–21, 1989-1 C.B. 842);

(b) an inter vivos CRAT providing for annuity payments payable consecutively for two measuring lives (see Rev. Proc. 2003–55, superceding section 4 of Rev. Proc. 90–32, 1990–1 C.B. 546);

(c) an inter vivos CRAT providing for annuity payments payable concurrently and consecutively for two measuring lives (see Rev. Proc. 2003-56, superceding section 5 of Rev. Proc. 90–32);

(d) a testamentary CRAT providing for annuity payments for one measuring life (see Rev. Proc. 2003–57, superceding section 6 of Rev. Proc. 90–32);

(e) a testamentary CRAT providing for annuity payments for a term of years (see Rev. Proc. 2003–58);

(f) a testamentary CRAT providing for annuity payments payable consecutively for two measuring lives (see Rev. Proc. 2003–59, superceding section 7 of Rev. Proc. 90–32); and

(g) a testamentary CRAT providing for annuity payments payable concurrently and consecutively for two measuring lives (see Rev. Proc. 2003–60, superceding section 8 of Rev. Proc. 90–32).

SECTION 3. SCOPE AND OBJECTIVE

Section 4 of this revenue procedure provides a sample declaration of trust for an inter vivos CRAT that is created by an individual who is a citizen or resident of the United States and that provides for a term of years annuity period. Section 5 of this revenue procedure provides annotations to the provisions of the sample trust. Section 6 of this revenue procedure provides samples of alternate provisions concerning: (.01) the statement of the annuity amount as a specific dollar amount; (.02) the payment of part of the annuity to an organization described in section 170(c); (.03) the apportionment of the annuity amount among members of a named class in the discretion of the trustee; (.04) a qualified contingency; (.05) the restriction of the charitable remainderman to a public charity; (.06) a retained right to substitute the charitable remainderman; and (.07) a power of appointment to designate the charitable remainderman.

For transfers to a qualifying CRAT, as defined in section 664(d)(1), the remainder interest will be deductible by a citizen or resident of the United States under sections 170(f)(2)(A), 2055(e)(2)(A), and 2522(c)(2)(A) for income, estate, and gift tax purposes, respectively, if the other requirements of sections 170(f)(2)(A), 2055(e)(2)(A), and 2522(c)(2)(A) (that is, the requirements not relating to the provisions of the governing instrument) are also met. The Service will recognize a trust as a qualified CRAT meeting all of the requirements of section 664(d)(1) if the trust operates in a manner consistent with the terms of the trust instrument, if the trust is a valid trust under applicable local law, and if the trust instrument: (i) is substantially similar to the sample in section 4 of this revenue procedure; or (ii) properly integrates one or more alternate provisions from section 6 of this revenue procedure into a document substantially similar to the sample in section 4 of this revenue procedure. A trust instrument that contains substantive provisions in addition to those provided in section 4 of this revenue procedure (other than properly integrated alternate provisions from section 6 of this revenue procedure, or provisions necessary to establish a valid trust under applicable local law that are not inconsistent with the applicable federal tax requirements), or that omits any of the provisions of section 4 of this revenue procedure (unless an alternate provision from section 6 of this revenue procedure is properly integrated), will not necessarily be disqualified, but neither will that trust be assured of qualification under the provisions of this revenue procedure. The Service generally will not issue a letter ruling on whether an inter vivos trust created by an individual and having a term of years annuity period qualifies as a CRAT. The Service, however, generally will issue letter rulings on the effect of substantive trust provisions, other than those contained in sections 4 and 6 of this revenue procedure, on the qualification of a trust as a CRAT.

SECTION 4. SAMPLE INTER VIVOS CHARITABLE REMAINDER ANNUITY TRUST—TERM OF YEARS

On this ___ day of ___ , 20___, I, ___ (hereinafter "the Donor"), desiring to establish a charitable remainder annuity trust, within the meaning of Rev. Proc. 2003–54 and section 664(d)(1) of the Internal Revenue Code (hereinafter "the Code"), hereby enter into this trust agreement with ___ as the initial trustee (hereinafter "the Trustee"). This trust shall be known as the ___ Charitable Remainder Annuity Trust.

1. Funding of Trust. The Donor hereby transfers and irrevocably assigns, on the above date, to the Trustee the property described in Schedule A, and the Trustee accepts the property and agrees to hold, manage, and distribute the property under the terms set forth in this trust instrument.

2. Payment of Annuity Amount. In each taxable year of the trust during the annuity period, the Trustee shall pay to [permissible recipient] (hereinafter "the Recipient") an annuity amount equal to [a number no less than 5 and no more than 50] percent of the initial net fair market value of all property transferred to the trust, valued as of the above date (that is, the date of the transfer). The annuity period is a term of [a number not more than 20] years. The first day of the annuity period shall be the date the property is transferred to the trust and the last day of the annuity period shall be the day preceding the [ordinal number corresponding to the length of the annuity period] anniversary of that date. The annuity amount shall be paid in equal quarterly installments at the end of each calendar quarter from income, and to the extent income is not sufficient, from principal. Any income of the trust for a taxable year in excess of the annuity amount shall be added to principal. If the initial net fair market value of the trust assets is incorrectly determined, then within a reasonable period after the value is finally determined for federal tax purposes, the Trustee shall pay to the Recipient (in the case of an undervaluation) or receive from the Recipient (in the case of an overvaluation) an amount equal to the difference between the annuity amount(s) properly payable and the annuity amount(s) actually paid.

3. Proration of Annuity Amount. The Trustee shall prorate the annuity amount on a daily basis for any short taxable year. In the taxable year of the trust during which the annuity period ends, the Trustee shall prorate the annuity amount on a daily basis for the number of days of the annuity period in that taxable year.

4. Distribution to Charity. At the termination of the annuity period, the Trustee shall distribute all of the then principal and income of the trust (other than any amount due the Recipient under the provisions above) to [designated remainderman] (hereinafter "the Charitable Organization"). If the Charitable Organization is not an organization described in sections 170(c), 2055(a), and 2522(a) of the Code at the time when any principal or income of the trust is to be distributed to it, then the Trustee shall distribute the then principal and income to one or more organizations described in sections 170(c), 2055(a), and 2522(a) of the Code as the Trustee shall select, and in the proportions as the Trustee shall decide, in the Trustee's sole discretion.

5. Additional Contributions. No additional contributions shall be made to the trust after the initial contribution.

6. Prohibited Transactions. The Trustee shall not engage in any act of self-dealing within the meaning of section 4941(d) of the Code, as modified by section 4947(a)(2)(A) of the Code, and shall not make any taxable expenditures within the meaning of section 4945(d) of the Code, as modified by section 4947(a)(2)(A) of the Code.

7.   Taxable Year. The taxable year of the trust shall be the calendar year.

8.   Governing Law. The operation of the trust shall be governed by the laws of the State of ___. However, the Trustee is prohibited from exercising any power or discretion granted under said laws that would be inconsistent with the qualification of the trust as a charitable remainder annuity trust under section 664(d)(1) of the Code and the corresponding regulations.

9.   Limited Power of Amendment. This trust is irrevocable. However, the Trustee shall have the power, acting alone, to amend the trust from time to time in any manner required for the sole purpose of ensuring that the trust qualifies and continues to qualify as a charitable remainder annuity trust within the meaning of section 664(d)(1) of the Code.

10. Investment of Trust Assets. Nothing in this trust instrument shall be construed to restrict the Trustee from investing the trust assets in a manner that could result in the annual realization of a reasonable amount of income or gain from the sale or disposition of trust assets.

SECTION 5. ANNOTATIONS REGARDING SAMPLE INTER VIVOS CHARITABLE REMAINDER ANNUITY TRUST -- TERM OF YEARS

.01 Annotations for Introductory Paragraph and Paragraph 1, Funding of Trust, of the Sample Trust.

(1) Factors concerning qualification of trust. A deduction must be allowable under section 170, section 2055, or section 2522 for property contributed to the trust. Section 1.664-1(a)(1)(iii)(a) of the Income Tax Regulations. The trust must meet the definition of and function exclusively as a charitable remainder trust from the creation of the trust. Section 1.664–1(a)(4). Solely for purposes of section 664, a trust is deemed created at the earliest time that neither the grantor nor any other person is treated as the owner of the entire trust under subpart E, part 1, subchapter J, chapter 1, subtitle A of the Code (subpart E), but in no event prior to the time property is first transferred to the trust. Neither the donor nor the donor's spouse shall be treated as the owner of the trust under subpart E merely because he or she is named as a recipient of the annuity amount. Section 1.664-1(a)(4). In addition, funding the trust with certain types of assets may disqualify it as a charitable remainder trust. See section 1.664–1(a)(7) and Rev. Rul. 73–610, 1973–2 C.B. 213.

(2) Valuation of unmarketable assets. If the trust is funded with unmarketable assets, the initial net fair market value of the assets must be determined exclusively by an independent trustee, as defined in section 1.664-1(a)(7)(iii), or must be determined by a current "qualified appraisal" from a "qualified appraiser," as defined in section 1.170A–13(c)(3) and (c)(5), respectively. Section 1.664–1(a)(7).

(3) Income tax deductibility limitations. The amount of the charitable deduction for income tax purposes is affected by a number of factors, including the type of property contributed to the trust, the type of charity receiving the property, whether the remainder interest is paid outright to charity or held in further trust, and the donor's adjusted gross income (with certain adjustments). See section 170 (b) and (e); section 1.170A-8; Rev. Rul. 80-38, 198G-1 C.B. 56; and Rev. Rul. 79-368, 1979-2 C.B. 109. See section 6.05 of this revenue procedure for an alternate provision that restricts the charitable remainderman to a public charity (as defined therein).

(4) Trustee provisions. Alternate or successor trustees may be designated in the trust instrument. In addition, the trust instrument may contain other administrative provisions relating to the trustee's duties and powers, as long as the provisions do not conflict with the rules governing charitable remainder trusts under section 664 and the regulations thereunder. Note that certain powers given to certain persons serving as the trustee may cause the trustee to be treated as the owner of the trust under subpart E and thus disqualify the trust as a charitable remainder trust. See section 1.664-1(a)(4). See section 6.03 of this revenue procedure for an alternate provision providing for the apportionment of the annuity amount among members of a named class in the discretion of the trustee.

(5) Identity of donor. For purposes of qualification under this revenue procedure, the donor may be an individual or a husband and wife. Appropriate adjustments should be made to the introductory paragraph if a husband and wife are the donors. Terms such as "grantor" or "settlor" may be substituted for "donor."

.02 Annotations for Paragraph 2, Payment of Annuity Amount, of the Sample Trust.

(1) Permissible term. The period for which the annuity amount is payable must not exceed 20 years. Section 1.664–2(a)(5)(i). Thus, for example, the annuity period of a CRAT for a term of 20 years will end on the day preceding the twentieth anniversary of the date the trust was created.

(2) Permissible recipients. For a CRAT having a term of years annuity period, the annuity amount must generally be paid to a named person or persons (within the meaning of section 7701(a)(1)). If the annuity amount is to be paid to an individual or individuals, all the individuals must be living at the time of the creation of the trust. The annuity amount may be payable to the estate or heirs of a named recipient who dies prior to the expiration of the term of years. See Rev. Rul. 74–39, 1974–1 C.B. 156. The annuity amount may be payable to members of a named class and, because the annuity period is for a term of years, all of the members of the class need not be living or ascertainable at the creation of the trust. An organization described in section 170(c) may receive part, but not all, of the annuity amount. Section 664(d)(1)(A) and section 1.664–2(a)(3)(i). See section 6.02 of this revenue procedure for an alternate provision that provides for payment of part of the annuity to an organization described in section 170(c).

(3) Multiple noncharitable recipients. Generally, if the annuity amount is payable to more than one person, the trust instrument should describe the interest of each person. See section 6.03 of this revenue procedure for an alternate provision providing for the apportionment of the annuity amount among members of a named class in the discretion of the trustee.

(4) Percentage requirements. The sum certain annuity amount must be at least 5 percent and not more than 50 percent of the initial net fair market value of the assets placed in trust. Section 664(d)(1)(A). In addition, the value (determined under section 7520) of the charitable remainder interest must be at least 10 percent of the initial net fair market value of all property placed in the trust. Section 664(d)(1)(D). See sections 1.7520–3(b) and 25.7520–3(b) for special rules that may be applicable in valuing interests transferred to CRATs.

(5) Payment of annuity amount in installments. Paragraph 2, Payment of Annuity Amount, of the sample trust specifies that the annuity amount is to be paid in equal quarterly installments at the end of each quarter. However, the trust instrument may specify that the annuity amount is to be paid to the recipient annually or in equal or unequal installments throughout the year. See section 1.664–2(a)(1)(i). The amount of the charitable deduction will be affected by the frequency of payment, by whether the installments are equal or unequal, and by whether each installment is payable at the beginning or end of the period. See section 1.664–2(c) and section 20.2031–7(d)(2)(iv).

(6) Payment of annuity amount by close of taxable year. Generally, the annuity amount for any taxable year must be paid before the close of the taxable year for which it is due. For circumstances under which the annuity amount may be paid within a reasonable time after the close of the taxable year, see section 1.664–2(a)(1)(i)(a).

(7) Early distributions to charity. The trust instrument may provide that an amount other than the annuity shall be paid (or may be paid in the discretion of the trustee) to an organization described in section 170(c). If such a distribution is made in kind, the adjusted basis of the property distributed must be fairly representative of the adjusted basis of the property available for distribution on the date of distribution. Section 1.664–2(a)(4).

.03 Annotation for Paragraph 3, Proration of Annuity Amount, of the Sample Trust.

(1) Prorating annuity amount. To compute the annuity amount in a short taxable year and in the taxable year in which the annuity period terminates, see section 1.664–2(a)(1)(iv)(a) and (b), respectively.

.04 Annotations for Paragraph 4, Distribution to Charity, of the Sample Trust.

(1) Minimum value of remainder. As noted in section 5.02(4) of this revenue procedure, the value (determined under section 7520) of the charitable remainder interest is required to be at least 10 percent of the initial net fair market value of all property placed in the trust. Section 664(d)(1)(D).

(2) Designated remainderman. Any named charitable remainderman must be an organization described in section 170(c) at the time of the transfer to the charitable remainder annuity trust. See section 664(d)(1)(C). Any named charitable remainderman also must be an organization described in section 2522(a) to qualify for the

gift tax charitable deduction and an organization described in section 2055(a) to qualify for the estate tax charitable deduction. See Rev. Rul. 77–385, 1977–2 C.B. 331. If it is determined a deduction under section 2055(a) will not be necessary in any event, all references to section 2055(a) in the trust instrument may be deleted. The trust instrument may restrict the charitable remainderman to an organization described in sections 170(c), 2055(a), and 2522(a), but grant to a trustee or other person the power to designate the actual charitable remainderman. The gift of the remainder interest will be incomplete for gift tax purposes if, for example: (i) the donor retains the power to substitute the charitable remainderman; or (ii) the trust instrument provides the trustee with the power to designate the charitable remainderman and the donor is not prohibited from serving as trustee. See section 25.2511–2(c). Note, however, that an income tax charitable deduction is available even if the donor has the authority to substitute the charitable remainderman or the trustee has the authority to designate the charitable remainderman. Rev. Rul. 68–417, 1968–2 C.B. 103; Rev. Rul. 79–368, 1979–2 C.B. 109. See section 6.06 of this revenue procedure for an alternate provision in which the donor retains the right to substitute the charitable remainderman. See section 6.07 of this revenue procedure for an alternate provision in which the recipient is granted a power of appointment to designate the charitable remainderman.

(3)   Multiple remaindermen. The remainder interest may pass to more than one charitable organization as long as each organization is described in sections 170(c), 2522(a), and, if needed, 2055(a). Section 1.664–2(a)(6)(i).

(4)   Alternative remaindermen. The trust instrument of a CRAT must provide a means for selecting alternative charitable remaindermen in the event the designated organization is not qualified at the time any payments are to be made to it from the trust. Section 1.664–2(a)(6)(iv).

.05 Annotations for Paragraph 6, Prohibited Transactions, of the Sample Trust.

(1)   Payment of the annuity amount. Payment of the annuity amount to the recipient is not considered an act of self-dealing within the meaning of section 4941(d), as modified by section 4947(a)(2)(A), or a taxable expenditure within the meaning of section 4945(d), as modified by section 4947(a)(2)(A). Section 53.4947–1(c)(2) of the Foundation and Similar Excise Taxes Regulations.

(2)   Prohibitions against certain investments and excess business holdings. Prohibitions against investments that jeopardize the exempt purpose of the trust for purposes of section 4944, as modified by section 4947(a)(2)(A), and against retaining any excess business holdings for purposes of section 4943, as modified by section 4947(a)(2)(A), are required if the trust provides for payment of part of an annuity amount to an organization described in section 170(c) and gift and estate tax charitable deductions are sought for this interest. See section 4947(b)(3). See section 6.02 of this revenue procedure for an alternate provision that provides for payment of part of the annuity to an organization described in section 170(c).

(3)   Trust to continue in existence for benefit of charity. The governing instrument requirements of section 508(e) must be included in the trust instrument if, after the termination of the annuity period: (i) the trust instrument provides that the trust shall continue in existence for the benefit of the charitable remainderman and, as a result, the trust will become subject to the provisions of section 4947(a)(1); and (H) the trust will be treated as a private foundation within the meaning of section 509(a), as modified by section 4947(a)(1). Except as provided in paragraph 6 of the sample trust, the trust instrument may limit the application of the provisions of section 508(e) to the period after the termination of the annuity period when the trust continues in existence for the benefit of the charitable remainderman. Note that when the trust provides for the trust corpus to be retained, in whole or in part, in trust for the charitable remainderman, the higher deductibility limitations in section 170(b)(1)(A) for the income tax charitable deduction will not be available (even if the charitable remainderman is restricted to a public charity) because the contribution of the trust corpus is made "for the use of" rather than "to" the charitable remainderman. See section 1.170A–8(b).

SECTION 6. ALTERNATE PROVISIONS FOR SAMPLE INTER VIVOS CHARITABLE REMAINDER ANNUITY TRUST—TERM OF YEARS

.01 Annuity Amount Stated as a Specific Dollar Amount.

(1)   Explanation. As an alternative to stating the annuity amount as a fraction or percentage of the initial net fair

market value of the assets transferred to the trust, the annuity amount may be stated as a specific dollar amount. Section 1.664-2(a)(1)(ii) and (iii). In either case, the annuity amount must be not less than 5 percent nor more than 50 percent of the initial net fair market value of all property placed in trust. Section 664(d)(1)(A).

(2) Instructions for use.

(a) Replace the first sentence of paragraph 2, Payment of Annuity Amount, of the sample trust with the following sentence:

In each taxable year of the trust during the annuity period, the Trustee shall pay to [permissible recipient] (hereinafter "the Recipient") an annuity amount equal to [the stated dollar amount].

(b) Delete the last sentence of paragraph 2, Payment of Annuity Amount, of the sample trust concerning the incorrect valuation of trust assets.

.02 Payment of Part of the Annuity to an Organization Described in section 170(c).

(1) Explanation. An organization described in section 170(c) may receive part, but not all, of any annuity amount. Section 664(d)(1)(A). If a gift tax charitable deduction and, if needed, an estate tax charitable deduction are sought for the present value of the annuity interest passing to a charitable organization, the trust instrument must contain additional provisions. First, the trust instrument must specify the portion of each annuity payment that is payable to the noncharitable recipient and to the charitable organization described in sections 170(c), 2522(a), and, if needed, section 2055(a). Second, the trust instrument must contain a means for selecting an alternative qualified charitable organization if the designated organization is not a qualified organization at the time when any annuity amount is to be paid to it. Third, the trust instrument must contain prohibitions against investments that jeopardize the exempt purpose of the trust for purposes of section 4944, as modified by section 4947(a)(2)(A), and against retaining any excess business holdings for purposes of section 4943, as modified by section 4947(a)(2)(A).

(2) Instructions for use.

(a) Replace paragraph 2, Payment of Annuity Amount, of the sample trust with the following paragraph:

Payment of Annuity Amount. The annuity amount is equal to [a number no less than 5 and no more than 50] percent of the initial net fair market value of all property transferred to the trust, valued as of the above date (that is, the date of the transfer). In each taxable year of the trust during the annuity period, the Trustee shall pay [the percentage of the annuity amount payable to the noncharitable recipient] percent of the annuity amount to [permissible recipient] (hereinafter "the Recipient") and [the percentage of the annuity amount payable to the charitable recipient] percent of the annuity amount to [an organization described in sections 170(c), 2055(a), and 2522(a) of the Code] (hereinafter "the Charitable Recipient"). The annuity period is a term of [not more than 20] years. The first day of the annuity period shall be the date the property is transferred to the trust and the last day of the annuity period shall be the day preceding the [ordinal number corresponding to the length of the annuity period] anniversary of that date. If the Charitable Recipient is not an organization described in sections 170(c), 2055(a), and 2522(a) of the Code at the time when any annuity payment is to be distributed to it, then the Trustee shall distribute that annuity payment to one or more organizations described in sections 170(c), 2055(a), and 2522(a) of the Code as the Trustee shall select, and in the proportions as the Trustee shall decide, in the Trustee's sole discretion. The annuity amount shall be paid in equal quarterly installments at the end of each calendar quarter from income, and to the extent income is not sufficient, from principal. Any income of the trust for a taxable year in excess of the annuity amount shall be added to principal. If the initial net fair market value of the trust assets is incorrectly determined, then within a reasonable period after the value is finally determined for federal tax purposes, the Trustee shall pay to the Recipient and the Charitable Recipient (in the case of an undervaluation) or receive from the Recipient and the Charitable Recipient (in the case of an overvaluation) an amount equal to the difference between the annuity amount(s) properly payable and the annuity amount(s) actually paid.

(b) Replace the first parenthetical in paragraph 4, Distribution to Charity, of the sample trust with the following parenthetical:

(other than any amount due the Recipient and the Charitable Recipient under the provisions above).

207

(c) Add the following sentence after the first and only sentence in paragraph 6, Prohibited Transactions, of the sample trust: The Trustee shall not make any investments that jeopardize the exempt purpose of the trust for purposes of section 4944 of the Code, as modified by section 4947(a)(2)(A) of the Code, or retain any excess business holdings for purposes of section 4943 of the Code, as modified by section 4947(a)(2)(A) of the Code.

.03 Apportionment of the Annuity Amount among Members of a Named Class in the Discretion of the Trustee.

(1)   Explanation. A trust is not a CRAT if any person has the power to alter the amount to be paid to any named person other than an organization described in section 170(c) if the power would cause any person to be treated as the owner of the trust, or any portion thereof, if subpart E were applicable to the trust. Section 1.664–2(a)(3)(ii), See Rev. Rul. 77–73, 1977–1 C.B. 175. For example, the donor would not be treated as the owner of any portion of a trust if the power is exercisable solely by an independent trustee or trustees, provided no person has the power to add beneficiaries to the class except to provide for after-born or after-adopted children. Section 674(c). Trustees are independent for purposes of section 674(c) if none of them is the donor or the donor's spouse and if no more than half of them are related or subordinate parties who are subservient to the wishes of the donor. However, an independent trustee's discretionary power, exercisable solely by that trustee, to allocate the annuity amount among the members of a class would cause the trustee to be treated as the owner of all or a portion of the trust under section 678(a) if the trustee is a member of the class, if the trustee may apply trust income or corpus to satisfy the trustee's own legal obligation, or if the trustee actually exercises the power to satisfy a support obligation owed by the trustee. Therefore, if any trustee is given the discretionary power exercisable solely by that trustee to allocate the annuity amount among members of a class, the trust instrument must provide that such trustee must be: (i) independent; (ii) not a member of the recipient class; and (iii) prohibited from applying any part of the annuity payment in satisfaction of the trustee's own legal obligation.

(2)   Instructions for use.

(a) Add the following sentence to the sample trust:

Any trustee who is authorized in the trustee's sole discretion to allocate the annuity amount among members of a Recipient class must be independent within the meaning of section 674(c) of the Code and must not be a member of the Recipient class.

(b) Replace the first sentence of paragraph 2, Payment of Annuity Amount, of the sample trust with the following three sentences:

In each taxable year of the trust during the annuity period, the Trustee shall pay to a member or members of a class of persons comprised of [designated members of class] (hereinafter "the Recipient") an annuity amount equal to [a number no less than 5 and no more than 50] percent of the initial net fair market value of all property transferred to the trust, valued as of the above date (that is, the date of the transfer). The Trustee may pay the annuity amount to one or more members of the class, in equal or unequal shares, as the Trustee, in the Trustee's sole discretion, may from time to time deem advisable. The Trustee may not, however, apply the payment for the Trustee's own benefit, or in satisfaction of any support or other legal obligation of the Trustee.

.04 Qualified Contingency.

(1)   Explanation. Under section 664(f), payment of the annuity amount may terminate upon the earlier of the occurrence of a qualified contingency (as defined in section 664(f)(3)) or the expiration of the term of years. The amount of the charitable deduction, however, will be determined without regard to a qualified contingency. See section 664(f)(2).

(2)   Instruction for use. Replace the second and third sentences of paragraph 2, Payment of Annuity Amount, of the sample trust with the following two sentences, respectively:

The annuity period is a term of [not more than 20] years, unless earlier terminated by the occurrence of [qualified contingency]. The first day of the annuity period shall be the date the property is transferred to the trust and the last day of the annuity period shall be the day preceding the [ordinal number corresponding to the length of the annuity period] anniversary of that date or, if earlier, the date on which occurs the [qualified contingency].

.05 Restricting the Charitable Remainderman to a Public Charity.

(1)   Explanation. The amount of the donor's income tax charitable deduction is more limited for gifts to certain private foundations than for other charitable organizations. Specifically, charitable organizations described in section 170(c) include private foundations that are not described in section 170(b)(1)(E). See section 170(b) and Rev. Rul. 79–368, 1979–2 C.B. 109. To avoid these more restrictive limitations, a donor of an inter vivos CRAT may wish to restrict the charitable remainderman to an organization that is described in section 170(b)(1)(A) as well as sections 170(c), 2055(a), and 2522(a) (referred to herein as a "public charity").

(2)   Instruction for use. To restrict the charitable remainderman to a public charity, each and every time the phrase "an organization described in sections 170(c), 2055(a), and 2522(a) of the Code" appears in the sample trust, replace it with the phrase "an organization described in sections 170(b)(1)(A), 170(c), 2055(a), and 2522(a) of the Code."

.06 Retaining the Right to Substitute the Charitable Remainderman.

(1)   Explanation. The donor may retain the right to substitute another charitable remainderman for the charitable remainderman named in the trust instrument. See Rev. Rul. 76–8, 1976–1 C.B. 179. Note, however, that the retention of this right will cause the gift of the remainder interest to be incomplete for gift tax purposes. See section 25.2511–2(c) and Rev. Rul. 77–275, 1977–2 C.B. 346.

(2)   Instruction for use. Insert the following sentence between the first and last sentences of paragraph 4, Distribution to Charity, of the sample trust:

209

The Donor reserves the right to designate, at any time and from time to time, in lieu of the Charitable Organization identified above, one or more organizations described in sections 170(c), 2055(a), and 2522(a) of the Code as the charitable remainderman, and shall make any such designation by giving written notice to the Trustee.

.07 Power of Appointment to Designate the Charitable Remainderman.

(1)   Explanation. The trust instrument may grant a recipient a power of appointment to designate the charitable remainderman. See Rev. Rul. 76–7, 1976–1 C.B. 179.

(2)   Instruction for use. Replace paragraph 4, Distribution to Charity, of the sample trust with the following paragraph:

Distribution to Charity. At the termination of the annuity period, the Trustee shall distribute all of the then principal and income of the trust (other than any amount due the Recipient under the provisions above) to one or more charitable organizations described in sections 170(c), 2055(a), and 2522(a) of the Code as the Recipient shall appoint and direct by specific reference to this power of appointment by inter vivos or testamentary instrument. To the extent the Recipient fails to effectively exercise the power of appointment, the principal and income not effectively appointed shall be distributed to one or more organizations described in sections 170(c), 2055(a), and 2522(a) of the Code as the Trustee shall select, and in the proportions as the Trustee shall decide, in the Trustee's sole discretion. If an organization fails to qualify as an organization described in sections 170(c), 2055(a), and 2522(a) of the Code at the time when any principal or income of the trust is to be distributed to it, then the Trustee shall distribute the then principal and income to one or more organizations described in sections 170(c), 2055(a), and 2522(a) of the Code as the Trustee shall select, and in the proportions as the Trustee shall decide, in the Trustee's sole discretion.

DRAFTING INFORMATION

The principal authors of this revenue procedure are Karlene M. Lesho and Stephanie N. Bland of the Office of Associate Chief Counsel (Passthroughs and Special Industries).

IRS SPECIMEN INTER VIVOS CRAT: PAYMENTS FOR TWO MEASURING LIVES—PAYABLE CONSECUTIVELY

Annotations and Alternative Provisions
Rev. Proc. 2003–55

SECTION 1. PURPOSE

This revenue procedure contains an annotated sample declaration of trust and alternate provisions that meet the requirements of section 664(d)(1) of the Internal Revenue Code for an inter vivos charitable remainder annuity trust (CRAT) providing for annuity payments payable consecutively for two measuring lives followed by the distribution of trust assets to a charitable remainderman.

SECTION 2. BACKGROUND

Previously, the Internal Revenue Service issued sample trust instruments for certain types of CRATs. The Service is updating the previously issued samples and issuing new samples for additional types of CRATs; annotations and alternate sample provisions are included as further guidance. In addition to the sample trust instrument included in this revenue procedure for an inter vivos CRAT providing for annuity payments payable consecutively for two measuring lives, samples are provided in separate revenue procedures for:

(a)   an inter vivos CRAT providing for annuity payments for one measuring life (see Rev. Proc. 2003–53, superceding Rev. Proc. 89–21, 1989-1 C.B. 842);

(b)   an inter vivos CRAT providing for annuity payments for a term of years (see Rev. Proc. 2003–54);

(c)   an inter vivos CRAT providing for annuity payments payable concurrently and consecutively for two measuring lives see Rev. Proc. 2003–56, superceding section 5 of Rev. Proc. 90–32, 1990–1 C.B. 546);

(d)   a testamentary CRAT providing for annuity payments for one measuring life (see Rev. Proc. 2003–57, superceding section 6 of Rev. Proc. 90-32);

(e)   a testamentary CRAT providing for annuity payments for a term of years (see Rev. Proc. 2003–58);

(f)   a testamentary CRAT providing for annuity payments payable consecutively for two measuring lives (see Rev. Proc. 2003–59, superceding section 7 of Rev. Proc. 90-32); and

(g)   a testamentary CRAT providing for annuity payments payable concurrently and consecutively for two measuring lives (see Rev. Proc. 2003–60, superceding section 8 of Rev. Proc. 90–32).

SECTION 3. SCOPE AND OBJECTIVE

Section 4 of this revenue procedure provides a sample declaration of trust for an inter vivos CRAT with consecutive interests for two measuring lives that is created by an individual who is a citizen or resident of the United States. Section 5 of this revenue procedure provides annotations to the provisions of the sample trust. Section 6 of this revenue procedure provides samples of alternate provisions concerning: (.01) the statement of the annuity amount as a specific dollar amount; (.02) the payment of part of the annuity to an organization described in section 170(c); (.03) a qualified contingency; (.04) the retained right to revoke the interest of the survivor recipient; (.05) the last annuity payments to the recipients; (.06) the restriction of the charitable remainderman to a public charity; (.07) the retained right to substitute the charitable remainderman; and (.08) a power of appointment to designate the charitable remainderman.

For transfers to a qualifying CRAT, as defined in section 664(d)(1), the remainder interest will be deductible by a citizen or resident of the United States under sections 170(f)(2)(A), 2055(e)(2)(A), and 2522(c)(2)(A) for income, estate, and gift tax purposes, respectively, if the other requirements of sections 170(f)(2)(A), 2055(e)(2)(A), and 2522(c)(2)(A) (that is, the requirements not relating to the provisions of the governing instrument) are also met. The Service will recognize a trust as a qualified CRAT meeting all of the requirements of section 664(d)(1) if the trust operates in a manner consistent with the terms of the trust instrument, if the trust is a valid trust under applicable local law, and if the trust instrument: (i) is substantially similar to the sample in section 4 of this revenue procedure; or (ii) properly integrates one or more alternate provisions from section 6 of this revenue procedure into a document substantially similar to the sample in section 4 of this revenue procedure. A trust instrument that contains substantive provisions in addition to those provided in section 4 of this revenue procedure (other than properly integrated alternate provisions from section 6 of this revenue procedure, or provisions necessary to establish a valid trust under applicable local law that are not inconsistent with the applicable federal tax requirements), or that omits any of the provisions of section 4 of this revenue procedure (unless an alternate provision from section 6 of this revenue procedure is properly integrated), will not necessarily be disqualified, but neither will that trust be assured of qualification under the provisions of this revenue procedure. The Service generally will not issue a letter ruling on whether an inter vivos trust created by an individual and with consecutive interests for two measuring lives qualifies as a CRAT. The Service, however, generally will issue letter rulings on the effect of substantive trust provisions, other than those contained in sections 4 and 6 of this revenue procedure, on the qualification of a trust as a CRAT.

SECTION 4. SAMPLE INTER VIVOS CHARITABLE REMAINDER ANNUITY TRUST -- TWO LIVES, CONSECUTIVE INTERESTS

On this ___ day of ___, 20___, I, ___ (hereinafter "the Donor"), desiring to establish a charitable remainder annuity trust, within the meaning of Rev. Proc. 2003–55 and section 664(d)(1) of the Internal Revenue Code (hereinafter "the Code"), hereby enter into this trust agreement with ___ as the initial trustee (hereinafter "the Trustee"). This trust shall be known as the ___ Charitable Remainder Annuity Trust.

1. Funding of Trust. The Donor hereby transfers and irrevocably assigns, on the above date, to the Trustee the property described in Schedule A, and the Trustee accepts the property and agrees to hold, manage, and distribute the property under the terms set forth in this trust instrument.

2. Payment of Annuity Amount. In each taxable year of the trust during the annuity period, the Trustee shall pay to [permissible recipient] (hereinafter "the Initial Recipient") until the Initial Recipient's death, and thereafter to [permissible recipient] (hereinafter "the Successor Recipient") (subject to any proration in paragraph 4), an annuity amount equal to [a number no less than 5 and no more than 50] percent of the initial net fair market value of all property transferred to the trust, valued as of the above date (that is, the date of the transfer). The first day of the annuity period shall be the date the property is transferred to the trust and the last day of the annuity period shall be the date of the death of the survivor of the Initial Recipient and the Successor Recipient. The annuity amount shall be paid in equal quarterly installments at the end of each calendar quarter from income, and to the extent income is not sufficient, from principal. Any income of the trust for a taxable year in excess of the annuity amount shall be added to principal. If the initial net fair market value of the trust assets is incorrectly determined, then within a reasonable period after the value is finally determined for federal tax purposes, the Trustee shall pay to the Initial Recipient and/or Successor Recipient (in the case of an undervaluation) or receive from the Initial Recipient and/or Successor Recipient (in the case of an overvaluation) an amount equal to the difference between the annuity amount(s) properly payable and the annuity amount(s) actually paid.

3. Payment of Federal Estate Taxes and State Death Taxes. The lifetime annuity interest of the Successor Recipient will take effect upon the death of the Initial Recipient only if the Successor Recipient furnishes the funds for payment of any federal estate taxes and state death taxes for which the Trustee may be liable upon the death of the Initial Recipient. If the funds are not furnished by the Successor Recipient, the annuity period shall terminate on the death of the Initial Recipient, notwithstanding any other provision in this instrument to the contrary.

4. Proration of Annuity Amount. The Trustee shall prorate the annuity amount on a daily basis for any short taxable year. If the Successor Recipient survives the Initial Recipient, the Trustee shall prorate on a daily basis the next regular annuity payment due after the death of the Initial Recipient between the estate of the Initial Recipient and the Successor Recipient. In the taxable year of the trust during which the annuity period ends, the Trustee shall prorate the annuity amount on a daily basis for the number of days of the annuity period in that taxable year.

5. Distribution to Charity. At the termination of the annuity period, the Trustee shall distribute all of the then principal and income of the trust (other than any amount due the Recipients or their estates under the provisions above) to [designated remainderman] (hereinafter "the Charitable Organization"). If the Charitable Organization is not an organization described in sections 170(c), 2055(a), and 2522(a) of the Code at the time when any principal or income of the trust is to be distributed to it, then the Trustee shall distribute the then principal and income to one or more organizations described in sections 170(c), 2055(a), and 2522(a) of the Code as the Trustee shall select, and in the proportions as the Trustee shall decide, in the Trustee's sole discretion.

6. Additional Contributions. No additional contributions shall be made to the trust after the initial contribution.

7. Prohibited Transactions. The Trustee shall not engage in any act of self-dealing within the meaning of section 4941(d) of the Code, as modified by section 4947(a)(2)(A) of the Code, and shall not make any taxable expenditures within the meaning of section 4945(d) of the Code, as modified by section 4947(a)(2)(A) of the Code.

8. Taxable Year. The taxable year of the trust shall be the calendar year.

9. Governing Law. The operation of the trust shall be governed by the laws of the State of ___. However, the Trustee is prohibited from exercising any power or discretion granted under said laws that would be inconsistent with the qualification of the trust as a charitable remainder annuity trust under section 664(d)(1) of the Code and the corresponding regulations.

10. Limited Power of Amendment. This trust is irrevocable. However, the Trustee shall have the power, acting alone, to amend the trust from time to time in any manner required for the sole purpose of ensuring that the trust qualifies and continues to qualify as a charitable remainder annuity trust within the meaning of section 664(d)(1) of the Code.

11. Investment of Trust Assets. Nothing in this trust instrument shall be construed to restrict the Trustee from investing the trust assets in a manner that could result in the annual realization of a reasonable amount of income or gain from the sale or disposition of trust assets.

SECTION 5. ANNOTATIONS REGARDING SAMPLE INTER VIVOS CHARITABLE REMAINDER ANNUITY TRUST -- TWO LIVES, CONSECUTIVE INTERESTS

.01 Annotations for Introductory Paragraph and Paragraph 1, Funding of Trust, of the Sample Trust.

(1) Factors concerning qualification of trust. A deduction must be allowable under section 170, section 2055, or section 2522 for property contributed to the trust. Section 1.664-1(a)(1)(iii)(a) of the Income Tax Regulations. The trust must meet the definition of and function exclusively as a charitable remainder trust from the creation of the trust. Section 1.664-1(a)(4). Solely for purposes of section 664, a trust is deemed created at the earliest time that neither the grantor nor any other person is treated as the owner of the entire trust under subpart E, part 1, subchapter J, chapter 1, subtitle A of the Code (subpart E), but in no event prior to the time property is first transferred to the trust. Neither the donor nor the donor's spouse shall be treated as the owner of the trust under subpart E merely because he or she is named as a recipient of the annuity amount. Section 1.664-1(a)(4). In addition, funding the trust with certain types of assets may disqualify it as a charitable remainder trust. See section 1.664-1(a)(7) and Rev. Rul. 73–610, 1973–2 C.B. 213.

(2) Valuation of unmarketable assets. If the trust is funded with unmarketable assets, the initial net fair market value of the assets must be determined exclusively by an independent trustee, as defined in section 1.664–1(a)(7)(iii), or must be determined by a current "qualified appraisal" from a "qualified appraiser," as defined in section 1.170A–13(c)(3) and (c)(5), respectively. Section 1.664–1(a)(7).

(3) Income tax deductibility limitations. The amount of the charitable deduction for income tax purposes is affected by a number of factors, including the type of property contributed to the trust, the type of charity receiving the property, whether the remainder interest is paid outright to charity or held in further trust, and the donor's adjusted gross income (with certain adjustments). See section 170(b) and (e); section 1.170A–8;

Rev. Rul. 80–38, 1980–1 C.B. 56; and Rev. Rul. 79–368, 1979–2 C.B. 109. See section 6.06 of this revenue procedure for an alternate provision that restricts the charitable remainderman to a public charity (as defined therein).

(4)   Trustee provisions. Alternate or successor trustees may be designated in the trust instrument. In addition, the trust instrument may contain other administrative provisions relating to the trustee's duties and powers, as long as the provisions do not conflict with the rules governing charitable remainder trusts under section 664 and the regulations thereunder.

(5)   Identity of donor. For purposes of qualification under this revenue procedure, the donor may be an individual or a husband and wife. Appropriate adjustments should be made to the introductory paragraph if a husband and wife are the donors. Terms such as "grantor" or "settlor" may be substituted for "donor."

.02 Annotations for Paragraph 2, Payment of Annuity Amount, of the Sample Trust.

(1)   Permissible recipients. For a CRAT with an annuity period based on the lives of two individuals, the annuity amount must generally be paid to those individuals and both must be living at the time of the creation of the trust. See Rev. Rul. 2002–20, 2002–1 C.B. 794, for situations in which the annuity amount may be paid to a trust for the benefit of an individual who is financially disabled. An organization described in section 170(c) may receive part, but not all, of the annuity amount. Section 664(d)(1)(A) and section 1.664–2(a)(3)(i). See section 6.02 of this revenue procedure for an alternate provision that provides for payment of part of the annuity to an organization described in section 170(c).

(2)   Percentage requirements. The sum certain annuity amount must be at least 5 percent and not more than 50 percent of the initial net fair market value of the assets placed in trust. Section 664(d)(1)(A). Even if the sum certain annuity amount is at least 5 percent and not more than 50 percent of the initial net fair market value of the assets placed in trust, no deduction will be allowable under section 2055 or section 2522 if the probability that the trust corpus will be exhausted before the death of the survivor of the recipients exceeds 5 percent. Rev. Rul. 77–374, 1977–2 C.B. 329, and Rev. Rul. 70–452, 1970–2 C.B. 199. See sections 1.7520–3(b) and 25.7520–3(b) for special rules that may be applicable in valuing interests transferred to CRATs. In addition, the value (determined under section 7520) of the charitable remainder interest must be at least 10 percent of the initial net fair market value of all property placed in the trust. Section 664(d)(1)(D).

(3)   Payment of annuity amount in installments. Paragraph 2, Payment of Annuity Amount, of the sample trust specifies that the annuity amount is to be paid in equal quarterly installments at the end of each quarter. However, the trust instrument may specify that the annuity amount is to be paid to the recipient annually or in equal or unequal installments throughout the year. See section 1.664–2(a)(1)(i). The amount of the charitable deduction will be affected by the frequency of payment, by whether the installments are equal or unequal, and by whether each installment is payable at the beginning or end of the period. See section 1.664–2(c) and section 20.2031–7(d)(2)(iv).

(4)   Payment of annuity amount by close of taxable year. Generally, the annuity amount for any taxable year must be paid before the close of the taxable year for which it is due. For circumstances under which the annuity amount may be paid within a reasonable time after the close of the taxable year, see section 1.664-2(a)(1)(i)(a).

(5)   Early distributions to charity. The trust instrument may provide that an amount other than the annuity shall be paid (or may be paid in the discretion of the trustee) to an organization described in section 170(c). If such a distribution is made in kind, the adjusted basis of the property distributed must be fairly representative of the adjusted basis of the property available for distribution on the date of distribution. Section 1.664–2(a)(4).

.03 Annotation for Paragraph 3, Payment of Federal Estate Taxes and State Death Taxes, of the Sample Trust.

(1)   Tax payment clause. If it is possible that all or part of the fair market value of the trust assets will be includible for federal estate tax purposes in the gross estate of the donor, the trust must contain a tax payment clause. If federal estate taxes and state death taxes are paid from other sources, the tax payment clause will never become operative. Nevertheless, the tax payment clause is necessary because it ensures that the trustee will never be required to pay federal estate taxes or state death taxes from the trust assets. See section 664(d)(1)(B); section 1.664-1 (a)(6), Example 3; and Rev. Rul. 82-128, 1982-2 C.B. 71.

.04 Annotations for Paragraph 4, Proration of Annuity Amount, of the Sample Trust.

(1) Prorating annuity amount. To compute the annuity amount in a short taxable year and in the taxable year in which the annuity period terminates, see section 1.664-2(a)(1)(iv)(a) and (b), respectively.

(2) Determining annuity amount payable in year of a recipient's death. Paragraph 4, Proration of Annuity Amount, of the sample trust specifies that the annuity amount shall be prorated on a daily basis. See section 6.05 of this revenue procedure for alternate provisions that provide for termination of the annuity amount with the last regular payment preceding the death of each recipient.

.05 Annotations for Paragraph 5, Distribution to Charity, of the Sample Trust.

(1) Minimum value of remainder. As noted in section 5.02(2) of this revenue procedure, the value (determined under section 7520) of the charitable remainder interest is required to be at least 10 percent of the initial net fair market value of all property placed in the trust. Section 664(d)(1)(D).

(2) Designated remainderman. Any named charitable remainderman must be an organization described in section 170(c) at the time of the transfer to the charitable remainder annuity trust. See section 664(d)(1)(C). Any named charitable remainderman also must be an organization described in section 2522(a) to qualify for the gift tax charitable deduction and an organization described in section 2055(a) to qualify for the estate tax charitable deduction. See Rev. Rul. 77–385, 1977–2 C.B. 331. If it is determined that a deduction under section 2055(a) will not be necessary in any event, all references to section 2055(a) in the trust instrument may be deleted. The trust instrument may restrict the charitable remainderman to an organization described in sections 170(c), 2055(a), and 2522(a), but grant to a trustee or other person the power to designate the actual charitable remainderman. The gift of the remainder interest will be incomplete for gift tax purposes if, for example: (i) the donor retains the power to substitute the charitable remainderman; or (ii) the trust instrument provides the trustee with the power to designate the charitable remainderman and the donor is not prohibited from serving as trustee. See section 25.2511–2(c). Note, however, that an income tax charitable deduction is available even if the donor has the authority to substitute the charitable remainderman or the trustee has the authority to designate the charitable remainderman. Rev. Rul. 68–417, 1968–2 C.B. 103; Rev. Rul. 79–368, 1979–2 C.B. 109. See section 6.07 of this revenue procedure for an alternate provision in which the donor retains the right to substitute the charitable remainderman. See section 6.08 of this revenue procedure for an alternate provision in which a recipient is granted a power of appointment to designate the charitable remainderman.

(3) Multiple remaindermen. The remainder interest may pass to more than one charitable organization as long as each organization is described in sections 170(c), 2522(a), and, if needed, section 2055(a). Section 1.664-2(a)(6)(i).

(4) Alternative remaindermen. The trust instrument of a CRAT must provide a means for selecting alternative charitable remaindermen in the event the designated organization is not qualified at the time any payments are to be made to it from the trust. Section 1.664–2(a)(6)(iv).

.06 Annotations for Paragraph 7, Prohibited Transactions, of the Sample Trust.

(1) Payment of the annuity amount. Payment of the annuity amount to the recipients is not considered an act of self-dealing within the meaning of section 4941(d), as modified by section 4947(a)(2)(A), or a taxable expenditure within the meaning of section 4945(d), as modified by section 4947(a)(2)(A). Section 53.4947–1(c)(2) of the Foundation and Similar Excise Taxes Regulations.

(2) Prohibitions against certain investments and excess business holdings. Prohibitions against investments that jeopardize the exempt purpose of the trust for purposes of section 4944, as modified by section 4947(a)(2)(A), and against retaining any excess business holdings for purposes of section 4943, as modified by section 4947(a)(2)(A), are required if the trust provides for payment of part of an annuity amount to an organization described in section 170(c) and gift and estate tax charitable deductions are sought for this interest. See section 4947(b)(3). See section 6.02 of this revenue procedure for an alternate provision that provides for payment of part of the annuity to an organization described in section 170(c).

(3)   Trust to continue in existence for benefit of charity. The governing instrument requirements of section 508(e) must be included in the trust instrument if, after the termination of the annuity period: (i) the trust instrument provides that the trust shall continue in existence for the benefit of the charitable remainderman and, as a result, the trust will become subject to the provisions of section 4947(a)(1); and (ii) the trust will be treated as a private foundation within the meaning of section 509(a), as modified by section 4947(a)(1). Except as provided in paragraph 7 of the sample trust, the trust instrument may limit the application of the provisions of section 508(e) to the period after the termination of the annuity period when the trust continues in existence for the benefit of the charitable remainderman. Note that when the trust provides for the trust corpus to be retained, in whole or in part, in trust for the charitable remainderman, the higher deductibility limitations in section 170(b)(1)(A) for the income tax charitable deduction will not be available (even if the charitable remainderman is restricted to a public charity) because the contribution of the trust corpus is made "for the use of" rather than "to" the charitable remainderman. See section 1.170A–8(b).

SECTION 6. ALTERNATE PROVISIONS FOR SAMPLE INTER VIVOS CHARITABLE REMAINDER ANNUITY TRUST—TWO LIVES, CONSECUTIVE INTERESTS

.01 Annuity Amount Stated as a Specific Dollar Amount.

(1)   Explanation. As an alternative to stating the annuity amount as a fraction or percentage of the initial net fair market value of the assets transferred to the trust, the annuity amount may be stated as a specific dollar amount. Section 1.664–2(a)(1)(ii) and (iii). In either case, the annuity amount must be not less than 5 percent nor more than 50 percent of the initial net fair market value of all property placed in trust. Section 664(d)(1)(A).

(2)   Instructions for use.

(a) Replace the first sentence of paragraph 2, Payment of Annuity Amount, of the sample trust with the following sentence:

In each taxable year of the trust during the annuity period, the Trustee shall pay to [permissible recipient] (hereinafter "the Initial Recipient") until the Initial Recipient's death and thereafter to [permissible recipient] (hereinafter "the Successor Recipient") (subject to any proration in paragraph 4), an annuity amount equal to [the stated dollar amount].

(b) Delete the last sentence of paragraph 2, Payment of Annuity Amount, of the sample trust concerning the incorrect valuation of trust assets.

.02 Payment of Part of the Annuity to an Organization Described in section 170(c).

(1)   Explanation. An organization described in section 170(c) may receive part, but not all, of any annuity amount. Section 664(d)(1)(A). If a gift tax charitable deduction, and, if needed, an estate tax charitable deduction are sought for the present value of the annuity interest passing to a charitable organization, the trust instrument must contain additional provisions. First, the trust instrument must specify the portion of each annuity payment that is payable to the noncharitable recipient and to the charitable organization described in sections 170(c), 2522(a), and, if needed, section 2055(a). Second, the trust instrument must contain a means for selecting an alternative qualified charitable organization if the designated organization is not a qualified organization at the time when any annuity amount is to be paid to it. Third, the trust instrument must contain prohibitions against investments that jeopardize the exempt purpose of the trust for purposes of section 4944, as modified by section 4947(a)(2)(A), and against retaining any excess business holdings for purposes of section 4943, as modified by section 4947(a)(2)(A).

(2)   Instructions for use.

(a) Replace paragraph 2, Payment of Annuity Amount, of the sample trust with the following paragraph:

Payment of Annuity Amount. The annuity amount is equal to [a number no less than 5 and no more than 50] percent of the initial net fair market value of all property transferred to the trust, valued as of the above date (that is, the date of transfer). In each taxable year of the trust during the annuity period, the Trustee shall pay [the percentage of the annuity amount payable to the noncharitable recipients] percent of the annuity amount to [permissible recipient] (hereinafter "the Initial Recipient") until the Initial Recipient's death, and thereafter to [permissible recipient] (hereinafter "the Successor Recipient") (subject to any proration in paragraph 4). In each taxable year of the trust during the annuity period, the Trustee shall pay [the percentage of the annuity amount payable to the charitable recipient] percent of the annuity amount to [an organization described in sections 170(c), 2055(a), and 2522(a) of the Code] (hereinafter "the Charitable Recipient"). The first day of the annuity period shall be the date the property is transferred to the trust and the last day of the annuity period shall be the date of the death of the survivor of the Initial Recipient and the Successor Recipient. If the Charitable Recipient is not an organization described in sections 170(c), 2055(a), and 2522(a) of the Code at the time when any annuity payment is to be distributed to it, then the Trustee shall distribute that annuity payment to one or more organizations described in sections 170(c), 2055(a), and 2522(a) of the Code as the Trustee shall select, and in the proportions as the Trustee shall decide, in the Trustee's sole discretion. The annuity amount shall be paid in equal quarterly installments at the end of each calendar quarter from income, and to the extent income is not sufficient, from principal. Any income of the trust for a taxable year in excess of the annuity amount shall be added to principal. If the initial net fair market value of the trust assets is incorrectly determined, then within a reasonable period after the value is finally determined for federal tax purposes, the Trustee shall pay to the Initial Recipient and/or the Successor Recipient and the Charitable Recipient (in the case of an undervaluation) or receive from the Initial Recipient and/or the Successor Recipient and the Charitable Recipient (in the case of an overvaluation) an amount equal to the difference between the annuity amount(s) properly payable and the annuity amount(s) actually paid.

(b) Replace the first parenthetical in paragraph 5, Distribution to Charity, of the sample trust with the following parenthetical:

(other than any amount due the Initial Recipient, the Successor Recipient, or their estates and the Charitable Recipient under the provisions above).

(c) Add the following sentence after the first and only sentence in paragraph 7, Prohibited Transactions, of the sample trust:

The Trustee shall not make any investments that jeopardize the exempt purpose of the trust for purposes of section 4944 of the Code, as modified by section 4947(a)(2)(A) of the Code, or retain any excess business holdings for purposes of section 4943 of the Code, as modified by section 4947(a)(2)(A) of the Code.

.03 Qualified Contingency.

(1) Explanation. Under section 664(f), payment of the annuity amount may terminate upon the earlier of the occurrence of a qualified contingency (as defined in section 664(f)(3)) or the death of the survivor of the initial recipient and the successor recipient. The amount of the charitable deduction, however, will be determined without regard to a qualified contingency. See section 664(f)(2).

(2) Instruction for use. Replace the second sentence of paragraph 2, Payment of Annuity Amount, of the sample trust with the following sentence:

The first day of the annuity period shall be the date the property is transferred to the trust and the last day of the annuity period shall be the date of the death of the survivor of the Initial Recipient and the Successor Recipient or, if earlier, the date on which occurs the [qualified contingency].

.04 Retaining the Right to Revoke the Interest of the Successor Recipient.

(1) Explanation. The donor may retain the right to revoke or terminate the interest of the successor recipient. This right is exercisable only by the donor's last will and testament. Section 1.664-2(a)(4). The retention of this right may have gift and estate tax consequences. It will affect the value of the annuity interests transferred. It may also cause a portion of the trust to be included in the donor's gross estate for federal estate tax purposes, even if it would otherwise not be includible. The following alternate provision provides for the donor's retention of the right to revoke when the donor is also a recipient.

(2) Instructions for use. To retain the right to revoke the successor recipient's interest by the donor's last will and testament:

(a) Designate the donor as the initial recipient in paragraph 2, Payment of Annuity Amount, of the sample trust.

(b) Replace the second sentence of paragraph 2, Payment of Annuity Amount, of the sample trust with the following two sentences:

The Donor hereby expressly reserves the power, exercisable only by the Donor's last will and testament, to revoke and terminate the interest of the Successor Recipient under this trust. The first day of the annuity period shall be the date the property is transferred to the trust and the last day of the annuity period shall be the date of the death of the survivor of the Initial Recipient and the Successor Recipient or, if the Donor revokes the interest of the Successor Recipient, the date of the Initial Recipient's death.

.05 Last Annuity Payments to the Recipients.

(1)   Explanation. As an alternative to prorating the annuity amount in the taxable year of the initial recipient's death, payment of the initial recipient's share of the annuity amount may terminate with the last regular payment preceding the initial recipient's death. Similarly, as an alternative to prorating the annuity amount in the taxable year of the termination of the annuity period, payment of the annuity amount may terminate with the last regular payment preceding the termination of the annuity period. However, the fact that a recipient may not receive the last payment shall not be taken into account for purposes of determining the present value of the remainder interest. Section 1.664–2(a)(5)(i).

(2)   Instructions for use.

(a) To add an alternate provision to terminate the payment of the initial recipient's share of the annuity amount with the last regular payment preceding his or her death, replace paragraph 4, Proration of Annuity Amount, of the sample trust with the following paragraph:

Proration of Annuity Amount. Except as provided below, the Trustee shall prorate the annuity amount on a daily basis for any short taxable year. The obligation of the Trustee to pay the annuity amount to the Initial Recipient shall terminate with the regular quarterly installment next preceding the Initial Recipient's death. In the taxable year of the trust during which the annuity period ends, the Trustee shall prorate the annuity amount on a daily basis for the number of days of the annuity period in that taxable year.

(b) To add an alternate provision to terminate the payment of the annuity amount with the last regular payment preceding the termination of the annuity period, replace paragraph 4, Proration of Annuity Amount, of the sample trust with the following paragraph:

Proration of Annuity Amount. Except as provided below, the Trustee shall prorate the annuity amount on a daily basis for any short taxable year. If the Successor Recipient survives the Initial Recipient, the Trustee shall prorate on a daily basis the next regular annuity payment due after the death of the Initial Recipient between the estate of the Initial Recipient and the Successor Recipient. In the taxable year of the trust during which the annuity period ends, the obligation of the Trustee to pay the annuity amount shall terminate with the regular quarterly installment next preceding the termination of the annuity period.

(c) To add an alternate provision terminating the payment of the initial recipient's share of the annuity amount with the last regular payment preceding his or her death, and terminating the payment of the annuity amount with the last regular payment preceding the termination of the annuity period, replace paragraph 4, Proration of Annuity Amount, of the sample trust with the following paragraph:

Proration of Annuity Amount. Except as provided below, the Trustee shall prorate the annuity amount on a daily basis for any short taxable year. The obligation of the Trustee to pay the annuity amount to the Initial Recipient shall terminate with the regular quarterly installment next preceding the Initial Recipient's death. In the taxable year of the trust during which the annuity period ends, the obligation of the Trustee to pay the annuity amount shall terminate with the regular quarterly installment next preceding the termination of the annuity period.

.06 Restricting the Charitable Remainderman to a Public Charity.

(1) Explanation. The amount of the donor's income tax charitable deduction is more limited for gifts to certain private foundations than for other charitable organizations. Specifically, charitable organizations described in section 170(c) include private foundations that are not described in section 170(b)(1)(E). See section 170(b) and Rev. Rul. 79–368, 1979–2 C.B. 109. To avoid these more restrictive limitations, a donor of an inter vivos CRAT may wish to restrict the charitable remainderman to an organization that is described in section 170(b)(1)(A) as well as sections 170(c), 2055(a), and 2522(a) (referred to herein as a "public charity").

(2) Instruction for use. To restrict the charitable remainderman to a public charity, each and every time the phrase "an organization described in sections 170(c), 2055(a), and 2522(a) of the Code" appears in the sample trust, replace it with the phrase "an organization described in sections 170(b)(1)(A), 170(c), 2055(a), and 2522(a) of the Code."

.07 Retaining the Right to Substitute the Charitable Remainderman.

(1) Explanation. The donor may retain the right to substitute another charitable remainderman for the charitable remainderman named in the trust instrument. See Rev. Rul. 76–8, 1976–1 C.B. 179. Note, however, that the retention of this right will cause the gift of the remainder interest to be incomplete for gift tax purposes. See section 25.2511–2(c) and Rev. Rul. 77–275, 1977–2 C.B. 346.

(2) Instruction for use. Insert the following sentence between the first and last sentences of paragraph 5, Distribution to Charity, of the sample trust:

The Donor reserves the right to designate, at any time and from time to time, in lieu of the Charitable Organization identified above, one or more organizations described in sections 170(c), 2055(a), and 2522(a) of the Code as the charitable remainderman and shall make any such designation by giving written notice to the Trustee.

.08 Power of Appointment to Designate the Charitable Remainderman.

(1) Explanation. The trust instrument may grant a recipient a power of appointment to designate the charitable remainderman. See Rev. Rul. 76–7, 1976–1 C.B. 179.

(2) Instruction for use. Replace paragraph 5, Distribution to Charity, of the sample trust with the following paragraph:

Distribution to Charity. At the termination of the annuity period, the Trustee shall distribute all of the then principal and income of the trust (other than any amount due the Recipients or their estates under the provisions above) to one or more charitable organizations described in sections 170(c), 2055(a) and 2522(a) of the Code as [one of the named permissible recipients] shall appoint and direct by specific reference to this power of appointment by inter vivos or testamentary instrument. To the extent this power of appointment is not effectively exercised, the principal and income not effectively appointed shall be distributed to one or more organizations described in sections 170(c), 2055(a), and 2522(a) of the Code as the Trustee shall select, and in the proportions as the Trustee shall decide, in the Trustee's sole discretion. If an organization fails to qualify as an organization described in sections 170(c), 2055(a), and 2522(a) of the Code at the time when any principal or income of the trust is to be distributed to it, then the Trustee shall distribute the then principal and income to one or more organizations described in sections 170(c), 2055(a), and 2522(a) of the Code as the Trustee shall select, and in the proportions as the Trustee shall decide, in the Trustee's sole discretion.

SECTION 7. EFFECT ON OTHER REVENUE PROCEDURES

Section 4 of Rev. Proc. 90–32 is superseded.

DRAFTING INFORMATION

The principal authors of this revenue procedure are Karlene M. Lesho and Stephanie N. Bland of the Office of Associate Chief Counsel (Passthroughs and Special Industries). For further information regarding this revenue procedure, contact Karlene M. Lesho or Stephanie N. Bland at (202) 622-7830 (not a toll-free call).

IRS SPECIMEN INTER VIVOS CRAT: PAYMENTS FOR TWO MEASURING LIVES—PAYABLE CONCURRENTLY AND CONSECUTIVELY

Annotations and Alternative Provisions
Rev. Proc. 2003–56

SECTION 1. PURPOSE

This revenue procedure contains an annotated sample declaration of trust and alternate provisions that meet the requirements of section 664(d)(1) of the Internal Revenue Code for an inter vivos charitable remainder annuity trust (CRAT) providing for annuity payments payable concurrently and consecutively for two measuring lives followed by the distribution of trust assets to a charitable remainderman.

SECTION 2. BACKGROUND

Previously, the Internal Revenue Service issued sample trust instruments for certain types of CRATs. The Service is updating the previously issued samples and issuing new samples for additional types of CRATs; annotations and alternate sample provisions are included as further guidance. In addition to the sample trust instrument included in this revenue procedure for an inter vivos CRAT providing for annuity payments payable concurrently and consecutively for two measuring lives, samples are provided in separate revenue procedures for:

(a)   an inter vivos CRAT providing for annuity payments for one measuring life (see Rev. Proc. 2003–53, superceding Rev. Proc. 89–21, 1989-1 C.B. 842);

(b)   an inter vivos CRAT providing for annuity payments for a term of years (see Rev. Proc. 2003–54);

(c)   an inter vivos CRAT providing for annuity payments payable consecutively for two measuring lives (see Rev. Proc. 2003–55, superceding section 4 of Rev. Proc. 90–32, 1990–1 C.B. 546);

(d)   a testamentary CRAT providing for annuity payments for one measuring life (see Rev. Proc. 2003–57, superceding section 6 of Rev. Proc. 90–32);

(e)   a testamentary CRAT providing for annuity payments for a term of years (see Rev. Proc. 2003-58);

(f)   a testamentary CRAT providing for annuity payments payable consecutively for two measuring lives (see Rev. Proc. 2003–59, superceding section 7 of Rev. Proc. 90–32); and

(g)   a testamentary CRAT providing for annuity payments payable concurrently and consecutively for two measuring lives (see Rev. Proc. 2003–60, superceding section 8 of Rev. Proc. 90–32).

SECTION 3. SCOPE AND OBJECTIVE

Section 4 of this revenue procedure provides a sample declaration of trust for an inter vivos CRAT with concurrent and consecutive interests for two measuring lives that is created by an individual who is a citizen or resident of the United States. Section 5 of this revenue procedure provides annotations to the provisions of the sample trust. Section 6 of this revenue procedure provides samples of alternate provisions concerning: (.01) the statement of the annuity amount as a specific dollar amount; (.02) the payment of part of the annuity to an organization described in section 170(c); (.03) a qualified contingency; (.04) the retained right to revoke the interest of the survivor recipient; (.05) the last annuity payments to the recipients; (.06) the restriction of the charitable remainderman to a public charity; (.07) the retained right to substitute the charitable remainderman; and (.08) a power of appointment to designate the charitable remainderman.

For transfers to a qualifying CRAT, as defined in section 664(d)(1), the remainder interest will be deductible by a citizen or resident of the United States under sections 170(f)(2)(A), 2055(e)(2)(A), and 2522(c)(2)(A) for income, estate, and gift tax purposes, respectively, if the other requirements of sections 170(f)(2)(A), 2055(e)(2)(A), and 2522(c)(2)(A) (that is, the requirements not relating to the provisions of the governing instrument) are also met. The Service will recognize a trust as a qualified CRAT meeting all of the requirements of section 664(d)(1) if the trust operates in a manner consistent with the terms of the trust instrument, if the trust is a valid trust under applicable local law, and if the trust instrument: (i) is substantially similar to the sample in section 4 of this revenue procedure; or (ii) properly integrates one or more alternate provisions from section 6 of this revenue procedure into a document substantially similar to the sample in section 4 of this revenue procedure. A trust instrument that contains substantive provisions in addition to those provided in section 4 of this revenue procedure (other than properly integrated alternate provisions from section 6 of this revenue procedure, or provisions necessary to establish a valid trust under applicable local law that are not inconsistent with the applicable federal tax requirements), or that omits any of the provisions of section 4 of this revenue procedure (unless an alternate provision from section 6 of this revenue procedure is properly integrated), will not necessarily be disqualified, but neither will that trust be assured of qualification under the provisions of this revenue procedure. The Service generally will not issue a letter ruling on whether an inter vivos trust created by an individual and with concurrent and consecutive interests for two measuring lives qualifies as a CRAT. The Service, however, generally will issue letter rulings on the effect of substantive trust provisions, other than those contained in sections 4 and 6 of this revenue procedure, on the qualification of a trust as a CRAT.

SECTION 4. SAMPLE INTER VIVOS CHARITABLE REMAINDER ANNUITY TRUST—TWO LIVES, CONCURRENT AND CONSECUTIVE INTERESTS

On this ___ day of ___, 20___, I, ___ (hereinafter "the Donor"), desiring to establish a charitable remainder annuity trust, within the meaning of Rev. Proc. 2003-56 and section 664(d)(1) of the Internal Revenue Code (hereinafter "the Code"), hereby enter into this trust agreement with ___ as the initial trustee (hereinafter "the Trustee"). This trust shall be known as the ___ Charitable Remainder Annuity Trust.

1. Funding of Trust. The Donor hereby transfers and irrevocably assigns, on the above date, to the Trustee the property described in Schedule A, and the Trustee accepts the property and agrees to hold, manage, and distribute the property under the terms set forth in this trust instrument.

2. Payment of Annuity Amount. In each taxable year of the trust during the annuity period, the Trustee shall pay to [permissible recipient] and to [permissible recipient] (hereinafter "the Recipients") in equal shares during their lifetimes, an annuity amount equal to [a number no less than 5 and no more than 50] percent of the initial net fair market value of all property transferred to the trust, valued as of the above date (that is, the date of the transfer), and upon the death of one (hereinafter "the Predeceasing Recipient"), the Trustee shall pay the entire annuity amount (subject to any proration in paragraph 4) to the survivor (hereinafter "the Survivor Recipient"). The first day of the annuity period shall be the date the property is transferred to the trust and the last day of the annuity period shall be the date of the Survivor Recipient's death. The annuity amount shall be paid in equal quarterly installments at the end of each calendar quarter from income, and to the extent income is not sufficient, from principal. Any income of the trust for a taxable year in excess of the annuity amount shall be added to principal. If the initial net fair market value of the trust assets is incorrectly determined, then within a reasonable period after the value is finally determined for federal tax purposes, the Trustee shall pay to the Recipients (in the case of an undervaluation) or receive from the Recipients (in the case of an overvaluation) an amount equal to the difference between the annuity amount(s) property payable and the annuity amount(s) actually paid.

3. Payment of Federal Estate Taxes and State Death Taxes. The lifetime annuity interest of the Survivor Recipient will continue in effect upon the death of the Predeceasing Recipient only if the Survivor Recipient furnishes the funds for payment of any federal estate taxes and state death taxes for which the Trustee may be liable upon the death of the Predeceasing Recipient. If the funds are not furnished by the Survivor Recipient, the annuity period shall terminate on the death of the Predeceasing Recipient, notwithstanding any other provision in this instrument to the contrary.

4. Proration of Annuity Amount. The Trustee shall prorate the annuity amount on a daily basis for any short taxable year. Upon the death of the Predeceasing Recipient, the Trustee shall prorate on a daily basis the Predeceasing Recipient's share of the next regular annuity payment between the estate of the Predeceasing Recipient and the Survivor Recipient. In the taxable year of the trust during which the annuity period ends, the Trustee shall prorate the annuity amount on a daily basis for the number of days of the annuity period in that taxable year.

5. Distribution to Charity. At the termination of the annuity period, the Trustee shall distribute all of the then principal and income of the trust (other than any amount due the Recipients or their estates under the provisions above) to [designated remainderman] (hereinafter "the Charitable Organization"). If the Charitable Organization is not an organization described in sections 170(c), 2055(a), and 2522(a) of the Code at the time when any principal or income of the trust is to be distributed to it, then the Trustee shall distribute the then principal and income to one or more organizations described in sections 1701(c), 2055(a), and 2522(a) of the Code as the Trustee shall select, and in the proportions as the Trustee shall decide, in the Trustee's sole discretion.

6. Additional Contributions. No additional contributions shall be made to the trust after the initial contribution.

7. Prohibited Transactions. The Trustee shall not engage in any act of self-dealing within the meaning of section 4941(d) of the Code, as modified by section 4947(a)(2)(A) of the Code, and shall not make any taxable expenditures within the meaning of section 4945(d) of the Code, as modified by section 4947(a)(2)(A) of the Code.

8. Taxable Year. The taxable year of the trust shall be the calendar year.

9. Governing Law. The operation of the trust shall be governed by the laws of the State of ___. However, the Trustee is prohibited from exercising any power or discretion granted under said laws that would be inconsistent with the qualification of the trust as a charitable remainder annuity trust under section 664(d)(1) of the Code and the corresponding regulations.

10. Limited Power of Amendment. This trust is irrevocable. However, the Trustee shall have the power, acting alone, to amend the trust from time to time in any manner required for the sole purpose of ensuring that the trust qualifies and continues to qualify as a charitable remainder annuity trust within the meaning of section 664(d)(1) of the Code.

11. Investment of Trust Assets. Nothing in this trust instrument shall be construed to restrict the Trustee from investing the trust assets in a manner that could result in the annual realization of a reasonable amount of income or gain from the sale or disposition of trust assets.

SECTION 5. ANNOTATIONS REGARDING SAMPLE INTER VIVOS CHARITABLE REMAINDER ANNUITY TRUST—TWO LIVES, CONCURRENT AND CONSECUTIVE INTERESTS

.01 Annotations for Introductory Paragraph and Paragraph 1, Funding of Trust, of the Sample Trust.

(1) Factors concerning qualification of trust. A deduction must be allowable under section 170, section 2055, or section 2522 for property contributed to the trust. Section 1.664–1(a)(1)(iii)(a) of the Income Tax Regulations. The trust must meet the definition of and function exclusively as a charitable remainder trust from the creation of the trust. Section 1.664–1(a)(4). Solely for purposes of section 664, a trust is deemed created at the earliest time that neither the grantor nor any other person is treated as the owner of the entire trust under subpart E, part 1, subchapter J, chapter 1, subtitle A of the Code (subpart E), but in no event prior to the time property is first transferred to the trust. Neither the donor nor the donor's spouse shall be treated as the owner of the trust under subpart E merely because he or she is named as a recipient of the annuity amount. Section 1.664–1(a)(4). In addition, funding the trust with certain types of assets may disqualify it as a charitable remainder trust. See section 1.664-1(a)(7) and Rev. Rul. 73–610, 1973–2 C.B. 213.

(2) Valuation of unmarketable assets. If the trust is funded with unmarketable assets, the initial net fair market value of the assets must be determined exclusively by an independent trustee, as defined in section 1.664-1(a)(7)(iii), or must be determined by a current "qualified appraisal" from a "qualified appraiser," as defined in section 1.170A–13(c)(3) and (c)(5), respectively. Section 1.664–1(a)(7).

(3) Income tax deductibility limitations. The amount of the charitable deduction for income tax purposes is affected by a number of factors, including the type of property contributed to the trust, the type of charity receiving the property, whether the remainder interest is paid outright to charity or held in further trust, and the donor's adjusted gross income (with certain adjustments). See section 170(b) and (e); section 1.170A–8;

Rev. Rul. 80–38, 1980–1 C.B. 56; and Rev. Rul. 79–368, 1979–2 C.B. 109. See section 6.06 of this revenue procedure for an alternate provision that restricts the charitable remainderman to a public charity (as defined therein).

(4) Trustee provisions. Alternate or successor trustees may be designated in the trust instrument. In addition, the trust instrument may contain other administrative provisions relating to the trustee's duties and powers, as long as the provisions do not conflict with the rules governing charitable remainder trusts under section 664 and the regulations thereunder.

(5) Identity of donor. For purposes of qualification under this revenue procedure, the donor may be an individual or a husband and wife. Appropriate adjustments should be made to the introductory paragraph if a husband and wife are the donors. Terms such as "grantor" or "settlor" may be substituted for "donor."

.02 Annotations for Paragraph 2, Payment of Annuity Amount, of the Sample Trust.

(1) Permissible recipients. For a CRAT having an annuity period based on the lives of two individuals, the annuity amount must generally be paid to those individuals, and both must be living at the time of the creation of the trust. See Rev. Rul. 2002–20, 2002–1 C.B. 794, for situations in which the annuity amount may be paid to a trust for the benefit of an individual who is financially disabled. An organization described in section 170(c) may receive part, but not all, of the annuity amount. Section 664(d)(1)(A) and section 1.664–2(a)(3)(i). See section 6.02 of this revenue procedure for an alternate provision that provides for payment of part of the annuity to an organization described in section 170(c).

(2) Division of annuity amount between recipients. The sample trust provides that while both recipients are alive they will share the annuity amount equally and upon the death of the predeceasing recipient the survivor recipient will receive all of the annuity amount, subject to any proration in paragraph 4. The annuity amount may be divided other than equally during the joint lives of the recipients. In addition, the share of the predeceasing recipient may be made payable to an organization described in section 170(c) for the rest of the survivor recipient's life.

(3) Percentage requirements. The sum certain annuity amount must be at least 5 percent and not more than 50 percent of the initial net fair market value of the assets placed in trust. Section 664(d)(1)(A). Even if the sum certain annuity amount is at least 5 percent and not more than 50 percent of the initial net fair market value of the assets placed in trust, no deduction will be allowable under section 2055 or section 2522 if the probability that the trust corpus will be exhausted before the death of the survivor of the recipients exceeds 5 percent. Rev. Rul. 77–37.4, 1977–2 C.B. 329 and Rev. Rul. 70–452, 1970–2 C.B. 199. See sections 1.7520–3(b) and 25.7520–3(b) for special rules that may be applicable in valuing interests transferred to CRATs. In addition, the value (determined under section 7520) of the charitable remainder interest must be at least 10 percent of the initial net fair market value of all property placed in the trust. Section 664(d)(1)(D).

(4) Payment of annuity amount in installments. Paragraph 2, Payment of Annuity Amount, of the sample trust specifies that the annuity amount is to be paid in equal quarterly installments at the end of each quarter. However, the trust instrument may specify that the annuity amount is to be paid to the recipients annually or in equal or unequal installments throughout the year. See section 1.664–2(a)(1)(i). The amount of the charitable deduction will be affected by the frequency of payment, by whether the installments are equal or unequal, and by whether each installment is payable at the beginning or end of the period. See section 1.664–2(c) and section 20.2031–7(d)(2)(iv).

(5) Payment of annuity amount by close of taxable year. Generally, the annuity amount for any taxable year must be paid before the close of the taxable year for which it is due. For circumstances under which the annuity amount may be paid within a reasonable time after the close of the taxable year, see section 1.664–2(a)(1)(i)(a).

(6) Early distributions to charity. The trust instrument may provide that an amount other than the annuity shall be paid (or may be paid in the discretion of the trustee) to an organization described in section 170(c). If such a distribution is made in kind, the adjusted basis of the property distributed must be fairly representative of the adjusted basis of the property available for distribution on the date of distribution. Section 1.664–2(a)(4).

222

.03 Annotation for Paragraph 3, Payment of Federal Estate Taxes and State Death Taxes, of the Sample Trust.

(1)   Tax payment clause. If it is possible that all or part of the fair market value of the trust assets will be includible for federal estate tax purposes in the gross estate of the donor, the trust must contain a tax payment clause. If federal estate taxes and state death taxes are paid from other sources, the tax payment clause will never become operative. Nevertheless, the tax payment clause is necessary because it ensures that the trustee will never be required to pay federal estate taxes or state death taxes from the trust assets. See section 664(d)(1)(B); section 1.664–1(a)(6), Example 3; and Rev. Rul. 82–128, 1982–2 C.B. 71.

.04 Annotations for Paragraph 4, Proration of Annuity Amount, of the Sample Trust.

(1)   Prorating annuity amount. To compute the annuity amount in a short taxable year and in the taxable year in which the annuity period terminates, see section 1.664–2(a)(1)(iv)(a) and (b), respectively.

(2)   Determining annuity amount payable in year of a recipient's death. Paragraph 4, Proration of Annuity Amount, of the sample trust specifies that the annuity amount shall be prorated on a daily basis. See section 6.05 of this revenue procedure for alternate provisions that provide for termination of the annuity amount with the last regular payment preceding the death of each recipient.

.05 Annotations for Paragraph 5, Distribution to Charity, of the Sample Trust.

(1) Minimum value of remainder. As noted in section 5.02(3) of this revenue procedure, the value (determined under section 7520) of the charitable remainder interest is required to be at least 10 percent of the initial net fair market value of all property placed in the trust. Section 664(d)(1)(D).

(2)   Designated remainderman. Any named charitable remainderman must be an organization described in section 170(c) at the time of the transfer to the charitable remainder annuity trust. See section 664(d)(1)(C). Any named charitable remainderman also must be an organization described in section 2522(a) to qualify for the gift tax charitable deduction and an organization described in section 2055(a) to qualify for the estate tax charitable deduction. See Rev. Rul. 77–385, 1977–2 C.B. 331. If it is determined that a deduction under section 2055(a) will not be necessary in any event, all references to section 2055(a) in the trust instrument may be deleted. The trust instrument may restrict the charitable remainderman to an organization described in sections 170(c), 2055(a), and 2522(a), but grant to a trustee or other person the power to designate the actual charitable remainderman. The gift of the remainder interest will be incomplete for gift tax purposes if, for example: (i) the donor retains the power to substitute the charitable remainderman; or (ii) the trust instrument provides the trustee with the power to designate the charitable remainderman and the donor is not prohibited from serving as trustee. See section 25.2511–2(c). Note, however, that an income tax charitable deduction is available even if the donor has the authority to substitute the charitable remainderman or the trustee has the authority to designate the charitable remainderman. Rev. Rul. 68–417, 1968–2 C.B. 103; Rev. Rul. 79–368, 1979–2 C.B. 109. See section 6.07 of this revenue procedure for an alternate provision in which the donor retains the fight to substitute the charitable remainderman. See section 6.08 of this revenue procedure for an alternate provision in which a recipient is granted a power of appointment to designate the charitable remainderman.

(3)   Multiple remaindermen. The remainder interest may pass to more than one charitable organization as long as each organization is described in sections 170(c), 2522(a), and, if needed, section 2055(a). Section 1.664-2(a)(6)(i).

(4)   Alternative remaindermen. The trust instrument of a CRAT must provide a means for selecting alternative charitable remaindermen in the event the designated organization is not qualified at the time any payments are to be made to it from the trust. Section 1.664–2(a)(6)(iv).

.06 Annotations for Paragraph 7, Prohibited Transactions, of the Sample Trust.

(1)   Payment of the annuity amount. Payment of the annuity amount to the recipients is not considered an act of self-dealing within the meaning of section 4941(d), as modified by section 4947(a)(2)(A), or a taxable expenditure within the meaning of section 4945(d), as modified by section 4947(a)(2)(A). Section 53.4947–1(c)(2) of the Foundation and Similar Excise Taxes Regulations.

(2)   Prohibitions against certain investments and excess business holdings. Prohibitions against investments that jeopardize the exempt purpose of the trust for purposes of section 4944, as modified by section 4947(a)(2)(A), and against retaining any excess business holdings for purposes of section 4943, as modified by section 4947(a)(2)(A), are required if the trust provides for payment of part of an annuity amount to an organization described in section 170(c) and gift and estate tax charitable deductions are sought for this interest. See section 4947(b)(3). See section 6.02 of this revenue procedure for an alternate provision that provides for payment of part of the annuity to an organization described in section 170(c).

(3)   Trust to continue in existence for benefit of charity. The governing instrument requirements of section 508(e) must be included in the trust instrument if, after the termination of the annuity period: (i) the trust instrument provides that the trust shall continue in existence for the benefit of the charitable remainderman and, as a result, the trust will become subject to the provisions of section 4947(a)(1); and (ii) the trust will be treated as a private foundation within the meaning of section 509(a), as modified by section 4947(a)(1). Except as provided in paragraph 7 of the sample trust, the trust instrument may limit the application of the provisions of section 508(e) to the period after the termination of the annuity period when the trust continues in existence for the benefit of the charitable remainderman. Note that when the trust provides for the trust corpus to be retained, in whole or in part, in trust for the charitable remainderman, the higher deductibility limitations in section 170(b)(1)(A) for the income tax charitable deduction will not be available (even if the charitable remainderman is restricted to a public charity) because the contribution of the trust corpus is made "for the use of" rather than "to" the charitable remainderman. See section 1.170A–8(b).

SECTION 6. ALTERNATE PROVISIONS FOR SAMPLE INTER VIVOS CHARITABLE REMAINDER ANNUITY TRUST—TWO LIVES, CONCURRENT AND CONSECUTIVE INTERESTS

.01 Annuity Amount Stated as a Specific Dollar Amount.

(1)   Explanation. As an alternative to stating the annuity amount as a fraction or percentage of the initial net fair market value of the assets transferred to the trust, the annuity amount may be stated as a specific dollar amount. Section 1.664–2(a)(1)(ii) and (iii). In either case, the annuity amount must be not less than 5 percent nor more than 50 percent of the initial net fair market value of all property placed in trust. Section 664(d)(1)(A).

(2)   Instructions for use.

(a)   Replace the first sentence of paragraph 2, Payment of Annuity Amount, of the sample trust with the following sentence:

In each taxable year of the trust during the annuity period, the Trustee shall pay to [permissible recipient] and to [permissible recipient] (hereinafter "the Recipients") in equal shares during their lifetimes an annuity amount equal to [the stated dollar amount], and upon the death of one (hereinafter "the Predeceasing Recipient"), the Trustee shall pay the entire annuity amount (subject to any proration in paragraph 4) to the survivor (hereinafter "the Survivor Recipient").

(b) Delete the last sentence of paragraph 2, Payment of Annuity Amount, of the sample trust concerning the incorrect valuation of trust assets.

.02 Payment of Part of the Annuity to an Organization Described in section 170(c).

(1)   Explanation. An organization described in section 170(c) may receive part, but not all, of any annuity amount. Section 664(d)(1)(A). If a gift tax charitable deduction and, if needed, an estate tax charitable deduction are sought for the present value of the annuity interest passing to a charitable organization, the trust instrument must contain additional provisions. First, the trust instrument must specify the portion of each annuity payment that is payable to the noncharitable recipients and to the charitable organization described in sections 170(c), 2522(a), and, if needed, section 2055(a). Second, the trust instrument must contain a means for selecting an alternative qualified charitable organization if the designated organization is not a qualified organization at the time when any annuity amount is to be paid to it. Third, the trust instrument must contain prohibitions against investments that jeopardize the exempt purpose of the trust for purposes of section 4944, as modified by section 4947(a)(2)(A), and against retaining any excess business holdings for purposes of section 4943, as modified by section 4947(a)(2)(A).

(2) Instructions for use.

(a) Replace paragraph 2, Payment of Annuity Amount, of the sample trust with the following paragraph:

Payment of Annuity Amount. The annuity amount is equal to [a number no less than 5 and no more than 50] percent of the initial net fair market value of all property transferred to the trust, valued as of the above date (that is, the date of the transfer). In each taxable year of the trust during the annuity period, the Trustee shall pay [the percentage of the annuity amount payable to the noncharitable recipients] percent of the annuity amount to [permissible recipient] and [permissible recipient] (hereinafter "the Recipients") in equal shares during their joint lives, and upon the death of one (hereinafter "the Predeceasing Recipient"), the Trustee shall pay that entire percentage of the annuity amount (subject to any proration in paragraph 4) to the survivor (hereinafter "the Survivor Recipient"). In each taxable year of the trust during the annuity period, the Trustee shall pay [the percentage of the annuity amount payable to the charitable recipient] percent of the annuity amount to [an organization described in sections 170(c), 2055(a), and 2522(a) of the Code] (hereinafter "the Charitable Recipient"). The first day of the annuity period shall be the date the property is transferred to the trust and the last day of the annuity period shall be the date of the Survivor Recipient's death. If the Charitable Recipient is not an organization described in sections 170(c), 2055(a), and 2522(a) of the Code at the time when any annuity payment is to be distributed to it, then the Trustee shall distribute that annuity payment to one or more organizations described in sections 170(c), 2055(a), and 2522(a) of the Code as the Trustee shall select, and in the proportions as the Trustee shall decide, in the Trustee's sole discretion. The annuity amount shall be paid in equal quarterly installments at the end of each calendar quarter from income, and to the extent income is not sufficient, from principal. Any income of the trust for a taxable year in excess of the annuity amount shall be added to principal. If the initial net fair market value of the trust assets is incorrectly determined, then within a reasonable period after the value is finally determined for federal tax purposes, the Trustee shall pay to the Recipients and the Charitable Recipient (in the case of an undervaluation) or receive from the Recipients and the Charitable Recipient (in the case of an overvaluation) an amount equal to the difference between the annuity amount(s) properly payable and the annuity amount(s) actually paid.

(b) Replace the first parenthetical in paragraph 5, Distribution to Charity, of the sample trust with the following parenthetical:

(other than any amount due the Recipients or their estates and the Charitable Recipient under the provisions above).

(c) Add the following sentence after the first and only sentence in paragraph 7, Prohibited Transactions, of the sample trust:

The Trustee shall not make any investments that jeopardize the exempt purpose of the trust for purposes of section 4944 of the Code, as modified by section 4947(a)(2)(A) of the Code, or retain any excess business holdings for purposes of section 4943 of the Code, as modified by section 4947(a)(2)(A) of the Code.

.03 Qualified Contingency.

(1) Explanation. Under section 664(f), payment of the annuity amount may terminate upon the earlier of the occurrence of a qualified contingency (as defined in section 664(f)(3)) or the death of the survivor recipient. The amount of the charitable deduction, however, will be determined without regard to a qualified contingency. See section 664(f)(2).

(2) Instruction for use. Replace the second sentence of paragraph 2, Payment of Annuity Amount, of the sample trust with the following sentence:

The first day of the annuity period shall be the date the property is transferred to the trust and the last day of the annuity period shall be the date of the Survivor Recipient's death or, if earlier, the date on which occurs the [qualified contingency].

.04 Retaining the Right to Revoke the Interest of the Survivor Recipient.

(1) Explanation. The donor may retain the right to revoke or terminate the interest of the other noncharitable recipient. This right is exercisable only by the donor's last will and testament. Section 1.664–2(a)(4). The re-

225

tention of this right may have gift and estate tax consequences. It will affect the value of the annuity interests transferred. It may also cause a portion of the trust to be included in the donor's gross estate for federal estate tax purposes, even if it would otherwise not be includible. The following alternate provision provides for the donor's retention of the right to revoke when the donor is also a recipient.

(2) Instructions for use. To retain the right to revoke the other noncharitable recipient's interest by the donor's last will and testament:

(a) Designate the donor as a recipient in paragraph 2, Payment of Annuity Amount, of the sample trust.

(b) Replace the second sentence of paragraph 2, Payment of Annuity Amount, of the sample trust with the following two sentences:

The Donor hereby expressly reserves the power, exercisable only by the Donor's last will and testament, to revoke and terminate the interest of [the name of permissible recipient who is not the Donor] under this trust. The first day of the annuity period shall be the date the property is transferred to the trust and the last day of the annuity period shall be the date of death of the Survivor Recipient, or on the earlier death of the Donor if the power to revoke [the name of permissible recipient who is not the Donor]'s interest is exercised.

.05 Last Annuity Payments to the Recipients.

(1) Explanation. As an alternative to prorating the annuity amount in the taxable year of the predeceasing recipient's death, payment of the predeceasing recipient's share of the annuity amount may terminate with the last regular payment preceding the predeceasing recipient's death. Similarly, as an alternative to prorating the annuity amount in the taxable year of the termination of the annuity period, payment of the annuity amount may terminate with the last regular payment preceding the termination of the annuity period. However, the fact that a recipient may not receive the last payment shall not be taken into account for purposes of determining the present value of the remainder interest. Section 1.664–2(a)(5)(i).

(2) Instructions for use.

(a) To add an alternate provision to terminate the payment of the predeceasing recipient's share of the annuity amount with the last regular payment preceding his or her death, replace paragraph 4, Proration of Annuity Amount, of the sample trust with the following paragraph:

Proration of Annuity Amount. Except as provided below, the Trustee shall prorate the annuity amount on a daily basis for any short taxable year. The obligation of the Trustee to pay a share of the annuity amount to the Predeceasing Recipient shall terminate with the regular quarterly installment next preceding the Predeceasing Recipient's death. In the taxable year of the trust during which the annuity period ends, the Trustee shall prorate the annuity amount on a daily basis for the number of days of the annuity period in that taxable year.

(b) To add an alternate provision to terminate the payment of the annuity amount with the last regular payment preceding the termination of the annuity period, replace paragraph 4, Proration of Annuity Amount, of the sample trust with the following paragraph:

Proration of Annuity Amount. Except as provided below, the Trustee shall prorate the annuity amount on a daily basis for any short taxable year. Upon the death of the Predeceasing Recipient, the Trustee shall prorate on a daily basis the Predeceasing Recipient's share of the next regular annuity payment between the estate of the Predeceasing Recipient and the Survivor Recipient. In the taxable year of the trust during which the annuity period ends, the obligation of the Trustee to pay the annuity amount shall terminate with the regular quarterly installment next preceding the termination of the annuity period.

(c) To add an alternate provision terminating the payment of the predeceasing recipient's share of the annuity amount with the last regular payment preceding his or her death, and terminating the payment of the annuity amount with the last regular payment preceding the termination of the annuity period, replace paragraph 4, Proration of Annuity Amount, of the sample trust with the following paragraph:

Proration of Annuity Amount. Except as provided below, the Trustee shall prorate the annuity amount on a daily basis for any short taxable year. The obligation of the Trustee to pay a share of the annuity amount to the Predeceasing Recipient shall terminate with the regular quarterly installment next preceding the Predeceasing Recipient's death. In the taxable year of the trust during which the annuity period ends, the obligation of the Trustee to pay the annuity amount shall terminate with the regular quarterly installment next preceding the termination of the annuity period.

.06 Restricting the Charitable Remainderman to a Public Charity.

(1)   Explanation. The amount of the donor's income tax charitable deduction is more limited for gifts to certain private foundations than for other charitable organizations. Specifically, charitable organizations described in section 170(c) include private foundations that are not described in section 170(b)(1)(E). See section 170(b) and Rev. Rul. 79–368, 1979–2 C.B. 109. To avoid these more restrictive limitations, a donor of an inter vivos CRAT may wish to restrict the charitable remainderman to an organization that is described in section 170(b)(1)(A) as well as sections 170(c), 2055(a), and 2522(a) (referred to herein as a "public charity").

(2)   Instructions for use. To restrict the charitable remainderman to a public charity, each and every time the phrase "an organization described in sections 170(c), 2055(a), and 2522(a) of the Code" appears in the sample trust, replace it with the phrase "an organization described in sections 170(b)(1)(A), 170(c), 2055(a), and 2522(a) of the Code."

.07 Retaining the Right to Substitute the Charitable Remainderman.

(1)   Explanation. The donor may retain the right to substitute another charitable remainderman for the charitable remainderman named in the trust instrument. See Rev. Rul. 76–8, 1976–1 C.B. 179. Note, however, that the retention of this right will cause the gift of the remainder interest to be incomplete for gift tax purposes. See section 25.2511–2(c) and Rev. Rul. 77–275, 1977–2 C.B. 346.

(2)   Instruction for use. Insert the following sentence between the first and last sentences of paragraph 5, Distribution to Charity, of the sample trust:

The Donor reserves the right to designate, at any time and from time to time, in lieu of the Charitable Organization identified above, one or more organizations described in sections 170(c), 2055(a), and 2522(a) of the Code as the charitable remainderman and shall make any such designation by giving written notice to the Trustee.

.08 Power of Appointment to Designate the Charitable Remainderman.

(1)   Explanation. The trust instrument may grant a recipient a power of appointment to designate the charitable remainderman. See Rev. Rul. 76–7, 1976–1 C.B. 179.

(2)   Instruction for use. Replace paragraph 5, Distribution to Charity, of the sample trust with the following paragraph:

Distribution to Charity. At the termination of the annuity period, the Trustee shall distribute all of the then principal and income of the trust (other than any amount due the Recipients or their estates under the provisions above) to one or more charitable organizations described in sections 170(c), 2055(a), and 2522(a) of the Code as [one of the named permissible recipients] shall appoint and direct by specific reference to this power of appointment by inter vivos or testamentary instrument. To the extent this power of appointment is not effectively exercised, the principal and income not effectively appointed shall be distributed to one or more organizations described in sections 170(c), 2055(a), and 2522(a) of the Code as the Trustee shall select, and in the proportions as the Trustee shall decide, in the Trustee's sole discretion. If an organization fails to qualify as an organization described in sections 170(c), 2055(a), and 2522(a) of the Code at the time when any principal or income of the trust is to be distributed to it, then the Trustee shall distribute the then principal and income to one or more organizations described in sections 170(c), 2055(a), and 2522(a) of the Code as the Trustee shall select, and in the proportions as the Trustee shall decide, in the Trustee's sole discretion.

SECTION 7. EFFECT ON OTHER REVENUE PROCEDURES

Section 5 of Rev. Proc. 90–32 is superseded.

DRAFTING INFORMATION

The principal authors of this revenue procedure are Karlene M. Lesho and Stephanie N. Bland of the Office of Associate Chief Counsel (Passthroughs and Special Industries). For further information regarding this revenue procedure, contact Karlene M. Lesho or Stephanie N. Bland at (202) 622-7830 (not a toll-free call).

IRS SPECIMEN TESTAMENTARY CRAT: PAYMENTS FOR ONE MEASURING LIFE

Annotations and Alternative Provisions
Rev. Proc. 2003–57

SECTION 1. PURPOSE

This revenue procedure contains an annotated sample declaration of trust and alternate provisions that meet the requirements of section 664(d)(1) of the Internal Revenue Code for a testamentary charitable remainder annuity trust (CRAT) providing for annuity payments for one measuring life followed by the distribution of trust assets to a charitable remainderman.

SECTION 2. BACKGROUND

Previously, the Internal Revenue Service issued sample trust instruments for certain types of CRATs. The Service is updating the previously issued samples and issuing new samples for additional types of CRATs; annotations and alternate sample provisions are included as further guidance. In addition to the sample trust instrument included in this revenue procedure for a testamentary CRAT providing for annuity payments for one measuring life, samples are provided in separate revenue procedures for:

(a) an inter vivos CRAT providing for annuity payments for one measuring life (see Rev. Proc. 2003–53, superceding Rev. Proc. 89–21, 1989–1 C.B. 842);

(b) an inter vivos CRAT providing for annuity payments for a term of years (see Rev. Proc. 2003–54);

(c) an inter vivos CRAT providing for annuity payments payable consecutively for two measuring lives (see Rev. Proc. 2003–55, superceding section 4 of Rev. Proc. 90–32, 1990–1 C.B. 546);

(d) an inter vivos CRAT providing for annuity payments payable concurrently and consecutively for two measuring lives (see Rev. Proc. 2003–56, superceding section 5 of Rev. Proc. 90–32);

(e) a testamentary CRAT providing for annuity payments for a term of years (see Rev. Proc. 2003–58);

(f) a testamentary CRAT providing for annuity payments payable consecutively for two measuring lives (see Rev. Proc. 2003–59, superceding section 7 of Rev. Proc. 90–32); and

(g) a testamentary CRAT providing for annuity payments payable concurrently and consecutively for two measuring lives (see Rev. Proc. 2003–60, superceding section 8 of Rev. Proc. 90–32).

SECTION 3. SCOPE AND OBJECTIVE

Section 4 of this revenue procedure provides a sample declaration of trust for a testamentary CRAT with one measuring life that is created by an individual who is a citizen or resident of the United States. Section 5 of this revenue procedure provides annotations to the provisions of the sample trust. Section 6 of this revenue procedure provides samples of alternate provisions concerning: (.01) the statement of the annuity amount as a specific dollar amount; (.02) the payment of part of the annuity to an organization described in section 170(c); (.03) a qualified contingency; (.04) the last annuity payment to the recipient; and (.05) a power of appointment to designate the charitable remainderman. For transfers to a qualifying CRAT, as defined in section 664(d)(1), the remainder interest will be deductible by the estate of a citizen or resident of the United States under section 2055(e)(2)(A) if the other requirements of section 2055(e)(2)(A) (that is, the requirements not relating to the provisions of the governing instrument) are also met. The Service will recognize a trust as a qualified CRAT meeting all of the requirements of section 664(d)(1) if the trust operates in a manner consistent with the terms of the trust instrument, if the trust is a valid trust under applicable local law, and if the trust instrument: (i) is substantially similar to the sample in section 4 of this revenue procedure; or (ii) properly integrates one or more alternate provisions from section 6 of this revenue procedure into a document substantially similar to the sample in section 4 of this revenue procedure. A trust instrument that contains substantive provisions in addition to those provided in section 4 of this revenue procedure (other than properly integrated alternate provisions from section 6 of this revenue procedure, or provisions necessary to establish a valid trust under applicable local law that are not inconsistent with the applicable federal tax requirements), or that omits any of the provisions of section 4 of this revenue procedure (unless an alternate provision from section 6 of this revenue procedure is properly integrated), will not necessarily be disqualified, but neither will that trust be assured of qualification under the provisions of this revenue procedure. The Service generally will not issue a letter ruling on whether a testamentary trust created by an individual and with one measuring life qualifies as a CRAT. The Service, however, generally will issue letter rulings on the effect of substantive trust provisions, other than those contained in sections 4 and 6 of this revenue procedure, on the qualification of a trust as a CRAT.

SECTION 4. SAMPLE TESTAMENTARY CHARITABLE REMAINDER ANNUITY TRUST—ONE LIFE

I give, devise, and bequeath [property bequeathed] to my Trustee in trust to be administered under this provision. I intend this bequest to establish a charitable remainder annuity trust, within the meaning of Rev. Proc. 2003–57 and section 664(d)(1) of the Internal Revenue Code (hereinafter "the Code"). The trust shall be known as the ___ Charitable Remainder Annuity Trust and I hereby designate ___ as the initial trustee (hereinafter "the Trustee").

1. Payment of Annuity Amount. In each taxable year of the trust during the annuity period, the Trustee shall pay to [permissible recipient] (hereinafter "the Recipient") an annuity amount equal to [a number no less than 5 and no more than 50] percent of the initial net fair market value of all property passing to this trust as finally determined for federal estate tax purposes. The first day of the annuity period shall be the date of my death and the last day of the annuity period shall be the date of the Recipient's death. The annuity amount shall be paid in equal quarterly installments at the end of each calendar quarter from income, and to the extent income is not sufficient, from principal. Any income of the trust for a taxable year in excess of the annuity amount shall be added to principal. If the initial net fair market value of the trust assets is incorrectly determined, then within a reasonable period after the value is finally determined for federal estate tax purposes, the Trustee shall pay to the Recipient (in the case of an undervaluation) or receive from the Recipient (in the case of an overvaluation) an amount equal to the difference between the annuity amount(s) properly payable and the annuity amount(s) actually paid.

2. Deferral Provision. The obligation to pay the annuity amount shall commence with the date of my death, but payment of the annuity amount may be deferred from this date until the end of the taxable year in which the trust is completely funded. Within a reasonable time after the end of the taxable year in which the trust is completely funded, the Trustee must pay to the Recipient (in the case of an underpayment) or receive from the Recipient (in the case of an overpayment) the difference between any annuity amounts actually paid, plus interest, and the annuity amounts payable, plus interest. The interest shall be computed for any period at the rate of interest, compounded annually, that the federal income tax regulations under section 664 of the Code prescribe for this computation.

3. Proration of Annuity Amount. The Trustee shall prorate the annuity amount on a daily basis for any short taxable year. In the taxable year of the trust during which the annuity period ends, the Trustee shall prorate the annuity amount on a daily basis for the number of days of the annuity period in that taxable year.

4. Distribution to Charity. At the termination of the annuity period, the Trustee shall distribute all of the then principal and income of the trust (other than any amount due the Recipient or the Recipient's estate under the provisions above) to [designated remainderman] (hereinafter "the Charitable Organization"). If the Charitable Organization is not an organization described in sections 170(c) and 2055(a) of the Code at the time when any principal or income of the trust is to be distributed to it, then the Trustee shall distribute the then principal and income to one or more organizations described in sections 170(c) and 2055(a) of the Code as the Trustee shall select, and in the proportions as the Trustee shall decide, in the Trustee's sole discretion.

5. Additional Contributions. No additional contributions shall be made to the trust after the initial contribution. The initial contribution, however, shall be deemed to consist of all property passing to the trust by reason of my death.

6. Prohibited Transactions. The Trustee shall not engage in any act of self-dealing within the meaning of section 4941(d) of the Code, as modified by section 4947(a)(2)(A) of the Code, and shall not make any taxable

expenditures within the meaning of section 4945(d) of the Code, as modified by section 4947(a)(2)(A) of the Code.

7. Taxable Year. The taxable year of the trust shall be the calendar year.

8. Governing Law. The operation of the trust shall be governed by the laws of the State of ___. However, the Trustee is prohibited from exercising any power or discretion granted under said laws that would be inconsistent with the qualification of the trust as a charitable remainder annuity trust under section 664(d)(1) of the Code and the corresponding regulations.

9. Limited Power of Amendment. This trust is irrevocable. However, the Trustee shall have the power, acting alone, to amend the trust from time to time in any manner required for the sole purpose of ensuring that the trust qualifies and continues to qualify as a charitable remainder annuity trust within the meaning of section 664(d)(1) of the Code.

10. Investment of Trust Assets. Nothing in this trust instrument shall be construed to restrict the Trustee from investing the trust assets in a manner that could result in the annual realization of a reasonable amount of income or gain from the sale or disposition of trust assets.

SECTION 5. ANNOTATIONS REGARDING SAMPLE TESTAMENTARY CHARITABLE REMAINDER ANNUITY TRUST—ONE LIFE

.01 Annotations for Introductory Paragraph of the Sample Trust.

(1) Factors concerning qualification of trust. A deduction must be allowable under section 2055 for property contributed to the trust. Section 1.664–1(a)(1)(iii)(a) of the Income Tax Regulations. The trust must meet the definition of and function exclusively as a charitable remainder trust from the creation of the trust. Section 1.664–1(a)(4). Solely for purposes of section 664, a trust is deemed created at the earliest time that no person is treated as the owner of the entire trust under subpart E, part 1, subchapter J, chapter 1, subtitle A of the Code (subpart E). Section 1.664–1(a)(4). For purposes of section 2055, a charitable remainder trust shall be deemed created at the date of death of the decedent (even though the trust is not funded until the end of a reasonable period of administration or settlement) if the obligation to pay the annuity amount with respect to the property passing in trust at the death of the decedent begins as of the date of death of the decedent, even though the requirement to pay this amount is deferred in accordance with section 1.664–1(a)(5)(i). Section 1.664–1(a)(5)(i). In addition, funding the trust with certain types of assets may disqualify it as a charitable remainder trust. See section 1.664–1(a)(7) and Rev. Rul. 73–610, 1973–2 C.B. 213.

(2) Valuation of unmarketable assets. If the trust is funded with unmarketable assets, the initial net fair market value of the assets must be determined exclusively by an independent trustee, as defined in section 1.664–1(a)(7)(iii), or must be determined by a current "qualified appraisal" from a "qualified appraiser," as defined in section 1.170A–13(c)(3) and (c)(5), respectively. Section 1.664–1(a)(7).

(3) Trustee provisions. Alternate or successor trustees may be designated in the trust instrument. In addition, the trust instrument may contain other administrative provisions relating to the trustee's duties and powers, as long as the provisions do not conflict with the rules governing charitable remainder trusts under section 664 and the regulations thereunder.

.02 Annotations for Paragraph 1, Payment of Annuity Amount, of the Sample Trust.

(1) Permissible recipients. For a CRAT with an annuity period based on the life of one individual, the annuity amount must generally be paid to that individual and the individual must be living at the time of the creation of the trust. See Rev. Rul. 2002–20, 2002–1 C.B. 794, for situations in which the annuity amount may be paid to a trust for the benefit of an individual who is financially disabled. An organization described in section 170(c) may receive part, but not all, of the annuity amount. Section 664(d)(1)(A) and section 1.664–2(a)(3)(i). See section 6.02 of this revenue procedure for an alternate provision that provides for payment of part of the annuity to an organization described in section 170(c).

(2) Percentage requirements. The sum certain annuity amount must be at least 5 percent and not more than 50 percent of the initial net fair market value of the assets placed in trust. Section 664(d)(1)(A). Even if the sum

certain annuity amount is at least 5 percent and not more than 50 percent of the initial net fair market value of the assets placed in trust, no deduction will be allowable under section 2055 if the probability that the trust corpus will be exhausted before the death of the recipient exceeds 5 percent. Rev. Rul. 77–374, 1977–2 C.B. 329. See section 20.7520–3(b) for special rules that may be applicable in valuing interests transferred to CRATs. In addition, the value (determined under section 7520) of the charitable remainder interest must be at least 10 percent of the initial net fair market value of all property placed in the trust. Section 664(d)(1)(D).

(3) Payment of annuity amount in installments. Paragraph 1, Payment of Annuity Amount, of the sample trust specifies that the annuity amount is to be paid in equal quarterly installments at the end of each quarter. However, the trust instrument may specify that the annuity amount is to be paid to the recipient annually or in equal or unequal installments throughout the year. See section 1.664–2(a)(1)(i). The amount of the charitable deduction will be affected by the frequency of payment, by whether the installments are equal or unequal, and by whether each installment is payable at the beginning or end of the period. See section 1.664–2(c) and section 20.2031–7(d)(2)(iv).

(4) Payment of annuity amount by close of taxable year. Generally, the annuity amount for any taxable year must be paid before the close of the taxable year for which it is due. For circumstances under which the annuity amount may be paid within a reasonable time after the close of the taxable year, see section 1.664–2(a)(1)(i)(a). In addition, section 1.664–1(a)(5)(i) provides a special rule applicable to charitable remainder trusts created by testamentary transfer that may defer the requirement to pay the annuity amount until the end of the taxable year in which the trust is completely funded. See section 5.03(1) of this revenue procedure for additional information regarding the deferral of the payment of the annuity amount until the end of the taxable year in which the trust is completely funded.

(5) Early distributions to charity. The trust instrument may provide that an amount other than the annuity shall be paid (or may be paid in the discretion of the trustee) to an organization described in section 170(c). If such a distribution is made in kind, the adjusted basis of the property distributed must be fairly representative of the adjusted basis of the property available for distribution on the date of distribution. Section 1.664–2(a)(4).

.03 Annotations for Paragraph 2, Deferral Provision, of the Sample Trust.

(1) Deferral of requirement to pay annuity amount. The deferral provision in paragraph 2 of the sample trust authorizes deferring the payment of the annuity amount until the end of the taxable year of the trust in which the trust is completely funded. Section 1.664–1(a)(5)(i) provides the operational rule for deferring payment of the annuity amount in this circumstance.

(2) Treatment of distributions. For the proper treatment of distributions to a charitable remainder trust or to the recipient during the period of administration of an estate or settlement of a trust that is not a charitable remainder trust, see section 1.664–1(a)(5)(iii).

.04 Annotations for Paragraph 3, Proration of Annuity Amount, of the Sample Trust.

(1) Prorating annuity amount. To compute the annuity amount in a short taxable year and in the taxable year in which the annuity period terminates, see section 1.664–2(a)(1)(iv)(a) and (b), respectively.

(2) Determining annuity amount payable in year of recipient's death. Paragraph 3, Proration of Annuity Amount, of the sample trust specifies that the annuity amount shall be prorated on a daily basis. See section 6.04 of this revenue procedure for an alternate provision that provides for the termination of the annuity amount with the last regular payment preceding the recipient's death.

.05 Annotations for Paragraph 4, Distribution to Charity, of the Sample Trust.

(1) Minimum value of remainder. As noted in section 5.02(2) of this revenue procedure, the value (determined under section 7520) of the charitable remainder interest is required to be at least 10 percent of the initial net fair market value of all property placed in the trust. Section 664(d)(1)(D).

(2)   Designated remainderman. Any named charitable remainderman must be an organization described in sections 170(c) and 2055(a) at the time of the transfer to the charitable remainder annuity trust. See section 664(d)(1)(C) and Rev. Rul. 77–385, 1977–2 C.B. 331. The trust instrument may restrict the charitable remainderman to an organization described in sections 170(c) and 2055(a), but grant to a trustee or other person the power to designate the actual charitable remainderman. See section 6.05 of this revenue procedure for an alternate provision in which the recipient is granted a power of appointment to designate the charitable remainderman.

(3)   Multiple remaindermen. The remainder interest may pass to more than one charitable organization as long as each organization is described in sections 170(c) and 2055(a). Section 1.664–2(a)(6)(i).

(4)   Alternative remaindermen. The trust instrument of a CRAT must provide a means for selecting alternative charitable remaindermen in the event the designated organization is not qualified at the time any payments are to be made to it from the trust. Section 1.664–2(a)(6)(iv).

.06 Annotations for Paragraph 6, Prohibited Transactions, of the Sample Trust.

(1)   Payment of the annuity amount. Payment of the annuity amount to the recipient is not considered an act of self-dealing within the meaning of section 4941(d), as modified by section 4947(a)(2)(A), or a taxable expenditure within the meaning of section 4945(d), as modified by section 4947(a)(2)(A). Section 53.4947–1(c)(2) of the Foundation and Similar Excise Taxes Regulations.

(2)   Prohibitions against certain investments and excess business holdings. Prohibitions against investments that jeopardize the exempt purpose of the trust for purposes of section 4944, as modified by section 4947(a)(2)(A), and against retaining any excess business holdings for purposes of section 4943, as modified by section 4947(a)(2)(A), are required if the trust provides for payment of part of an annuity amount to an organization described in section 170(c) and an estate tax charitable deduction is sought for this interest. See section 4947(b)(3). See section 6.02 of this revenue procedure for an alternate provision that provides for payment of part of the annuity to an organization described in section 170(c).

(3)   Trust to continue in existence for benefit of charity. The governing instrument requirements of section 508(e) must be included in the trust instrument if, after the termination of the annuity period: (i) the trust instrument provides that the trust shall continue in existence for the benefit of the charitable remainderman and, as a result, the trust will become subject to the provisions of section 4947(a)(1); and (ii) the trust will be treated as a private foundation within the meaning of section 509(a), as modified by section 4947(a)(1). Except as provided in paragraph 6 of the sample trust, the trust instrument may limit the application of the provisions of section 508(e) to the period after the termination of the annuity period when the trust continues in existence for the benefit of the charitable remainderman.

SECTION 6. ALTERNATE PROVISIONS FOR SAMPLE TESTAMENTARY CHARITABLE REMAINDER ANNUITY TRUST—ONE LIFE

.01 Annuity Amount Stated as a Specific Dollar Amount.

(1)   Explanation. As an alternative to stating the annuity amount as a fraction or percentage of the initial net fair market value of the assets transferred to the trust, the annuity amount may be stated as a specific dollar amount. Section 1.664–2(a)(1)(ii) and (iii). In either case, the annuity amount must be not less than 5 percent nor more than 50 percent of the initial net fair market value of all property placed in trust. Section 664(d)(1)(A).

(2)   Instructions for use.

(a) Replace the first sentence of paragraph 1, Payment of Annuity Amount, of the sample trust with the following sentence:

In each taxable year of the trust during the annuity period, the Trustee shall pay to [permissible recipient] (hereinafter "the Recipient") an annuity amount equal to [the stated dollar amount].

(b) Delete the last sentence of paragraph 1, Payment of Annuity Amount, of the sample trust concerning the incorrect valuation of trust assets.

.02 Payment of Part of the Annuity to an Organization Described in section 170(c).

(1)   Explanation. An organization described in section 170(c) may receive part, but not all, of any annuity amount. Section 664(d)(1)(A). If an estate tax charitable deduction is sought for the present value of the annuity interest passing to a charitable organization, the trust instrument must contain additional provisions. First, the trust instrument must specify the portion of each annuity payment that is payable to the noncharitable recipient and to the charitable organization described in sections 170(c) and 2055(a). Second, the trust instrument must contain a means for selecting an alternative qualified charitable organization if the designated organization is not a qualified organization at the time when any annuity amount is to be paid to it. Third, the trust instrument must contain prohibitions against investments that jeopardize the exempt purpose of the trust for purposes of section 4944, as modified by section 4947(a)(2)(A), and against retaining any excess business holdings for purposes of section 4943, as modified by section 4947(a)(2)(A).

(2)   Instructions for use.

(a) Replace paragraph 1, Payment of Annuity Amount, of the sample trust with the following paragraph:

Payment of Annuity Amount. The annuity amount is equal to [a number no less than 5 and no more than 50] percent of the initial net fair market value of all property passing to this trust as finally determined for federal estate tax purposes. In each taxable year of the trust during the annuity period, the Trustee shall pay [the percentage of the annuity amount payable to the noncharitable recipient] percent of the annuity amount to [permissible recipient] (hereinafter "the Recipient") and [the percentage of the annuity amount payable to the charitable recipient] percent of the annuity amount to [an organization described in sections 170(c) and 2055(a) of the Code] (hereinafter "the Charitable Recipient"). The first day of the annuity period shall be the date of my death and the last day of the annuity period shall be the date of the Recipient's death. If the Charitable Recipient is not an organization described in sections 170(c) and 2055(a) of the Code at the time when any annuity payment is to be distributed to it, then the Trustee shall distribute that annuity payment to one or more organizations described in sections 170(c) and 2055(a) of the Code as the Trustee shall select, and in the proportions as the Trustee shall decide, in the Trustee's sole discretion. The annuity amount shall be paid in equal quarterly installments at the end of each calendar quarter from income, and to the extent income is not sufficient, from principal. Any income of the trust for a taxable year in excess of the annuity amount shall be added to principal. If the initial net fair market value of the trust assets is incorrectly determined, then within a reasonable period after the value is finally determined for federal estate tax purposes, the Trustee shall pay to the Recipient and the Charitable Recipient (in the case of an undervaluation) or receive from the Recipient and the Charitable Recipient (in the case of an overvaluation) an amount equal to the difference between the annuity amount(s) properly payable and the annuity amount(s) actually paid.

(b) In paragraph 2, Deferral Provision, of the sample trust, replace each reference to "the Recipient" with a reference to "the Recipient and the Charitable Recipient."

(c) Replace the first parenthetical in paragraph 4, Distribution to Charity, of the sample trust with the following parenthetical:

(other than any amount due the Recipient or the Recipient's estate and the Charitable Recipient under the provisions above).

(d) Add the following sentence after the first and only sentence in paragraph 6, Prohibited Transactions, of the sample trust:

The Trustee shall not make any investments that jeopardize the exempt purpose of the trust for purposes of section 4944 of the Code, as modified by section 4947(a)(2)(A) of the Code, or retain any excess business holdings for purposes of section 4943 of the Code, as modified by section 4947(a)(2)(A) of the Code.

.03 Qualified Contingency.

(1)   Explanation. Under section 664(f), payment of the annuity amount may terminate upon the earlier of the occurrence of a qualified contingency (as defined in section 664(f)(3)) or the death of the recipient. The amount of the charitable deduction, however, will be determined without regard to a qualified contingency. See section 664(f)(2).

(2)   Instruction for use. Replace the second sentence of paragraph 1, Payment of Annuity Amount, of the sample trust with the following sentence:

The first day of the annuity period shall be the date of my death and the last day of the annuity period shall be the date of the Recipient's death or, if earlier, the date on which occurs the [qualified contingency].

.04 Last Annuity Payment to the Recipient.

(1)   Explanation. As an alternative to prorating the annuity amount in the taxable year of the recipient's death, payment of the annuity amount may terminate with the last regular payment preceding the recipient's death. However, the fact that the recipient may not receive the last payment shall not be taken into account for purposes of determining the present value of the remainder interest. Section 1.664–2(a)(5)(i).

(2)   Instruction for use. Replace the second sentence of paragraph 3, Proration of Annuity Amount, of the sample trust with the following sentence:

In the taxable year of the trust during which the annuity period ends, the obligation of the Trustee to pay the annuity amount shall terminate with the regular quarterly installment next preceding the death of the Recipient.

.05 Power of Appointment to Designate the Charitable Remainderman.

(1)   Explanation. The trust instrument may grant the recipient a power of appointment to designate the charitable remainderman. See Rev. Rul. 76–7, 1976–1 C.B. 179.

(2)   Instruction for use. Replace paragraph 4, Distribution to Charity, of the sample trust with the following paragraph:

Distribution to Charity. At the termination of the annuity period, the Trustee shall distribute all of the then principal and income of the trust (other than any amount due the Recipient or the Recipient's estate under the provisions above) to one or more charitable organizations described in sections 170(c) and 2055(a) of the Code as the Recipient shall appoint and direct by specific reference to this power of appointment by inter vivos or testamentary instrument. To the extent the Recipient fails to effectively exercise the power of appointment, the principal and income not effectively appointed shall be distributed to one or more organizations described in sections 170(c) and 2055(a) of the Code as the Trustee shall select, and in the proportions as the Trustee shall decide, in the Trustee's sole discretion. If an organization fails to qualify as an organization described in sections 170(c) and 2055(a) of the Code at the time when any principal or income of the trust is to be distributed to it, then the Trustee shall distribute the then principal and income to one or more organizations described in sections 170(c) and 2055(a) of the Code as the Trustee shall select, and in the proportions as the Trustee shall decide, in the Trustee's sole discretion.

SECTION 7. EFFECT ON OTHER REVENUE PROCEDURES

Section 6 of Rev. Proc. 90–32 is superseded.

DRAFTING INFORMATION

The principal authors of this revenue procedure are Karlene M. Lesho and Stephanie N. Bland of the Office of Associate Chief Counsel (Passthroughs and Special Industries). For further information regarding this revenue procedure, contact Karlene M. Lesho or Stephanie N. Bland at (202) 622-7830 (not a toll-free call).

IRS SPECIMEN TESTAMENTARY CRAT:
PAYMENTS FOR A TERM OF YEARS

Annotations and Alternative Provisions
Rev. Proc. 2003–58

SECTION 1. PURPOSE

This revenue procedure contains an annotated sample declaration of trust and alternate provisions that meet the requirements of section 664(d)(1) of the Internal Revenue Code for a testamentary charitable remainder annuity trust (CRAT) providing for annuity payments for a term of years followed by the distribution of trust assets to a charitable remainderman.

SECTION 2. BACKGROUND

Previously, the Internal Revenue Service issued sample trust instruments for certain types of CRATs. The Service is updating the previously issued samples and issuing new samples for additional types of CRATs; annotations and alternate sample provisions are included as further guidance. In addition to the sample trust instrument included in this revenue procedure for a testamentary CRAT providing for annuity payments for a term of years, samples are provided in separate revenue procedures for:

(a) an inter vivos CRAT providing for annuity payments for one measuring life (see Rev. Proc. 2003–53, superceding Rev. Proc. 89–21, 1989–1 C.B. 842);

(b) an inter vivos CRAT providing for annuity payments for a term of years (see Rev. Proc. 2003–54);

(c) an inter vivos CRAT providing for annuity payments payable consecutively for two measuring lives (see Rev. Proc. 2003–55, superceding section 4 of Rev. Proc. 90–32, 1990–1 C.B. 546);

(d) an inter vivos CRAT providing for annuity payments payable concurrently and consecutively for two measuring lives (see Rev. Proc. 2003–56, superceding section 5 of Rev. Proc. 90–32);

(e) a testamentary CRAT providing for annuity payments for one measuring life (see Rev. Proc. 2003–57, superceding section 6 of Rev. Proc. 90–32);

(f) a testamentary CRAT providing for annuity payments payable consecutively for two measuring lives (see Rev. Proc. 2003–59, superceding section 7 of Rev. Proc. 90–32); and

(g) a testamentary CRAT providing for annuity payments payable concurrently and consecutively for two measuring lives (see Rev. Proc. 2003–60, superceding section 8 of Rev. Proc. 90–32).

SECTION 3. SCOPE AND OBJECTIVE

Section 4 of this revenue procedure provides a sample declaration of trust for a testamentary CRAT that is created by an individual who is a citizen or resident of the United States and that provides for a term of years annuity period. Section 5 of this revenue procedure provides annotations to the provisions of the sample trust. Section 6 of this revenue procedure provides samples of alternate provisions concerning: (.01) the statement of the annuity amount as a specific dollar amount; (.02) the payment of part of the annuity to an organization described in section 170(c); (.03) the apportionment of the annuity amount among members of a named class in the discretion of the trustee; (.04) a qualified contingency; and (.05) a power of appointment to designate the charitable remainderman.

For transfers to a qualifying CRAT, as defined in section 664(d)(1), the remainder interest will be deductible by the estate of a citizen or resident of the United States under section 2055(e)(2)(A) if the other requirements of section 2055(e)(2)(A) (that is, the requirements not relating to the provisions of the governing instrument) are also met. The Service will recognize a trust as a qualified CRAT meeting all of the requirements of section 664(d)(1) if the trust operates in a manner consistent with the terms of the trust instrument, if the trust is a valid trust under applicable local law, and if the trust instrument: (i) is substantially similar to the sample in section 4 of this revenue procedure;

or (ii) properly integrates one or more alternate provisions from section 6 of this revenue procedure into a document substantially similar to the sample in section 4 of this revenue procedure. A trust instrument that contains substantive provisions in addition to those provided in section 4 of this revenue procedure (other than properly integrated alternate provisions from section 6 of this revenue procedure, or provisions necessary to establish a valid trust under applicable local law that are not inconsistent with the applicable federal tax requirements), or that omits any of the provisions of section 4 of this revenue procedure (unless an alternate provision from section 6 of this revenue procedure is properly integrated), will not necessarily be disqualified, but neither will that trust be assured of qualification under the provisions of this revenue procedure. The Service generally will not issue a letter ruling on whether a testamentary trust created by an individual and having a term of years annuity period qualifies as a CRAT. The Service, however, generally will issue letter rulings on the effect of substantive trust provisions, other than those contained in sections 4 and 6 of this revenue procedure, on the qualification of a trust as a CRAT.

SECTION 4. SAMPLE TESTAMENTARY CHARITABLE REMAINDER ANNUITY TRUST -- TERM OF YEARS

I give, devise, and bequeath [property bequeathed] to my Trustee in trust to be administered under this provision. I intend this bequest to establish a charitable remainder annuity trust, within the meaning of Rev. Proc. 2003–58 and section 664(d)(1) of the Internal Revenue Code (hereinafter "the Code"). The trust shall be known as the ___ Charitable Remainder Annuity Trust and I hereby designate ___ as the initial trustee (hereinafter "the Trustee").

1. Payment of Annuity Amount. In each taxable year of the trust during the annuity period, the Trustee shall pay to [permissible recipient] (hereinafter "the Recipient") an annuity amount equal to [a number no less than 5 and no more than 50] percent of the initial net fair market value of all property passing to this trust as finally determined for federal estate tax purposes. The annuity period is a term of [a number not more than 20] years. The first day of the annuity period shall be the date of my death and the last day of the annuity period shall be the day preceding the [ordinal number corresponding to the length of the annuity period] anniversary of that date. The annuity amount shall be paid in equal quarterly installments at the end of each calendar quarter from income, and to the extent income is not sufficient, from principal. Any income of the trust for a taxable year in excess of the annuity amount shall be added to principal. If the initial net fair market value of the trust assets is incorrectly determined, then within a reasonable period after the value is finally determined for federal estate tax purposes, the Trustee shall pay to the Recipient (in the case of an undervaluation) or receive from the Recipient (in the case of an overvaluation) an amount equal to the difference between the annuity amount(s) properly payable and the annuity amount(s) actually paid.

2. Deferral Provision. The obligation to pay the annuity amount shall commence with the date of my death, but payment of the annuity amount may be deferred from this date until the end of the taxable year in which the trust is completely funded. Within a reasonable time after the end of the taxable year in which the trust is completely funded, the Trustee must pay to the Recipient (in the case of an underpayment) or receive from the Recipient (in the case of an overpayment) the difference between any annuity amounts actually paid, plus interest, and the annuity amounts payable, plus interest. The interest shall be computed for any period at the rate of interest, compounded annually, that the federal income tax regulations under section 664 of the Code prescribe for this computation.

3. Proration of Annuity Amount. The Trustee shall prorate the annuity amount on a daily basis for any short taxable year. In the taxable year of the trust during which the annuity period ends, the Trustee shall prorate the annuity amount on a daily basis for the number of days of the annuity period in that taxable year.

4. Distribution to Charity. At the termination of the annuity period, the Trustee shall distribute all of the then principal and income of the trust (other than any amount due the Recipient under the provisions above) to [designated remainderman] (hereinafter "the Charitable Organization"). If the Charitable Organization is not an organization described in sections 170(c) and 2055(a) of the Code at the time when any principal or income of the trust is to be distributed to it, then the Trustee shall distribute the then principal and income to one or more organizations described in sections 170(c) and 2055(a) of the Code as the Trustee shall select, and in the proportions as the Trustee shall decide, in the Trustee's sole discretion.

5. Additional Contributions. No additional contributions shall be made to the trust after the initial contribution. The initial contribution, however, shall be deemed to consist of all property passing to the trust by reason of my death.

6. Prohibited Transactions. The Trustee shall not engage in any act of self-dealing within the meaning of section 4941(d) of the Code, as modified by section 4947(a)(2)(A) of the Code, and shall not make any taxable expenditures within the meaning of section 4945(d) of the Code, as modified by section 4947(a)(2)(A) of the Code.

7. Taxable Year. The taxable year of the trust shall be the calendar year.

8. Governing Law. The operation of the trust shall be governed by the laws of the State of ___. However, the Trustee is prohibited from exercising any power or discretion granted under said laws that would be inconsistent with the qualification of the trust as a charitable remainder annuity trust under section 664(d)(1) of the Code and the corresponding regulations.

9. Limited Power of Amendment. This trust is irrevocable. However, the Trustee shall have the power, acting alone, to amend the trust from time to time in any manner required for the sole purpose of ensuring that the trust qualifies and continues to qualify as a charitable remainder annuity trust within the meaning of section 664(d)(1) or the Code.

10. Investment of Trust Assets. Nothing in this trust instrument shall be construed to restrict the Trustee from investing the trust assets in a manner that could result in the annual realization of a reasonable amount of income or gain from the sale or disposition of trust assets.

SECTION 5. ANNOTATIONS REGARDING SAMPLE TESTAMENTARY CHARITABLE REMAINDER ANNUITY TRUST -- TERM OF YEARS

.01 Annotations for Introductory Paragraph of the Sample Trust.

(1) Factors concerning qualification of trust. A deduction must be allowable under section 2055 for property contributed to the trust. Section 1.664–1(a)(1)(iii)(a) of the Income Tax Regulations. The trust must meet the definition of and function exclusively as a charitable remainder trust from the creation of the trust. Section 1.664–1(a)(4). Solely for purposes of section 664, a trust is deemed created at the earliest time that no person is treated as the owner of the entire trust under subpart E, part 1, subchapter J, chapter 1, subtitle A of the Code (subpart E). Section 1.664–1(a)(4). For purposes of section 2055, a charitable remainder trust shall be deemed created at the date of death of the decedent (even though the trust is not funded until the end of a reasonable period of administration or settlement) if the obligation to pay the annuity amount with respect to the property passing in trust at the death of the decedent begins as of the date of death of the decedent, even though the requirement to pay this amount is deferred in accordance with section 1.664-1(a)(5)(i). Section 1.664–1(a)(5)(i). In addition, funding the trust with certain types of assets may disqualify it as a charitable remainder trust. See section 1.664–1(a)(7) and Rev. Rul, 73–610, 1973–2 C.B. 213.

(2) Valuation of unmarketable assets. If the trust is funded with unmarketable assets, the initial net fair market value of the assets must be determined exclusively by an independent trustee, as defined in section 1.664–1(a)(7)(iii), or must be determined by a current "qualified appraisal" from a "qualified appraiser," as defined in section 1.170A–13(c)(3) and (c)(5), respectively. Section 1.664–1(a)(7).

(3) Trustee provisions. Alternate or successor trustees may be designated in the trust instrument. In addition, the trust instrument may contain other administrative provisions relating to the trustee's duties and powers, as long as the provisions do not conflict with the rules governing charitable remainder trusts under section 664 and the regulations thereunder. Note that certain powers given to certain persons serving as the trustee may cause the trustee to be treated as the owner of the trust under subpart E and thus disqualify the trust as a charitable remainder trust. See section 1.664–1(a)(4). See section 6.03 of this revenue procedure for an alternate provision providing for the apportionment of the annuity amount among members of a named class in the discretion of the trustee.

.02 Annotations for Paragraph 1, Payment of Annuity Amount, of the Sample Trust.

(1) Permissible term. The period for which the annuity amount is payable must not exceed 20 years. Section 1.664–2(a)(5)(i). Thus, for example, the annuity period of a CRAT for a term of 20 years will end on the day preceding the twentieth anniversary of the date the trust was created.

(2)   Permissible recipients. For a CRAT having a term of years annuity period, the annuity amount must generally be paid to a named person or persons (within the meaning of section 7701(a)(1)). If the annuity amount is to be paid to an individual or individuals, all the individuals must be living at the time of the creation of the trust. The annuity amount may be payable to the estate or heirs of a named recipient who dies prior to the expiration of the term of years. See Rev. Rul. 74–39, 1974–1 C.B. 156. The annuity amount may be payable to members of a named class and, because the annuity period is for a term of years, all of the members of the class need not be living or ascertainable at the creation of the trust. An organization described in section 170(c) may receive part, but not all, of the annuity amount. Section 664(d)(1)(A) and section 1.664–2(a)(3)(i). See section 6.02 of this revenue procedure for an alternate provision that provides for payment of part of the annuity to an organization described in section 170(c).

(3)   Multiple noncharitable recipients. Generally, if the annuity amount is payable to more than one person, the trust instrument should describe the interest of each person. See section 6.03 of this revenue procedure for an alternate provision providing for the apportionment of the annuity amount among members of a named class in the discretion of the trustee.

(4)   Percentage requirements. The sum certain annuity amount must be at least 5 percent and not more than 50 percent of the initial net fair market value of the assets placed in trust. Section 664(d)(1)(A). In addition, the value (determined under section 7520) of the charitable remainder interest must be at least 10 percent of the initial net fair market value of all property placed in the trust. Section 664(d)(1)(D). See section 20.7520–3(b) for special rules that may be applicable in valuing interests transferred to CRATs.

(5)   Payment of annuity amount in installments. Paragraph 1, Payment of Annuity Amount, of the sample trust specifies that the annuity amount is to be paid in equal quarterly installments at the end of each quarter. However, the trust instrument may specify that the annuity amount is to be paid to the recipient annually or in equal or unequal installments throughout the year. See section 1.664–2(a)(1)(i). The amount of the charitable deduction will be affected by the frequency of payment, by whether the installments are equal or unequal, and by whether each installment is payable at the beginning or end of the period. See section 1.664–2(c) and section 20.2031–7(d)(2)(iv).

(6)   Payment of annuity amount by close of taxable year. Generally, the annuity amount for any taxable year must be paid before the close of the taxable year for which it is due. For circumstances under which the annuity amount may be paid within a reasonable time after the close of the taxable year, see section 1.664–2(a)(1)(i)(a). In addition, section 1.664–1(a)(5)(i) provides a special rule applicable to charitable remainder trusts created by testamentary transfer that may defer the requirement to pay the annuity amount until the end of the taxable year in which the trust is completely funded. See section 5.03(1) of this revenue procedure for additional information regarding the deferral of the payment of the annuity amount until the end of the taxable year in which the trust is completely funded.

(7)   Early distributions to charity. The trust instrument may provide that an amount other than the annuity shall be paid (or may be paid in the discretion of the trustee) to an organization described in section 170(c). If such a distribution is made in kind, the adjusted basis of the property distributed must be fairly representative of the adjusted basis of the property available for distribution on the date of distribution. Section 1.664–2(a)(4).

.03 Annotations for Paragraph 2, Deferral Provision, of the Sample Trust.

(1)   Deferral of requirement to pay annuity amount. The deferral provision in paragraph 2 of the sample trust authorizes deferring the payment of the annuity amount until the end of the taxable year of the trust in which the trust is completely funded. Section 1.664–1(a)(5)(i) provides the operational rule for deferring payment of the annuity amount in this circumstance.

(2)   Treatment of distributions. For the proper treatment of distributions to a charitable remainder trust or to the recipient during the period of administration of an estate or settlement of a trust that is not a charitable remainder trust, see section 1.664–1(a)(5)(iii).

.04 Annotation for Paragraph 3, Proration of Annuity Amount, of the Sample Trust.

(1)   Prorating annuity amount. To compute the annuity amount in a short taxable year and in the taxable year in which the annuity period terminates, see section 1.664–2(a)(1)(iv)(a) and (b), respectively.

.05 Annotations for Paragraph 4, Distribution to Charity, of the Sample Trust.

(1) Minimum value of remainder. As noted in section 5.02(4) of this revenue procedure, the value (determined under section 7520) of the charitable remainder interest is required to be at least 10 percent of the initial net fair market value of all property placed in the trust. Section 664(d)(1)(D).

(2) Designated remainderman. Any named charitable remainderman must be an organization described in sections 170(c) and 2055(a) at the time of the transfer to the charitable remainder annuity trust. See section 664(d)(1)(C) and Rev. Rul. 77–385, 1977–2 C.B. 331. The trust instrument may restrict the charitable remainderman to an organization described in sections 170(c) and 2055(a), but grant to a trustee or other person the power to designate the actual charitable remainderman. See section 605 of this revenue procedure for an alternate provision in which a recipient is granted a power of appointment to designate the charitable remainderman.

(3) Multiple remainderman. The remainder interest may pass to more than one charitable organization as long as each organization is described in sections 170(c) and 2055(a). Section 1.664–2(a)(6)(i).

(4) Alternative remaindermen. The trust instrument of a CRAT must provide a means for selecting alternative charitable remaindermen in the event the designated organization is not qualified at the time any payments are to be made to it from the trust. Section 1.664–2(a)(6)(iv).

.06 Annotations for Paragraph 6, Prohibited Transactions, of the Sample Trust.

(1) Payment of the annuity amount. Payment of the annuity amount to the recipient is not considered an act of self-dealing within the meaning of section 4941(d), as modified by section 4947(a)(2)(A), or a taxable expenditure within the meaning of section 4945(d), as modified by section 4947(a)(2)(A). Section 53.4947–1(c)(2) of the Foundation and Similar Excise Taxes Regulations.

(2) Prohibitions against certain investments and excess business holdings. Prohibitions against investments that jeopardize the exempt purpose of the trust for purposes of section 4944, as modified by section 4947(a)(2)(A), and against retaining any excess business holdings for purposes of section 4943, as modified by section 4947(a)(2)(A), are required if the trust provides for payment of part of an annuity amount to an organization described in section 170(c) and an estate tax charitable deduction is sought for this interest. See section 4947(b)(3). See section 6.02 of this revenue procedure for an alternate provision that provides for payment of part of the annuity to an organization described in section 170(c).

(3) Trust to continue in existence for benefit of charity. The governing instrument requirements of section 508(e) must be included in the trust instrument if, after the termination of the annuity period: (i) the trust instrument provides that the trust shall continue in existence for the benefit of the charitable remainderman and, as a result, the trust will become subject to the provisions of section 4947(a)(1); and (ii) the trust will be treated as a private foundation within the meaning of section 509(a), as modified by section 4947(a)(1). Except as provided in paragraph 6 of the sample trust, the trust instrument may limit the application of the provisions of section 508(e) to the period after the termination of the annuity period when the trust continues in existence for the benefit of the charitable remainderman.

SECTION 6. ALTERNATE PROVISIONS FOR SAMPLE TESTAMENTARY CHARITABLE REMAINDER ANNUITY TRUST—TERM OF YEARS

.01 Annuity Amount Stated as a Specific Dollar Amount.

(1) Explanation. As an alternative to stating the annuity amount as a fraction or percentage of the initial net fair market value of the assets transferred to the trust, the annuity amount may be stated as a specific dollar amount. Section 1.664–2(a)(1)(ii) and (iii). In either case, the annuity amount must be not less than 5 percent nor more than 50 percent of the initial net fair market value of all property placed in trust. Section 664(d)(1)(A).

(2) Instructions for use.

(a) Replace the first sentence of paragraph 1, Payment of Annuity Amount, of the sample trust with the following sentence:

In each taxable year of the trust during the annuity period, the Trustee shall pay to [permissible recipient] (hereinafter "the Recipient") an annuity amount equal to [the stated dollar amount].

(b) Delete the last sentence of paragraph 1, Payment of Annuity Amount, of the sample trust concerning the incorrect valuation of trust assets.

.02 Payment of Part of the Annuity to an Organization Described in section 170(c).

(1) Explanation. An organization described in section 170(c) may receive part, but not all, of any annuity amount. Section 664(d)(1)(A). If an estate tax charitable deduction is sought for the present value of the annuity interest passing to a charitable organization, the trust instrument must contain additional provisions. First, the trust instrument must specify the portion of each annuity payment that is payable to the noncharitable recipient and to the charitable organization described in sections 170(c) and 2055(a). Second, the trust instrument must contain a means for selecting an alternative qualified charitable organization if the designated organization is not a qualified organization at the time when any annuity amount is to be paid to it. Third, the trust instrument must contain prohibitions against investments that jeopardize the exempt purpose of the trust for purposes of section 4944, as modified by section 4947(a)(2)(A), and against retaining any excess business holdings for purposes of section 4943, as modified by section 4947(a)(2)(A).

(2) Instructions for use.

(a) Replace paragraph 1, Payment of Annuity Amount, of the sample trust with the following paragraph:

Payment of Annuity Amount. The annuity amount is equal to [a number no less than 5 and no more than 50] percent of the initial net fair market value of all property passing to this trust as finally determined for federal estate tax purposes. In each taxable year of the trust during the annuity period, the Trustee shall pay [the percentage of the annuity amount payable to the noncharitable recipient] percent of the annuity amount to [permissible recipient] (hereinafter "the Recipient") and [the percentage of the annuity amount payable to the charitable recipient] percent of the annuity amount to [an organization described in sections 170(c) and 2055(a) of the Code] (hereinafter "the Charitable Recipient"). The annuity period is a term of [not more than 20] years. The first day of the annuity period shall be the date of my death and the last day of the annuity period shall be the day preceding the [ordinal number corresponding to the length of the annuity period] anniversary of that date. If the Charitable Recipient is not an organization described in sections 170(c) and 2055(a) of the Code at the time when any annuity payment is to be distributed to it, then the Trustee shall distribute that annuity payment to one or more organizations described in sections 170(c) and 2055(a) of the Code as the Trustee shall select, and in the proportions as the Trustee shall decide, in the Trustee's sole discretion. The annuity amount shall be paid in equal quarterly installments at the end of each calendar quarter from income, and to the extent income is not sufficient, from principal. Any income of the trust for a taxable year in excess of the annuity amount shall be added to principal. If the initial net fair market value of the trust assets is incorrectly determined, then within a reasonable period after the value is finally determined for federal estate tax purposes, the Trustee shall pay to the Recipient and the Charitable Recipient (in the case of an undervaluation) or receive from the Recipient and the Charitable Recipient (in the case of an overvaluation) an amount equal to the difference between the annuity amount(s) properly payable and the annuity amount(s) actually paid.

(b) In paragraph 2, Deferral Provision, and paragraph 4, Distribution to Charity, of the sample trust, replace each reference to "the Recipient" with a reference to "the Recipient and the Charitable Recipient."

(c) Add the following sentence after the first and only sentence in paragraph 6, Prohibited Transactions, of the sample trust:

The Trustee shall not make any investments that jeopardize the exempt purpose of the trust for purposes of section 4944 of the Code, as modified by section 4947(a)(2)(A) of the Code, or retain any excess business holdings for purposes of section 4943 of the Code, as modified by section 4947(a)(2)(A) of the Code.

.03 Apportionment of the Annuity Amount among Members of a Named Class in the Discretion of the Trustee.

(1) Explanation. A trust is not a CRAT if any person has the power to alter the amount to be paid to any named person other than an organization described in section 170(c) if the power would cause any person to be

241

treated as the owner of the trust, or any portion thereof, if subpart E were applicable to the trust. Section 1.664-2(a)(3)(ii). See Rev. Rul. 77–73, 1977–1 C.B. 175. A trustee's discretionary power, exercisable solely by that trustee, to allocate the annuity amount among the members of a class would cause the trustee to be treated as the owner of all or a portion of the trust under section 678(a) if the trustee is a member of the class, if the trustee may apply trust income or corpus to satisfy the trustee's own legal obligation, or if the trustee actually exercises the power to satisfy a support obligation owed by the trustee. Therefore, if any trustee is given the discretionary power exercisable solely by that trustee to allocate the annuity amount among members of a class, the trust instrument must provide that such trustee must be: (i) not a member of the recipient class; and (ii) prohibited from applying any part of the annuity payment in satisfaction of the trustee's own legal obligation.

(2) Instructions for use.

(a) Add the following sentence to the sample trust:

Any trustee who is authorized in the trustee's sole discretion to allocate the annuity amount among members of a Recipient class must not be a member of the Recipient class.

(b) Replace the first sentence of paragraph 1, Payment of Annuity Amount, of the sample trust with the following three sentences:

In each taxable year of the trust during the annuity period, the Trustee shall pay to a member or members of a class of persons comprised of [designated members of class] (hereinafter "the Recipient") an annuity amount equal to [a number no less than 5 and no more than 50] percent of the initial net fair market value of all property passing to this trust as finally determined for federal estate tax purposes. The Trustee may pay the annuity amount to one or more members of the class, in equal or unequal shares, as the Trustee, in the Trustee's sole discretion, may from time to time deem advisable. The Trustee may not, however, apply the payment for the Trustee's own benefit, or in satisfaction of any support or other legal obligation of the Trustee.

.04 Qualified Contingency.

(1) Explanation. Under section 664(f), payment of the annuity amount may terminate upon the earlier of the occurrence of a qualified contingency (as defined in section 664(f)(3)) or the expiration of the term of years. The amount of the charitable deduction, however, will be determined without regard to a qualified contingency. See section 664(f)(2).

(2) Instruction for use. Replace the second and third sentences of paragraph 1, Payment of Annuity Amount, of the sample trust with the following two sentences, respectively:

The annuity period is a term of [not more than 20] years, unless earlier terminated by the occurrence of [qualified contingency]. The first day of the annuity period shall be the date of my death and the last day of the annuity period shall be the day preceding the [ordinal number corresponding to the length of the annuity period] anniversary of that date or, if earlier, the date on which occurs the [qualified contingency].

.05 Power of Appointment to Designate the Charitable Remainderman.

(1) Explanation. The trust instrument may grant a recipient a power of appointment to designate the charitable remainderman. See Rev. Rul. 76–7, 1976–1 C.B. 179.

(2) Instruction for use. Replace paragraph 4, Distribution to Charity, of the sample trust with the following paragraph:

Distribution to Charity. At the termination of the annuity period, the Trustee shall distribute all of the then principal and income of the trust (other than any amount due the Recipient under the provisions above) to one or more charitable organizations described in sections 170(c) and 2055(a) of the Code as the Recipient shall appoint and direct by specific reference to this power of appointment by inter vivos or testamentary instrument. To the extent the Recipient fails to effectively exercise the power of appointment, the principal and income not effectively appointed shall be distributed to one or more organizations described in sections 170(c) and 2055(a) of the Code as the Trustee shall select, and in the proportions as the Trustee shall decide, in the Trustee's sole discretion. If an organization fails to qualify as an organization described in sections 170(c) and 2055(a) of the Code at the time when any principal or income of the trust is to be distributed to it, then the Trustee shall distribute the then principal and income to one or more organizations described in sections 170(c) and 2055(a) of the Code as the Trustee shall select, and in the proportions as the Trustee shall decide, in the Trustee's sole discretion.

DRAFTING INFORMATION

The principal authors of this revenue procedure are Karlene M. Lesho and Stephanie N. Bland of the Office of Associate Chief Counsel (Passthroughs and Special Industries). For further information regarding this revenue procedure, contact Karlene M. Lesho or Stephanie N. Bland at (202) 622-7830 (not a toll free call).

IRS SPECIMEN TESTAMENTARY CRAT: PAYMENTS FOR TWO MEASURING LIVES—PAYABLE CONSECUTIVELY

Annotations and Alternative Provisions
Rev. Proc. 2003–59

SECTION 1. PURPOSE

This revenue procedure contains an annotated sample declaration of trust and alternate provisions that meet the requirements of section 664(d)(1) of the Internal Revenue Code for a testamentary charitable remainder annuity trust (CRAT) providing for annuity payments payable consecutively for two measuring lives followed by the distribution of trust assets to a charitable remainderman.

SECTION 2. BACKGROUND

Previously, the Internal Revenue Service issued sample trust instruments for certain types of CRATs. The Service is updating the previously issued samples and issuing new samples for additional types of CRATs; annotations and alternate sample provisions are included as further guidance. In addition to the sample trust instrument included in this revenue procedure for a testamentary CRAT providing for annuity payments payable consecutively for two measuring lives, samples are provided in separate revenue procedures for:

(a)   an inter vivos CRAT providing for annuity payments for one measuring life (see Rev. Proc. 2003–53, superceding Rev. Proc. 89–21, 1989–1 C.B. 842);

(b)   an inter vivos CRAT providing for annuity payments for a term of years (see Rev. Proc. 2003–54);

(c)   an inter vivos CRAT providing for annuity payments payable consecutively for two measuring lives (see Rev. Proc. 2003–55, superceding section 4 of Rev. Proc. 90–32, 1990–4 C.B. 546);

(d)   an inter vivos CRAT providing for annuity payments payable concurrently and consecutively for two measuring lives (see Rev. Proc. 2003–56, superceding section 5 of Rev. Proc. 90–32);

(e)   a testamentary CRAT providing for annuity payments for one measuring life (see Rev. Proc. 2003–57, superceding section 6 of Rev. Proc. 90–32);

(f)   a testamentary CRAT providing for annuity payments for a term of years (see Rev. Proc. 2003–59); and

(g)   a testamentary CRAT providing for annuity payments payable concurrently and consecutively for two measuring lives (see Rev. Proc. 2003–60, superceding section 8 of Rev. Proc. 90–32).

SECTION 3. SCOPE AND OBJECTIVE

Section 4 of this revenue procedure provides a sample declaration of trust for a testamentary CRAT with consecutive interests for two measuring lives that is created by an individual who is a citizen or resident of the United States. Section 5 of this revenue procedure provides annotations to the provisions of the sample trust. Section 6 of this revenue procedure provides samples of alternate provisions concerning: (.01) the statement of the annuity amount as a specific dollar amount; (.02) the payment of part of the annuity to an organization described in section 170(c); (.03) a qualified contingency; (.04) the last annuity payments to the recipients; and (.05) a power of appointment to designate the charitable remainderman.

For transfers to a qualifying CRAT, as defined in section 664(d)(1), the remainder interest will be deductible by the estate of a citizen or resident of the United States under section 2055(e)(2)(A) if the other requirements of section 2055(e)(2)(A) (that is, the requirements not relating to the provisions of the governing instrument) are also met. The Service will recognize a trust as a qualified CRAT meeting all of the requirements of section 664(d)(1) if the trust operates in a manner consistent with the terms of the trust instrument, if the trust is a valid trust under applicable local law, and if the trust instrument: (i) is substantially similar to the sample in section 4 of this revenue procedure; or (ii) properly integrates one or more alternate provisions from section 6 of this revenue procedure into a document substantially similar to the sample in section 4 of this revenue procedure. A trust instrument that contains substantive provisions in addition to those provided in section 4 of this revenue procedure (other than properly integrated alternate provisions from section 6 of this revenue procedure, or provisions necessary to establish a valid trust under applicable local law that are not inconsistent with the applicable federal tax requirements), or that omits any of the provisions of section 4 of this revenue procedure (unless an alternate provision from section 6 of this revenue procedure is properly integrated), will not necessarily be disqualified, but neither will that trust be assured of qualification under the provisions of this revenue procedure. The Service generally will not issue a letter ruling on whether a testamentary trust created by an individual and with consecutive interests for two measuring lives qualifies as a CRAT. The Service, however, generally will issue letter rulings on the effect of substantive trust provisions, other than those contained in sections 4 and 6 of this revenue procedure, on the qualification of a trust as a CRAT.

SECTION 4. SAMPLE TESTAMENTARY CHARITABLE REMAINDER ANNUITY TRUST -- TWO LIVES, CONSECUTIVE INTERESTS

I give, devise, and bequeath [property bequeathed] to my Trustee in trust to be administered under this provision. I intend this bequest to establish a charitable remainder annuity trust, within the meaning of Rev. Proc. 2003–59 and section 664(d)(1) of the Internal Revenue Code (hereinafter "the Code"). The trust shall be known as the ___ Charitable Remainder Annuity Trust and I hereby designate ___ as the initial trustee (hereinafter "the Trustee").

1. Payment of Annuity Amount. In each taxable year of the trust during the annuity period, the Trustee shall pay to [permissible recipient] (hereinafter "the Initial Recipient") until the Initial Recipient's death, and thereafter to [permissible recipient] (hereinafter "the Successor Recipient") (subject to any proration in paragraph 3), an annuity amount equal to [a number no less than 5 and no more than 50] percent of the initial net fair market value of all property passing to this trust as finally determined for federal estate tax purposes. The first day of the annuity period shall be the date of my death and the last day of the annuity period shall be the date of the death of the survivor of the Initial Recipient and the Successor Recipient. The annuity amount shall be paid in equal quarterly installments at the end of each calendar quarter from income, and to the extent income is not sufficient, from principal. Any income of the trust for a taxable year in excess of the annuity amount shall be added to principal. If the initial net fair market value of the trust assets is incorrectly determined, then within a reasonable period after the value is finally determined for federal estate tax purposes, the Trustee shall pay to the Initial Recipient and/or Successor Recipient (in the case of an undervaluation) or receive from the Initial Recipient and/or Successor Recipient (in the case of an overvaluation) an amount equal to the difference between the annuity amount(s) properly payable and the annuity amount(s) actually paid.

2. Deferral Provision. The obligation to pay the annuity amount shall commence with the date of my death, but payment of the annuity amount may be deferred from this date until the end of the taxable year in which the trust is completely funded. Within a reasonable time after the end of the taxable year in which the trust is completely funded, the Trustee must pay to the Initial Recipient and/or the Successor Recipient (in the case of an underpayment) or receive from the Initial Recipient and/or the Successor Recipient (in the case of an overpayment) the difference between any annuity amounts actually paid, plus interest, and the annuity amounts payable, plus interest. The interest shall be computed for any period at the rate of interest, compounded annually, that the federal income tax regulations under section 664 of the Code prescribe for this computation.

3. Proration of Annuity Amount. The Trustee shall prorate the annuity amount on a daily basis for any short taxable year. If the Successor Recipient survives the Initial Recipient, the Trustee shall prorate on a daily basis the next regular annuity payment due after the death of the Initial Recipient between the estate of the Initial Recipient and the Successor Recipient. In the taxable year of the trust during which the annuity period ends, the Trustee shall prorate the annuity amount on a daily basis for the number of days of the annuity period in that taxable year.

4. Distribution to Charity. At the termination of the annuity period, the Trustee shall distribute all of the then principal and income of the trust (other than any amount due the Recipients or their estates under the provisions above) to [designated remainderman] (hereinafter "the Charitable Organization"). If the Charitable Organization is not an organization described in sections 170(c) and 2055(a) of the Code at the time when any principal or income of the trust is to be distributed to it, then the Trustee shall distribute the then principal

245

and income to one or more organizations described in sections 170(c) and 2055(a) of the Code as the Trustee shall select, and in the proportions as the Trustee shall decide, in the Trustee's sole discretion.

5. Additional Contributions. No additional contributions shall be made to the trust after the initial contribution. The initial contribution, however, shall be deemed to consist of all property passing to the trust by reason of my death.

6. Prohibited Transactions. The Trustee shall not engage in any act of self-dealing within the meaning of section 4941(d) of the Code, as modified by section 4947(a)(2)(A) of the Code, and shall not make any taxable expenditures within the meaning of section 4945(d) of the Code, as modified by section 4947(a)(2)(A) of the Code.

7. Taxable Year. The taxable year of the trust shall be the calendar year.

8. Governing Law. The operation of the trust shall be governed by the laws of the State of . However, the Trustee is prohibited from exercising any power or discretion granted under said laws that would be inconsistent with the qualification of the trust as a charitable remainder annuity trust under section 664(d)(1) of the Code and the corresponding regulations.

9. Limited Power of Amendment. This trust is irrevocable. However, the Trustee shall have the power, acting alone, to amend the trust from time to time in any manner required for the sole purpose of ensuring that the trust qualifies and continues to qualify as a charitable remainder annuity trust within the meaning of section 664(d)(1) of the Code.

10. Investment of Trust Assets. Nothing in this trust instrument shall be construed to restrict the Trustee from investing the trust assets in a manner that could result in the annual realization of a reasonable amount of income or gain from the sale or disposition of trust assets.

246

SECTION 5. ANNOTATIONS REGARDING SAMPLE TESTAMENTARY CHARITABLE REMAINDER ANNUITY TRUST -- TWO LIVES, CONSECUTIVE INTERESTS

.01 Annotations for Introductory Paragraph of the Sample Trust.

(1) Factors concerning qualification of trust. A deduction must be allowable under section 2055 for property contributed to the trust. Section 1.664–1(a)(1)(iii)(a) of the Income Tax Regulations. The trust must meet the definition of and function exclusively as a charitable remainder trust from the creation of the trust. Section 1.664–1(a)(4). Solely for purposes of section 664, a trust is deemed created at the earliest time that no person is treated as the owner of the entire trust under subpart E, part 1, subchapter J, chapter 1, subtitle A of the Code (subpart E). Section 1.664–1(a)(4). For purposes of section 2055, a charitable remainder trust shall be deemed created at the date of death of the decedent (even though the trust is not funded until the end of a reasonable period of administration or settlement) if the obligation to pay the annuity amount with respect to the property passing in trust at the death of the decedent begins as of the date of death of the decedent, even though the requirement to pay this amount is deferred in accordance with section 1.664-1(a)(5)(i). Section 1.664–1(a)(5)(i). In addition, funding the trust with certain types of assets may disqualify it as a charitable remainder trust. See section 1.664–1(a)(7) and Rev. Rul. 73–610, 1973–2 C.B. 213.

(2) Valuation of unmarketable assets. If the trust is funded with unmarketable assets, the initial net fair market value of the assets must be determined exclusively by an independent trustee, as defined in section 1.664–1(a)(7)(iii), or must be determined by a current "qualified appraisal" from a "qualified appraiser," as defined in section 1.170A–13(c)(3) and (c)(5), respectively. Section 1.664–1(a)(7).

(3) Trustee provisions. Alternate or successor trustees may be designated in the trust instrument. In addition, the trust instrument may contain other administrative provisions relating to the trustee's duties and powers, as long as the provisions do not conflict with the rules governing charitable remainder trusts under section 664 and the regulations thereunder.

.02 Annotations for Paragraph 1, Payment of Annuity Amount, of the Sample Trust.

(1) Permissible recipients. For a CRAT with an annuity period based on the lives of two individuals, the annuity amount must generally be paid to those individuals and both must be living at the time of the creation of the

trust. See Rev. Rul. 2002–20, 2002–1 C.B. 794, for situations in which the annuity amount may be paid to a trust for the benefit of an individual who is financially disabled. An organization described in section 170(c) may receive part, but not all, of the annuity amount. Section 664(d)(1)(A) and section 1.664–2(a)(3)(i). See section 6.02 of this revenue procedure for an alternate provision that provides for payment of part of the annuity to an organization described in section 170(c).

(2) Percentage requirements. The sum certain annuity amount must be at least 5 percent and not more than 50 percent of the initial net fair market value of the assets placed in trust. Section 664(d)(1)(A). Even if the sum certain annuity amount is at least 5 percent and not more than 50 percent of the initial net fair market value of the assets placed in trust, no deduction will be allowable under section 2055 if the probability that the trust corpus will be exhausted before the death of the survivor of the recipients exceeds 5 percent. Rev. Rul. 77–374, 1977–2 C.B. 329. See section 20.7520–3(b) for special rules that may be applicable in valuing interests transferred to CRATs. In addition, the value (determined under section 7520) of the charitable remainder interest must be at least 10 percent of the initial net fair market value of all property placed in the trust. Section 664(d)(1)(D).

(3) Payment of annuity amount in installments. Paragraph 1, Payment of Annuity Amount, of the sample trust specifies that the annuity amount is to be paid in equal quarterly installments at the end of each quarter. However, the trust instrument may specify that the annuity amount is to be paid to the recipient annually or in equal or unequal installments throughout the year. See section 1.664–2(a)(1)(i). The amount of the charitable deduction will be affected by the frequency of payment, by whether the installments are equal or unequal, and by whether each installment is payable at the beginning or end of the period. See section 1-664–2(c) and section 20.2031–7(d)(2)(iv).

(4) Payment of annuity amount by close of taxable year. Generally, the annuity amount for any taxable year must be paid before the close of the taxable year for which it is due. For circumstances under which the annuity amount may be paid within a reasonable time after the close of the taxable year, see section 1.664–2(a)(1)(i)(a). In addition, section 1.664–1(a)(5)(i) provides a special rule applicable to charitable remainder trusts created by testamentary transfer that may defer the requirement to pay the annuity amount until the end of the taxable year in which the trust is completely funded. See section 5.03(1) of this revenue procedure for additional information regarding the deferral of the payment of the annuity amount until the end of the taxable year in which the trust is completely funded.

(5) Early distributions to charity. The trust instrument may provide that an amount other than the annuity shall be paid (or may be paid in the discretion of the trustee) to an organization described in section 170(c). If such a distribution is made in kind, the adjusted basis of the property distributed must be fairly representative of the adjusted basis of the property available for distribution on the date of distribution. Section 1.664–2(a)(4).

.03 Annotations for Paragraph 2, Deferral Provision, of the Sample Trust.

(1) Deferral of requirement to pay annuity amount. The deferral provision in paragraph 2 of the sample trust authorizes deferring the payment of the annuity amount until the end of the taxable year of the trust in which the trust is completely funded. Section 1.664–1(a)(5)(i) provides the operational rule for deferring payment of the annuity amount in this circumstance.

(2) Treatment of distributions. For the proper treatment of distributions to a charitable remainder trust or to the recipient during the period of administration of an estate or settlement of a trust that is not a charitable remainder trust, see section 1.664–1(a)(5)(iii).

.04 Annotations for Paragraph 3, Proration of Annuity Amount, of the Sample Trust.

(1) Prorating annuity amount. To compute the annuity amount in a short taxable year and in the taxable year in which the annuity period terminates, see section 1.664–2(a)(1)(iv)(a) and (b), respectively.

(2) Determining annuity amount payable in year of a recipient's death. Paragraph 3, Proration of Annuity Amount, of the sample trust specifies that the annuity amount shall be prorated on a daily basis. See section 6.04 of this revenue procedure for alternate provisions that provide for termination of the annuity amount with the last regular payment preceding the death of each recipient.

.05 Annotations for Paragraph 4, Distribution to Charity, of the Sample Trust.

(1) Minimum value of remainder. As noted in section 5.02(2) of this revenue procedure, the value (determined under section 7520) of the charitable remainder interest is required to be at least 10 percent of the initial net fair market value of all property placed in the trust. Section 664(d)(1)(D).

(2) Designated remainderman. Any named charitable remainderman must be an organization described in sections 170(c) and 2055(a) at the time of the transfer to the charitable remainder annuity trust. See section 664(d)(1)(C) and Rev. Rul. 77–385, 1977–2 C.B. 331. The trust instrument may restrict the charitable remainderman to an organization described in sections 170(c) and 2055(a), but grant to a trustee or other person the power to designate the actual charitable remainderman. See section 6.05 of this revenue procedure for an alternate provision in which a recipient is granted a power of appointment to designate the charitable remainderman.

(3) Multiple remaindermen. The remainder interest may pass to more than one charitable organization as long as each organization is described in sections 170(c) and 2055(a). Section 1.664–2(a)(6)(i).

(4) Alternative remaindermen. The trust instrument of a CRAT must provide a means for selecting alternative charitable remaindermen in the event the designated organization is not qualified at the time any payments are to be made to it from the trust. Section 1.664–2(a)(6)(iv).

.06 Annotations for Paragraph 6, Prohibited Transactions, of the Sample Trust.

(1) Payment of the annuity amount. Payment of the annuity amount to the recipients is not considered an act of self-dealing within the meaning of section 4941(d), as modified by section 4947(a)(2)(A), or a taxable expenditure within the meaning of section 4945(d), as modified by section 4947(a)(2)(A). Section 53.4947–1(c)(2) of the Foundation and Similar Excise Taxes Regulations.

(2) Prohibitions against certain investments and excess business holdings. Prohibitions against investments that jeopardize the exempt purpose of the trust for purposes of section 4944, as modified by section 4947(a)(2)(A), and against retaining any excess business holdings for purposes of section 4943, as modified by section 4947(a)(2)(A), are required if the trust provides for payment of part of an annuity amount to an organization described in section 170(c) and an estate tax charitable deduction is sought for this interest. See section 4947(b)(3). See section 6.02 of this revenue procedure for an alternate provision that provides for payment of part of the annuity to an organization described in section 170(c).

(3) Trust to continue in existence for benefit of charity. The governing instrument requirements of section 508(e) must be included in the trust instrument if, after the termination of the annuity period: (i) the trust instrument provides that the trust shall continue in existence for the benefit of the charitable remainderman and, as a result, the trust will become subject to the provisions of section 4947(a)(1); and (ii) the trust will be treated as a private foundation within the meaning of section 509(a), as modified by section 4947(a)(1). Except as provided in paragraph 6 of the sample trust, the trust instrument may limit the application of the provisions of section 508(e) to the period after the termination of the annuity period when the trust continues in existence for the benefit of the charitable remainderman.

SECTION 6. ALTERNATE PROVISIONS FOR SAMPLE TESTAMENTARY CHARITABLE REMAINDER ANNUITY TRUST -- TWO LIVES, CONSECUTIVE INTERESTS

.01 Annuity Amount Stated as a Specific Dollar Amount.

(1) Explanation. As an alternative to stating the annuity amount as a fraction or percentage of the initial net fair market value of the assets transferred to the trust, the annuity amount may be stated as a specific dollar amount. Section 1.664–2(a)(1)(ii) and (iii). In either case, the annuity amount must be not less than 5 percent nor more than 50 percent of the initial net fair market value of all property placed in trust. Section 664(d)(1)(A).

(2) Instructions for use.

(a) Replace the first sentence of paragraph 1, Payment of Annuity Amount, of the sample trust with the following sentence:

In each taxable year of the trust during the annuity period, the Trustee shall pay to [permissible recipient] (hereinafter "the Initial Recipient") until the Initial Recipient's death and thereafter to [permissible recipient] (hereinafter "the Successor Recipient") (subject to any proration in paragraph 3), an annuity amount equal to [the stated dollar amount].

(b) Delete the last sentence of paragraph 1, Payment of Annuity Amount, of the sample trust concerning the incorrect valuation of trust assets.

.02 Payment of Part of the Annuity to an Organization Described in section 170(c).

(1) Explanation. An organization described in section 170(c) may receive part, but not all, of any annuity amount. Section 664(d)(1)(A). If an estate tax charitable deduction is sought for the present value of the annuity interest passing to a charitable organization, the trust instrument must contain additional provisions. First, the trust instrument must specify the portion of each annuity payment that is payable to the noncharitable recipient and to the charitable organization described in sections 170(c) and 2055(a). Second, the trust instrument must contain a means for selecting an alternative qualified charitable organization if the designated organization is not a qualified organization at the time when any annuity amount is to be paid to it. Third, the trust instrument must contain prohibitions against investments that jeopardize the exempt purpose of the trust for purposes of section 4944, as modified by section 4947(a)(2)(A), and against retaining any excess business holdings for purposes of section 4943, as modified by section 4947(a)(2)(A).

(2) Instructions for use.

(a) Replace paragraph 1, Payment of Annuity Amount, of the sample trust with the following paragraph:

Payment of Annuity Amount. The annuity amount is equal to [a number no less than 5 and no more than 50] percent of the initial net fair market value of all property passing to this trust as finally determined for federal estate tax purposes. In each taxable year of the trust during the annuity period, the Trustee shall pay [the percentage of the annuity amount payable to the noncharitable recipients] percent of the annuity amount to [permissible recipient] (hereinafter "the Initial Recipient") until the Initial Recipient's death, and thereafter to [permissible recipient] (hereinafter "the Successor Recipient") (subject to any proration in paragraph 3). In each taxable year of the trust during the annuity period, the Trustee shall pay [the percentage of the annuity amount payable to the charitable recipient] percent of the annuity amount to [an organization described in sections 170(c) and 2055(a) of the Code] (hereinafter "the Charitable Recipient"). The first day of the annuity period shall be the date of my death and the last day of the annuity period shall be the date of the death of the survivor of the Initial Recipient and the Successor Recipient. If the Charitable Recipient is not an organization described in sections 170(c) and 2055(a) of the Code at the time when any annuity payment is to be distributed to it, then the Trustee shall distribute that annuity payment to one or more organizations described in sections 170(c) and 2055(a) of the Code as the Trustee shall select, and in the proportions as the Trustee shall decide, in the Trustee's sole discretion. The annuity amount shall be paid in equal quarterly installments at the end of each calendar quarter from income, and to the extent income is not sufficient, from principal. Any income of the trust for a taxable year in excess of the annuity amount shall be added to principal. If the initial net fair market value of the trust assets is incorrectly determined, then within a reasonable period after the value is finally determined for federal estate tax purposes, the Trustee shall pay to the Initial Recipient and/or the Successor Recipient and the Charitable Recipient (in the case of an undervaluation) or receive from the Initial Recipient and/or the Successor Recipient and the Charitable Recipient (in the case of an overvaluation) an amount equal to the difference between the annuity amount(s) properly payable and the annuity amount(s) actually paid.

(b) In paragraph 2, Deferral Provision, of the sample trust, replace each reference to "the Initial Recipient and/or the Successor Recipient" with a reference to "the Initial Recipient and/or the Successor Recipient and the Charitable Recipient."

(c) Replace the first parenthetical in paragraph 4, Distribution to Charity, of the sample trust with the following parenthetical:

(other than any amount due the Initial Recipient, the Successor Recipient, or their estates and the Charitable Recipient under the provisions above).

(d) Add the following sentence after the first and only sentence in paragraph 6, Prohibited Transactions, of the sample trust:

The Trustee shall not make any investments that jeopardize the exempt purpose of the trust for purposes of section 4944 of the Code, as modified by section 4947(a)(2)(A) of the Code, or retain any excess business holdings for purposes of section 4943 of the Code, as modified by section 4947(a)(2)(A) of the Code.

.03 Qualified Contingency.

(1) Explanation. Under section 664(f), payment of the annuity amount may terminate upon the earlier of the occurrence of a qualified contingency (as defined in section 664(f)(3)) or the death of the survivor of the initial recipient and the successor recipient. The amount of the charitable deduction, however, will be determined without regard to a qualified contingency. See section 664(f)(2).

(2) Instructions for use. Replace the second sentence of paragraph 1, Payment of Annuity Amount, of the sample trust with the following sentence:

The first day of the annuity period shall be the date of my death and the last day of the annuity period shall be the date of the death of the survivor of the Initial Recipient and the

Successor Recipient or, if earlier, the date on which occurs the [qualified contingency].

.04 Last Annuity Payments to the Recipients.

(1) Explanation. As an alternative to prorating the annuity amount in the taxable year of the initial recipient's death, payment of the initial recipient's share of the annuity amount may terminate with the last regular payment preceding the initial recipient's death. Similarly, as an alternative to prorating the annuity amount in the taxable year of the termination of the annuity period, payment of the annuity amount may terminate with the last regular payment preceding the termination of the annuity period. However, the fact that a recipient may not receive the last payment shall not be taken into account for purposes of determining the present value of the remainder interest. Section 1.664–2(a)(5)(i).

(2) Instruction for use.

(a) To add an alternate provision to terminate the payment of the initial recipient's share of the annuity amount with the last regular payment preceding his or her death, replace paragraph 3, Proration of Annuity Amount, of the sample trust with the following paragraph:

Proration of Annuity Amount. Except as provided below, the Trustee shall prorate the annuity amount on a daily basis for any short taxable year. The obligation of the Trustee to pay the annuity amount to the Initial Recipient shall terminate with the regular quarterly installment next preceding the Initial Recipient's death. In the taxable year of the trust during which the annuity period ends, the Trustee shall prorate the annuity amount on a daily basis for the number of days of the annuity period in that taxable year.

(b) To add an alternate provision to terminate the payment of the annuity amount with the last regular payment preceding the termination of the annuity period, replace paragraph 3, Proration of Annuity Amount, of the sample trust with the following paragraph:

Proration of Annuity Amount. Except as provided below, the Trustee shall prorate the annuity amount on a daily basis for any short taxable year. If the Successor Recipient survives the Initial Recipient, the Trustee shall prorate on a daily basis the next regular annuity payment due after the death of the Initial Recipient between the estate of the Initial Recipient and the Successor Recipient. In the taxable year of the trust during which the annuity period ends, the obligation of the Trustee to pay the annuity amount shall terminate with the regular quarterly installment next preceding the termination of the annuity period.

(c) To add an alternate provision terminating the payment of the initial recipient's share of the annuity amount with the last regular payment preceding his or her death, and terminating the payment of the annuity amount with the last regular payment preceding the termination of the annuity period, replace paragraph 3, Proration of Annuity Amount, of the sample trust with the following paragraph:

Proration of Annuity Amount. Except as provided below, the Trustee shall prorate the annuity amount on a daily basis for any short taxable year. The obligation of the Trustee to pay the annuity amount to the Initial Recipient shall terminate with the regular quarterly installment next preceding the Initial Recipient's death. In the taxable year of the trust during which the annuity period ends, the obligation of the Trustee to pay the annuity amount shall terminate with the regular quarterly installment next preceding the termination of the annuity period.

.05 Power of Appointment to Designate the Charitable Remainderman.

(1)   Explanation. The trust instrument may grant a recipient a power of appointment to designate the charitable remainderman. See Rev. Rul. 76–7, 1976–1 C.B. 179.

(2)   Instruction for use. Replace paragraph 4, Distribution to Charity, of the sample trust with the following paragraph:

Distribution to Charity. At the termination of the annuity period, the Trustee shall distribute all of the then principal and income of the trust (other than any amount due the Recipients or their estates under the provisions above) to one or more charitable organizations described in sections 170(c) and 2055(a) of the Code as [one of the named permissible recipients] shall appoint and direct by specific reference to this power of appointment by inter vivos or testamentary instrument. To the extent this power of appointment is not effectively exercised, the principal and income not effectively appointed shall be distributed to one or more organizations described in sections 170(c) and 2055(a) of the Code as the Trustee shall select, and in the proportions as the Trustee shall decide, in the Trustee's sole discretion. If an organization fails to qualify as an organization described in sections 170(c) and 2055(a) of the Code at the time when any principal or income of the trust is to be distributed to it, then the Trustee shall distribute the then principal and income to one or more organizations described in sections 170(c) and 2055(a) of the Code as the Trustee shall select, and in the proportions as the Trustee shall decide, in the Trustee's sole discretion.

251

SECTION 7. EFFECT ON OTHER REVENUE PROCEDURES

Section 7 of Rev. Proc. 90–32 is superseded.

DRAFTING INFORMATION

The principal authors of this revenue procedure are Karlene M. Lesho and Stephanie N. Bland of the Office of Associate Chief Counsel (Passthroughs and Special Industries). For further information regarding this revenue procedure, contact Karlene M. Lesho or Stephanie N. Bland at (202) 622-7830 (not a toll-free call).

IRS SPECIMEN TESTAMENTARY CRAT: PAYMENTS FOR TWO MEASURING LIVES—PAYABLE CONCURRENTLY AND CONSECUTIVELY

Annotations and Alternative Provisions
Rev. Proc. 2003–60

SECTION 1. PURPOSE

This revenue procedure contains an annotated sample declaration of trust and alternate provisions that meet the requirements of section 664(d)(1) of the Internal Revenue Code for a testamentary charitable remainder annuity trust (CRAT) providing for annuity payments payable concurrently and consecutively for two measuring lives followed by the distribution of trust assets to a charitable remainderman.

SECTION 2. BACKGROUND

Previously, the Internal Revenue Service issued sample trust instruments for certain types of CRATs. The Service is updating the previously issued samples and issuing new samples for additional types of CRATs; annotations and alternate sample provisions are included as further guidance. In addition to the sample trust instrument included in this revenue procedure for a testamentary CRAT providing for annuity payments payable concurrently and consecutively for two measuring lives, samples are provided in separate revenue procedures for:

(a) an inter vivos CRAT providing for annuity payments for one measuring life (see Rev. Proc. 2003–53, superceding Rev. Proc. 89–21, 1989–1 C.B. 842);

(b) an inter vivos CRAT providing for annuity payments for a term of years (see Rev. Proc. 2003–54);

(c) an inter vivos CRAT providing for annuity payments payable consecutively for two measuring lives (see Rev. Proc. 2003–55, superceding section 4 of Rev. Proc. 90–32, 1990–1 C.B. 546);

(d) an inter vivos CRAT providing for annuity payments payable concurrently and consecutively for two measuring lives (see Rev. Proc. 2003–56, superceding section 5 of Rev. Proc. 90–32);

(e) a testamentary CRAT providing for annuity payments for one measuring life (see Rev. Proc. 2003–57, superceding section 6 of Rev. Proc. 90–32);

(f) a testamentary CRAT providing for annuity payments for a term of years (see Rev. Proc. 2003–58); and

(g) a testamentary CRAT providing for annuity payments payable consecutively for two measuring lives (see Rev. Proc. 2003–59, superceding section 7 of Rev. Proc. 90–32).

SECTION 3. SCOPE AND OBJECTIVE

Section 4 of this revenue procedure provides a sample declaration of trust for a testamentary CRAT with concurrent and consecutive interests for two measuring lives that is created by an individual who is a citizen or resident of the United States. Section 5 of this revenue procedure provides annotations to the provisions of the sample trust. Section 6 of this revenue procedure provides samples of alternate provisions concerning: (.01) the statement of the annuity amount as a specific dollar amount; (.02) the payment of part of the annuity to an organization described in section 170(c); (.03) a qualified contingency; (.04) the last annuity payments to the recipients; and (.05) a power of appointment to designate the charitable remainderman.

For transfers to a qualifying CRAT, as defined in section 664(d)(1), the remainder interest will be deductible by the estate of a citizen or resident of the United States under section 2055(e)(2)(A) if the other requirements of section 2055(e)(2)(A) (that is, the requirements not relating to the provisions of the governing instrument) are also met. The Service will recognize a trust as a qualified CRAT meeting all of the requirements of section 664(d)(1) if the trust operates in a manner consistent with the terms of the trust instrument, if the trust is a valid trust under applicable local law, and if the trust instrument: (i) is substantially similar to the sample in section 4 of this revenue procedure; or (ii) properly integrates one or more alternate provisions from section 6 of this revenue procedure into a document substantially similar to the sample in section 4 of this revenue procedure. A trust instrument that contains substantive provisions in addition to those provided in section 4 of this revenue procedure (other than properly integrated alternate provisions from section 6 of this revenue procedure, or provisions necessary to establish a valid trust under applicable local law that are not inconsistent with the applicable federal tax requirements), or that omits any of the provisions of section 4 of this revenue procedure (unless an alternate provision from section 6 of this revenue procedure is properly integrated), will not necessarily be disqualified, but neither will that trust be assured of qualification under the provisions of this revenue procedure. The Service generally will not issue a letter ruling on whether a testamentary trust created by an individual and with concurrent and consecutive interests for two measuring lives qualifies as a CRAT. The Service, however, generally will issue letter rulings on the effect of substantive trust provisions, other than those contained in sections 4 and 6 of this revenue procedure, on the qualification of a trust as a CRAT.

SECTION 4. SAMPLE TESTAMENTARY CHARITABLE REMAINDER ANNUITY TRUST -- TWO LIVES, CONCURRENT AND CONSECUTIVE INTERESTS

I give, devise, and bequeath [property bequeathed] to my Trustee in trust to be administered under this provision. I intend this bequest to establish a charitable remainder annuity trust, within the meaning of Rev. Proc. 2003–60 and section 664(d)(1) of the Internal Revenue Code (hereinafter "the Code"). The trust shall be known as the ___ Charitable Remainder Annuity Trust and I hereby designate ___ as the initial trustee (hereinafter "the Trustee").

1. Payment of Annuity Amount. In each taxable year of the trust during the annuity period, the Trustee shall pay to [permissible recipient] and to [permissible recipient] (hereinafter "the Recipients") in equal shares during their lifetimes, an annuity amount equal to [a number no less than 5 and no more than 50] percent of the initial net fair market value of all property passing to this trust as finally determined for federal estate tax purposes, and upon the death of one (hereinafter "the Predeceasing Recipient"), the Trustee shall pay the entire annuity amount (subject to any proration in paragraph 3) to the survivor (hereinafter "the Survivor Recipient"). The first day of the annuity period shall be the date of my death and the last clay of the annuity period shall be the date of the Survivor Recipient's death. The annuity amount shall be paid in equal quarterly installments at the end of each calendar quarter from income, and to the extent income is not sufficient, from principal. Any income of the trust for a taxable year in excess of the annuity amount shall be added to principal. If the initial net fair market value of the trust assets is incorrectly determined, then within a reasonable period after the value is finally determined for federal estate tax purposes, the Trustee shall pay to the Recipients (in the case of an undervaluation) or receive from the Recipients (in the case of an overvaluation) an amount equal to the difference between the annuity amount(s) properly payable and the annuity amount(s) actually paid.

2. Deferral Provision. The obligation to pay the annuity amount shall commence with the date of my death, but payment of the annuity amount may be deferred from this date until the end of the taxable year in which the trust is completely funded. Within a reasonable time after the end of the taxable year in which the trust is completely funded, the Trustee must pay to the Recipients (in the case of an underpayment) or receive from the Recipients (in the case of an overpayment) the difference between any annuity amounts actually paid, plus interest, and the annuity amounts payable, plus interest. The interest shall be computed for any period at the rate of interest, compounded annually, that the federal income tax regulations under section 664 of the Code prescribe for this computation.

3. Proration of Annuity Amount. The Trustee shall prorate the annuity amount on a daily basis for any short taxable year. Upon the death of the Predeceasing Recipient, the Trustee shall prorate on a daily basis the Predeceasing Recipient's share of the next regular annuity payment between the estate of the Predeceasing Recipient and the Survivor Recipient. In the taxable year of the trust during which the annuity period ends, the Trustee shall prorate the annuity amount on a daily basis for the number of days of the annuity period in that taxable year.

4. Distribution to Charity. At the termination of the annuity period, the Trustee shall distribute all of the then principal and income of the trust (other than any amount due the Recipients or their estates under the provisions above) to [designated remainderman] (hereinafter "the Charitable Organization"). If the Charitable Organization is not an organization described in sections 170(c) and 2055(a) of the Code at the time when any principal or income of the trust is to be distributed to it, then the Trustee shall distribute the then principal

and income to one or more organizations described in sections 170(c) and 2055(a) of the Code as the Trustee shall select, and in the proportions as the Trustee shall decide, in the Trustee's sole discretion.

5.   Additional Contributions. No additional contributions shall be made to the trust after the initial contribution. The initial contribution, however, shall be deemed to consist of all property passing to the trust by reason of my death.

6.   Prohibited Transactions. The Trustee shall not engage in any act of self-dealing within the meaning of section 4941(d) of the Code, as modified by section 4947(a)(2)(A) of the Code, and shall not make any taxable expenditures within the meaning of section 4945(d) of the Code, as modified by section 4947(a)(2)(A) of the Code.

7.   Taxable Year. The taxable year of the trust shall be the calendar year.

8.   Governing Law. The operation of the trust shall be governed by the laws of the State of ___. However, the Trustee is prohibited from exercising any power or discretion granted under said laws that would be inconsistent with the qualification of the trust as a charitable remainder annuity trust under section 664(d)(1) of the Code and the corresponding regulations.

9.   Limited Power of Amendment. This trust is irrevocable. However, the Trustee shall have the power, acting alone, to amend the trust from time to time in any manner required for the sole purpose of ensuring that the trust qualifies and continues to qualify as a charitable remainder annuity trust within the meaning of section 664(d)(1) of the Code.

10. Investment of Trust Assets. Nothing in this trust instrument shall be construed to restrict the Trustee from investing the trust assets in a manner that could result in the annual realization of a reasonable amount of income or gain from the sale or disposition of trust assets.

SECTION 5. ANNOTATIONS REGARDING SAMPLE TESTAMENTARY CHARITABLE REMAINDER ANNUITY TRUST -- TWO LIVES, CONCURRENT AND CONSECUTIVE INTERESTS

.01 Annotations for Introductory Paragraph of the Sample Trust.

(1) Factors concerning qualification of trust. A deduction must be allowable under section 2055 for property contributed to the trust. Section 1.664–1(a)(1)(iii)(a) of the Income Tax Regulations. The trust must meet the definition of and function exclusively as a charitable remainder trust from the creation of the trust. Section 1.664–1(a)(4). Solely for purposes of section 664, a trust is deemed created at the earliest time that no person is treated as the owner of the entire trust under subpart E, part 1, subchapter J, chapter 1, subtitle A of the Code (subpart E). Section 1.664–1(a)(4). For purposes of section 2055, a charitable remainder trust shall be deemed created at the date of death of the decedent (even though the trust is not funded until the end of a reasonable period of administration or settlement) if the obligation to pay the annuity amount with respect to the property passing in trust at the death of the decedent begins as of the date of death of the decedent, even though the requirement to pay this amount is deferred in accordance with section 1.664–1(a)(5)(i). Section 1.664–1(a)(5)(i). In addition, funding the trust with certain types of assets may disqualify it as a charitable remainder trust. See section 1.664–1(a)(7) and Rev. Rul. 73–610, 1973–2 C.B. 213.

(2) Valuation of unmarketable assets. If the trust is funded with unmarketable assets, the initial net fair market value of the assets must be determined exclusively by an independent trustee, as defined in section 1.664-1(a)(7)(iii), or must be determined by a current "qualified appraisal" from a "qualified appraiser," as defined in section 1.170A–13(c)(3) and (c)(5), respectively. Section 1.664–1(a)(7).

(3) Trustee provisions. Alternate or successor trustees may be designated in the trust instrument. In addition, the trust instrument may contain other administrative provisions relating to the trustee's duties and powers, as long as the provisions do not conflict with the rules governing charitable remainder trusts under section 664 and the regulations thereunder.

.02 Annotations for Paragraph 1, Payment of Annuity Amount, of the Sample Trust.

(1) Permissible recipients. For a CRAT having an annuity period based on the lives of two individuals, the annuity amount must generally be paid to those individuals, and both must be living at the time of the creation of the

trust. See Rev. Rul. 2002–20, 2002–1 C.B. 794, for situations in which the annuity amount may be paid to a trust for the benefit of an individual who is financially disabled. An organization described in section 170(c) may receive part, but not all, of the annuity amount. Section 664(d)(1)(A) and section 1.664-2(a)(3)(i). See section 6.02 of this revenue procedure for an alternate provision that provides for payment of part of the annuity to an organization described in section 170(c).

(2) Division of annuity amount between recipients. The sample trust provides that while both recipients are alive they will share the annuity amount equally and upon the death of the predeceasing recipient the survivor recipient will receive all of the annuity amount, subject to any proration in paragraph 3. The annuity amount may be divided other than equally during the joint lives of the recipients. In addition, the share of the predeceasing recipient may be made payable to an organization described in section 170(c) for the rest of the survivor recipient's life.

(3) Percentage requirements. The sum certain annuity amount must be at least 5 percent and not more than 50 percent of the initial net fair market value of the assets placed in trust. Section 664(d)(1)(A). Even if the sum certain annuity amount is at least 5 percent and not more than 50 percent of the initial net fair market value of the assets placed in trust, no deduction will be allowable under section 2055 if the probability that the trust corpus will be exhausted before the death of the survivor of the recipients exceeds 5 percent. Rev. Rul. 77–374, 1977–2 C.B. 329. See section 20.7520–3(b) for special rules that may be applicable in valuing interests transferred to CRATs. In addition, the value (determined under section 7520) of the charitable remainder interest must be at least 10 percent of the initial net fair market value of all property placed in the trust. Section 664(d)(1)(D).

(4) Payment of annuity amount in installments. Paragraph 1, Payment of Annuity Amount, of the sample trust specifies that the annuity amount is to be paid in equal quarterly installments at the end of each quarter. However, the trust instrument may specify that the annuity amount is to be paid to the recipients annually or in equal or unequal installments throughout the year. See section 1.664–2(a)(1)(i). The amount of the charitable deduction will be affected by the frequency of payment, by whether the installments are equal or unequal, and by whether each installment is payable at the beginning or end of the period. See section 1.664–2(c) and section 20.2031–7(d)(2)(iv).

(5) Payment of annuity amount by close of taxable year. Generally, the annuity amount for any taxable year must be paid before the close of the taxable year for which it is due. For circumstances under which the annuity amount may be paid within a reasonable time after the close of the taxable year, see section 1.664–2(a)(1)(i)(a). In addition, section 1.664–1(a)(5)(i) provides a special rule applicable to charitable remainder trusts created by testamentary transfer that may defer the requirement to pay the annuity amount until the end of the taxable year in which the trust is completely funded. See section 5.03(1) of this revenue procedure for additional information regarding the deferral of the payment of the annuity amount until the end of the taxable year in which the trust is completely funded.

(6) Early distributions to charity. The trust instrument may provide that an amount other than the annuity shall be paid (or may be paid in the discretion of the trustee) to an organization described in section 170(c). If such a distribution is made in kind, the adjusted basis of the property distributed must be fairly representative of the adjusted basis of the property available for distribution on the date of distribution. Section 1.664–2(a)(4).

.03 Annotations for Paragraph 2, Deferral Provision, of the Sample Trust.

(1) Deferral of requirement to pay annuity amount. The deferral provision in paragraph 2 of the sample trust authorizes deferring the payment of the annuity amount until the end of the taxable year of the trust in which the trust is completely funded. Section 1.664–1(a)(5)(i) provides the operational rule for deferring payment of the annuity amount in this circumstance.

(2) Treatment of distributions. For the proper treatment of distributions to a charitable remainder trust or to the recipients during the period of administration of an estate or settlement of a trust that is not a charitable remainder trust, see section 1.664–1(a)(5)(iii).

.04 Annotations for Paragraph 3, Proration of Annuity Amount, of the Sample Trust.

(1) Prorating annuity amount. To compute the annuity amount in a short taxable year and in the taxable year in which the annuity period terminates, see section 1.664–2(a)(1)(iv)(a) and (b), respectively.

(2) Determining annuity amount payable in year of a recipient's death. Paragraph 3, Proration of Annuity Amount, of the sample trust specifies that the annuity amount shall be prorated on a daily basis. See section 6.04 of this revenue procedure for alternate provisions that provide for termination of the annuity amount with the last regular payment preceding the death of each recipient.

.05 Annotations for Paragraph 4, Distribution to Charity, of the Sample Trust.

(1) Minimum value of remainder. As noted in section 5.02(3) of this revenue procedure, the value (determined under section 7520) of the charitable remainder interest is required to be at least 10 percent of the initial net fair market value of all property placed in the trust. Section 664(d)(1)(D).

(2) Designated remainderman. Any named charitable remainderman must be an organization described in sections 170(c) and 2055(a) at the time of the transfer to the charitable remainder annuity trust. See section 664(d)(1)(C) and Rev. Rul. 77–385, 1977–2 C.B. 331. The trust instrument may restrict the charitable remainderman to an organization described in sections 170(c) and 2055(a), but grant to a trustee or other person the power to designate the actual charitable remainderman. See section 6.05 of this revenue procedure for an alternate provision in which a recipient is granted a power of appointment to designate the charitable remainderman.

(3) Multiple remaindermen. The remainder interest may pass to more than one charitable organization as long as each organization is described in sections 170(c) and 2055(a). Section 1.664–2(a)(6)(i).

(4) Alternative remaindermen. The trust instrument of a CRAT must provide a means for selecting alternative charitable remaindermen in the event the designated organization is not qualified at the time any payments are to be made to it from the trust. Section 1.664–2(a)(6)(iv).

.06 Annotations for Paragraph 6, Prohibited Transactions, of the Sample Trust.

(1) Payment of the annuity amount. Payment of the annuity amount to the recipients is not considered an act of self-dealing within the meaning of section 4941(d), as modified by section 4947(a)(2)(A), or a taxable expenditure within the meaning of section 4945(d), as modified by section 4947(a)(2)(A). Section 53.4947–1(c)(2) of the Foundation and Similar Excise Taxes Regulations.

(2) Prohibitions against certain investments and excess business holdings. Prohibitions against investments that jeopardize the exempt purpose of the trust for purposes of section 4944, as modified by section 4947(a)(2)(A), and against retaining any excess business holdings for purposes of section 4943, as modified by section 4947(a)(2)(A), are required if the trust provides for payment of part of an annuity amount to an organization described in section 170(c) and an estate tax charitable deduction is sought for this interest. See section 4947(b)(3). See section 6.02 of this revenue procedure for an alternate provision that provides for payment of part of the annuity to an organization described in section 170(c).

(3) Trust to continue in existence for benefit of charity. The governing instrument requirements of section 508(e) must be included in the trust instrument if, after the termination of the annuity period: (i) the trust instrument provides that the trust shall continue in existence for the benefit of the charitable remainderman and, as a result, the trust will become subject to the provisions of section 4947(a)(1); and (ii) the trust will be treated as a private foundation within the meaning of section 509(a), as modified by section 4947(a)(1). Except as provided in paragraph 6 of the sample trust, the trust instrument may limit the application of the provisions of section 509(e) to the period after the termination of the annuity period when the trust continues in existence for the benefit of the charitable remainderman.

SECTION 6. ALTERNATE PROVISIONS FOR SAMPLE TESTAMENTARY CHARITABLE REMAINDER ANNUITY TRUST—TWO LIVES, CONCURRENT AND CONSECUTIVE

.01 Annuity Amount Stated as a Specific Dollar Amount.

(1) Explanation. As an alternative to stating the annuity amount as a fraction or percentage of the initial net fair market value of the assets transferred to the trust, the annuity amount may be stated as a specific dollar amount. Section 1.664-2(a)(1)(ii) and (iii). In either case, the annuity amount must be not less than 5 percent nor more than 50 percent of the initial net fair market value of all property placed in trust. Section 664(d)(1)(A).

(2) Instructions for use.

(a) Replace the first sentence of paragraph 1, Payment of Annuity Amount, of the sample trust with the following sentence:

In each taxable year of the trust during the annuity period, the Trustee shall pay to [permissible recipient] and to [permissible recipient] (hereinafter "the Recipients") in equal shares during their lifetimes an annuity amount equal to [the stated dollar amount], and upon the death of one (hereinafter "the Predeceasing Recipient"), the Trustee shall pay the entire annuity amount (subject to any proration in paragraph 3) to the survivor (hereinafter "the Survivor Recipient").

(b) Delete the last sentence of paragraph 1, Payment of Annuity Amount, of the sample trust concerning the incorrect valuation of trust assets.

.02 Payment of Part of the Annuity to an Organization Described in section 170(c).

(1) Explanation. An organization described in section 170(c) may receive part, but not all, of any annuity amount. Section 664(d)(1)(A). If an estate tax charitable deduction is sought for the present value of the annuity interest passing to a charitable organization, the trust instrument must contain additional provisions. First, the trust instrument must specify the portion of each annuity payment that is payable to the noncharitable recipients and to the charitable organization described in sections 170(c) and 2055(a). Second, the trust instrument must contain a means for selecting an alternative qualified charitable organization if the designated organization is not a qualified organization at the time when any annuity amount is to be paid to it. Third, the trust instrument must contain prohibitions against investments that jeopardize the exempt purpose of the trust for purposes of section 4944, as modified by section 4947(a)(2)(A), and against retaining any excess business holdings for purposes of section 4943, as modified by section 4947(a)(2)(A).

(2) Instructions for use.

(a) Replace paragraph 1, Payment of Annuity Amount, of the sample trust with the following paragraph:

Payment of Annuity Amount. The annuity amount is equal to [a number no less than 5 and no more than 50] percent of the initial net fair market value of all property passing to this trust as finally determined for federal estate tax purposes. In each taxable year of the trust during the annuity period, the Trustee shall pay [the percentage of the annuity amount payable to the noncharitable recipients] percent of the annuity amount to [permissible recipient] and [permissible recipient] (hereinafter "the Recipients") in equal shares during their joint lives, and upon the death of one hereinafter "the Predeceasing Recipient"), the Trustee shall pay that entire percentage of the annuity amount (subject to any proration in paragraph 3) to the survivor (hereinafter "the Survivor Recipient"). In each taxable year of the trust during the annuity period, the Trustee shall pay [the percentage of the annuity amount payable to the charitable recipient] percent of the annuity amount to [an organization described in sections 170(c) and 2055(a) of the Code] (hereinafter "the Charitable Recipient"). The first day of the annuity period shall be the date of my death and the last day of the annuity period shall be the date of the Survivor Recipient's death. If the Charitable Recipient is not an organization described in sections 170(c) and 2055(a) of the Code at the time when any annuity payment is to be distributed to it, then the Trustee shall distribute that annuity payment to one or more organizations described in sections 170(c) and 2055(a) of the Code as the Trustee shall select, and in the proportions as the Trustee shall decide, in the Trustee's sole discretion. The annuity amount shall be paid in equal quarterly installments at the end of each calendar quarter from income, and to the extent income is not sufficient, from principal. Any income of the trust for a taxable year in excess of the annuity amount shall be added to principal. If the initial net fair market value of the trust assets is incorrectly determined, then within a reasonable period after the value is finally determined for federal estate tax purposes, the Trustee shall pay to the Recipients and the Charitable Recipient (in the case of an undervaluation) or receive from the Recipients and the Charitable Recipient (in the case of an overvaluation) an amount equal to the difference between the annuity amount(s) properly payable and the annuity amount(s) actually paid.

(b) In paragraph 2, Deferral Provision, of the sample trust, replace each reference to "the Recipients" with a reference to "the Recipients and the Charitable Recipient."

(c) Replace the first parenthetical in paragraph 4, Distribution to Charity, of the sample trust with the following parenthetical:

(other than any amount due the Recipients or their estates and the Charitable Recipient under the provisions above).

(d) Add the following sentence after the first and only sentence in paragraph 6, Prohibited Transactions, of the sample trust:

The Trustee shall not make any investments that jeopardize the exempt purpose of the trust for purposes of section 4944 of the Code, as modified by section 4947(a)(2)(A) of the Code, or retain any excess business holdings for purposes of section 4943 of the Code, as modified by section 4947(a)(2)(A) of the Code.

.03 Qualified Contingency.

(1)   Explanation. Under section 664(f), payment of the annuity amount may terminate upon the earlier of the occurrence of a qualified contingency (as defined in section 664(f)(3)) or the death of the survivor recipient. The amount of the charitable deduction, however, will be determined without regard to a qualified contingency. See section 664(f)(2).

(2)   Instruction for use. Replace the second sentence of paragraph 1, Payment of Annuity Amount, of the sample trust with the following sentence:

The first day of the annuity period shall be the date of my death and the last day of the annuity period shall be the date of the Survivor Recipient's death or, if earlier, the date on which occurs the [qualified contingency].

.04 Last Annuity Payments to the Recipients.

(1)   Explanation. As an alternative to prorating the annuity amount in the taxable year of the predeceasing recipient's death, payment of the predeceasing recipient's share of the annuity amount may terminate with the last regular payment preceding the predeceasing recipient's death. Similarly, as an alternative to prorating the annuity amount in the taxable year of the termination of the annuity period, payment of the annuity amount may terminate with the last regular payment preceding the termination of the annuity period. However, the fact that a recipient may not receive the last payment shall not be taken into account for purposes of determining the present value of the remainder interest. Section 1.664–2(a)(5)(i).

(2)   Instructions for use.

(a) To add an alternate provision to terminate the payment of the predeceasing recipient's share of the annuity amount with the last regular payment preceding his or her death, replace paragraph 3, Proration of Annuity Amount, of the sample trust with the following paragraph:

Proration of Annuity Amount. Except as provided below, the Trustee shall prorate the annuity amount on a daily basis for any short taxable year. The obligation of the Trustee to pay a share of the annuity amount to the Predeceasing Recipient shall terminate with the regular quarterly installment next preceding the Predeceasing Recipient's death. In the taxable year of the trust during which the annuity period ends, the Trustee shall prorate the annuity amount on a daily basis for the number of days of the annuity period in that taxable year.

(b) To add an alternate provision to terminate the payment of the annuity amount with the last regular payment preceding the termination of the annuity period, replace paragraph 3, Proration of Annuity Amount, of the sample trust with the following paragraph:

Proration of Annuity Amount. Except as provided below, the Trustee shall prorate the annuity amount on a daily basis for any short taxable year. Upon the death of the Predeceasing Recipient, the Trustee shall prorate on a daily basis the Predeceasing Recipient's share of the next regular annuity payment between the estate of the Predeceasing Recipient and the Survivor Recipient. In the taxable year of the trust during which the annuity period ends, the obligation of the Trustee to pay the annuity amount shall terminate with the regular quarterly installment next preceding the termination of the annuity period.

(c) To add an alternate provision terminating the payment of the predeceasing recipient's share of the annuity amount with the last regular payment preceding his or her death, and terminating the payment of the annuity amount with the last regular payment preceding the termination of the annuity period, replace paragraph 3, Proration of Annuity Amount, of the sample trust with the following paragraph:

Proration of Annuity Amount. Except as provided below, the Trustee shall prorate the annuity amount on a daily basis for any short taxable year. The obligation of the Trustee to pay a share of the annuity amount to the Predeceasing Recipient shall terminate with the regular quarterly installment next preceding the Predeceasing Recipient's death. In the taxable year of the trust during which the annuity period ends, the obligation of the Trustee to pay the annuity amount shall terminate with the regular quarterly installment next preceding the termination of the annuity period.

.05 Power of Appointment to Designate the Charitable Remainderman.

(1) Explanation. The trust instrument may grant a recipient a power of appointment to designate the charitable remainderman. See Rev. Rul. 76–7, 1976–1 C.B. 179.

(2) Instruction for use. Replace paragraph 4, Distribution to Charity, of the sample trust with the following paragraph:

Distribution to Charity. At the termination of the annuity period, the Trustee shall distribute all of the then principal and income of the trust (other than any amount due the Recipients or their estates under the provisions above) to one or more charitable organizations described in sections 170(c) and 2055(a) of the Code as [one of the named permissible recipients] shall appoint and direct by specific reference to this power of appointment by inter vivos or testamentary instrument. To the extent this power of appointment is not effectively exercised, the principal and income not effectively appointed shall be distributed to one or more organizations described in sections 170(c) and 2055(a) of the Code as the Trustee shall select, and in the proportions as the Trustee shall decide, in the Trustee's sole discretion. If an organization fails to qualify as an organization described in sections 170(c) and 2055(a) of the Code at the time when any principal or income of the trust is to be distributed to it, then the Trustee shall distribute the then principal and income to one or more organizations described in sections 170(c) and 2055(a) of the Code as the Trustee shall select, and in the proportions as the Trustee shall decide, in the Trustee's sole discretion.

259

SECTION 7. EFFECT ON OTHER REVENUE PROCEDURES

Section 8 of Rev. Proc. 90–32 is superseded.

DRAFTING INFORMATION

The principal authors of this revenue procedure are Karlene M. Lesho and Stephanie N. Bland of the Office of Associate Chief Counsel (Passthroughs and Special Industries). For further information regarding this revenue procedure, contact Karlene M. Lesho or Stephanie N. Bland at (202) 622-7830 (not a toll-free call).

Split-Interest Trust Information Return

Form 5227

Department of the Treasury
Internal Revenue Service

Split-Interest Trust Information Return

► See separate instructions.

OMB No. 1545-0196

2004

Full name of trust	**A** Employer identification number

Name of trustee	**B** Type of Entity

Number, street, and room or suite no. (If a P.O. box, see page 3 of the instructions.)

(1) ☐ Charitable lead trust

City, state, and ZIP code

(2) ☐ Charitable remainder annuity trust described in section 664(d)(1)

C Fair market value (FMV) of assets at end of tax year	**D** Date the trust was created

(3) ☐ Charitable remainder unitrust described in section 664(d)(2)

E **Check applicable boxes** (see instructions)
☐ Initial return ☐ Final return ☐ Amended return
Change in trustee's ► ☐ Name ☐ Address

(4) ☐ Pooled income fund described in section 642(c)(5)

(5) ☐ Other

F Did the split-interest trust have any unrelated business taxable income (section 664 trusts only)? If "Yes," file Form 1041 . . . . ☐ Yes ☐ No

Part I — Ordinary Income (Section 664 trust only)

1	Interest income	**1**
2a	Qualified dividends (see instructions) **2a**	
b	Ordinary dividends (including qualified dividends)	**2b**
3	Business income or (loss) (attach Schedule C or C-EZ (Form 1040)).	**3**
4	Rents, royalties, partnerships, other estates and trusts, etc. (attach Schedule E (Form 1040)) .	**4**
5	Farm income or (loss) (attach Schedule F (Form 1040))	**5**
6	Ordinary gain or (loss) (attach Form 4797)	**6**
7	Other income (state nature of income)	**7**
8	**Total** ordinary income (combine lines 1, 2b, and 3 through 7)	**8**

Deductions Allocable to Ordinary Income

9	Interest	**9**
10	Taxes	**10**
11	Other deductions (attach a separate sheet listing deductions)	**11**
12	**Total** deductions (add lines 9 through 11)	**12**
13	Ordinary income less deductions (subtract line 12 from line 8). Enter here and on line 21, column (a)	**13**

Capital Gains (Losses) and Allocable Deductions

14	Total short-term capital gain or (loss) for tax year (attach Schedule D (Form 1041))	**14**	
15	Deductions allocable to short-term capital gains	**15**	
16	**Balance** (subtract line 15 from line 14). Enter here and on line 21, column (b)		**16**
17a	Total long-term capital gain or (loss) for tax year (attach Schedule D (Form 1041))	**17a**	
b	28% rate gain or (loss) **17b**		
c	Unrecaptured section 1250 gain **17c**		
18	Deductions allocable to long-term capital gains	**18**	
19	**Balance** (subtract line 18 from line 17a). Enter here and on line 21, column (c)		**19**

Part II — Accumulation Schedule (Section 664 trust only)

Accumulations	(a) Ordinary income	Capital gains and (losses)		(d) Nontaxable income
		(b) Net short-term	(c) Net long-term	
20 Undistributed from prior tax years				
21 Current tax year (before distributions)				
22 **Total** (add lines 20 and 21)				
23 Undistributed at end of tax year				

Part III — Current Distributions Schedule (Section 664 trust only)

Name of recipient	Identifying number	(a) Ordinary income	Capital gains		(d) Nontaxable income	(e) Corpus
			(b) Short-term	(c) Long-term		
24a						
b						
c						

For Paperwork Reduction Act Notice, see page 10 of the instructions.   Cat. No. 13227T   Form **5227** (2004)

Form 5227 (2004)   Page **2**

Part IV	**Balance Sheet** (see page 6 of the instructions)			
		(a) Beginning-of-Year Book Value	**(b)** End-of-Year Book Value	**(c)** FMV (see instructions)
	Assets			
25	Cash — non-interest-bearing **25**			
26	Savings and temporary cash investments **26**			
27a	Accounts receivable **27a**			
b	Less: allowance for doubtful accounts . . . **27b**			
28	Receivables due from officers, directors, trustees, and other disqualified persons (attach schedule) **28**			
29a	Other notes and loans receivable **29a**			
b	Less: allowance for doubtful accounts **29b**			
30	Inventories for sale or use **30**			
31	Prepaid expenses and deferred charges **31**			
32a	Investments — U.S. and state government obligations (attach schedule) **32a**			
b	Investments — corporate stock (attach schedule) **32b**			
c	Investments — corporate bonds (attach schedule) **32c**			
33a	Investments — land, buildings, and equipment: basis (attach schedule) **33a**			
b	Less: accumulated depreciation **33b**			
34	Investments — other (attach schedule) **34**			
35a	Land, buildings, and equipment: basis . . . **35a**			
b	Less: accumulated depreciation **35b**			
36	Other assets (describe ▶ ---------------------------------) **36**			
37	**Total assets** (add lines 25 through 36) (must equal line 47) **37**			
	Liabilities			
38	Accounts payable and accrued expenses **38**			
39	Deferred revenue **39**			
40	Loans from officers, directors, trustees, and other disqualified persons **40**			
41	Mortgages and other notes payable (attach schedule) **41**			
42	Other liabilities (describe ▶ ---------------------------------) **42**			
43	**Total liabilities** (add lines 38 through 42) **43**			
	Net Assets			
44	Trust principal or corpus **44**			
45a	Undistributed income **45a**			
b	Undistributed capital gains **45b**			
c	Undistributed nontaxable income **45c**			
46	**Total net assets** (add lines 44 through 45c) **46**			
47	**Total liabilities and net assets** (add lines 43 and 46) **47**			

Part V-A	**Charitable Remainder Annuity Trust Information** (to be completed **only** by a section 664 charitable remainder annuity trust)	
48a	Enter the initial fair market value (FMV) of the property placed in the trust	**48a**
b	Enter the total annual annuity amounts for all recipients (attach schedule showing the amount for each recipient if more than one)	**48b**

Part V-B	**Charitable Remainder Unitrust Information** (to be completed **only** by a section 664 charitable remainder unitrust)	
49a	Enter the unitrust fixed percentage to be paid to the recipients	**49a** %
	If there is more than one recipient, attach a schedule showing the percentage of the total unitrust dollar amount payable to each recipient.	
b	**Unitrust amount.** Subtract line 43, column (c), from line 37, column (c), and multiply the result by the percentage on line 49a	**49b**
	Note: Complete lines 50a through 51b only for those unitrusts whose governing instruments provide for determining required distributions with reference to the unitrust's income. Otherwise, enter the amount from line 49b on line 52.	
50a	Trust's accounting income for 2004	**50a**
b	Enter the smaller of line 49b or line 50a here, and on line 52 on page 3, unless the **Caution** below applies	**50b**
	Caution: Lines 51a and b need to be completed by those unitrusts whose governing instruments provide for current distributions to make up for any distribution deficiencies in previous years due to the trust income limit. See Regulations section 1.664-3(a)(1)(i)(b)(2). For these trusts, when completing line 52 enter the smaller of line 50a or line 51b.	

Form **5227** (2004)

51a	Total accrued distribution deficiencies from previous years (see page 8 of the instructions) . . .	**51a**
b	Add lines 49b and 51a	**51b**
52	Unitrust distributions for 2004.	**52**
53	Carryover of distribution deficiency (subtract line 52 from line 51b)	**53**

54 Did the trustee change the method of determining the fair market value of the assets? . . . . . . ☐ Yes ☐ No
If "Yes," attach an explanation.

55 Were any additional contributions received by the trust during 2004? . . . . ☐ Yes ☐ No
If "Yes," attach a schedule that lists the assets and the date(s) received.

Part VI-A   Statements Regarding Activities (see page 8 of the instructions)

		Yes	No
1	Are the requirements of section 508(e) satisfied either: • By the language in the governing instrument; or • By state legislation that effectively amends the governing instrument so that no mandatory directions that conflict with the state law remain in the governing instrument? **1**		
2	Are you using this return only to report the income and assets of a segregated amount under section 4947(a)(2)(B)? **2**		

Part VI-B   Statements Regarding Activities for Which Form 4720 May Be Required

File Form 4720 if any item is checked in the "Yes" column (to the right), unless an exception applies.

Yes | No

1 Self-dealing (section 4941):

a During 2004, did the trust (either directly or indirectly):

(1) Engage in the sale or exchange, or leasing of property with a disqualified person?. ☐ Yes ☐ No

(2) Borrow money from, lend money to, or otherwise extend credit to (or accept it from) a disqualified person? . . . . ☐ Yes ☐ No

(3) Furnish goods, services, or facilities to (or accept them from) a disqualified person? ☐ Yes ☐ No

(4) Pay compensation to, or pay or reimburse the expenses of, a disqualified person? ☐ Yes ☐ No

(5) Transfer any income or assets to a disqualified person (or make any of either available for the benefit or use of a disqualified person)? . . . . ☐ Yes ☐ No

(6) Agree to pay money or property to a government official? (**Exception.** Check "No" if the trust agreed to make a grant to or to employ the official for a period after termination of government service, if terminating within 90 days.) . . . . ☐ Yes ☐ No

b If any answer is "Yes" to 1a(1)—(6), did **any** of the acts fail to qualify under the exceptions described in Regulations sections 53.4941(d)-3 and 4, or in a current Notice regarding disaster assistance (see page 9 of the instructions)? **1b**
Organizations relying on a current Notice regarding disaster assistance, check here . . . . ▶ ☐

c Did the trust engage in a prior year in any of the acts described in 1a, other than excepted acts, that were not corrected before January 1, 2004?. **1c**

2 Does section 4947(b)(3)(A) or (B) apply? (See page 9 of the instructions.) (If "Yes," check the "N/A" box in questions 3 and 4.) . . . . ☐ Yes ☐ No

3 Taxes on excess business holdings (section 4943): ☐ **N/A**

a Did the trust hold more than a 2% direct or indirect interest in any business enterprise at any time during 2004? . . . . ☐ Yes ☐ No

b If "Yes," did the trust have excess business holdings in 2004 as a result of **(1)** any purchase by the trust or disqualified persons after May 26, 1969; **(2)** the lapse of the 5-year period (or longer period approved by the Commissioner under section 4943(c)(7)) to dispose of holdings acquired by gift or bequest; or **(3)** the lapse of the 10-, 15-, or 20-year first phase holding period? **3b**
Use Schedule C, Form 4720, to determine if the trust had excess business holdings in 2004.

4 Taxes on investments that jeopardize charitable purposes (section 4944): ☐ **N/A**

a Did the trust invest during 2004 any amount in a manner that would jeopardize its charitable purpose?. **4a**

b Did the trust make any investment in a prior year (but after December 31, 1969) that could jeopardize its charitable purpose that had not been removed from jeopardy before January 1, 2004? **4b**

5 Taxes on taxable expenditures (section 4945) and political expenditures (section 4955):

a During 2004 did the trust pay or incur any amount to:

(1) Carry on propaganda, or otherwise attempt to influence legislation (section 4945(e))? ☐ Yes ☐ No

(2) Influence the outcome of any specific public election (see section 4955); or to carry on, directly or indirectly, any voter registration drive?. . . . . ☐ Yes ☐ No

(3) Provide a grant to an individual for travel, study, or other similar purposes? . . . ☐ Yes ☐ No

(4) Provide a grant to an organization other than a charitable, etc., organization described in section 509(a)(1), (2), or (3), or section 4940(d)(2)? . . . . ☐ Yes ☐ No

(5) Provide for any purpose other than religious, charitable, scientific, literary, or educational, or for the prevention of cruelty to children or animals?. . . . . . ☐ Yes ☐ No

263

Form **5227** (2004)

		Yes	No
5b	If any answer is "Yes" to 5a(1)—(5), did **any** of the transactions fail to qualify under the exceptions described in Regulations section 53.4945, or in a current Notice regarding disaster assistance (see page 9 of the instructions)? **5b**		

Organizations relying on a current Notice regarding disaster assistance, check here . . . . ▶ ☐

c If the answer is "Yes" to question 5a(4), does the trust claim exemption from the tax because it maintained expenditure responsibility for the grant? (See page 9 of the instructions.) . . . . ☐ **Yes** ☐ **No**

If "Yes," attach the statement required by Regulations section 53.4945-5(d).

6 Personal benefit contracts (section 170(f)(10)):

a Did the trust, during the year, receive any funds, directly or indirectly, to pay premiums on a personal benefit contract? . . . . ☐ **Yes** ☐ **No**

b Did the trust, during the year, pay premiums, directly or indirectly, on a personal benefit contract? . . **6b**
If "Yes" to 6b, file Form 8870 (see instructions).

Part VII **Questionnaire for Charitable Lead Trusts, Pooled Income Funds, and Charitable Remainder Trusts**

Section A—Charitable Lead Trusts

1 Does the governing instrument require income in excess of the required annuity or unitrust payments to be paid for charitable purposes? . . . . ☐ **Yes** ☐ **No**

2	Enter the amount of any excess income required to be paid for charitable purposes for 2004 . . .	**2**	
3	Enter the amount of annuity or unitrust payments required to be paid to charitable beneficiaries for 2004	**3**	
4	Enter the amount of annuity or unitrust payments required to be paid to private beneficiaries for 2004	**4**	

Section B—Pooled Income Funds

1	Enter the amount of contributions received during 2004	**1**	
2	Enter the amount required to be distributed for 2004 to satisfy the remainder interest	**2**	
3	Enter any amounts that were required to be distributed to the remainder beneficiary that remain undistributed	**3**	
4	Enter the amount of income required to be paid to private beneficiaries for 2004	**4**	
5	Enter the amount of income required to be paid to the charitable remainder beneficiary for 2004	**5**	

Section C—Charitable Remainder Trusts and Other Information
(All split-interest trusts, check applicable boxes.)

1 Check this box if you are filing for a charitable remainder annuity trust or a charitable remainder unitrust whose charitable interests involve only cemeteries or war veterans' posts . . . . ▶ ☐

2 Check this box if you are making an election under Regulations section 1.664-2(a)(1)(i)(a)(2) or 1.664-3(a)(1)(i)(g)(2) to treat income generated from certain property distributions (other than cash) by the trust as occurring on the last day of the tax year. (See page 10 of the instructions.) . . . . ▶ ☐

3 Check this box if any of the split-interest trust's income interests expired during 2004 . . . . ▶ ☐

Sign Here

Under penalties of perjury, I declare that I have examined this return, including accompanying schedules and statements, and to the best of my knowledge and belief, it is true, correct, and complete. Declaration of preparer (other than trustee) is based on all information of which preparer has any knowledge.

▶ _____   ▶ _____
Signature of trustee or officer representing trustee   Date

Paid Preparer's Use Only

Preparer's ▶ signature		Date	Check if self-employed ☐	Preparer's SSN or PTIN
Firm's name (or yours if self-employed), address, and ZIP code ▶			EIN	
			Phone no. ( )	

Form **5227** (2004)

U.S. Income Tax Return for Estates and Trusts

Form **1041**

Department of the Treasury—Internal Revenue Service

U.S. Income Tax Return for Estates and Trusts 2004

OMB No. 1545-0092

A Type of entity (see instr.):

☐ Decedent's estate
☐ Simple trust
☐ Complex trust
☐ Qualified disability trust
☐ ESBT (S portion only)
☐ Grantor type trust
☐ Bankruptcy estate–Ch. 7
☐ Bankruptcy estate–Ch. 11
☐ Pooled income fund

For calendar year 2004 or fiscal year beginning _____ , 2004, and ending _____ , 20 _____

Name of estate or trust (If a grantor type trust, see page 12 of the instructions.)

Name and title of fiduciary

Number, street, and room or suite no. (If a P.O. box, see page 12 of the instructions.)

City or town, state, and ZIP code

C Employer identification number

D Date entity created

E Nonexempt charitable and split-interest trusts, check applicable boxes (see page 13 of the instr.):

☐ Described in section 4947(a)(1)
☐ Not a private foundation
☐ Described in section 4947(a)(2)

B Number of Schedules K-1 attached (see instructions) ▶

F Check applicable boxes:
☐ Initial return ☐ Final return ☐ Amended return
☐ Change in fiduciary ☐ Change in fiduciary's name
☐ Change in trust's name
☐ Change in fiduciary's address

G Pooled mortgage account (see page 14 of the instructions): ☐ Bought ☐ Sold Date:

Income

1	Interest income	1
2a	Total ordinary dividends	2a
b	Qualified dividends allocable to: **(1)** Beneficiaries _____ **(2)** Estate or trust _____	
3	Business income or (loss) (attach Schedule C or C-EZ (Form 1040))	3
4	Capital gain or (loss) (attach Schedule D (Form 1041))	4
5	Rents, royalties, partnerships, other estates and trusts, etc. (attach Schedule E (Form 1040))	5
6	Farm income or (loss) (attach Schedule F (Form 1040))	6
7	Ordinary gain or (loss) (attach Form 4797)	7
8	Other income. List type and amount _____	8
9	**Total income.** Combine lines 1, 2a, and 3 through 8 ▶	9

Deductions

10	Interest. Check if Form 4952 is attached ▶ ☐	10
11	Taxes	11
12	Fiduciary fees	12
13	Charitable deduction (from Schedule A, line 7)	13
14	Attorney, accountant, and return preparer fees	14
15a	Other deductions **not** subject to the 2% floor (attach schedule)	15a
b	Allowable miscellaneous itemized deductions subject to the 2% floor	15b
16	**Total.** Add lines 10 through 15b	16
17	Adjusted total income or (loss). Subtract line 16 from line 9. Enter here and on Schedule B, line 1 ▶	17
18	Income distribution deduction (from Schedule B, line 15) (attach Schedules K-1 (Form 1041))	18
19	Estate tax deduction (including certain generation-skipping taxes) (attach computation)	19
20	Exemption	20
21	**Total deductions.** Add lines 18 through 20 ▶	21

Tax and Payments

22	Taxable income. Subtract line 21 from line 17. If a loss, see page 19 of the instructions	22
23	**Total tax** (from Schedule G, line 7)	23
24	**Payments: a** 2004 estimated tax payments and amount applied from 2003 return	24a
b	Estimated tax payments allocated to beneficiaries (from Form 1041-T)	24b
c	Subtract line 24b from line 24a	24c
d	Tax paid with extension of time to file: ☐ Form 2758 ☐ Form 8736 ☐ Form 8800	24d
e	Federal income tax withheld. If any is from Form(s) 1099, check ▶ ☐	24e
	Other payments: **f** Form 2439 _____ ; **g** Form 4136 _____ ; Total ▶	24h
25	**Total payments.** Add lines 24c through 24e, and 24h ▶	25
26	Estimated tax penalty (see page 20 of the instructions)	26
27	**Tax due.** If line 25 is smaller than the total of lines 23 and 26, enter amount owed	27
28	**Overpayment.** If line 25 is larger than the total of lines 23 and 26, enter amount overpaid	28
29	Amount of line 28 to be: **a** Credited to 2005 estimated tax ▶ _____ ; **b** Refunded ▶	29

Sign Here

Under penalties of perjury, I declare that I have examined this return, including accompanying schedules and statements, and to the best of my knowledge and belief, it is true, correct, and complete. Declaration of preparer (other than taxpayer) is based on all information of which preparer has any knowledge.

▶ _____ Signature of fiduciary or officer representing fiduciary   Date   ▶ _____ EIN of fiduciary if a financial institution

May the IRS discuss this return with the preparer shown below (see instr.)? ☐ Yes ☐ No

Paid Preparer's Use Only

Preparer's signature ▶ _____ Date _____ Check if self-employed ☐   Preparer's SSN or PTIN

Firm's name (or yours if self-employed), address, and ZIP code ▶ _____ EIN _____ Phone no. ( )

For Privacy Act and Paperwork Reduction Act Notice, see the separate instructions.   Cat. No. 11370H   Form **1041** (2004)

Form 1041 (2004)   Page **2**

Schedule A   Charitable Deduction. Do not complete for a simple trust or a pooled income fund.

1	Amounts paid or permanently set aside for charitable purposes from gross income (see page 20)	1	
2	Tax-exempt income allocable to charitable contributions (see page 20 of the instructions) . .	2	
3	Subtract line 2 from line 1	3	
4	Capital gains for the tax year allocated to corpus and paid or permanently set aside for charitable purposes	4	
5	Add lines 3 and 4	5	
6	Section 1202 exclusion allocable to capital gains paid or permanently set aside for charitable purposes (see page 20 of the instructions)	6	
7	**Charitable deduction.** Subtract line 6 from line 5. Enter here and on page 1, line 13	7	

Schedule B   Income Distribution Deduction

1	Adjusted total income (see page 21 of the instructions)	1	
2	Adjusted tax-exempt interest	2	
3	Total net gain from Schedule D (Form 1041), line 15, column (1) (see page 21 of the instructions)	3	
4	Enter amount from Schedule A, line 4 (reduced by any allocable section 1202 exclusion) . .	4	
5	Capital gains for the tax year included on Schedule A, line 1 (see page 21 of the instructions)	5	
6	Enter any gain from page 1, line 4, as a negative number. If page 1, line 4, is a loss, enter the loss as a positive number	6	
7	**Distributable net income (DNI).** Combine lines 1 through 6. If zero or less, enter -0- . . .	7	
8	If a complex trust, enter accounting income for the tax year as determined under the governing instrument and applicable local law 8		
9	Income required to be distributed currently	9	
10	Other amounts paid, credited, or otherwise required to be distributed	10	
11	Total distributions. Add lines 9 and 10. If greater than line 8, see page 22 of the instructions	11	
12	Enter the amount of tax-exempt income included on line 11	12	
13	Tentative income distribution deduction. Subtract line 12 from line 11	13	
14	Tentative income distribution deduction. Subtract line 2 from line 7. If zero or less, enter -0-	14	
15	**Income distribution deduction.** Enter the smaller of line 13 or line 14 here and on page 1, line 18	15	

Schedule G   Tax Computation (see page 22 of the instructions)

1	**Tax: a** Tax on taxable income (see page 22 of the instructions) . .	1a		
	b Tax on lump-sum distributions (attach Form 4972)	1b		
	c Alternative minimum tax (from Schedule I, line 56)	1c		
	d Total. Add lines 1a through 1c . . . . ▶		1d	
2a	Foreign tax credit (attach Form 1116)	2a		
b	Other nonbusiness credits (attach schedule)	2b		
c	General business credit. Enter here and check which forms are attached: ☐ Form 3800 ☐ Forms (specify) ▶	2c		
d	Credit for prior year minimum tax (attach Form 8801)	2d		
3	**Total credits.** Add lines 2a through 2d . . . . ▶		3	
4	Subtract line 3 from line 1d. If zero or less, enter -0-		4	
5	Recapture taxes. Check if from: ☐ Form 4255 ☐ Form 8611		5	
6	Household employment taxes. Attach Schedule H (Form 1040)		6	
7	**Total tax.** Add lines 4 through 6. Enter here and on page 1, line 23 . . . . . ▶		7	

Other Information

		Yes	No
1	Did the estate or trust receive tax-exempt income? If "Yes," attach a computation of the allocation of expenses Enter the amount of tax-exempt interest income and exempt-interest dividends ▶ $		
2	Did the estate or trust receive all or any part of the earnings (salary, wages, and other compensation) of any individual by reason of a contract assignment or similar arrangement?		
3	At any time during calendar year 2004, did the estate or trust have an interest in or a signature or other authority over a bank, securities, or other financial account in a foreign country? . . . . See page 24 of the instructions for exceptions and filing requirements for Form TD F 90-22.1. If "Yes," enter the name of the foreign country ▶		
4	During the tax year, did the estate or trust receive a distribution from, or was it the grantor of, or transferor to, a foreign trust? If "Yes," the estate or trust may have to file Form 3520. See page 24 of the instructions .		
5	Did the estate or trust receive, or pay, any qualified residence interest on seller-provided financing? If "Yes," see page 24 for required attachment		
6	If this is an estate or a complex trust making the section 663(b) election, check here (see page 24) . . ▶ ☐		
7	To make a section 643(e)(3) election, attach Schedule D (Form 1041), and check here (see page 24) . ▶ ☐		
8	If the decedent's estate has been open for more than 2 years, attach an explanation for the delay in closing the estate, and check here ▶ ☐		
9	Are any present or future trust beneficiaries skip persons? See page 24 of the instructions		

Form **1041** (2004)

Schedule I	**Alternative Minimum Tax** (see pages 25 through 31 of the instructions)			

Part I—Estate's or Trust's Share of Alternative Minimum Taxable Income

1	Adjusted total income or (loss) (from page 1, line 17)	**1**		
2	Interest	**2**		
3	Taxes	**3**		
4	Miscellaneous itemized deductions (from page 1, line 15b)	**4**		
5	Refund of taxes	**5**	(	)
6	Depletion (difference between regular tax and AMT)	**6**		
7	Net operating loss deduction. Enter as a positive amount	**7**		
8	Interest from specified private activity bonds exempt from the regular tax	**8**		
9	Qualified small business stock (see page 26 of the instructions)	**9**		
10	Exercise of incentive stock options (excess of AMT income over regular tax income)	**10**		
11	Other estates and trusts (amount from Schedule K-1 (Form 1041), line 9)	**11**		
12	Electing large partnerships (amount from Schedule K-1 (Form 1065-B), box 6)	**12**		
13	Disposition of property (difference between AMT and regular tax gain or loss)	**13**		
14	Depreciation on assets placed in service after 1986 (difference between regular tax and AMT)	**14**		
15	Passive activities (difference between AMT and regular tax income or loss)	**15**		
16	Loss limitations (difference between AMT and regular tax income or loss)	**16**		
17	Circulation costs (difference between regular tax and AMT)	**17**		
18	Long-term contracts (difference between AMT and regular tax income)	**18**		
19	Mining costs (difference between regular tax and AMT)	**19**		
20	Research and experimental costs (difference between regular tax and AMT)	**20**		
21	Income from certain installment sales before January 1, 1987	**21**	(	)
22	Intangible drilling costs preference	**22**		
23	Other adjustments, including income-based related adjustments	**23**		
24	Alternative tax net operating loss deduction (See the instructions for the limitation that applies.)	**24**	(	)
25	Adjusted alternative minimum taxable income. Combine lines 1 through 24	**25**		

Note: *Complete Part II below before going to line 26.*

26	Income distribution deduction from Part II, line 44	**26**		
27	Estate tax deduction (from page 1, line 19)	**27**		
28	Add lines 26 and 27	**28**		
29	Estate's or trust's share of alternative minimum taxable income. Subtract line 28 from line 25	**29**		

If line 29 is:

- $22,500 or less, stop here and enter -0- on Schedule G, line 1c. The estate or trust is not liable for the alternative minimum tax.
- Over $22,500, but less than $165,000, go to line 45.
- $165,000 or more, enter the amount from line 29 on line 51 and go to line 52.

Part II—Income Distribution Deduction on a Minimum Tax Basis

30	Adjusted alternative minimum taxable income (see page 29 of the instructions)	**30**		
31	Adjusted tax-exempt interest (other than amounts included on line 8)	**31**		
32	Total net gain from Schedule D (Form 1041), line 15, column (1). If a loss, enter -0-	**32**		
33	Capital gains for the tax year allocated to corpus and paid or permanently set aside for charitable purposes (from Schedule A, line 4)	**33**		
34	Capital gains paid or permanently set aside for charitable purposes from gross income (see page 29 of the instructions)	**34**		
35	Capital gains computed on a minimum tax basis included on line 25	**35**	(	)
36	Capital losses computed on a minimum tax basis included on line 25. Enter as a positive amount	**36**		
37	Distributable net alternative minimum taxable income (DNAMTI). Combine lines 30 through 36. If zero or less, enter -0-	**37**		
38	Income required to be distributed currently (from Schedule B, line 9)	**38**		
39	Other amounts paid, credited, or otherwise required to be distributed (from Schedule B, line 10)	**39**		
40	Total distributions. Add lines 38 and 39	**40**		
41	Tax-exempt income included on line 40 (other than amounts included on line 8)	**41**		
42	Tentative income distribution deduction on a minimum tax basis. Subtract line 41 from line 40	**42**		
43	Tentative income distribution deduction on a minimum tax basis. Subtract line 31 from line 37. If zero or less, enter -0-	**43**		
44	**Income distribution deduction on a minimum tax basis.** Enter the smaller of line 42 or line 43. Enter here and on line 26	**44**		

Form **1041** (2004)

Form 1041 (2004)   Page **4**

Part III—Alternative Minimum Tax

45	Exemption amount	**45**	$22,500	00
46	Enter the amount from line 29	**46**		
47	Phase-out of exemption amount	**47**	$75,000	00
48	Subtract line 47 from line 46. If zero or less, enter -0-	**48**		
49	Multiply line 48 by 25% (.25)	**49**		
50	Subtract line 49 from line 45. If zero or less, enter -0-	**50**		
51	Subtract line 50 from line 46	**51**		

52 Go to Part IV of Schedule I to figure line 52 if the estate or trust has qualified dividends or has a gain on lines 14a and 15 of column (2) of Schedule D (Form 1041) (as refigured for the AMT, if necessary). Otherwise, if line 51 is—
- $175,000 or less, multiply line 51 by 26% (.26).
- Over $175,000, multiply line 51 by 28% (.28) and subtract $3,500 from the result . . . . | **52** | | |

53	Alternative minimum foreign tax credit (see page 29 of the instructions)	**53**	
54	Tentative minimum tax. Subtract line 53 from line 52	**54**	
55	Enter the tax from Schedule G, line 1a (minus any foreign tax credit from Schedule G, line 2a)	**55**	
56	**Alternative minimum tax.** Subtract line 55 from line 54. If zero or less, enter -0-. Enter here and on Schedule G, line 1c	**56**	

Part IV—Line 52 Computation Using Maximum Capital Gains Rates

Caution: *If you did not complete Part V of Schedule D (Form 1041), the Schedule D Tax Worksheet, or the Qualified Dividends Tax Worksheet, see page 31 of the instructions before completing this part.*

57	Enter the amount from line 51	**57**		
58	Enter the amount from Schedule D (Form 1041), line 22, line 13 of the Schedule D Tax Worksheet, or line 4 of the Qualified Dividends Tax Worksheet, whichever applies (as refigured for the AMT, if necessary)	**58**		
59	Enter the amount from Schedule D (Form 1041), line 14b, column (2) (as refigured for the AMT, if necessary). If you did not complete Schedule D for the regular tax or the AMT, enter -0-	**59**		
60	If you did not complete a Schedule D Tax Worksheet for the regular tax or the AMT, enter the amount from line 58. Otherwise, add lines 58 and 59 and enter the **smaller** of that result or the amount from line 10 of the Schedule D Tax Worksheet (as refigured for the AMT, if necessary)	**60**		
61	Enter the **smaller** of line 57 or line 60	**61**		
62	Subtract line 61 from line 57	**62**		
63	If line 62 is $175,000 or less, multiply line 62 by 26% (.26). Otherwise, multiply line 62 by 28% (.28) and subtract $3,500 from the result . . . . ▶	**63**		
64	Maximum amount subject to the 5% rate	**64**	$1,950	00
65	Enter the amount from line 23 of Schedule D (Form 1041), line 14 of the Schedule D Tax Worksheet, or line 5 of the Qualified Dividends Tax Worksheet, whichever applies (as figured for the regular tax). If you did not complete Schedule D or either worksheet for the regular tax, enter -0-	**65**		
66	Subtract line 65 from line 64. If zero or less, enter -0-	**66**		
67	Enter the **smaller** of line 57 or line 58	**67**		
68	Enter the **smaller** of line 66 or line 67	**68**		
69	Multiply line 68 by 5% (.05) . . . . ▶	**69**		
70	Subtract line 68 from line 67	**70**		
71	Multiply line 70 by 15% (.15) . . . . ▶	**71**		

If line 59 is zero or blank, skip lines 72 and 73 and go to line 74. Otherwise, go to line 72.

72	Subtract line 67 from line 61	**72**	
73	Multiply line 72 by 25% (.25) . . . . ▶	**73**	
74	Add lines 63, 69, 71, and 73	**74**	
75	If line 57 is $175,000 or less, multiply line 57 by 26% (.26). Otherwise, multiply line 57 by 28% (.28) and subtract $3,500 from the result	**75**	
76	Enter the **smaller** of line 74 or line 75 here and on line 52	**76**	

Form **1041** (2004)

Printed on recycled paper

6611

SCHEDULE K-1 (Form 1041) Department of the Treasury Internal Revenue Service	**Beneficiary's Share of Income, Deductions, Credits, etc.** for the calendar year 2004, or fiscal year beginning .... , 2004, ending .... , 20 .... ▶ Complete a separate Schedule K-1 for each beneficiary.	OMB No. 1545-0092 **2004**

Name of trust or decedent's estate

☐ Amended K-1
☐ Final K-1

Beneficiary's identifying number ▶   Estate's or trust's EIN ▶

Beneficiary's name, address, and ZIP code	Fiduciary's name, address, and ZIP code

(a) Allocable share item		(b) Amount	(c) Calendar year 2004 Form 1040 filers enter the amounts in column (b) on:
1 Interest	**1**		Form 1040, line 8a
2a Qualified dividends	**2a**		Form 1040, line 9b
b Total ordinary dividends	**2b**		Form 1040, line 9a
3 Net short-term capital gain	**3**		Schedule D, line 5, column (f)
4a Net long-term capital gain	**4a**		Schedule D, line 12, column (f)
b Unrecaptured section 1250 gain	**4b**		Line 11 of the worksheet for Schedule D, line 19
c 28% rate gain	**4c**		Line 4 of the worksheet for Schedule D, line 18
5a Annuities, royalties, and other nonpassive income before directly apportioned deductions	**5a**		Schedule E, Part III, column (f)
b Depreciation	**5b**		Include on the applicable line of the appropriate tax form
c Depletion	**5c**		
d Amortization	**5d**		
6a Trade or business, rental real estate, and other rental income before directly apportioned deductions (see instructions)	**6a**		Schedule E, Part III
b Depreciation	**6b**		Include on the applicable line of the appropriate tax form
c Depletion	**6c**		
d Amortization	**6d**		
7 Income for minimum tax purposes	**7**		
8 Income for regular tax purposes (add lines 1, 2b, 3, 4a, 5a, and 6a)	**8**		
9 Adjustment for minimum tax purposes (subtract line 8 from line 7)	**9**		Form 6251, line 14
10 Estate tax deduction (including certain generation-skipping transfer taxes)	**10**		Schedule A, line 27
11 Foreign taxes	**11**		Form 1040, line 46 or Schedule A, line 8
12 Adjustments and tax preference items (itemize):			
a Accelerated depreciation	**12a**		Include on the applicable line of Form 6251
b Depletion	**12b**		
c Amortization	**12c**		
d Exclusion items	**12d**		2005 Form 8801
13 Deductions in the final year of trust or decedent's estate:			
a Excess deductions on termination (see instructions)	**13a**		Schedule A, line 22
b Short-term capital loss carryover	**13b** ( )		Schedule D, line 5, column (f)
c Long-term capital loss carryover	**13c** ( )		Sch. D, line 12, col. (f); line 5 of the wksht. for Sch. D, line 18; and line 16 of the wksht. for Sch. D, line 19
d Net operating loss (NOL) carryover for regular tax purposes	**13d** ( )		Form 1040, line 21
e NOL carryover for minimum tax purposes	**13e**		See the instructions for Form 6251, line 27
f	**13f**		Include on the applicable line of the appropriate tax form
g	**13g**		
14 Other (itemize):			
a Payments of estimated taxes credited to you	**14a**		Form 1040, line 64
b Tax-exempt interest	**14b**		Form 1040, line 8b
c	**14c**		
d	**14d**		
e	**14e**		Include on the applicable line of the appropriate tax form
f	**14f**		
g	**14g**		
h	**14h**		

For Paperwork Reduction Act Notice, see the Instructions for Form 1041.   Cat. No. 11380D   Schedule K-1 (Form 1041) 2004

269

Instructions for Beneficiary Filing Form 1040

Note: *The fiduciary's instructions for completing Schedule K-1 are in the Instructions for Form 1041.*

General Instructions

Purpose of Form

The fiduciary of a trust or decedent's estate uses Schedule K-1 to report your share of the trust's or estate's income, credits, deductions, etc. Keep it for your records. Do not file it with your tax return. A copy has been filed with the IRS.

Inconsistent Treatment of Items

Generally, you must report items shown on your Schedule K-1 (and any attached schedules) the same way that the estate or trust treated the items on its return.

If the treatment on your original or amended return is inconsistent with the estate's or trust's treatment, or if the estate or trust was required to but has not filed a return, you must file Form 8082, Notice of Inconsistent Treatment or Administrative Adjustment Request (AAR), with your original or amended return to identify and explain any inconsistency (or to note that an estate or trust return has not been filed).

If you are required to file Form 8082 but fail to do so, you may be subject to the accuracy-related penalty. This penalty is in addition to any tax that results from making your amount or treatment of the item consistent with that shown on the estate's or trust's return. Any deficiency that results from making the amounts consistent may be assessed immediately.

Errors

If you believe the fiduciary has made an error on your Schedule K-1, notify the fiduciary and ask for an amended or a corrected Schedule K-1. Do not change any items on your copy. Be sure that the fiduciary sends a copy of the amended Schedule K-1 to the IRS. If you are unable to reach an agreement with the fiduciary regarding the inconsistency, you must file Form 8082.

Tax Shelters

If you receive a copy of Form 8271, Investor Reporting of Tax Shelter Registration Number, see the Instructions for Form 8271 to determine your reporting requirements.

Beneficiaries of Generation-Skipping Trusts

If you received Form 706-GS(D-1), Notification of Distribution From a Generation-Skipping Trust, and paid a generation-skipping transfer (GST) tax on Form 706-GS(D), Generation-Skipping Transfer Tax Return for Distributions, you can deduct the GST tax paid on income distributions on Schedule A (Form 1040), line 8. To figure the deduction, see the Instructions for Form 706-GS(D).

Specific Instructions

Lines 3 and 4a

If there is an attachment to this Schedule K-1 reporting a disposition of a passive activity, see the Instructions for Form 8582, Passive Activity Loss Limitations, for information on the treatment of dispositions of interests in a passive activity.

Lines 6b through 6d

The deductions on lines 6b through 6d may be subject to the passive loss limitations of Internal Revenue Code section 469, which generally limits deductions from passive activities to the income from those activities. The rules for applying these limitations to beneficiaries have not yet been issued. For more details, see Pub. 925, Passive Activity and At-Risk Rules.

Line 12d

If you pay alternative minimum tax in 2004, the amount on line 12d will help you figure any minimum tax credit for 2005. See the 2005 Form 8801, Credit for Prior Year Minimum Tax—Individuals, Estates, and Trusts, for more information.

Line 14a

To figure any underpayment and penalty on Form 2210, Underpayment of Estimated Tax by Individuals, Estates, and Trusts, treat the amount entered on line 14a as an estimated tax payment made on January 15, 2005.

Lines 14c through 14h

The amount of gross farming and fishing income is included on line 6a. This income is also separately stated on line 14 to help you determine if you are subject to a penalty for underpayment of estimated tax. Report the amount of gross farming and fishing income on Schedule E (Form 1040), line 42.

Form W-9
(Rev. January 2005)
Department of the Treasury
Internal Revenue Service

Request for Taxpayer
Identification Number and Certification

Give form to the requester. Do not send to the IRS.

Print or type
See Specific Instructions on page 2.

Name (as shown on your income tax return)

Business name, if different from above

Check appropriate box:
☐ Individual/Sole proprietor ☐ Corporation ☐ Partnership ☐ Other ▶ ....

☐ Exempt from backup withholding

Address (number, street, and apt. or suite no.)

Requester's name and address (optional)

City, state, and ZIP code

List account number(s) here (optional)

Part I — Taxpayer Identification Number (TIN)

Enter your TIN in the appropriate box. The TIN provided must match the name given on Line 1 to avoid backup withholding. For individuals, this is your social security number (SSN). However, for a resident alien, sole proprietor, or disregarded entity, see the Part I instructions on page 3. For other entities, it is your employer identification number (EIN). If you do not have a number, see *How to get a TIN* on page 3.

Note. *If the account is in more than one name, see the chart on page 4 for guidelines on whose number to enter.*

Social security number

or

Employer identification number

Part II — Certification

Under penalties of perjury, I certify that:

1. The number shown on this form is my correct taxpayer identification number (or I am waiting for a number to be issued to me), and

2. I am not subject to backup withholding because: (a) I am exempt from backup withholding, or (b) I have not been notified by the Internal Revenue Service (IRS) that I am subject to backup withholding as a result of a failure to report all interest or dividends, or (c) the IRS has notified me that I am no longer subject to backup withholding, and

3. I am a U.S. person (including a U.S. resident alien).

Certification instructions. You must cross out item 2 above if you have been notified by the IRS that you are currently subject to backup withholding because you have failed to report all interest and dividends on your tax return. For real estate transactions, item 2 does not apply. For mortgage interest paid, acquisition or abandonment of secured property, cancellation of debt, contributions to an individual retirement arrangement (IRA), and generally, payments other than interest and dividends, you are not required to sign the Certification, but you must provide your correct TIN. (See the instructions on page 4.)

Sign Here
Signature of U.S. person ▶

Date ▶

Purpose of Form

A person who is required to file an information return with the IRS, must obtain your correct taxpayer identification number (TIN) to report, for example, income paid to you, real estate transactions, mortgage interest you paid, acquisition or abandonment of secured property, cancellation of debt, or contributions you made to an IRA.

U.S. person. Use Form W-9 only if you are a U.S. person (including a resident alien), to provide your correct TIN to the person requesting it (the requester) and, when applicable, to:

1. Certify that the TIN you are giving is correct (or you are waiting for a number to be issued),

2. Certify that you are not subject to backup withholding, or

3. Claim exemption from backup withholding if you are a U.S. exempt payee.

Note. *If a requester gives you a form other than Form W-9 to request your TIN, you must use the requester's form if it is substantially similar to this Form W-9.*

For federal tax purposes you are considered a person if you are:

● An individual who is a citizen or resident of the United States,

● A partnership, corporation, company, or association created or organized in the United States or under the laws of the United States, or

● Any estate (other than a foreign estate) or trust. See Regulations sections 301.7701-6(a) and 7(a) for additional information.

Foreign person. If you are a foreign person, do not use Form W-9. Instead, use the appropriate Form W-8 (see Publication 515, Withholding of Tax on Nonresident Aliens and Foreign Entities).

Nonresident alien who becomes a resident alien. Generally, only a nonresident alien individual may use the terms of a tax treaty to reduce or eliminate U.S. tax on certain types of income. However, most tax treaties contain a provision known as a "saving clause." Exceptions specified in the saving clause may permit an exemption from tax to continue for certain types of income even after the recipient has otherwise become a U.S. resident alien for tax purposes.

If you are a U.S. resident alien who is relying on an exception contained in the saving clause of a tax treaty to claim an exemption from U.S. tax on certain types of income, you must attach a statement to Form W-9 that specifies the following five items:

1. The treaty country. Generally, this must be the same treaty under which you claimed exemption from tax as a nonresident alien.

2. The treaty article addressing the income.

3. The article number (or location) in the tax treaty that contains the saving clause and its exceptions.

4. The type and amount of income that qualifies for the exemption from tax.

5. Sufficient facts to justify the exemption from tax under the terms of the treaty article.

Example. Article 20 of the U.S.-China income tax treaty allows an exemption from tax for scholarship income received by a Chinese student temporarily present in the United States. Under U.S. law, this student will become a resident alien for tax purposes if his or her stay in the United States exceeds 5 calendar years. However, paragraph 2 of the first Protocol to the U.S.-China treaty (dated April 30, 1984) allows the provisions of Article 20 to continue to apply even after the Chinese student becomes a resident alien of the United States. A Chinese student who qualifies for this exception (under paragraph 2 of the first protocol) and is relying on this exception to claim an exemption from tax on his or her scholarship or fellowship income would attach to Form W-9 a statement that includes the information described above to support that exemption.

If you are a nonresident alien or a foreign entity not subject to backup withholding, give the requester the appropriate completed Form W-8.

What is backup withholding? Persons making certain payments to you must under certain conditions withhold and pay to the IRS 28% of such payments (after December 31, 2002). This is called "backup withholding." Payments that may be subject to backup withholding include interest, dividends, broker and barter exchange transactions, rents, royalties, nonemployee pay, and certain payments from fishing boat operators. Real estate transactions are not subject to backup withholding.

You will not be subject to backup withholding on payments you receive if you give the requester your correct TIN, make the proper certifications, and report all your taxable interest and dividends on your tax return.

Payments you receive will be subject to backup withholding if:

1. You do not furnish your TIN to the requester, or

2. You do not certify your TIN when required (see the Part II instructions on page 4 for details), or

3. The IRS tells the requester that you furnished an incorrect TIN, or

4. The IRS tells you that you are subject to backup withholding because you did not report all your interest and dividends on your tax return (for reportable interest and dividends only), or

5. You do not certify to the requester that you are not subject to backup withholding under 4 above (for reportable interest and dividend accounts opened after 1983 only).

Certain payees and payments are exempt from backup withholding. See the instructions below and the separate Instructions for the Requester of Form W-9.

Penalties

Failure to furnish TIN. If you fail to furnish your correct TIN to a requester, you are subject to a penalty of $50 for each such failure unless your failure is due to reasonable cause and not to willful neglect.

Civil penalty for false information with respect to withholding. If you make a false statement with no reasonable basis that results in no backup withholding, you are subject to a $500 penalty.

Criminal penalty for falsifying information. Willfully falsifying certifications or affirmations may subject you to criminal penalties including fines and/or imprisonment.

Misuse of TINs. If the requester discloses or uses TINs in violation of federal law, the requester may be subject to civil and criminal penalties.

Specific Instructions

Name

If you are an individual, you must generally enter the name shown on your social security card. However, if you have changed your last name, for instance, due to marriage without informing the Social Security Administration of the name change, enter your first name, the last name shown on your social security card, and your new last name.

If the account is in joint names, list first, and then circle, the name of the person or entity whose number you entered in Part I of the form.

Sole proprietor. Enter your individual name as shown on your social security card on the "Name" line. You may enter your business, trade, or "doing business as (DBA)" name on the "Business name" line.

Limited liability company (LLC). If you are a single-member LLC (including a foreign LLC with a domestic owner) that is disregarded as an entity separate from its owner under Treasury regulations section 301.7701-3, enter the owner's name on the "Name" line. Enter the LLC's name on the "Business name" line. Check the appropriate box for your filing status (sole proprietor, corporation, etc.), then check the box for "Other" and enter "LLC" in the space provided.

Other entities. Enter your business name as shown on required Federal tax documents on the "Name" line. This name should match the name shown on the charter or other legal document creating the entity. You may enter any business, trade, or DBA name on the "Business name" line.

Note. You are requested to check the appropriate box for your status (individual/sole proprietor, corporation, etc.).

Exempt From Backup Withholding

If you are exempt, enter your name as described above and check the appropriate box for your status, then check the "Exempt from backup withholding" box in the line following the business name, sign and date the form.

Generally, individuals (including sole proprietors) are not exempt from backup withholding. Corporations are exempt from backup withholding for certain payments, such as interest and dividends.

Note. If you are exempt from backup withholding, you should still complete this form to avoid possible erroneous backup withholding.

Exempt payees. Backup withholding is not required on any payments made to the following payees:

1. An organization exempt from tax under section 501(a), any IRA, or a custodial account under section 403(b)(7) if the account satisfies the requirements of section 401(f)(2),

2. The United States or any of its agencies or instrumentalities,

3. A state, the District of Columbia, a possession of the United States, or any of their political subdivisions or instrumentalities,

4. A foreign government or any of its political subdivisions, agencies, or instrumentalities, or

5. An international organization or any of its agencies or instrumentalities.

Other payees that may be exempt from backup withholding include:

6. A corporation,

7. A foreign central bank of issue,

8. A dealer in securities or commodities required to register in the United States, the District of Columbia, or a possession of the United States,

9. A futures commission merchant registered with the Commodity Futures Trading Commission,

10. A real estate investment trust,

11. An entity registered at all times during the tax year under the Investment Company Act of 1940,

12. A common trust fund operated by a bank under section 584(a),

13. A financial institution,

14. A middleman known in the investment community as a nominee or custodian, or

15. A trust exempt from tax under section 664 or described in section 4947.

The chart below shows types of payments that may be exempt from backup withholding. The chart applies to the exempt recipients listed above, 1 through 15.

IF the payment is for . . .	THEN the payment is exempt for . . .
Interest and dividend payments	All exempt recipients except for 9
Broker transactions	Exempt recipients 1 through 13. Also, a person registered under the Investment Advisers Act of 1940 who regularly acts as a broker
Barter exchange transactions and patronage dividends	Exempt recipients 1 through 5
Payments over $600 required to be reported and direct sales over $5,000 [1]	Generally, exempt recipients 1 through 7 [2]

[1] See Form 1099-MISC, Miscellaneous Income, and its instructions.

[2] However, the following payments made to a corporation (including gross proceeds paid to an attorney under section 6045(f), even if the attorney is a corporation) and reportable on Form 1099-MISC are not exempt from backup withholding: medical and health care payments, attorneys' fees; and payments for services paid by a Federal executive agency.

Part I. Taxpayer Identification Number (TIN)

Enter your TIN in the appropriate box. If you are a resident alien and you do not have and are not eligible to get an SSN, your TIN is your IRS individual taxpayer identification number (ITIN). Enter it in the social security number box. If you do not have an ITIN, see *How to get a TIN* below.

If you are a sole proprietor and you have an EIN, you may enter either your SSN or EIN. However, the IRS prefers that you use your SSN.

If you are a single-owner LLC that is disregarded as an entity separate from its owner (see *Limited liability company (LLC)* on page 2), enter your SSN (or EIN, if you have one). If the LLC is a corporation, partnership, etc., enter the entity's EIN.

Note. See the chart on page 4 for further clarification of name and TIN combinations.

How to get a TIN. If you do not have a TIN, apply for one immediately. To apply for an SSN, get Form SS-5, Application for a Social Security Card, from your local Social Security Administration office or get this form online at *www.socialsecurity.gov/online/ss-5.pdf*. You may also get this form by calling 1-800-772-1213. Use Form W-7, Application for IRS Individual Taxpayer Identification Number, to apply for an ITIN, or Form SS-4, Application for Employer Identification Number, to apply for an EIN. You can apply for an EIN online by accessing the IRS website at *www.irs.gov/businesses/* and clicking on Employer ID Numbers under Related Topics. You can get Forms W-7 and SS-4 from the IRS by visiting *www.irs.gov* or by calling 1-800-TAX-FORM (1-800-829-3676).

If you are asked to complete Form W-9 but do not have a TIN, write "Applied For" in the space for the TIN, sign and date the form, and give it to the requester. For interest and dividend payments, and certain payments made with respect to readily tradable instruments, generally you will have 60 days to get a TIN and give it to the requester before you are subject to backup withholding on payments. The 60-day rule does not apply to other types of payments. You will be subject to backup withholding on all such payments until you provide your TIN to the requester.

Note. Writing "Applied For" means that you have already applied for a TIN or that you intend to apply for one soon.

Caution: *A disregarded domestic entity that has a foreign owner must use the appropriate Form W-8.*

273

Part II. Certification

To establish to the withholding agent that you are a U.S. person, or resident alien, sign Form W-9. You may be requested to sign by the withholding agent even if items 1, 4, and 5 below indicate otherwise.

For a joint account, only the person whose TIN is shown in Part I should sign (when required). Exempt recipients, see *Exempt From Backup Withholding* on page 2.

Signature requirements. Complete the certification as indicated in 1 through 5 below.

1. Interest, dividend, and barter exchange accounts opened before 1984 and broker accounts considered active during 1983. You must give your correct TIN, but you do not have to sign the certification.

2. Interest, dividend, broker, and barter exchange accounts opened after 1983 and broker accounts considered inactive during 1983. You must sign the certification or backup withholding will apply. If you are subject to backup withholding and you are merely providing your correct TIN to the requester, you must cross out item 2 in the certification before signing the form.

3. Real estate transactions. You must sign the certification. You may cross out item 2 of the certification.

4. Other payments. You must give your correct TIN, but you do not have to sign the certification unless you have been notified that you have previously given an incorrect TIN. "Other payments" include payments made in the course of the requester's trade or business for rents, royalties, goods (other than bills for merchandise), medical and health care services (including payments to corporations), payments to a nonemployee for services, payments to certain fishing boat crew members and fishermen, and gross proceeds paid to attorneys (including payments to corporations).

5. Mortgage interest paid by you, acquisition or abandonment of secured property, cancellation of debt, qualified tuition program payments (under section 529), IRA, Coverdell ESA, Archer MSA or HSA contributions or distributions, and pension distributions. You must give your correct TIN, but you do not have to sign the certification.

What Name and Number To Give the Requester

For this type of account:	Give name and SSN of:
1. Individual	The individual
2. Two or more individuals (joint account)	The actual owner of the account or, if combined funds, the first individual on the account [1]
3. Custodian account of a minor (Uniform Gift to Minors Act)	The minor [2]
4. a. The usual revocable savings trust (grantor is also trustee)	The grantor-trustee [1]
b. So-called trust account that is not a legal or valid trust under state law	The actual owner [1]
5. Sole proprietorship or single-owner LLC	The owner [3]

For this type of account:	Give name and EIN of:
6. Sole proprietorship or single-owner LLC	The owner [3]
7. A valid trust, estate, or pension trust	Legal entity [4]
8. Corporate or LLC electing corporate status on Form 8832	The corporation
9. Association, club, religious, charitable, educational, or other tax-exempt organization	The organization
10. Partnership or multi-member LLC	The partnership
11. A broker or registered nominee	The broker or nominee
12. Account with the Department of Agriculture in the name of a public entity (such as a state or local government, school district, or prison) that receives agricultural program payments	The public entity

[1] List first and circle the name of the person whose number you furnish. If only one person on a joint account has an SSN, that person's number must be furnished.

[2] Circle the minor's name and furnish the minor's SSN.

[3] You must show your individual name and you may also enter your business or "DBA" name on the second name line. You may use either your SSN or EIN (if you have one). If you are a sole proprietor, IRS encourages you to use your SSN.

[4] List first and circle the name of the legal trust, estate, or pension trust. (Do not furnish the TIN of the personal representative or trustee unless the legal entity itself is not designated in the account title.)

Note. If no name is circled when more than one name is listed, the number will be considered to be that of the first name listed.

Privacy Act Notice

Section 6109 of the Internal Revenue Code requires you to provide your correct TIN to persons who must file information returns with the IRS to report interest, dividends, and certain other income paid to you, mortgage interest you paid, the acquisition or abandonment of secured property, cancellation of debt, or contributions you made to an IRA, or Archer MSA or HSA. The IRS uses the numbers for identification purposes and to help verify the accuracy of your tax return. The IRS may also provide this information to the Department of Justice for civil and criminal litigation, and to cities, states, and the District of Columbia to carry out their tax laws. We may also disclose this information to other countries under a tax treaty, to federal and state agencies to enforce federal nontax criminal laws, or to federal law enforcement and intelligence agencies to combat terrorism.

You must provide your TIN whether or not you are required to file a tax return. Payers must generally withhold 28% of taxable interest, dividend, and certain other payments to a payee who does not give a TIN to a payer. Certain penalties may also apply.

 Printed on recycled paper

Instructions for the Requester of Form W-9

Department of the Treasury
Internal Revenue Service

(Rev. October 2004)

Request for Taxpayer Identification Number and Certification

Section references are to the Internal Revenue Code unless otherwise noted.

What's New

- The backup withholding rate is reduced to 28% for reportable payments.
- The IRS website offers TIN Matching e-services for payers to validate name and TIN combinations. See *Taxpayer Identification Number (TIN) Matching* on page 4.
- Certain payment card transactions made by a qualified payment card agent have been added to the list of payments exempt from backup withholding on page 3.

How Do I Know When To Use Form W-9?

Use Form W-9 to request the taxpayer identification number (TIN) of a U.S. person (including a resident alien) and to request certain certifications and claims for exemption. (See Purpose of Form on Form W-9.) Withholding agents may require signed Forms W-9 from U.S. exempt recipients to overcome any presumptions of foreign status. For federal purposes, a U.S. person includes:

- an individual who is a citizen or resident of the United States,
- a partnership, corporation, company, or association created or organized in the United States or under the laws of the United States,
- any estate (other than a foreign estate) or trust.

See Regulations section 301.7701-6(a) for additional information.

Advise foreign persons to use the appropriate Form W-8. See Publication 515, Withholding of Tax on Nonresident Aliens and Foreign Entities, for more information and a list of the W-8 forms.

Also, a nonresident alien individual may, under certain circumstances, claim treaty benefits on scholarships and fellowship grant income. See Publication 515 or Publication 519, U.S. Tax Guide for Aliens, for more information.

Electronic Submission of Forms W-9

Requesters may establish a system for payees and payees' agents to submit Forms W-9 electronically, including by fax. A requester is anyone required to file an information return. A payee is anyone required to provide a taxpayer identification number (TIN) to the requester.

Payee's agent. A payee's agent can be an investment advisor (corporation, partnership, or individual) or an introducing broker. An investment advisor must be registered with the Securities Exchange Commission (SEC) under the Investment Advisers Act of 1940. The introducing broker is a broker-dealer that is regulated by the SEC and the National Association of Securities Dealers, Inc., and that is not a payer. Except for a broker who acts as a payee's agent for "readily tradable instruments," the advisor or broker must show in writing to the payer that the payee authorized the advisor or broker to transmit the Form W-9 to the payer.

Electronic system. Generally, the electronic system must:

- Ensure the information received is the information sent, and document all occasions of user access that result in the submission;
- Make reasonably certain that the person accessing the system and submitting the form is the person identified on Form W-9, the investment advisor, or the introducing broker;
- Provide the same information as the paper Form W-9;
- Be able to supply a hard copy of the electronic Form W-9 if the Internal Revenue Service requests it; and
- Require as the final entry in the submission an electronic signature by the payee whose name is on Form W-9 that authenticates and verifies the submission. The electronic signature must be under penalties of perjury and the perjury statement must contain the language of the paper Form W-9.

For Forms W-9 that are not required to be signed, the electronic system need not provide for an electronic signature or a perjury statement.

For more details, see the following.
- Announcement 98-27, 1998-1 C.B. 865 on page 30 of Internal Revenue Bulletin (I.R.B.)1998-15 available at *www.irs.gov/pub/irs-irbs/irb98-15.pdf.*
- Announcement 2001-91 on page 221 of I.R.B. 2001-36 available at *www.irs.gov/pub/irs-irbs/irb01-36.pdf.*

Individual Taxpayer Identification Number (ITIN)

Form W-9 (or an acceptable substitute) is used by persons required to file information returns with the IRS to get the payee's (or other person's) correct name and TIN. For individuals, the TIN is generally a social security number (SSN).

However, in some cases, individuals who become U.S. resident aliens for tax purposes are not eligible to obtain an SSN. This includes certain resident aliens who must receive information returns but who cannot obtain an SSN.

These individuals must apply for an ITIN on Form W-7, Application for IRS Individual Taxpayer Identification Number, unless they have an application pending for an SSN. Individuals who have an ITIN must provide it on Form W-9.

Substitute Form W-9

You may develop and use your own Form W-9 (a substitute Form W-9) if its content is substantially similar to the official IRS Form W-9 and it satisfies certain certification requirements.

You may incorporate a substitute Form W-9 into other business forms you customarily use, such as account signature cards. However, the certifications on the substitute Form W-9 must clearly state (as shown on the official Form W-9) that under penalties of perjury:

   1. The payee's TIN is correct,
   2. The payee is not subject to backup withholding due to failure to report interest and dividend income, and
   3. The payee is a U.S. person.

  You may not:

   1. Use a substitute Form W-9 that requires the payee, by signing, to agree to provisions unrelated to the required certifications, or
   2. Imply that a payee may be subject to backup withholding unless the payee agrees to provisions on the substitute form that are unrelated to the required certifications.

A substitute Form W-9 that contains a separate signature line just for the certifications satisfies the requirement that the certifications be clearly stated.

If a single signature line is used for the required certifications and other provisions, the certifications must be highlighted, boxed, printed in bold-face type, or presented in some other manner that causes the language to stand out from all other information contained on the substitute form. Additionally, the following statement must be presented to stand out in the same manner as described above and must appear immediately above the single signature line:

"The Internal Revenue Service does not require your consent to any provision of this document other than the certifications required to avoid backup withholding."

If you use a substitute form, you are encouraged (but not required) to provide Form W-9 instructions to the payee. However, if the IRS has notified the payee that backup withholding applies, then you must instruct the payee to strike out the language in the certification that relates to underreporting. This instruction can be given orally or in writing. See item 2 of the *Certification* on Form W-9. For more information see Revenue Procedure 83-89,1983-2, C.B. 613; amplified by Revenue Procedure

96-26 which is on page 22 of I.R.B. 1996-8 at *www.irs.gov/pub/irs-irbs/irb96-08.pdf.*

TIN Applied for

For interest and dividend payments and certain payments with respect to readily tradable instruments, the payee may return a properly completed, signed Form W-9 to you with "Applied For" written in Part I. This is an "awaiting- TIN" certificate. The payee has 60 calendar days, from the date you receive this certificate, to provide a TIN. If you do not receive the payee's TIN at that time, you must begin backup withholding on payments.

Reserve rule. You must backup withhold on any reportable payments made during the 60-day period if a payee withdraws more than $500 at one time, unless the payee reserves 28 percent of all reportable payments made to the account.

Alternative rule. You may also elect to backup withhold during this 60-day period, after a 7-day grace period, under one of the two alternative rules discussed below.

  Option 1. Backup withhold on any reportable payments if the payee makes a withdrawal from the account after the close of 7 business days after you receive the awaiting-TIN certificate. Treat as reportable payments all cash withdrawals in an amount up to the reportable payments made from the day after you receive the awaiting-TIN certificate to the day of withdrawal.

  Option 2. Backup withhold on any reportable payments made to the payee's account, regardless of whether the payee makes any withdrawals, beginning no later than 7 business days after you receive the awaiting-TIN certificate.

 The 60-day exemption from backup withholding does not apply to any payment other than interest, dividends, and certain payments relating to readily tradable instruments. Any other reportable payment, such as nonemployee compensation, is subject to backup withholding immediately, even if the payee has applied for and is awaiting a TIN.

Even if the payee gives you an awaiting-TIN certificate, you must backup withhold on reportable interest and dividend payments if the payee does not certify, under penalties of perjury, that the payee is not subject to backup withholding.

Payees Exempt From Backup Withholding

Even if the payee does not provide a TIN in the manner required, you are not required to backup withhold on any payments you make if the payee is:

   1. An organization exempt from tax under section 501(a), any IRA, or a custodial account under section 403(b)(7) if the account satisfies the requirements of section 401(f)(2,
   2. The United States or any of its agencies or instrumentalities,
   3. A state, the District of Columbia, a possession of the United States, or any of their political subdivisions or instrumentalities,

276

4. A foreign government or any of its political subdivisions, agencies, or instrumentalities, or

5. An international organization or any of its agencies or instrumentalities.

Other payees that may be exempt from backup withholding include:

6. A corporation,

7. A foreign central bank of issue,

8. A dealer in securities or commodities required to register in the United States, the District of Columbia, or a possession of the United States,

9. A futures commission merchant registered with the Commodity Futures Trading Commission,

10. A real estate investment trust,

11. An entity registered at all times during the tax year under the Investment Company Act of 1940,

12. A common trust fund operated by a bank under section 584(a),

13. A financial institution,

14. A middleman known in the investment community as a nominee or custodian, or

15. A trust exempt from tax under section 664 or described in section 4947.

The following types of payments are exempt from backup withholding as indicated for items 1 through 15 above.

Interest and dividend payments. All listed payees are exempt except the payee in item 9.

Broker transactions. All payees listed in items 1 through 13 are exempt. A person registered under the Investment Advisers Act of 1940 who regularly acts as a broker is also exempt.

Barter exchange transactions and patronage dividends. Only payees listed in items 1 through 5 are exempt.

Payments reportable under sections 6041 and 6041A. Only payees listed in items 1 through 7 are generally exempt.

However, the following payments made to a corporation (including gross proceeds paid to an attorney under section 6045(f), even if the attorney is a corporation) and reportable on Form 1099-MISC, Miscellaneous Income, are not exempt from backup withholding.

- Medical and health care payments.
- Attorneys' fees.
- Payments for services paid by a federal executive agency. (See Revenue Ruling 2003-66 on page 1115 in Internal Revenue Bulletin 2003-26 at *www.irs.gov/pub/irs-irbs/irb03-26.pdf.*)

Payments Exempt From Backup Withholding

Payments that are not subject to information reporting also are not subject to backup withholding. For details, see sections 6041, 6041A, 6042, 6044, 6045, 6049, 6050A, and 6050N, and their regulations. The following payments are generally exempt from backup withholding.

Dividends and patronage dividends
- Payments to nonresident aliens subject to withholding under section 1441.
- Payments to partnerships not engaged in a trade or business in the United States and that have at least one nonresident alien partner.
- Payments of patronage dividends not paid in money.
- Payments made by certain foreign organizations.
- Section 404(k) distributions made by an ESOP.

Interest payments
- Payments of interest on obligations issued by individuals. However, if you pay $600 or more of interest in the course of your trade or business to a payee, you must report the payment. Backup withholding applies to the reportable payment if the payee has not provided a TIN or has provided an incorrect TIN.
- Payments of tax-exempt interest (including exempt-interest dividends under section 852).
- Payments described in section 6049(b)(5) to nonresident aliens.
- Payments on tax-free covenant bonds under section 1451.
- Payments made by certain foreign organizations.
- Mortgage or student loan interest paid to you.

Other types of payment
- Wages.
- Distributions from a pension, annuity, profit-sharing or stock bonus plan, any IRA, an owner-employee plan, or other deferred compensation plan.
- Distributions from a medical or health savings account and long-term care benefits.
- Certain surrenders of life insurance contracts.
- Distribution from qualified tuition programs or Coverdell ESAs.
- Gambling winnings if regular gambling winnings withholding is required under section 3402(q). However, if regular gambling winnings withholding is not required under section 3402(q), backup withholding applies if the payee fails to furnish a TIN.
- Real estate transactions reportable under section 6045(e).
- Cancelled debts reportable under section 6050P.
- Fish purchases for cash reportable under section 6050R.
- Certain payment card transactions if the payment is made on or after January 1, 2005, by a qualified payment card agent (as described in Rev. Proc. 2004-42 and Regulations section 31.3406(g)-1(f) and if the requirements under Regulations section 31.3406(g)-1(f) are met. Rev. Proc. 2004-42 is available at *www.irs.gov/irb/2004-31_IRB*).

Joint Foreign Payees

If the first payee listed on an account gives you a Form W-8 or a similar statement signed under penalties of perjury, backup withholding applies unless:

1. Every joint payee provides the statement regarding foreign status, or

2. Any one of the joint payees who has not established foreign status gives you a TIN.

277

If any one of the joint payees who has not established foreign status gives you a TIN, use that number for purposes of backup withholding and information reporting.

For more information on foreign payees, see the Instructions for the Requester of Forms W-8BEN, W-8ECI, W-8EXP, and W-8IMY.

Names and TINs To Use for Information Reporting

Show the full name and address as provided on Form W-9 on the information return filed with the IRS and on the copy furnished to the payee. If you made payments to more than one payee or the account is in more than one name, enter on the first name line only the name of the payee whose TIN is shown on the information return. You may show the names of any other individual payees in the area below the first name line.

Sole proprietor. Enter the individual's name on the first name line. On the second name line, enter the business name or "doing business as (DBA)" if provided. You may not enter only the business name. For the TIN, you may enter either the individual's SSN or the employer identification number (EIN) of the business. However, the IRS encourages you to use the SSN.

LLC. For an LLC that is disregarded as an entity separate from its owner, you must show the owner's name on the first name line. On the second name line, you may enter the LLC's name. Use the owner's TIN.

Notices From the IRS

The IRS will send you a notice if the payee's name and TIN on the information return you filed do not match the IRS's records. (*See Taxpayer Identification Number (TIN) Matching* below.) You may have to send a "B" notice to the payee to solicit another TIN. Publications 1679 and 1281 contain copies of the two types of "B" notices.

Taxpayer Identification Number (TIN) Matching

TIN Matching allows a payer or authorized agent who is required to file Forms 1099-B, DIV, INT, MISC, OID, and /or PATR to match TIN and name combinations with IRS records before submitting the forms to the IRS. TIN Matching is one of the e-services products that is offered, and is accessible through the IRS website at *www.irs.gov/taxpros*. It is anticipated that payers who validate the TIN and name combinations before filing information returns will receive fewer backup withholding (CP2100) "B"notices and penalty notices.

Additional Information

For more information on backup withholding, see:
- Publication 1679, A Guide to Backup Withholding or
- Publication 1281, Backup Withholding on Missing and Incorrect Name/TIN(s).

278

Form **8282**
(Rev. September 1998)
Department of the Treasury
Internal Revenue Service

Donee Information Return

(Sale, Exchange, or Other Disposition of Donated Property)

▶ **See instructions on back.**

OMB No. 1545-0908

Give a Copy to Donor

Please Print or Type	Name of charitable organization (donee)	**Employer identification number**
	Address (number, street, and room or suite no.)	
	City or town, state, and ZIP code	

Part I	**Information on ORIGINAL DONOR and DONEE Receiving the Property**

1a Name(s) of the original donor of the property	**1b** Identifying number

Note: *Complete lines 2a–2d only if you gave this property to another charitable organization (successor donee).*

2a Name of charitable organization	**2b** Employer identification number
2c Address (number, street, and room or suite no.)	
2d City or town, state, and ZIP code	

Note: *If you are the original donee, skip Part II and go to Part III now.*

Part II	**Information on PREVIOUS DONEES—Complete this part only if you were not the first donee to receive the property.** If you were the second donee, leave lines 4a–4d blank. If you were a third or later donee, complete lines 3a–4d. On lines 4a–4d, give information on the preceding donee (the one who gave you the property).

3a Name of original donee	**3b** Employer identification number
3c Address (number, street, and room or suite no.)	
3d City or town, state, and ZIP code	
4a Name of preceding donee	**4b** Employer identification number
4c Address (number, street, and room or suite no.)	
4d City or town, state, and ZIP code	

Part III	**Information on DONATED PROPERTY—**If you are the original donee, leave column (c) blank.

(a) Description of donated property sold, exchanged, or otherwise disposed of (if you need more space, attach a separate statement)	**(b)** Date you received the item(s)	**(c)** Date the first donee received the item(s)	**(d)** Date item(s) sold, exchanged, or otherwise disposed of	**(e)** Amount received upon disposition

For Paperwork Reduction Act Notice, see back of form.   Cat. No. 62307Y   Form **8282** (Rev. 9-98)

General Instructions

Section references are to the Internal Revenue Code.

Purpose of Form

Donee organizations use Form 8282 to report information to the IRS about dispositions of certain charitable deduction property made within 2 years after the donor contributed the property.

Definitions

Note: *For Form 8282 and these instructions, the term "donee" includes all donees, unless specific reference is made to "original" or "successor" donees.*

Original donee. The first donee to or for which the donor gave the property. The original donee is required to sign an Appraisal Summary presented by the donor for charitable deduction property.

Successor donee. Any donee of property other than the original donee.

Appraisal summary. Section B of **Form 8283,** Noncash Charitable Contributions.

Charitable deduction property. Property (other than money or certain publicly traded securities) for which the original donee signed, or was presented with for signature, the Appraisal Summary (Form 8283, Section B).

Generally, only items or groups of similar items for which the donor claimed a deduction of more than $5,000 are included on the Appraisal Summary. There is an exception if a donor gives similar items to more than one donee organization and the total deducted for these similar items exceeds $5,000. For example, if a donor deducts $2,000 for books given to a donee organization and $4,000 for books to another donee organization, the donor must present a separate Appraisal Summary to each organization. For more information, see the Instructions for Form 8283.

Who Must File

Original and successor donee organizations must file Form 8282 if they sell, exchange, consume, or otherwise dispose of (with or without consideration) charitable deduction property within 2 years after the date the original donee received the property. See **Charitable deduction property** earlier.

Exceptions. There are two situations where Form 8282 does not have to be filed.

1. Items valued at $500 or less. You do not have to file Form 8282 if, at the time the original donee signed the Appraisal Summary, the donor had signed a statement on Form 8283 that the appraised value of the specific item was not more than $500. If Form 8283 contains more than one similar item, this exception applies only to those items that are clearly identified as having a value of $500 or less. However, for purposes of the donor's

determination of whether the appraised value of the item exceeds $500, all shares of nonpublicly traded stock, or items that form a set, are considered one item. For example, a collection of books written by the same author, components of a stereo system, or six place settings of a pattern of silverware are considered one item.

2. Items consumed or distributed for charitable purpose. You do not have to file Form 8282 if an item is consumed or distributed, without consideration, in fulfilling your purpose or function as a tax-exempt organization. For example, no reporting is required for medical supplies consumed or distributed by a tax-exempt relief organization in aiding disaster victims.

When To File

If you dispose of charitable deduction property within 2 years of the date the original donee received it and you do not meet exception **1** or **2** above, you must file Form 8282 within 125 days after the date of disposition.

Exception. If you did not file because you had no reason to believe the substantiation requirements applied to the donor, but you later become aware that they did apply, file Form 8282 within 60 days after the date you become aware you are liable. For example, this exception would apply where an Appraisal Summary is furnished to a successor donee after the date that donee disposes of the charitable deduction property.

Missing Information

If Form 8282 is filed by the due date, you must enter your organization's name, address, and EIN and complete at least Part III, column (a). You do not have to complete the remaining items if the information is not available. For example, you may not have the information necessary to complete all entries if the donor's Appraisal Summary is not available to you.

Where To File

Send Form 8282 to the Internal Revenue Service, Ogden, UT 84201-0027.

Penalty

You may be subject to a penalty if you fail to file this form by the due date, fail to include all of the information required to be shown on this form, or fail to include correct information on this form (see **Missing Information** above). The penalty is generally $50. For more details, see section 6721.

Other Requirements

Information you must give a successor donee. If the property is transferred to another charitable organization within the 2-year period discussed earlier, you must give your successor donee all of the following information.

1. The name, address, and EIN of your organization.

2. A copy of the Appraisal Summary (the Form 8283 that you received from the donor or a preceding donee).

3. A copy of this Form 8282, within 15 days after you file it.

You must furnish items **1** and **2** above within 15 days after the latest of the date:

● You transferred the property,

● The original donee signed the Appraisal Summary, or

● You received a copy of the Appraisal Summary from the preceding donee if you are also a successor donee.

Information the successor donee must give you. The successor donee organization to whom you transferred this property is required to give you their organization's name, address, and EIN within 15 days after the later of:

● The date you transferred the property, or

● The date they received a copy of the Appraisal Summary.

Information you must give the donor. You must give a copy of your Form 8282 to the original donor of the property.

Recordkeeping. You must keep a copy of the Appraisal Summary in your records.

Paperwork Reduction Act Notice. We ask for the information on this form to carry out the Internal Revenue laws of the United States. You are required to give us the information. We need it to ensure that you are complying with these laws and to allow us to figure and collect the right amount of tax.

You are not required to provide the information requested on a form that is subject to the Paperwork Reduction Act unless the form displays a valid OMB control number. Books or records relating to a form or its instructions must be retained as long as their contents may become material in the administration of any Internal Revenue law. Generally, tax returns and return information are confidential, as required by section 6103.

The time needed to complete this form will vary depending on individual circumstances. The estimated average time is:

Recordkeeping. . . . . 3 hr., 7 min

Learning about the law or the form . . . . 35 min.

Preparing and sending the form to the IRS . . . . . 41 min.

If you have comments concerning the accuracy of these time estimates or suggestions for making this form simpler, we would be happy to hear from you. You can write to the Tax Forms Committee, Western Area Distribution Center, Rancho Cordova, CA 95743-0001. **DO NOT** send the form to this address. Instead, see **Where To File** on this page.

Form 8283

(Rev. October 1998)

Department of the Treasury
Internal Revenue Service

Noncash Charitable Contributions

▶ Attach to your tax return if you claimed a total deduction
of over $500 for all contributed property.

▶ See separate instructions.

OMB No. 1545-0908

Attachment
Sequence No. **55**

Name(s) shown on your income tax return	Identifying number

Note: *Figure the amount of your contribution deduction before completing this form. See your tax return instructions.*

Section A—List in this section **only** items (or groups of similar items) for which you claimed a deduction of $5,000 or less. Also, list certain publicly traded securities even if the deduction is over $5,000 (see instructions).

Part I   Information on Donated Property—If you need more space, attach a statement.

1	(a) Name and address of the donee organization	(b) Description of donated property
A		
B		
C		
D		
E		

Note: *If the amount you claimed as a deduction for an item is $500 or less, you do not have to complete columns (d), (e), and (f).*

	(c) Date of the contribution	(d) Date acquired by donor (mo., yr.)	(e) How acquired by donor	(f) Donor's cost or adjusted basis	(g) Fair market value	(h) Method used to determine the fair market value
A						
B						
C						
D						
E						

Part II   Other Information—Complete line 2 if you gave less than an entire interest in property listed in Part I. Complete line 3 if conditions were attached to a contribution listed in Part I.

2   If, during the year, you contributed less than the entire interest in the property, complete lines a–e.

   a   Enter the letter from Part I that identifies the property ▶ _____ . If Part II applies to more than one property, attach a separate statement.

   b   Total amount claimed as a deduction for the property listed in Part I: **(1)** For this tax year   ▶ _____ .

                                             (2) For any prior tax years ▶ _____ .

   c   Name and address of each organization to which any such contribution was made in a prior year (complete only if different from the donee organization above):

     Name of charitable organization (donee)

     Address (number, street, and room or suite no.)

     City or town, state, and ZIP code

   d   For tangible property, enter the place where the property is located or kept ▶ _____

   e   Name of any person, other than the donee organization, having actual possession of the property ▶ _____

3   If conditions were attached to any contribution listed in Part I, answer questions a – c and attach the required statement (see instructions).

		Yes	No
a	Is there a restriction, either temporary or permanent, on the donee's right to use or dispose of the donated property?		
b	Did you give to anyone (other than the donee organization or another organization participating with the donee organization in cooperative fundraising) the right to the income from the donated property or to the possession of the property, including the right to vote donated securities, to acquire the property by purchase or otherwise, or to designate the person having such income, possession, or right to acquire?		
c	Is there a restriction limiting the donated property for a particular use?		

For Paperwork Reduction Act Notice, see page 4 of separate instructions.   Cat. No. 62299J   Form **8283** (Rev. 10-98)

Form 8283 (Rev. 10-98) Page 2

Name(s) shown on your income tax return	Identifying number

Section B—Appraisal Summary—List in this section only items (or groups of similar items) for which you claimed a deduction of more than $5,000 per item or group. **Exception.** Report contributions of certain publicly traded securities only in Section A.

If you donated art, you may have to attach the complete appraisal. See the **Note** in Part I below.

Part I   Information on Donated Property—To be completed by the taxpayer and/or appraiser.

4   Check type of property:

☐ Art* (contribution of $20,000 or more)   ☐ Real Estate   ☐ Gems/Jewelry   ☐ Stamp Collections
☐ Art* (contribution of less than $20,000)   ☐ Coin Collections   ☐ Books   ☐ Other

*Art includes paintings, sculptures, watercolors, prints, drawings, ceramics, antique furniture, decorative arts, textiles, carpets, silver, rare manuscripts, historical memorabilia, and other similar objects.

Note: *If your total art contribution deduction was $20,000 or more, you must attach a complete copy of the signed appraisal. See instructions.*

5	(a) Description of donated property (if you need more space, attach a separate statement)	(b) If tangible property was donated, give a brief summary of the overall physical condition at the time of the gift	(c) Appraised fair market value
A			
B			
C			
D			

	(d) Date acquired by donor (mo., yr.)	(e) How acquired by donor	(f) Donor's cost or adjusted basis	(g) For bargain sales, enter amount received	(h) Amount claimed as a deduction	(i) Average trading price of securities
					See instructions	
A						
B						
C						
D						

Part II   Taxpayer (Donor) Statement—List each item included in Part I above that the appraisal identifies as having a value of $500 or less. See instructions.

I declare that the following item(s) included in Part I above has to the best of my knowledge and belief an appraised value of not more than $500 (per item). Enter identifying letter from Part I and describe the specific item. See instructions. ▶ _____

Signature of taxpayer (donor) ▶   Date ▶

Part III   Declaration of Appraiser

I declare that I am not the donor, the donee, a party to the transaction in which the donor acquired the property, employed by, or related to any of the foregoing persons, or married to any person who is related to any of the foregoing persons. And, if regularly used by the donor, donee, or party to the transaction, I performed the majority of my appraisals during my tax year for other persons.

Also, I declare that I hold myself out to the public as an appraiser or perform appraisals on a regular basis; and that because of my qualifications as described in the appraisal, I am qualified to make appraisals of the type of property being valued. I certify that the appraisal fees were not based on a percentage of the appraised property value. Furthermore, I understand that a false or fraudulent overstatement of the property value as described in the qualified appraisal or this appraisal summary may subject me to the penalty under section 6701(a) (aiding and abetting the understatement of tax liability). I affirm that I have not been barred from presenting evidence or testimony by the Director of Practice.

Sign Here   Signature ▶   Title ▶   Date of appraisal ▶

Business address (including room or suite no.)	Identifying number
City or town, state, and ZIP code	

Part IV   Donee Acknowledgment—To be completed by the charitable organization.

This charitable organization acknowledges that it is a qualified organization under section 170(c) and that it received the donated property as described in Section B, Part I, above on ▶ _____
(Date)

Furthermore, this organization affirms that in the event it sells, exchanges, or otherwise disposes of the property described in Section B, Part I (or any portion thereof) within 2 years after the date of receipt, it will file **Form 8282,** Donee Information Return, with the IRS and give the donor a copy of that form. This acknowledgment does not represent agreement with the claimed fair market value.

Does the organization intend to use the property for an unrelated use? . . . . ▶ ☐ Yes   ☐ No

Name of charitable organization (donee)	Employer identification number
Address (number, street, and room or suite no.)	City or town, state, and ZIP code
Authorized signature	Title	Date

INDEX

NOTES

NOTES

NOTES

NOTES

NOTES